Dispute Settlement in the UN Convention the Law of the Sea

The United Nations Convention on the Law ___ ___ ___ __ ___ __ ___ most important constitutive instruments in international law. Not only does this treaty regulate the uses of the world's largest resource, but it also contains a mandatory dispute settlement system – an unusual phenomenon in international law. While some scholars have lauded this development as a significant achievement, others have been highly skeptical of its comprehensiveness and effectiveness. This book explores whether a compulsory dispute settlement mechanism is necessary for the regulation of the oceans under the Convention. The requisite role of dispute settlement in the Convention is determined through an assessment of its relationship to the substantive provisions. Klein firstly describes the dispute settlement procedure in the Convention. She then takes each of the issue areas subject to limitations or exceptions to compulsory procedures entailing binding decisions, and analyzes the inter-relationship between the substantive and procedural rules.

NATALIE KLEIN is a Lecturer at Macquarie University in Sydney, Australia. She obtained her law degree from the University of Adelaide, where she went on to teach international law. She completed her Doctorate at Yale Law School in 2003. Klein was recently an Associate at the New York office of Debevoise and Plimpton LLP, where she practiced in international litigation and arbitration. Klein has also worked as counsel to the Government of Eritrea on the Eritrea/Yemen maritime boundary arbitration and the Eritrea/Ethiopia boundary dispute, and as a consultant in the Codification Division of the Office of Legal Affairs at the United Nations.

CAMBRIDGE STUDIES IN INTERNATIONAL AND COMPARATIVE LAW

Established in 1946, this series produces high quality scholarship in the fields of public and private international law and comparative law. Although these are distinct legal subdisciplines, developments since 1946 confirm their interrelation.

Comparative law is increasingly used as a tool in the making of law at national, regional, and international levels. Private international law is now often affected by international conventions, and the issues faced by classical conflicts rules are frequently dealt with by substantive harmonisation of law under international auspices. Mixed international arbitrations, especially those involving state economic activity, raise mixed questions of public and private international law, while in many fields (such as the protection of human rights and democratic standards, investment guarantees and international criminal law) international and national systems interact. National constitutional arrangements relating to 'foreign affairs,' and to the implementation of international norms, are a focus of attention.

The Board welcomes works of a theoretical or interdisciplinary character, and those focusing on the new approaches to international or comparative law or conflicts of law. Studies of particular institutions or problems are equally welcome, as are translations of the best work published in other languages.

A list of books in the series can be found at the end of this volume.

Dispute Settlement in the UN Convention on the Law of the Sea

Natalie Klein

CAMBRIDGE
UNIVERSITY PRESS

CAMBRIDGE UNIVERSITY PRESS
Cambridge, New York, Melbourne, Madrid, Cape Town, Singapore, São Paulo, Delhi

Cambridge University Press
The Edinburgh Building, Cambridge CB2 8RU, UK

Published in the United States of America by Cambridge University Press, New York

www.cambridge.org
Information on this title: www.cambridge.org/9780521118323

First published 2005
This digitally printed version 2009

A catalogue record for this publication is available from the British Library

Library of Congress Cataloguing in Publication data
Klein, Natalie (Natalie S.)
The role of dispute settlement in the UN Convention on the Law of the Sea / Natalie
Klein.
   p.   cm. – (Cambridge studies in international and comparative law ; 39)
Includes bibliographical references and index.
ISBN 0 521 83520 8 (hardback)
1. United Nations Convention on the Law of the Sea (1982)   2. Law of the sea.
3. Arbitration, International.   I. Title.   II. Cambridge studies in international and
comparative law (Cambridge, England : 1996) ; 39.
KZA1120.3.K58   2004
341.4′5–dc22   2004051862

ISBN 978-0-521-83520-6 hardback
ISBN 978-0-521-11832-3 paperback

Contents

Acknowledgements

From the inception of this work, I had the extreme good fortune of working under the supervision of Professor Michael Reisman. His advice and guidance throughout this project have been invaluable and I am very grateful for all of the time and consideration he has given to my work. This work was also significantly improved because of the intellectual contributions of Professor Lea Brilmayer and Professor Ruth Wedgwood. Professor Brilmayer has indelibly influenced my life through our work for the Government of Eritrea. To me, she epitomizes what it means to be a teacher, scholar, and international lawyer. Professor Wedgwood always pushed me to think more critically and to take into account a political dynamic that I might well have otherwise overlooked. Most of all, Professors Reisman, Brilmayer, and Wedgwood fundamentally changed my understanding of public international law and as a result, their instruction has greatly enriched my scholarship.

As a student of international law at the University of Adelaide in Australia, Professor Hilary Charlesworth, Dr. Judith Gardam, and Gerald McGinley first introduced me to the world of international law and opened up many possibilities for me. I am particularly grateful for the ongoing support and advice of Dr. Gardam.

This book is based on my dissertation prepared in fulfillment of the requirements for the Doctor of the Science of Law at Yale Law School. My residence at Yale Law School was made possible through the award of the Howard M. Holtzmann Fellowship in International Arbitration and a Lillian Goldman Fellowship. Many people at Yale Law School provided assistance to me in a myriad of ways, resolving a range of administrative, technical and financial issues, and in this regard, I would like to thank Judy Couture, Associate Dean Barbara Safriet, Judith Miller, John Davie, Cina Santos, Paddy Spiegelhalter, Marge Camera, and Yvonne Squeri.

The transformation from dissertation to book was completed during my time as an associate at Debevoise and Plimpton LLP, and I am grateful for the support of Donald Francis Donovan throughout this undertaking. My thanks also to Lorraine Cali for her assistance during the final editing of the text.

Essential to me throughout this undertaking, and all leading up to it, are those who have provided indispensable moral support. My family, especially Sue Klein, Stephen Klein, Grant Klein, and Ann Coates, has been a constant source of support that I have relied on at all stages of my education, probably more than I truly realize. Matthew Kelly, Daniel Bonilla, Kirsten Edwards, Annette Florance, Kate Hewson, Marica Ilich, Victoria Langmaid, Tracy Macdonald, Jonathan Marshall, Kate Melvin, Nathalia Mendieta, Nicole Pettitt, Radoslav Prochazka, Elizabeth Reed, Esteban Restrepo, Karina Rook, Ralf Sauer, Andrei Stoica, and Paul Wisch have been unfailing in their enthusiasm and encouragement, and their ongoing support has been absolutely invaluable. I could not have completed this book without them.

Abbreviations

1994 Agreement	Agreement Relating to the Implementation of Part XI of the United Nations Convention on the Law of the Sea, 1994.
CCAMLR	Convention on the Conservation of Antarctic Marine Living Resources, 1980.
CCSBT	Convention for the Conservation of Southern Bluefin Tuna, 1993.
Codification Conference	Rosenne, Shabtai ed., League of Nations, Conference for the Codification of International Law [1930] (1975).
Continental Shelf Convention	Convention on the Continental Shelf, 1958.
Dispute Resolving Agreement	Agreement Concerning Interim Arrangements Relating to Polymetallic Nodules of the Deep Sea Bed, 1982.
DSHMR Act	Deep Seabed Hard Mineral Resources Act.
EC, or Community	European Community.
EEZ	Exclusive Economic Zone.
First Conference	First United Nations Conference on the Law of the Sea (1958).
Fishing and Conservation Convention	Convention on Fishing and Conservation of the Living Resources of the High Seas, 1958.

FSA, or Fish Stocks Agreement	Agreement for the Implementation of the Provisions of the United Nations Convention on the Law of the Sea Relating to the Conservation and Management of Straddling Fish Stocks and Highly Migratory Fish Stocks.
High Seas Convention	Convention on the High Seas, 1958.
ICJ	International Court of Justice.
ITLOS	International Tribunal for the Law of the Sea.
NIEO	New International Economic Order.
OSPAR Convention	1992 Convention for the Protection of the Marine Environment of the North-East Atlantic.
PCIJ	Permanent Court of International Justice.
Prepcom	Preparatory Commission established under Resolution I of the Final Act of the Conference.
Second Conference	Second United Nations Conference on the Law of the Sea (1960).
Territorial Sea Convention	Convention on the Territorial Sea and Contiguous Zone, 1958.
Third Conference	Third United Nations Conference on the Law of the Sea (1974–82).
UN	United Nations.
UNCLOS, or Convention	United Nations Convention on the Law of the Sea, 1982.
WTO	World Trade Organization.

Table of treaties and other international instruments

Table of cases

1   Introduction

Introduction

The oceans cover five-sevenths of the earth's surface and play a vital role in supporting the human population. They are without doubt the most important resource on the planet. Every State in the world has economic, political, strategic, and social interests in the oceans. These interests are manifest in a variety of maritime activities – including fishing, shipping of goods, hydrocarbon and mineral extraction, naval missions, and scientific research. The uses of the oceans have significantly evolved from times when maritime areas were primarily important as trading routes and considered as a common resource of limitless quantities of fish. The oceans are no longer immense barriers separating the nations of the world. All States now share interests in the way the oceans are used. These changes have led to the development of a complex pattern of ownership of maritime space and control of maritime activities over the last fifty years. The multiplicity of maritime claims has resulted in a high degree of regulation in the international system.

The primary instrument governing the conduct of States in their uses of the oceans is the 1982 United Nations Convention on the Law of the Sea ("UNCLOS" or "Convention").[1] The importance of this treaty cannot be underestimated. UNCLOS is a constitutive treaty, setting out the rights and obligations of States and other international actors in different maritime areas and in relation to various uses of the oceans. The significance of UNCLOS is not only found in its far-reaching control over activities in all maritime zones, but also in the procedures it provides for States to resolve their differences in respect of competing claims.

---

[1] United Nations Convention on the Law of the Sea, opened for signature December 10, 1982, 1833 UNTS 397.

UNCLOS is one of an extremely small number of global treaties that prescribe mandatory jurisdiction for disputes arising from the interpretation and application of its terms.[2] International disputes are typically settled through diplomatic efforts and only submitted to adjudication or arbitration with the consent of the parties involved. To create a treaty that includes a mechanism for compulsory arbitration or adjudication for such a fundamentally important resource was a distinct deviation from the norm in international law and politics.

The creation of a dispute resolution system entailing compulsory procedures in the body of the Convention has been hailed by governments and commentators alike as one of the most significant developments in dispute settlement in international law, even as important as the entry into force of the United Nations Charter.[3] Charney, for example, considered that the Convention contains "the most significant regime for the settlement of disputes, in general, found in modern multilateral agreements."[4] At the conclusion of the conference on the negotiations of the Convention, the President of the conference proclaimed, "The world community's interest in the peaceful settlement of disputes and the prevention of use of force in the settlement of disputes between States have been advanced by the mandatory system of dispute settlement in the Convention."[5] The significance of the dispute settlement mechanism has also been emphasized because of its role in protecting the integrity of the compromise reached in formulating the substantive provisions. The binding and compulsory dispute settlement procedures were to be "the pivot upon which the delicate equilibrium of the compromise must be balanced";[6] "the cement which should hold the whole structure together and guarantee its continued acceptability

---

[2] The only other two treaties within this category are the United Nations Charter and the World Trade Organization Agreement. The UN Charter could even be excluded from this group, as the means of dispute resolution available under Chapter VII do not typically include mandatory adjudication or arbitration.

[3] See, e.g., Alan E. Boyle, "Dispute Settlement and the Law of the Sea Convention: Problems of Fragmentation and Jurisdiction," 46 *Int'l & Comp. L.Q.* 37 (1997); Louis B. Sohn, "Settlement of Law of the Sea Disputes," 10 *Int'l J. Marine & Coastal L.* 205 (1995); John Warren Kindt, "Dispute Settlement in International Environmental Issues: The Model Provided by the 1982 Convention on the Law of the Sea," 22 *Vand. J. Transnat'l L.* 1097, 1098–99 (1989).

[4] Jonathan I. Charney, "Entry into Force of the 1982 Convention on the Law of the Sea," 35 *Va. J. Int'l L.* 381, 389–90 (1995).

[5] Statement by the President, in 17 *Third United Nations Conference on the Law of the Sea: Official Records* at 13, ¶ 48, UN Sales No. E.84.V.3 (1984).

[6] Memorandum by the President of the Conference on doc. A/CONF.62/WP.9, UN Doc. A/CONF.62/WP.9/Add.1 (1976), reprinted in 5 *Third United Nations Conference on the Law of*

and endurance for all parties."[7] Other commentators have been more cautious, or indeed skeptical, about the transformation of international dispute resolution through the conclusion of UNCLOS. Oda has argued that the exceptions and ambiguities render the mechanism comparable to traditional consent-based methods of dispute settlement.[8] Doubts have also been expressed about how inclusive the available procedures truly are. Notably, the assertion that UNCLOS provides a comprehensive and effective dispute settlement system has been undermined by one of the very tribunals constituted under the Convention.[9]

UNCLOS, with its complex regulation of ocean uses, assignment of maritime zones, and compulsory dispute settlement procedures, certainly reflects a new era in international relations generally and in law of the sea and dispute resolution specifically. Yet the extent that the Convention represents a reconfiguration of dispute resolution in international law may not be quite as dramatic as some commentators predict. This book tests the cogency of these diametric views by asking whether compulsory dispute settlement is requisite for the operation of the Convention. Such an appraisal requires an exploration of the interaction between the substantive provisions of the Convention and the procedural devices available to resolve differences in the interpretation and application of those substantive rules. The connection between substance and procedure can be discerned through an analysis of what the drafters of the Convention intended, what was actually produced in the Convention and what is likely to happen in the future. In this way, it is clear that in some issue areas, the substantive principles share a symbiotic relationship with the procedures and are therefore dependent on

---

the Sea: Official Records at 122, ¶ 6, UN Sales No. E.76.V.8 (1984) (explaining his initiative in preparing an informal single negotiating text on the settlement of disputes).

[7] Boyle, "Dispute Settlement," at 38.

[8] Shigeru Oda, "Some Reflections on the Dispute Settlement Clauses in the United Nations Convention on the Law of the Sea," in Essays in International Law in Honour of Judge Manfred Lachs 645, 655 (Jerzy Makarczyk ed., 1984). See also John King Gamble, Jr., "The Law of the Sea Conference: Dispute Settlement in Perspective," 9 Vand. J. Int'l L. 323, 341 (1976) (noting that the tendency of States is to claim more sovereignty over the oceans rather than relinquish that sovereignty to third-party dispute settlement); Gilbert Guillaume, "The Future of International Judicial Institutions," 44 Int'l & Comp. L.Q. 848 (1995).

[9] Southern Bluefin Tuna Cases, Australia and New Zealand v. Japan, Award on Jurisdiction and Admissibility, (Australia v. Japan; New Zealand v. Japan) (Arbitral Tribunal constituted under Annex VII of the United Nations Convention on the Law of the Sea, August 4, 2000), 39 ILM 1359 (2000), para. 62. ("It thus appears to the Tribunal that UNCLOS falls significantly short of establishing a truly comprehensive regime of compulsory jurisdiction entailing binding decisions.")

the dispute settlement system for their effective functioning. In many other instances, the availability of compulsory dispute settlement is irrelevant to the functioning of the normative provisions of the Convention. States need not rely on an external source of review but can regulate their relationships regardless of any available procedures and only resort to traditional means of dispute settlement if needed. As one commentator has noted, "It is not obvious that dispute settlement will be necessary or even helpful in putting together an effective treaty package."[10] The analysis set forth in this book demonstrates that compulsory dispute procedures are only required in some issue areas when particular conditions are met whereas disputes in other issue areas remain to be settled through traditional consent-based methods.

This first chapter sketches the interrelated developments in international relations, dispute resolution, and the law of the sea that preceded the adoption of UNCLOS. A brief historical perspective describes the changing nature of international relations from a community of sovereign, independent States where issues were typically regulated within a bilateral framework to a system of highly interdependent actors that share a commonality of interests in a variety of areas. The evolution in international politics is reflected in the ways States resolve disputes – from reliance on the use of force to an increasing confidence in third-party processes – and in the law of the sea – as an inclusive system that has accounted for escalating demands of exclusive rights. This background illustrates how UNCLOS reinforces as well as considerably develops the substantive law of the sea and the methods of international dispute resolution. In light of this development, the final section of Chapter 1 further evaluates the opposing views on the significance and effectiveness of the dispute settlement system in the Convention.

The subsequent chapters examine in detail the way that particular issue areas are subject to the dispute settlement system in the Convention. Chapter 2 describes the procedures for dispute settlement as set out in Part XV of the Convention. Chapters 3 and 4 then closely analyze Articles 297 and 298 of UNCLOS, which specify how mandatory jurisdiction applies with respect to the freedoms of navigation, overflight, and the laying of submarine cables and pipelines; protection and preservation of the marine environment; fishing; marine scientific research; maritime delimitation; and, finally, military activities, law enforcement, and disputes in respect of which the Security Council is exercising its functions. These chapters thus explore in what situations compulsory

---

[10] Gamble, "Dispute Settlement in Perspective," at 323 and 325.

jurisdiction entailing binding decisions is essential for the operation of the normative provisions of the Convention. Chapter 5 examines the role of dispute settlement in the deep seabed mining regime under the Convention, and compares the position of a dispute resolution mechanism in the alternative regime that was developed outside the Convention. Chapter 6 summarizes these arguments and suggests what conditions must be present for mandatory jurisdiction to play a viable and requisite role in regulating the behavior of actors in the law of the sea. A final assessment of the impact of the dispute settlement mechanism in UNCLOS in law of the sea, as well as in international law and international relations more generally, concludes the book.

Historical Perspective

The law of the sea has been based on the fundamental principle of *mare liberum* for the last five centuries. Although some States had sought to establish sovereignty over the high seas in order to monopolize trade and fishing,[11] these attempts failed in favor of the establishment of *mare liberum*, the freedom of the seas, for the benefit of every State.[12] The system of open waters meant that the oceans were available for all users, a *res communis*, and every State had the right to navigate and fish freely.[13] This view, which predominated from the seventeenth century, was jurisprudentially grounded in the writings of a Dutch scholar, Hugo Grotius, who asserted that things that cannot be seized or enclosed cannot become property.[14] *Mare liberum* was thus advocated in order to uphold the right of the Dutch to navigation and commerce with

[11] In 1493, Pope Alexander VI divided ownership of all oceans and unexplored territories between Spain and Portugal, despite England and Denmark's earlier claims over the seas adjacent to their shores. See Richard B. McNees, "Freedom of Transit Through International Straits," 6 *J. Mar. L. & Com.* 175, 176 (1974–75) (describing King Edgar the Peaceful's claim to being "Sovereign of the Brittanic Oceans" from the tenth century through to the fourteenth century as well as Denmark's claims to the Baltic on the principle that possession of the opposite shores carried with it sovereignty over the intervening seas).

[12] See Arthur H. Dean, "The Second Geneva Conference on the Law of the Sea: The Fight for Freedom of the Seas," 54 *Am. J. Int'l L.* 751, 757–61 (1960); Carl M. Franklin, "The Law of the Sea: Some Recent Developments (With Particular Reference to the United Nations Conference of 1958)," 53 *Int'l L. Studies* 1, 54 (1959–60).

[13] "[T]he principle of the freedom of the high seas was the fundamental tenet of the law of the sea as a whole." *United Nations Conference on the Law of the Sea*, 2nd Comm., at 27, ¶ 5 (Israel), UN Doc. A/CONF.13/40, UN Sales No. 58.V.4, vol. IV (1958).

[14] Hugo Grotius, *The Freedom of the Seas or the Right which Belongs to the Dutch to Take Part in the East Indian Trade* (Ralph Magoffin trans., James Brown Scott ed., 1916) (1633), pp. 22–44.

the Indies in the face of Portuguese claims to a monopoly.[15] Grotius noted that use of the oceans for fishing or for navigation by one did not preclude their use by others. The oceans were created by nature in such a state that their usage could not be exclusive but belonged to all humankind.[16]

Mare liberum applied to all the high seas, with the exception of a narrow belt of territorial sea adjacent to the coasts of States. These belts of water close to the coast existed for the protection of local fishing interests and for security.[17] Throughout the nineteenth century, the freedoms of the high seas meant that the oceans constituted a common resource whereby all States had equal access. By virtue of the shared use of maritime areas, States could promote their economic well-being through transportation, navigation, and exploitation of natural resources.[18] Economic interests in the movement of goods and people were thus enhanced by the freedom of navigation into the twentieth century. This approach favored nations with significant maritime fleets that could use the waters for communication with overseas colonies and dominions and for the transport of goods and people. Nations with considerable naval fleets were also able to rely on the *mare liberum* system to their advantage as it allowed uninterrupted passage of warships around areas of political and military influence.

The *res communis* approach to governing the use of the oceans was both typical and atypical of the relations between States over several centuries. The Peace of Westphalia, which ended the Thirty Years War

[15] Kenneth Booth, "The Military Implications of the Changing Law of the Sea," in *Law of the Sea: Neglected Issues* (John King Gamble, Jr., ed., 1979), pp. 328, 335. See also "Introduction" to Hugo Grotius, *The Rights of War and Peace* 5 (A. C. Campbell trans., introduction by David J. Hill, Universal Classic Library ed., 1901) (1646).

[16] See generally Grotius, *Freedom of the Seas*, pp. 28–29. A British legal scholar, John Selden, argued that the sea and its resources were capable of being subject to appropriation and dominion. See John Selden, *Of the Dominion, Or, Ownership of the Sea* (Marchamont Nedham trans., 1972) (1635). Although Selden's view attracted some support, it was ultimately discarded in favor of *mare liberum*.

[17] It was established in 1703 that a State could extend its dominion over the adjacent waters to a distance of three miles, which was said to be equivalent to the range of a cannon at the time. Dean debunks this theory by noting that no cannon was known to have such a range at the time but that Bynkershoek, who is credited with the theory, actually stated that "the territorial sovereignty ends where the power of arms ends." See Dean, "Second Geneva Conference," at 759–60.

[18] McDougal and Burke describe the value of "wealth" in claims to the ocean as "a goal in the great congeries of claims relating to transportation, navigation, fishing and mineral exploitation." Myres S. McDougal and William T. Burke, "Crisis in the Law of the Sea: Community Perspectives Versus National Egoism," 67 *Yale L.J.* 539, 549 (1958).

in 1648, is typically viewed as the moment that the modern nation State was first created.[19] It was at this point that assortments of communities could first be said to have been recognized as "sovereign entities possessed of the centralized structures typical of the modern State."[20] Traditionally, public international law was based on the notion of a community of independent, sovereign States in which the sovereignty of a State could only be restricted through its consent. The hallmark of the modern State, according to this conventional understanding, has always been its exclusive sovereignty over a defined territory. This emphasis on exclusive dominion was incompatible with the use of the oceans. States were not physically able to control large expanses of maritime areas in a similar way to land territory. Nonetheless, the *mare liberum* system permitted each State to use the oceans as it was able in pursuing its interests. As with international relations on land, on the oceans, States had a minimum interest in cooperation and would only be bound by rules to which they had consented. In the "anarchical" international system, no superior force existed to coerce States into compliance if it was not in their interest to act so. In this context, international law endorsed the existing power relationships.[21] States were solely interested in augmenting their power to ensure their survival. There was no joint interest in compliance with the law within the international system and international law was only relevant in governing inter-State relations to the extent that it coincided with State interests.[22] Military power was a primary source of legitimation and as such, States were not bound by norms but remained free to violate international law with impunity whenever it was in their interest to do so. Thus when disputes arose,

---

[19] See, e.g., Antonio Cassese, *International Law in a Divided World* (1986), pp. 34–38.

[20] *Ibid.*, 38.

[21] The scholars that have classically represented this approach include Hans Morgenthau, Georg Schwarzenberger, and George Kennan. See generally Hans Morgenthau, *Politics Among Nations* (5th ed., 1973); Ian Brownlie, "The Relation of Law and Power," in *Contemporary Problems of International Law: Essays in Honour of Georg Schwarzenberger* (Bin Cheng and E. D. Brown eds., 1988), p. 19.

[22] Morgenthau, for example, argues that the:

> great majority of rules of international law are generally observed by all nations without actual compulsion, for it is generally in the nature of all nations concerned to honor their obligations under international law . . . [When] compliance with international law and its enforcement have a direct bearing upon the relative power of the nations concerned . . . considerations of power rather than of law determine compliance and enforcement.

Morgenthau, pp. 290–91. See also Francis Anthony Boyle, *Foundations of World Order: The Legalist Approach to International Relations, 1898–1922* (1999), pp. 7–8.

the use of force was a valid means of settling the matter along with consent-based methods.

The use of third-party dispute settlement finds its genesis at the end of the eighteenth century with the adoption of the Jay Treaty.[23] The Jay Treaty, which was signed by the United States and the United Kingdom in 1794, established an arbitral procedure that became the model for subsequent attempts at peaceful third-party dispute resolution.[24] From this time, a recognized procedure existed that was available to States to settle disputes without resorting to armed force and instances of arbitration became more common. A change in attitude towards the use of force occurred at the end of the nineteenth century with the convocation of the Hague Peace Conferences. These two Conferences were intended to consider the reduction of arms and the maintenance of general peace through alternative means of dispute settlement.[25] There was insufficient political will at this time to accept a multilateral agreement providing for obligatory arbitration of any international disputes. States nonetheless agreed in 1899 to the establishment of the Permanent Court of Arbitration, which provided a procedure for States to select designated arbitrators and utilize an established arbitral procedure if they wished.[26] Article 19 of the 1899 Convention regarding the Pacific Settlement of International Disputes reserved the right of contracting parties to conclude obligatory arbitration agreements between themselves and thereby provided the impetus for a number of bilateral arbitration agreements.

[23] Treaty of Amity, Commerce and Navigation, November 19, 1794, US–UK, 1794, 8 Stat. 116. Although the settlement of disputes on the basis of law can be traced back to Greek antiquity, the majority of commentators consider the Jay Treaty as the starting point for the development of international arbitration. See, e.g., J. L. Simpson and Hazel Fox, *International Arbitration: Law and Practice* (1959), p. 1.

[24] The Jay Treaty was a precedent for the settlement of the *Alabama* claims of the United States against the United Kingdom with respect to construction of vessels in British ports during the American Civil War. The success of the *Alabama* tribunal provided "the momentum propelling the international movement for the obligatory arbitration of international disputes throughout the rest of the nineteenth century and well into the First Hague Peace Conference." Boyle, *Foundations of World Order*, p. 26. See also Simpson and Fox, p. 8 (describing the *Alabama* arbitration as giving new impetus to international arbitration).

[25] See Boyle, *Foundations of World Order*, pp. 27–32.

[26] The availability of good offices and mediation by third parties was also instituted at this time, as well as a voluntary procedure for the formation of international commissions of inquiry. See Convention [No. 1] Regarding the Pacific Settlement of International Disputes, July 29, 1899, Title II, art. 2, 32 Stat. 1779, 1 Bevans 230, and *ibid.*, Title III, arts. 9–14.

Throughout the twentieth century, arbitration was often incorporated as a dispute settlement mechanism in treaties, particularly as compromissory clauses. The inclusion of compromissory clauses did not create mandatory jurisdiction but rather established an obligation to negotiate for the institution of a dispute settlement procedure.[27] Certain disputes were categorized as acceptable for third-party resolution whereas other disputes were too closely tied to the "vital interests, independence or honour" of the State to be left to the decision of a third party.[28] While the availability of this mode of dispute settlement was increasingly recognized, the inclusion of a mechanism for third-party dispute resolution in bilateral and multilateral treaties did not actually result in a large number of arbitrations or conciliations.[29]

Changes in the international system away from the "Westphalian" model of international relations advanced after World War I with the creation of the League of Nations. A new enthusiasm was voiced for international law and organizations, collective security, open diplomacy, free trade, arms control, and national self-determination.[30] The establishment of the League of Nations demonstrated a move against the acceptability of the use of military force as a means of dispute resolution. Although the resort to force was not outlawed, conditions were imposed on its use.[31] Instead, peaceful modes of third-party dispute settlement were to constitute viable substitutes to recourse to war. The Covenant of the League of Nations required States to submit any dispute likely to lead to a rupture either to arbitration or judicial settlement or to inquiry by the League's Council. The Covenant also called for the establishment of a permanent court to hear and determine any dispute of an international character.[32] The Permanent Court of International Justice ("PCIJ") was thus established at this time but was neither endowed with compulsory jurisdiction nor constituted an integral part of the League of Nations Covenant. Instead, the PCIJ had jurisdiction over all cases

---

[27] See Manley O. Hudson, *International Tribunals* (1944), p. 75.

[28] See Simpson and Fox, pp. 15–16 (describing the phrase as a "stock formula for bilateral arbitration treaties" at this time).

[29] See Christine Gray and Benedict Kingsbury, "Developments in Dispute Settlement Inter-State Arbitration Since 1945," 63 *Brit. Y.B. Int'l L.* 97, 101 (1992).

[30] See Boyle, *Foundations of World Order*, pp. 8–9.

[31] League of Nations Covenant, art. 12 (requiring States to wait three months prior to resorting to force following the submission of the dispute to arbitration or adjudication).

[32] *Ibid.*, art. 14.

the parties referred to it as well as all matters specially provided for in treaties and conventions in force.[33]

The impact of these changes was only marginal in the development of the law of the sea. The League of Nations decision to initiate a project on the progressive codification of international law in 1924 could have been influential because the topic of territorial waters was one of the areas of international law considered "ripe" for codification.[34] The issues examined included the nature and limits of territorial waters, the contiguous zone, and the passage of foreign ships through territorial waters. Rather than being "ripe" for codification, the general debate revealed that there was no agreement on the breadth of the territorial sea and related issues. The only documents produced on this topic were a report on the legal status of the territorial waters and articles with commentaries on the delimitation of the territorial sea. Additional resolutions on inland waters and the protection of fisheries were adopted.[35] As so many outstanding questions remained, the Committee decided that the League of Nations Council should recommend the convocation of a new conference.[36] No such conference was ever held under the auspices of the League of Nations.

A watershed moment in international law and politics occurred at the end of World War II with the creation of the United Nations ("UN"). The adoption of the UN Charter signaled several significant changes in the international system. Following the devastation of World War II, States were prepared to accept some form of control on military power. Of particular note in this regard was the express prohibition on the use of force (except in cases of self-defense)[37] and the collective enforcement

---

[33] PCIJ Statute, art. 36.

[34] See generally Shabtai Rosenne ed., *League of Nations, Conference for the Codification of International Law [1930]* (1975).

[35] Report Adopted by the Committee on April 10, 1930, reprinted in 4 *Codification Conference*, at 1411.

[36] Rosenne has considered why the Conference did not succeed in the task as originally envisaged. He posits:

> The League itself was far from being representative of the international community of States as it then existed, and the codification effort itself was largely the work of a few devoted individuals with most of the initiative coming from one single geographical region. Governments, too, with few exceptions do not seem to have shown great interest in codification. Running through the records of both the Council and the Assembly, there is an almost built-in political and ideological imbalance.

1 *Codification Conference*, at xl.

[37] UN Charter, art. 2(4) and art. 51.

mechanism established in Chapter VII of the UN Charter. Under Chapter VII, the Security Council is authorized to respond to threats to the peace, breaches of the peace, and acts of aggression and these decisions are binding on all Member States.[38] Chapter VII thus represents a form of compulsory third-party dispute settlement. The International Court of Justice ("ICJ") was created as the primary judicial organ of the UN, as a successor to the PCIJ.[39] Like the Permanent Court, the ICJ does not have compulsory jurisdiction over all Member States.[40] The Charter also addressed economic and social issues that had previously been left to the sole responsibility of States and hence began the process for greater recognition of human rights in the international system.[41] Finally, the Charter created the Trusteeship Council as a mechanism to facilitate the self-determination of colonized territories.[42] The effectiveness of the UN, as envisaged at the adoption of the Charter, was largely thwarted by the onset of the Cold War and the nuclear arms race between the United States and the Soviet Union. Consequently, the collective security system was left in desuetude and the functions of the Security Council were largely rendered redundant.

With the arrival of the Cold War, international politics became largely polarized between the superpowers and their respective supporters. An ideological divide formed between the western democratic States and the socialist bloc. A third voice in this sphere came from the States achieving independence after World War II through the decolonization process. The newly independent States were able to utilize the bipolar divide for their own economic and political objectives. In particular, the decolonized States sought to overcome the economic disadvantages of colonization and to reclaim their rights over resources to secure their development.[43] Each group influenced the development of the law through their divergent socio-economic philosophies, ideologies, and political motivations. The dominance of the bipolar dynamic in regulating all aspects of international relations refuted the idealistic

---

[38] Ibid., arts. 39, 41, 42, and 48.   [39] Ibid., art. 92.   [40] ICJ Statute, art. 36.

[41] See UN Charter, arts. 55–72 (setting out obligations of international economic and social cooperation as well as establishing the Economic and Social Council).

[42] UN Charter, Chapter XII.

[43] A particular outlet for this goal was the development of the New International Economic Order. The basic goals of the New International Economic Order were the reconstruction of the existing international economic system to improve development and welfare in developing countries, to narrow disparities between developing and developed states, and to give developing countries more control over their political, social, and economic destinies. See Edwin P. Reubens, "An Overview of the NIEO," in The Challenge of the New International Economic Order (Edwin P. Reubens ed., 1981), p. 1.

visions of world governance. Instead, the nuclear era, involving successive policies of deterrence, created a fragile balance of international stability.

It was in this political context that the First United Nations Conference on the Law of the Sea ("First Conference") was held. Rapid civilian technological developments facilitated extensive use of ocean resources, while military technology had increased the utility of submarine naval power.[44] The discovery of offshore hydrocarbons in the seabed and subsoil, and the means to exploit these resources, led to increasing claims of exclusive control over wider areas of sea adjacent to coastal States. Claims to the continental shelf led some States to assert claims to other ocean resources, most particularly fish. Increased interest in the seas as a source of food had led to the development of distant water fishing fleets with highly mechanized cannery ships and advanced sonar-equipped fishing vessels that could track the large migrations of fish.[45] Coastal States became very anxious to protect these resources and developing States particularly considered their geographical advantage as the opportunity to achieve economic development. For these developing States, it was insufficient to consider the seas as a common resource because their technological under-development meant that the established maritime States could continue to profit tremendously from the existing rules whereas the developing States would struggle to compete.[46] These economic interests came to challenge the interests of the developed States in maintaining the traditional freedoms of the oceans. Increasing claims to ocean space had the potential to interfere with the freedom of navigation, including the passage of warships, submarines, and other naval vessels. This tension between inclusive and exclusive uses came to a head during the First Conference.

Pursuant to resolution 1105 (XI), the General Assembly decided in 1957 to convoke an international conference "to examine the law of the sea, taking account not only of the legal, but also of the technical, biological, economic and political aspects of the problem, and to embody the results of its work in one or more international conventions or such other instruments as it may deem appropriate."[47] A report of the International

---

[44] Booth, at 338.   [45] McNees, at 188.

[46] "They viewed some aspects of freedom of the high seas as a fiction invented by the maritime nations to rob them of their living resources off their coasts." Charles Swan and James Ueberhorst, "The Conference on the Law of the Sea: A Report," 56 *Mich. L. Rev.* 1132 (1958). See also Shigeru Oda, "The Territorial Sea and Natural Resources," 4 *Int'l L. & Comp. Q.* 415, 424 (1955).

[47] GA Res. 1105, UN GAOR, 11th Sess., Supp. No. 17 at 54, ¶ 2, UN Doc. A/3572 (1957).

Law Commission containing draft articles and commentaries, as well as the records of debates in various bodies of the General Assembly, formed the bases of discussions at the First Conference.[48] This Conference, which was held in Geneva, was designed to codify the law of the sea in respect of four different maritime zones: the territorial sea, the contiguous zone, the continental shelf, and the high seas.

The participants at the First Conference succeeded in adopting four conventions: the Convention on the Territorial Sea and Contiguous Zone ("Territorial Sea Convention"); the Convention on the High Seas ("High Seas Convention"); the Convention on Fishing and Conservation of the Living Resources of the High Seas ("Fishing and Conservation Convention"); and the Convention on the Continental Shelf ("Continental Shelf Convention").[49] The High Seas Convention is the only convention of the four that purports to be generally declaratory of international law. In addition to these conventions, States attending the First Conference adopted an Optional Protocol on the Settlement of Disputes.[50]

---

[48] *Ibid.*, ¶ 9. The First Conference relied heavily on the preparatory work of the International Law Commission. The Commission had decided to include the regime of the high seas and the regime of the territorial sea on its agenda at its first session in 1949. The continental shelf was subsequently included amongst these topics because the Commission recognized the economic and social importance of the exploitation of the resources of the seabed and subsoil and did not believe that legal concepts should hamper a development that could benefit all mankind. Report of the International Law Commission to the General Assembly, UN GAOR at 384, UN Doc. A/1316 (1950), reprinted in *Documents of the Second Session including the Report of the Commission to the General Assembly,* [1950] 2 Y.B. Int'l L. Comm'n 364, UN Doc. A/CN.4/Ser.A/1950/Add.1, UN Sales No. 1957.V.3, vol. II (1957). The General Assembly also specifically requested that the International Law Commission examine the question of conservation of the living resources in connection with its work on the regime of the high seas. GA Res. 900, UN GAOR, 9th Sess., Supp. No. 21, at 51, UN Doc. A/2890 (1954). Work on the draft articles culminated in 1956 when the International Law Commission submitted a final report to the General Assembly containing seventy-three articles with commentaries for use at an international conference of plenipotentiaries. See Report of the International Law Commission to the General Assembly, UN GAOR, at 254–301, UN Doc. A/3159 (1956), reprinted in *Documents of the Eighth Session including the Report of the Commission to the General Assembly,* [1956] 2 Y.B. Int'l L. Comm'n 253, UN Doc. A/CN.4/Ser.A/1956/Add.1, UN Sales No. 1956.V.3, vol. II (1957).

[49] Convention on the Territorial Sea and Contiguous Zone, April 29, 1958, 15 UST 1606, 516 UNTS 205; Convention on the High Seas, April 29 1958, 13 UST 2312, 450 UNTS 82; Convention on Fishing and Conservation of the Living Resources of the High Seas, April 29, 1958, 17 UST 138, 559 UNTS 285; Convention on the Continental Shelf, April 29, 1958, 15 UST 1171, 499 UNTS 311.

[50] Optional Protocol of Signature Concerning the Compulsory Settlement of Disputes, Adopted by the United Nations Conference on the Law of the Sea, April 29, 1958, 450 UNTS 172.

Despite the success in codifying many rules regulating the use of the seas, the First Conference failed to reach an agreement on fixing a breadth either for the territorial sea or for fishery limits. Instead, a resolution was adopted requesting the General Assembly to convene a second international conference to address these particular issues.[51] Further to this proposal, the General Assembly decided, "that a second international conference of plenipotentiaries on the law of the sea should be called for the purpose of considering further the questions of the breadth of the territorial sea and fishery limits."[52] These two questions were considered simultaneously in 1960 at the Second United Nations Conference on the Law of the Sea ("Second Conference"), first in a Committee of the Whole and then in plenary meetings. The bulk of the time in the Committee of the Whole was spent on general debate, during which delegations mostly reiterated the concerns that had been expressed throughout the course of the First Conference. Again, economic interests were considered of paramount importance among the eighty-eight States in attendance along with the concomitant security interests of the coastal State over the waters adjacent to its coast. The Second Conference also failed to resolve the question of either fishery limits or the breadth of the territorial sea.

The question of dispute settlement in relation to the law of the sea was initially raised at the First Conference in the context of the Continental Shelf Convention.[53] Some delegations at the First Conference were strongly in favor of the inclusion of a dispute settlement mechanism,[54]

---

[51] Resolution VIII, UN Doc. A/CONF.13/L.56, reprinted in *United Nations Conference on the Law of the Sea*, Plenary Meetings, at 145, UN Doc. A/CONF.13/38, UN Sales No. 58.V.4, vol. II (1958).

[52] GA Res. 1307, UN GAOR, 13th Sess., Supp. No. 18, at 54, UN Doc. A/4090 (1958), para. 1.

[53] The draft articles adopted by the International Law Commission proposed that any disputes between States concerning the interpretation or application of the continental shelf provisions would be submitted to the ICJ at the request of any of the parties, unless agreement was reached on another method of settlement. Articles 67 to 73 of the Draft of the International Law Commission, UN Doc. A/3159, reprinted in *United Nations Conference on the Law of the Sea*, 4th Comm., at 125 (art. 73), UN Doc. A/CONF.13/42, UN Sales No. 58.V.4, vol. VI (1958). See also Kwang Lim Koh, "The Continental Shelf and the International Law Commission," 35 *B.U.L. Rev.* 523, 535 (1955) (describing the advantages of compulsory jurisdiction for the continental shelf regime).

[54] *First Conference*, 4th Comm., at 7, ¶18 (Netherlands); *ibid.*, at 7, ¶ 22 (Spain); *ibid.*, at 10, ¶ 13 (Colombia); *ibid.*, at 12, ¶ 9 (India) (provided it was subject to a declaration under art. 36 of the Court's Statute); *ibid.*, at 20, ¶ 14 (United States); *ibid.*, at 30, ¶ 31 (Canada) (acknowledging, however, that difficulties might arise for technical disputes); *ibid.*, at 101, ¶ 27 (Federal Republic of Germany); *ibid.*, at 100, ¶15 (Sweden); *ibid.*, at 101, ¶ 30 (Uruguay); *ibid.*, at 6, ¶ 8 (Greece).

particularly because of some of the vague expressions used in the articles.[55] As one delegate remarked, "In the absence of a proper definition of a continental shelf, and without any judicial body to whom points of interpretation could be referred, States would place on the provision whatever construction suited them."[56] This was especially the case "since they embodied new rules of law, which were a result of compromises between conflicting interests."[57] However, the very newness of the articles on the continental shelf was another reason as to why compulsory adjudication was considered inappropriate, as they had not been put "to the test of experience."[58] A further justification for the inclusion of mandatory jurisdiction was the perception that it was a way of protecting less powerful States when dealing with this new subject area in international law.[59]

Referral of disputes to the ICJ was resisted by other States because that forum had optional jurisdiction and it was thus considered inappropriate to be according it mandatory jurisdiction.[60] Argentina stated a common view:

His government did not accept the idea that it should be obliged to have recourse to the International Court for disputes in which agreement had not previously been reached between the parties. It preferred to have complete freedom to resort to normal methods of settlement and, where those methods proved unavailing, to be able to choose whether to refer the dispute to the Court or to any other arbitration body.[61]

Arguments were also presented that compulsory settlement went against the general trend in international law, which was "developing in the direction of option, rather than compulsory recourse to the International Court, a fact which should be taken into account in drafting an international instrument."[62] Despite arguments to the contrary, the use of compulsory jurisdiction was still viewed as detrimental to smaller States because it potentially gave powerful States the opportunity to

---

[55] *Ibid.*, at 9, ¶ 4 (Dominican Republic).   [56] *Ibid.*, at 44, ¶ 46 (Germany).

[57] *Ibid.*, at 99, ¶ 13 (Sweden).   [58] *Ibid.*, at 99, ¶ 7 (USSR).

[59] See, e.g., *ibid.*, at 101, ¶ 30 (Uruguay) ("international law was the only protection on which a small country could rely in cases of dispute").

[60] India, by way of compromise, proposed that a proviso be added to the article to the effect that the jurisdiction of the ICJ should be subject to art. 36 of the Court's Statute. India: proposal, UN Doc. A/CONF.13/C.4/L.61, reprinted in *ibid.*, at 142.

[61] *Ibid.*, at 99, ¶ 1 (Argentina).

[62] *Ibid.*, at 101, ¶ 32 (Romania). See also *ibid.*, at 100, ¶ 25 (Byelorussian Soviet Socialist Republic).

take unnecessary legal action as a means of bringing pressure to bear on others.[63]

Instead of relying on the jurisdiction of the ICJ, States supported the traditional means of dispute settlement that were set forth in Article 33 of the UN Charter.[64] In advocating a simple reference to Article 33 of the Charter, States were effectively arguing that the status quo should be maintained and that the conventions under consideration should be subjected to the traditional modes of dispute settlement. In response to these arguments, the United States pointed out that a reference to Article 33 was redundant, as nearly all States at the First Conference had accepted the UN Charter so that there was no need to repeat existing obligations.[65]

Ultimately, there was insufficient support at the First Conference for any form of compulsory dispute settlement: "while compulsory jurisdiction in international law represented a noble ideal, the time was not yet ripe for the inclusion of compulsory settlement clauses in all multilateral treaties."[66] The First Conference thus voted in favor of the adoption of an Optional Protocol.[67] The Optional Protocol covered all disputes arising out of the interpretation and application of the 1958 Conventions, except for the provisions subject to the dispute resolution mechanism in the Fishing and Conservation Convention. The disputes covered by the Optional Protocol were subject to the compulsory jurisdiction of the ICJ, unless the parties instead agreed to arbitration or conciliation. In the event that conciliation failed (i.e. the recommendations of the conciliation commission were not accepted), the matter could be taken to the Court. There was no procedure for the appointment of the arbitral tribunal or conciliation commission and no other rules of procedure

---

[63] *Ibid.*, at 99, ¶ 4 (ROK). See also *ibid.*, at 23–24, ¶ 12 (ROK).

[64] *Ibid.*, at 16, ¶ 16 (Chile). See also *ibid.*, at 23, ¶ 3 (Poland); *ibid.*, at 19, ¶ 8 (Pakistan). In support of the methods of dispute settlement under art. 33, ROK noted that the ICJ had optional jurisdiction and thus could be used under the terms of the Charter. *Ibid.*, at 23, ¶ 11(ROK). For those in favor of the art. 33 approach, Argentina produced a proposal providing: "Any disputes that may arise between States concerning the interpretation or application of the preceding articles shall be settled by the procedure provided for in the Charter of the United Nations." Argentina: Second Revised Proposal, UN Doc. A/CONF.13/C.4/L.51, reprinted in *ibid.*, at 140 (supported by Bulgaria, ROK, Soviet Union).

[65] *Ibid.*, at 100, ¶ 21 (United States). See also *ibid.*, at 101, ¶ 36 (China).

[66] *First Conference*, Plenary Meetings, at 33, ¶ 36 (Iran). See also *ibid.*, at 10, ¶ 28 (Canada); *ibid.*, at 31, ¶ 14 (France); *ibid.*, at 31, ¶ 8 (USSR).

[67] *Ibid.*, at 55 (considering the Eighth Report of the Drafting Committee of the Conference on the judicial settlement of disputes).

were stipulated within the Optional Protocol. No procedure was linked to any particular type of dispute and no reservations or exceptions to the Optional Protocol were envisaged.

States thus maintained their traditional stance on consent-based, non-compulsory methods of dispute settlement during the First and Second Conferences.[68] This attitude continued despite the growing awareness of the demands of interdependence in the international system. Techno-logical advances, growing environmental awareness, and interconnected security policies marked the beginning of an era of interdependence. States had increasingly recognized the need to coordinate responses to particular matters on a global or regional basis and became more willing to sacrifice some degree of sovereignty in favor of participation in coop-erative arrangements that would further their interests. The result was an increase in the creation of international institutions and regimes to regulate various aspects of international relations. International regimes are formed when actors' expectations converge in a given area of interna-tional relations.[69] Particular issues become conducive for regime forma-tion when there is widespread, general recognition that cooperation is essential to achieve particular goals.[70] States will participate in a multi-lateral regime when the problems that the regime is designed to address cannot be resolved on a unilateral basis and are sufficiently important to

---

[68] The stalemate reached on substantive provisions at the Second Conference meant that questions of dispute settlement were never discussed.

[69] Stephen Krasner has defined regimes as:

> ... implicit or explicit principles, norms, rules and decision-making procedures around which actors' expectations converge in a given area of international relations. Principles are beliefs of fact, causation and rectitude. Norms are standards of behavior defined in terms of rights and obligations. Rules are specific prescriptions or proscriptions for action. Decision-making procedures are prevailing practices for making and implementing collective choice.

Stephen D. Krasner, "Structural Causes and Regime Consequences: Regimes as Intervening Variables," in *International Regimes* (Stephen D. Krasner ed., 1983), pp. 1, 2. Robert Keohane has defined regimes more simply as, "institutions with explicit rules, agreed upon by governments, that pertain to particular sets of issues in international relations." Robert O. Keohane, *International Institutions and State Power: Essays in International Relations Theory* (1989), p. 4. Krasner's definition has been criticized because of the difficulties in precisely identifying, and distinguishing between, the relevant procedures. See, e.g., Stephan Haggard and Beth A. Simmons, "Theories of International Regimes," 41 *Int'l Org.* 491, 493 (1987); Oran R. Young, "International Regimes: Toward a New Theory of Institutions," 39 *World Pol.* 104, 106 (1986).

[70] "The creation of international rules, regimes and institutions is seen as a purposeful activity designed to improve unsatisfactory situations." Kenneth W. Abbot, "Modern International Relations Theory: A Prospectus for International Lawyers," 14 *Yale J. Int'l L.* 335, 354 (1989).

warrant participation.[71] Once established, regime maintenance requires the ongoing collaboration of participants, including exchanges of information and avenues to alter the rules of the regime as required to meet changing expectations arising from new circumstances. These systems enhance compliance with international agreements as they establish legitimate standards of behavior for States to follow by reducing the incentives to cheat and enhancing the value of reputation.[72] Regimes do not require the inclusion of a mandatory system of dispute resolution. Instead, the theories espoused have accounted for the fact that there has typically not been compulsory jurisdiction available to States, nor any enforcement mechanisms. Cooperative arrangements could be sustained because of the joint interests in the common goal, the inbuilt means to vary the process as needed and through the benefits of iteration and concomitant reputational aspects.

These dynamics shaped the process involved in the elaboration of UNCLOS. After the failure of the Second Conference to settle the breadth of the territorial sea, the two superpowers wished to resolve their navigational rights in territorial seas, particularly in international straits. The Soviet Union circulated a diplomatic note to sixty countries to inquire about the possibility of a new conference to fix the breadth of the territorial sea at twelve miles.[73] As the Soviet Union's military capabilities, particularly its submarine fleet, improved and enlarged, it developed a correspondingly greater interest in guaranteeing navigational rights through international straits. The United States recognized that claims to twelve-mile territorial seas would be increasingly difficult to resist – both diplomatically and as a practical matter. The Soviet Union and the United States thus decided to circulate draft articles on the territorial sea and straits.[74] Claims to fishing rights in waters adjacent to territorial seas were also gathering momentum, and received support

---

[71] Elliot L. Richardson, "Dispute Settlement under the Convention on the Law of the Sea: A Flexible and Comprehensive Extension of the Rule of the Law to Ocean Space," in *Contemporary Issues in International Law, Essays in Honor of Louis B. Sohn* (Thomas Buergenthal ed., 1984), p. 149.

[72] See Robert O. Keohane, *After Hegemony: Cooperation and Discord in the World Political Economy* (1984), pp. 244–45.

[73] Elmar Rauch, "Military Uses of the Oceans" [1984] 28 *German. Y.B. Int'l L.*, 229, 233 (1985).

[74] Bernard H. Oxman, "The Third United Nations Conference on the Law of the Sea: The Tenth Session," 76 *Am. J. Int'l L.* 1, 4 (1982). See also Bernard H. Oxman, "The Regime of Warships Under the United Nations Convention on the Law of the Sea," 24 *Va. J. Int'l L.* 809, 810 (1984). ("[P]rotecting the mobility and use of warships was a central motivating force in organizing the Third United Nations Conference on the Law of the Sea.")

from the ICJ in the *Icelandic Fisheries* decision.[75] When the technology was developed to recover the mineral resources found in manganese nodules lying on the floor of the oceans, a new opportunity was open to coastal States to claim yet another ocean resource. The economic opportunities afforded by the development of deep seabed mining technology prompted Ambassador Arvid Pardo of Malta to propose that the UN declare the seabed and ocean floor "underlying the seas beyond the limits of present national jurisdiction" to be "the common heritage of mankind," not subject to appropriation by any State for its sole use.[76] Developing States did not want to be excluded from this new resource and thus advocated for the creation of an international institution that would share the benefits from this enterprise with all States. The efforts of the superpowers to focus on draft texts relating to the territorial sea and straits were resisted, as developing States wished to prioritize an international agreement creating a multilateral institution to regulate deep seabed mining.

Following Ambassador Pardo's proposal that the deep seabed and ocean floor be declared as a common heritage area, the General Assembly established an Ad Hoc Committee to study the peaceful uses of the seabed and the ocean floor beyond the limits of national jurisdiction.[77] These interests in maritime spaces, and the resources contained therein, prompted consideration of a range of law of the sea issues within an international forum. As different groups of States were interested in particular aspects of ocean use, it became immediately obvious that the formulation of rules relating to one use would have to incorporate consideration of other usages. States shared an interest in creating a new international agreement to address this range of ocean uses.

Preparations for the Third United Nations Conference on the Law of the Sea ("Third Conference") thus began in 1967 within the UN Seabed Committee, which was organized under the auspices of the First Committee of the General Assembly. Instead of relying on the International Law Commission again, an Ad Hoc Committee and then a permanent Seabed Committee was entrusted with the responsibility of formulating draft texts to be used as the bases of discussion at the Third Conference.

[75] Fisheries Jurisdiction (*United Kingdom* v. *Iceland*; *Federal Republic of Germany* v. *Iceland*) 1974 ICJ 3, 175 (July 25).

[76] The complete address is in UN GAOR 1st Comm., 22d Sess., 1515th mtg. at 1–68, UN Doc. A/C.1/PV.1515 (1967) and UN GAOR 1st Comm., 22d Sess. 1515th mtg. at 1–6, UN Doc. A/C.1/PV.1516 (1967). See also UN GAOR 1st Comm., 22d Sess., UN Doc. A/6695 (1967) (Malta's Memorandum to the Secretary-General).

[77] GA Res. 2340, UN GAOR, 22d Sess., Supp. No. 16, at 14, UN Doc. A/6716 (1967).

One of the main tasks of the Committee was to establish the rules and regulations of the international authority that would regulate, supervise, and control all seabed activities. In 1970, the General Assembly adopted resolution 2750 C at its XXV session wherein it decided to convene an adequately prepared conference on the law of the sea. This conference was particularly intended to develop and implement the concept of the common heritage of mankind; stabilize the breadth of the territorial sea; and establish an effective regime for the exploitation of the living resources of the sea in the area adjacent to the territorial sea.

The Third Conference was convened in Caracas in 1974 and its work spanned eight years. The Third Conference negotiations were extremely complex because of the range of issues being considered, the number of States involved, and the importance of the interests at stake. "Nearly every issue at the Conference raised short-term or long-term implications for States and every proposal at the Conference had adverse or beneficial consequences for States."[78] In addition to the traditional blocs of States (western, socialist, developing), States' allegiances varied in relation to the particular issue area. Groupings of States for negotiation purposes cut across geographic, economic, and ideological lines when particular geographic features (length of coast, width of continental shelf) were specially relevant or when regional, economic, or military interests came into play. A further complicating factor was the interrelated nature of many of the provisions on the law of the sea. States were hesitant to commit to certain positions on one issue for fear that it would affect their negotiating position on another issue that was still being discussed.

Dispute settlement provisions were initially neglected during the early negotiations at the Third Conference.[79] Each of the Main Committees was meant to address the question of dispute resolution but it was often not mentioned during debates nor included in draft texts. As a result, an informal group was established to consider the main dispute settlement issues and present alternative texts. In drafting these texts, four fundamental aims were espoused as the basis of the dispute

---

[78] Tommy T. B. Koh and Shanmugam Jayakumar, "The Negotiating Process of the Third United Nations Conference on the Law of the Sea," in 1 *United Nations Convention on the Law of the Sea 1982: A Commentary* (Myron H. Nordquist et al. eds., 1989), pp. 29, 42.

[79] Discussions about dispute settlement in the UN Seabed Committee were predominantly in relation to deep seabed mining, more so than law of the sea generally, or in relation to a range of specific issue areas.

settlement procedures.[80] First, the settlement of disputes was to be based on law to avoid disputes being settled through the political and economic pressures of the more powerful States. Second, the greatest possible uniformity in the interpretation of the Convention would be sought through compulsory dispute settlement. Third, exceptions would be carefully determined in order to enhance the obligatory character of the settlement regime. Finally, the system of dispute settlement had to constitute an integral part of the Convention rather than be included as an optional protocol. The President of the Conference then took the initiative in 1976 to include a set of provisions relating to dispute settlement in the Informal Single Negotiating Text as a procedural device to serve as the basis of discussions.[81] The most difficult issues to be resolved during the ensuing negotiations were the available fora for dispute settlement as well as procedures in relation to the delimitation of extended maritime zones and the exercise of coastal States' sovereign rights in the Exclusive Economic Zone ("EEZ"). As negotiations on dispute settlement progressed, the interconnection beteen substance and procedure became more pronounced. Questions of substance were left unresolved until questions of dispute settlement were settled, or were concurrently finalized.

Eight years of negotiations culminated in the adoption of the Convention in New York on April 30, 1982 by a vote of 130 to 4, with 17 abstentions. The four negative votes were cast by the United States, Israel, Venezuela, and Turkey. The States abstaining at that time included the United Kingdom, the Netherlands, Belgium, the Federal Republic of Germany, Italy, Spain, and the majority of eastern European countries. The Convention was then opened for signature in December 1982.[82] The United States, along with the majority of industrialized nations, decided not to sign UNCLOS at this time because of their dissatisfaction with the provisions in Part XI of the Convention relating to the deep

---

[80] Ambassador R. Galindo Pohl summarized these themes in 1974, cited in A. O. Adede, *The System for Settlement of Disputes Under the United Nations Convention on the Law of the Sea* (1987), p. 39.

[81] Memorandum by the President of the Conference on doc. A/CONF.62/WP.9, UN Doc. A/CONF.62/WP.9/Add.1 (1976), reprinted in 5 *Third United Nations Conference on the Law of the Sea: Official Records* at 122, ¶ 6, UN Sales No. E.76.V.8 (1984).

[82] One hundred and seventeen countries and a UN body representing Namibia and the Cook islands signed the Convention; twenty-three countries attending the ceremony did not sign, including the United States, and twenty-four countries did not even attend the ceremony.

seabed mining regime.[83] To enter into force, sixty States had to ratify UNCLOS.[84] When it became apparent that the Convention could enter into force without the participation of the United States and other industrialized States, negotiations on deep seabed mining were reopened. In 1994, these negotiations resulted in the UN General Assembly adopting the Agreement Relating to the Implementation of Part XI ("the 1994 Agreement") on July 28, 1994.[85] The Convention entered into force on November 16, 1994.

UNCLOS provides a complex regime with respect to ocean space and uses. It deals with the delimitation of and jurisdiction over all marine areas through provisions on the territorial sea, archipelagic waters, straits, contiguous zone, the EEZ, continental shelf, high seas, deep seabed, and the airspace above the oceans. The Convention also sets out the rights and obligations of States with respect to these areas. Activities such as fishing, mining, navigation, and marine scientific research are all addressed. The Convention also includes provisions on the protection and preservation of the marine environment and the transfer of technology. As stated in the Preamble to the Convention, the States parties were "[p]rompted by a desire to settle . . . *all* issues related to the law of the sea."[86] Yet issues are neither completely nor comprehensively regulated by the Convention. In some instances, the Convention does directly regulate the rights and duties of States with respect to particular activities and particular zones (as with rights of passage and the deep seabed). In other instances, it provides a framework for States to cooperate and negotiate further agreements for certain issues (such as the marine environment; the transfer of technology; delimitation of maritime boundaries; and fishing of straddling stocks and highly migratory species). For disputes relating to the interpretation or application

---

[83] Agreement on the United States' Actions Concerning the Conference on the Law of the Sea, II PUB. PAPERS 911 (July 9, 1982). Colson reports that the United Kingdom and Germany also refused to sign UNCLOS because of their opposition to Part XI, whereas France, Japan, Italy, Belgium, and the Netherlands signed but issued statements that ratification would not occur until an acceptable solution was found to the seabed mining section. David A. Colson, "US Accession to the UNCLOS," 7 *Geo. Int'l Envtl. L. Rev.* 651, 657 (1995).

[84] UNCLOS, art. 308(1).

[85] Agreement Relating to the Implementation of Part XI of the United Nations Convention on the Law of the Sea, November 16, 1994, S. TREATY Doc. No. 104–24, 1836 UNTS 3 (1995).

[86] UNCLOS, Preamble (emphasis added).

of the Convention, States parties may have recourse to the procedural mechanism set out in Part XV.[87]

Section 1 of Part XV, entitled "General Provisions," essentially requires States to settle disputes through diplomatic channels prior to referring the matter to the compulsory procedures found in Section 2 of Part XV.[88] All traditional methods of dispute resolution are available to States and alternative dispute settlement procedures may take priority over those in UNCLOS. When disputant States have not settled their differences through the various means available under Section 1 of Part XV, the dispute is to be submitted at the request of any party to the appropriate forum under the terms of the Convention.[89] Only disputes falling within the limitations and exceptions set out in Section 3 need not be submitted for compulsory settlement by binding decision.

By the time the Convention entered into force, there was a new era in international relations. The Cold War had ended, resulting in the disintegration of the socialist bloc and the emergence of the United States as the sole superpower. Further technological advancements accelerated and deepened interdependence. Many traditional international barriers have been broken down with the growth in communication between a variety of actors in the international system. There has been a continuing emphasis on a range of issues being organized through international processes, particularly through the use of global and regional institutions.

Dispute resolution in international relations has also altered to some extent. The most significant change in this regard was the revitalization of the Security Council with the end of the Cold War. The obligatory measures that can be adopted under Chapter VII of the Charter have now been exercised in a range of situations. This system remains limited, however, as the interests of the permanent members of the Security Council do not consistently coalesce in addressing particular issues.

Avenues for dispute settlement are also now available in a range of issue specific tribunals. The World Trade Organization ("WTO") has mandatory jurisdiction over allegations of nullification or impairment

---

[87] *Ibid.*, arts. 186–191. Part XV is divided into three sections: first, general provisions; second, compulsory procedures entailing binding decisions; and, third, the limitations and exceptions to the compulsory procedures. A special dispute settlement regime is established for deep seabed mining under Part XI and the Agreement.

[88] *Ibid.*, art. 279.   [89] *Ibid.*, art. 286.

of the benefits parties expect to derive under the WTO Agreement.[90] Tribunals have also been established with compulsory jurisdiction to deal with trade disputes on a regional basis.[91] Human rights courts, international criminal tribunals, and compensation commissions have all been created as part of the recognition of the rights and duties of individuals in the international system. The number of cases being submitted to the ICJ has been steadily increasing and *ad hoc* tribunals have resolved a range of diverse matters. The proliferation of consent-based tribunals and the burgeoning ICJ docket indicates a greater willingness on the part of States to refer questions to third-party review and decision. The use of formal dispute settlement procedures remains the exception rather than the rule, however, with the bulk of conflicts or differences being resolved through diplomatic and political avenues.

In this context, the entry into force of UNCLOS may be viewed as another instance of using international tribunals as part of a current trend in international relations to rely more on the rule of law than on political or economic pressures. What makes the Convention more exceptional in this regard is that it sets out compulsory procedures entailing binding decisions for subjects that touch on the interests of all States. To accept such a procedural mechanism is a significant departure from the methods States have traditionally relied on for resolving disputes. Because the Convention's dispute settlement provisions appear so divergent from the norm in international politics, it must be asked whether such a deviation was warranted and how this new approach is likely to work given the habits of old.

Present Perspective

The entry into force of UNCLOS has been lauded as "the most important development in the settlement of international disputes since the adoption of the UN Charter and the Statute of the International Court of Justice."[92] The Convention could even be "important in preparing the

---

[90] Agreement on Trade-Related Aspects of Intellectual Property Rights, April 15, 1994, Marrakesh Agreement Establishing the World Trade Organization, Annex 1C, *Legal Instruments – Results of the Uruguay Round* vol. 31; 33 ILM 81 (1994).

[91] Examples include the Court of the Common Market for Eastern and Southern Africa and the Court of Justice of the European Communities. See John Collier and Vaughan Lowe, *The Settlement of Disputes in International Law* (1999), pp. 105–09.

[92] Boyle, "Dispute Settlement," at 37. Professor Sohn asserts that the Convention constitutes the "first time such a complete system of conflict resolution has been embodied in a global treaty." He considers the system to be both comprehensive and

ground for compulsory third party settlement in other areas of international cooperation."[93] Many benefits have been identified in what is generally described as a flexible, comprehensive, and binding dispute settlement system for the oceans. One claim is that the availability of compulsory arbitration or adjudication may prevent the destabilization of the Convention by unilateral action in the absence of agreed authoritative collective mechanisms for interpretation.[94] Dispute settlement proceedings could further prove useful to States in political matters, as it would provide a means of resolving a crisis without imposing direct responsibility upon the governments involved.[95] In this regard, States could be provided with a "graceful retreat" as they "yield to the rule of law as embodied in the binding judgment of a disinterested tribunal" rather than the political or economic pressure of another State.[96] The availability of compulsory procedures under the Convention is meant to provide States with another means, in addition to coercive economic or military measures, to enforce their rights or to prevent violations of the Convention.[97] For these assorted reasons a system of compulsory,

---

pioneering. Sohn, "Settlement of Law of the Sea Disputes," at 205. The degree of consensus reached and the inclusion of the regime in the main text are "unique." Kindt, at 1098–99.

[93] Marcel M. T. A. Brus, *Third Party Dispute Settlement in an Interdependent World* (1995), p. 23.

[94] Bernard H. Oxman, "Commentary," in *Implementation of the Law of the Sea Convention Through International Institutions* (Alfred H. A. Soons ed., 1990), pp. 648, 651. Binding procedures for dispute resolution were considered necessary in order to avoid any instability or uncertainty that could eventuate if parties to UNCLOS were left to interpret the provisions of the Convention unilaterally. Kindt, at 1116. A compulsory regime was also needed so that States would not lose the compromise achieved in the course of negotiations. The dispute settlement provisions were thus designed to guarantee the integrity of the text as well as to control the implementation and development of the Convention by States parties. Boyle, "Dispute Settlement," at 38–39.

[95] Guillaume, at 851.

[96] Statement by Expert Panel, "U.S. Policy on the Settlement of Disputes in the Law of the Sea," 81 *Am. J. Int'l L.* 438, 440 (1987). The establishment of a binding dispute settlement regime would "induce greater self-restraint, encourage officials to seek legal advice before acting, and . . . impel lawyers to be cautious in their advice." *Ibid.* See also Mark E. Rosen, "Military Mobility and the 1982 UN Law of the Sea Convention," 7 *Geo. Int'l Envtl. L. Rev.* 717, 718 (1995) ("written convention [is] the preferable method of protecting our current operating environment rather than the customary practice of gunboat diplomacy").

[97] In considering the United States position on the ratification of UNCLOS, Schachte comments that "as a nation committed to the rule of law, the use of military force to resolve legal conflicts between parties and non-parties to the Convention should not be the preferred method of challenging excessive coastal state claims."

impartial third-party adjudication was deemed essential to the overall structure of the Convention.[98]

Despite this enthusiasm, it has also been argued that the Convention does not meet these many expectations but lacks both comprehensiveness and effectiveness. Oda, for example, has noted that UNCLOS was "not so very different from the 1958 [Conventions on the Law of the Sea], in that not all ocean disputes are necessarily made subject to compulsory settlement."[99] The exceptions to and limitations on the mandatory system in UNCLOS may demonstrate that the system in Part XV is unlikely to function well, if at all. Courts and tribunals will only be vested with mandatory jurisdiction if States fail to resolve any differences through diplomatic channels.[100] In accordance with Article 281, for States Parties to institute compulsory proceedings entailing binding decisions under Section 2 when a separate agreement governs an aspect of the oceans, they must have exhausted attempts at dispute settlement under the separate agreement and that agreement cannot exclude resort to the procedures in UNCLOS. Furthermore, if States are parties to a general, regional, or bilateral agreement that provides for a dispute settlement procedure entailing a binding decision, then that procedure applies in lieu of the mechanism in the Convention.[101] These exclusions were necessary in light of the large number of multilateral, regional, and bilateral treaties that relate to the law of the sea and often have their own dispute settlement procedures. In the *Southern Bluefin Tuna* case, the Tribunal reasoned that since States had adopted these agreements with the idea that there would not be a unilateral resort to compulsory procedures, it was contrary to what these States had consented to permit recourse to the mandatory UNCLOS mechanism.[102] In taking

---

William J. Schachte, Jr., "National Security: Customary International Law and the Convention on the Law of the Sea," 7 *Geo. Int'l Envtl. L. Rev.* 709, 713 (1995).

[98] John R. Stevenson and Bernard H. Oxman, "The Preparations for the Law of the Sea Conference," 68 *Am. J. Int'l L.* 1, 31 (1974).

[99] Shigeru Oda, "Dispute Settlement Prospects in the Law of the Sea," 44 *Int'l & Comp. L.Q.* 863, 863 (1995).

[100] See UNCLOS, arts. 279 and 280.   [101] *Ibid.*, art. 282.

[102] The Tribunal stated:

> The Tribunal is of the view that the existence of such a body of treaty practice – postdating as well as antedating the conclusion of UNCLOS – tends to confirm the conclusion that States parties to UNCLOS may, by agreement, preclude subjection of their disputes to section 2 procedures in accordance with Article 281(1). To hold that disputes implicating obligations under both UNCLOS and an implementing treaty such as the [Convention on the Conservation of Southern Bluefin Tuna] – as such disputes typically may – must

this approach, the Tribunal effectively rejected arguments that UNCLOS created a comprehensive and effective regime for the resolution of all disputes, as well as the argument that decisions on jurisdiction "should lean in favour of the effectiveness and comprehensive character of the dispute settlement regime, itself a key aspect of the UNCLOS regime."[103]

Views supporting the comprehensive nature of the Convention are further undercut by Section 3 of Part XV of the Convention, which specifically sets out the limitations and exceptions to the applicability of compulsory procedures entailing a binding decision in Articles 297 and 298.[104] Rather than allowing all disputes of interpretation and application of the Convention to be submitted to mandatory third-party procedures, Part XV had to be designed to protect the primary interests at stake for each issue area. Richardson has noted as much:

> Various forms of dispute settlement . . . fall along a continuum of strength that is defined by the degree to which the particular form of dispute settlement intrudes upon a nation's sovereignty. The more comprehensive, mandatory, and binding the form of dispute settlement, the less willing nations will be to submit to its jurisdiction when the substantive interests involved are considered too important an aspect of sovereignty to risk an unfavorable outcome. Thus, the particular form of dispute resolution must be tailored to the problems it is intended to deal with. Otherwise, nations will refuse to utilize the procedures.[105]

From this perspective, mandatory jurisdiction will only be necessary for a limited number of disputes arising under the Convention.

This book analyzes when compulsory procedures are indispensable for the issues explicitly addressed in Articles 297 and 298, as well as for the deep seabed.[106] An examination of the different issue areas referred to in Part XV indicates whether the dispute settlement system in the

be brought within the reach of section 2 of Part XV of UNCLOS would be effectively to deprive of substantial effect the dispute settlement provisions of those implementing agreements which prescribe disputes resolution by means of the parties' choice.
Southern Bluefin Tuna, Jurisdiction, para. 63.

[103] Southern Bluefin Tuna Case, *Australia and New Zealand v. Japan*, Australia and New Zealand, Reply on Jurisdiction, vol. 1, Text, March 31, 2000, para. 31.

[104] See Oda, "Dispute Settlement Prospects," at 863 (noting that the provisions of Part XV are not sufficiently comprehensive to cover all disputes relating to interpretation and application and that some disputes are expressly exempted from compulsory settlement by the judicial and arbitral tribunals).

[105] Richardson, "Dispute Settlement," at 153.

[106] As such, questions such as the delimitation of the outer limits of the continental shelf, the rights and duties of land-locked and geographically disadvantaged States, and the transfer of marine technology are outside the scope of this study.

Convention is the "pivot" or "cement" of the new law of the sea. The answer cannot be provided in a manichean fashion. The dispute settlement system in UNCLOS relies on a spectrum of resolution techniques – ranging from formal adjudication or arbitration, to compulsory conciliation (of varying impact), to voluntary conciliation, to diplomatic initiatives and negotiation. What procedure is available depends on the substantive question in dispute. Clearly, States were not of the view that mandatory jurisdiction was essential for every issue regulated under the Convention. In some instances, mandatory jurisdiction is an essential complement in the regulation of specific issue areas – either to guarantee the substantive rules formulated in the Convention or to elaborate on the provisions of the Convention if no other international forum is available. In other instances, the emphasis has been placed on national decision-making rather than the use of international processes. A preference for diplomatic settlement or other consent-based methods of dispute resolution also remains evident with respect to a range of issues.

Part XV had to be constructed to reflect the political dynamic of the Third Conference and while the result cannot be described as perfect, it is evident that the dispute settlement regime is carefully tailored to specific issue areas to ensure the greatest workability possible. Although resort to mandatory arbitration or adjudication has been excluded for some questions when this avenue could have served a valuable purpose, States rejected this approach because it did not accord with political realities or because binding dispute settlement was not necessary. Such a selective approach does not undermine the viability of the Convention for those issues. International regimes have been able to function quite successfully regardless of the availability of a system of mandatory jurisdiction. Instead, external regulating factors, mutual interests, and diplomatic avenues facilitate dispute settlement. The normative rules governing the uses of the oceans thus remain effective regardless of whether there is mandatory jurisdiction available or not. The Convention certainly represents the new law of the sea but compulsory dispute settlement procedures entailing binding decisions are only essential to some aspects of this law and not others.

2   The Dispute Settlement Procedure under UNCLOS

Part XV of UNCLOS is a complex dispute settlement system that entails both traditional consent-based processes as well as mandatory procedures. In both respects, flexibility for States parties is a key feature. Section 1 of Part XV anticipates that States will pursue a range of dispute settlement options both within and outside the UNCLOS framework, reflecting that States have been accustomed to settling disputes in a variety of ways as those disputes arose and as demanded by the situation – not through predetermined means. Typically, diplomatic initiatives and negotiation have been the most efficient way to resolve a conflict. Resolution through political channels prior to judicial settlement is promoted in UNCLOS through the obligation to proceed expeditiously to an exchange of views when differences over the interpretation and application of the Convention emerge. States also retain the right to resolve conflicts through alternative (bilateral, regional, or general) agreements. This allowance was necessary in light of the large number of treaties that are specific to a particular issue area in the law of the sea and that incorporate their own dispute settlement systems.

Reliance is not entirely placed on consent-based methods of dispute resolution, however. The scope and complexity of UNCLOS as a constitutive instrument demanded procedural guarantees. For States to enjoy the benefits of the Convention, they simultaneously consent to binding and mandatory dispute resolution procedures. The large number of participants at the Third Conference meant that referral to a distinct international process was needed to safeguard the balances and compromises achieved in negotiating the Convention. Yet the procedure for dispute settlement had to be constructed very carefully to make it acceptable to States. There were considerable differences of opinion on alternative third-party methods for settling disputes. Some States, for example, had traditionally preferred arbitration whereas others wanted to prevent the proliferation of international tribunals in favor of bestowing the necessary competence on the ICJ. The procedure selected had to be sufficiently flexible to cater to these preferences. The way the States parties anticipated the dispute settlement procedures working reflects on whether compulsory procedures entailing binding decisions are requisite for the operation of the normative provisions of the Convention. It will be demonstrated that Part XV is integral to UNCLOS in that the dispute settlement procedures are closely related to the substantive provisions of the Convention. These links are particularly evident when considering Section 3 of Part XV, which sets out the limitations and exceptions to the compulsory procedures in relation to specific issue areas. While compulsory dispute settlement is integral to the effective operation of the Convention, the emphasis in Part XV is on consent-based modes of dispute settlement and choice of procedures. The compulsory dispute settlement mechanism in UNCLOS is thus clearly limited on a procedural level – in terms of deference to traditional consent-based methods – and on a substantive level – with respect to the disputes that are excluded from mandatory jurisdiction.

The first section of this chapter describes the general obligations imposed on States relating to the pacific settlement of disputes. It illustrates the emphasis that remains on traditional consent-based methods of dispute resolution. In particular, the relationship of dispute settlement provisions in other treaties to the procedures available in UNCLOS is examined. The jurisdictional decision in *Southern Bluefin Tuna* is highly instructive in this regard. That Tribunal's decision on jurisdiction demonstrates that Part XV is not an entirely comprehensive mechanism and that alternative, consent-based, procedures remain valid in regulating aspects of the law of the sea. The second section of this chapter then considers how the compulsory procedures entailing binding decisions operate with respect to disputes not excluded from Part XV proceedings. In particular, the complementary role of provisional measures to compulsory procedures is examined. The final part of this section then turns to the specialized, compulsory procedure of prompt release of vessels. Certain disputes arising from the failure to release vessels promptly upon the payment of a reasonable bond are subject to their own particular mechanism under the Convention. The resolution of these disputes has been one of the main tasks of the International Tribunal for the

Law of the Sea ("ITLOS") in its initial years. These early decisions are shaping the jurisprudence in this area as the Tribunal works through questions of jurisdiction and admissibility, as well as determining the scope of what constitutes a reasonable bond. The final section of this chapter outlines what disputes are potentially excluded from mandatory jurisdiction. These exceptions and limitations are then explored in detail in the two subsequent chapters.

General Obligations Relating to the Pacific Settlement of Disputes

Prior to the resort to compulsory procedures entailing binding decisions, States parties must have recourse to alternative methods of dispute settlement. Section 1 of Part XV permits States to utilize a range of peaceful methods, including settlement under separate agreements. This Section highlights the continuing relevance of traditional, consent-based modes of dispute resolution in relation to the interpretation and application of UNCLOS and emphasizes the flexibility that must be accorded to States in choosing methods for dispute resolution. Negotiation and settlement through diplomatic channels is emphasized through the obligation to exchange views. The use of conciliation is also encouraged through the inclusion of a separate procedure in Annex V of the Convention. Furthermore, certain deference is accorded to alternate modes of dispute settlement that may be available in other international agreements. States may pursue peaceful means of their own choice and only utilize the UNCLOS system once this agreement does not exclude any further procedure. The jurisdictional decision in *Southern Bluefin Tuna* is exemplary in this regard. States also have the flexibility to utilize procedures entailing binding decisions under general, regional or bilateral agreements in lieu of the process in Part XV. The interaction of those procedures with UNCLOS was considered in the provisional measures stage of the *MOX Plant case* between Ireland and the United Kingdom, and at the June, 2003 hearings in the merits phase of the case.

Preliminary Means of Dispute Settlement under UNCLOS

Section 1 of Part XV, entitled "General Provisions," essentially requires States to settle disputes through diplomatic channels prior to reference to the compulsory procedures of Section 2 of Part XV. There is a fundamental obligation on States to settle any dispute between them by peaceful means.[1] The main emphasis in this regard is on the right of States to choose any mode of dispute settlement (other than the use of force). Article 279 of the Convention refers to the range of dispute settlement methods set out under Article 33(1) of the UN Charter.[2] As such, this obligation adds little to the duties that are already imposed on States, as virtually all States are members of the UN, and the UNCLOS provision thus carries as much weight as Article 33 of the UN Charter in the resolution of disputes.[3] What is important about the reference to Article 33 of the UN Charter is that it emphasizes the variety of consent-based modes of dispute settlement that remain open to States prior to the institution of mandatory procedures entailing binding decisions. Article 280 reinforces this view by stipulating that the right of States parties to agree to any peaceful means of dispute settlement of their own choice is not impaired by any of the provisions in Part XV. States remain the "complete masters" of how their disputes are settled.[4]

The right of States to use methods of their choosing prior to resort to arbitration or adjudication conforms to political and diplomatic practice. Certainly the resolution of a conflict through diplomatic channels or negotiations is likely to be perceived as the preferable mode of dispute settlement even with the alternative avenues of third-party intervention available. "States are reluctant to give up their control over diplomatic and political options for resolving their disputes, and . . . are more comfortable seeking political legitimization, rather than declarations of

---

[1] UNCLOS, art. 279.

[2] Article 33, para. 1 reads: "The parties to any dispute, the continuance of which is likely to endanger the maintenance of international peace and security, shall, first of all, seek a solution by negotiation, enquiry, mediation, conciliation, arbitration, judicial settlement, resort to regional agencies or arrangements, or other peaceful means of their own choice." UN Charter, art. 33(1). By referring only to the "means" of dispute settlement set out in Article 33, the Convention avoids the possible restriction of Part XV only applying to disputes "the continuance of which is likely to endanger the maintenance of international peace and security", as stipulated in Article 33. 5 *United Nations Convention on the Law of the Sea 1982 A Commentary*, p. 18.

[3] Gamble, "Dispute Settlement in Perspective," at 326.

[4] 5 *United Nations Convention on the Law of the Sea 1982: A Commentary*, p. 20. See also A. L. C. De Mestral, "Compulsory Dispute Settlement in the Third United Nations Convention on the Law of the Sea: A Canadian Perspective," in *Contemporary Issues in International Law, Essays in Honor of Louis B. Sohn* (Thomas Buergenthal ed., 1984), pp. 169, 181 (noting that the general provisions of Section 1 reflect the desire of the socialist States to utilize the traditional body of international law dealing with the voluntary settlement of international disputes).

legal validity, for their actions."[5] Dispute resolution through negotiations received "overwhelming support" at the Third Conference.[6]

The importance of resolving disputes through negotiations is reaffirmed through Article 283, which reads: "When a dispute arises between States parties concerning the interpretation or application of the Convention, the parties to the dispute shall proceed expeditiously to an exchange of views regarding its settlement by negotiation or other peaceful means."[7] This obligation is intended to be a continuing obligation applicable at every stage of the dispute,[8] and even extends to the manner of implementing any settlement reached.[9] The inclusion of an obligation to exchange views was designed to cater to the wishes of delegations that the primary obligation of parties to a dispute should be to make every effort to settle the matter through negotiations.[10] Whether the exchange has been undertaken is a subjective determination, however. ITLOS has taken the position that the requirement is satisfied when one party concludes that the possibilities of settlement have been exhausted.[11] In the *Southern Bluefin Tuna* case, the Tribunal deciding on jurisdiction did not adopt the subjective perspective of ITLOS, but considered that this obligation had been fulfilled because negotiations had been "prolonged, intense and serious" and that during the course of those negotiations the Applicants had invoked UNCLOS (even though Japan denied its relevance).[12] The Tribunal was not purporting to set out criteria to meet the requirement under Article 283, but rather that these facts were sufficient to indicate that the obligation to exchange views for settlement by negotiation or other peaceful means had been satisfied.

This emphasis on negotiations as a means of dispute settlement does not preclude the use of different consent-based third-party procedures,

---

[5] John E. Noyes, "Compulsory Third-Party Adjudication and the 1982 United Nations Convention on the Law of the Sea," 4 *Conn. J. Int'l L.* 675, 678 (1989) ("Noyes, Compulsory Adjudication"). See also John E. Noyes, "The International Tribunal for the Law of the Sea," 32 *Cornell Int'l L.J.* 109, 119 (1999) ("Noyes, ITLOS"). ("The primacy accorded informal dispute settlement mechanisms in the Convention reflects the reality of interstate diplomatic practice.")

[6] Gurdip Singh, *United Nations Convention on the Law of the Sea: Dispute Settlement Mechanisms* (1985), p. 202 (referring to statements by the USSR, the United Kingdom, Italy, Romania, Venezuela, and Romania at the fourth session of the Third Conference).

[7] UNCLOS, art. 283(2).

[8] 5 *United Nations Convention on the Law of the Sea 1982: A Commentary*, p. 29.

[9] UNCLOS, art. 283(2).

[10] 5 *United Nations Convention on the Law of the Sea 1982: A Commentary*, p. 29.

[11] See further pp. 62–63.   [12] Southern Bluefin Tuna, Jurisdiction, para. 55.

such as inquiry, mediation, and conciliation. Singh considers that "tremendous importance" is attached to conciliation because of an express provision and an Annex on this procedure.[13] States may voluntarily opt for a conciliation commission where one party to a dispute invites the other to submit a matter to conciliation.[14] If that party refuses to do so then the conciliation procedure ends. Otherwise, the procedure continues in accordance with the provisions in Annex V, Section 1 of the Convention or another conciliation procedure. The prominence given to voluntary conciliation seems to be attributable to the fact that a separate procedure is provided in the Convention rather than expecting States to determine their own procedure. It is still anticipated, however, that States could formulate their own procedure if desired – thus reinforcing once more the freedom of States parties to choose their own procedures. Conciliation is also imposed as a compulsory procedure for certain disputes that would otherwise be excluded from mandatory jurisdiction.[15] The import of compulsory conciliation is assessed in the following chapters in relation to the particular disputes in question.

Dispute Settlement through Procedures Other than UNCLOS

Articles 281 and 282 envisage the resolution of disputes outside the framework of Part XV if certain specified conditions are met. If States have selected their own means of dispute settlement, the procedure available through Part XV will only apply if, according to Article 281, no resolution is reached through that means and if the parties did not exclude any further procedure in so choosing.[16] In accordance with the emphasis on the free choice of States in selecting the means to resolve disputes, the alternative agreement may provide, either explicitly or implicitly, the exclusive method of dispute settlement. In that case, the dispute is not subject to Part XV's mandatory jurisdiction if no resolution was reached because it would run contrary to the wishes of the parties to utilize the (probably non-compulsory) procedures in the alternative agreement.[17] Article 282 also permits States to refer disputes concerning the interpretation or application of the Convention to procedures that produce a binding decision under general, regional,

---

[13] Singh, p. 205. See also Noyes, ITLOS, at 123, n. 73. ("Several features of the Convention's conciliation articles suggest that the goal of the conciliation procedure is to promote dispute settlement.")

[14] UNCLOS, art. 284.

[15] *Ibid.*, art. 297(2) and (3); *ibid.*, art. 298(1)(a).   [16] *Ibid.*, art. 281.

[17] 5 *United Nations Convention on the Law of the Sea 1982: A Commentary*, p. 24.

or bilateral agreements. The alternative agreements will again apply in lieu of Part XV's compulsory procedures unless the parties to the dispute agree otherwise.

Article 281 – Procedure Where No Settlement has been Reached by the Parties

The potential effect of Article 281 was tested in *Southern Bluefin Tuna*.[18] In that case, a controversy had arisen between the Applicants (Australia and New Zealand) and Japan over the conservation and management of southern bluefin tuna, a highly migratory species.[19] Australia and New Zealand sought to bring the dispute within the compulsory jurisdiction of an arbitral tribunal established under Annex VII of the Convention in order to address Japan's alleged violations of UNCLOS provisions relating to high seas fisheries through the institution of an experimental fishing program. Japan maintained that the arbitral tribunal lacked jurisdiction since the conservation and management of southern bluefin tuna were regulated by the trilateral Convention for the Conservation of Southern Bluefin Tuna ("CCSBT")[20] and that agreement, including its non-compulsory dispute settlement clause, should govern the dispute.

The primary question thus addressed by the *ad hoc* Tribunal was whether it had jurisdiction under UNCLOS to decide the dispute concerning the conservation of southern bluefin tuna. The Tribunal had regard to the substantive obligations contained in the CCSBT as well as in UNCLOS. Japan took the view that the provisions of the CCSBT covered all of the relevant articles of UNCLOS relied on by the Applicants.[21] Japan emphasized the fact that UNCLOS was an "umbrella" agreement whereby its effectiveness was dependent on the conclusion of further, specific agreements in order to give substance to the more general obligations it imposes on States parties.[22] Japan further argued:

The CCSBT is one product of the recognition by all three of its Parties of their obligations under UNCLOS to cooperate in the development of practical arrangements for the conservation and management of highly migratory and high seas fisheries. The CCSBT is significant in two respects. First, it is in itself a fulfillment by the three States Parties to it of the duty to cooperate in relation to

---

[18] Southern Bluefin Tuna, Jurisdiction.   [19] UNCLOS, Annex 1.

[20] Convention for the Conservation of Bluefin Tuna, May 10, 1993, Australia-New Zealand-Japan, May 10, 1993, 1819 UNTS 360 (entered into force May 30, 1994).

[21] Southern Bluefin Tuna Case – *Australia and New Zealand v. Japan*, Government of Japan, Memorial on Jurisdiction, para. 36.

[22] *Ibid.*, para. 119.

the southern bluefin tuna fishery. Second, by laying down, in a legally binding instrument, the procedures by which the Parties will implement their commitments to cooperate, the CCSBT particularized their obligations in relation to cooperation regarding southern bluefin tuna.[23]

Japan strongly argued that the CCSBT dispute settlement clause governed the way that the dispute over southern bluefin tuna was to be resolved. The Tribunal summarized this argument as follows:

If the approach of Australia and New Zealand in espousing the governance of the dispute settlement provisions of UNCLOS were to apply to these treaties, parties to those treaties who had no intention of entering into compulsory jurisdiction would find themselves so bound . . . Clearly the parties chose to avoid, and not implicitly to undertake, obligations for compulsory adjudication or arbitration, i.e., the intention was to exclude recourse to the compulsory jurisdiction of UNCLOS. It cannot reasonably be presumed that States concluded treaties containing such clauses which are useless because they are overridden by UNCLOS Part XV . . . If this Tribunal were to find that UNCLOS Part XV overrides the specific terms of Article 16 of the CCSBT, it would profoundly disturb the host of dispute settlement provisions in treaties – whether antedating or postdating UNCLOS – that relate to matters embraced by UNCLOS.[24]

By contrast, Australia and New Zealand asserted that the parties had not intended to depart from the binding procedures of Part XV of UNCLOS in relation to UNCLOS obligations when adopting the CCSBT.[25] The CCSBT implemented obligations found in UNCLOS and should not be used as a means of escaping those obligations. The Applicants pointed to a possible consequence of Japan's arguments whereby the parties to implementation agreements would be accountable to third parties for breaching the general principles of the head agreement but would not be accountable to each other for UNCLOS violations once they concluded a treaty embodying the principles of their cooperation.[26] Instead, Australia and New Zealand advocated that UNCLOS created a comprehensive and effective regime for the resolution of disputes concerning the law of the sea generally and the conservation and management of highly migratory species particularly.[27] Furthermore, the nature of UNCLOS was such that any tribunal exercising jurisdiction under Part XV "should lean in favour of the effectiveness and comprehensive character of the dispute settlement regime, itself a key aspect of the UNCLOS regime."[28]

The Tribunal accepted Australia and New Zealand's arguments that there can be an accretion and cumulation of treaty law as a fact

---

[23] Ibid., para. 118.   [24] Southern Bluefin Tuna, Jurisdiction, para. 38(i).
[25] See ibid., para. 41(g).   [26] Ibid., para. 41(k).
[27] Southern Bluefin Tuna, Applicants' Reply, para. 30.   [28] Ibid., para. 31.

of international relations.[29] It was therefore accepted that obligations could be in dispute under both UNCLOS and the CCSBT and that was the case with respect to Australia and New Zealand's disagreement with Japan over the conservation of the southern bluefin tuna and Japan's experimental fishing program.[30] However, the Tribunal did not then conclude that two distinct disputes would necessarily exist but could be one dispute arising under more than one convention.[31] The relevant question was then what dispute settlement procedure would apply.[32]

For States parties to institute compulsory proceedings entailing binding decisions under Section 2 when a separate agreement governs an aspect of the oceans, Article 281 stipulates two criteria. First, the parties must have exhausted attempts at dispute settlement under the separate agreement and, second, that agreement cannot exclude resort to the procedures in UNCLOS. The Tribunal determined that the negotiations pursued between the parties did amount to attempts to resolve the dispute through the separate proceedings.[33] While the Tribunal found that the first criterion had been met, the majority determined that the second criterion had not.

The majority of the Tribunal concluded that Article 16 of the CCSBT did exclude recourse to the compulsory procedures in UNCLOS. The absence of an express exclusion of the UNCLOS procedure was not decisive,[34] but instead the terms of Article 16 were intended to prevent disputes relating to the CCSBT from being included in the UNCLOS mechanism.[35] Article 16 of the CCSBT envisaged that the consent of

---

[29] See Southern Bluefin Tuna, Jurisdiction, para. 52.   [30] *Ibid.*

[31] *Ibid.*, para. 54. ("To find that, in this case, there is a dispute actually arising under UNCLOS which is distinct from the dispute that arose under the CCSBT would be artificial.")

[32] Japan submitted, "Part XV was drafted in such a way as to preserve the right of States to settle their disputes by means of their own choosing." However, unlike the Tribunal, Japan emphasized Articles 279 and 288 in this regard. See Southern Bluefin Tuna Case, Japan's Memorial, para. 148 *et seq.*

[33] Southern Bluefin Tuna, Jurisdiction, para. 55.

[34] *Ibid.*, para. 57. Sir Kenneth Keith, in the dissent, considered that clear wording was needed to exclude the obligation to submit to the UNCLOS binding procedure. *Ibid.*, paras. 17–22 (dissenting opinion of Sir Kenneth Keith). Japan took the converse approach to the Tribunal in arguing that if the parties had truly intended the CCSBT to be supplemented by recourse to the procedure in UNCLOS then that would have been expressly stated. Southern Bluefin Tuna, Japan's Memorial, para. 138.

[35] Commentators have questioned how it will be possible to determine what dispute settlement procedures in separate treaties will exclude UNCLOS procedures, and which will not. See, e.g., Barbara Kwiatkowska, "Southern Bluefin Tuna (Australia and New Zealand v. Japan). Jurisdiction and Admissibility," 95 *Am. J. Int'l L.* 162, 169–170 (2001); Deborah Horowitz, "The Catch of Poseidon's Trident: The Fate of High Seas Fisheries in the Southern Bluefin Tuna Case," 25 *Melb. Univ. L.R.* 810, 820–21 (2001).

States was necessary for resort to arbitration and adjudication.[36] The importance of this consent was underlined by the fact that the States parties were obliged to continue to make every effort to resolve the dispute under the variety of peaceful means mentioned in the CCSBT even if that consent was not forthcoming.[37] In the event that the parties did consent to arbitration, then the arbitral proceedings were to be held in accordance with the Annex to the CCSBT, which was an integral part of the treaty.[38]

The majority of the Tribunal was fortified in its view by noting that many treaties addressed topics relating to the law of the sea and that these typically had their own dispute settlement provisions.[39] Other treaties that might exclude reference to UNCLOS compulsory procedures on this reasoning would include those that provide generally for the parties to resolve disputes by mutually agreeable means, or by consultations or negotiations, or that have more detailed clauses providing for dispute settlement by a variety of peaceful means, including binding third-party settlement.[40] The majority was of the opinion that since States had adopted these agreements with the idea that there would not be a unilateral resort to compulsory procedures, it was counter to what these States had consented by permitting the UNCLOS mechanism to be applied. The Tribunal stated:

The Tribunal is of the view that the existence of such a body of treaty practice – postdating as well as antedating the conclusion of UNCLOS – tends to confirm the conclusion that States Parties to UNCLOS may, by agreement, preclude subjection of their disputes to section 2 procedures in accordance with Article 281(1). To hold that disputes implicating obligations under both UNCLOS and an implementing treaty such as the [CCSBT] – as such disputes typically may – must be brought within the reach of section 2 of Part XV of UNCLOS

---

[36] Japan had argued that the *travaux préparatoires* that were available for the drafting of the CCSBT indicated that a deliberate decision was taken to exclude compulsory jurisdiction. Southern Bluefin Tuna – Japan's Memorial, para. 38.

[37] CCSBT, art. 16(2).   [38] *Ibid.*, art. 16(3).

[39] Southern Bluefin Tuna, Jurisdiction, para. 63. Perhaps as a note of caution to the Tribunal of the possible consequences of a finding in favor of the Applicants, Japan had observed in its Memorial that Article 16 of the CCSBT was similar or virtually identical to dispute settlement clauses in the 1959 Antarctic Treaty, the 1980 Convention on the Conservation of Antarctic Marine Living Resources, the 1994 Convention on the Conservation and Management of Pollock Resources in the Central Bering Sea, and the 1996 Agreement on the Conservation of Cetaceans of Black Sea, Mediterranean Sea and Contiguous Atlantic Oceans. Southern Bluefin Tuna, Japan's Memorial, para. 37.

[40] Kwiatkowska, "Jurisdiction and Admissibility," at 169–70.

would be effectively to deprive of substantial effect the dispute settlement provisions of those implementing agreements which prescribe dispute resolution by means of the parties' choice.[41]

Article 281 of UNCLOS thus reinforced the importance of States' freedom of choice for methods of dispute settlement.

This holding essentially restrains the potential applicability of the UNCLOS compulsory dispute settlement procedure.[42] It recognizes that States may enter into regional agreements with near identical substantive obligations to UNCLOS but with non-binding dispute settlement mechanisms as a means of avoiding the procedural obligations accepted under UNCLOS. The decision prevents a range of treaties being swept into the UNCLOS regime against the intentions of the signatories to those other agreements. This approach effectively grants priority to the States' wishes in staying away from compulsory dispute settlement, the traditional approach in international relations. The Tribunal considered that Article 281(1) confined "the applicability of compulsory procedures of section 2 of Part XV to cases where all parties to the dispute have agreed upon submission of their dispute to such compulsory procedures."[43] The decision underscores the importance attributed to States being "complete masters" of what methods will be used to resolve disputes.

This case represents a very deliberate effort not to open the proverbial flood-gates. The position of the Tribunal is that a cumulation of substantive obligations relating to the law of the sea does not mean that those obligations arising under separate agreements should be considered as automatically subject to the procedures in UNCLOS, against the wishes of the parties. The judgment can be viewed as a reaffirmation of the fundamental importance attributed to the role of consent in international dispute settlement.[44] Through the institutionalization of a mandatory

---

[41] Southern Bluefin Tuna, Jurisdiction, para. 63.

[42] Oxman has criticized the award for this very reason. See Bernard H. Oxman, "Complementary Agreements and Compulsory Jurisdiction," 95 *Am. J. Int'l L.* 277, 304 (2001). However, given the varying roles accorded to the compulsory dispute settlement procedures in relation to the substantive provisions of the Convention, such criticism is unwarranted. The decision correctly emphasizes the importance of States' freedom of choice and the continuing relevance of traditional consent-based methods of dispute settlement in the law of the sea.

[43] Southern Bluefin Tuna, Jurisdiction, para. 62.

[44] "It is well-established in international law that no state can, without its consent, be compelled to submit its dispute with other states either to mediation or to arbitration, or to any other kind of pacific settlement." Status of Eastern Carelia, Advisory Opinion No. 5, 1923 PCIJ (ser. B) No. 5, p. 27 (July 23).

dispute settlement system in UNCLOS, the barrier posed by consent to jurisdiction had been overcome to some extent – once a State became a party to UNCLOS, it agreed to compulsory jurisdiction for the settlement of disputes.[45] No separate instrument of ratification or accession is required, nor is dispute settlement sequestered in a separate, optional, protocol to the "main" substantive convention. The jurisdictional decision of *Southern Bluefin Tuna* therefore provides a stark reminder of the traditional barriers to inter-State adjudication or arbitration.

If the consent of a State party is not determinative of whether the dispute settlement procedure of a separate agreement excludes recourse to the procedures in Part XV of UNCLOS, a tribunal may be well-advised to undertake a contextual analysis, and consider how the dispute should be characterized.[46] Clearly the facts of *Southern Bluefin Tuna* did give the impression that the question was more obviously one related to the CCSBT. Australia and New Zealand acted under the cadre of the CCSBT in the first instance when Japan unilaterally initiated its experimental fishing program, requesting urgent consultations under the CCSBT and establishing a special working group to report to the CCSBT Commission on its evaluation of the program.[47] The dispute was essentially based on Japan's implementation of the experimental fishing program as a violation of the allocations accorded under the CCSBT, and this fact

---

[45] This issue was touched on in the Applicants' Reply on Jurisdiction:

> There is an underlying theme in Japan's Memorial on Jurisdiction that a State cannot be taken to binding dispute settlement unless it has consented to that course, that Japan has not consented to compulsory procedures in respect of this dispute and that [Australia and New Zealand] have somehow acted in an underhand way by instituting proceedings in these circumstances. But it is a central contention of [Australia and New Zealand] that by becoming a party to UNCLOS, Japan has in fact consented to compulsory and binding dispute settlement procedures for this dispute. Because of the importance of the obligations contained in the new regime, there was general agreement that the UNCLOS dispute settlement regime needed to be both mandatory and comprehensive.

Southern Bluefin Tuna, Applicants' Reply, para. 28, fn. 29.

[46] Evans supports this view:

> It is not difficult to imagine that parties to a regional convention that seeks to lend substance to the general obligations in [UNCLOS] might quite legitimately deem it appropriate to require agreement on a proposed course of action in a particular matter . . . It may, therefore, be necessary to adopt a more rigorous approach to the question of what constitutes the essence of a case.

Malcolm D. Evans, "The *Southern Bluefin Tuna* Dispute: Provisional Thinking on Provisional Measures?," 10 *Y.B. Int'l Envtl L.* 7, 9 (1999).

[47] See "Moritaka Hayashi, The Southern Bluefin Tuna Cases: Prescription of Provisional Measures by the International Tribunal for the Law of the Sea," 13 *Tul. Envtl L.J.* 361 (2000).

triggered the legal proceedings instituted by Australia and New Zealand. The statement of claims, the relief requested, as well as the facts giving rise to the dispute may be indicative of what treaty rights and duties are at stake, and concomitantly what dispute settlement scheme is applicable.

The *Southern Bluefin Tuna* decision also indicates that when implementing agreements are adopted as a means of fulfilling the general obligations set out in UNCLOS then the more detailed agreements should be subject to their own dispute settlement provisions. Such a result is reasonable if one accepts the view that the mandatory dispute settlement procedures are necessary in the Convention as a means of fleshing out certain substantive provisions. If normative content is given to the UNCLOS obligations through separate agreements then it could well be argued that compulsory dispute settlement procedures are less essential for that particular issue. Perhaps the distinction should be one between a separate convention that implements and supplements the obligations under UNCLOS and one that closely follows, or replicates, the obligations in the Convention. Compulsory dispute settlement would be necessary for the latter, not the former. The question that arises is whether the decision in *Southern Bluefin Tuna* might have been different if the obligations in UNCLOS dealing with high seas fisheries contained more specific norms of conduct rather than exhortations of cooperation without any substance as to what that cooperation should involve.

The majority of the Tribunal further garnered support for its decision that the CCSBT dispute settlement mechanism was applicable from the fact that Section 3 of Part XV of UNCLOS sets out a series of exceptions and limitations to the applicability of the compulsory procedures entailing binding decisions.[48] The majority pointed at the significance of the exclusions in that Section and concluded that UNCLOS is not actually a comprehensive regime, but rather "falls significantly short of establishing a truly comprehensive regime of compulsory jurisdiction entailing binding decisions."[49] This argument quite cuts to the truth of

---

[48] Southern Bluefin Tuna, Jurisdiction, paras. 60 and 61. Oxman has also criticized this decision for allowing the exceptions to compulsory jurisdiction to affect the strength accorded to compulsory dispute settlement in other respects. Oxman, "Complementary Agreements," p. 297.

[49] Southern Bluefin Tuna, Jurisdiction, para. 62. Sir Kenneth Keith, in his dissenting opinion, pointed to the central importance of the dispute settlement provisions in the drafting of UNCLOS. He noted that a number of statements were made to the effect that the dispute settlement provisions were an integral part of the treaty and that the treaty was to be regarded as comprehensive. *Ibid.*, Dissenting Opinion of Sir Kenneth Keith, paras. 23–28.

the matter. A large number of controversial areas of inter-State relations dealing with the uses of the oceans have been excluded from compulsory dispute settlement. This fact demonstrates that compulsory dispute settlement procedures are not considered essential for the operation of all of the substantive principles of the Convention. The use of implementing agreements may then indicate that States consider that mandatory jurisdiction is no longer needed to regulate certain issues in the law of the sea.

From this perspective, the majority of the Tribunal was correct in its holding that it lacked jurisdiction to decide the case. The facts before the Tribunal indicated that the primary source of controversy arose from obligations set forth in the CCSBT and that Article 16 of that convention was intended by the parties to deal with those disputes. It was contemplated in UNCLOS that high seas fishing would primarily be governed by a general principle of cooperation and would be substantively regulated through separate agreements. In the absence of those agreements, the use of third-party dispute settlement could fill the gaps in determining the appropriate standards of conduct for States parties. Hortatory obligations could be included in UNCLOS because there was the safeguard of compulsory and binding dispute settlement in cases where there was blatant disregard of the guidelines included in the Convention. The result of this approach is that the three parties to the CCSBT could now all bring claims against States like Indonesia and Korea under the compulsory procedures in UNCLOS for failing to cooperate.[50] An additional incentive is thus provided to these States to sign on to implementing agreements like the CCSBT so that there is less likelihood that they would be part of compulsory procedures in this matter. The disincentive is that the implementing agreements are likely to set out far more detailed obligations than those found in UNCLOS. Article 281 protects States' freedom to choose between dispute settlement regimes and may influence any balancing process in this regard.

A possible loophole to the application of Article 281 is, however, signaled by the Tribunal through reference to Article 300. Article 300 requires that States parties fulfil in good faith the obligations assumed under the Convention as well as exercise the rights, jurisdiction, and freedoms recognized in UNCLOS in a manner that would not constitute an abuse of right. Through reference to this provision, the Tribunal "does

---

[50] Both Indonesia and the Republic of Korea, which fish for southern bluefin tuna, are parties to UNCLOS.

not exclude the possibility that there might be instances in which the conduct of a State Party to UNCLOS and to a fisheries treaty implementing it would be so egregious, and risk consequences of such gravity, that a Tribunal might find that the obligations of UNCLOS provide a basis for jurisdiction."[51] If these conditions of egregious conduct and grave consequences are met, then the parties could be compelled to use the Part XV mechanism in the Convention regardless of alternative consent-based procedures in implementing treaties. The freedom of choice would be curtailed in these circumstances despite the stipulations of Article 281. Through this statement, the Tribunal has effectively imported conditions into the Convention that were not expressly stated, nor anticipated in the operation of Article 281.

Article 282 – Obligations Under General, Regional, or Bilateral Agreements

Alternative means of resolving UNCLOS disputes are also anticipated in Article 282. Dispute settlement options under Section 2 of Part XV may not be available to States when they are parties to a general, regional, or bilateral agreement under which a binding decision could be reached in relation to disputes concerning the interpretation and application of the Convention, as these agreements take precedence over the Convention's regime.[52] This primacy is not accorded, however, if the general, regional, or bilateral agreement does not provide a mechanism for producing a binding decision. (Separate conciliation or mediation agreements are thereby excluded from this category.)

If the States in dispute have both accepted in advance the compulsory jurisdiction of the ICJ by virtue of Article 36(2) of that Court's Statute, then Article 282 would preclude these States from pursuing compulsory procedures under the Convention without agreement by the parties to the contrary.[53] An argument to counter this view is that the declarations accepting the jurisdiction of the ICJ are unilateral actions and thus cannot constitute a "general, regional or bilateral agreement." Rosenne has taken the position that "[t]he mere acceptances do not, of course, constitute any agreement as between States forcing them to refer a given

---

[51] Southern Bluefin Tuna, Jurisdiction, para. 64.   [52] UNCLOS, art. 282.

[53] See Hayashi, "Southern Bluefin Tuna," at 363 (noting that this argument had been raised by Japan in the provisional measures stage of *Southern Bluefin Tuna*, but was not addressed by the Tribunal). See also 5 *United Nations Convention on the Law of the Sea 1982: A Commentary*, pp. 26–27 (stating that reference to an agreement being "otherwise" reached was intended to include declarations accepting the compulsory jurisdiction of the ICJ under Article 36(2) of the Court's Statute).

dispute to [the ICJ]. The declarations express a willingness to accept the jurisdiction if another State having made a declaration institutes proceedings. That was clearly the intention behind those words."[54] This view suggests that the declarations accepting the Court's compulsory jurisdiction under Article 36(2) of the ICJ Statute are thus relevant in respect of the choice of procedure under Article 286 of UNCLOS, and not for the purposes of Article 282. However, Article 286 constitutes a means to accept the Court's jurisdiction consistently with Article 36(1) of the ICJ Statute. If a State had accepted the compulsory jurisdiction of the Court, but then opted for arbitration or for ITLOS under Article 286, then this choice would normally prevail either for being later in time or being a more specific agreement. The breadth of Article 282, referring to "a general, regional or bilateral agreement or otherwise" means it is more likely that Article 282 is triggered when both States have accepted the compulsory jurisdiction of the ICJ under Article 36(2) of the Court's Statute.

Consideration was given to the interpretation and application of Article 282 in the context of provisional measures proceedings in *MOX Plant*.[55] The discussion in this case is of particular interest as it followed the jurisdictional decision in *Southern Bluefin Tuna* and involved the same procedural posture as *Southern Bluefin Tuna* where provisional measures were sought from ITLOS pending the constitution of an *ad hoc* arbitral tribunal and ITLOS had to decide if that tribunal had jurisdiction on a *prima facie* basis. ITLOS determined that there was *prima facie* jurisdiction in both *Southern Bluefin Tuna* and *MOX Plant*. The *ad hoc* tribunal constituted for *MOX Plant* confirmed its *prima facie* jurisdiction but suspended its proceedings to allow for resolution of potentially conflicting international obligations and dispute settlement procedures under the European Community legal order so as to determine the applicability of Article 282.[56]

---

[54] Shabtai Rosenne, "The Case-Law of ITLOS (1997–2001): An Overview," in *Current Marine Environmental Issues and the International Tribunal for the Law of the Sea* (Myron H. Nordquist and John Norton Moore, eds, 2001), p. 127, p. 139, n.17.

[55] The MOX Plant Case, Request for Provisional Measures (*Ireland v. United Kingdom*) (Order of December 3, 2001) 41 ILM 405 (2002).

[56] The College of Commissioners of the European Community decided to authorize the institution of proceedings against Ireland in respect of Community law issues on October 15, 2003. As a result, Ireland requested that the *MOX Plant* tribunal suspend the hearings in the proceedings until the Europeran Court of Justice gave judgment in the matter. The tribunal so ordered on November 14, 2003. Arbitral Tribunal Constituted Pursuant to Article 287, and Article 1 of Annex VII, of the United Nations

MOX Plant concerned Ireland's claims against the United Kingdom following the United Kingdom's authorization to open a new MOX facility in Sellafield.[57] Ireland considered that the duties that the United Kingdom owed to it under the Convention concerned obligations: (1) to cooperate with Ireland in taking measures to protect and preserve the Irish Sea; (2) to carry out a prior environmental assessment of the effects on the environment of the MOX plant and of international movements of radioactive materials associated with the operation of the plant; and (3) to protect the marine environment of the Irish Sea, including by taking all necessary measures to prevent, reduce, and control further radioactive pollution of the Irish Sea.[58] To this end, Ireland invoked Article 123, relating to cooperation of States bordering semi-enclosed seas, and Article 197, requiring cooperation on a global or regional basis as appropriate for the protection and preservation of the marine environment. Ireland also relied on Article 206, which sets forth the requirement that States assess the potential effects of activities that may cause substantial pollution or significant and harmful changes to the marine environment and communicate the results of such assessments. Finally, Ireland relied on Articles 192, 193, 194, 207, 211, and 213 in support of its argument that the United Kingdom had violated its obligations to protect the marine environment of the Irish Sea.

As the countries had not selected the same procedure for dispute settlement under Article 287, they were deemed to have accepted arbitration in accordance with Annex VII of the Convention. Prior to the constitution of the arbitral tribunal, Ireland sought the prescription of provisional measures from ITLOS under Article 290(5). The United Kingdom requested that ITLOS reject Ireland's requests for provisional measures on the basis that, *inter alia*, Ireland was precluded from having recourse to the Annex VII arbitral tribunal by virtue of Article 282 of the Convention. The United Kingdom argued that Ireland had already

---

Convention on the Law of the Sea for the Dispute Concerning the MOX Plant, International Movements of Radioactive Materials, and the Protection of the Marine Environment of the Irish Sea, The MOX Plant Case (*Ireland v. United Kingdom*) Order No. 4, Further Suspension of Proceedings on Jurisdiction and Merits, November 14, 2003, para. 1, available at http://www.pca-cpa.org/ENGLISH/RPC/.

[57] MOX refers to mixed oxide fuel, which is produced from the reprocessing of spent nuclear fuel.

[58] In the Dispute Concerning the MOX Plant, International Movements of Radioactive Materials, and the Protection of the Marine Environment of the Irish Sea (*Ireland v. United Kingdom*) Request for Provisional Measures and Statement of Case of Ireland, November 9, 2001, para. 55, available at http://www.pca-cpa.org/ENGLISH/RPC/.

submitted its complaints concerning access to information to an arbitral tribunal under the 1992 Convention for the Protection of the Marine Environment of the North-East Atlantic ("OSPAR Convention") and that Ireland's other allegations were governed by European treaties, which conferred jurisdiction on the Court of Justice of the European Communities.[59] According to the United Kingdom, Ireland had already announced publicly that it intended to pursue proceedings before the European Court of Justice as well.[60]

In response, Ireland submitted that the question put forward under the OSPAR Convention concerned solely the disclosure of information, and did not cover the range of "detailed legal obligations as are prescribed by the [Convention]."[61] Article 282 specifically speaks to general, regional or bilateral agreements that provide for the settlement of disputes concerning the interpretation or application of UNCLOS. Here, Ireland argued, the other fora referred to by the United Kingdom would not be addressing the terms of UNCLOS specifically. Further, the other dispute settlement mechanisms would not extend to all the matters in the dispute before the UNCLOS arbitral tribunal.

ITLOS accepted Ireland's view that the other dispute settlement bodies under the different treaties referred to by the parties would not be resolving a dispute related to the interpretation or application of UNCLOS. Even if those treaties contained similar rights or duties, the "application of international law rules on interpretation of treaties to identical or similar provisions of different treaties may not yield the same results, having regard to, *inter alia*, differences in the respective contexts, objects and purposes, subsequent practice of parties and *travaux préparatoires*."[62] Given the focus on the interpretation and application of UNCLOS, ITLOS determined that Article 282 was not applicable. The Tribunal thus concluded that the arbitral tribunal would have *prima facie* jurisdiction.

The separate opinions of several of the judges examined in more detail the interpretation and application of Article 282. One concern was that Article 282 should not be read in such a way as to render it almost otiose. Both Vice-President Nelson and Judge Treves emphasized that Article 282 applies to disputes *concerning the interpretation or application of the*

---

[59] MOX Plant, Provisional Measures, para. 40.   [60] *Ibid.*, para. 41.

[61] MOX Plant, Provisional Measures, Statement of Case of Ireland, para. 137.

[62] MOX Plant, Provisional Measures, para. 51. In his Separate Opinion, Vice President Nelson entertained doubts about the reach of this paragraph and voiced concern that it might render Articles 281 or 282 ineffective. *Ibid.*, Separate Opinion of Vice-President Nelson, para. 7.

Convention being referred to settlement under general, regional, or bilateral agreements.[63] But Vice-President Nelson also considered that Article 282 had to be understood in the context of the role of Section 1 of Part XV of the Convention, whereby: "The whole object of section 1 of Part XV of the Convention is to ensure that disputes concerning the interpretation or application of the Convention are settled by peaceful means and not necessarily by the mechanism for dispute settlement embodied in the Convention."[64] Article 282 had to be read in this context and "the bar created by [Articles 281 and 282] can only be circumvented when the requirements are met."[65] At most, his Opinion could be interpreted as wanting a balance to be struck so that Articles 281 and 282 are not read so broadly as to emasculate the mandatory dispute settlement mechanism in Section 2 of UNCLOS, but nor should decisions be taken that would undermine the purpose of these articles to allow States a wide choice of diplomatic or alternative means of dispute settlement prior to instituting compulsory adjudication or arbitration.

None of the ITLOS judges referred to the jurisdictional decision in *Southern Bluefin Tuna* directly, but it clearly influenced Judge Wolfrum, who commented:

It is well known in international law and practice that more than one treaty may bear upon a particular dispute. The development of a plurality of international norms covering the same topic or right is a reality. There is frequently a parallelism of treaties, both in their substantive content and in their provisions for settlement of disputes arising thereunder. However, a dispute under one agreement, such as the OSPAR Convention does not become a dispute under [UNCLOS] by the mere fact that both instruments cover the issue. If the OSPAR Convention, the Euratom Treaty or the EC treaty were to set out rights and obligations similar or even identical to those of [UNCLOS], these still arise from rules having a separate existence from the ones of [UNCLOS].[66]

In line with this emphasis on disputes relating to the interpretation or application of UNCLOS, he stated: "An intention to entrust the settlement of disputes concerning the interpretation and application of the Convention to other institutions must be *expressed explicitly* in respective agreements."[67] In requiring an express exclusion of UNCLOS dispute

---

[63] *Ibid.*, Separate Opinion of Judge Treves, para. 3, and Separate Opinion of Vice President Nelson, para. 2.
[64] *Ibid.*, Separate Opinion of Vice-President Nelson, para. 2.
[65] *Ibid.*, Separate Opinion of Vice-President Nelson, para. 6.
[66] *Ibid.*, Separate Opinion of Judge Wolfrum, p. 2.
[67] *Ibid.*, Separate Opinion of Judge Wolfrum, p. 2 (emphasis added).

settlement procedures, Judge Wolfrum has taken the opposite view to the majority in the jurisdictional decision of *Southern Bluefin Tuna*.[68]

As with Article 281, it is proposed that a court or tribunal deciding on jurisdiction should have regard to the facts of the case and the claims of the parties and consider if they can be more fairly characterized as a dispute concerning the interpretation or application of UNCLOS or of another multilateral treaty. For the *MOX Plant* tribunal, this task could mean that the particular facts and claims relating to access to information are more closely related to the OSPAR Convention than to more general obligations under UNCLOS. Further, a court or tribunal should consider the types of obligations at issue and the designated role of dispute settlement in relation to those obligations. In *Southern Bluefin Tuna*, the CCSBT set out more detailed rules about the conservation and management of southern bluefin tuna compared with UNCLOS. The relevant provisions of UNCLOS were broadly worded and it would be anticipated that third-party dispute settlement would perform a vital role in elaborating on the content of those rules. When such elaboration has already taken place in the form of an implementing treaty, or other agreement that deals with an issue more specifically than UNCLOS, then the need for the procedures under UNCLOS is less and greater weight should be attributed to the State's choice of an alternative mechanism set forth in that other treaty.

Before the *MOX Plant ad hoc* arbitral tribunal, the parties argued at greater length about the potential applicability of Article 282. The written pleadings predominantly discussed Ireland's reliance on a range of international instruments, including provisions of European Community and Euratom law, and whether those international law agreements were outside the jurisdiction of the tribunal, or whether the reference to those instruments demonstrated that the dispute did not solely relate to the interpretation and application of UNCLOS.[69] In its Rejoinder, the United Kingdom focused on the application of Article 282 in light of the Convention's status as a "mixed agreement" whereby the European

---

[68] See note 34 and accompanying text. Judge Treves sought to reconcile the ITLOS approach from that of the *ad hoc* arbitral tribunal in *Southern Bluefin Tuna* in distinguishing art. 282 from art. 281. See MOX Plant, Provisional Measures, Separate Opinion of Judge Treves, para. 4.

[69] See The MOX Plant Case (*Ireland* v. *United Kingdom*) Counter-Memorial of the United Kingdom, January 9, 2003, Chapter 4, available at http://www.pca-cpa.org/ENGLISH/RPC/; In the Dispute Concerning the MOX Plant, International Movements of Radioactive Materials, and the Protection of the Marine Environment of the Irish Sea (*Ireland* v. *United Kingdom*), Reply of Ireland, March 7, 2003, Chapter 4, available at http://www.pca-cpa.org/ENGLISH/RPC/.

Community ("EC" or "Community") and its members are parties to a treaty.[70] The United Kingdom considered that there was a restriction on jurisdiction by virtue of Article 282 for disputes between Member States of the EC when the dispute concerns a matter over which competence has been transferred to the Community. The United Kingdom took the position that virtually all of the claims of Ireland fell within the competence of the EC and that to the extent that provisions of international agreements impose obligations or confer rights on the Community, then the European Court of Justice has jurisdiction to interpret such provisions. On this basis, the United Kingdom argued, the European Court of Justice was entitled to interpret and apply the relevant provisions of UNCLOS that were in dispute between EC Member States, as UNCLOS had become part of Community law and was justiciable before that Court.

Ireland maintained that the obligations in question were not within the exclusive competence of the Community. The declaration of the Community provided:

With regard to the provisions on maritime transport, safety of shipping and the prevention of marine pollution . . . , the Community has exclusive competence only to the extent that such provisions of the Convention or legal instruments adopted in implementation thereof affect common rules established by the Community. When Community rules exist but are not affected, in particular in cases of Community provisions establishing only minimum standards, the Member States have competence, without prejudice to the competence of the Community to act in this field. Otherwise competence rests with the Member States.[71]

[70] The MOX Plant Case (*Ireland* v. *United Kingdom*), Rejoinder of the United Kingdom, April 24, 2003, Chapter 4, available at http://www.pca-cpa.org/ENGLISH/RPC/. International organizations may become parties to UNCLOS if a majority of its member States are signatories. See UNCLOS, art. 305 and Annex IX, art. 2. The Convention defines "international organizations" as "an intergovernmental organization constituted by States to which its member States have transferred competence over matters governed by this Convention, including the competence to enter into treaties in respect of those matters." *Ibid.*, Annex IX, art. 1. An international organization is then required to file a declaration at the time of its signature specifying the matters governed by the Convention in respect of which competence has been transferred to that organization by its member States, and the nature and extent of that competence. *Ibid.*, Annex IX, art. 2. The European Community, established by the First Treaty of Rome of March 25, 1957, had the necessary competence to sign UNCLOS and thus filed a declaration designating the matters over which it has exclusive competence and what matters over which it shares competence with Member States.

[71] Declaration concerning the competence of the European Community with regard to matters governed by the United Nations Convention on the Law of the Sea of 10 December 1982 and the Agreement of 28 July 1994 relating to the implementation of Part XI of the Convention, available at http://www.un.org/Depts/los/convention_agreements/convention_declarations.htm#European%20Community%20Declaration%20made%20upon%20formal%20confirmation.

Ireland maintained that the questions before the Tribunal concerned environmental obligations that laid down minimum standards under Community rules. In such a situation, the EC would not have exclusive competence but Member States would be free to establish higher standards or more stringent measures.[72] Nonetheless, the European Commission issued a statement shortly before the oral arguments whereby it noted that the UNCLOS provisions on which Ireland relied were provisions of EC law, either generally or to the extent that they fell within EC competence. The Commission was thus considering whether it should institute proceedings under the EC Treaty before the European Court of Justice while the arbitral proceedings under the UNCLOS dispute settlement regime were pending.

Following oral arguments on jurisdiction, the President of the *ad hoc* Tribunal issued a statement whereby the Tribunal noted that to decide on the jurisdictional objections of the United Kingdom, the Tribunal would be compelled to assess, *inter alia*, whether the EC or its Member States had competence in respect of all or some of the matters raised by the UNCLOS provisions invoked in the case.[73] If the interpretation of the Convention fell entirely within the exclusive competence of the European Court of Justice as between members of the Community, then it would preclude the jurisdiction of the *ad hoc* Tribunal completely by virtue of Article 282.[74] The Tribunal acknowledged that the European Court of Justice could embark on the same process of assessing competence, leading to the risk of two final and binding, yet contradictory, decisions being issued.[75] In view of this situation, the Tribunal decided as a matter of "mutual respect and comity which should prevail between judicial institutions both of which may be called upon to determine

---

[72] Ireland supported its argument through Articles 175 and 176 of the EC Treaty (formerly Articles 130s and 130t), where Article 176 reads: "The protective measures adopted pursuant to Article 175 shall not prevent any Member State from maintaining or introducing more stringent protective measures." Treaty on European Union (Maastricht) February 7, 1992, (1992) 31 ILM 247.

[73] MOX Plant, Statement of the President, June 13, 2003, available at http://www.pca-cpa.org/ENGLISH/RPC/STATEMENT% 20BY%20THE%20PRESIDENT.pdf, para. 9. See also Arbitral Tribunal Constituted Pursuant to Article 287, and Article 1 of Annex VII, of the United Nations Convention on the Law of the Sea for the Dispute Concerning the MOX Plant, International Movements of Radioactive Materials, and the Protection of the Marine Environment of the Irish Sea, The MOX Plant Case (*Ireland* v. *United Kingdom*) Order No. 3, Suspension of Proceedings on Jurisdiction and Merits, and Request for Further Provisional Measures, June 24, 2003, para. 21.

[74] MOX Plant, Order No. 3, para. 22.   [75] *Ibid.*, para. 27.

rights and obligations as between two States" that it should suspend its own proceedings.[76]

The decision was not based on any legal doctrine of *lis pendens* – and could not be so based given that no actual proceedings had been instituted before the European Court of Justice. As such, the stance of the Tribunal can be criticized as overly cautious and premature. UNCLOS requires that a tribunal constituted under Part XV will determine its own competence,[77] so the *ad hoc* Tribunal should have proceeded to assess whether the criteria of Article 282 had been met. Yet given the absence of any mechanism in the international system at present to resolve situations of overlapping jurisdiction, falling back on comity was the most realistic tool for reconciling potential conflict between judicial proceedings.[78] The decision to suspend its hearings was also consistent with Section 1 of Part XV, which anticipate States utilizing a range of dispute settlement mechanisms prior to resorting to the compulsory procedures under the Convention. This deference may also discourage States from "forum shopping" by submitting disputes to third-party settlement through a range of available mechanisms in order to increase the likelihood that the desired result will be obtained (either through different judicial opinions, or through the increase in diplomatic pressure as a result of the multiplicity of proceedings).

The inclusion of Article 282 indicates the flexibility that is accorded to the choices of the parties and is in line with the prevailing view at the Third Conference that parties usually prefer to settle their disputes through procedures previously agreed upon by them.[79] It is only when no voluntary settlement has been reached by the parties and no agreement between the parties excludes any alternative procedure that

---

[76] *Ibid.*, para. 28. The President of the Tribunal had earlier stated: "The Tribunal considers that a situation in which there might be two conflicting decisions on the same issues would not be helpful to the resolution of this international dispute. Nor would such a situation be in accord with the dictates of mutual respect and comity that should exist between judicial institutions deciding on rights and obligations as between States, and entrusted with the function of assisting States in the peaceful settlement of disputes that arise between them." MOX Plant, Statement of the President, para. 11.

[77] UNCLOS, art. 288(4).

[78] This approach was taken in *SPP* v. *Egypt* where two international arbitral tribunals were constituted to hear the same dispute, and one of the tribunals decided "in its discretion and as a matter of comity" that it would "stay the exercise of its jurisdiction pending a decision by the other tribunal." *SPP(ME) Ltd.* v. *Egypt* (First Decision on Jurisdiction), November 27, 1985, 106 ILR 502, 529, para. 84.

[79] 5 *United Nations Convention on the Law of the Sea 1982: A Commentary*, p. 26.

referral to the compulsory procedures entailing binding decisions found in Section 2 of Part XV becomes relevant.

Compulsory Procedures Entailing Binding Decisions

One of the most common reasons proffered for the inclusion of compulsory dispute settlement provisions in UNCLOS has been the need for a mechanism that could guarantee the "integrity" of the text.[80] The availability of a third-party process was considered a deterrent for unilateral interpretations of the terms of the Convention that would lose the compromise achieved during negotiations. Unilateral interpretations were viewed as potentially rendering the Convention unstable and uncertain.[81] As will be seen in the following chapters, this need for compulsory dispute settlement is certainly justified with respect to some issues under the Convention whereas other issues were too politically sensitive and required flexibility, and so remain subject to traditional modes of dispute settlement.

Compulsory dispute settlement also had an appeal to some States because of the impact the availability of these procedures would have on the political dynamic of a dispute. Developing States believed that a binding regime would reduce the risk of more powerful States using political, economic, and military pressures to force the developing States to give up rights guaranteed under the Convention.[82] Equally, third-party dispute settlement was considered advantageous because it could provide an alternative option to expending military, political, or economic capital to protect maritime interests.[83] Moreover, the binding nature

---

[80] Boyle, "Dispute Settlement," at 38–39. See also De Mestral, at 171 ("The underlying purpose of compulsory dispute settlement was to guarantee the integrity of the bargains struck between all the states of the world. Some saw it as a defence, others saw it as a means of enforcement, while others still viewed it with profound skepticism or hostility"); Noyes, "Compulsory Adjudication," at 682 (citing a statement by the President of the Conference, H. S. Amerasinghe).

[81] Kindt, at 1116.

[82] Noyes, "Compulsory Adjudication," at 681. See also Andreas J. Jacovides, "Peaceful Settlement of Disputes in Ocean Conflicts: Does UNCLOS III Point the Away?," in *Contemporary Issues in International Law, Essays in Honor of Louis B. Sohn* (Thomas Buergenthal ed., 1984), pp. 165, 166 (citing his statement made on April 6, 1976 where he propounded the need for dispute settlement "by reason of our national self-interest as a small and militarily weak state which needs the protection of the law, impartially and effectively administered, in order to safeguard its legitimate rights" under UNCLOS).

[83] Statement by Expert Panel, at 439–40.

of the regime was hoped to give less powerful States equal standing before the law.[84] In this manner, compulsory dispute settlement could be used as a tool of diplomacy. Recourse to international processes was viewed as dual purpose as it could provide a check on powers granted to States as well as provide a means to protect those powers.

To make the system of mandatory jurisdiction workable for States, there is an emphasis on flexibility and freedom of choice in the Convention. The discussion below describes the range of procedures that are open to States once mandatory proceedings are instituted. This choice includes the selection of an international forum, requests for provisional measures of protection prior to the resolution of a dispute by arbitration or adjudication, and a special procedure to facilitiate the prompt release of vessels that are seized under the terms of the Convention.

Choice of Procedure

When States have not settled their differences through the various means available under Section 1 of Part XV, disputes can be submitted at the request of any party to the appropriate forum subject to the terms of the Convention.[85] No additional form of consent is required once a State is party to the Convention – consent to be bound by UNCLOS includes consent to compulsory procedures entailing binding decisions (subject to Sections 1 and 3 of Part XV). Under Section 2, the States in dispute do not need (both or all) to consent to the referral of the dispute to a court or tribunal, but the dispute can be submitted at the behest of just one of the disputant States. "Unilateral action is sufficient to vest the court or tribunal with jurisdiction, and that court or tribunal may render a decision whether or not the other party participates in the process."[86]

The particular procedure that can be utilized by States parties is largely a matter of choice. States may select their preferred forum at the time they sign, ratify, or accede to the Convention, or at any time thereafter.[87] Under Article 287(1), States may choose between:

---

[84] Adede, *System for Settlement of Disputes*, pp. 39 and 241. See also Noyes, "Compulsory Adjudication," at 681.

[85] UNCLOS, art. 286. Local remedies must be exhausted "where this is required by international law" as a further precondition to the resort to compulsory procedure under Section 2. *Ibid.*, art. 295. See Singh, at 196–98 (discussing the scope of the rule of exhaustion of local remedies in UNCLOS).

[86] 5 *United Nations Convention on the Law of the Sea 1982: A Commentary*, at 39.

[87] UNCLOS, art. 287(1).

- the International Tribunal for the Law of the Sea established in accordance with Annex VI;
- the International Court of Justice;
- an arbitral tribunal constituted in accordance with Annex VII; and
- a special arbitral tribunal constituted in accordance with Annex VIII for one or more of the categories of disputes specified therein.[88]

Such flexibility as to the choice of fora available to States parties was required in order to achieve consensus on compulsory dispute settlement at the Third Conference. States are provided with a choice between two courts, the ICJ and a new permanent international court, ITLOS. During negotiations, it was considered that a new tribunal was needed with judges who would be more familiar with the development of the new principles set forth in UNCLOS than the ICJ, which was perceived by some States as not understanding the new law of the sea.[89] Developing States were very critical of the jurisprudence, structure, and membership of the ICJ and were unwilling to accept formal mechanisms of international adjudication.[90] This sentiment is illustrated in Cuba's choice of procedure upon its ratification of the Convention. Cuba did not specify a preference for ITLOS or arbitration but expressly stated that it does not accept the jurisdiction of the ICJ under Article 287.[91] The creation of ITLOS was also viewed as necessary because only States have standing

---

[88] UNCLOS, art. 287(1). The order of listing of the available choices has been said to have no significance. 5 *United Nations Convention on the Law of the Sea 1982: A Commentary*, p. 44. However, the President of the Third Conference considered that the creation of ITLOS as a new judicial organ with comprehensive jurisdiction over all disputes pertaining to the law of the sea merited it being listed as the first alternative. See Oda, "Some Reflections," at 646–47.

[89] 5 *United Nations Convention on the Law of the Sea 1982: A Commentary*, pp. 8 and 42. Oda believes that the desire for the creation of ITLOS lay in the ulterior motives of those proposing it: "it is regrettable that the idea of ITLOS seems to have been reinforced by the personal desires of some delegates to UNCLOS III and the Preparatory Commission and other jurists, who appear to have been personally interested in obtaining posts in international judicial organs". Oda, "Dispute Settlement Prospects," at 865.

[90] Noyes, "Compulsory Adjudication," at 679. Judge Guillaume notes that the negotiations for the choice of procedure took place in 1975 when developing States still resented judgments rendered by the ICJ in the *South West Africa* cases and the *Northern Cameroons* case. Guillaume, at 854. Moreover, Judge Guillaume considers that if the Third Conference was undertaken today it would be less certain that the ITLOS would still be created. *Ibid.*, at 855.

[91] See *Multilateral Treaties Deposited with the Secretary-General*, UN Doc. ST/LEG/SER.E/15, http://www.un.org/Depts/los/los_decl.htm (updated November 13, 2003). See also declarations by Algeria and Guinea-Bissau. *Ibid.*

before the ICJ[92] whereas ITLOS is open to "entities other than States parties" as well as States.[93] Other States considered that the ICJ was an appropriate forum precisely because it had already rendered several judgments relating to the law of the sea.[94] It was further argued that as the ICJ is the principal judicial organ of the UN,[95] it should have the opportunity to expand its jurisdiction over such an important area of international law.[96]

Scholarly concern has been expressed about the establishment of ITLOS as a new judicial body in parallel with the ICJ because it may cause the fragmentation of the law of the sea from the jurisprudence on international law as a whole.[97] In response, Charney has argued that ITLOS and the other fora are likely to take appropriate account of public international law.[98] Certainly the few cases already decided under the UNCLOS procedures have made reference to principles of international law and relied on judgments of the ICJ.[99] Moreover, Charney has recalled that the ICJ is one of the proposed fora and as such, "if the ICJ gives the best service, it will be selected by the disputants in their initial declarations."[100] These notions of market competition are understandable

---

[92] ICJ Statute, art. 34.

[93] Other entities may have access to ITLOS "in any case expressly provided for in Part XI or in any case submitted pursuant to any other agreement conferring jurisdiction on the Tribunal which is accepted by all the parties to that case." UNCLOS, Annex VI, art. 20(2).

[94] See, e.g., North Sea Continental Shelf (*Federal Republic of Germany v. Denmark; Federal Republic of Germany v. Netherlands*), 1969 ICJ 3 (February 20); Icelandic Fisheries; Continental Shelf (*Tunisia v. Libya*), 1982 ICJ 18 (February 24).

[95] UN Charter, art. 92.

[96] 5 *United Nations Convention on the Law of the Sea 1982: A Commentary*, p. 41.

[97] Oda, "Dispute Settlement Prospects," at 864. Oda believes that "[i]f the development of the law of the sea were to be separated from the general rules of international law and placed under the jurisdiction of a separate judicial authority, this could lead to the destruction of the very foundation of international law." *Ibid.*

[98] Jonathan I. Charney, "The Implications of Expanding International Dispute Settlement Systems: The 1982 Convention on the Law of the Sea," 90 *Am. J. Int'l L.* 69, 72 (1996). Rosenne has also dismissed this argument in stating that there is "no evidence to support the view that a multiplicity of international judicial institutions for the settlement of disputes seriously impairs the unity of jurisprudence (a difficult proposition at the best of times)." Shabtai Rosenne, "Establishing the International Tribunal for the Law of the Sea," 89 *Am. J. Int'l L.* 806, 814 (1995).

[99] For example, dicta from ICJ decisions on interim measures have been cited by the parties in M/V "Saiga" and Southern Bluefin Tuna. The judgments have reflected consideration of the ICJ jurisprudence and it has been directly cited in separate opinions.

[100] Charney, "Implications," at 71 (arguing that the competition may promote the best reasoning and solutions).

since States' participation in this aspect of the law of the sea regime was dependent on an accommodation of their diverse views on appropriate means of dispute resolution for particular issues.

Arbitration is offered as an alternative to adjudication. Some States preferred arbitration to adjudication because it allows for a more flexible procedure enabling disputes to be settled more expeditiously.[101] The preference for arbitration is in accordance with an increasing trend to include arbitral clauses in treaties.[102] The appeal of arbitration may be found in the possibility of secrecy, party control over the composition of the tribunal and the questions addressed to the tribunal as well as the ability to avoid a third State's intervention in the proceedings.[103] States may opt for arbitration under Annex VII or Annex VIII. For Annex VII arbitration, the arbitrators are to be "persons experienced in maritime affairs and enjoying the highest reputation for fairness, competence and integrity." Unlike the ITLOS and the ICJ, no legal qualifications are specified for the members of the arbitral tribunal under Annex VII.[104]

The option of special arbitration under Annex VIII allows parties access to a forum that is specialized in specific types of dispute.[105] The Convention, being drafted in the 1970s, had to accommodate the views of the socialist States that perceived western international tribunals as bourgeois.[106] The socialist States instead favored special arbitration where States could have significant influence in the settlement process by being able to select expert members of the arbitral panel.[107] Annex VIII provides that a list of experts shall be drawn up in relation to the fields of (1) fisheries, (2) protection and preservation of the marine environment, (3) marine scientific research, and (4) navigation, including pollution

---

[101] 5 *United Nations Convention on the Law of the Sea 1982: A Commentary*, p. 42.

[102] Gray and Kingsbury, at 101.   [103] *Ibid.*

[104] By comparison, the ITLOS Statute requires members who enjoy "the highest reputation for fairness and integrity and of recognized competence in the field of law." UNCLOS, Annex VI, art. 2.

[105] George A. Pierce, "Dispute Settlement Mechanisms in the Draft Convention on the Law of the Sea," 10 *Denv. J. Int'l L. & Pol'y* 331, 333 (1981).

[106] Noyes, "Compulsory Adjudication," at 679.

[107] *Ibid.*, at 684–85. De Mestral notes:

> Initially, this provision was essential to ensure that the Soviet bloc came along with the principle of compulsory dispute settlement. Now however, it is likely to be an embarrassment and an impediment to the smooth operation of the Convention.

De Mestral, at 185.

from vessels and by dumping[108] and at least four members of the five member tribunal will constitute these experts.[109]

Technical experts from specialized agencies were considered as the best qualified to decide disputes in their particular areas. Oda has also argued that it is appropriate to leave questions involving the discretion of the coastal State to a special tribunal in matters related to fishing, marine scientific research, and the prevention of pollution since considerations of equity rather than law may be involved.[110] The special arbitral panels may conduct fact-finding alone that is conclusive between the parties.[111] Annex VIII procedures remain subject to the limitations and exceptions in Part XV.[112] States are not obliged to use special arbitration for the specified disputes but may still utilize Annex VII arbitration, ITLOS,[113] or the ICJ.

A State party may institute compulsory procedures by unilateral application if the parties in dispute have chosen the same forum in their declaration. For States that have not specifically selected their preferred choice of procedure, there is a default clause in the Convention. It is deemed that these States have accepted arbitration.[114] When this issue was being debated, it was initially accepted that the parties would use the tribunal chosen by the defendant.[115] However, dissatisfaction was expressed because some States were not prepared to accept the jurisdiction of the ICJ if the defendant selected this forum.[116] Arbitration was thus preferred as the alternative in the event that States parties have not specifically pre-selected a procedure. This default clause also applies in the event that the States in dispute have accepted different procedures for settlement.[117]

---

[108] UNCLOS, Annex VIII, art. 2. These lists have now been established for each of these fields. See Lists of Experts for the purposes of article 2 of Annex VIII (Special Arbitration) to the Convention, available at http://www.un.org/Depts/los/settlement_of_disputes/experts_ special_arb.htm (as at June 24, 2003).

[109] UNCLOS, Annex VIII, art. 3(b) and (c). Under Article 3(d), the president of the special arbitral tribunal shall be "chosen preferably from the appropriate list." As it is simply a preference that the president be selected from the expert list, this provision indicates that a person not on the expert list may act as president of the tribunal.

[110] Oda, "Dispute Settlement Prospects," at 868.

[111] UNCLOS, Annex VIII, art. 5.   [112] Ibid., Annex VIII, art. 1.

[113] It is notable in this regard that ITLOS has formed two standing special chambers to deal with fisheries and the marine environment for cases requiring specific expertise.

[114] UNCLOS, art. 287(3).

[115] Sohn, "Settlement of Law of the Sea Disputes," at 206.   [116] Ibid.

[117] UNCLOS, art. 287(5). Professor Sohn provides an interesting insight into the negotiation process in working out this default provision:

The particular forum for dispute settlement is not greatly dependent on the subject matter of the claims asserted. The ICJ, ITLOS, and the arbitral tribunals all have jurisdiction over any dispute concerning the interpretation or application of the Convention.[118] Article 293 provides that the applicable law is the Convention and other rules of international law not incompatible with UNCLOS. Various articles of UNCLOS, particularly those addressing the protection and preservation of the marine environment, incorporate by reference "generally accepted international rules and standards," thereby increasing the sources of law that may be applicable to a dispute.[119] A hierarchy is created whereby the foremost law governing the dispute is the Convention and in the case of conflict between UNCLOS and existing law, the Convention must prevail. Article 293 applies to all courts and tribunals exercising jurisdiction under Section 2, Part XV.

Disputes relating to the interpretation or application of any other international agreement that pertains to the law of the sea may also be submitted to the courts or tribunals listed under Article 287.[120] The courts or tribunals will have jurisdiction over these disputes provided the submission is expressly authorized and any conditions are fulfilled in accordance with the agreement.[121] The overlap of subject matter jurisdiction has been criticized on the basis that it could lead to "unnecessary multiplicity of jurisdictions and conflicting jurisprudence."[122] Multiplicity of jurisdiction is not of itself a tremendous problem, provided

> the informal rapporteur of the working group suggested a non-binding secret ballot, on which each participant would list both a first choice and a second one. The result was that while the first choice listed all four dispute settlement methods, almost all of those who did not list arbitration as their first choice selected it as their second choice. It was agreed, therefore, that where the parties do not agree on a first choice, the parties would have to resort to arbitration. A complex issue was resolved by a simple procedural devise, and the full meeting accepted it by consensus.

Sohn, "Settlement of Law of the Sea Disputes," at 212.

[118] UNCLOS, art. 288(1).

[119] See further pp. 148–152.

[120] UNCLOS, art. 288(2). See also *ibid.*, Annex VI, arts. 21 and 22 (conferring jurisdiction on ITLOS over all disputes and all applications submitted to it in accordance with the Convention as well as disputes outside the terms of the Convention provided agreements specifically confer jurisdiction on ITLOS).

[121] *Ibid.*, art. 288(2). See also 5 *United Nations Convention on the Law of the Sea 1982: A Commentary*, pp. 47–48.

[122] Marianne P. Gaertner, "The Dispute Settlement Provisions of the Convention on the Law of the Sea: Critique and Alternatives to the International Tribunal for the Law of the Sea," 19 *San Diego L. Rev.* 577, 593 (1982). See also Oda, "Some Reflections," at 649.

proceedings on the same dispute are not instituted in more than one forum. If a dispute involves the same parties, the same claims, and the same object, then by virtue of the principle of *lis pendens*, a second tribunal or court may not exercise jurisdiction. In any event, UNCLOS anticipates the need to avoid duplicative proceedings to some extent through Articles 281 and 282. It may not be terribly cost effective to have several fora with the same subject matter jurisdiction but the variety of available procedures was necessary to make the adoption of a system of mandatory jurisdiction politically acceptable.

The potential for conflicting jurisprudence should not be overestimated either, and these concerns have been rightly criticized. Consistency is necessary for predictability in States choosing procedures under Article 287. States will prefer to submit matters to a tribunal or court where they can reasonably predict how a matter will be handled based on previous decisions. Courts and tribunals thus have an incentive to take other international bodies' opinions into account. Cases involving maritime boundaries or fishing have been resolved by the ICJ and by arbitral tribunals without any overt conflicts between their decisions.[123] Boyle has noted that in these cases the "jurisprudence may not be a seamless web, but it is more impressive for its continuity than for its discord."[124] Consistency of decision-making is also important for the dispute settlement procedures to fulfill their role vis-à-vis the substantive provisions. The substantive rules could be undermined if third-party procedures produce inconsistent interpretations and applications of the Convention. Overall, "[a]lthough different fora may have jurisdiction in similar disputes, the possibility of inconsistent rulings seems unlikely to present significant new problems for international law and process."[125]

Provisional Measures

Provisional measures, sometimes called interim measures of protection, provide safeguards to States in litigation so that their rights will be preserved pending the outcome of the case. The justification for provisional measures derives from the "elementary juridical principle that the judgment of a court should be effective and that to ensure this it may, while a case is before the Court, be essential to restrain either party, or both, from disrupting the situation, or attempting to present its adversary with a *fait accompli*."[126] Provisional measures are typically most effective

---

[123] Boyle, "Dispute Settlement," at 40–41. [124] *Ibid.*, at 41. [125] Noyes, "ITLOS," at 175.
[126] J. G. Merrills, *International Dispute Settlement* (3rd ed., 1998), p. 129.

when the disputant States recognize the value of judicial intervention in the matter.[127] The ICJ has the power "to indicate" provisional measures "if it considers that circumstances so require."[128] While controversy had previously arisen over the binding nature of interim measures indicated by the ICJ,[129] no such ambiguity exists under UNCLOS. A court or tribunal with jurisdiction under UNCLOS has power to "prescribe" provisional measures and is similar in this regard to the European Court of Justice.[130] The language of the Convention clearly demonstrates that the provisional measures ordered in UNCLOS disputes are binding as a matter of law.

Article 290, paragraph 1 of the Convention permits a court or tribunal with *prima facie* jurisdiction to prescribe provisional measures that are "appropriate under the circumstances to preserve the respective rights of the parties to the dispute or to prevent serious harm to the marine environment, pending the final decision." This formulation requires certain conditions to be fulfilled prior to the prescription of provisional measures. The first basic prerequisite is that the relevant court or tribunal has *prima facie* jurisdiction. This condition limits parties to a dispute from acting unilaterally to exert pressure through the prescription of provisional measures.[131] The standard that must then be met is whether the circumstances warrant the prescription of measures pending the final decision of the court or tribunal in order to preserve the rights of the parties or whether there is a need to prevent serious harm to the marine environment. Once prescribed, the measures may be modified or revoked if the circumstances justifying their prescription have been changed or cease to exist.[132] Measures may also be sought pending the constitution of an arbitral tribunal under the procedure in paragraph 5 of Article 290.[133] An additional standard stipulated in that paragraph is

---

[127] *Ibid.*, at 130.   [128] ICJ Statute, art. 41.

[129] This question was resolved in favor of the binding nature of provisional measures in LaGrand. See LaGrand (*Federal Republic of Germany* v. *United States*) 2001 ICJ (June 27), available at http://www.icj-cij.org/icj/www/idocket/igus/igusframe.htm.

[130] See Treaty Establishing the European Economic Community, March 25, 1957, art. 186, 298 UNTS 3.

[131] John King Gamble, Jr., "The 1982 UN Convention on the Law of the Sea: Binding Dispute Settlement?," 9 *B.U. Int'l L.J.* 39, 42 (1991).

[132] UNCLOS, art. 290(2).

[133] Prior to the constitution of an arbitral tribunal, provisional measures can be sought under art. 290(5) from "any court or tribunal agreed upon by the parties or, failing such agreement within two weeks from the date of the request for provisional measures, the International Tribunal for the Law of the Sea or, with respect to activities in the Area, the Seabed Disputes Chamber." UNCLOS, art. 290(5).

one of the "urgency of the situation." The requirements for *prima facie* jurisdiction and other conditions to be met for the grant of provisional measures are discussed below, along with the types of orders that may be issued.

Determining *Prima Facie* Jurisdiction

If a court or tribunal is determining whether provisional measures should be prescribed pursuant to Article 290(1) or Article 290(5), it must assess *prima facie* whether the court or tribunal deciding the substance of the case has jurisdiction. In respect of paragraph 1 of Article 290, the court or tribunal makes this determination on its own account whereas under paragraph 5, the court or tribunal asked to prescribe provisional measures makes this decision for the *ad hoc* arbitral tribunal that is yet to be constituted. A request under Article 290(5) must indicate the legal grounds upon which the arbitral tribunal to be constituted would have jurisdiction.[134] In assessing whether treaty provisions invoked appear on their face to afford a basis on which jurisdiction might be based for the indication of interim measures, the ICJ has stated that the relevant inquiry is whether "the dispute appears, *prima facie*, to afford a possible basis on which the jurisdiction of the Court might be founded."[135] In explaining this standard in *Interhandl*, Judge Lauterpacht stated: "The Court may properly act under the terms of article 41 provided that there is in existence an instrument . . . which prima facie confers jurisdiction upon the Court and which incorporates no reservations obviously excluding its jurisdiction."[136] In the same vein, the *ad hoc* tribunal in *MOX Plant* considered that there was *prima facie* jurisdiction where

---

[134] Rules of the Tribunal, art. 89(4), available at http://www.un.org/Depts/los/ITLOS/Rules-Tribunal.htm.

[135] Fisheries Jurisdiction (*United Kingdom v. Iceland; Federal Republic of Germany v. Iceland*), Request for the Indication of Interim Measures of Protection, Order, 1972 ICJ 12, and 30, paras. 15 and 17 (August 17). See also Vienna Convention on Consular Relations (*Paragway v. United States*), Request for the Indication of Provisional Measures, Order, 1998 ICJ, para. 23 (April 9); LaGrand (*Federal Republic of Germany v. United States*), Request for the Indication of Provisional Measures, Order, 1999 ICJ, para. 13 (March 3).

[136] Interhandl Case (*Switzerland v. United States*) 1957 ICJ 105, at 118–19 (October 24). Writing extra-judicially, Judge Ndiaye stated that *prima facie* jurisdiction "arises only if it is reasonably probable that the arbitral tribunal would have jurisdiction on the merits." Tafsir Malick Ndiaye, "Provisional Measures Before the International Tribunal for the Law of the Sea," in *Current Marine Environmental Issues and the International Tribunal for the Law of the Sea* (Myron Nordquist and John Norton Moore eds., 2001), pp. 95, 97.

"there is nothing which manifestly and in terms excludes the Tribunal's jurisdiction."[137]

The first provisional measures decisions taken by ITLOS have considered possible bars to a finding that no jurisdiction exists on a *prima facie* basis. These hurdles include the requirement in Article 283 to proceed expeditiously to an exchange of views; the existence of alternative dispute settlement procedures to be utilized in lieu of those in UNCLOS; and whether the exclusions and limitations in Section 3 of Part XV would prevent a finding of jurisdiction on a *prima facie* basis. These questions are considered immediately below.

Violation of the Obligation to Exchange Views under Article 283

States are required to proceed expeditiously to an exchange of views regarding the settlement of a dispute by negotiation or other peaceful means prior to resorting to the compulsory procedures entailing binding decisions under Section 2.[138] In the provisional measures stages of *Southern Bluefin Tuna*, *MOX Plant*, and *Land Reclamation*, the respondent States submitted that the applicants had failed to fulfill this obligation and thus jurisdiction for compulsory adjudication or arbitration was not *prima facie* established.

In *Southern Bluefin Tuna*, in response to Japan's arguments on Article 283,[139] Australia and New Zealand submitted that they had made extensive efforts to resolve the dispute through negotiations but the main obstacle to such discussions was Japan's refusal to suspend its experimental fishing program during negotiation and mediation efforts.[140] The Tribunal took the view that the requirements for invoking the compulsory procedures in the Convention were satisfied when a State Party concluded that the possibilities of settlement under Section 1 of Part XV

---

[137] MOX Plant, Order No. 3, para. 14. See also Rosenne, "An Overview," p. 133 (noting that a finding of *prima facie* jurisdiction is a very low threshold and allows the prescription of provisional measures provided "the absence of jurisdiction is not manifest").

[138] See notes 7–12 and accompanying text.

[139] Southern Bluefin Tuna, Requests for Provisional Measures (*New Zealand v. Japan*; *Australia v. Japan*) (Order of August 27, 1999), Verbatim Records, ITLOS/PV.99/23, p. 9, available at http://www.itlos.org/start2_en.html.

[140] Southern Bluefin Tuna, Requests for Provisional Measures (*New Zealand v. Japan*; *Australia v. Japan*) (Order of August 27, 1999), Verbatim Records, ITLOS/PV.99/20, p. 23, available at http://www.itlos.org/start2_en.html.

had been exhausted.[141] ITLOS then confirmed the use of this test in *MOX Plant* and *Land Reclamation*.[142]

These decisions indicate that the standard for satisfying Article 283 has been set in a subjective manner. It is sufficient for one of the disputant States to conclude that efforts under Section 1 have been exhausted to entitle that State to invoke Section 2 by way of unilateral application. In *Land Reclamation*, however, ITLOS did indicate that the assessment of the requesting State still had to be reviewed by the court or tribunal determining whether it could exercise jurisdiction over the dispute. After reviewing the communications between Malaysia and Singapore, ITLOS referred to the earlier standard and stated that "in the view of the Tribunal, in the circumstances of the present case Malaysia was not obliged to continue with an exchange of views when it concluded that this exchange could not yield a positive result."[143] The reference to its own assessment of the facts of the case, rather that just referring to the subjective determination of one of the parties, illustrates a reviewing role of the court or tribunal under Article 283 has been maintained.[144]

---

[141] Southern Bluefin Tuna, Requests for Provisional Measures (*New Zealand v. Japan; Australia v. Japan*) (Order of August 27, 1999), available at http://www.itlos.org/start2_en.html, paras. 60 and 61. Kwaitkowska considers that this decision reflects the practice of international tribunals to give applicants the benefit of the doubt in provisional measures proceedings. Barbara Kwiatkowska, "The Southern Bluefin Tuna (New Zealand v Japan; Australia v Japan) Cases," 15 *Int'l J. Marine & Coastal L.* 1, 33 (2000).

[142] MOX Plant, Provisional Measures, para. 68; Case concerning Land Reclamation by Singapore in and around the Straits of Johor (*Malaysia v. Singapore*), Request for Provisional Measures (Order of October 8, 2003), available at http://www.itlos.org/start2_en.html, para. 48.

[143] Land Reclamation, Provisional Measures, para. 48.

[144] Singapore had argued that a State party's assessment that the possibilities of settlement had been exhausted was "by its nature, a determination ultimately made by ITLOS." Case Concerning Land Reclamation by Singapore in and around the Straits of Johor (*Malaysia v. Singapore*), Request for Provisional Measures, Verbatim Record, ITLOS/PV.03/03, p. 31, available at http://www.itlos.org/start2_en.html. In his Separate Opinion, Judge Chandrasekhara Rao endorsed Singapore's view that the Tribunal had the ultimate role in assessing whether the determination of the disputant State to abandon further exchanges of view could be accepted. Land Reclamation, Provisional Measures, Separate Opinion of Judge Chandrasekhara Rao, para. 11. ("The requirement of this article regarding exchange of views is not an empty formality, to be dispensed with at the whims of a disputant. The obligation in this regard must be discharged in good faith, and it is the duty of the Tribunal to examine whether this is being done.")

In *MOX Plant*, the United Kingdom took the position that correspondence between itself and Ireland did not amount to an exchange of views and that Ireland had rejected the United Kingdom's request for such an exchange.[145] The United Kingdom seemed to consider that a formal invitation to exchange views for the express purpose of settling by negotiation or other peaceful means any alleged dispute arising under UNCLOS was required. Ireland relied on a range of letters sent to and from the United Kingdom and noted that it was only after the United Kingdom failed to indicate its willingness to consider the immediate suspension of the authorization of the MOX plant and a halt to related international transports that it instituted proceedings.[146] ITLOS did not require a formalized process but considered that an exchange of correspondence relating to the dispute under UNCLOS will be sufficient to meet this requirement.

One requirement under Article 283 appears to be that the invocation of UNCLOS provisions as a basis for the dispute should be made in the context of this exchange. The respondent States in both *Southern Bluefin Tuna* and *MOX Plant* complained that the reliance on UNCLOS had happened belatedly, thereby suggesting that the reference to the Convention in the later correspondence was simply a matter of posturing in anticipation of legal proceedings. While the reference to UNCLOS must necessarily occur in the course of the correspondence, the timing of these claims should be irrelevant. It would be surprising if a State was barred from utilizing the mandatory dispute settlement mechanism in UNCLOS on the sole basis that the first notices of complaint did not stipulate all legal bases for its claims.

Alternative Dispute Settlement Procedures to UNCLOS Available
Prima facie jurisdiction may be lacking if either Articles 281 or 282 clearly bar recourse to the compulsory procedures in Section 2 of Part XV, or if the dispute does not involve the interpretation or application of UNCLOS. In the provisional measures phase of *Southern Bluefin Tuna*, Japan did not rely specifically on Article 281 but argued that for jurisdiction to be *prima facie* established the dispute had to concern the interpretation and application of UNCLOS rather than some other international agreement. Here, Japan submitted, the dispute was one arising under the CCSBT. In supporting this claim, Japan pointed to the fact that the obligations in UNCLOS concerning the conservation of highly migratory species, and

---

[145] MOX Plant, Provisional Measures, paras. 56–57.   [146] *Ibid.*, paras. 58–59.

high seas fisheries, generally do not prescribe specific conservation measures, principles of conservation, nor principal factors to be considered when deciding such matters.[147] As such, UNCLOS had to be regarded as a framework convention for these matters, leaving the specific conservation requirements to be determined on a regional or species-specific basis.[148] Allegations of violations of the specific requirements, as set out in the CCSBT, did not automatically constitute allegations of violations of UNCLOS.[149]

Australia and New Zealand emphasized that for the prescription of provisional measures only *prima facie* jurisdiction was necessary and that the Applicants had raised a substantial claim under particular provisions of the Convention and that the facts supported that claim on a *prima facie* basis.[150] The Applicants did not consider that the obligations in the CCSBT were intended to give effect to UNCLOS and thereby replace or exclude the UNCLOS obligations.[151] Instead, they argued that the Convention was a comprehensive, overarching regime whereby subsidiary processes were envisaged as the means to give effect to some of its provisions.[152] This argument applied to both the substantive obligations and the dispute settlement procedures in each of the treaties. According to the Applicants, the CCSBT was not meant to deal with disputes relating to the interpretation or application of UNCLOS nor did it provide for binding and compulsory third-party settlement.[153] The dispute settlement provision in the CCSBT thus encouraged the peaceful resolution of disputes but did not preclude the parties from resorting to the procedures available under UNCLOS that related to that Convention.[154] The Tribunal in granting provisional measures agreed that the fact that the CCSBT applied between the parties did not exclude their right to invoke the provisions of the Convention in regard to the conservation and management of southern bluefin tuna,[155] nor did it preclude recourse to the dispute procedures of the Convention.[156] ITLOS therefore concluded that it had *prima facie* jurisdiction to prescribe provisional measures.

In *Land Reclamation*, Singapore submitted that Malaysia had failed to comply with Article 281 on the basis that Malaysia had an obligation to negotiate in situations in which two States both allege different and potentially incompatible rights in the same resource.[157] On this

---

[147] Southern Bluefin Tuna, ITLOS/PV.99/23, at 7.   [148] *Ibid.*   [149] *Ibid.*
[150] ITLOS/PV.99/20, at 20.   [151] *Ibid.*   [152] *Ibid.*, at 20–21.   [153] *Ibid.*, at 22.
[154] *Ibid.*, at 22–23.   [155] Southern Bluefin Tuna, Provisional Measures, para. 51.
[156] *Ibid.*, para. 55.   [157] Land Reclamation, ITLOS/PV.03/03, at 33.

basis, Singapore argued, "both States had embarked upon a course of negotiation under Article 281 in an effort to arrive at an amicable solution of the dispute between them."[158] Further, "[h]aving selected a mode of dispute resolution, Malaysia cannot unilaterally terminate it without the consent of Singapore before the negotiation has an opportunity to achieve a settlement."[159] In response to this "astonishing" argument, Malaysia distinguished the present case from the jurisdictional decision in *Southern Bluefin Tuna* where a specific trilateral agreement existed between the parties and that included its own dispute settlement clause.[160] Malaysia further refuted that there had been any agreement to negotiate that had the effect of contracting the parties out of their rights under Section 2 of Part XV.

The Tribunal did not consider whether Singapore's argument on Article 281 was correct as a matter of law, but took the position that it could not be established as a matter of fact. In the Tribunal's view, Malaysia had accepted an invitation to meetings after it had filed its Statement of Claim without prejudice to Malaysia's right to proceed with the arbitration. There was no basis for applying Article 281 in these circumstances.[161] Given the jurisdictional decision in *Southern Bluefin Tuna* that there is no requirement for compulsory procedures to be excluded expressly for Article 281 to apply,[162] the decision in *Land Reclamation* leaves open the possibility that an agreement to negotiate could preclude jurisdiction for the institution of mandatory adjudication or arbitration under Section 2 of Part XV. An assessment of the facts will be required to determine whether such an agreement has precluded recourse to other dispute settlement procedures. If it is not clear that the parties had agreed to negotiate to settle their differences to the exclusion of other dispute settlement procedures then a finding of *prima facie* jurisdiction should be warranted and any further challenge on this basis should be held over for a full hearing.

ITLOS also had to address the question of alternative dispute settlement procedures in *MOX Plant* and whether those procedures would prevent a finding that jurisdiction was afforded on a *prima facie* basis

---

[158] *Ibid.*, at 34.   [159] *Ibid.*, at 35.

[160] Case concerning Land Reclamation by Singapore in and around the Straits of Johor, Request for Provisional Measures, *Malaysia v. Singapore*, Verbatim Record, ITLOS/PV.03/05, p. 10, available at http://www.itlos.org/start2_en.html.

[161] Land Reclamation, Provisional Measures, para. 57.

[162] See note 34 and accompanying text.

under the Convention. The United Kingdom contended that Ireland was precluded from having recourse to mandatory dispute settlement under Section 2 of UNCLOS by virtue of Article 282 of the Convention. Article 282 provides that the procedures under UNCLOS are not available if the States parties have agreed "through a general, regional or bilateral agreement or otherwise, that such dispute shall . . . be submitted to a procedure that entails a binding decision." The United Kingdom pointed to a pending arbitration under the OSPAR Convention and to Ireland's intention to pursue proceedings before the European Court of Justice as well for alleged violations of other European treaties. Ireland responded that the dispute concerned the interpretation and application of UNCLOS and the other fora would not be specifically addressing all the terms of UNCLOS at issue in this case.

In affirming *prima facie* jurisdiction,[163] ITLOS noted that the other dispute settlement bodies under the different treaties would not resolve specifically a dispute related to the interpretation or application of UNCLOS. Even if those treaties contained similar rights or duties, the "application of international law rules on interpretation of treaties to identical or similar provisions of different treaties may not yield the same results, having regard to, *inter alia*, differences in the respective contests, objects and purposes, subsequent practice of parties and *travaux préparatoires*."[164] ITLOS has thus taken the position that the dispute before the alternative forum must expressly deal with violations of UNCLOS to prevent a *prima facie* finding of jurisdiction.

Section 3 Exceptions and Limitations
The issue of whether the exceptions and limitations to compulsory procedures entailing binding decisions, set out in Section 3 of Part XV, could prevent even a *prima facie* finding of jurisdiction was addressed in the provisional measures phase of *M/V "Saiga" (No. 2)*. That case concerned Guinea's arrest and seizure of a bunkering vessel registered to Saint Vincent and the Grenadines. Saint Vincent and the Grenadines

---

163 The *ad hoc* tribunal constituted under Annex VII in *MOX Plant* subsequently affirmed that there was *prima facie* jurisdiction when ordering provisional measures. See MOX Plant, Order No. 3, para. 17.

164 MOX Plant, Provisional Measures, para. 51. In his Separate Opinion, Vice-President Nelson entertained doubts about the reach of this paragraph and voiced concern that it might render Articles 281 or 282 ineffective. *Ibid.*, Separate Opinion of Vice-President Nelson, para. 7.

first filed an application with ITLOS requesting the prompt release of the vessel.[165] An order was made to this effect, conditional upon the payment of a bond.[166] Following the judgment, Saint Vincent and the Grenadines posted a US$400,000 bank guarantee. Guinea did not release the M/V "Saiga" at that time because it did not accept the terms of the Bank Guarantee and requested changes to those terms. Saint Vincent and the Grenadines considered Guinea's request for changes to be unreasonable or irrelevant. On December 22, 1997, Saint Vincent and the Grenadines notified Guinea that it was instituting arbitral proceedings on the merits of the dispute,[167] and filed a request for the prescription of provisional measures with ITLOS.[168]

In challenging Saint Vincent and the Grenadines' request for provisional measures, Guinea argued that ITLOS lacked *prima facie* jurisdiction. Guinea sought to take advantage of the Tribunal's decision on the prompt release of vessels and the manner by which it characterized Guinea's actions as falling within the Convention provisions on the exploring and exploiting, conserving and managing of natural resources within the EEZ.[169] On this basis, Guinea was put in a position to argue that the dispute fell within the terms of Article 297(3), which effectively excludes all disputes related to fishing in the EEZ from the compulsory dispute procedures of the Convention.[170] Guinea took the position that the possible application of one of the exceptions to the compulsory resolution of a dispute was sufficient to deprive the Tribunal of even *prima facie* jurisdiction.

Saint Vincent and the Grenadines instead relied on Article 297(1) as the basis for jurisdiction, which allows compulsory dispute settlement for matters relating to the sovereign rights of States in relation to the freedom of navigation in the EEZ in Article 58.[171] The Tribunal

---

[165] See The M/V "Saiga", Request for Prompt Release (St. Vincent v. Guinea) (Dec. 4, 1997), available at http://www.itlos.org/start2_en.html.

[166] *Ibid.*, para. 81.

[167] Saint Vincent and the Grenadines Requests Provisional Measures in respect of the M/V "Saiga", ITLOS/Press 11, January 13, 1998, available at http://www.itlos.org/start2_en.html.

[168] *Ibid.* Prior to the hearing on provisional measures, the parties agreed to submit the dispute on the merits to ITLOS, rather than to arbitration, through an Exchange of Letters. As a procedural issue, the parties agreed that the request for provisional measures be considered as submitted in accordance with Article 290(1).

[169] See further, pp. 103–108.   [170] See further, pp. 176–190.

[171] See further, pp. 135–138.

decided that this article afforded a *prima facie* basis of jurisdiction.[172] Such a conclusion was drawn on the basis that the parties had agreed to resolve issues of jurisdiction during a single phase of proceedings in the Exchange of Letters.[173] In addition, the Tribunal noted that it was not required fully to satisfy itself that it had jurisdiction on the merits of the case.[174] On this basis, ITLOS did not hobble the provisional measures proceedings by allowing a dispute to be excluded from its scope by a simple assertion that it may fall within the exceptions of Section 3 of Part XV.[175] In light of the complexity of the dispute settlement provisions and the varying interpretations of the Convention that might be submitted for adjudication, the parties should be able to argue the matter fully and the court or tribunal has the opportunity to consider the issues raised. Such a determination is more likely to meet the expectations of the parties in determining how the dispute settlement system intersects with the substantive norms of the Convention.

Standard for Prescribing Provisional Measures under Article 290

Given the temporal distinction between paragraphs 1 and 5 of Article 290, the question arises as to whether the conditions under paragraph 1 are limited to that provision, or whether those criteria are to be read into decisions on provisional measures being decided under Article 290(5). A higher standard must clearly be met under paragraph 5 since the need for protection is more imminent or immediate, and cannot wait for the constitution of the *ad hoc* arbitral tribunal. The temporal distinction between the two paragraphs (namely, measures required pending final decision, as opposed to pending the constitution of a separate international body) justifies a higher standard being imposed on the requesting

---

[172] The M/V "Saiga" (No. 2), Order on Provisional Measures (*Saint Vincent v. Guinea*) (March 11, 1998) available at http://www.itlos.org/start2_en.html, para. 30. Rosenne appears to consider this issue as somewhat redundant. He states: "Actually, once the parties had agreed to submit the dispute to the Tribunal, that agreement was sufficient to confer jurisdiction on the Tribunal, and made it unnecessary for the Tribunal to look for any other basis for its jurisdiction to prescribe provisional measures." Shabtai Rosenne, "International Tribunal for the Law of the Sea: 1998 Survey," 14 *Int'l J. Marine & Coastal L.* 453, 461 (1999).

[173] M/V "Saiga" (No. 2), Provisional Measures, para. 28.   [174] *Ibid.*, para. 29.

[175] In *Land Reclamation*, the Tribunal noted in its Order that none of the exceptions under Article 298 applied when considering if there was *prima facie* jurisdiction. Land Reclamation, Provisional Measures, para. 28. Article 298 declarations could well fall into Lauterpacht's category of a reservation obviously excluding jurisdiction. See note 136 and accompanying text. If jurisdiction was not "obviously excluded" by Article 298, a full jurisdictional hearing would be warranted.

State under Article 290(5); the urgency must necessarily be greater when a shorter period of time is at stake. Judge Treves, in his separate opinion in the provisional measures stage of *Southern Bluefin Tuna*, commented on the differing application of "urgency" in paragraphs 1 and 5 of Article 290 as follows:

> The requirement of urgency is stricter when provisional measures are requested under paragraph 5 than it is when they are requested under paragraph 1 of article 290 as regards the moment in which the measures may be prescribed. In particular, there is no "urgency" under paragraph 5 if the measures requested could, without prejudice to the rights to be protected, be granted by the arbitral tribunal once constituted. As regards the moment up to which it is needed that the measures be complied with, the only urgency which is relevant is that of paragraph 1 of article 290.[176]

In discussing the difference between paragraphs 1 and 5 of Article 290 in *MOX Plant*, Judge Mensah highlighted that for measures to be prescribed under paragraph 5 it had to be borne in mind that the tribunal or court doing so was not the body that would ultimately decide the substance of the case (warranting a certain degree of self-discipline so that matters outside of that forum's competence would not be addressed).[177] He also emphasized that the measures prescribed under paragraph 5 were those necessary to protect the rights of the parties only until the arbitral tribunal was constituted, not until a final decision on the case was reached.[178]

In *Land Reclamation*, ITLOS clarified that provisional measures under Article 290(5) did not immediately expire upon the constitution of the tribunal. The Tribunal clearly stated that while it could prescribe provisional measures pending the constitution of the arbitral tribunal under Article 290(5), that limitation did not mean that the measures ordered would only be applicable until the arbitral tribunal was constituted.[179] On this basis, the "urgency" was not to be assessed in relation to the period between the provisional measures being ordered by ITLOS and the exact moment the arbitral tribunal is constituted, but rather the "urgency of the situation must be assessed taking into account the period during which the Annex VII arbitral tribunal is not yet in a position to 'modify, revoke or affirm those provisional measures',"[180] as

---

[176] Southern Bluefin Tuna, Provisional Measures, Separate Opinion of Judge Treves.
[177] MOX Plant, Provisional Measures, Separate Opinion of Judge Mensah, at 3.
[178] *Ibid.*, at 3.   [179] Land Reclamation, Provisional Measures, para. 67.
[180] *Ibid.*, para. 68.

well as the fact that the measures may remain applicable beyond that period.[181]

In *MOX Plant*, Ireland alleged that the United Kingdom's authorization of the MOX plant on the coast of the Irish Sea and accompanying international movement of radioactive materials violated various provisions of UNCLOS and that provisional measures were necessary pending the constitution of the arbitral tribunal to address these claims. In presenting their cases, both Ireland and the United Kingdom addressed the standards set forth in Article 290(1) as well as Article 290(5), and thus considered whether Ireland's rights needed to be preserved or whether there was a need to to prevent serious harm to the marine environment, as required under Article 290(1). The question of urgency pending the constitution of the arbitral tribunal was dealt with in addition to these criteria.

In addressing this question, the Tribunal linked the criteria under Article 290(5) with those under Article 290(1) so that what would constitute "urgency" would be understood to involve action prejudicial to the rights of either party or serious harm being caused to the marine environment pending the constitution of the arbitral tribunal.[182] Reading these paragraphs together was considered appropriate on the understanding that paragraph 1 "sets out the parameters and conditions for the prescription of provisional measures in general."[183] Following this decision, parties seeking provisional measures under Article 290(5) must therefore demonstrate urgency not only from a temporal perspective, but also in relation to the criteria set forth in paragraph 1 of Article 290.

Thus far, ITLOS has not spelled out more specific standards or criteria in addition to the Convention that must be met in this regard (avoiding qualifications of irreparable or irreversible harm). The assessment has

---

[181] *Ibid.*, para. 69.

[182] MOX Plant, Provisional Measures, para. 64 ("if the Tribunal considers that the urgency of the situation so requires in the sense that action prejudicial to the rights of either party or causing serious harm to the marine environment is likely to be taken before the constitution of the Annex VII arbitral tribunal").

[183] *Ibid.*, Separate Opinion of Judge Mensah, p. 1. This approach overlooks, however, that para. 1 provides that a court or tribunal to which a "dispute has been duly submitted" may prescribe provisional measures, which distinguishes the role played by ITLOS under para. 5. See Hayashi, "Southern Bluefin Tuna," at 381. Nonetheless, given the absence of standards otherwise set forth in the Convention, and the reticence of the Tribunal to use the standard of irreparable harm, as discussed below, the linkage at least ensures consistency of standards for the prescription of provisional measures under UNCLOS.

largely been dependent on the facts of each case. For example, in *M/V "Saiga" (No. 2)*,[184] the main concern of Saint Vincent and the Grenadines in the provisional measures stage was the release of the M/V "Saiga" and the vessel's crew, as well as ensuring that municipal judicial decisions relating to the M/V "Saiga" be suspended and not enforced.[185] In conjunction with these requests, Saint Vincent and the Grenadines sought orders to prevent Guinea from interfering with rights of navigation, that certain customs laws of Guinea not be applied or enforced in the EEZ, and that Guinea cease and desist from undertaking hot pursuit of Saint Vincent and the Grenadines' vessels unless that pursuit complied with the conditions laid down in Article 111 of the Convention. Guinea argued that the factual premise for establishing an urgent need for provisional measures was lacking. Guinea submitted that there was no evidence that the owners of the M/V "Saiga" were incurring great financial cost or that other bunkering vessels flying the Saint Vincent and the Grenadines flag risked interference from Guinean authorities.[186] In relation to the release of the M/V "Saiga," Guinea argued that the bank guarantee was not "reasonable" security.[187] Guinea otherwise considered that the measures requested were not provisional or that the Tribunal lacked competence to issue orders to the requested effect.

The Tribunal's decision on provisional measures was unanimous. In deciding what provisional measures to prescribe, the Tribunal had to take into account the fact that the M/V "Saiga" had been released from detention in Conakry and berthed in Senegal.[188] As a result, the most urgent request was rendered moot. However, the Tribunal still considered that measures needed to be prescribed in order to preserve fully the rights of Saint Vincent and the Grenadines pending the final decision on the merits, and to avoid aggravation or extension of the dispute.[189] By virtue of Article 89(5) of the Tribunal's Rules, the Tribunal "may

---

[184] M/V "Saiga" (No. 2), Provisional Measures, para. 20 (request from Notification of December 22, 1997). See also *ibid.*, para. 21 (measures in Request dated January 13, 1998 and revised in the Reply of February 13, 1998) and para. 23 (final submissions presented at public sitting).

[185] The Court of Appeal of Conakry sentenced the Master of the ship to a six month suspended prison sentence. Saint Vincent and the Grenadines was also held to be civilly liable.

[186] The M/V "Saiga" (No. 2), Order on Provisional Measures (*Saint Vincent v. Guinea*) (March 11, 1998), Verbatim Record, ITLOS/PV.98/2, pp. 7–8, available at http://www.itlos.org/start2_en.html.

[187] The very fact that the bank refused to pay the bond when no appeal from a Guinean court was possible was deemed to be unreasonable. *Ibid.*, at 8.

[188] M/V "Saiga" (No. 2), Provisional Measures, para. 36.   [189] *Ibid.*, paras. 41–43.

prescribe measures different in whole or in part from those requested."
The Tribunal therefore decided that:

Guinea shall refrain from taking or enforcing any judicial or administrative
measure against the M/V Saiga, its Master and the other members of the crew, its
owners or operators, in connection with the incidents leading to the arrest and
detention of the vessel on 28 October 1997 and to the subsequent prosecution
and conviction of the Master.

This order basically gives effect to Saint Vincent and the Grenadines'
request in relation to the municipal judicial proceedings taken in Guinea
in respect of the vessel.[190] Presumably, the judicial or administrative
measures could not have been remedied purely by payment of compensation, if necessary, at the merits stage. Saint Vincent and the Grenadine's
other requests were rightly deferred as issues to be resolved until the
merits and not warranted to protect Saint Vincent and the Grenadine's
rights pending the final decision.

The standards for prescribing provisional measures were explored further in *Southern Bluefin Tuna*. There, Australia and New Zealand considered that provisional measures were necessary on an urgent basis
in light of Japan's adoption of an experimental fishing program that
involved Japan harvesting more tuna than had been agreed as part of
national allocations under the CCSBT. The CCSBT establishes a Commission that has the power to decide the total allowable catch and its allocation among the parties unless other appropriate, or additional, measures
are decided on in light of the recommendations of the Commission's Scientific Committee.[191] In 1994, the Commission fixed the national quotas as had been agreed between the parties in 1989 and these quotas
remained in effect until 1997. During discussions in 1998, Japan proposed an experimental fishing program that was meant to improve the
understanding of the southern bluefin tuna stock and reduce uncer-
tainties about the state of the stock. Such a program required Japan
to increase the amount of southern bluefin tuna it harvested under the
CCSBT. When disagreement on an experimental program continued and
no agreement could be reached on changing the total allowable catch,
Japan unilaterally implemented the experimental fishing program for a
three-year period.

---

[190] Judge Warioba, in his declaration, took the view that the order had actually gone
"far beyond" the request of the Applicants in terms of the type of action prohibited
and the category of persons protected. *Ibid.*, Declaration of Judge Warioba.
[191] CCSBT, art. 8(3).

In challenging Australia and New Zealand's request for provisional measures, Japan argued that there was no urgency requiring the prescription of provisional measures. According to Japan, any urgency had to be determined in accordance with the requirement that irreparable harm or damage be imminent.[192] Japan's proposed standard of an irreparability requirement applying with respect to both the element of urgency and the need to preserve the rights of the parties was consistent with the jurisprudence of the ICJ in this regard.[193] Japan was of the view that no such harm was imminent – if so, then Australia and New Zealand would be restraining their own catches of southern bluefin tuna rather than just demanding that Japan's level of catch be controlled.[194]

The Applicants submitted that the grant of jurisdiction to ITLOS for the prescription of provisional measures was broader than that granted to the ICJ and so circumscriptions through the use of a standard of irreparable harm or prejudice were inappropriate.[195] Instead, the Applicants referred to a procedural and substantive urgency. The procedural urgency related to the time delay that existed between the decision to institute arbitral proceedings and the actual establishment of the arbitral tribunal.[196] The substantive urgency related to a question of whether in the circumstances of the case the measures would be appropriate to preserve the respective rights of the parties.[197] A test of what was appropriate would set a lower threshold compared with a standard of irreparable harm. Australia and New Zealand argued that there was an immediate urgency to prevent further fishing by Japan because Japan had already exceeded its national quota for 1999 and the Applicants considered that there was a need to prevent the further decline in numbers of tuna.[198] The parties informed the Tribunal that commercial fishing

---

[192] Southern Bluefin Tuna, ITLOS/PV.99/23, at 10.

[193] See Karin Oellers-Frahm, Interim Measures of Protection, in 1 *Encylcopedia of Public International Law* (Rudolf Bernhardt ed., 1986), p. 70 (referring to the jurisprudence of the ICJ and PCIJ and stating, "Unanimity exists for the view that interim protection can only be awarded if irreparable damage is imminent").

[194] Southern Bluefin Tuna, ITLOS/PV.99/23, at 10–11.

[195] Southern Bluefin Tuna, Requests for Provisional Measures (*New Zealand v. Japan; Australia v. Japan*) (Order of August 27, 1999), Verbatim Records, ITLOS/PV.99/21, p. 24, available at http://www.itlos.org/start2_en.html.

[196] *Ibid.*, at 25.   [197] *Ibid.*, at 25–26 and 27.

[198] *Ibid.*, at 26. In his separate opinion, Judge Treves noted that the urgency was not to stop the actual collapse in the stock but to stop the trend towards such a collapse. See Southern Bluefin Tuna, Provisional Measures, para. 8 (separate opinion of Judge Treves).

was anticipated in 1999 and non-parties to the CCSBT were expected to continue to fish the species as well.[199]

A majority of the Tribunal noted that all the parties agreed that the stock of southern bluefin tuna was severely depleted and was at its historically lowest levels.[200] The Tribunal stated: "although the Tribunal cannot conclusively assess the scientific evidence presented by the parties, it finds that measures should be taken as a matter of urgency to preserve the rights of the parties and to avert further deterioration of the southern bluefin tuna stock."[201] No reference was made to the possibility of "irreparable harm" or "irreparable damage" as the reason for prescribing measures.[202] The Tribunal granted Australia and New Zealand's request that Japan should be prohibited from continuing the experimental fishing program, but this measure to avert deterioration of the stock was directed at all of the parties.

Environmental concerns and differences of opinion over scientific information also influenced the Tribunal's decision on what provisional measures to prescribe in *MOX Plant*.[203] In seeking to establish that such urgency existed, Ireland relied on a range of facts addressing the dangers of radioactive leaks and the irreversibility of commissioning the plant or of introducing plutonium to the marine environment.[204] The United Kingdom maintained that the risk of pollution was "infinitesimally small,"[205] security risks were "negligible,"[206] and that neither the introduction of plutonium nor the commissioning of the plant (while causing technical and financial difficulties) was irreversible.[207] The Tribunal reached the conclusion that the urgency of the situation did not require the prescription of the measures requested by Ireland.

---

[199] *Southern Bluefin Tuna*, Provisional Measures, paras. 72–76.

[200] *Ibid.*, para. 71.   [201] *Ibid.*, para. 80.

[202] Judge Laing endorsed this approach in his separate opinion:

> Instead of irreparability, the key to UNCLOS provisional measures is the discretionary element of appropriateness . . . Along with appropriateness, the formulation of preservation of the respective rights of the parties underscores the discretionary nature of provisional measures.

Ibid., Separate Opinion of Judge Laing para. 5.

[203] Although parties have argued for the application of the precautionary principle, ITLOS has not expressly endorsed or applied this principle in its Orders. It is nonetheless arguable that some statements seem to favor the essential elements of the principle. See Alexander Yankov, "Current Fisheries Disputes and the International Tribunal for the Law of the Sea," in *Current Marine Environmental Issues and the International Tribunal for the Law of the Sea* (Myron H. Nordquist and John Norton Moore eds., 2001), pp. 223, 230.

[204] MOX Plant, Provisional Measures, paras. 68–70.

[205] *Ibid.*, para. 72.   [206] *Ibid.*, para. 76.   [207] *Ibid.*, para. 74.

In reaching its decision on the question of urgency, the Tribunal took account of the United Kingdom's assurances to the Tribunal that there would be no additional marine transports of radioactive material either to or from the MOX plant as a result of the commissioning of the plant; nor would there be any export of MOX fuel or imports of spent nuclear fuel in the following eleven months. Perhaps without such assurances, a specific order would have been warranted in this case. The Tribunal did not comment on the standard to be met in establishing what constitutes "serious harm to the marine environment" under Article 290(1), but simply referred to the "circumstances of this case."[208] Judge Mensah, in his Separate Opinion, similarly refused to undertake this task, but still stated, "that a court or tribunal will not prescribe provisional measures if it is not satisfied that some irreversible prejudice of rights or serious harm to the marine environment might occur in the absence of such measures."[209]

Despite arguments of the parties referring to standards of "irreparable" harm in *Land Reclamation*, ITLOS again refrained from endorsing this standard in its reasoning. Malaysia had sought orders from ITLOS requiring Singapore to suspend all land reclamation activities in the vicinity of their mutual maritime boundary, provide Malaysia with full information as to the current and projected works, afford Malaysia a full opportunity to comment upon the works and their potential impacts, and agree to negotiate with Malaysia concerning any remaining unresolved issues. Relying on jurisprudence from the ICJ, Singapore submitted, "the essential condition for provisional measures 'presupposes that the circumstances of the case disclose the risk of an irreparable prejudice to rights in issue in the proceedings'."[210] As with Singapore, Malaysia did not adhere to the exact terminology of Article 290 but drew on the standards more typically applied for provisional measures. Malaysia thus argued that for the prescription of provisional measures "there must be some threat of irreparable harm to the rights involved or the interests protected; that is, some threat if the conduct in question is not enjoined,

---

[208] *Ibid.*, para. 81.

[209] *Ibid.*, Separate Opinion of Judge Mensah, p. 2. He later equates irreversibility with irreparability. *Ibid.*, Separate Opinion of Judge Mensah, p. 4.

[210] Case Concerning Land Reclamation by Singapore In and around the Straits of Johor (*Malaysia v. Singapore*), Request for the Prescription of Provisional Measures under Article 290, Paragraph 5, of the United Nations Convention on the Law of the Sea, Response of Singapore (September 20), para. 88, available at http://www.itlos.org/start2_en.html (citing the ICJ interim measures order in the *Aegean Sea Continental Shelf* case).

and the matter must be urgent, not distant or remote."[211] Malaysia considered that there was clearly a risk of irreparable harm on the basis that "Singapore is working hard to establish a *fait accompli.*"[212]

Through the course of the written and oral pleadings, Singapore offered various assurances to Malaysia that satisfied three of Malaysia's requested measures. Malaysia was prepared to accept these assurances, provided that ITLOS made them a matter of formal judicial record.[213] The Tribunal did so for those assurances, as well as Singapore's further assurance that no irreversible action would be taken in what was known as Area D, pending the completion of a joint study by independent experts for the two parties.[214] Ultimately, the Tribunal did not address the urgency of the matter with respect to Malaysia's specific requests in light of the assurances that were recorded in the Order. Instead, the Tribunal referred to the ongoing lack of cooperation between the parties and stated, "that it is urgent to build on the commitments made to ensure prompt and effective cooperation of the parties in the implementation of their commitments."[215] Judge Anderson was critical of the Tribunal's assessment of urgency and considered the "urgent" need to cooperate was "less than self-evident."[216] He did not see what urgency could exist when parties were to be expected to carry out their obligations in good faith.[217]

ITLOS proceeded to consider what measures should be put in place to ensure that no action would be taken that might aggravate or extend the dispute, and referred to "possible implications of land reclamation on the marine environment." This language tends to indicate that "serious harm to the marine environment" had not been established to warrant an order of provisional measures. Moreover, there was no other discussion of the standards to be met for the prescription of provisional measures in the *consideranda*, but the *dispositif* unanimously directed Singapore "not to conduct its land reclamation in ways that might cause irreparable prejudice to the rights of Malaysia or serious harm to the

---

[211] Case Concerning Land Reclamation by Singapore in and around the Straits of Johor (*Malaysia* v. *Singapore*), Request for Provisional Measures, Verbatim Record, ITLOS/PV.03/02/Corr.1, p. 23, available at http://www.itlos.org/start2_en.html.

[212] *Ibid.*, p. 23.   [213] Land Reclamation, Provisional Measures, para. 79.

[214] *Ibid.*, para. 88.   [215] *Ibid.*, para. 98.

[216] *Ibid.*, Declaration of Judge Anderson, para. 3. Judge Chandrasekhara Rao also considered that there was no urgency in respect of Malaysia's request for an order suspending Singapore's land reclamation activities. *Ibid.*, Separate Opinion of Judge Chandrasekhara Rao, para. 38.

[217] *Ibid.*, Declaration of Judge Anderson, para. 3.

marine environment."[218] As such, there is no indication that a risk of "irreparable" prejudice to Malaysia's rights or serious harm to the marine environment existed as the predicate for this Order. Rather, this measure was a specific requirement of conduct on Singapore's behalf. The Tribunal's desire to facilitate the parties' agreements reached during the course of the proceedings obscured how, or if, the criteria of Article 290 were met.

Counter to this stance, the *ad hoc* Tribunal in *MOX Plant* adopted the standard of urgency and irreparable harm in considering provisional measures pending the final resolution of the dispute. In referring to the protection of the rights of the parties under Article 290(1), the Tribunal stated: "International judicial practice confirms that a general requirement for the prescription of provisional measures to protect the rights of the Parties is that there needs to be a showing both of urgency and of irreparable harm to the claimed rights."[219] Having made this statement, the *ad hoc* Tribunal did not examine any further whether this standard had been met with regard to the measures of cooperation required by ITLOS and then confirmed in their own order.

No definitive view has therefore emerged from ITLOS on whether the general requirement of irreparable harm in international law is applicable in respect of the provisional measures to be ordered under the Convention. Any conclusions on this point must be drawn from what was not said. Thus, in *Southern Bluefin Tuna* and *Land Reclamation*, the Tribunal did not clearly endorse a standard of irreparability, and in *MOX Plant*, again, reference was only made to the circumstances of the case. Judge Mensah is presently a lone voice in ITLOS utilizing this standard in *MOX Plant*.[220] The *ad hoc* Tribunal in *MOX Plant*, of which Judge Mensah is President, then sought to apply this requirement and presumably considered that it was met in respect of ITLOS's initial order through its confirmation of that order. Whether the conditions are met for the prescription of provisional measures is ultimately highly fact dependent. Nonetheless, the Convention sets out the applicable legal standards for the prescription or provisional measures. It is for the requesting party to show that this standard is met in the application of the relevant facts, and for the Tribunal to adhere to that standard. In light of the temporal considerations and the conditions set out in Article 290 itself, it does not seem necessary for a tribunal or court prescribing provisional measures under UNCLOS to imply any additional legal standard.

---

[218] *Ibid.*, para. 106(2).   [219] MOX Plant, Order No. 3, para. 58.
[220] Judge Ndiaye has endorsed this standard writing extrajudicially. See Ndiaye, at 98.

Types of Provisional Measures

In UNCLOS proceedings requesting provisional measures, the court or tribunal is not constrained to order only the measures requested by the parties, but may vary the requests, or devise new measures, as that court or tribunal sees fit. ITLOS has thus far acted in accordance with one of the central themes of the dispute settlement provisions in the Convention – namely, that of flexibility – through its willingness to prescribe measures different to those requested by the parties but still intended to prevent aggravation of the dispute pending arbitration or adjudication of the merits.[221] The parties have routinely requested measures requiring the parties not to aggravate the dispute or to prejudice the rights of the parties pending resolution of the dispute. In addition to prescribing specific measures, ITLOS has also taken the position that its power under Article 290 encompasses the authority to make recommendations as well as issue orders to parties. Despite requests that the other party pay costs of the proceedings, ITLOS has so far split the costs between the parties.[222]

The practice of ITLOS has been to prescribe certain measures, and then supplement those orders through a reporting order, which would presumably be intended to enhance the likelihood of compliance. In *M/V "Saiga" (No. 2)*, for example, ITLOS issued an order that Guinea refrain from taking or enforcing various judicial or administrative measures relating to the arrest and detention of the M/V "Saiga" along with associated legal proceedings. The enforcement of this order was then supported by a further decision of the Tribunal to require the parties to submit reports and information on compliance with the prescribed measures.[223] A similar approach was adopted in *MOX Plant*. There, while rejecting Ireland's requests for specific orders about the commissioning of the MOX plant and associated marine transports, the Tribunal nonetheless considered it appropriate to prescribe certain measures of cooperation. It specifically required the parties to enter into consultations in order to:

---

[221] The *ad hoc* Tribunal in *MOX Plant* considered that it was also competent to prescribe provisional measures other than those sought by any party in light of ITLOS's power to do so, a comparable authority accorded to the ICJ, and the lack of disagreement from the parties to the dispute. MOX Plant, Order No. 3, para. 43.

[222] "In inter-State proceedings it is usual for each State to bear its own costs, and for the costs of the tribunal to be divided equally between the parties." Collier and Lowe, p. 253.

[223] The Tribunal has power to make such a decision under Article 95(1) of its Rules.

    (a)   exchange further information with regard to possible consequences for the Irish Sea arising out of the commissioning of the MOX plant;

    (b)   monitor risks or the effects of the operation of the MOX plant for the Irish Sea;

    (c)   devise, as appropriate, measures to prevent pollution of the marine environment which might result from the operation of the MOX plant.[224]

The Tribunal then required that Ireland and the United Kingdom submit an initial report on these measures and authorized the President of the Tribunal to request further reports and information as appropriate.[225] When the *ad hoc* Tribunal affirmed this Order, it also decided that the States should continue their reporting obligations.[226]

    The duty to cooperate to prevent pollution of the marine environment and the concomitant rights that arise from this duty were also recognized in *Land Reclamation*.[227] The Tribunal affirmed that these were rights that may need to be preserved through the prescription of provisional measures. Considering the different positions of the parties on the possible repercussions of Singapore's land reclamation works and the lack of cooperation between the parties prior to the institution of third-party proceedings,[228] the Tribunal prescribed that Malaysia and Singapore cooperate and enter into consultations in respect of the prompt establishment of a group of experts,[229] the exchange of information on and assessment of risks or effects of Singapore's land reclamation works, and the implementation of the commitments noted in the Order. Similar to the decision in *MOX Plant*, ITLOS also ordered the parties to report on the actions taken both to the Tribunal, as well as the arbitral tribunal unless the arbitral tribunal decided differently.[230]

    In *Southern Bluefin Tuna*, the Applicants sought provisional orders that largely reflected the requests on the merits of the case.[231] More

---

[224] MOX Plant, Provisional Measures, para. 89(1).

[225] *Ibid.*, para. 89(2). The *ad hoc* Tribunal confirmed the continuation of this measure when it decided to suspend the proceedings. See MOX Plant, Order No. 3.

[226] MOX Plant, Order No. 3, para. 68 (noting that it was consistent with the practice of ITLOS for each party to submit reports and information on compliance with provisional measures orders).

[227] Land Reclamation, Provisional Measures, para. 92 (citing *MOX Plant*).

[228] *Ibid.*, paras. 93–97.

[229] *Ibid.*, para. 106(1) (Singapore accepted Malaysia's proposal to this effect during the oral arguments).

[230] *Ibid.*, para. 106(3).

[231] In its Statement of Claim instituting arbitral proceedings, Australia requested that Japan refrain from experimental fishing without the agreement of Australia and

particularly, Australia and New Zealand requested an order that Japan immediately cease unilateral experimental fishing for southern bluefin tuna and restrict its catch in any given fishing year to the previously agreed national quota, minus a reduction for the fish caught from the experimental fishing. While objecting to the prescription of provisional measures for the *prima facie* lack of jurisdiction, Japan requested *arguendo* that the Tribunal prescribe that the Applicants recommence negotiations for a six-month period with any differences left unresolved to be referred to a panel of independent scientists.

ITLOS decided that all of the parties had to adhere to the annual national allocations that had last been agreed upon unless the parties were able to agree otherwise.[232] This order was also strengthened by the requirement that each party submit a report upon the steps it had taken, or proposed to take, to ensure prompt compliance with the measures prescribed.[233] The prescription of fish catch totals was quite a striking decision as it was an exercise of authority that more normally takes place on a national basis,[234] or cooperatively between the relevant States.[235] The Convention itself emphasizes the need for cooperation and agreement between States for high seas fishing. Here, the Tribunal has carved out an important role for third-party decision-making with respect to these

New Zealand; that it negotiate and cooperate in good faith in order to agree on future conservation measures; that its nationals and persons subject to its jurisdiction not harvest more fish than the previously agreed national quota; and that its catch should be limited to the last agreed national allocation, with reductions for the catch taken during the experimental fishing program. See In the Dispute Concerning Southern Bluefin Tuna, *Australia v. Japan*, Statement of Claim and Grounds on Which it is Based, para. 69.

[232] Judge Warioba, in his separate declaration, dissented on this point because he considered there was no basis for the Tribunal to set quotas when it had acknowledged that the scientific evidence could not be assessed conclusively. Southern Bluefin Tuna, Provisional Measures, Declaration of Judge Warioba.

[233] ITLOS Rules, art. 96(1). By 21 votes to 1, ITLOS decided in *Southern Bluefin Tuna* that each party was to submit an initial report six weeks after the measures were ordered.

[234] The restriction of Australia and New Zealand's catches impinged on the catch occurring almost entirely in their respective EEZs, an area under the exclusive jurisdiction of the coastal State with respect to fishing. See Donald L. Morgan, "Emerging Fora for International Litigation (part 1): Implications of the Proliferation of International Legal Fora: The Example of the *Southern Bluefin Tuna Cases*," 43 *Harv. Int'l L.J.* 541, 546 (2002).

[235] Japan, for example, took the position in *Southern Bluefin Tuna* that no party can be subject to a quota to which it did not consent since the total allowable catch and quotas must be set by consensus. See Hayashi, "Southern Bluefin Tuna," at 367 (referring to Japan's response to Australia and New Zealand's position that the parties had to maintain previously agreed quotas in the absence of consensus on new quotas).

obligations. When this cooperation breaks down (or cannot be reached in the first place), the tribunal or courts in Part XV have the power to step in and fill a gap, albeit temporarily, through the prescription of pro-visional measures. The availability of this measure is even more potent as a tribunal or court need only establish that it has *prima facie* juris-diction to play this role. Further, the urgency criterion was established through a risk of depleting a fish stock, even in the face of uncertain scientific evidence.[236]

It can be noted that in *Southern Bluefin Tuna*, ITLOS did not set totals different to those last agreed by the parties and this aspect may indi-cate some reticence, or limitation, on the decision-making power of an international court or tribunal in this regard.[237] Nonetheless, the totals ordered by the Tribunal could only be altered through agreement by all the parties, or by the arbitral tribunal once constituted. ITLOS created an ongoing role for third-party decision-making due to the potential for circumstances to change and thereby require modifications in the allo-cation ordered. At the jurisdictional stage of *Southern Bluefin Tuna*, the arbitral tribunal revoked ITLOS' Order but still noted that the revocation did "not mean that the Parties may disregard the effects of the Order or their own decisions made in conformity with it."[238] This recognition reinforces the impact that provisional measures can have in regulating fishing activity under UNCLOS.

The decision that international courts and tribunals have the power to prescribe fish catch totals through provisional proceedings and thereby exercise authority traditionally reserved to coastal States is the one most likely to impact on substantive obligations under the Convention because it demonstrates what role a third-party decision-maker can play when States fail to meet their duties of cooperation and agreement with respect to high seas fishing and bring the issue to an international forum. Furthermore, a logical extension of the reasoning in *Southern*

---

[236] Fabra states that the risk of depleting a fish stock would be sufficient grounds for prescribing provisional measures even if there was no need to preserve the rights of the parties. Adriana Fabra, "The LOSC and the Implementation of the Precautionary Principle," 10 Y.B. Int'l Envtl L. 15, 22 (1999). However, the rights to be preserved would be those relating to the previously agreed total allowable catch amounts. See Evans, "Southern Bluefin Tuna," at 13.

[237] Cf. Douglas M. Johnston, "Fishery Diplomacy and Science and the Judicial Function," 10 Y.B. Int'l Envtl L. 33, 38 (1999) (arguing that the decision on fish catch quantities reflects a commitment to the principle of good faith in negotiating rather than involvement in the merits of regulatory decision-making).

[238] Southern Bluefin Tuna, Jurisdiction, para. 67.

Bluefin Tuna can be drawn to fishing in the EEZ. The fact that the Tribunal did not accept Guinea's argument in *M/V "Saiga" (No. 2)* that a case falling under the exception in Article 297(3) was automatically indicative of a *prima facie* lack of jurisdiction could mean that a court or tribunal may prescribe the allowable catch for fishing in the EEZ. The EEZ provisions of the Convention stipulate that the coastal State has the authority to set the allowable catch in its zone but conceivably, in accordance with the provisional measures decision in *Southern Bluefin Tuna*, there are circumstances that may vest this control, at least on an interim basis, in international decision-makers instead.

An activist role was also taken by ITLOS in *MOX Plant* in that it set forth a requirement that the parties undertake consultations on specific topics as part of their obligations to cooperate. Judges Caminos, Yamamoto, Park, Akl, Marsit, Eiriksson, and Jesus considered that this measure was "the most effective measure that the Tribunal could have adopted."[239] In requiring the parties to enter into consultations about information exchange, risk monitoring, and pollution prevention measures, these judges hoped to improve the common understanding of the scientific evidence and appreciation of the required measures to prevent harm to the marine environment.[240] On this basis, it would seem that these judges were of the view that they had a valuable role to play in requiring the parties to take certain actions in line with their duty to cooperate.

The activist role of the Tribunal in *Southern Bluefin Tuna* can be compared with its role in *Land Reclamation*. A notable feature of the provisional measures phase of that case was the extent that the parties reached agreement on a number of issues during the course of the oral and written proceedings. As noted above,[241] Singapore offered various assurances during the course of the proceedings that were placed on record by ITLOS and that responded to Malaysia's requested measures. The parties further agreed that they jointly sponsor and fund a scientific study by independent experts on terms of reference to be agreed by the two sides. In this regard, the Tribunal was not the instigator of these initiatives but the availability of its procedures and its potential to order binding provisional measures was a catalyst for these agreements being reached. Through this process, the function of ITLOS can be viewed as predominantly facilitative, as it provided a forum for the parties to reach

---

[239] MOX Plant, Provisional Measures, Joint Declaration of Judges Caminos, Yamamoto, Park, Akl, Marsit, Eiriksson, and Jesus, p. 2.
[240] *Ibid.*   [241] See notes 213–215 and accompanying text.

these agreements after their discussions were otherwise stalemated. In addition, ITLOS also carried with it the threat of imposing measures on the parties that would not accord precisely with the wishes of either of the parties, since it may vary the orders sought by the requesting State. These coercive powers may have further persuaded the parties to reach agreement on certain issues that may not have been possible without such intervention.

As well as prescribing particular measures, ITLOS may recommend measures to the disputant parties. The Tribunal in *M/V "Saiga" (No. 2)* chose to recommend that the parties enter into provisional arrangements to ensure that there would be no aggravation of the dispute pending its final settlement. A distinction was drawn here between the Tribunal's power to decide or prescribe measures and its power to recommend measures. This question was evidently discussed during deliberations,[242] but no explanation for this split between mandatory and discretionary measures is provided in the majority judgment. Judge Vukas, in his separate declaration, considered the nature of the measures recommended and commented that "[t]he reason for including such measures without characterising them as provisional remain obscure."[243] Judge Vukas expressed reservations about the Tribunal's power to make recommendations in light of the provisions of the Tribunal's Statute and Rules:

Under all the rules on provisional measures in the United Nations Convention on the Law of the Sea (Article 290), the Statute of the International Tribunal for the Law of the Sea (Article 25) and the Rules of the Tribunal (Articles 89–95), the Tribunal is not entitled to take any other decision, make any suggestion or recommendation, express any wish, etc.; its only task and competence is to "prescribe provisional measures" which it considers appropriate under the circumstances of the dispute.[244]

Recommendations may be a more realistic option when it is considered less likely that the parties will comply, or the Tribunal does not

---

[242] M/V "Saiga" (No. 2), Provisional Measures, para. 3 (declaration of Judge Vukas).
("[I]n the course of deliberations it was decided that the only provisional measure prescribed by the Tribunal would be the one formulated in subparagraph 1, and that the contents of subparagraph 2 would be drafted and adopted in the form of a recommendation.")

[243] *Ibid*, para. 4.

[244] *Ibid.*, para. 3. See also Rosenne, "1998 Survey," at 463–64 (considering that the Tribunal's reasoning was "thin" and that recommendations should only be used when they relate to the rights of the parties in the dispute before the Tribunal, and do not extend to other parties or other issues).

want to create a situation where a sanction under international law for violations of a prescription would be available to the injured State. Instead, the hope may have been that the recommendation would have a persuasive value in subsequent negotiations between the parties or during deliberations in subsequent litigation. Recommendations may provide useful guidance for the conduct of the parties without creating the burden of sanctions under international law should any conduct be viewed askance. Such an approach indicates an ongoing deference to State sovereignty as well as the facilitative function that third-party decision-making may play as part of a broader international process.

Conclusion

The first provisional measures decisions under UNCLOS predominantly demonstrate a willingness to grant such measures, albeit not always consistently with the requests of the applicant State. This approach can be viewed as consistent with the jurisprudence of the ICJ in that the applicant State is given the benefit of the doubt in assessing *prima facie* jurisdiction.[245] Questions of *prima facie* jurisdiction have not proved insurmountable as restrictions found in Sections 1 and 3 of Part XV have been interpreted in favor of applicant States, setting a low threshold for finding *prima facie* jurisdiction. The only other criteria to be met are those set out in Article 290 itself, assessed against the facts of the case. The main control exercised by ITLOS has been in its decisions on what measures to order. The Tribunal does not usually follow the requests of applicant States precisely but has ordered, or recommended, measures appropriate for the circumstances of the case. In so deciding, the Tribunal has arrogated responsibility to itself that was traditionally in the domain of State decision-making. In this regard, the attitude to provisional measures evinced thus far is proactive, giving rise to the question of whether this trend will be evident in other proceedings under Part XV.

Prompt Release of Vessels

Although Section 2 of Part XV sets out procedures for compulsory dispute settlement for disputes relating to the interpretation and application of UNCLOS in general, a specific procedure is laid out in Article 292 to deal with particular cases involving the arrest and detention of

---

[245] See Barbara Kwiatkowska, "The Australia and New Zealand v. Japan Southern Bluefin Tuna (Jurisdiction and Admissibility) Award of the First Law of the Sea Convention Annex VII Arbitral Tribunal," 16 *Int'l J. Marine & Coastal L.* 239, 244 (2001) (citing to Judge Schwebel's dissenting opinion in the provisonal measures phase of *Nicaragua*).

foreign vessels and crews. UNCLOS permits coastal States to exercise enforcement jurisdiction through the seizure of vessels and crews in certain limited circumstances. Since the adoption of the Convention, coastal States have addressed with increasing urgency the problem of illegal, unregulated, and unreported fishing in their maritime zones. A coastal State is entitled to board and inspect any vessel in its EEZ in order to enforce its laws and regulations with respect to its living resources.[246] When a vessel and its crew are arrested, the coastal State is required promptly to release them upon the posting of a bond or other security.[247] Lengthy detention of a fishing vessel may result in that vessel missing a considerable amount of harvest during a fishing season. Coastal States must also adhere to prompt release obligations where a vessel is detained because there is evidence that it has violated laws and regulations with respect to the prevention, reduction, and control of pollution in the coastal State's EEZ or territorial sea,[248] or where the vessel has been delayed for the purpose of investigation under Articles 216, 218, and 220 in relation to the enforcement of rules for the protection and preservation of the marine environment.[249] As Articles 73 and 220 provide "wide openings to a coastal State to interfere with the freedom of navigation beyond the outer limits of its territorial sea . . . enforceable guarantees for the freedom of navigation became essential."[250] The inclusion of a provision on the prompt release of vessels in Section 2 of Part XV is this procedural safeguard to these particular substantive provisions on the detention of vessels. Such a procedure was considered necessary at the Third Conference to balance against any overly enthusiastic implementation of the coastal State's enforcement powers.[251]

Where a vessel has been detained and the detaining State has not complied with the provisions of the Convention for the prompt release of the vessel or its crew upon the posting of a reasonable bond or other financial security, Article 292 permits the flag State of the detained vessel to institute proceedings before ITLOS.[252] The Tribunal has residual jurisdiction for situations where there is no other international court or tribunal with jurisdiction over the case at the time of arrest or detention.

---

[246] UNCLOS, art. 73(1).   [247] *Ibid.*, art. 73(2).   [248] *Ibid.*, art. 220.

[249] *Ibid.*, art. 226(1)(b). Brown notes that detentions under Article 226(1)(c) would not be subject to Article 292 because it does not refer to the posting of security, and it would necessarily involve consideration of questions other than release. See E. D. Brown, "The M/V 'Saiga' case on prompt release of detained vessels: the first Judgment of the International Tribunal for the Law of the Sea," 22 *Marine Pol'y* 307, 316 (1998).

[250] Rosenne, "Establishing ITLOS," at 813.   [251] Oxman, "Commentary," at 648.

[252] UNCLOS, art. 292(1).

The Tribunal must deal with the application for release without delay,[253] and must only address the question of release, without prejudice to the merits of any case before the domestic forum.[254] The Tribunal can determine the amount, nature, and form of the bond or financial security to be posted for the release of the vessel or crew.[255] The first prompt release decisions under Article 292 have gradually elaborated on the contours of these procedures. Particular issues that have been addressed, and that are discussed in this section, are jurisdiction, admissibility, the scope of the procedure, and the reasonableness of the bond.

Jurisdiction under Article 292

Several procedural conditions must be met for a flag State to make an application for the release of a vessel under Article 292. Questions of jurisdiction and admissibility are not addressed in a separate phase to assessing whether an allegation that a detaining State has not complied with a relevant provision of the Convention is well-founded, whether a reasonable bond has been assessed, and the appropriate amount and form of the bond.[256] The accelerated procedures anticipated in the Convention and the Tribunal's Rules for the prompt release of vessels necessitates that these challenges be raised and resolved as part of the submissions on detention and conditions of release of the vessel.

An application may be submitted to ITLOS, or to a court or tribunal accepted by the detaining State under Article 287, failing agreement of the parties to submit the question of release from detention to another court or tribunal within ten days from the time the vessel was detained.[257] As such, the ICJ could determine a dispute under Article 292 if it has been selected as the procedure of choice of the detaining State under Article 287. While Article 292 anticipates prompt release applications to be presented to a range of courts or tribunals at the parties' choosing, ITLOS has been the preferred forum in default of agreement to the contrary.

---

[253] *Ibid.*, art. 292(3). See also ITLOS Rules, art. 122.   [254] UNCLOS, art. 292(3).

[255] ITLOS Rules, art. 113(2).

[256] Prior to the hearings in *Grand Prince*, France argued that the application was without object since the case had been resolved on the merits before French courts and had to be rejected without proceeding to any hearings. The Tribunal decided, without prejudice to any decision on jurisdiction and admissibility, that the matter required a full examination. "Grand Prince," Application for Prompt Release (*Belize* v. *France*) (Judgment of April 20, 2001), available at http://www.itlos.org/start2_en.html, para. 15.

[257] UNCLOS, art. 292(1).

The Flag State of the Seized Vessel

An application may be submitted by or on behalf of the flag State of the vessel. In accordance with Article 110(2) of the Rules of the Tribunal, a State party may notify the Tribunal of its State authorities competent to authorize persons to make applications on its behalf under Article 292. Alternatively, Article 110(2) of the Tribunal's Rules allows the flag State directly to authorize persons to make an application on its behalf. With the exercise of this authority, a flag State is only nominally involved in proceedings and so in reality the owners of the seized vessels are able to pursue international proceedings in order to protect their investments. While the detaining State may question the ownership of particular vessels, as happened in *M/V "Saiga"*[258] and the *Volga*,[259] the court or tribunal will have jurisdiction under Article 292 if the applicant State is the flag State of the vessel at the time the application is filed.

The issue of whether the applicant State was the flag State of a vessel was central, and decisive, in the *Grand Prince*.[260] The "Grand Prince" was a fishing vessel flying under the flag of Belize when it was arrested in the EEZ of the Kerguelen Islands by a French frigate on 26 December 2000. The vessel and its crew were escorted to Réunion where the Master was charged with failure to announce either his entry into the EEZ or his on-board cargo as well as fishing without authorization in the EEZ of the Kerguelen Islands. The Master of the vessel admitted the violations with which he was charged. At the conclusion of the criminal proceedings in Réunion, Belize filed an application under Article 292 at ITLOS.

The Tribunal raised *proprio motu* the question of whether Belize was the flag State of the "Grand Prince" for the purposes of filing the application. This question was relevant because the vessel had been issued a provisional patent of navigation on October 16, 2000 and the date of its expiration was December 29, 2000. Although Belize was clearly the flag State at the time of the arrest of the vessel, the Tribunal asked whether it was the flag State when the application was filed on March 21, 2001. In support of its right to submit the claim on behalf of the "Grand Prince," Belize pointed to the provisional patent of navigation, a letter from its Attorney General authorizing the Agent to institute the proceedings before ITLOS in which the vessel was described as

---

[258] M/V "Saiga," Prompt Release, para. 25 (setting out the submissions of Guinea; the issue was not addressed by the Tribunal).

[259] The "Volga" Case, Application for Prompt Release (*Russia* v. *Australia*) (Judgment of December 23, 2002), available at http://www.itlos.org/start2_en.html, para. 75.

[260] Grand Prince, para. 30.

"of Belize flag" and a certification from the International Merchant Marine Registry of Belize.[261] The latter document, dated March 30, 2001, stated that the vessel was still considered as registered in Belize pending the result of the proceedings and that the cancellation of the vessel's status was suspended. France instead drew the Tribunal's attention to a note verbale, dated January 4, 2001, in which the Ministry of Foreign Affairs of Belize notified the Embassy of France that in light of the second reported violation committed by the vessel, the punitive measure being imposed was its de-registration effective the day of the note.[262] In a subsequent letter, dated March 25, 2001, the Registry of Belize wrote that while they were "in the process of canceling ex-officio the vessel's status, the owners requested an opportunity to defend themselves of the accusations by submitting an appeal to the Tribunal for the Law of the Sea."[263]

The nationality of ships is governed by Article 91, paragraph 1 of the Convention. This Article was described as codifying a well-established rule of general international law in the merits stage of *M/V "Saiga" (No. 2)*,[264] and reads:

Every State shall fix the conditions for the grant of its nationality to ships, for the registration of ships in its territory, and for the right to fly its flag. Ships have the nationality of the State whose flag they are entitled to fly. There must exist a genuine link between the State and the ship.

In accordance with its decision in *M/V "Saiga" (No. 2)*,[265] the Tribunal noted that the nationality of a ship is a question of fact to be determined on the basis of evidence adduced by the parties and that the conduct of the flag State at all times material to the dispute was an important consideration.[266] The majority of the Tribunal in *Grand Prince* considered that the Registry letter and certification were administrative in nature and could not be considered as documents that entitle a ship to fly its flag in the meaning of Article 91, paragraph 2.[267] The note

---

[261] *Ibid.*, para. 67.   [262] *Ibid.*, para. 72.

[263] *Ibid.*, para. 74. Judge Anderson, in his separate opinion, noted that this letter confused the true nature of the Article 292 proceedings. *Ibid.*, Separate Opinion of Judge Anderson.

[264] *M/V "Saiga" (No. 2)*, Merits (*Saint Vincent v. Guinea*) (Judgment of July 1, 1999), available at http://www.itlos.org/start2_en.html, para. 63.

[265] *Ibid.*, paras. 66 and 68.

[266] Grand Prince, paras. 81 and 89 (citing *M/V "Saiga" (No. 2)*, paras. 66 and 68 respectively).

[267] *Ibid.*, paras. 85–86.

verbale was instead taken as "an official communication from Belize to France, setting out the legal position of the Government of Belize with respect to the registration of the vessel."[268] The Tribunal effectively accorded more weight to the note verbale than to the other documents presented, particularly when the laws relating to de-registration and combating illegal fishing were taken into account.[269] The conclusion reached was that Belize did not act at all times material to the dispute as the flag State based on the expiration of the provisional patent of navigation, the note verbale, and an overall assessment of the material placed before the Tribunal.[270] The Tribunal took the view, "the assertion that the vessel is 'still considered as registered in Belize' contains an element of fiction and does not provide sufficient basis for holding that Belize was the flag State of the vessel for the purposes of making an application under article 292 of the Convention."[271] As the majority decided it did not have jurisdiction to determine the application, no further matter was addressed. The nine judges in dissent took the view that the documents before the Tribunal were sufficient to discharge the initial burden of establishing that the vessel had Belize nationality.[272] They further noted that the consequence of the Tribunal's decision was that flag States could effectively be absolved of responsibility from exercising jurisdiction and control in administrative, technical, and social matters over vessels by simply revoking, without more, the registration of ships flying their flags.[273] The focus of the majority had been more on the efforts of Belize to curb the practice of illegal fishing by strengthening the powers of the Registrar to de-register vessels.[274]

What is notable about this decision is that the Tribunal is prepared to take decisions on questions that have formerly been within the purview of national decision-making rather than external review. The question of nationality was considered at some length in the judgment on the merits of *M/V "Saiga" (No. 2)* and the Tribunal was similarly prepared to exercise this authority in the *Grand Prince*. As noted by Judge Wolfrum in his Declaration in *Grand Prince*, to accept that a vessel was registered under a particular flag solely on the ground that a State so claimed

---

[268] *Ibid.*, para. 87.   [269] *Ibid.*, paras. 90–91.
[270] *Ibid.*, paras. 89 and 93.   [271] *Ibid.*, para. 85.
[272] *Ibid.*, Dissenting Opinion of Judges Caminos, Marotta Rangel, Yankov, Yamamoto, Akl, Vukas, Marsit, Eiriksson, and Jesus, para. 14.
[273] *Ibid.*, Dissenting Opinion of Judges Caminos, Marotta Rangel, Yankov, Yamamoto, Akl, Vukas, Marsit, Eiriksson, and Jesus, para. 16.
[274] *Ibid.*, para. 91.

would render registration devoid of substance.[275] He further noted that to accept such an approach whereby jurisdiction would "depend upon a decision of national officials without the State concerned assuming the responsibilities of a flag State in substance . . . would be incompatible with the role and function of the tribunal and would erode the flag State system."[276] The rights of States to exercise certain powers over vessels flying their flags has the potential to be subjected to international scrutiny in circumstances where a dispute over those powers finds its way into the proceedings set out in Section 2 of Part XV of UNCLOS. Although France had raised some doubts over the flagging history of the vessel in *Camouco*, the Tribunal did not address this history as there was no question of nationality at the relevant times of the proceedings. The decision in *Grand Prince* reinforces the authority of international decision-makers to assess the actions of States in this regard.

Whether an Allegation of Non-Compliance is "Well-Founded"
Another preliminary question under Article 292 is "whether or not the allegation made by the applicant that the detaining State has not complied with a provision of the Convention for the prompt release of the vessel or the crew upon the posting of a reasonable bond or other financial security is well-founded."[277] ITLOS grappled with the requirement of a well-founded allegation of non-compliance in its earliest decisions. In assessing the standard for meeting this requirement for the purposes of Article 292, the Tribunal must take into account the possibility of further third-party settlement relating to the merits as well as the accelerated nature of the Article 292 proceedings. In *M/V "Saiga,"* the majority of the Tribunal considered these characteristics of prompt release proceedings and decided that an appropriate "standard of appreciation" could be based on "assessing whether the allegations made are arguable or are of a sufficiently plausible character in the sense that the Tribunal may rely upon them for present purposes."[278] One reason given for this standard was that it did not foreclose a conclusion on the merits of a

---

[275] *Ibid.*, Declaration of Judge Wolfrum, para. 3.
[276] *Ibid.*, Declaration of Judge Wolfrum, para. 4.   [277] ITLOS Rules, art. 113(1).
[278] *M/V "Saiga,"* Prompt Release, para. 51. Judge Anderson, in the dissent, noted that the standard of a "sufficiently plausible character" was drawn from the decision of the ICJ in *Ambatielos* where the Court considered whether Greece's interpretation of the treaty was of a sufficiently plausible character to warrant a conclusion that the claim was based on the treaty and should be referred to another tribunal for arbitration. *Ibid.*, Dissenting Opinion of Judge Anderson.

possible future decision.[279] Another reason was that Article 292 required the Tribunal to examine the "allegation" that the detaining State had not complied with the Convention and thus indicated a lower standard of appreciation.[280]

Judge Anderson considered that the majority's standard was inappropriate because the proceedings on the release of vessels would not be referred to another body but were discrete and definitive; they did not form the first phase of a case advancing to the merits.[281] Moreover, the "standard of appreciation" utilized by the majority of ITLOS in M/V "Saiga" ran counter to the Rules of the Tribunal, which demand that the allegations be "well-founded,"[282] not just arguable or sufficiently plausible. The dissenting judges applied the standard specified in the Rules. Judges Park, Nelson, Chandrasekhara Rao, Vukas, and Ndiaye, in a joint dissenting Opinion, stated that the burden on Saint Vincent and the Grenadines to establish that its allegation was "well-founded" could only be discharged where there was a "direct connection" between the arrest of the vessel and the actions taken by Guinea under Article 73 of the Convention.[283] This interpretation was consistent with the Rules of the Tribunal,[284] and took account of the relationship of Article 292 to the relevant substantive provisions of the Convention.

In subsequent decisions, the Tribunal effectively abandoned its standard of arguable or sufficiently plausible and utilized the standard set

---

[279] M/V "Saiga," Prompt Release, para. 51. See also Eli Lauterpacht, "The First Decision of the International Tribunal for the Law of the Sea," in *Liber Amicorum: Professor Ignaz Seidl-Hohenveldern* (Gerhard Hafner *et al.*, eds., 1998), pp. 395, 416 (supporting the use of this standard for this reason).

[280] M/V "Saiga," Prompt Release, para. 51.

[281] *Ibid.*, paras. 4–5 (dissenting opinion of Judge Anderson). See also *ibid.*, Dissenting Opinion of President Mensah, para. 5, and *ibid.*, Dissenting Opinion of Vice-President Wolfrum and Judge Yamamoto, paras. 5 and 6. See also Vaughan Lowe, "The M/V Saiga: The First Case in the International Tribunal for the Law of the Sea," 48 *Int'l & Comp. L.Q.* 187, 191 (1999); Brown, "M/V 'Saiga,'" at 321 (both commenting that the tone of the majority suggested that it considered the proceedings as akin to applications for provisional measures in the ICJ).

[282] ITLOS Rules, art. 113(1).

[283] M/V "Saiga," Prompt Release, Dissenting Opinion of Judges Park, Nelson, Chandrasekhara Rao, Vukas, and Ndiaye, para. 9. See also *ibid.*, Dissenting Opinion of President Mensah, para. 7; *ibid.*, Dissenting Opinion of Vice-President Wolfrum and Judge Yamamoto, para. 4 (referring to a "genuine connection" between the detention of the vessel and the laws and regulations of the detaining state relating to Article 73); *ibid.*, Dissenting Opinion of Vice-President Wolfrum and Judge Yamamoto, para. 8; *ibid.*, Dissenting Opinion of Judge Anderson, paras. 2 and 3.

[284] But see Lauterpacht, at 408 (objecting to the use of the Tribunal's Rules of Procedure as a controlling element in interpreting the Convention).

forth in Article 113 of its Rules.[285] Judge Mensah, in his separate declaration in *Camouco*, supported reliance on this standard in view of the fact that the Rules represented "the well-considered understanding of the Tribunal regarding what is expected of it when dealing with disputes regarding the interpretation or application of article 292 of the Convention."[286] Utilizing the standard in the Rules was a way of elaborating on certain UNCLOS provisions to the extent necessary in order to give effect to their object and purpose.[287] In *Monte Confurco*, as with *Camouco*, the Tribunal again considered its task as determining whether the allegation of the Applicant relating to non-compliance with Article 73(2) was well-founded.[288] It now seems unlikely that the Tribunal will revert to a consideration of whether an allegation is "arguable" or "sufficiently plausible."

Posting of Bond as Precondition to Application
ITLOS has considered whether an applicant State must post a bond prior to the institution of proceedings under Article 292 in order to exercise jurisdiction. This issue was addressed in *M/V "Saiga,"* as Saint Vincent and the Grenadines had not offered Guinea any bond or financial security but asked the Tribunal to determine that the vessel should be released without requiring any such payment. Saint Vincent and the Grenadines was otherwise "prepared to provide any security reasonably imposed by the Tribunal to the Tribunal itself."[289] Guinea argued that since Saint Vincent and the Grenadines had not paid any bond, an application could not be instituted under Article 292. The Tribunal did not consider that the posting of a bond had to be effected in fact as a precondition of the applicability of Article 292.[290]

---

[285] See "Camouco," Application for Prompt Release (*Panama* v. *France*) (Judgment of February 7, 2000), available at http://www.itlos.org/start2_en.html, para. 61. See also The "Volga" Case, Statement in Response of Australia, December 7, 2002, available at http://www.itlos.org/start2_en.html, paras. 2–6 (arguing that Russia's claim may not have been well-founded for the purposes of Article 292 because of its allegations concerning the violation of the right of hot pursuit).

[286] Camouco, Declaration of Judge Mensah, para. 3.

[287] *Ibid.*, Declaration of Judge Mensah, para. 4.

[288] Judge Laing, however, preferred the standard of "arguable or sufficiently plausible" from *M/V "Saiga,"* although he considered that his view was still tenable on a different standard of appreciation. See "Monte Confurco," Application for Prompt Release (*Seychelles* v. *France*), (Judgment of December 18, 2000), available at http://www.itlos.org/start2_en.html., Dissenting Opinion of Judge Laing, para. 2.

[289] M/V "Saiga," Prompt Release, para. 23.   [290] *Ibid.*, para. 76.

France also argued in *Camouco* that the allegations under Article 73 were not well-founded on the basis that no bond or other security had been posted and this act was a necessary condition to be satisfied before a vessel and its crew could be released.[291] The Tribunal referred back to its *dicta* in the *M/V "Saiga"* where it had noted that the posting of a bond or other security was not necessarily a condition precedent to the filing of an application under Article 292 as the posting may not have been possible, had been rejected, was not provided for under the laws of the coastal State, or was unreasonable.[292] Moreover, the Tribunal could look to Article 292(4), which provides: "Upon the posting of the bond or other financial security determined by the court or tribunal, the authorities of the detaining State shall comply promptly with the decision of the court or tribunal concerning the release of the vessel or its crew." This provision allows for the possibility that a bond would not be paid prior to the order of the court or tribunal and thus would not be a prerequisite for an application under Article 292. Nonetheless, the posting of a bond or financial security was seen to be necessary for the release of the vessel, and thus could not be waived in its entirety, in view of the nature of the prompt release proceedings.[293]

Issues of Admissibility in Prompt Release Proceedings

In addition to ascertaining whether a court or tribunal has jurisdiction to entertain an application under Article 292, the detaining State may raise various challenges to the admissibility of an application.[294] Issues outside the scope of the specific provisions on prompt release are inadmissible for purposes of Article 292 procedures. Other admissibility issues addressed by ITLOS in its early jurisprudence have been closely related to the parallel nature of Article 292 proceedings and domestic court proceedings. The timing of the application, problems of *lis pendens* and the requirement to exhaust local remedies were all argued by France as reasons to find an application inadmissible under Article 292 in the *Camouco* case.

---

[291] Camouco, para. 62.

[292] *Ibid.*, para. 64. See also Brown, "M/V 'Saiga,'" at 325.

[293] M/V "Saiga," Prompt Release, para. 81.

[294] An objection to the admissibility of a claim is "a plea that the tribunal should rule the claim to be inadmissible on some ground other than its ultimate merits," whereas an objection to the jurisdiction of a court is "a plea that the tribunal itself is incompetent to give any ruling at all whether as to the merits or as to the admissibility of the claim." Gerald Fitzmaurice, "The Law and Procedure of the International Court of Justice, 1951–54: Questions of Jurisdiction, Competence and Procedure," [1958] *Brit. Y.B. Int'l L.* 1, 12–13.

Questions Besides the Release of the Vessel

The seizure of a vessel for violation of fisheries or environmental laws might provoke challenges relating to different provisions of the Convention, beyond the requirements to release a vessel or its crew promptly upon posting of a reasonable bond or other financial security. ITLOS has thus far strictly adhered to the limits of its jurisdiction under Article 292, and refused to consider questions that could be viewed as incidental to the arrest of vessels and crews. Nor has the Tribunal allowed challenges to the exercise of enforcement jurisdiction or hot pursuit to color its consideration of what constitutes a reasonable bond.

In *Camouco*, Panama argued that France had violated paragraphs 3 and 4 of Article 73. These paragraphs provide that the coastal State cannot prescribe imprisonment or corporal punishment as penalties for violations of fisheries laws and regulations in the EEZ and that the coastal State is required to notify promptly the flag State of actions taken and penalties imposed in cases of arrest or detention of vessels. The Tribunal did not consider that these provisions could be challenged through the Article 292 proceedings since these were not provisions "for the prompt release of the vessel or its crew upon the posting of a reasonable bond or other financial security." As such, Panama's claims under these paragraphs were deemed inadmissible.[295] The Tribunal similarly refused to deal with the questions relating to Article 73, paragraphs 3 and 4 relating to the detention of the Master and the need to provide proper notification of the arrest respectively in *Monte Confurco*.[296] These submissions were again deemed to be inadmissible as ITLOS was only to address non-compliance with Article 73, paragraph 2 of the Convention. The Tribunal's holding was unanimous on this point.

These decisions mean that the Tribunal has elected to read Article 292 narrowly so that the only issues to be resolved concern the actual release and the question of bond. Issues that could be related to those questions (perhaps questions of fairness of trial of a Master of the vessel, use of force used in arresting the vessel, the validity of fishing laws and regulations being enforced) will be outside the scope of proceedings under Article 292.[297]

---

[295] Camouco, para. 59.   [296] Monte Confurco, para. 63.

[297] Certainly, such a position seems reasonable in light of Panama's argument during the oral round of proceedings that a question arose as to whether the Master had received a fair trial within a reasonable period of time under Article 6(1) of the European Convention on Human Rights. "Camouco," Application for Prompt Release (*Panama* v. *France*), Verbatim Record, ITLOS PV-00/1, p. 26, available at http://www.itlos.org/start2_en.html.

Not only will the Tribunal exclude consideration of matters that may be incidental to the arrest and detention of vessels and their crews, but the court or tribunal will not trespass on other questions that could, or should, be resolved in separate merits proceedings under the Convention. For example, the Tribunal in *M/V "Saiga"* explicitly recognized that it could only deal with the question of release, since a case concerning the merits of the situation that led to the detention of the M/V "Saiga" may be subject to dispute resolution under the other provisions of Part XV of the Convention. The Tribunal would only consider those aspects of the merits necessary to reach a decision on the question of release of the vessel.[298]

A similar issue arose in the *Volga*,[299] which concerned the seizure of a long-line fishing vessel flying under the flag of the Russian Federation. The "Volga" was boarded by Australian military personnel beyond the limits of Australia's EEZ around the Australian Territory of Heard Island and the McDonald Islands. The Applicant submitted that the vessel had received no communication from Australian authorities prior to it entering the high seas. In its Memorial, the Russian Federation alleged that Australia was in breach of the right of hot pursuit under Article 111 of UNCLOS when it boarded the vessel and that the apprehension of the vessel was also in violation of Article 87(1)(a) of the Convention.[300] Australia responded that such communications had been made when the vessel was seen fleeing from Australian waters, and it was only upon subsequent calculations that it was discovered that the "Volga" was several hundred meters beyond the EEZ when that communication was made.[301]

The Tribunal, however, was not willing to comment on the circumstances of the seizure of the "Volga" since they were not relevant for the prompt release proceedings.[302] The Russian Federation had also argued that the circumstances of the arrest should be weighed against the gravity of the offences committed.[303] The Tribunal further constrained its considerations of the merits of the dispute in stating that

---

[298] M/V "Saiga," Prompt Release, para. 50.   [299] See The "Volga" Case, para. 32.

[300] "Volga," Application for Prompt Release, (*Russia v. Australia*), Memorial of the Russian Federation, available at http://www.itlos.org/start2_en.html, p. 10. Article 87(1)(a) concerns the freedom of navigation on the high seas.

[301] The "Volga" Case, para. 33.   [302] *Ibid.*, para. 83.

[303] "The Applicant has made a clear allegation against the Respondent of a serious breach of the international obligations owed to the Applicant . . . The Respondent has offered no reparation or tenable justification for its actions." The Volga, Russian Memorial, p. 16.

the circumstances surrounding the seizure were not even relevant for assessing the reasonableness of the bond.[304]

Impact of Domestic Court Proceedings

Challenges to the admissibility of an application under Article 292 have also been derived from the fact that domestic courts are usually dealing with matters concerning the release of the vessel and the crew, as well as the prosecution of the offenses for which they were arrested. Respondent States have challenged the timing of applications, particularly where they have been submitted at an advanced stage of the domestic court proceedings. The parallel nature of Article 292 cases and domestic court proceedings have led to questions of *lis pendens* and abuse of process, and whether domestic proceedings should have been exhausted. ITLOS' treatment of these questions is discussed immediately below. The key factor in these decisions is that Article 292 provides for a discreet procedure that does not preempt a national court's determination of the merits of the dispute.

In *Camouco*, France claimed that Panama had waited more than three months since the seizure to file the application before ITLOS and Panama's delay amounted to a situation akin to estoppel. France argued that the procedure in Article 292 concerned a "prompt release" and this designation connoted a sense of dispatch and urgency in filing an application.[305] The "Camouco" was seized on September 29, 1999 and its bond was set nine days later. The request for the release of seized items and a reduction in the amount of the bond was filed on October 22, 1999. The court of first instance rejected this request on December 14, 1999. Panama's application was then filed with ITLOS a month later, while the court of appeal decision was pending. France considered that the delay in instituting proceedings created an estoppel against Panama. The Applicant argued that there was no time limit for making an application under Article 292 and that, in any event, there had not been any delay from the point that the court of first instance had affirmed its earlier decision.[306]

The Tribunal decided that there was "no merit" in arguments based on the delay in bringing the matter before ITLOS; Article 292 did not

---

[304] The "Volga" Case, para. 83.
[305] Camouco, para. 51. See further "Camouco," Application for Prompt Release (*Panama* v. *France*), Verbatim Record, ITLOS PV-00/2, p. 17, available at http://www.itlos.org/start2_en.html.
[306] Camouco, para. 52.

require the flag State to file an application within any specified period of time following the detention of a vessel and its crew.[307] Although no comment was made on this point by the Tribunal, it would seem there was a certain inconsistency in the arguments of France. On the one hand, it asserted that there had been a delay in submitting the Application but, on the other hand, the second ground of inadmissibility argued was that Panama should not have brought the application so soon as proceedings were still pending before the national court. In any event, the position clearly established on this point is that there are no arbitrary deadlines for filing applications under Article 292 vis-à-vis domestic court proceedings.

The one possible exception is where proceedings before the national courts have been concluded before an action is presented under Article 292. This issue arose in the *Grand Prince*, but was ultimately not considered by the Tribunal. In that case, the court of first instance confirmed the arrest of the "Grand Prince" and fixed for its release. Eleven days after this decision, the criminal court found that the "Grand Prince" had entered the EEZ without giving notice of its entry or declaring the tonnage of fish on board, engaged in illegal fishing, and that the Master had knowingly engaged in illegal fishing. The court fined the Master and ordered the confiscation of the vessel, its equipment and gear, as well as the fishing products seized, and that the order should be immediately enforceable notwithstanding the lodging of an appeal. The ship owners then submitted an application to the court of first instance for the release of the vessel upon the presentation of a bank guarantee but this application was rejected since the criminal court had already ordered the confiscation of the vessel with immediate execution. In light of this decision, the court of first instance no longer had jurisdiction to order the return of the vessel in consideration of a bank guarantee.

Three weeks subsequent to the decision of the criminal court, Belize submitted an application to ITLOS under Article 292 of the Convention. Belize alleged that France had "evaded the requirement of prompt release . . . by not allowing the release of the vessel upon the posting of a reasonable, or any kind of, guarantee alleging that the vessel is confiscated and the decision of confiscation has been provisionally executed."[308] The prompt confiscation of the vessel, it was argued, amounted to a "trick" or a "fraud of law," as it would render Article 73 redundant.[309] The Applicant instead asked that the Tribunal promptly

---

[307] *Ibid.*, para. 54.

[308] Grand Prince, para. 30 (setting out the submissions of Belize).   [309] *Ibid.*, para. 54.

release the "Grand Prince" upon the posting of a bond or other security determined by the Tribunal.

France took the position that it was no longer possible for Belize to file an application under Article 292, as the competent domestic forum had delivered judgment on the merits and ordered the confiscation of the vessel.[310] In particular, France pointed to paragraph 3 of Article 292, which stipulates that the prompt release proceedings under the Convention are without prejudice to the merits of any case before the appropriate domestic forum. France further argued that Article 292 proceedings could not be used to challenge the procedural fairness or due process in relation to judicial proceedings in France and that the case had been conducted in full compliance with the provisions of French law. According to France:

> the power to confiscate under French law flowed from article 73 of the Convention which empowered the coastal State to define fishing offences and to establish penalties applicable to those who commit such offences and the only limit placed upon this power was the one stated in article 73, paragraph 3, which excluded penalties of imprisonment and corporal punishment.[311]

France considered the case to be one relating to law enforcement, which would be excluded by virtue of Article 298, and not one of prompt release.

As the Tribunal decided it lacked jurisdiction because Belize was no longer the flag State of the detained vessel at the time of its application,[312] there was no consideration of this question in the Tribunal's Order.[313] Given the object and purpose of Article 292 and the anticipated context of Article 292 proceedings, it would seem inappropriate for an international court or tribunal to order the prompt release of a vessel upon payment of a reasonable bond when a decision on the merits has already been reached before domestic courts. If the flag State of a detained vessel or crew considered the exercise of enforcement jurisdiction violated the application of the Convention then such a challenge would have to be pursued as any other dispute concerning

---

[310] *Ibid.*, para. 57.   [311] *Ibid.*, para. 59.

[312] See notes 260–74 and accompanying text.

[313] Judge *ad hoc* Cot agreed with France's argument that a rapid prosecution of a vessel and its crew was not a "fraud" on the Convention but was consistent with creating a situation that eliminated the need for Article 292 procedures. See Camouco, Declaration of Judge *ad hoc* Cot, para. 7. By contrast, Judge Laing did not consider that the confiscation of a vessel should not be accepted by an international court or tribunal if it excludes jurisdiction of that body. See Camouco, Separate Opinion of Judge Laing, para. 16.

the interpretation or application of the Convention, rather than under Article 292. Article 292 provides a procedure for the "question of release from detention" and is "without prejudice to the merits of any case before the appropriate domestic forum."[314] It is clearly an interim proceeding inasmuch as it allows the vessel to continue its business while the legal processes are completed. Detention ends once a vessel is confiscated; the decision to do so is the final result of the proceedings and constitutes the merits of the enforcement action. There is no room for proceedings under Article 292 in this situation. The stricture on an international court or tribunal to hear a dispute once a domestic court has reached the merits of a decision serves the purpose of requiring flag States to pursue Article 292 proceedings promptly and not being allowed to hedge their bets by waiting for a decision in one forum before turning to an alternative forum that may produce what the flag State views as a better result.

An application for prompt release under Article 292 during the pendency of domestic court proceedings also raises the issue of whether the principles of *lis pendens* or abuse of process render the dispute inadmissible. For *lis pendens* to apply there must be identity of parties, of claims, and of object.[315] There can be no strict application of *lis pendens* between the prompt release proceedings under Article 292 and the national court processes because the parties and bases of claims will not be identical.

Rather than rely on the technical principle of *lis pendens*, a detaining State may submit that an application is an abuse of process under general principles of law in light of the procedures being undertaken by its domestic courts.[316] France took this approach in *Camouco* by reference to what it considered as the object and purpose of Article 292. To this end, France submitted that:

These provisions were adopted in order to avoid injustices which might result from the seizure of a foreign vessel by a coastal state if no domestic judicial proceedings have been instituted in that state after the seizure or if the domestic legal system of the state having seized or detained the vessel did not provide for its release by the posting of a bond.[317]

---

[314] UNCLOS, art. 292(1) and (3).

[315] See Bin Cheng, *General Principles of Law as Applied by International Courts and Tribunals* (1987), p. 340.

[316] A detaining State cannot rely on Article 294, which permits a State to claim that an application is an abuse of process in respect of claims under Article 297 only. Article 300 is a more general obligation requiring States to exercise the rights, jurisdiction, and freedoms recognized in the Convention in a manner that would not constitute an abuse of right.

[317] Camouco, ITLOS PV-00/2, at 13.

France therefore argued that the parallel proceedings on the release of the vessel cast doubt on the admissibility of Panama's application.[318] France further relied on the decision of ITLOS in *M/V "Saiga"* where it was stated that the Tribunal should take "great care" not to interfere with functions of national courts seized of the same question.[319] In view of the procedures being undertaken in its courts in Réunion, France submitted that there was no need for the proceedings under UNCLOS as well. France thus argued that Panama's application was an abuse of process.[320]

The Tribunal in *Camouco* did not address either the technical doctrine of *lis pendens* or France's alternative reliance on abuse of process as independent points. Judge Vukas discussed the doctrine of litispendence in his dissenting opinion and took the view that the Article 292 proceedings and proceedings for the release of a vessel and its crew before national courts were separate.[321] In this regard, he reasoned that Panama had chosen to initiate proceedings before French courts, not the Tribunal, to secure the release of the vessel and its crew and that Panama's use of the Tribunal on these facts was not in line with the object and purpose of Article 292.[322] The thrust of Judge Vukas' opinion was that Panama's application could have amounted to an abuse of process, but he did not use this terminology in his opinion.

Panama took the approach that the prompt release procedure under the Convention was a special process that was concurrent with the process existing in the French national system.[323] Although not directly discussed by ITLOS in *Camouco*, it would seem that Panama's view on this issue has prevailed. Decisions on prompt release under Article 292 subsequent to *Camouco* have been taken concurrently with procedures in domestic fora, rather than only in the absence of such procedures.

A further argument affecting the admissibility of an application under Article 292 in light of ongoing proceedings in a domestic court concerns the exhaustion of local remedies. In *Camouco*, the Tribunal considered whether the rule requiring the exhaustion of local remedies prior to the institution of international proceedings had to be met under Article 292 in order to avoid the overlap with domestic proceedings. France noted in that case that the requirement to exhaust local remedies, included

---

[318] Camouco, para. 55. See further Camouco, ITLOS PV-00/2, at 16.

[319] Camouco, ITLOS PV-00/2, at 18 (referring to para. 49 of the *M/V "Saiga"* decision in the prompt release proceedings).

[320] *Ibid.*, at 15.   [321] Camouco, Dissenting Opinion of Judge Vukas, at 3–4.

[322] *Ibid.*, Dissenting Opinion of Judge Vukas, at 4.   [323] Camouco, ITLOS PV-00/1, at 27.

in the Convention in Article 295,[324] was not a necessary prerequisite for the institution of proceedings under Article 292.[325] The majority of the Tribunal agreed that it was "not logical to read the requirement of exhaustion of local remedies or any other analogous rule into article 292."[326] Article 292 proceedings are without prejudice to the merits of the case in the domestic forum as well as the international forum. This approach "neither requires nor discourages exhaustion of local remedies."[327]

In a dissenting opinion, Judge Anderson took the view that judicial restraint should be exercised on an international level when the national court system had not been completely or exhaustively used.[328] He read Article 295 as applying to Article 292 procedures since the former provision applied "to the procedures provided for in this section," thereby including Article 292.[329] Judge Anderson did not conclude that the rule on the exhaustion of local remedies was directly applicable to Article 292 proceedings, but he instead thought that the outstanding domestic remedy was a relevant factor in a decision on whether to grant relief.[330]

The majority of the Tribunal took the view that the procedure for the prompt release of vessels and crews under the Convention was an independent remedy and not a form of appeal against a national court decision.[331] To imply that the rule of exhaustion of local remedies applied to prompt release proceedings would effectively defeat the object and purpose of Article 292.[332] This approach is consistent with the view of

---

[324] Article 295 reads: "Any dispute between States parties concerning the interpretation or application of this Convention may be submitted to the procedures provided for in [Section 2 of Part XV] only after local remedies have been exhausted where this is required by international law." UNCLOS, art. 295.

[325] Camouco, para. 55.

[326] *Ibid.*, para. 57. Oxman agrees: "Insofar as vessel release proceedings are concerned, there is no lack of persuasive arguments that Article 295 does not require exhaustion of local remedies, that Article 294 regarding preliminary proceedings is not relevant, and that other provisions of Part XV that might frustrate or delay the proceedings are inapposite. But the analysis is simplified by the reference to the 10-day period and the command to proceed 'without delay' and 'deal only with the question of release'." Bernard H. Oxman, "Observations on Vessel Release under the United Nations Convention on the Law of the Sea," 11 *Int'l J. Marine & Coastal L.* 201, 211 (1996). See also Brown, "M/V 'Saiga,'" at 310.

[327] Bernard H. Oxman and Vincent P. Bantz, "The 'Camouco' (Panama v. France) (Judgment)," 94 *Am. J. Int'l L.* 713, 719 (2000).

[328] Camouco, Dissenting Opinion of Judge Anderson, at 1–2.

[329] *Ibid.*, Dissenting Opinion of Judge Anderson, at 2.

[330] *Ibid.* Dissenting Opinion of Judge Anderson, at 2.   [331] *Ibid.*, para. 58.

[332] *Ibid.* Vice President Nelson considered that any requirement that the Tribunal refrain from giving judgment on prompt release applications while the matter was before a

Vice-President Wolfrum and Judge Yamamoto from the *M/V "Saiga,"* where they described Article 292 as a unique and self-contained procedure with specific rules and very precise limits.[333]

Types of Vessel Seizures Subject to Proceedings under Article 292

There are two key substantive questions to be addressed by an international court or tribunal under Article 292: whether there has been a violation of a prompt release provision of UNCLOS, and whether the bond set is reasonable. In the first instance, the flag State must bring an application with respect to the provisions in UNCLOS that specifically require the prompt release of vessels and crews upon posting of a reasonable bond, and that the applicant State claims have been violated.

In the very first prompt release case under the Convention, the *M/V "Saiga,"* the Tribunal was faced with the question of whether any arrest and detention of a vessel and its crew could be subject to proceedings under Article 292 or whether those proceedings were only available in respect of the specific UNCLOS provisions that expressly require States promptly to release vessels and/or crews upon the posting of a reasonable bond. Saint Vincent and the Grenadines filed a case against Guinea over a dispute relating to the prompt release of the M/V "Saiga," an oil tanker sailing under the flag of Saint Vincent and the Grenadines that served as a bunkering vessel (i.e. supplied fuel) to fishing and other vessels off the coast of Guinea. The M/V "Saiga" entered the EEZ of Guinea to supply fuel to three fishing vessels but was arrested outside Guinea's EEZ by Guinean customs patrol boats. Guinea asserted that the arrest of the M/V "Saiga" had been executed following a hot pursuit motivated by a violation of its customs laws in the contiguous zones of Guinea. The M/V "Saiga," Guinea claimed, had been involved in smuggling in the sense of illegally supplying fuel to fishing vessels in violation of Guinea's customs legislation and that Article 292 was not applicable to an arrest for a case of smuggling.

In instituting proceedings, Saint Vincent and the Grenadines submitted that Guinea had violated the Convention by failing to comply with the relevant provisions for the prompt release of the vessel. Saint Vincent and the Grenadines asserted that the arrest of the M/V "Saiga" and its crew was within the exercise of Guinea's sovereign jurisdiction over its

national court would "fly in the face of the very object and purpose of article 292."
Ibid., Separate Opinion of Vice President Nelson, at 2.

[333] M/V "Saiga," Prompt Release, Dissenting Opinion of Vice-President Wolfrum and Judge Yamamoto, para. 16.

living resources in the EEZ in order to link the arrest and detention of the vessel with Article 73.

In addressing the applicability of Article 73 of the Convention, the Tribunal initially asked whether bunkering of a fishing vessel within the EEZ fell within the scope of the coastal State's exercise of its sovereign rights with respect to exploring, exploiting, conserving and managing the living resources of the EEZ. Bunkering could be viewed as an activity ancillary to fishing,[334] or be classed as an independent activity falling within the scope of freedom of navigation.[335] No decision on the issue was reached as the majority of the Tribunal concluded that the allegation that bunkering fell within Article 73 was arguable or sufficiently plausible.[336] The Tribunal then considered Guinea's laws and regulations, and how they connected with the provisions of UNCLOS, particularly Article 73. The majority stated that Guinea's reference to Article 40 of its Maritime Code, which enacted the concept of the EEZ into Guinea's domestic law, served to bring the arrest of the vessel within the scope of Article 73. The majority reasoned that Article 73 was said to be part of a group of provisions in the Convention that develop in detail the rule in Article 56 and consequently, a reference to Article 40 of the Maritime Code should be read as dealing with the matters covered by Article 73.[337]

Dissenting Judges Park, Nelson, Chandrasekhara Rao, Vukas, and Ndiaye thought that Article 40 of the Maritime Code could not be viewed in isolation from the other legislation on which the arrest of the M/V "Saiga" was based.[338] They noted that Guinea had also relied on provisions of its Customs Code and Penal Code, which dealt with the prohibition of unauthorized distribution of fuel and the punishment and

---

[334] M/V "Saiga," Prompt Release, para. 57. The Tribunal considered two examples of State practice in this regard: art. 1 of the Convention for the Prohibition of Fishing with Long Driftnets in the South Pacific of 23 November 1989 and domestic laws of Guinea Bissau, Sierra Leone, and Morocco.

[335] Ibid., para. 58. In support of this argument, the Tribunal considered that the absence of laws and regulations on the bunkering of fishing vessels might mean that States do not regard bunkering of fishing vessels as connected to fishing activities.

[336] Ibid., para. 59. The dissenting judges did not consider the majority's characterization of bunkering to be appropriate. One view was that the issue required fuller argumentation. Ibid., Dissenting Opinion of Vice-President Wolfrum and Judge Yamamoto, paras. 20–25. President Mensah described the discussion as "unwarranted obiter dictum." See ibid., Dissenting Opinion of President Mensah, para. 6. Judge Anderson chose to define bunkering as "an internationally lawful use of the sea related to navigation." Ibid., Dissenting Opinion of Judge Anderson, para. 14.

[337] Ibid., para. 66. See also ibid., para. 68.

[338] Ibid., Dissenting Opinion of Judges Park, Nelson, Chandrasekhara Rao, Vukas, and Ndiaye, para. 14.

penalties for such an act.[339] President Mensah was similarly critical of the majority's reliance on Article 40 of the Maritime Code and asserted that the reference to Article 40 was simply intended to establish the geographical area in which the offenses were alleged to have been committed.[340] Certainly the provisions referred to in the Proces-Verbal, as Judge Anderson set out, indicated that the arrest was made in terms of smuggling and the enforcement of Guinean customs laws.

The majority of the Tribunal did not accept Guinea's classification of its laws, however. The reason for this rejection was justified as follows:

> the classification as "customs" of the prohibition of bunkering of fishing vessels makes it very arguable that . . . the Guinean authorities acted from the beginning in violation of international law, while the classification under article 73 permits the assumption that Guinea was convinced that in arresting the M/V Saiga it was acting within its rights under the Convention. It is the opinion of the Tribunal that given the choice between a legal classification that implies a violation of international law and one that avoids such implication it must opt for the latter.[341]

President Mensah commented that the reasoning of the majority means that the Tribunal is claiming the right to determine the laws on which a State should have based itself to make its actions justifiable under international law.[342] Judges Park, Nelson, Chandrasekhara Rao, Vukas, and Ndiaye similarly considered it inappropriate for the Tribunal to comment on the validity of Guinean actions under international law and that the Tribunal should not "appear to be better custodians of

---

[339] They further noted that the arrest of the M/V "Saiga" was not established as part of an anti-bunkering operation to protect fishing stocks in Guinea's EEZ. *Ibid.*, Dissenting Opinion of Judges Park, Nelson, Chandrasekhara Rao, Vukas, and Ndiaye, para. 13.

[340] *Ibid.*, Dissenting Opinion of President Mensah, para. 13. Judge Anderson also supported this view, stating that "article 40 appears simply to supply the 200 mile limit . . . [and] does not appear to create any fisheries offenses. Accordingly, the relevant provisions of the legislation can be characterized or classified only as customs or fiscal, not fisheries legislation." *Ibid.*, Dissenting Opinion of Judge Anderson, para. 6.

[341] *Ibid.*, para. 72.

[342] *Ibid.*, Dissenting Opinion of President Mensah, para. 20. President Mensah also considered that the reasoning led to the conclusion that bunkering could be assimilated to a fishing activity and thus would be an activity falling within the coastal State's exercise of sovereign jurisdiction. This implication could be drawn even though the majority had stated that it would not reach a decision on whether bunkering constituted an activity with respect to the exploration, exploitation, conservation, and management of living resources of the EEZ. *Ibid.*, Dissenting Opinion of President Mensah, paras. 21 and 22.

Guinean interests than Guinea itself."[343] In so deciding, the Tribunal arrogated to itself the power to characterize the actions of Guinea and thus classified the actions under Article 73.[344]

As the majority of ITLOS determined that an application could be made on the basis of Article 73, the Tribunal did not consider Saint Vincent and the Grenadines' alternative argument in relation to Article 292. Saint Vincent and the Grenadines had submitted that Article 292 could be argued without reference to a specific provision of the Convention for the prompt release of vessels or their crews on the basis that "it would be strange that the procedure for prompt release should be available in cases in which detention is permitted by the Convention . . . and not in cases in which it is not permitted by it."[345] The Tribunal termed this construction as a "non-restrictive interpretation" of Article 292.[346]

In their joint dissenting opinion, Judges Park, Nelson, Chandrasekhara Rao, Vukas, and Ndiaye examined Saint Vincent and the Grenadines' contention that a violation of Article 56 of the Convention would be an appropriate basis for an application under Article 292. Through a textual analysis of Article 292 and reference to its legislative history, Judges Park, Nelson, Chandrasekhara Rao, Vukas, and Ndiaye decided that the procedure under Article 292 is only available where the Convention contains specific provisions concerning the prompt release of the vessel or its crew upon the posting of a reasonable bond or other financial security.[347] The specific provisions in the Convention are Articles 73, 220, and 226.

Vice-President Wolfrum and Judge Yamamoto went beyond a textual analysis and considered Article 292 in relation to the dispute settlement regime of the Convention as a whole. Section 2 of Part XV of

---

[343] Ibid., Dissenting Opinion of Judges Park, Nelson, Chandrasekhara Rao, Vukas, and Ndiaye, para. 20. This decision to override Guinea's plea has been described as "objectionable at every level." Lowe, "M/V Saiga," at 194. Not only did it infringe the right of States to choose how they would present their case, but it also has the potential to impede the development of new rules and institutions as well as undermine the standing of ITLOS. Ibid. See also Brown, "M/V 'Saiga,'" at 323 (describing the arrogation of the right to classify the nature of the relevant Guinean laws as "indefensible").

[344] But see Lauterpacht, at 411 (arguing that "assessment must take place not by reference to the legislation which the detaining State itself invokes as the basis of its conduct, but rather by reference to what objectively must be seen as a likely or possible basis," otherwise the detaining State could too easily circumvent Article 292).

[345] M/V "Saiga," Prompt Release, para. 53.   [346] Ibid.

[347] Ibid., Dissenting Opinion of Judges Park, Nelson, Chandrasekhara Rao, Vukas, and Ndiaye, para. 23.

the Convention addresses compulsory procedures entailing binding decisions and, under Article 286, any dispute relating to the interpretation
and application of the Convention must be settled in accordance with
the procedures available in the Convention. Section 3 limits the applicability of the compulsory dispute settlement procedures to certain disputes. In Section 3, Article 297, paragraph 3, specifies that disputes relating to the coastal State's exercise of its sovereign rights in the EEZ in
relation to living resources are excluded from the compulsory procedures under Section 2.[348] A situation may arise where a vessel and its
crew are arrested because of non-compliance with the coastal State's
laws regarding fishing in the EEZ. The dispute may then be excluded
from the procedures in Section 2 in accordance with Article 297(3), and
may also fall under the optional exception of law enforcement activities with respect to fisheries.[349] The question thus arises as to whether
proceedings could still be instituted under Article 292, as Section 3 is
intended to limit the application of Section 2 of Part XV. Oda has criticized the role of courts or tribunals in securing the prompt release of
vessels on this basis.[350] He notes that the "question of prompt release is
inevitably linked with the content of the rules and regulations of the
coastal State concerning the fisheries in its exclusive economic zone, and
the way in which these rules are enforced."[351] From this characterization, Oda concludes that the issue of prompt release cannot be isolated
from the competence of the coastal State with respect to fisheries in
the EEZ and thus the issue before the courts or tribunals is not simply a matter of securing prompt release.[352] Vice-President Wolfrum and
Judge Yamamoto took the view in *M/V "Saiga"* that Article 292, which
is found in Section 2, was a unique and self-contained procedure with
specific rules and very precise limits.[353] Its procedure was meant to complement normal procedures under Part XV.[354] As such, the Article 292
procedure could "be seen as an exception to the limitations on applicability as contained in Article 297 of the Convention."[355] Since proceedings under Article 292 are only meant to address the question of
release and not the merits, the limitations in Article 297 should not
affect the operation of Article 292. As Article 292 is thus an "exception"

---

[348] UNCLOS, art. 297(3)(a).   [349] *Ibid.*, art. 298(1)(b).
[350] Oda, "Dispute Settlement Prospects," at 865–67.   [351] *Ibid.*, at 866.   [352] *Ibid.*
[353] M/V "Saiga," Prompt Release, Dissenting Opinion of Vice-President Wolfrum and
Judge Yamamoto, para. 16.
[354] *Ibid.*, Dissenting Opinion of Vice-President Wolfrum and Judge Yamamoto, para. 18.
[355] *Ibid.*, Dissenting Opinion of Vice-President Wolfrum and Judge Yamamoto.

to Article 297, Vice-President Wolfrum and Judge Yamamoto preferred a narrow construction of Article 292 whereby the procedure for the release of vessels would only be available for the express substantive provisions in the Convention.

Assessing the Reasonableness of the Bond

In assessing whether the bond imposed is reasonable or not, a court or tribunal operating under Article 292 will take into account a variety of factors, including "the gravity of the alleged offences, the penalties imposed or imposable under the laws of the detaining State, the value of the detained vessel and of the cargo seized, the amount of the bond imposed by the detaining State and its form."[356] This list is not exhaustive but indicates what factors are likely to be most relevant for Article 292 proceedings. To date, ITLOS has only assessed the reasonableness of bonds in the context of seizures under Article 73 but presumably these factors would be equally pertinent in respect of Articles 220 and 226, as well as Article 73.

Gravity of the Alleged Offences

In assessing the reasonableness of the bond, an international court or tribunal must recognize the need to balance coastal State interests in upholding the right to enforce laws in the EEZ and flag State interests in maintaining the freedom of navigation. The Tribunal observed in *Monte Confurco* that paragraph 1 of Article 73 referred to the right of the coastal State to take measures as may be necessary to ensure conformity with its laws and regulations adopted in the exercise of its sovereign rights to explore, exploit, conserve, and manage the living resources of the EEZ. Paragraph 2, requiring the prompt release of arrested vessels and their crews upon posting of a reasonable bond, then protected the interest of the flag State as a balance to the interests of the coastal State recognized in paragraph 1.[357] A comparable balance is seen in Articles 220 and 226. This balance is then found again in Article 292 with respect to the need to release the arrested vessels and crews versus the need to ensure the appearance in court of the Master as well as the payment of the penalties.[358]

---

[356] Camouco, para. 67.

[357] Monte Confurco, para. 70. See also *ibid.*, Dissenting Opinion of Judge Jesus (supporting the observation of the balance in the Convention).

[358] *Ibid.*, para. 71. The Tribunal reaffirmed this view in the *Volga*. See The "Volga" Case, para. 65 (citing the *Monte Confurco* decision, para. 71).

The competing interests of coastal States and flag States have been evident in prompt release cases that have arisen in relation to coastal States efforts to curb the practice of illegal, unregulated, and unreported fishing of Patagonian toothfish in the Antarctic Ocean. These cases, *Camouco*, *Monte Confurco*, and *Volga*, have also highlighted the tension between coastal State efforts to protect and conserve fish stocks in the context of a specific multilateral regime (the Convention on the Conservation of Antarctic Marine Living Resources ("CCAMLR"))[359] and the enduring importance of the freedom of navigation as upheld in Article 292 proceedings. These typically opposing interests have impacted on the assessment of the reasonableness of bonds as judges have grappled with their appraisal of the gravity of the offence.

In *Camouco*, several judges in their separate or dissenting opinions emphasized that weight should be accorded to the conservation of the living resources of the oceans and the effective enforcement of national fisheries laws and regulations, particularly in a remote and extensive EEZ.[360] Vice-President Nelson, for example, considered that regard should be had to the "factual matrix" of the case, particularly the illegal, uncontrolled, and undeclared fishing in the Antarctic Ocean.[361] These judges were of the view that the rights of the coastal State to enforce its fisheries laws should not be reduced to an "empty shell" through prompt release proceedings.[362] When taking into account the interests and rights of the coastal State, Judge Wolfrum wrote in this regard:

> These discretionary powers or margin of appreciation on the side of the coastal state limit the powers of the Tribunal on deciding whether a bond set by national authorities was reasonable or not. It is not for the Tribunal to establish a system of its own which does not take into account the enforcement policy by the coastal State in question.[363]

---

[359] Convention on the Conservation of Antarctic Marine Living Resources, May 21, 1980, 33 UST 3476.

[360] See, e.g., Camouco, Dissenting Opinion of Judge Anderson. Judge Wolfrum took a similar approach in his Dissenting Opinion when commenting that the fact that Article 73 of the Convention was at issue indicated that the rights and interests of the coastal State in the living resources should form the background to the proceedings. See *ibid.*, Dissenting Opinion of Judge Wolfrum, para. 5.

[361] *Ibid.*, Separate Opinion of Vice President Nelson, at 3. Judge Wolfrum also took the view that the Tribunal should have taken into account the fishing regime in effect between over thirty States under the CCAMLR. *Ibid.*, Dissenting Opinion of Judge Wolfrum, para. 17.

[362] *Ibid.*, Dissenting Opinion of Judge Wolfrum, para. 8.

[363] *Ibid.*, Dissenting Opinion of Judge Wolfrum, para. 11.

These separate opinions acknowledge the wider impact the prompt release proceedings could have on the rules regulating fishing conservation and management in the EEZ.

Both parties in *Camouco* addressed the issue of illegal fishing, particularly in violation of the CCAMLR, in their arguments. France had drawn the Tribunal's attention to the economic and ecological problems associated with the illegal fishing of Patagonian toothfish in the southern oceans.[364] Panama resisted these arguments on the grounds that that particular issue was before other international fora.[365] This submission reflected a very narrow perspective on the questions involved in relation to the prompt release of vessels and emphasized the inclusive navigational interests over the exclusive rights of the coastal State to protect its living resources. ITLOS did not seemingly take account of these factors in assessing the reasonableness of the bond, however.

When considering the gravity of the offences in *Monte Confurco*, the Tribunal took note of France's arguments concerning the threats posed by illegal fishing and the measures taken under the CCAMLR for the conservation of toothfish,[366] as well as the range of penalties imposable under French law for the alleged offences.[367] These observations thus incorporated some of the considerations that were raised by judges in their separate and dissenting opinions in the *Camouco* case. Judge Anderson particularly emphasized the importance of the conservation of the resources of the EEZ and the CCAMLR in his dissenting opinion and considered it "material in forming a view of what is a 'reasonable' bond within the *overall* scheme of the Convention."[368] The Tribunal's reasoning in this regard indicated greater awareness of the importance of the coastal State's enforcement powers than had been evident in *Camouco*.

In *Volga*, the respondent State, Australia, similarly to France in *Monte Confurco* and *Camouco*, referred to the continuing illegal fishing in the area covered by the CCAMLR and the serious depletion of the stocks of Patagonian toothfish.[369] The Tribunal acknowledged the level of international concern about the dangers posed to the conservation of the fisheries in the area and that the maintenance of the ecological balance

---

[364] Camouco, ITLOS PV-00/2, at 8–12 (estimating that 90,000 tons of toothfish had been unlawfully harvested from areas covered by the CCAMLR).

[365] "Camouco," Application for Prompt Release (*Panama* v. *France*), Verbatim Record, ITLOS PV-00/3, p. 5, available at http://www.itlos.org/start2_en.html.

[366] Monte Confurco, para. 79.   [367] *Ibid.*, para. 80.

[368] Monte Confurco, Dissenting Opinion of Judge Anderson (emphasis in original).

[369] Australia emphasized this international concern in its Response. The "Volga" Case, Australian Response, paras. 42–47.

of the environment warranted serious penalties, including a high level of bond, as had been incorporated into Australian legislation.[370] However, "[t]he purpose of the procedure provided for in article 292 of the Convention is to secure the prompt release of the vessel and crew upon the posting of a reasonable bond, pending completion of the judicial procedures before the courts of the detaining State."[371] In this way, the Tribunal affirmed that the Article 292 proceedings are aimed at upholding the freedom of navigation and a certain emphasis on this side of the equation is warranted in balancing the rights of States with detained vessels and crews with the rights of States seeking to uphold their fisheries conservation efforts.

In addressing issues of enforcement under the CCAMLR, ITLOS is right to take the view that the prompt release provisions were included as part of the balance to protect rights of navigation in these zones.[372] The importance of the navigational interest could be diminished, however, in situations where the owners of vessels have specifically sought to avoid certain fishing limitations imposed through cooperative regimes, such as the CCAMLR, through the use of flags of convenience.[373] While this practice is outside of the scope of Article 292 proceedings, evidence of this behavior may reinforce the gravity of the offence in determining what bond or financial security is reasonable in particular cases. In its first decisions, ITLOS should have accorded more weight to the fact that the enforcement powers of the coastal State have to be protected in order to maintain the effectiveness of established cooperative regimes.[374] Effectively curtailing the enforcement powers of coastal States in relation to detained vessels fishing illegally could undermine the efforts of conservation of particular States cooperating under an international agreement. Coastal States were granted enforcement powers under the Convention in order to protect their newly attributed rights to manage

---

[370] The "Volga" Case, para. 67.   [371] Ibid., para. 69.

[372] "It is my view that, while the commercial importance of maritime transportation and marine exploitation are the primary motivating forces, the prompt release institution is undergirded somewhat by the venerable freedom of the high seas including, *inter alia*, the freedom of navigation." Camouco, Separate Opinion of Judge Laing, at 2.

[373] France brought to the attention of the Tribunal the fact that the "Camouco" had previously sailed under the French flag as the "Saint Jean" and then registered under the flag of Panama in 1999. Camouco, ITLOS PV-00/2, at 5. The Tribunal did not refer to this fact in its judgment or in the separate opinions as the relevant jurisdictional question was whether Panama was the flag State at the time the vessel was seized and when the proceedings were before ITLOS.

[374] See Camouco, Dissenting Opinion of Judge Wolfrum, para. 17. See further Camouco, ITLOS PV-00/2, at 9–10.

and conserve the living resources of the EEZ. When a situation has been reached that compels coastal States to embark on serious or drastic conservation regimes, particularly in a cooperative context, greater weight should be accorded to the enforcement powers of the coastal State in assessing a reasonable bond than might otherwise be accorded to a coastal State dealing with less serious threats to its living resources in its maritime zone.

Penalties Imposed or Imposable by the Detaining State

In assessing what bonds should be paid, detaining States frequently take into account the amount of the fines or other penalties that may be incurred for violations of its fisheries or pollution laws. The fines may be imposed on the owners of the vessel and/or on the members of the crew. In this regard, the bond for the release of the vessel and crew constitutes a surety that any fines imposed through domestic court proceedings will be paid. In *Camouco*, for example, France stated that the essential purpose of the bond was to ensure that the fines levied would be paid,[375] as well as payment for any damage and interest.[376] The bond also needed to be high enough to serve as a sufficient deterrent against illegal fishing.[377] France further submitted that the amount it had fixed was reasonable since it was comparable to the practice of other States in the region.[378] By comparison, in *Monte Confurco*, there was no disagreement between the parties on the fines themselves,[379] but the Applicant submitted that the maximum penalties should not have been imposed in light of the facts of the case and the practice of French courts in the imposition of these penalties.[380] As the fine could have been as high as FF 30 million or more, France argued that the fact that the amount demanded (namely, FF 20 million) was less indicated the reasonableness of the bond.[381] Assessing the bond as an amount equivalent to the fine tends to preempt the necessity of a vessel and its crew from returning for further domestic legal proceedings once they are released.

In determining the penalties imposed or imposable, ITLOS must necessarily examine the domestic proceedings that have been undertaken with respect to the vessel and its crew. The assessment of evidence by

---

[375] Camouco, ITLOS PV-00/2, at 18 (explaining that the Master was liable for four fines: fishing without authorization in the French EEZ; failing to give notice of his entry into the EEZ; concealing the vessel's identification marks; and attempting to evade control).

[376] *Ibid.*, at 19.   [377] *Ibid.*   [378] *Ibid.*

[379] Monte Confurco, para. 83.   [380] *Ibid.*, para. 83.   [381] *Ibid.*

each court or tribunal may lead to different results and so an issue to consider is how these conflicts may be reconciled. In *Monte Confurco*,[382] for example, ITLOS assessed what value should be accorded to the toothfish found on the vessel at the time of its arrest. The Tribunal noted that the court of first instance in Réunion had assumed that the fines imposed by a trial judge could correspond to the value of one half of the catch, but disagreed with that court's assessment of the evidence:

> The Tribunal is aware that the expert opinion of the scientist [called on behalf of the Respondents] suggests that not all the fish on board could have been fished outside the exclusive economic zone of the Kerguelen Islands. The Tribunal does not, however, consider the assumption of the court of first instance at Saint-Paul as being entirely consistent with the information before this Tribunal. Such information does not give an adequate basis to assume that the entire catch on board, or a substantial part of it, was taken in the exclusive economic zone of the Kerguelen Islands; nor does it provide clear indications as to the period of time the vessel was in the exclusive economic zone before its interception.[383]

This statement effectively questioned the basis of the decision made by the court of first instance and criticized the manner by which the domestic court assessed the evidence before it.

Judge Mensah, in his declaration, considered this criticism to be "both unjustified and inappropriate in the circumstances."[384] France had explained in its submissions that the court of first instance had made a presumption of fact (and not utilized a legal presumption) prior to a decision by the trial court on whether the alleged facts were correct.[385] Judge Mensah took the view that the Tribunal was in no better position to determine what figure could be validated by the "facts" at this stage of the proceedings.[386] In this situation, he considered, the Tribunal should not appear to be making any decisions that related to the merits of the case but should be limited to the facts and circumstances necessary for a proper appreciation of the reasonablenss of the bond.[387] Judge Jesus expressed similar reservations about the majority's qualifications of facts and law applicable to the case and maintained that the Tribunal should

---

[382] *Ibid.*, paras. 27–46 (setting out the facts of the case).

[383] *Ibid.*, para. 88.   [384] *Ibid.*, Declaration of Judge Mensah.

[385] "Monte Confurco," Application for Prompt Release (*Seychelles* v. *France*), (Judgment of December 18, 2000), Verbatim Record, ITLOS PV.00/8, p.11, available at http://www.itlos.org/start2_en.html, paras. 14–17.

[386] Monte Confurco, Declaration of Judge Mensah.

[387] *Ibid.*, Declaration of Judge Mensah.

only "determine under the concrete circumstances of each case if the bond imposed by the domestic court is or is not reasonable."[388]

The difficulty here is determining where the appropriate line should be drawn between which facts and circumstances can be taken into account and which ones impinge on the decision on the merits. The detrimental impact of the Tribunal's approach in *Monte Confurco* is nonetheless limited if reference is made to the earlier view expressed in *M/V "Saiga"* that, "domestic courts, in considering the merits of the case, are not bound by any findings of fact or law that the Tribunal may have made in order to reach its conclusions."[389] Given the availability of an international forum to deal with applications for the prompt release of vessels and to assess what constitutes a reasonable bond, the way certain factors are considered in that forum may influence decision-making on a national level precisely to avoid the situation that the flag State of the vessel will pursue international proceedings. The interaction between the international and domestic fora on this issue could promote an international standard for the assessment of bonds or other financial security for arrested vesels.

Value of the Detained Vessel and the Cargo or Equipment Seized
A court or tribunal will not only have to consider what fines or other financial penalties are imposed or imposable on a vessel owner or crew member guilty of violating laws in the maritime zones of a coastal State in assessing the bond, but also the value of the arrested vessel and any other cargo or equipment seized.[390] This value may be able to offset the amount of the bond that is otherwise required. Panama made this submission in *Camouco*, arguing that the bond should be fixed at FF 1.3 million, with a reduction for the value of the seized cargo. France argued that the seized cargo and equipment should not be taken into account as it was subject to a different proceeding under French law than that of the vessel.[391] In addition to the vessel and its cargo and equipment, ITLOS took into account the seizures of fish catch as a factor relevant in the assessment of a reasonable bond. Similarly, in *Monte Confurco*, the Tribunal set the bond at FF 18 million, with half of that amount

---

[388] *Ibid.*, Dissenting Opinion of Judge Jesus, para. 10.
[389] M/V "Saiga," Prompt Release, para. 49.
[390] Under art. 111(2)(b) of the Tribunal's Rules, the prompt release application may provide information concerning the vessel's "tonnage, cargo capacity and data relative to the determination of its value" if it is "appropriate."
[391] Camouco, para. 85.

accounted for as the monetary value of the toothfish and the other half to be posted with France in the form of a bank guarantee.[392] By contrast, in *Volga*, the Tribunal stated that it did not take into account the amount derived from the proceeds of the sale of the fish and bait because it was irrelevant to the bond to be set for the release of the vessel and its crew members.[393] In taking this view, the Tribunal slightly distanced itself from its decisions in *Camouco* and *Monte Confurco*.[394] The bond favored was thus one that was based on the value of the vessel and its equipment only.

Amount of Bond Imposed by the Detaining State
In the first prompt release cases before ITLOS, the Tribunal consistently set lower amounts for the bond than that imposed by the detaining State. For example, in *Volga*, in taking note of the value of the vessel and its fuel, lubricants, and equipment, as well as the amount of the catch and bait sold by the Australian authorities, the Tribunal set the bond for the "Volga" at AU$1.92 million – a reduction of AU$1,412,500 from the bond requested by Australia.[395] After looking at the range of factors in *Camouco*, the Tribunal concluded that France's bond of FF 20 million was not reasonable,[396] but instead, the majority of ITLOS set the amount at FF 8 million.[397] No details were provided as to what weight was given to any of the specific factors or how the precise figure was finally determined. In his separate opinion, Judge Laing compared the amounts of the required bonds in *M/V "Saiga"* to *Camouco* by contrasting the amounts as percentages of potential liability to which the ship owners were exposed.[398] Using this form of calculation, Judge Laing cautioned that consistency and proportionality in Article 292 proceedings should be adhered to in determinations of reasonableness.[399] In *Monte*

---

[392] Monte Confurco, para. 93.
[393] The "Volga" Case, para. 86. Australia had submitted: "It is indisputable in international practice as reflected in the domestic laws of States that States may require the forfeiture of a vessel *and* the forfeiture of the catch. If a bond set for the vessel is reduced by the value of the catch, the Tribunal would effectively be eliminating the right of a State under its domestic legislation to the effective forfeiture of the vessel as such. This means the bond would not provide the intended security." The "Volga" Case, Australian Response, para. 50 (emphasis in original).
[394] See The "Volga" Case, Dissenting Opinion of Judge *ad hoc* Shearer, para. 15.
[395] *Ibid.*, paras. 71 and 73.   [396] *Ibid.*, para. 70.   [397] *Ibid.*, para. 74.
[398] Camouco, Separate Opinion of Judge Laing, at 3 (calculating that the bond set in *M/V "Saiga"* was 9 percent of the potential liability to which the ship owners were exposed whereas the amount chosen in *Camouco* was 40 percent).
[399] *Ibid.*, Separate Opinion of Judge Laing.

Confurco, the court of first instance explicitly referred to the provisions of Articles 73(2) and 292 of UNCLOS and observed the holding of ITLOS in the *Camouco* case as to what factors should be taken into account in the determination of a "reasonable" bond. On this basis, the total bond was fixed at FF 56.4 million. ITLOS instead decided that the bond or other security should consist of FF 9 million as the monetary equivalent of the catch seized, and a further amount of FF 9 million as bond. Thus far, the discrepancies between the bond amounts can best be attributed to different weight being accorded to the factors considered in assessing what a reasonable bond might be.

Greater consistency between national and international decision-making on bonds may be possible if there is a clearer explication of the weight attributed to factors considered by the Tribunal in setting a bond. ITLOS plainly has the opportunity to initiate a clear international jurisprudence of reasonable bonds in situations of unlawful fishing. Judge Laing and Judge Treves in *Camouco* both considered the possibility of creating an international standard for bonds.[400] Judge Treves thought that an international standard would reflect equally the interests of the coastal State in the enforcement of its fishing laws and regulations as well as the interests of the flag State in protecting the freedom of navigation and the commercial interests thereby at stake.[401] Such an international standard could be determined through regard to the practice of States in the region in enforcing their fisheries laws and regulations. France certainly argued that its bond was reasonable when the fines imposed by Australia and New Zealand could be compared with the bonds typically imposed by the French court in Réunion.[402]

Oda has been critical of the possibility of ITLOS being able to create a universal standard for fines, particularly since reasonableness can never be proved from an objective point of view.[403] Oda writes: "since there is no international standard for such financial penalties, it seems that the degree of these penalties would fall exclusively within the domestic jurisdiction of each coastal state, unless otherwise provided in international law."[404] He continues:

---

[400] See *ibid.*, Separate Opinion of Judge Laing, at 2, and Dissenting Opinion of Judge Treves, para. 4.

[401] *Ibid.*, Dissenting Opinion of Judge Treves, paras. 4 and 6.

[402] Camouco, ITLOS PV-00/2, at 19.

[403] Oda, Some Reflections, at 651. See also Oda, "Dispute Settlement Prospects," at 866.

[404] Shigeru Oda, "Fisheries under the United Nations Convention on the Law of the Sea," 77 *Am. J. Int'l L.* 739, 747 (1983).

Indeed, no rules exist in international law that suggest a universal standard for fines to be imposed for violations of coastal regulations by foreign vessels, so that it would be extremely difficult for any court or tribunal to carry out the suggestion in the 1982 Convention that it determine the reasonableness of the bond or other financial security to be deposited.[405]

This task may, however, be accomplished as ITLOS jurisprudence on this issue evolves. The formulation of an international standard for the release of fishing vessels has the advantage of creating a common expectation in the way vessels and their crews should be treated as a reflection of both the importance of the freedom of navigation and the conservation and management of living resources. Under UNCLOS, States have assigned this role to third-party institutions under Article 292 and have thereby surrendered a decision typically made within national fora. This transfer of authority will only prove successful if the international courts and tribunals assigned this task can establish clear guidelines as to what factors are to be considered in setting an amount. The guidelines must remain flexible to allow for a variety of conditions but still sufficiently defined to create continuity and consistency in this process.

Non-Financial Conditions of a Bond
The factors suggested by the Tribunal thus far have all been indicators relevant for determining the amount of the bond. In *Volga*, the Australian Fisheries Management Authority sought to impose a security of AU$3,332,500 for the release of the "Volga," which was based on the assessed value of the vessel, fuel, lubricants, and fishing equipment, potential fines, and also as security for the carriage of a fully operational Vessel Monitoring System and observance of the CCAMLR.[406] When considering the additional, non-monetary conditions imposed by the Australian authorities, the Tribunal decided that "it is not appropriate in the present proceedings to consider whether a coastal State is entitled to impose such conditions in the exercise of its sovereign rights under the Convention."[407] It instead formulated the question as one concerning whether the "bond or other security" to be applied under Article 73(2) could include such conditions.[408] In interpreting these words, the Tribunal had regard to references to bonds and other security in other provisions of the Convention, including the seizure of vessels under Articles 220 and 226, as well as Article 292. By reference to these other

---

[405] *Ibid.*, at 749.   [406] The "Volga" Case, para. 53.
[407] *Ibid.*, para. 76. See also *ibid.*, para. 79.   [408] *Ibid.*, para. 76.

provisions, it was evident to the Tribunal that bonds and other security were to be of a financial nature only, otherwise the object and purpose of Article 73(2) could not be achieved if it was not possible to assess the reasonableness of the bond in financial terms.[409] "In the view of the Tribunal, a 'good behaviour bond' to prevent future violations of the laws of a coastal State cannot be considered as a bond or security within the meaning of article 73, paragraph 2, of the Convention read in conjunction with article 292 of the Convention."

While reading the other references to bond and other security in the Convention indicates that non-financial terms are not supposed to be part of any bond or security for the release of the vessel, the reasoning that the object and purpose of Article 73(2) when read in conjunction with Article 292 would be defeated with the addition of non-financial terms is not persuasive. Given the flexibility inherent in the qualifier "reasonable," there is no reason for the Tribunal *not* to assess the reasonableness of non-financial bonds that are designed to enhance the enforcement aspects of Article 73(1). The prompt release proceedings clearly provide the avenue to reassess these conditions if and when necessary.

Conclusion

Although Article 292 only applies to limited situations, those situations reflect the most fundamental tensions existing between States in the exercise of rights in the EEZ. The role of ITLOS under Article 292 is to reconcile States' competing interests and to preserve a workable balance as States exercise their respective rights under the Convention. Comparable issues will presumably arise with the intersection of Article 292 proceedings and the enforcement of laws and regulations relating to the protection and preservation of the marine environment under Articles 220 and 226.

---

[409] *Ibid.*, para. 26. ("The object and purpose of article 73, paragraph 2, read in conjunction with article 292 of the Convention, is to provide the flag State with a mechanism for obtaining the prompt release of a vessel and crew arrested for alleged fisheries violations by posting a security of a financial nature whose reasonableness can be assessed in financial terms. The inclusion of additional non-financial conditions in such a security would defeat this object and purpose.") Judge Anderson thought that the legislative history of the different provisions, especially the relationship of the environmental provisions to international standards under other multilateral treaties, demanded separate treatment. *Ibid.*, Dissenting Opinion of Judge Anderson, para. 17.

The availability of an international mechanism to deal with the question of prompt release of vessels and crews undoubtedly impacts on the substantive rules of the Convention. The main effect on coastal State authority to be discerned so far has been through the assessment of the reasonableness of bonds set by domestic courts. Contrasting views have come out of the Tribunal on this point. On the one hand, Judge Wolfrum considers that the discretionary powers of the coastal State limit the powers of the Tribunal on deciding whether a bond set by national authorities was reasonable or not and that the Tribunal should not establish a system of its own that would not take into account the enforcement policy by the coastal State in question.[410] The arrogation of this responsibility by ITLOS could counter the provisions in the Convention favoring State authority over fishing in the EEZ. This approach is only appropriate when States are cooperating to conserve and manage species that are particularly threatened through over-fishing. By contrast, Vice-President Nelson has instead stated:

it must be remarked that the Tribunal has in fact been invested with the competence to limit – to put a brake on – the discretionary power of the coastal State with respect to the fixing of bonds in certain specific circumstances. That is a necessary consequence which arises from the very nature of the mechanism contained in article 292.[411]

Except where there is a need to support cooperative fishing regimes, this view correctly emphasizes the role of Article 292 in protecting navigational rights of States in foreign EEZs.

Conclusion

The purpose of Section 2 of Part XV is to set out a flexible mechanism for the interpretation and application of the Convention that accommodates the different preferences of States for international dispute resolution. In establishing a structure for third-party dispute settlement, UNCLOS incorporates rules that traditionally govern the operation of international courts and tribunals – such as the rule of exhaustion of local remedies, availability of provisional measures and authority

---

410 Camouco, Dissenting Opinion of Judge Wolfrum, para. 11. Judge Anderson, in his Dissenting Opinion in *"Monte Confurco"* also noted that it is "for the legislators and the courts of States Parties to lay down fines for illegal fishing." Monte Confurco, Dissenting Opinion of Judge Anderson.
411 *Ibid.*, Separate Opinion of Vice-President Nelson, p. 1.

to settle jurisdictional challenges.[412] The system in Section 2 demonstrates the sensitivity of States when it comes to involvement in a mandatory international judicial or arbitral mechanism. The extent that this sensitivity is heeded by the fora available under UNCLOS will be played out in their decision-making processes. The provisional measures cases and prompt release proceedings decided by ITLOS thus far do indicate that aspects of State decision-making power will be subsumed by international processes (particularly with ITLOS' power to prescribe fish catch totals as a provisional measure, assessing nationality of vessels, and in establishing what constitutes a reasonable bond as part of fisheries enforcement). In other respects, these particular procedures advance the goals of Part XV by supporting the peaceful settlement of disputes through recommended provisional measures and not expanding Article 292 to encompass matters that must be decided on the merits. The workability of compulsory dispute settlement entailing binding decisions is therefore not only attributable to deference to States' freedom of choice and flexibility, but also to limitations that inhere in these procedures.

Even with these concessions, some allowance still had to be made for a specific range of disputes that States were unwilling to submit to compulsory procedures entailing binding decisions. As Gamble notes, "It is clear that whenever one makes the quantum jump from non-binding to binding modes of dispute settlement a whole new set of considerations is introduced necessitating many qualifications and escape clauses."[413] These exceptions and limitations are set out in Section 3 of Part XV of UNCLOS. They are briefly outlined below before a more thorough examination in the next two chapters.

---

[412] UNCLOS, arts. 295, 290 and 288, respectively. Article 294 stipulates separately that challenges can be raised by the parties, or the court or tribunal *proprio motu*, as to whether a claim constitutes an abuse of legal process or whether *prima facie* it is well-founded for the disputes referred to in Article 297. This preliminary proceeding was included in Part XV because of coastal State "fears that they might be forced to defend too many cases before international courts or tribunals, stretching thin their financial resources and skilled manpower, and that they should be protected against harassment through frivolous complaints." 5 *United Nations Convention on the Law of the Sea 1982: A Commentary*, at 76. The inclusion of Article 294 could attenuate the force of the compulsory proceedings. De Mestral, at 182. See generally Tullio Treves, "Preliminary Proceedings in the Settlement of Disputes under the United Nations Law of the Sea Convention: Some Observations," in *Liber Amicorum Judge Shigeru Oda* (N. Ando *et al.* eds, 2002), p. 749.

[413] Gamble, "Dispute Settlement in Perspective," at 331.

Limits on Compulsory Procedures Entailing Binding Decisions

The vast majority of States at the Third Conference were "in favour of some form and some degree of compulsory dispute settlement, but placed less priority upon achieving a comprehensive system, and in many cases approached the problem of establishing a workable compulsory dispute settlement system with reservations on certain issues."[414] A system of exceptions and limitations had to be allowed since Article 309 prohibits States from entering reservations to the terms of the Convention. The limitations on the application of the compulsory dispute settlement system are thus incorporated into Part XV itself. Section 3, entitled "Limitations and Exceptions to Section 2," identifies some of the disputes to which Section 2 is specifically applicable and how certain disputes are excepted from mandatory adjudication and arbitration.

The exceptions and limitations primarily relate to the exercise of the traditional freedoms of the high seas in the EEZ and on the continental shelf. Article 297(1) provides that Section 2 of Part XV is applicable to the exercise of the freedoms of navigation, overflight, or the laying of submarine cables and pipelines, and other internationally lawful uses of the sea related to these freedoms in areas subject to the coastal State's sovereign rights or jurisdiction.[415] Section 2 is also specifically applicable to certain disputes regarding the protection and preservation of the marine environment,[416] marine scientific research,[417] and fishing.[418] Article 297 sets out which of these disputes are subject to compulsory procedures entailing binding decisions, which disputes are subject to compulsory conciliation, and which disputes are not subject to the UNCLOS dispute settlement regime at all.

For disputes subject to compulsory conciliation, only the procedure itself is compulsory as there is no obligation to comply with the recommendations of the conciliation commission. At most, the reports of the conciliation commissions may constitute a form of pressure on the State to conform to the commission's recommendations.[419] The use of

---

[414] De Mestral, at 170.

[415] UNCLOS, art. 297(1)(a) and (b). Although this provision does not strictly constitute an exception or limitation, the drafting history shows how any dispute relating to the exercise of the coastal State's sovereign rights, exclusive rights or executive jurisdiction was to be excluded from compulsory procedures and then this provision was to be an exception to the exclusion. See E. D. Brown, "Dispute settlement and the law of the sea: the UN Convention regime," 21 *Marine Pol'y* 17, 22 (1997).

[416] UNCLOS, art. 297(1)(c).   [417] *Ibid.*, art. 297(2).

[418] *Ibid.*, art. 297(3).   [419] See Charney, "Implications," at 73.

compulsory conciliation in this regard struck a compromise between States wanting some form of third-party settlement to be available and those States refusing the possibility of a binding decision in certain situations.[420] Noyes describes this balance as follows:

Maritime powers achieved agreement that the substantive articles of the Convention would allow them some rights in the coastal zones concerning fishing and marine scientific research, as well as navigation and other rights. They wanted treaty provisions for compulsory binding third-party adjudication to protect their rights from unilateral usurpation by the coastal states. The developing coastal states, on the other hand, had strongly asserted claims to control fishing and marine scientific research in their EEZs, and they resisted provisions that would enable other states to assert claims before third parties relating to EEZ fishing rights or marine scientific research. The coastal states feared vexatious suits alleging violations of their obligations concerning the rights of maritime powers.[421]

Basically, States are not obliged to submit matters that are considered of vital national concern to any binding dispute settlement system.[422] Instead, compulsory conciliation was viewed as an appropriate compromise in light of the broad discretionary powers granted to coastal States and the lack of substantive law on particular questions.[423] Although useful as a compromise, non-binding procedures are only likely to have any force to the extent that the opinion of the international community or bilateral responses can influence the behavior of the relevant State.[424]

Optional exceptions to compulsory dispute settlement may also be made by States "when signing, ratifying or acceding or at any time thereafter" with respect to specified categories of disputes.[425] These exceptions were formulated as "an attempt to balance the desire to be a judge in one's own cause against the principle of binding third party settlement."[426] States may choose to exclude disputes concerning boundary delimitations and historic title,[427] military and law enforcement activities,[428] and disputes in respect of which the Security Council

---

[420] See Sohn, "Settlement of Law of the Sea Disputes," at 214.

[421] Noyes, "Compulsory Adjudication," at 686–87.

[422] Guillaume, at 855. Gaertner considers that such a situation reflected an inequitable bias in favor of the Group of 77 and the aims of the New International Economic Order. Gaertner, at 586.

[423] See Brus, p. 19.   [424] See Charney, "Entry into Force," at 391.

[425] UNCLOS, art. 298(1).

[426] Merrills, at 121. See also Richardson, "Dispute Settlement," at 159. ("The mandatory and optional exceptions to mandatory binding resolution reflect the balance between sovereignty and cooperation in the Convention.").

[427] UNCLOS, art. 298(1)(a).   [428] Ibid., art. 298(1)(b).

is exercising its functions under the Charter of the United Nations.[429] These exceptions are not self-judging and cannot serve as a simple bar to proceedings under Section 2.[430] It is for the court or tribunal to determine whether it has jurisdiction to decide a particular matter.[431] Even if a State has opted to exclude a certain category of dispute, the disputant parties may still agree to use the Convention's procedures.[432]

Conclusion

Disputes concerning the interpretation and application of the Convention may only be settled by a compulsory procedure entailing a binding decision if they do not fall within the exceptions and limitations of Section 3 of Part XV and when no settlement has been reached through diplomatic channels or otherwise in accordance with Section 1. The main emphasis in Section 1 is that parties are free to choose whatever peaceful means they prefer for dispute settlement. This selection may include non-binding and non-compulsory procedures. *Southern Bluefin Tuna* confirmed that the UNCLOS mechanism would not override the dispute settlement provisions in other law of the sea treaties to which the parties have consented in accordance with Article 281. A preference for traditional, consent-based modes of dispute resolution is evident in this regard.

If the matter is not resolved under Section 1, a unilateral application may be utilized to institute proceedings under UNCLOS. For the compulsory settlement of disputes, States parties have a choice of two courts and two arbitral tribunals. If a State has failed to declare its preferred forum or the choices of the disputant States are different, the default choice of procedure is arbitration. The subject matter of a dispute is only relevant for the choice of procedure to the extent that States parties may wish to take advantage of the technical expertise available through the special arbitration procedure.[433] Otherwise, the ICJ, the ITLOS and the arbitral tribunals all have jurisdiction over any dispute concerning the interpretation or application of UNCLOS and it is unlikely that this overlapping jurisdiction should prove problematic.

---

[429] *Ibid.*, art. 298(1)(c).

[430] 5 *United Nations Convention on the Law of the Sea 1982: A Commentary*, p. 140.

[431] UNCLOS, art. 288(4).   [432] *Ibid.*, art. 299.

[433] It should also be noted that under Article 289, the ICJ, ITLOS, and the arbitral tribunal constituted under Annex VII may also select experts listed in Annex VIII to sit with the court or tribunal either at the request of a party or *proprio motu* in any dispute involving scientific or technical matters.

The compulsory procedures envisaged under the Convention include the prescription of provisional measures and a specialized mechanism for the prompt release of vessels and their crews. The first decisions of ITLOS have provided some indication of how international processes will (and will not) influence the interpretation and application of the normative aspects of UNCLOS. Limitations on compulsory procedures entailing binding decisions are set out in Section 3 of Part XV, indicating that not every dispute can be submitted to mandatory processes entailing binding decisions. Articles 297 and 298 stipulate which disputes may be excepted from the procedures in Section 2. These articles illustrate the anticipated role of compulsory dispute settlement in regulating the uses of the oceans under UNCLOS, and are explored in the next two chapters.

3 Limitations on Applicability of Compulsory Procedures Entailing Binding Decisions

The regulation of the uses of the oceans has demanded a high degree of cooperation between States in order to formulate a system that meets the needs and expectations of the greatest number of users. This regime requires an accommodation of both inclusive and exclusive interests – a balance between the freedoms of the high seas and certain economic rights inhering to coastal States. The far-reaching implications of oceans policies within the internal affairs of States have created a sufficient incentive for States to participate in an international regime and to transfer a certain degree of authority to the operation of the international system. Through participation, States may both control the interpretation and application of rules and standards as well as expect a certain degree of protection from the way that external control may be manipulated. This approach is manifest in the dispute settlement mechanism in Part XV. The dispute settlement procedures are intimately linked to the elaborate legal relationships set forth in UNCLOS, yet the necessity for dispute settlement procedures in relation to the normative framework of the Convention varies depending on the particular issue area in question. The complicated formulation of exceptions and limitations to the mandatory procedures established in the Convention indicates when dispute settlement is necessary for the functioning of the substantive rules. Also evident is when matters had to be left outside the purview of third-party adjudication and arbitration in favor of non-binding international processes, political settlement or unilateral decision-making.

Article 297 of the Convention, which deals with some of the limitations and exceptions to mandatory dispute resolution, predominantly addresses how the dispute settlement system will apply and operate with respect to the freedoms of the high seas in the EEZ and on the continental shelf. In these extended maritime zones, which now cover significant expanses of the oceans, the exclusive interests of the coastal State had to be carefully balanced with the inclusive interests of other users. Coastal States wanted to ensure control over the resources in these areas whereas third States wanted to protect their traditional freedoms to the greatest extent possible. This chapter examines how Article 297 intersects with the relevant substantive provisions of UNCLOS and how disputes are likely to be settled under this Article. Each section addresses, respectively, the freedoms of navigation, overflight, and the laying of submarine cables and pipelines; the protection and preservation of the marine environment; fishing; and, finally, marine scientific research.

Freedom of Navigation, Overflight, and the Laying of Submarine Cables and Pipelines

The freedoms of navigation, overflight, and the laying of submarine cables and pipelines existed across huge expanses of ocean space until the middle of the twentieth century. At this time, States began to claim a greater number of rights over extended maritime zones in pursuit of their economic interests. This practice led to the recognition of coastal State rights over the seabed and subsoil at the First Conference with the adoption of the Continental Shelf Convention. The unilateral actions of States in claiming special interests over the living resources of the superjacent waters resulted in the creation of the EEZ in UNCLOS. The accumulation of coastal State rights over extended maritime areas had to be countered by the preexisting interests of third States to retain the freedoms of the high seas. A number of rules were adopted to balance the freedoms of navigation, overflight, and the laying of submarine cables and pipelines with the newly acquired rights of the coastal States. The means to resolve conflicts over these competing interests was an essential part of the overall regulation of these freedoms of the high seas in the EEZ and on the continental shelf. Standards for resolving disputes were formulated within the text of UNCLOS and disputes pertaining to acts in contravention of the freedoms of navigation, overflight, and the laying of submarine cables and pipelines were rendered subject to compulsory dispute settlement. This section discusses how this new system of exclusive rights in high seas areas evolved and the way that compulsory dispute settlement became necessary to guarantee the continued exercise of the traditional freedoms of the high seas in the face of expanding coastal State jurisdiction. The available dispute settlement procedures play an essential role to protect these inclusive interests both through the provision of a mechanism to elaborate on duties of due regard and as an external source of review.

Increasing Attribution of Exclusive Maritime Rights over High Seas Areas

The result of the increasing claims of coastal States was the diminution in area that consisted of high seas and accordingly the diminution in areas wherein States were entitled to exercise the assorted freedoms of the high seas. States with significant merchant and naval fleets (often referred to as "maritime States") were anxious to preserve the *mare liberum* system to the greatest extent possible while still recognizing the entitlement of coastal States over the natural resources of the extended maritime zones. The desire to balance the demands of coastal States wishing to benefit fully from the ocean resources adjacent to their coasts with the long-held interests of the maritime States led to the development of a new system for the attribution of rights. First, with respect to the continental shelf, States developed a regime to allow for the exploration and exploitation of the seabed and subsoil while still preserving the status of the superjacent waters. This regime was largely crystallized with the adoption of the 1958 Continental Shelf Convention and was then reaffirmed in UNCLOS. Second, States sought increasingly to regulate the conservation, management, and exploitation of the living resources of the superjacent waters through the creation of a special function-oriented zone where States would have either sovereign rights or jurisdiction with respect to specific activities while still preserving aspects of the traditional freedoms of the high seas. This first part addresses these two developments of attribution of rights over the continental shelf and then the EEZ.

Attribution of Rights over the Continental Shelf

International recognition of legal rights over the continental shelf occurred through a system of allocation by virtue of legal norms formulated at the First Conference. There was a willingness on the part of States to rely on juridical processes to construct a legal regime that would allocate continental shelf areas and thereby facilitate the exploitation of natural resources from maritime areas.[1] All coastal States shared an interest in acquiring and recognizing exclusive rights over the natural resources of the seabed and subsoil. Developing countries envisaged the continental shelf as a potential source of economic power and thus wanted to protect this resource and profit from its exploitation. The continental shelf presented great financial potential for coastal States if ownership over offshore hydrocarbons could be claimed by virtue of geographic position rather than economic and technical capabilities. As an area that had been open to all users, developed States did not have any vested interests in the continental shelf and remained anxious to protect their freedom to navigate the oceans. The industrialized States were eager to create a legal regime that would only modify the freedoms of the high seas to the extent necessary to allow for the exploration and exploitation of the seabed and subsoil.

The exploitation of hydrocarbon resources from the seabed became a viable option in the 1940s when the oil industry developed offshore drilling techniques. Interest in the continental shelf had been manifested in 1942 in the delimitation of the Gulf of Paria between the British island of Trinidad and Venezuela.[2] This treaty purported to delimit the "submarine areas" of the Gulf on the basis that the seabed lying beyond the limits of territorial waters was *res nullius* and could therefore be acquired by occupation.[3] It was three years subsequent to this treaty that the President of the United States issued a proclamation on the continental shelf that sparked off a series of claims throughout the world. The Truman Proclamation asserted "jurisdiction and control" over the "natural resources" of the seabed and subsoil.[4] This claim was justified on the grounds of the global need for new sources of petroleum and other resources, the presence of these resources in the seabed, and the existence of the necessary technology to exploit them, as well as the need for some form of recognized jurisdiction in the interest of their conservation and utilization.[5] Many States followed suit in issuing claims to the

---

[1] See Lea Brilmayer and Natalie Klein, "Land and Sea: Two Sovereignty Regimes in Search of a Common Denominator," 33 *NYUJ. Int'l L. & Pol.* 703, 732–36 (2001).

[2] Treaty between His Majesty in Respect of the United Kingdom and the President of the United States of Venezuela Relating to the Submarine Areas of the Gulf of Paria, February 26, 1942, 1942 UKTS No. 10.

[3] J. A. C. Gutteridge, "The 1958 Geneva Convention on the Continental Shelf," 35 *Brit. Y.B. Int'l L.* 102, 103 (1959).

[4] Presidential Proclamation No. 2667, September 28, 1945, 59 Stat. 884.   [5] *Ibid.*

continental shelf, with variations on the type of rights being claimed.[6] The rapid development of the law in this area led to the International Law Commission including the continental shelf as part of its studies on the codification of the regime of the high seas.[7]

The recognition of legal rights over the continental shelf was thus inevitable but was cast in terms of derogation from the traditional freedoms of the high seas.[8] The primary goal in formulating the Continental Shelf Convention was to create a regime that would allow maximum exploitation of the natural resources of the continental shelf while retaining adequate protection for other uses of the high seas.[9] Statements during the First Conference were to the effect that continental shelf rights would not result in the abolition of the freedom of the high seas, "which was one of the main foundations of peaceful relations between countries and was in the interests of all nations."[10] To allay concerns that the development of the continental shelf as a legal institution would interfere with the high seas, a number of provisions were included to circumscribe the rights granted in the Continental Shelf Convention.[11] In particular, the Continental Shelf Convention provides for the coastal State to have "sovereign rights" over the continental shelf rather than "sovereignty." The use of this term was a "justifiable and realistic modification of the freedom of the high seas."[12] It conferred upon the coastal State all the rights necessary for and connected with the exploration and exploitation of the natural resources of the continental shelf while not granting full sovereignty.[13] The characterization of ownership as "sovereign rights" was considered as "based on general principles corresponding to the present needs of the international community and was in no way incompatible with the principle of the freedom of the seas."[14] Article 77(1) of UNCLOS repeats the language of

---

[6] See Hersch Lauterpacht, "Sovereignty Over Submarine Areas," 27 *Brit. Y.B. Int'l L.* 376, 380–82 (1950).

[7] See Report of the International Law Commission to the General Assembly, UN, GAOR at 296, UN Doc. A/3159 (1956), reprinted in *ILC Yearbook*, (1956), vol. II.

[8] Indeed, the Commission stated that the freedom of the high seas was a "paramount principle" and no modifications or exceptions to the principle were to be considered "unless expressly provided for in the present articles." *Ibid.*, at 298.

[9] See Franklin, at 13.   [10] *First Conference*, 4th Comm., at 20, ¶ 21 (USSR).

[11] See notes 31–39 and accompanying text.

[12] *First Conference*, 4th Comm., at 23, ¶ 9 (ROK).

[13] See Report of the International Law Commission to the General Assembly, UN GAOR at 297, UN Doc. A/3159 (1956), reprinted in *ILC Yearbook*, (1956), vol. II.

[14] *First Conference*, 4th Comm., at 59, ¶ 13 (Indonesia).

the 1958 Convention in recognizing the sovereign rights of the coastal State over the continental shelf.[15]

Attribution of Rights over the Exclusive Economic Zone

With the creation of the legal regime of the EEZ in UNCLOS, States agreed that an even larger maritime area should be subjected to coastal State control. Rather than limiting coastal States' rights to the seabed and subsoil, rights were conferred over the superjacent waters as well. As with the development of the legal regime for the continental shelf, States, particularly the industrialized nations, were very wary of permitting too many restrictions over maritime spaces due to the potential effect on international navigation and other high seas freedoms. To cater for States that remained committed to the freedom of navigation, the rights of coastal States in the EEZ were carefully constructed. Despite some efforts to the contrary, sovereignty was not attributed to the coastal State. Instead, a system of "sovereign rights" and "jurisdiction" was preferred. The coastal State has sovereign rights "for the purpose of exploring and exploiting, conserving and managing the natural resources, whether living or non-living, of the waters superjacent to the sea-bed and of the sea-bed and its subsoil."[16] Rights in the EEZ thus encompass all natural resources in and on the seabed and the superjacent waters. In addition, a coastal State has sovereign rights "with regard to other activities for the economic exploitation and exploration of the zone."[17] Jurisdiction is then accorded to the coastal State with regard to the establishment and use of artificial islands, installations and structures, marine scientific research, and the protection and preservation of the marine environment.[18]

Through the specification of a range of activities over which the coastal State has sovereign rights or jurisdiction, the EEZ is a type of "multifunctional" zone in which the coastal State has an "unprecedented

---

[15] UNCLOS also changed the legal definition of the continental shelf. In the Continental Shelf Convention, the continental shelf was defined by a depth criterion (down to 200 meters) and an exploitability criterion (allowing sovereign rights over the continental shelf to extend as far as technology would permit). See Continental Shelf Convention, art. 1. UNCLOS instead allows for a continental shelf of 200 miles regardless of technological capabilities and geological formations. Only in cases of the geological construct of the continental shelf extending beyond 200 miles may a legal continental shelf of up to 350 miles be recognized. Article 76 of the Convention sets out a complex formula to determine a coastal State's entitlement to this breadth of continental shelf.

[16] UNCLOS, art. 56(1)(a).   [17] Ibid., art. 56(1)(a).   [18] Ibid., art. 56(1)(b).

cumulation of resource-related powers."[19] States negotiating UNCLOS differed on the question as to whether the EEZ is still the high seas with an overlay of coastal State rights in this area or whether it is a *sui generis* zone. In favor of the EEZ being *sui generis*, it has been argued that both State practice and the work of the Third Conference in drafting UNCLOS reveal, "the aggregate of rights and duties" of the coastal State "constitutes a more complete, integral regime than a mere projection of competences."[20] Furthermore, the rights and duties that other States have in the zone are not viewed as a continuity of the high seas regime, but represent a different approach integrated within the EEZ regime.[21] The regime of the EEZ is "sufficiently complete and integrated as to justify its own juridical individuality."[22] The contrasting view is that although greater regulation of the freedoms of the high seas has been introduced in the Convention, the EEZ remains an "overlay" on the high seas since it does not eliminate the traditional role of the flag State.[23] Instead, "different states will have jurisdiction over different activities in the same area; not infrequently, there will be concurrent jurisdiction, usually for different purposes."[24] Full freedoms could thus be considered as preserved to some extent rather than setting up a regime of passage through a discrete maritime zone. Richardson argues that the freedoms of the high seas within the 200-mile zone are qualitatively and quantitatively the same as the high seas freedoms outside the zone.[25] National legislation has typically recognized the continued exercise of

[19] Barbara Kwiatkowska, *The 200 Mile Exclusive Economic Zone in the New Law of the Sea* (1989), p. 4.

[20] Francisco Orrego Vicuña, *The Exclusive Economic Zone: Regime and Legal Nature under International Law* (1989), p. 41.

[21] *Ibid.*   [22] *Ibid.*, at 42.

[23] Bernard H. Oxman, "The Third United Nations Conference on the Law of the Sea: The 1976 New York Session," 71 *Am. J. Int'l L.* 247, 263 (1977).

[24] *Ibid.*, at 259–60. See also John R. Stevenson and Bernard H. Oxman, "The Third United Nations Conference on the Law of the Sea: The 1975 Geneva Session," 69 *Am. J. Int'l L.* 763, 775 (1975); Bernard H. Oxman, "The Third United Nation's Conference on the Law of the Sea: The 1977 New York Session," 72 *Am. J. Int'l L.* 57, 74 (1978). ("Whether the high seas regime is in effect the applicable regime when one crosses into an economic zone depends on what one is doing.") Attard also notes: "The applicable legal regime is no longer dependent on the geographic area in question; rather, it is the activity in question that will determine the operative regime." David Joseph Attard, *The Exclusive Economic Zone in International Law* (1987), p. 66.

[25] Elliot L. Richardson, "Power, Mobility and the Law of the Sea," 58 *For. Aff.* 902, 907 (1979–80) ("they must be qualitatively the same in the sense that the nature and extent of the right is the same as the traditional high-seas freedoms; they must be quantitatively the same in the sense that the included uses of the sea must embrace a range no less complete – and allow for future uses no less inclusive – than traditional

the freedom of navigation and other internationally lawful uses of the
sea related to navigation and communication, but often qualifies this
recognition by rendering it subject to the rights of the coastal State
in the EEZ.[26] Ultimately, the terms of the Convention itself allow arguments to be made in favor of the EEZ being either high seas or *sui
generis*.[27]

The characterization of the EEZ is an important issue to the extent
that it impacts on the interpretation and application of States' powers
in this large body of water. It further has bearing on the question as
to what residual rights exist in this maritime area. Residual rights refer
to the rights in the EEZ that are not specifically assigned to the coastal
State or to other States under the Convention. Depending on whether
the zone is high seas or a *sui generis* functional zone, the right to control certain activities within the EEZ may rest with coastal States or
with flag States. Such ambiguity is bound to lead to disputes between
users. For example, in the *M/V "Saiga,"* in support of its control over
bunkering activities, Guinea raised the argument that the *sui generis*
nature of the EEZ meant that it could not be assumed that rights not
expressly attributed to coastal States were automatically part of the freedoms of the high seas.[28] "Accordingly, while recognizing the utility of

high-seas freedoms"). See also Kwiatkowska, *Exclusive Economic Zone*, p. 5. See also
William T. Burke, "National Legislation on Ocean Authority Zones and the
Contemporary Law of the Sea," 9 *Ocean Dev. & Int'l L.* 289, 302–03 (1981) (agreeing that
the coastal State has no greater rights over high seas freedoms in the EEZ than it does
in the high seas except as specifically provided in the Convention).

[26] Burke, "National Legislation," at 299.

[27] Commentators have relied on the text and the drafting history of the Convention to
reach each conclusion. In support of the EEZ being *sui generis*, Orrego Vicuña has
stated that this thesis is "the one that in reality best coincides with the sense of
equilibrium reflected in the provisions of the Convention and in its drafting history."
Orrego Vicuña, *Exclusive Economic Zone Regime*, p. 44. See also Jorge Castañeda,
"Negotiations on the Exclusive Economic Zone at the Third United Nations Conference
on the Law of the Sea," in *Essays in International Law in Honour of Judge Manfred Lachs*
(Jerzy Makarczyk ed., 1984), pp. 605, 613 (arguing that the *sui generis* thesis "finally
prospered and was incorporated in the draft convention"). Oxman's account of the
negotiations is that the text represented an attempt to accommodate the two sets of
views. See Oxman, "1977 New York Session," at 67. Oxman further argues: "The
implication that high seas freedoms and high seas law are not preserved in the
economic zone is contradicted by a close reading of the text, and even more
importantly, by the basic assumptions surrounding the negotiation of the economic
zone." Oxman, "1976 Session," at 265. See also Stevenson and Oxman, "Preparations,"
at 15. ("One underlying assumption of all these proposals seems to have been that the
nonresource uses referred to in the High Seas Convention will be protected beyond a
12-mile territorial sea.")

[28] M/V "Saiga" (No. 2), Merits, para. 125.

the general principle of accommodating freedom of navigation with protection of coastal interests, there is still reason to be wary of allocating exclusive decision making to the coastal state to choose how and where this accommodation is to be made."[29] The extent of the coastal State's power to determine how it may regulate or interfere with the freedoms of navigation, overflight, and the laying of submarine cables and pipelines depends on not only the types of rights attributed to States but also the substantive and procedural protections afforded these freedoms.

Regulation of the Freedoms of Navigation, Overflight, and the Laying of Submarine Cables and Pipelines in Extended Maritime Zones

UNCLOS creates a detailed regime for the regulation of coastal State and flag State rights in the areas designated as part of the continental shelf or the EEZ. "One basic characteristic of the economic zone is that it does not entail an unfettered discretion for any state."[30] This regime consists of substantive rules specifically protecting some of the traditional freedoms of the high seas in these zones, general obligations of due regard, and substantive and procedural rules for the resolution of disputes. Each of these elements is essential for the overall balance between the economic interests of coastal States and the interests of third States in preserving the freedoms of navigation, overflight, and the laying of submarine cables and pipelines.

The main substantive protections afforded to third States in continental shelf areas were settled during the First Conference and then affirmed through their inclusion in UNCLOS with only minor modification. The EEZ, as a creature of UNCLOS, included provisions in that Convention to address the impact of the conferral of sovereign rights and jurisdiction over the living resources on the high seas freedoms. These principles are described immediately below.

Substantive Provisions for the Protection of the Freedoms of Navigation, Overflight, and the Laying of Submarine Cables and Pipelines on the Continental Shelf

One of the most basic stipulations in the Continental Shelf Convention is that the rights of the coastal State over the continental shelf do not affect the legal status of the superjacent waters as high seas nor the

---

[29] Burke, "National Legislation," at 307.   [30] Oxman, "1976 Session," at 260.

air space above the waters.[31] This designation was slightly modified in
UNCLOS to allow for the establishment of the EEZ so that the rights
over the continental shelf do not affect the status of the superjacent
waters without specifying the actual status of those waters.[32] UNCLOS
again protects the status of the air above in order to preserve the freedom of overflight. A further paragraph stipulates that the exploration
and exploitation of the continental shelf is not to interfere unjustifiably with navigation and other rights and freedoms of other States as
provided in the Convention.[33] The International Law Commission had
deliberately chosen the reference to "unjustifiable" interference when
drafting articles on the continental shelf prior to the First Conference:

The progressive development of international law, which takes place against
the background of established rules, must often result in the modification
of those rules by reference to new interests or needs. The extent of that modification must be determined by the relative importance of the needs and interests
involved. To lay down, therefore, that the exploration and exploitation of the
continental shelf must never result in any interference whatsoever with navigation and fishing might result in many cases in rendering somewhat nominal
both the sovereign rights of exploration and exploitation and the very purpose
of the articles as adopted. The case is clearly one of assessment of the relative importance of the interests involved. Interference, even if substantial, with
navigation and fishing might, in some cases, be justified. On the other hand,
interference even on an insignificant scale would be unjustified if unrelated to
reasonably conceived requirements of exploration and exploitation of the continental shelf.[34]

In this regard, the freedoms of the high seas are both protected from and
limited by the rights of coastal States to explore and exploit the continental shelf. The Commission clearly envisaged that a balance would have to
be struck between the competing interests depending on the importance
of the respective activities. The suggestion is that the coastal State may
determine what actions may be taken in restricting navigation for the

---

[31] Continental Shelf Convention, art. 3. The ILC text protecting the legal status of the
waters superjacent to the continental shelf was adopted in the Fourth Committee by
fifty-four votes to none, with eight abstentions. *First Conference*, 4th Comm., at 78.

[32] UNCLOS, art. 78(1).

[33] *Ibid.*, art. 78(2). The Continental Shelf Convention had prohibited unjustifiable
interference with "fishing or the conservation of the living resources of the sea" as
well as "fundamental oceanographic or other scientific research" but again this
provision was modified to account for the creation of the EEZ.

[34] Report of the International Law Commission to the General Assembly, UN GAOR at 299,
UN Doc. A/3159 (1956), reprinted in *ILC Yearbook*, (1956), vol. II.

purposes of hydrocarbon exploration and exploitation and if the third State considers that its rights of navigation are being interfered with unjustifiably, then there could be recourse to third-party settlement. The United States commented during the debate in the Fourth Committee at the First Conference that even though the word "unjustifiable" was vague, it gave the article a proper balance between the interests of navigation and exploitation.[35] This term was ultimately retained in the Continental Shelf Convention as well as in UNCLOS.[36]

The freedom of States to lay submarine cables and pipelines was similarly restricted. Article 79, paragraph 1 of UNCLOS affirms the entitlement of States to lay submarine cables and pipelines on the continental shelf. This entitlement is then subject to the other provisions of Article 79. In particular, the right of States to lay submarine cables and pipelines on the continental shelf has been curtailed to allow for "reasonable measures for the exploration of the continental shelf, the exploitation of its natural resources and the prevention, reduction and control of pollution from pipelines."[37] UNCLOS grants further control to the coastal State by providing that the delineation of the course of the pipelines or cables is subject to the consent of the coastal State.[38] Express protection is further granted to the coastal State with respect to its entitlement to establish conditions for cables or pipelines entering its territorial sea and for its jurisdiction over cables and pipelines constructed or used for hydrocarbon extraction.[39] The rights of the coastal State are thus cast in terms of derogation from the overarching high seas freedoms and indicate a preference in favor of the latter.

Substantive Provisions for the Protection of the Freedoms of Navigation, Overflight, and the Laying of Submarine Cables and Pipelines in the EEZ

The EEZ presented a new challenge in determining the balance between coastal States and third States since the creation of this maritime zone presented another threat to developed States with large merchant and naval fleets wanting to guarantee their rights of navigation.[40] This protection is primarily afforded in Article 58 of UNCLOS, which addresses

---

[35] *First Conference*, 4th Comm., at 88, ¶ 12 (United States).
[36] Continental Shelf Convention, arts. 4 and 5; UNCLOS, arts. 78 and 79.
[37] UNCLOS, art. 79. See also Continental Shelf Convention, art. 4.
[38] UNCLOS, art. 79(3).   [39] *Ibid.*, art. 79(4).
[40] The size of the EEZ means that navigation is inevitably affected: "Use of this region for navigation is simply indispensable to the normal conduct of world shipping." Burke, "National Legislation," at 301.

the rights and duties of other States in the EEZ. Richardson, the United States Ambassador to the Third Conference, described the negotiations of Article 58 as "particularly difficult":

Article 58 was the subject of particularly difficult negotiations in the informal group. Every word and comma was exposed to extensive debate. It was understood from the outset that the willingness of the maritime States to back off their insistence on explicit high-seas status for the exclusive economic zone must be compensated for by coastal State recognition that the high-seas freedoms exercisable in the zone are qualitatively and quantitatively the same as the traditional high-seas freedoms recognized by international law.[41]

Article 58, paragraph 1 thus reads:

In the exclusive economic zone, all States, whether coastal or land-locked, enjoy, subject to the relevant provisions of this Convention, the freedoms referred to in Article 87 of navigation and overflight and of the laying of submarine cables and pipelines, and other internationally lawful uses of the sea related to these freedoms, such as those associated with the operation of ships, aircraft and submarine cables and pipelines, and compatible with the other provisions of this Convention.

A broad category of high seas freedoms is thus anticipated as coexisting with the rights of the coastal State in the EEZ, particularly through the reference to "other internationally lawful uses of the sea related to these freedoms." It is the extent of the modification that provides the potential source of conflict with respect to the freedoms being exercised. In accordance with Article 87, the freedom of laying submarine cables and pipelines is made subject to the articles on the continental shelf. No restriction is placed on the freedom of overflight through Article 87. The greatest threat is to the freedom of navigation in light of the rights accorded to the coastal State for the conservation and utilization of the living resources of the zone. As the coastal State is authorized to detain foreign vessels and their crews in the enforcement of its laws and regulations relating to living resources in the EEZ and relating to the protection and preservation of the environment,[42] the potential for interference in the freedom of navigation is considerable.[43] Burke considers that some effect on the freedom of navigation is inevitable in order to promote the optimal utilization of the living resources: "Where the

[41] Elliot L. Richardson, "Law of the Sea: Navigation and Other Traditional National Security Considerations," 19 *San Diego L. Rev.* 553, 572–73 (1982).
[42] UNCLOS, arts. 73, 220(6), and 226(1)(c) respectively.
[43] Rosenne, "Establishing ITLOS," at 813.

fisheries are vital to national well being because of this dependency, and enforcement is difficult yet critical to effective realization of financial benefit, it is appropriate to allow slight modification of total freedom of movement in order to facilitate effective management."[44]

Other high seas freedoms are incorporated into the EEZ provided that they are not incompatible with the EEZ regime in Part V of the Convention.[45] This cross-reference was intended to accommodate the conflicting positions of adherents to a *sui generis* or high seas regime of the EEZ.[46] In particular, the rights and duties located in Articles 88 to 115 are deemed to apply to the EEZ provided they are not incompatible with Part V. Articles 88 to 115, which are located in Part VII of the Convention dealing with the high seas, address not only navigation and the laying of submarine cables but also include the nationality and status of ships,[47] piracy,[48] slavery,[49] drug trafficking,[50] and unauthorized broadcasting.[51]

In addition to those rights and duties incorporated through reference to Part V of the Convention, a range of activities not specifically referred to in the Convention may constitute "other internationally lawful uses" enjoyed by all States in the EEZ. In the *M/V "Saiga" (No. 2)* decision on the merits, ITLOS was faced with the question as to whether bunkering fishing vessels fell within the freedom of navigation or other internationally lawful uses of the sea pursuant to Article 58, paragraph 1 or whether it was an activity inherent in the sovereign rights attributed to the coastal State under Article 56. Guinea argued that the supply of gas oil to fishing vessels was not part of the freedom of navigation, nor an internationally lawful use of the sea related to the freedom of navigation, but was to be considered as a commercial activity.[52] Saint Vincent and the Grenadines maintained that Guinea was not entitled to extend its customs laws to the EEZ and that the Guinean action had interfered with the right to the freedom of navigation as the supply of fuel oil fell within "other internationally lawful uses of the sea related to" the freedom of navigation. The Tribunal determined that the application of customs laws to parts of the EEZ was contrary to UNCLOS.[53] On this basis, the majority did not need to make any findings on the status of bunkering in the

---

[44] William T. Burke, "Exclusive Fisheries Zones and Freedom of Navigation," 20 *San Diego L. Rev.* 595, 600 (1983).

[45] UNCLOS, art. 58(2).   [46] See Kwiatkowska, *Exclusive Economic Zone*, p. 200.

[47] UNCLOS, arts. 91 (nationality of ships), 92 (ships to sail under one flag), 93 (ships employed in the official services of the UN), 95 (immunity of warships), and 96 (immunity of ships used only on government non-commercial service).

[48] *Ibid.*, arts. 100–07.   [49] *Ibid.*, art. 99.   [50] *Ibid.*, art. 108.   [51] *Ibid.*, art. 109.

[52] M/V "Saiga" (No. 2), Merits, para. 128.   [53] *Ibid.*, para. 136.

merits stage of the case. The decision is nonetheless indicative of the controversies that can arise in determining the regulation of conduct not specifically addressed in the Convention.

The freedoms of navigation, overflight, and the laying of submarine cables and pipelines have now been circumscribed to varying extents to allow for the exercise of the coastal State's exclusive rights in both the EEZ and the continental shelf. These provisions were carefully crafted to cater to the competing interests at stake in these maritime zones. Coastal States ensured recognition of their rights over the natural resources of the EEZ and continental shelf in the Convention and thereby successfully protected their economic interests. States interested in maintaining the traditional freedoms of the high seas managed to restrain coastal State ambitions to guarantee the continuing existence of inclusive interests within the substantive rules allocating the extended maritime zones. Even with these substantive principles in place, without an external process of review the balance of interests formulated in the Convention clearly risks being undone.

Dispute Settlement and the Freedoms of Navigation, Overflight, and the Laying of Submarine Cables and Pipelines on the Continental Shelf and in the EEZ

The formulation of the substantive rules allocating rights and responsibilities to different users only forms part of the overall regime for the freedoms of navigation, overflight, and the laying of pipelines and cables. Compromises on the rights to be attributed and those to be protected were conditioned on the inclusion of compulsory dispute settlement to minimize the impact of surrendered interests in the extended maritime zones. Part XV of UNCLOS specifically addresses what disputes relating to the exercise of these high seas freedoms in the extended maritime zones may be subject to compulsory procedures entailing binding decisions. A mandatory dispute settlement mechanism was perceived as the most effective method of preserving the delicate balance of interests achieved during negotiations. States not only wanted to establish certain standards to be applied in the event of conflicts over rights, but also provide for a specific procedure for dispute settlement.

Applicable Standards Pertaining to Dispute Settlement

In determining the appropriate balance between the freedoms of navigation, overflight, and the laying of submarine cables and pipelines and the rights of coastal States in the extended maritime zones, it was anticipated that conflicts between the respective rights set forth in the Convention would arise. The question of whether a presumption exists in favor of the coastal State or in favor of a third State depends on the use under consideration. No order of priorities between coastal States' rights and third States' rights in the EEZ were established in the Convention.[54] As a result, States negotiating UNCLOS recognized that some sort of resolution of concurrent uses and rights of the area would have to be made.[55] The Convention does set out a broad obligation requiring due regard of users to the coastal State's rights and duties, and for the coastal State to have due regard to other users in the exercise of its rights and duties.[56] As these duties of due regard are mutually applicable, the potential for them to regulate a dispute between users is slight. It is only when due regard obligations can be subjected to third-party procedures that the possibility exists for these duties to have a meaningful application that would take into account the differing circumstances.[57] An international court or tribunal could examine the nature of the interests at stake in assessing how and what content should be ascribed to mutual obligations of due regard.

A further conflict could arise between coastal States and other users in respect of certain activities (possibly relating to navigation or other economic uses) that have not been specifically addressed in the Convention. These unattributed rights could "refer to future activities, such as uses of the sea not yet discovered or certain military uses not contemplated in the . . . Convention, but traditionally practiced without any restriction by military powers in the high seas."[58] An anticipated response to this problem is found in Article 59, which refers to the circumstances to be taken into account for the resolution of disputes between coastal States and third States.[59] Article 59 reads:

In cases where this Convention does not attribute rights or jurisdiction to the coastal State or to other States within the exclusive economic zone, and a conflict arises between the interests of the coastal State and any other State or States, the conflict should be resolved on the basis of equity and in the light of all the

---

[54] Attard, pp. 64, 66.   [55] Castañeda, p. 615.

[56] UNCLOS, arts. 56(2) and 58(3). See Kwiatkowska, *Exclusive Economic Zone*, pp. 6, 214–15 (commenting that the careful balance between the exclusive and inclusive uses of the sea within the EEZ is governed by an overarching general duty of States to pay mutual, due regard to their respective rights and obligations) and Oxman, "1976 Session," at 260–61. ("It can be anticipated that these balanced duties will provide the juridical basis for resolving many practical problems of competing uses.")

[57] Oxman, "1976 Session," at 261.   [58] Castañeda, p. 620.

[59] See Orrego Vicuña, *Exclusive Economic Zone Regime*, p. 35.

relevant circumstances, taking into account the respective importance of the interests involved to the parties as well as the international community as a whole.

From Article 59, it is clear that "in the case of unattributed rights, there is no presumption in favour of either the coastal State or other States: each case, as it arises, will have to be decided on its own merits on the basis of the criteria set out in article 59."[60] While neutrality is achieved through the fact that no presumption exists in favor of any particular State, Article 59 provides an overly broad spectrum of factors. The lack of specificity as to what considerations might prevail, or might be more important than others, means that Article 59 effectively lacks any normative content without its concrete application through third-party processes. A similar observation is true of the articles requiring due regard between States. It is only when these provisions are applied in the context of mandatory Part XV procedures that their intended purpose can be attained.

Dispute Settlement under Part XV of the Convention

The dispute settlement system in Part XV of the Convention has been described as designed to protect the freedoms of the high seas.[61] Compulsory jurisdiction was a form of control in this respect because it had the potential to protect the interests of third States in light of the considerable discretion granted to coastal States. For this very reason, coastal States resisted compulsory dispute settlement. These States "insisted that the hard-won exclusive jurisdiction of the coastal state in the economic zone should not be jeopardized by its submission to third-party adjudication."[62] Concerns were expressed that compulsory dispute settlement would internationalize the EEZ by opening up the possibility of disputing the decisions of the coastal States.[63] However, it was precisely for

---

[60] R. R. Churchill and A. V. Lowe, *The Law of the Sea* (1983), p. 136.

[61] Sohn, "Settlement of Law of the Sea Disputes," at 205. Rosenne writes: "The essential safeguard for the freedoms of navigation, overflight and the laying of submarine cables and pipelines is supplied by the intricate provisions for the prevention and settlement of disputes contained in Part XV of the Convention." Rosenne, "Establishing ITLOS," at 812. See also Boyle, "Dispute Settlement," at 42 (noting that compulsory dispute settlement was intended to reinforce the balance established by Parts V and XII of the Convention in favor of the freedom of navigation).

[62] 5 *United Nations Convention on the Law of the Sea 1982: A Commentary*, p. 93 and n.7. Those States opposed to compulsory dispute settlement were Iceland, Kenya, Brazil, Mauritius, Venezuela, Pakistan, and the Democratic People's Republic of Korea. *Ibid.*

[63] *Ibid.*, at 93.

these reasons that a mandatory mechanism was required. It would provide maritime States with further protection of their navigation rights in creating an avenue for challenging excessive acts of jurisdiction over maritime space that impinge on high seas freedoms.[64]

The use of compulsory dispute settlement to regulate the coastal State's exercise of sovereign rights or jurisdiction underpinned the balance of interests achieved. A clear distinction is drawn between disputes concerning, on the one hand, the coastal State's infringement of freedoms and rights and, on the other hand, infringement by other States with interests in high seas freedoms. Article 297(1) thus reads, in part:

Disputes concerning the interpretation or application of this Convention with regard to the exercise by a coastal State of its sovereign rights or jurisdiction provided for in this Convention shall be subject to the procedures provided for in section 2 in the following cases:

a) when it is alleged that a coastal State has acted in contravention of the provisions of this Convention in regard to the freedoms and rights of navigation, overflight or the laying of submarine cables and pipelines, or in regard to other internationally lawful uses of the sea specified in article 58;

b) when it is alleged that a State in exercising the aforementioned freedoms, rights or uses has acted in contravention of this Convention or of laws or regulations adopted by the coastal State in conformity with this Convention and other rules of international law not incompatible with this Convention.[65]

The freedoms and rights specifically subject to compulsory dispute settlement are those relating to navigation, overflight, the laying of submarine cables and pipelines, and "other internationally lawful uses of the sea specified in article 58" in areas over which the coastal State exercises sovereign rights and jurisdiction. Although included in a section entitled "Limitations and Exceptions to Applicability of Section 2," Article 297(1)(a) reaffirms the applicability of compulsory procedures, rather than limits them. The scope of this provision is sufficiently large that any dispute concerning the exercise of high seas freedoms in the extended maritime zones (not related to the living resources there) will be subject to mandatory jurisdiction.

It has been argued that Article 297(1) does not purport to limit compulsory dispute settlement in relation to the exercise of high seas freedoms solely to the exercise of those rights in the EEZ but is available for

[64] Richardson, "Power," at 916.   [65] UNCLOS, art. 297(1).

disputes arising in other maritime zones where flag States have those rights.[66] Furthermore, disputes arising in the EEZ or on the continental shelf are not necessarily excluded simply because they do not fall within the express wording of Article 297(1). De Mestral explains why this is the case:

> The justification for [Article 297] was the guarantee of the integrity of rights to be exercised in the Exclusive Economic Zone . . . But a close reading of the text leads to the conclusion that it is likely to be something of a paper tiger and is unlikely to restrict the generality of Section II of Part XV . . . [O]ne cannot read [Article 297, paragraph 1] as implying a broad exclusion of the application of compulsory dispute settlement to disputes arising in the Zone *per se* . . . [T]he fundamental objective is to protect the integrity of certain rights and jurisdictions exercised by coastal states in the Exclusive Economic Zone and, in fact, this article faithfully reflects the nature of these rights.[67]

Article 297(1) essentially reflects the balance of the Convention through the reference to coastal State rights as well as the rights of other users.

The formulation of Article 297(1) is intended to provide safeguards against an abuse of power by a coastal State and at the same time to avoid an abuse of legal process by other States.[68] When the dispute settlement provisions were being drafted, it was proposed that the concept of abuse of right should be included as a means of conditioning the exceptions designed to benefit the coastal State.[69] It was ultimately included in Article 300 as a general provision to apply to the Convention as a whole. "In this way, the abuse of right is no longer a tool to weaken the exceptions indicated or the coastal State's discretionary power, but a more ample concept that seeks to avoid distortions in the exercise of the rights recognized by the Convention."[70] Moreover, Article 294 permits a court or tribunal to determine at the request of a party or *proprio motu*

---

[66] W. Riphagen, "Dispute Settlement in the 1982 United Nations Convention on the Law of the Sea," in *The New Law of the Sea* (C. L. Rozakis and C. A. Stephanou eds., 1983), pp. 281, 288 ("The Exclusive Economic Zone is, of course, not the only area in which the coastal State *and* the flag States have rights, and it would seem beyond doubt that flag State rights in those other areas and the corresponding obligations of the coastal State (such as the right of innocent passage) can also be 'implemented' through recourse to compulsory dispute settlement by a court or tribunal." [Emphasis in original]).

[67] De Mestral, at 183. But see Orrego Vicuña, *Exclusive Economic Zone Regime*, p. 126 (arguing that this interpretation is "exaggerated, since it would mean that the sovereignty and jurisdiction of the coastal State could be subject to continuous judicial confrontation, which certainly is not the scope of the provision").

[68] 5 *United Nations Convention on the Law of the Sea 1982: A Commentary*, p. 98.

[69] See Orrego Vicuña, *Exclusive Economic Zone Regime*, p. 132.   [70] *Ibid.*

whether a claim under Article 297 is an abuse of process or whether *prima facie* it is well-founded. This question is to be resolved in preliminary proceedings, and does not exclude other objections to the admissibility of the dispute or the jurisdiction of the court or tribunal. This explicit condition for the resolution of a dispute under Section 2 of Part XV provides a modicum of protection to coastal States. Coastal States lacking the military or diplomatic power to prevent abuses of high seas freedoms in their EEZ may gain greater political influence through an established third-party process to reaffirm and uphold their economic rights in the extended maritime zones.

What is important here is the need for these mandatory procedures. States clearly perceived that external review, or the threat thereof, was essential to protect these interests in high seas freedoms. The stakes in the inclusive, non-resource uses of these ocean spaces were too great to entrust the continued preservation of the relevant high seas freedoms to traditional forms of dispute settlement. While some States could rely on military or political power to enforce rights of navigation, the costs (economic and diplomatic) have become overly burdensome to rely solely on such exertions of authority to maintain high seas rights. States insisting on compulsory dispute settlement clearly signaled that despite the new emphasis on coastal State control in large areas of the oceans, certain elements of the traditional law of the sea should be upheld. The new development in UNCLOS is that these traditional rights are now undergirded and complemented through mandatory third-party proceedings.

It must finally be noted that further protection of the freedom of navigation is accorded through the prompt release proceedings for detained vessels under Article 292. As discussed in Chapter 2, Article 292 was included as part of the overall regime to protect the rights of navigation in the face of increasing coastal State jurisdiction.[71] Indeed, in the *Monte Confurco* decision, the Tribunal expressly noted that the prompt release requirement upon the payment of a reasonable bond or other financial security protected the interest of the flag State as a balance to the interests of the coastal State to enforce its laws and regulations.[72] This balance is reinforced in Article 292 with respect to the need to release the arrested vessels and crews versus the need to ensure the appearance in court of the Master as well as the payment of the penalties.[73]

[71] See further pp. 108–112.
[72] Monte Confurco, para. 70. See also *ibid.*, Dissenting Opinion of Judge Jesus (supporting the observation of the balance in the Convention).
[73] *Ibid.*, para. 71.

These proceedings do not involve any decisions on the merits of the dispute between the vessel and the coastal State authorities. Nonetheless, the potential clearly exists for Article 292 proceedings to impact on the decision-making processes of national courts and legislatures in assessing what bond or other financial security is reasonable in the application of domestic laws that impact on the freedom of navigation. The decisions of ITLOS in this regard will influence the exercise of coastal States' rights in the EEZ.

Conclusion

The development of the law of the sea in recognizing exclusive rights to extended maritime zones has been a laborious and difficult process. The open waters policy was so entrenched in the international system – and was so favorable to the interests of the most powerful States – that there was initially little support to replace entirely the *mare liberum* system with a brand new regime. Coastal States that were predominantly interested in the financial benefits to be derived from ocean resources envisaged a *sui generis* construct with the institution of the EEZ. However, the long-held and ongoing interests in promoting the freedom of navigation (as well as the freedoms of overflight and the laying of submarine cables and pipelines to a lesser extent) meant that a modification, or some sort of balance, was the only viable option. Regardless of whether the EEZ is regarded as a *sui generis* zone or as a modified high seas area, States with significant merchant and naval fleets had a particular interest in incorporating an effective dispute settlement mechanism as a necessary guarantee for the continuing rights of navigation, overflight, the laying of submarine cables and pipelines, and related uses. The acceptability of dispute settlement provisions in this regard is understandable since western States, which had a vested interest in protecting these freedoms, have been traditionally more receptive to formalized dispute settlement resolution. Developing States were also willing to accept dispute settlement procedures in this instance because it provided an avenue for disputes to be resolved that could reduce industrialized States' exertions of military or economic pressure. A clear role has been ascribed to international processes in regulating the freedoms of navigation, overflight, and the laying of submarine cables and pipelines in zones where coastal States exercise sovereign rights. There is an expectation that international decision-making, including dispute settlement, will be required to uphold these freedoms in accordance with the nature of the extended maritime zones and within the limits subscribed in the substantive provisions of the Convention.

Protection and Preservation of the Marine Environment

The establishment of norms and guidelines for the global protection and preservation of the marine environment was a product of the UNCLOS negotiating process.[74] Throughout the 1970s, global attention became focused on the implications of environmental degradation. A particular impetus was the adoption of the Stockholm Declaration and the Action Plan for the Human Environment whereby actions were initiated to deal with environmental problems in a legal framework and to develop a comprehensive, global, and future-oriented approach to solving these problems.[75] UNCLOS followed this initiative by setting out a regime for environmental protection and preservation that applies throughout the marine environment and covers all sources of pollution. Part XII of UNCLOS consists of articles dealing with general provisions,[76] global and regional cooperation,[77] technical assistance,[78] monitoring and environmental assessment,[79] international rules, and national legislation to prevent, reduce, and control pollution of the marine environment from various sources,[80] and enforcement of those provisions (including safeguards).[81] The provisions on the protection and preservation of the marine environment have been described as "the most complex regime" regulating the coastal State's rights in the EEZ.[82] The range of environmental issues covered in UNCLOS led Charney to proclaim, "the Convention probably contains the most comprehensive and progressive international environmental law of any modern international agreement."[83]

While complex in its shifting emphasis between States' interests, Part XII retains several features that are hallmarks of the Convention overall. First, Part XII reflects the tension between the protection of coastal State interests and the protection of the freedom of navigation that is prevalent throughout the Convention. A second characteristic of the Convention found in Part XII is the inclusion of a series of obligations

---

[74] This regime can be contrasted to the 1958 Conventions, which were too general and fragmentary to constitute a global framework. See High Seas Convention, arts. 24 and 25, and Continental Shelf Convention, art. 5(7). Moreover, these conventions did not provide for effective implementation measures but left States with a large amount of discretion and thus freedom to pollute. Kwiatkowska, *Exclusive Economic Zone*, p. 160.

[75] Kwiatkowska, *Exclusive Economic Zone*, p. 161.   [76] UNCLOS, arts. 192–96.

[77] *Ibid.*, arts. 197–201.   [78] *Ibid.*, arts. 202 and 203.

[79] *Ibid.*, arts. 204–06.   [80] *Ibid.*, arts. 207–12.

[81] *Ibid.*, arts. 213–35. Section XII also contains provisions on ice-covered areas and sovereign immunity. *Ibid.*, arts. 234 and 236 respectively.

[82] Orrego Vicuña, *Exclusive Economic Zone Regime*, p. 84.

[83] Jonathan I. Charney, "The Marine Environment and the 1982 United Nations Convention on the Law of the Sea," 28 *Int'l Law.* 879, 882 (1994).

ranging in determinacy – from soft law to duties of cooperation to rules with more definite normative content. Further, the recognition of the special interests of developing States is reaffirmed through flexible standards concomitant with State resources as well as specific assistance in defined areas. Finally, in crafting this system, certain reliance was placed on the prospect of diplomatic conferences that could later elaborate on the general obligations included in UNCLOS.[84]

States at the Third Conference recognized that there was a mutual interest in developing standards to protect the marine environment. The Convention basically reflects "a fundamental shift from power to duty as the central controlling principle of the legal regime for the protection of the marine environment."[85] The norms and principles required in this regard are not only incorporated into the Convention itself but are to be supplemented through separate international processes to be held subsequent to the adoption of the Convention. Through such an approach, Adede has argued that more effort was directed toward "developing techniques for *dispute avoidance* as opposed to focusing upon the formulation of procedures for *dispute settlement*."[86] Multilateral cooperative regimes in international environmental law have come to rely on different types of international institutions to provide mechanisms for exchange of information, monitoring, and reputation building to ensure compliance with the accepted norms.

UNCLOS does not follow the same type of cooperative, institutional approach but instead requires mandatory third-party review. Clearly, the regulatory and compliance regimes formulated in other areas of international environmental law were not perceived as workable, or perhaps adequate, for the protection and preservation of the marine environment within the context of UNCLOS. The difference with UNCLOS is that the articles on the protection and preservation of the marine environment have to be considered in the broader law of the sea context. The entrenched *mare liberum* system was the context for a range of trade-offs in creating the EEZ and garnering international recognition of different rights and duties with respect to a wide range of marine activities. The right of coastal States to exercise jurisdiction in respect of the marine environment in the extended maritime zones thus coexists

---

[84] *Ibid.*, at 884.

[85] Alan. E. Boyle, "Marine Pollution under the Law of the Sea Convention," 79 *Am. J. Int'l L.* 347, 350 (1985).

[86] A. O. Adede, "Environmental Disputes under the Law of the Sea Convention," 7 *Envtl. Pol'y & L.* 63, 64 (1981) (emphasis in original).

with the continuing right of third States to exercise their rights of navigation through these areas. Interlocking compromises in the Convention required external third-party review to maintain the guarantees for inclusive interests in the EEZ and on the continental shelf.

Article 297 of UNCLOS refers to limitations on the applicability of the compulsory dispute settlement mechanism for a certain category of disputes related to the protection and preservation of the marine environment with regard to the exercise of a coastal State's sovereign rights or jurisdiction. The language in the chapeau to Article 297(1) indicates that these limitations apply only to the EEZ and the continental shelf, rather than including the territorial sea and high seas areas as well. In maritime spaces where the coastal State has sovereign rights or jurisdiction, disputes may be referred to mandatory and binding procedures:

when it is alleged that a coastal state has acted in contravention of specified international rules and standards for the protection and preservation of the marine environment which are applicable to the coastal state and which have been established by this Convention or through a competent international organization or diplomatic conference in accordance with this Convention.[87]

In other words, the applicability of Section 2 of Part XV to marine environment disputes arising in the EEZ and on the continental shelf depends on a demonstration that certain international standards exist and that these standards can be applied to the coastal State. The relevant standards are established either under UNCLOS or in accordance with UNCLOS through international conferences or competent organizations. Standards under the latter may be rare if Article 297 is read unduly narrowly to require that a conference expressly refer to UNCLOS in some manner, rather than just generally being compatible with the principles set forth in UNCLOS. Given the general standards set forth in the substantive provisions, such a reading would seem unjustified.

UNCLOS provides for a range of general duties related to the protection and preservation of the marine environment as well as dealing specifically with pollution from a variety of sources. Different standards are applicable depending on the source or pollution, whether a State is a coastal State, flag State, or port State and whether the EEZ or some other maritime zone is involved. These standards are reinforced through the authorization to exercise enforcement jurisdiction at the national level. This section considers what "specified international rules and standards" are envisaged for the protection and preservation of the marine

---

[87] UNCLOS, art. 297(1)(c).

environment in the EEZ and on the continental shelf – in terms of general obligations and then specific sources of pollution – as well as the role third-party dispute settlement must play with respect to these standards.

Disputes Related to General Rules and Standards for the Protection and Preservation of the Marine Environment in the EEZ and on the Continental Shelf

The first two articles of Part XII set out the fundamental rights and duties of States for the protection and preservation of the marine environment. A general obligation is imposed on States to protect and preserve the marine environment,[88] which is then balanced by the sovereign rights of States to exploit their natural resources.[89] These articles thus establish an overarching framework for the rights and duties subsequently listed in the Convention. For disputes that arise in relation to the protection and preservation of the marine environment, these articles may apply in the nature of a residual category for activities not specifically envisaged in other provisions of the Convention. Such broad principles may provide considerable scope for the jurisdiction of the courts and tribunals constituted under Part XV. To the extent that these provisions can determine the conduct of States, they represent the key interests at stake and in that regard may provide guidance in defining the applicable international standards to which a coastal State must adhere.

The general obligations in the Convention contemplate regional action, as well as global action, for the protection and preservation of the marine environment.[90] Such an emphasis on regionalism is a common feature of environmental cooperation: "[T]he main trend in international regulation is an increasing emphasis on regionalism as a functional compromise between a necessarily generalized global response and unpredictable and uncertain unilateral responses."[91] The "functional compromise" found in UNCLOS consists of provisions requiring action in the event of environmental damage as well as stipulations of cooperation to formulate rules. Article 197, for example, envisages that States will cooperate either directly or through competent international organizations to formulate and elaborate international rules and standards for the protection and preservation of the marine environment.

---

[88] *Ibid.*, art. 192.   [89] *Ibid.*, art. 193.   [90] See *ibid.*, art. 197.

[91] Moira L. McConnell and Edgar Gold, "The Modern Law of the Sea: Framework for the Protection and Preservation of the Marine Environment?," 23 *Case W. Res. J. Int'l L.* 83, 85 (1991).

Similarly, States are to develop and promote contingency plans to deal with environmental emergencies.[92] Cooperation is further required for the promotion of certain activities – such as studies, scientific research, and exchange of information and data about pollution of the environment as well as programs for the assistance of developing States.[93]

If the Convention's obligations are implemented in a regional treaty with its own dispute settlement clause then, according to the decision in *Southern Bluefin Tuna*, the dispute may not be subject to compulsory resolution under UNCLOS if Article 281 applies, but must be resolved under the regional treaty. Moreover, the use of the alternate forum may be more politically acceptable to disputant States given the ambiguity of the UNCLOS provisions in this regard.

The Convention oscillates between precatory goals and more definite rules of conduct when setting out general obligations relating to marine pollution. The standard expected of States is relatively indeterminate with respect to monitoring the risks or effects of pollution. Article 204 requires States to "endeavor, as far as practicable" to observe, measure, evaluate, and analyze the risks or effects of pollution of the marine environment. More concrete obligations are laid down with respect to notification and environmental assessment. The Convention specifically stipulates that States must immediately notify potentially affected States when aware that the marine environment is in imminent danger of being damaged or has been damaged by pollution.[94] States in the affected area must then cooperate, to the extent possible, in eliminating the effects of the pollution and preventing or minimizing damage.[95] Assessment of potential effects of planned activities in areas under the control or jurisdiction of a State must be undertaken and reported to the competent international organization.[96]

When examining the Convention provisions for the protection and preservation of the marine environment it is readily apparent that little detail as to the substance of the duties imposed on States is provided in the Convention itself. Instead, it is more common for there to be exhortations of cooperation or for reliance on future international conferences.

Therefore, the provisions in Part XII are best viewed as guiding or interpretive principles, rather than standard setting principles. The provisions assume the existence of agreed standards, rules and practices external to the 1982 Convention. Considered as a whole, Part XII can be regarded as a "blueprint"

---

[92] UNCLOS, art. 199.   [93] *Ibid.*, arts. 200 and 202.
[94] UNCLOS, art. 198.   [95] *Ibid.*, art. 199.   [96] *Ibid.*, art. 206.

or "umbrella" for other more locally or situationally responsive legislation and activities.[97]

As such, it is assumed that "specific or local legislation exists to give it substance,"[98] or that the substance may otherwise be derived from different international agreements. Any dispute based on these substantive provisions of the Convention would necessarily have to rely on sources extraneous to the Convention in order to assess whether a treaty violation had occurred. The Convention on its own terms provides insufficient content to many of the provisions requiring cooperation, or other hortatory action. The availability of a third-party process allows for the concretization of applicable standards. The dispute settlement procedures thus provide an avenue to elaborate on the content of these provisions in specific cases.

In the pleadings for the jurisdiction and merits phase of *MOX Plant*, Ireland argued that the Tribunal should consider provisions of some "non-UNCLOS" instruments as an aid to the interpretation of UNCLOS articles.[99] The reason for this approach was that some of the articles are "phrased in very general terms,"[100] many of which are not defined in the Convention. To interpret these sorts of provisions and decide what they would mean in the context of the dispute before the Tribunal, Ireland proposed that it was natural to have regard to "the mass of detailed regulation in other treaties that deal with law of the sea matters" given that UNCLOS was not drafted in a vacuum but in full knowledge of these other international instruments.[101] To refer to another international agreement to determine whether there was a breach of an UNCLOS provision, was not a determination that the other international agreement was also violated.[102]

Ireland further considered that non-UNCLOS instruments would be relevant where there is a *renvoi* to other instruments. Such a *renvoi* existed where UNCLOS provisions, such as Articles 213 and 222, refer explicitly to the implementation of applicable international rules and standards established through competent international organizations or diplomatic conferences. Ireland therefore submitted:

There is a range of possible interpretations which would extend at the one extreme from those rules and standards that are already legally binding on

---

[97] McConnell and Gold, at 88.   [98] *Ibid.*, at 98.

[99] MOX Plant, Day 2 Transcript, p. 40, available at http://www.pca-cpa.org/PDF/MOX%20-%20Day%20 Two.pdf.

[100] *Ibid.*, at 39.   [101] *Ibid.*   [102] *Ibid.*, at 40.

the parties to the UNCLOS dispute, Britain and Ireland in this case, to at the other extreme rules and standards adopted by international or regional organizations or conferences in which the disputing states may not even have been entitled to participate. Ireland has relied in this case on the narrowest interpretation.[103]

Ireland maintained that this interpretation was correct based on the substantive provisions without having to rely on Article 293, which sets forth the applicable law for disputes under UNCLOS.[104] The United Kingdom rejected this approach, arguing that Ireland was effectively proposing "the wholesale incorporation into and application as part of UNCLOS of every far flung rule of customary or conventional international law merely by reference to a test of compatibility with UNCLOS."[105] The Tribunal did not definitively resolve this issue prior to the suspension of the proceedings after the jurisdictional hearing.[106]

It is submitted that Ireland's approach is completely consistent with the substantive obligations dealing with the protection and preservation of the marine environment, as it accounts for the preexisting and evolving body of international environmental law. Any third-party determination of international rules and standards relevant to the general obligations for the protection and preservation of the marine environment through Part XV processes must take account of the flexible terminology used in many of the provisions in Part XII. The Convention does not create a complete system that automatically implements all necessary environmental rules and standards.[107] A number of the

---

[103] *Ibid.*, at 41.

[104] *Ibid.*, at 40. Ireland nonetheless argued that art. 293 confirmed this approach as it "directs the Annex VII Tribunal to apply all the relevant rules of international law in identifying the nature and extent of each State's obligations, and in determining whether a State's behaviour is in conformity with those obligations." In the Dispute Concerning the MOX Plant, International Movements of Radioactive Materials, and the Protection of the Marine Environment of the Irish Sea, Ireland Memorial, Part II, para. 6.7 (July 26, 2002), available at http://www.pca-cpa.org/PDF/Ireland%20Memorial%20Part%20II.pdf.

[105] MOX Plant, United Kingdom's Rejoinder, para. 5.15.

[106] The Tribunal simply acknowledged that the scope of jurisdiction had to be distinguished from the applicable law, and that "to the extent that any aspects of Ireland's claims arise directly under legal instruments other than the Convention, such claims may be inadmissible." MOX Plant, Order No. 3, para. 19. This decision does not eliminate the possible use of different international instruments to interpret and apply the provisions in Part XII of the Convention.

[107] Jonathan I. Charney, "The Protection of the Marine Environment by the 1982 United Nations Convention on the Law of the Sea," 7 *Geo. Int'l Envtl. L. Rev.* 731, 735 (1995).

provisions in Part XII are in the nature of soft law,[108] imposing very flexible standards that are not conducive to third-party settlement. For example, many qualifiers ("as appropriate," "the best practicable means," "in accordance with their capabilities") are included in the provisions in order to accommodate the economic position of developing States. States must "endeavor" to cooperate in research programs,[109] "endeavor" to monitor the risks or effects of pollution,[110] and "endeavor" to establish and harmonize regional rules.[111] The result is that only an extremely indeterminate standard is in place should a State wish to challenge another State's application of this obligation. At best, it could be argued that States must not ignore soft law guidelines in their implementing measures.[112] This approach does not entirely alleviate difficulties relating to the indeterminacy of the standard. More problematic, it tends to contradict the point that States use soft law provisions in conventions precisely because they do not wish a concrete obligation to be imposed while still desiring an indication of how the law on an issue should develop. One way that a dispute may be resolved in relation to such provisions is if a very low threshold is imposed on a State in terms of its required cooperation and "endeavors," and the discretion of the State in determining what is "feasible" or "appropriate" may be given considerable latitude. A balance needs to be struck whereby it is acknowledged that these sorts of obligations are indeed soft law and are thus not strictly enforceable but the hortatory aspects of these obligations must not be ignored to render the provisions entirely otiose.

Disputes Related to International Rules and Standards Regarding Pollution of the Marine Environment in the EEZ and on the Continental Shelf

The significant increase in maritime commerce throughout the nineteenth and twentieth centuries led to concomitant concern about the likelihood of marine pollution from vessels. Concern about pollution from ships was voiced as early as 1926 when a draft convention was

---

[108] But see Lee A. Kimball, "The Law of the Sea Convention and Marine Environment Protection, 7 *Geo. Int'l Envtl. L. Rev.* 745, 746" (1995) (arguing that the UNCLOS establishes unqualified obligations to protect the entire marine environment because of the mandatory language used, unlike the language in other environmental conventions).

[109] UNCLOS, art. 200.   [110] *Ibid.*, art. 204.   [111] *Ibid.*, arts. 207, 208, 210, and 212.

[112] Kimball, "Marine Environment Protection," at 747.

drawn up and led to the first convention controlling pollution of ships on the basis of an oily water discharge formula.[113] Further efforts were undertaken to elaborate the legal standards to address this international problem and culminated in the adoption of the 1954 International Convention for the Prevention of the Pollution of the Sea by Oil.[114] The International Maritime Organization has since provided a forum for the adoption of numerous treaties dealing with the problem of marine pollution.[115] UNCLOS both complements and supplements these international obligations. It provides a framework in which the earlier conventions can be placed and develops the law on this matter by addressing a wider range of pollution sources. Article 194(1) sets out the general standard to be met by States:

States shall take, individually or jointly as appropriate, all measures consistent with this Convention that are necessary to prevent, reduce and control pollution of the marine environment from any source, using for this purpose the best practicable means at their disposal and in accordance with their capabilities, and they shall endeavor to harmonize their policies in this connection.

While a flexible standard is obviously created ("the best practicable means at their disposal and in accordance with their capabilities"), Section 5 of Part XII elaborates on this obligation with respect to each source of pollution. Among the various sources, "there are differences in the extent to which States have discretion in their implementation responsibilities."[116] These differences are described immediately below, along with the requirements dealing with the enforcement of laws and regulations for the protection and preservation of the marine environment. The following section analyzes the impact of these different rules on dispute settlement.

---

[113] Patricia Birnie, "Law of the Sea and Ocean Resources: Implications for Marine Scientific Research," 10 Int'l J. Marine & Coastal L. 229, 232 (1995).

[114] International Convention for the Prevention of the Pollution of the Sea by Oil, May 12, 1954, 12 UST 2989; 327 UNTS 3.

[115] See, e.g., International Convention for the Prevention of the Pollution of the Sea by Oil, May 12, 1954, 12 UST 2989, 327 UNTS 3; International Convention Relating to Intervention on the High Seas in Cases of Oil Pollution Casualties, November 29, 1969, 26 UST 765; Convention on the Prevention of Marine Pollution by Dumping of Wastes and Other Matter, December 29, 1972, 26 UST 2403, 1046 UNTS 120; International Convention for the Prevention of Pollution from Ships, May 18, 1967, 17 UST 1523, 600 UNTS 332, as modified by the Protocol of 1978 relating thereto, June 1, 1978, 17 ILM 546 (1978); International Convention on Oil Pollution Preparedness, Response and Co-operation, November 30 1990, 30 ILM 773 (1991).

[116] McConnell and Gold, at 92.

Substantive Provisions Dealing with Pollution of the Marine Environment

The jurisdictional framework established in the Convention "systematically differentiates between national measures and international rules and standards concerning particular sources of pollution."[117] Such a distinction is made with respect to both the prescription of rules to prevent, reduce, and control pollution as well as the rights of States to enforce those rules and standards. As one commentator has noted, the provisions on pollution control "must be taken as an inseparable whole if they are to constitute a workable and stable system."[118]

The Convention's provisions on pollution differentiate between the different sources of pollution: from land-based sources; seabed activities subject to national jurisdiction; activities in the Area; by dumping; from vessels; and from or through the atmosphere. States are to adopt national laws and regulations that take into account internationally agreed rules and standards, as well as take other measures that are necessary to prevent, reduce, and control these sorts of pollution. Action is required on an international level, as well as nationally. For land-based sources of pollution, dumping, and pollution from or through the atmosphere, States must "endeavour" to establish global and regional rules and standards. In respect of land-based sources of pollution, these rules and standards are to take into account "characteristic regional features, the economic capacity of developing States and their need for economic development."[119] For the other sources of pollution, States have a primary obligation to establish the rules instead of an obligation to attempt to establish the rules in the future.

In some instances, the Convention sets out further specific rules for certain sources of pollution. For example, the laws to be established by States with respect to dumping must ensure that dumping is not carried out without the permission of the competent authorities of States and express prior approval must be sought from a coastal State for dumping in its territorial sea, EEZ, or on its continental shelf.[120] As a further example, if the rules States establish to prevent, reduce, and control pollution from vessels through international organizations or conferences are inadequate to meet the particular circumstances, the possibility exists

---

[117] Kwiatkowska, *Exclusive Economic Zone*, p. 169.

[118] Horace B. Robertson, "Navigation in the Exclusive Economic Zone," 24 *Va. J. Int'l L.* 865, 905–06 (1984).

[119] UNCLOS, art. 207(4).   [120] *Ibid.*, art. 210(3) and (5).

for coastal States to adopt more stringent measures. This right is very narrowly drawn in order to prevent interference with navigation and is only allowed when there are:

special circumstances and coastal States have reasonable grounds for believing that a particular, clearly defined area of their respective exclusive economic zones is an area where the adoption of special mandatory measures for the prevention of pollution from vessels is required for recognized technical reasons in relation to its oceanographical and ecological conditions, as well as its utilization or the protection of its resources and the particular character of its traffic . . .[121]

Coastal States wanting to impose such measures must undertake appropriate consultations through the competent international organization with any other States concerned and that organization then has the competence to determine whether the conditions for special mandatory measures are met. These laws may relate to discharges and navigational practices but may not require that design, construction, manning, and equipment standards differ from the generally accepted international rules and standards.[122] UNCLOS specifically envisages that one of the international rules to be observed under this article is prompt notification to coastal States that may have their coastlines or related interests affected by pollution.[123] A less determinate obligation is further imposed on States to "promote the adoption" of routing systems "where appropriate" to minimize the threat of accidents.[124] Acting on the national level, States must adopt laws and regulations that have the same effect as the international standard and that are applicable to vessels flying their flags or of their registry.[125] The Convention anticipates that States will also seek to regulate foreign vessels that enter their ports, internal waters, or off-shore terminals and these laws must be given due publicity.[126]

Enforcement of Laws and Regulations Relating to Pollution of the Marine Environment

The right to enforce the laws and regulations for each source of pollution is plainly stated in the Convention. However, one issue of controversy concerned the powers of coastal States to enforce environmental

---

[121] Ibid., art. 211(6)(a).   [122] Ibid., art. 211(6)(c).
[123] Ibid., art. 211(7).   [124] Ibid., art. 211(1).   [125] Ibid., art. 211(2).
[126] Ibid., art. 211(3). This provision further sets out notice requirements for coastal States to harmonize their policies on entry in this regard.

laws through the detention of vessels or other legal proceedings. Traditionally, the flag State would be the only State with the authority to take action against one of its vessels. Flag States were concerned that coastal States would interfere with the freedom of navigation on the pretext of enforcing environmental rules and regulations. Coastal States, however, considered that enforcement by the flag State could well prove inadequate as it would lack sufficient concern to ensure that anti-pollution measures would be adequately enforced.[127] The enforcement provisions were intended to balance the rights of coastal and port States to guard against harm to their adjacent marine environments with the interests of flag States in protecting the freedom of navigation. This balance was achieved to some extent by accommodating "the interests of states in the freedom of navigation by varying the coastal state's unilateral enforcement authority based upon the severity of the actual or potential damage to the environment and the distance of the event from the shore."[128] Overall, there is a bias in favor of flag State jurisdiction due to the restrictions placed on the rights of coastal States to pursue enforcement action against foreign vessels.

Flag States must provide effective enforcement of applicable rules, standards, laws, and regulations wherever the violation occurs.[129] Enforcement by flag States involves immediate inspection and institution of proceedings in instances of violations as well as a certification system, including periodic inspections, to ensure that vessels flying their flag or of their registry do not sail if they are not in compliance with relevant environmental standards.[130] Port States have jurisdiction to undertake investigations and, where warranted, institute proceedings in respect of discharges from vessels outside the internal waters, territorial sea, or EEZ of that State.[131] Proceedings may not be instituted if the discharge occurred in the internal waters, territorial sea, or EEZ of another State unless that State, or a State damaged or threatened by the discharge violation, so requests.[132] The enforcement jurisdiction of the port State has been described as "the most important innovation of the enforcement system":

The universal enforcement jurisdiction of a port state is the most important innovation of the enforcement system established by the LOS Convention with

---

[127] J. C. Phillips, "The Exclusive Economic Zone as a Concept in International Law," 26 *Int'l & Comp. L.Q.* 585, 593 (1977).
[128] Charney, "Marine Environment," at 891.   [129] UNCLOS, art. 217(1).
[130] *Ibid.*, art. 217(2)–(8).   [131] *Ibid.*, art. 218(1).   [132] *Ibid.*, art. 218(2).

regard to pollution from ships and a notable achievement of that Convention from an environmental perspective. This is particularly so because – unlike coastal state enforcement, the port state's enforcement, while strengthening compliance, involves no interference with the freedom of navigation, for it applies only to vessels being voluntarily in the port of that state.[133]

In addition to flag and port States, coastal States are also entitled to exercise enforcement jurisdiction in certain circumstances with respect to vessels voluntarily in their ports, when in passage through its territorial sea, or when navigating in its EEZ.[134] The coastal State is entitled to exercise enforcement jurisdiction for violations of laws and regulations of that State adopted in accordance with either the Convention or applicable international rules and standards for the prevention, reduction, and control of pollution from vessels in the following ways:

- Institute proceedings against a vessel voluntarily in its port when that violation has occurred within the territorial sea or the EEZ of that State.[135]
- Physical inspections of vessels and, where warranted, institution of proceedings against vessels navigating the territorial sea when there are clear grounds for believing that a violation has occurred.[136]
- Obtain information from a vessel navigating in its territorial sea or EEZ when there are clear grounds for believing that a violation has occurred.[137]
- Physical inspection of vessels that have refused to supply information or the information supplied is manifestly at variance with the evident factual situation and circumstances so justify when a violation in the EEZ by a vessel navigating the territorial sea or the EEZ has resulted in a substantial discharge causing or threatening significant pollution of the marine environment.[138]
- Institute proceedings, including detention of the vessel, for violations in the EEZ by a vessel navigating the territorial sea or the EEZ that has resulted in a discharge causing major damage or threat of major damage to the coastline or related interest of the coastal State, or to any resource of its territorial sea or EEZ.[139]

The Convention thus sets high standards to justify physical inspections by the coastal State in respect of violations occurring in the EEZ. As

---

[133] Kwiatkowska, *Exclusive Economic Zone*, p. 180. See also Jon M. Van Dyke, *Consensus and Confrontation: the United States and the Law of the Sea Convention* (1985), p. 462.

[134] UNCLOS, art. 220.   [135] *Ibid.*, art. 220(1).

[136] *Ibid.*, art. 220(2).   [137] *Ibid.*, art. 220(3).   [138] *Ibid.*, art. 220(5).

[139] *Ibid.*, art. 220(6). A vessel must be allowed to proceed wherever appropriate procedures have been established for compliance with requirements for bonds or other financial security. *Ibid.*, art. 220(7).

a further protection, coastal State enforcement actions, as well as laws adopted pursuant to the Convention, are then subject to external third-party review under Part XV of UNCLOS should disputes arise.

Resolution of Disputes Relating to Sources of Pollution

One of the serious threats to the freedom of navigation comes from the grant of rights to the coastal State for the protection and preservation of the marine environment from pollution. It was recognized at the Third Conference that coastal States had a special interest in protecting against pollution of their maritime areas but there was an unwillingness to cede a general competence to coastal States.[140] "Rather, the Convention creates a carefully circumscribed set of coastal state rights, tied in large measure to generally accepted international rules and standards, balanced by clearly stated safeguards against arbitrary enforcement measures."[141] One such safeguard is evident in Article 292, which authorizes the flag State to institute proceedings for failure to release promptly a detained vessel upon payment of a reasonable bond in accordance with Articles 220 and 226.[142]

In order to limit the jurisdiction granted to the coastal State with respect to the protection and preservation of the marine environment, developed States also emphasized the need to adopt internationally agreed standards of pollution control.[143] The rationale for such an approach was based in practicalities:

At present, shipbuilders knew the standard of construction they had to adopt to meet internationally agreed discharge regulations, it would be virtually impossible to design ships that could move through all the areas that were regulated. Consequently, the economy of ship movement would be drastically reduced and the cost of world trade significantly increased.[144]

Article 297(1)(c) thus reflects the requirement that coastal State behavior in relation to the protection and preservation of the marine environment conform to international standards – standards that would account for navigational and commercial interests.

The dispute settlement mechanism for environmental disputes in Article 297 contributes to this system as coastal States' acts are to be judged in accordance with the rules and standards that are expressly included

---

[140] Robertson, at 896.   [141] Ibid.
[142] See further pp. 85–119.   [143] Phillips, at 590.
[144] Third United Nations Conference on the Law of the Sea, Official Records, vol. II, p. 200 (Speech of Sir Robert Jackling, United Kingdom), cited in Phillips, at 590.

in UNCLOS or formulated through diplomatic conferences or competent international organizations as required by the Convention. Through this mechanism, maritime States have an additional safeguard available, namely, resort to (or the threat of) binding and mandatory dispute settlement, to control the actions of the coastal State in taking measures to prevent, reduce, or control the pollution of the marine environment and the potential interference with the freedom of navigation. Denials, or unauthorized restrictions, of the freedom of navigation are meant to be kept in check through Article 297(1)(c).[145]

While third-party review of coastal State action may have been deemed necessary in this regard, the effectiveness of dispute settlement under Article 297(1)(c) in controlling the balance of authority granted to the coastal State vis-à-vis the rights of maritime States depends on a determination of what constitutes the relevant standards to which States must adhere.

The balance between the conflicting interests in the freedom of navigation and in the need for environmental protection is in particular ensured by the general requirement that national measures with regard to marine-based sources of pollution . . . must be no less effective or have the same effect as international rules and standards which states are obliged to establish, enforce and re-examine.[146]

The obligation to meet a certain international minimum standard does not overcome the problem of determining what that standard might be, however. Riphagen observes that, "Since the wording of the subparagraph presupposes that the 1982 Law of the Sea Convention itself has also established 'specified international rules and standards' the required degree of specification cannot be very high."[147] Obligations are imposed on States to hold international conferences to determine what international rules and standards should apply.[148] A court or tribunal is faced with a difficult situation if such conferences have not actually been held. What is more likely is that any decision-making process on the appropriate standard will have to refer to environmental conventions and agreements as an indicator of the "specified international rules and standards." Consequently, it is possible that multilateral environmental conventions regulating aspects of the marine environment could be incorporated within the scope of the dispute settlement provisions of the Convention if that convention was considered as establishing the

---

[145] See Kwiatkowska, *Exclusive Economic Zone*, pp. 170–71.   [146] *Ibid.*, p. 189.
[147] Riphagen, p. 289.   [148] See Charney, "Marine Environment," at 884.

"global rules and standards" for a particular issue.[149] This interpretation is facilitated through reference to Article 237, which provides that the obligations in Part XII are without prejudice to specific obligations assumed by States under special conventions and agreement concluded previously or in furtherance of the general principles in the Convention. Both obligations should be read together to determine what standard is applicable. When a disputant State is not a party to the other international conventions, the international rule imposed in that convention is applicable to the State in dispute under UNCLOS only to the extent that the other agreement reflects customary international law.[150]

In addition to international treaties or other international agreements as indicative of the relevant rules and standards, a court or tribunal could consider what action has, or has not been, taken by a State party in its domestic law. There may be a sufficiently consistent practice amongst States in one region, or among similarly economically situated States, to discern an applicable standard for that region or group of States. "Standard" need not be equated with assessing the existence of a customary law rule as the Convention refers to both rules and standards in Article 297(1)(c). The distinction may accord a court or tribunal more flexibility in assessing a State's behavior in this regard.

A question that arises here is the reach of the dispute settlement regime with respect to States' obligations to adopt national laws and regulations to prevent, reduce, and control pollution of the marine environment from various sources. Could a State challenge the content of such laws and regulations as taking insufficient account of international standards and practices? Such a dispute is most likely to arise between neighboring States where the neglect of one State may prove harmful to its neighbors. A challenge to the content of domestic laws must be admitted. It is well-established in international law that a State may not rely on its internal legislation to avoid international responsibility.[151]

---

[149] Roach considers this hypothetical with respect to the 1972 London Dumping Convention and Article 210 of UNCLOS and argues that ultimately the test relates to the protection of the marine environment and not identifying between national laws and global standards. J. Ashley Roach, "Dispute Settlement in Specific Situations," 7 *Geo. Int'l Envtl. L. Rev.* 775, 789 (1995).

[150] Cf. Noyes, "ITLOS," at 124 (stating that the reference to "generally accepted international rules and standards" renders those rules and standards binding on States parties to UNCLOS even if they have not separately accepted them).

[151] *See, e.g.,* Treatment of Polish Nationals and Other Persons of Polish Origin or Speech in the Danzig Territory, Advisory Opinion, 1932, PCIJ, Series A/B, No. 44, p. 4; Free Zones of Upper Savoy and the District of Gex, Judgment, 1932, PCIJ, Series A/B, No. 46,

States are required to accept certain minimum standards established through international organizations and may exceed that minimum to the extent that there would be no unreasonable interference with other legitimate maritime interests.[152] More controversial is the use of the dispute settlement mechanism with respect to States' inaction in their domestic law-making activities. Then could a State's failure to adopt such legislation give rise to a dispute concerning the interpretation and application of the Convention? An omission to perform treaty obligations can entail State responsibility and so should be justiciable under Part XV. In the UNCLOS context, such inaction would constitute *prima facie* evidence that no "endeavors" have been undertaken. These questions indicate that the potential role for the mandatory procedures in the Convention for the protection and preservation of the marine environment is quite pervasive – perhaps more so than the drafters fully anticipated.

A final issue in this regard is whether any State could challenge a coastal State's failure to implement national legislation for the protection and preservation of the marine environment even if that challenging State is not directly affected by the failure to take measures but has a general interest in protecting the environment. A State may attempt to take up this issue with a coastal State as a way of gaining political leverage in some other aspect of their bilateral relations. It is questionable as to whether a State would be likely to have standing to bring such claims and whether an *actio popularis*, a right resident in any member of a community to take legal action in vindication of a public interest, would be accepted in such a situation. Charney has argued that "[b]ecause a violation by any state party is a legal injury to every other state party, any state party may bring an action in dispute settlement to enforce compliance."[153] He considers that the resolution of environmental disputes provides the means to enforce environmentally favorable positions by ensuring that States' actions are consistent with the Convention's protection of the marine environment.[154] It is not evident whether such a

---

p. 167; Difference Relating to Immunity from Legal Process of a Special Rapporteur of the Commission on Human Rights, Advisory Opinion, 1999 ICJ para. 62 (April 29).

[152] Charney, "Marine Environment," at 889.

[153] Charney, "Protection of the Marine Environment," at 737.

[154] *Ibid.*, at 737–38. Cf. Clifton E. Curtis, "The United Nations Convention on the Law of the Sea and the Marine Environment: A Non-Governmental Perspective," 7 *Geo. Int'l Envtl. L. Rev.*739, 743 (1995) (suggesting effective safeguards be in place to ensure that dispute settlement is not used to vitiate or curtail more stringent national environment conservation measures).

broad basis of standing would be acceptable before the courts and tribunals available under the Convention. In the *South West Africa* cases, the ICJ expressly rejected the notion that an *actio popularis* is part of international law.[155] It could well be argued that the ICJ's position on this issue of standing is outdated, particularly in light of global environmental concerns. Nonetheless, any consideration of this type of claim would still have to uphold inclusive interests in the freedom of navigation, as well as deal with the question of whether the matter was inadmissible for being an abuse of process.[156]

Overall, it seems unlikely that a dispute relating to the pollution of the marine environment would not be resolved for lack of a specified international rule or standard. The question of what that standard is remains one of interpretation, the content and purpose of that task being dependent on the state of international environmental law at the time the matter is being resolved as well as the respective capabilities of the disputant States in accordance with the aims of the States parties in drafting the regime for the protection and preservation of the marine environment. A determination of the interests at stake must also take into account the fact that compulsory dispute settlement was included as part of an overall system of checks and balances on the power of the coastal State in the EEZ in respect of the marine environment. Mandatory and binding procedures for the protection and preservation of the marine environment are necessary to prevent the coastal State from exceeding its powers within areas over which it has jurisdiction or sovereign rights.

Conclusion

Dispute settlement procedures available for controversies arising over the interpretation and application of the provisions on the protection and preservation of the marine environment perform an important lawmaking function. Charney is very positive about the value of mandatory dispute settlement for conflicts over the environment:

The LOS Convention's articles on dispute settlement are the strongest of any environmental treaty to date. It is the only international agreement to establish a broad compulsory dispute settlement system for environmental issues . . . The compulsory dispute settlement system is the best guarantee possible that

---

[155] South West Africa (Second Phase) (*Ethiopia* v. *South Africa*; *Liberia* v. *South Africa*) 1966 ICJ 6 (July 18).
[156] See UNCLOS, art. 294.

states parties will fulfill their LOS Convention-based obligations with regard to the environment. Not only will states that are parties to those procedures be compelled to do so, but states parties will be encouraged to abide by their LOS Convention-based obligations since failure to perform those obligations exposes them to compulsory dispute settlement procedures.[157]

The importance of compulsory dispute settlement, however, is not so much the "guarantee" that States will fulfill their obligations under UNCLOS with respect to the protection and preservation of the marine environment. Rather, it is the case that without the availability of third-party procedures, many of the environmental obligations imposed on States are far from determinate and to this extent lack clarity of content. Part XII contains a number of soft law obligations, or permits flexible standards to be applied and so the availability of the dispute settlement proceedings is an essential complement to the regime in reinforcing the importance of the soft law or setting relevant standards. Any international process under Part XV of UNCLOS must ultimately take into account the policies at stake in the Convention in order to balance challenged rights, such as the freedom of navigation, with the protection and preservation of the marine environment.

Through the dispute settlement procedures, UNCLOS could also collaterally strengthen the obligations found in other international environmental treaties. The norms set out in other international treaties must be applied through Part XV proceedings in light of the references to international standards and rules as the benchmarks for conduct in accordance with UNCLOS. A potential side-effect from this system is that States parties to these other environmental treaties could use the compulsory proceedings under the Convention as a means to seek reparations for violations of these other treaties through reliance on the broad provisions in UNCLOS. Consideration would have to be given to the interplay between UNCLOS and other international conventions dealing with specific questions: can Part XV serve as a dispute settlement mechanism for these treaties as well? Such a tactic could well be viewed as an abuse of process – but how clearly could the motives of the applicant State be discerned before a court or tribunal constituted under UNCLOS? The indication from *Southern Bluefin Tuna* is that these cases must be resolved under the dispute settlement clauses of those other

---

[157] Charney, "Marine Environment," at 894–95. See also Oxman, "Complementary Agreements," at 287 (stating that "compulsory jurisdiction is central both to realizing and to accommodating" the protection of the marine environment); *ibid.*, at 298–99.

treaties if the requirements of Article 281 are met. Challenging violations of general environmental law obligations in UNCLOS would thus be
limited in favor of non-binding, non-compulsory dispute settlement for
specific provisions in other multilateral treaties. Arguably, however, the
express reference to international rules and standards in Article 297(1)(c)
creates a different situation to that existing in *Southern Bluefin Tuna*. A
court or tribunal must go beyond UNCLOS in its decision-making on
the international rules and standards relevant to the protection and
preservation of the marine environment. On this basis, the existence
of other international agreements and their relevance to any given dispute would not necessarily deprive the court or tribunal of mandatory
jurisdiction. The specific grant of authority to refer to external sources
should promote dispute settlement under the Convention's procedures.

Fishing

The traditional freedom of fishing has faced enormous pressure throughout the twentieth century. Economic and conservation incentives have
provided an impetus in favor of international regulation and coastal
State control over *laissez-faire* policies and *res communis*. With the adoption of UNCLOS, States instituted the EEZ and thereby recognized coastal
States' rights over living resources in a new maritime zone in the law of
the sea. A large degree of power was vested in the coastal State in light
of the variety of circumstances existing between States with respect to
their fish stock, coastal geography, and economic conditions as well as
the importance of commercial and conservation interests. Coastal State
interests have also been recognized in the Convention to varying degrees
with respect to the fishing of stocks or species that are located in more
than one zone or between the EEZ and the high seas (namely, highly
migratory species, straddling stock, and anadromous and catadromous
species). In high seas areas, State control is limited to its national vessels and the freedom of fishing is primarily curtailed by general obligations of cooperation relating to conservation and management.

   The Convention's dispute settlement provisions reflect the decisions
taken on substantive matters with respect to the different maritime
zones and types of fish species and stock. It is the purpose of this section to explore the development of rules governing fishing activities and
then consider the interplay of dispute settlement provisions with these
norms. In particular, the role of dispute settlement for conflicts relating to fishing in the EEZ, on the high seas, and between these zones

will be examined. For the EEZ, virtually all disputes are excluded from compulsory procedures entailing binding decisions, especially if they concern the discretionary power of the coastal State. While not an optimal system, the role accorded to third-party review in the Convention acknowledges the predominate interest of the coastal State in the conservation and management of living resources in the EEZ as well as anticipating in some ways the political forces that impact on national decision-making processes.

By contrast, greater international cooperation and regulation is now required for fishing on the high seas. The availability of compulsory dispute settlement allows courts and tribunals to perform a facilitative function in the implementation of these rules and this international process may fulfil the purpose of elaborating on the content of norms governing this activity. Alternatively, States may enter into implementation agreements to flesh out the high seas fishing obligations in UNCLOS. These agreements may have their own dispute settlement clauses that prevail over the mandatory jurisdiction of Part XV. A similar situation could arise with respect to straddling stock and highly migratory species. For disputes relating to the fishing of these species, it is unclear on the terms of UNCLOS whether compulsory dispute settlement entailing binding decisions is available or not. The 1995 Agreement for the Implementation of the Provisions of the United Nations Convention on the Law of the Sea Relating to the Conservation and Management of Straddling Fish Stocks and Highly Migratory Fish Stocks ("Fish Stocks Agreement" or "FSA"),[158] while elaborating on the international principles addressing straddling stock and highly migratory species, did not clarify the availability of compulsory dispute settlement for conflicts relating to these fish. It is argued here that courts or tribunals faced with jurisdictional challenges in relation to straddling stock and highly migratory species should not underestimate the valuable contribution an international third party process could make in this traditionally problematic area.

Increasing Regulation of the Freedom of Fishing

What was once one of the most important freedoms of the oceans has become one of the more complex legal regimes within UNCLOS. The attitudes of States towards the traditional freedom of fishing have changed

---

[158] Agreement for the Implementation of the Provisions of the United Nations Convention on the Law of the Sea Relating to the Conservation and Management of Straddling Fish Stocks and Highly Migratory Fish Stocks, UN Doc. A/CONF.164/37.

considerably as technology has developed and as information about environmental concerns has increased and improved. Under the *mare liberum* system, States were entitled to fish in any area of the high seas and could harvest as large a supply of fish as possible. These amounts were necessarily limited by virtue of the fishing equipment available, the lack of refrigeration, and the size and design of boats. As technology improved, the amount of fish harvested increased dramatically. At the same time, an international awareness developed that supplies of fish were not unlimited and that conservation measures were thus required in order to maintain the commercial benefits derived from the fishing industry. The development of States' fishing industries and their knowledge and concern over conservation issues has occurred to varying degrees at different times for different States. The predominant trend in this development has been a preference for obtaining international recognition of exclusive interests in larger maritime areas. The international law of fishing has shifted from an absolute freedom to fish, to an acknowledgement that coastal States had a "special interest" in the Fishing and Conservation Convention, to the recognition of "preferential interests" by the International Court of Justice in the *Icelandic Fisheries* case, and has culminated in the attribution of sovereign rights over the living resources in the EEZ under UNCLOS. The discussion immediately below traces this progression to illustrate the changing expectations of States towards the freedom of fishing and briefly describes how fishing is currently regulated under UNCLOS.

Increasing Regulation of Fishing Prior to UNCLOS

In accordance with *mare liberum*, States were free to fish in any area of the high seas. Any legal regulation was limited to protection of nascent fishing industries in the belt of territorial waters immediately adjacent to the coast of the State.[159] The available equipment and technology of the time limited the amount of fish that could be harvested in one fishing season. It was only at the start of the twentieth century that States began to perceive a mutual interest in curtailing the numbers of fish and other marine resources being harvested on the high sea.[160] Coastal

---

[159] It was on this basis that the Scandinavian countries claimed a breadth of one marine league (equivalent to four nautical miles) from the middle of the eighteenth century. This claim was recognized by other maritime States. See Dean, "Second Geneva Conference," at 758–59.

[160] One of the first conventions on conservation of marine resources, the Bering Fur Seal Convention, was adopted in 1911. Treaty between Great Britain and the United States

States subsequently employed conservation as the primary vehicle to claim extended rights over the living resources of the oceans.[161]

The emergence of the concept of a fishery zone occurred at the end of World War II, most notably when the United States issued a presidential proclamation in 1945 stressing the need for fisheries conservation zones.[162] This proclamation claimed conservation zones in areas of the high seas contiguous to the coasts of the United States wherein fishing by United States nationals occurred on a substantial scale. For areas where nationals other than those from the United States also actively fished, the proclamation recommended that conservation zones be established by agreement with the relevant States. This proclamation was made in response to the failure of international measures to protect the Alaskan salmon fisheries from exploitation by Japanese fishermen.[163] Although this proclamation was never applied in practice, these claims by the United States resulted in a number of other States asserting rights over larger maritime areas.

At the First and Second Conferences, the competing economic interests at stake were those of States with established long-distance fishing fleets and those of coastal States wishing to protect their resources from this industry and thereby promote their own economic prosperity through exclusive entitlement to the area directly adjacent to their coast.[164] States wishing to protect their long-distance fishing industries argued that conservation was a more appropriate mechanism than granting increased exclusive interests to coastal States in order to balance the competing interests.[165] To this end, various proposals were considered that would have allowed for States to claim a wider zone of

for the Protection of Fur Seals, February 7, 1911, United Kingdom-United States, 37 Stat. 1538. Modified by Convention between Great Britain, Japan, Russia and the United States respecting Measures for the Preservation and Protection of Fur Seals in the North Pacific Ocean, July 7, 1911, 37 Stat. 1542.

[161] See, e.g., Franklin, at 35; Acts of the Conference for the Codification of International Law, Meetings of the Committee, vol. III, Minutes of the Second Committee, Territorial Waters, reprinted in 4 *Codification Conference*, at 1336 (referring to Portugal's views about extending the application of conservation regulations).

[162] Presidential Proclamation No. 2668, September 28, 1945, 59 Stat. 885.

[163] See R. P. Anand, "The Politics of a New Legal Order for Fisheries," 11 *Ocean Dev. & Int'l L.* 265, 271 (1982).

[164] Even if a coastal State lacked a sufficiently advanced fishing industry to harvest fish at optimum levels, financial gains could still accrue through licensing agreements allowing access to exclusive maritime areas.

[165] *United Nations Conference on the Law of the Sea*, 1st Comm., at 8, ¶ 26 (United Kingdom), UN Doc. A/CONF.13/39, UN Sales No. 58.V.4, vol. III (1958). ("If the Conference could concentrate on conservation and devise measures which would give all countries

control in order to protect fisheries interests without having to extend the territorial sea to a breadth of twelve miles.[166] Attempts were also made to ensure the ongoing recognition of the rights of States with long-distance fishing fleets.[167] The ultimate failure to resolve this issue at the First and Second Conferences meant that the lawful breadth of the territorial sea remained unsettled in international law for a number of years.[168]

confidence that stocks of fish would be maintained at an adequate level, and that everyone would receive a fair share of them, the need for exclusive rights should no longer make itself felt.") See also *United Nations Second Conference on the Law of the Sea – Official Records, Summary Records of Plenary Meetings and of Meetings of the Committee of the Whole, Annexes and Final Act*, at 40, 16 (Cuba), UN Doc. A/CONF.19/8, UN Sales No. 60.V.6 (1960).

[166] For example, in an attempt to reach a compromise between these different positions in 1958, the United States introduced a proposal setting the maximum breadth of the territorial sea at six miles. This proposal also allowed for the regulation and exploitation of fisheries up to a limit of twelve miles from the coastal State's baselines provided that nationals of other States that had fished there in the ten years previous could continue to do so in the outer area. United States of America: proposal, UN Doc. A/CONF.13/C.1/L.159, reprinted in *First Conference*, 1st Comm., at 253. This proposal sought to protect the economic interests of States dependent on their fishing industries while thwarting those States that wanted a twelve-mile territorial sea for strategic purposes. Arthur H. Dean, "The Geneva Conference on the Law of the Sea: What was Accomplished," 52 *Am. J. Int'l L.* 607, 614 (1958).

Canada proposed the retention of a three-mile territorial sea with the addition of a contiguous zone that gave the same right of control over fishing throughout that zone. Canada: Proposal, UN Doc. A/CONF.13/C.1/L.77/Rev.1, *First Conference*, 1st Comm., at 232. See also *ibid.*, at 89–91 (introducing the proposal and explaining its rationale).

[167] For example, the United States and Canada submitted a joint proposal to the Second Conference that sought to balance coastal State and long distance fishing States' interests:

The joint proposal provided for a maximum limit of six miles for the breadth of the territorial sea, and for an exclusive fishing zone contiguous to the territorial sea, extending twelve miles from the baseline. It would also permit foreign States whose nationals had made a practice of fishing in the outer six-mile zone during the five years preceding 1 January 1958 to continue to do so for a period of ten years from 31 October 1960.

Second Conference, at 121, ¶2 (United States). This joint proposal was rejected by one vote at the end of the Second Conference. *Ibid.*, at 30 (fifty-four in favor, twenty-eight against, and five abstentions).

[168] The Territorial Sea Convention failed to specify the breadth of the territorial sea. It skirted around the issue by referring only to the method by which the outer limit of the territorial sea would be measured. See Territorial Sea Convention, art. 6. Despite the polemic surrounding the breadth of the territorial sea at previous conferences on the law of the sea, the issue was quickly resolved during the Third Conference. Once assurances on the rights of passage through international straits had been achieved, States were willing to set the breadth at twelve miles measured from the coastal State's baselines.

Rather than insist on an extension of the lawful breadth of the territorial sea, States also considered whether certain rights accrued to the coastal State for the purposes of controlling the exploitation of the living resources in high seas areas adjacent to the territorial sea. The rights of coastal States and other users in this regard were established at the First Conference with the adoption of the Fishing and Conservation Convention. Article 1 sets out the basic principle of freedom of fishing on the high seas as well as how it is to be curtailed. States were required to adopt, or to cooperate with other States in adopting, measures that would be necessary for the conservation of the living resources of the high seas. The general view was that the freedom of fishing without restrictions conflicted with the rights of coastal States to exercise sovereignty for the purposes of conserving and utilizing their marine resources.[169] As such, the principle of the freedom of the high seas was seen as the starting point from which derogation in favor of economic interests could be made.

The primary question involved here was which State would be best placed to make decisions about the conservation of fish stocks – States with experience in fishing the stocks and equipped with the necessary technology to make the relevant scientific assessments or those States in geographic proximity? Developed States, particularly those with long-distance fishing fleets, argued against the assertion that the coastal State was in a better position to determine conservation measures and control access to resources outside of its territorial sea.[170] The arguments in this context focused on traditional principles whereby the stock of fish in the sea was a natural resource common to all and that all States fishing in an area had an interest in the living resources of that sea area. On this basis, it could be asserted that coastal States did not necessarily have a greater interest in maintaining the stock than other countries.[171]

By contrast, the need to develop such programs of conservation was the vehicle used by coastal States to assert their entitlement to control resource utilization adjacent to the territorial sea. One rationale was,

---

[169] *First Conference*, 2nd Comm., at 17, ¶ 29 (Peru). See also *ibid.*, at 18, ¶ 38 (Peru); *ibid.*, at 31, ¶ 11 (Chile); *United Nations Conference on the Law of the Sea*, 3rd Comm., at 19, ¶ 21 (Republic of Korea), UN Doc. A/CONF.13/41, UN Sales No. 58.V.4, vol. V (1958). ("Korea subscribed to the principle of the freedom of the high seas but considered that no State had a right to the unlimited exercise of that freedom to the detriment of the interests of other States, particularly in the matter of fishing.")

[170] See, e.g., *First Conference*, 3rd Comm., at 7, ¶ 3 (Japan). ("The mere geographical position of a coastal State did not by itself constitute evidence of an interest in the conservation of the living resources, or proof of superior scientific knowledge.")

[171] *Ibid.*, at 12, ¶¶ 24–25 (Netherlands).

"[r]egulatory arrangements for a particular fishery can best be made by the states whose continued use of, or relative proximity to, the affected resources gives them both the interests and the intimate knowledge necessary for wise and effective control."[172] Coastal State measures could be more appropriately enforced by that State and attempts to enforce conservation measures by any other State could lead to political, legal, and other disputes between the States concerned.[173] Controlling resources was viewed as a way for developing States to redress the existing economic imbalance in the international system.[174]

The compromise reached is evidenced in Article 6 of the Fishing and Conservation Convention, which refers to the "special interest" of coastal States in the living resources of the high seas adjacent to their coasts regardless of their involvement in the fishing of those resources. Burke is very critical of the attribution of a "special interest" to the coastal State and describes it as a "product of a collective imagination." He continues: "It hardly seems likely to promote the goal of maximum productivity of fishing resources to permit states so ill-equipped with the necessary talent and equipment unilaterally to prescribe conservation measures."[175]

The Fisheries and Conservation Convention ultimately failed to establish a successful conservation regime. Only thirty-seven States ever ratified this treaty. The main reasons attributed for its lack of success were the failure to agree on restraints on foreign fishing; unilateral conservation measures were solely based on stocks of fish and did not take into account other scientific data; management objectives were poorly defined; there was no balance between the freedom to fish and the responsibility to conserve; and, finally, the question of the scale of priorities in determining allocation of resources was not addressed.[176]

---

[172] William W. Bishop, Jr., "International Law Commission Draft Articles on Fisheries," 50 *Am. J. Int'l L.* 627, at 629 (1956).

[173] *First Conference*, 3rd Comm., at 5, ¶ 21 (India). Korea considered that the coastal State was entitled to priority because of the "sacrifices and efforts made by the coastal State to apply and enforce such conservation measures." *Ibid.*, at 20, ¶ 25 (Republic of Korea). See also *ibid.*, at 56, ¶ 7.

[174] "What was required was that countries which possessed great economic wealth should consent to the sacrifice of a small share of their interests for the sake of those who were less fortunate, in order to allow the latter to breathe more easily and lead a better existence." *First Conference*, 3rd Comm., at 119, ¶ 52 (Uruguay). Cf. William T. Burke, Some Comments on the 1958 Conventions, in *Proceedings of the American Society of International Law at its Fifty-Third Annual Meeting, April 30–May 2, 1959* (1959), pp. 197, 199 (arguing that the hope that exclusive authority would produce food, employment or capital had "little foundation in reality in practically all circumstances").

[175] Burke, "Some Comments," p. 205.   [176] Attard, p. 147.

States instead undertook a variety of unilateral measures to protect their fishing interests. One such measure was the creation of the
"patrimonial sea", which was defined as including:

both the territorial sea as well as a zone beyond it the extension of which is determined unilaterally – but not arbitrarily – by the coastal state. The jurisdiction
of the coastal state to regulate the exploration, conservation, and exploitation
of the marine resources contained within the patrimonial sea is extended over
the adjacent waters, the seabed and subsoil thereof.[177]

The patrimonial sea was considered as a compromise between
"territorialist" States demanding full sovereignty over a 200-mile zone
and the major fishing States that favored a system of preferential rights
or only rights to resources within the capability of the coastal State to
harvest.[178] In the *Icelandic Fisheries* case, the ICJ decided that there was
sufficient practice to indicate that coastal States had preferential rights
over areas adjacent to their coasts in situations of special dependence
on coastal fisheries vis-à-vis other States involved in the exploitation of
the same fisheries.[179] The competing views thus ranged from extended
rights tantamount to an enlarged territorial sea, to a zone with exclusive rights over living and non-living rights, to a system of preferential,
rather than exclusive, rights.

The evolution of claims to all of the natural resources in the area
adjacent to the coast was significantly accelerated by developments in
international environmental law and international economic law.[180] The
concept of a special fisheries zone, which came to be known as the
"exclusive economic zone," emerged from discussions at several regional
fora, particularly in Latin America and in Africa. In introducing the
"Exclusive Zone Concept" to the 1972 Geneva Session of the UN Seabed
Committee, the Kenyan delegate explained the rationale for the proposal
as follows:

The exclusive economic zone concept is an attempt at creating a framework to
resolve the conflict of interests between the developed and developing countries
in the utilization of the sea. It is an attempt to formulate a new jurisdictional
basis which will ensure a fair balance between the coastal states and other users
of the neighboring waters.[181]

---

[177] Orrego Vicuña, *Exclusive Economic Zone Regime*, p. 11 (citing Edmundo Vargas, *Informe
Preliminarsobre el derecho del Mar, Mar Territorial y Mar Patrimonial*, Inter-American Juridical
Committee, April 1971, mimeo).
[178] Castañeda, pp. 608–09.   [179] Icelandic Fisheries, para. 52.
[180] Kwiatkowska, *Exclusive Economic Zone*, p. 2.
[181] Anand, at 278 (1982) (citing Njega (Kenya), *Asia-Africa Legal Consultative Committee, Report
of the 13th Session at Lagos*, January 18–25, 1972, p. 24).

In the final years of the Preparatory Committee of the Third Conference, nine States submitted a proposal that formed the basis of the EEZ regime created in the Convention.[182] This proposal envisaged the coastal State being accorded sovereign rights over natural resources as well as other rights and duties with respect to the protection and preservation of the marine environment and scientific research. Moreover, provisions were included to guarantee certain high seas rights in the new zone.[183] These developments laid the groundwork for the fishing regime established during the Third Conference.

Regulation of Fishing under UNCLOS

Fishing is regulated to varying degrees in UNCLOS depending on the maritime zone in question. States have complete authority to regulate fishing in their territorial seas by virtue of their sovereignty over this zone of water.[184] Coastal State control over fishing in the territorial sea is reinforced by Article 19, which states that any fishing activities during the passage of a foreign ship is prejudicial to the peace, good order, or security of the coastal State and thus outside the regime of innocent passage.[185] Furthermore, the coastal State may adopt laws and regulations relating to innocent passage to prevent infringement of its fisheries laws.[186] Similar rights are granted to States bordering straits subject to the regime of transit passage.[187] Although archipelagic States have sovereignty over archipelagic waters,[188] a narrow limit is imposed whereby these States are required to recognize traditional fishing rights of the immediately adjacent neighboring States.[189] The regulation of fishing under UNCLOS becomes more complex in areas not subject to the sovereignty of the coastal State.

The substantive articles relating to fishing in the EEZ are found in Articles 61 to 71 of Part V of the Convention. The creation of the EEZ in the Convention grants to coastal States sovereign rights over natural resources in a zone extending 200 miles from a State's coast.[190] The EEZ is defined as an "area beyond and adjacent to the territorial sea, subject to the specific legal regime established" in the Convention.[191]

---

[182] UN Doc. A/CONF.62/L.4/July 26, 1974 (Canada, Chile, India, Indonesia, Iceland, Mauritius, Mexico, Norway, and New Zealand), reprinted in 3 *Third United Nations Conference on the Law of the Sea: Official Records*, at 81, UN Sales No. E.75.V.5 (1974).
[183] See Castañeda, p. 608.
[184] Article 2 provides that the sovereignty of a coastal State extends beyond its land territory to an adjacent belt of sea. UNCLOS, art. 2.
[185] See *ibid.*, art. 19.   [186] *Ibid.*, art. 21.   [187] *Ibid.*, art. 42.   [188] *Ibid.*, art. 49.
[189] *Ibid.*, art. 51.   [190] *Ibid.*, art. 57.   [191] *Ibid.*, art. 55.

States parties to the Convention are accorded sovereign rights for the purpose of exploring, exploiting, conserving, and managing the natural resources of the waters superjacent to the seabed and of the seabed and its subsoil.[192] The coastal State is responsible for both the conservation and the management of the living resources found in the EEZ. It must determine the allowable catch in the EEZ and ensure through proper conservation and management measures that the maintenance of the living resources in the EEZ is not endangered by over-exploitation.[193] These measures are to be taken to ensure "a maximum sustainable yield" of the living resources.[194] Without prejudice to these conservation measures, the coastal State "shall promote the objective of optimum utilization of the living resources" in the EEZ.[195] The coastal State can determine its capacity to harvest the living resources and where it does not harvest the entire allowable catch, it is to enter into agreements with other States allowing access to the surplus of the allowable catch.[196] In the event that a coastal State decides a surplus exists, it is to have particular regard to the rights of land-locked and geographically disadvantaged States, which have the right to exploit "an appropriate part of the surplus."[197] Coastal States are not required to consider land-locked and geographically disadvantaged States when its own economy is overwhelmingly dependent on the exploitation of the living resources in its EEZ.[198] This regime is designed to restrain competition among coastal States for limited ocean space and finite living resources in that space but it significantly favors coastal States in their conservation, management, and exploitation efforts by granting a large degree of discretionary power.

The provisions on fisheries in UNCLOS also address certain stocks and species of fish that are not found exclusively in one zone of a coastal State. These provisions address straddling stocks,[199] highly migratory species,[200] anadromous stocks,[201] and catadromous species.[202] These provisions set out the rights of coastal States with respect to these different species and impose duties of cooperation between the relevantly affected

---

[192] *Ibid.*, art. 56(1)(a).   [193] *Ibid.*, art. 61(1) and (2).
[194] *Ibid.*, art. 61(3).   [195] *Ibid.*, art. 62(1).
[196] *Ibid.*, art. 62(2). The major fishing States had originally advocated a system whereby the coastal State would have the right to harvest the resources within its means but this right would not extend to all resources so that fishing States would remain entitled, without charge, to the surplus. See Castañeda, p. 608.
[197] UNCLOS, arts. 62(3), 69, and 70.   [198] *Ibid.*, art. 71.
[199] *Ibid.*, art. 63.   [200] *Ibid.*, art. 64.   [201] *Ibid.*, art. 66.   [202] *Ibid.*, art. 67.

States. It is "generally recognized that any law of the sea treaty will necessarily have to be accompanied by continuing international fisheries arrangements of a bilateral, regional, or special global character."[203]

Sedentary species continue to be regulated by the continental shelf regime rather than the provisions of the EEZ.[204] The regulation of sedentary species had been settled in the Continental Shelf Convention. Some commentators have considered the result of this provision is that sedentary fisheries are excluded from the application of the conservation and utilization provisions of Articles 61 and 62, particularly with respect to the granting of access to the surplus of these species.[205] On this basis, while coastal States have sovereign rights over both sedentary species and fish in the superjacent waters, greater control appears to be granted for the former than the latter because of the different rights granted and duties imposed under the continental shelf regime.

Fishing on the high seas has also been subjected to regulation in the Convention. Several proposals were made during the debates on UNCLOS that fishing be dropped entirely from the list of "freedoms" in the provisions on the high seas.[206] Nonetheless, the freedom of fishing is still included in UNCLOS but is made subject to obligations under other treaties, to the rights, duties, and interests of the coastal State with respect to resources found in the EEZ and the high seas and also to duties of management and conservation described in UNCLOS.[207] Article 117 sets out a broad duty for all States "to take, or to cooperate with other States in taking, such measures for their respective nationals as may be necessary for the conservation of the living resources of the high seas." States are required to enter into negotiations with a view to taking the necessary conservation measures with States fishing the same resource or in the same areas.[208] "An obligation to negotiate is a more demanding burden than simple cooperation, . . . it does not require an agreement, but it does mandate good faith in the attempt to remove differences and reach substantive agreement."[209] This cooperation could extend to the establishment of fisheries organizations on a regional or subregional level in order to facilitate the necessary conservation measures.[210]

---

[203] Stevenson and Oxman, "Preparations," at 19–20.   [204] UNCLOS, art. 68.

[205] But see Kwiatkowska, *Exclusive Economic Zone*, p. 75.   [206] Oda, "Fisheries," at 741.

[207] UNCLOS, art. 116. Article 116 reproduces the obligation of conservation set out in Article 1 of the Fishing and Conservation Convention. See Fishing and Conservation Convention, art. 1.

[208] UNCLOS, art. 118.

[209] William T. Burke, *The New International Law of Fisheries: UNCLOS 1982 and Beyond* (1994), p. 125.

[210] UNCLOS, art. 118.

The generality of the provisions relating to high seas fishing allows for a broad scope of interpretation and application. Article 119 states the general goal of the measures to be taken for conservation but a range of subjective factors is left for determination. The measures stipulated under Article 119 must produce, for example, the maximum sustainable yield, as qualified by "relevant environmental and economic factors" as well as "the special requirements of developing States." This situation has led one commentator to note, "the major shortcoming of UNCLOS is its attachment of vague duties and restrictions to high seas fishing without suggesting any parameters for these duties, let alone an enforcement regime or a list of appropriate sanctions that may be sought for violation of these duties."[211] The Convention does set out certain basic principles, but "the articles are phrased in hortatory language which appears to be primarily concerned with accommodation of conflicting interests and none of the relevant provisions provide a remedy if agreement is not forthcoming."[212] The exact substance of these obligations and possible remedies and sanctions are to be formulated in separate agreements or are to be elaborated through the processes available in Part XV of the Convention.

Overall, the balance of interests has clearly shifted to favor coastal State control over the traditional inclusive approach. Considerable coastal State authority has been recognized in the EEZ to decide how much fish can be caught and who can catch it, and these interests are also recognized to some degree in fisheries occurring beyond its EEZ. The extent that coastal State power is controlled – or reinforced – through dispute settlement procedures is next examined.

Resolution of Disputes Relating to Fishing

The increasing regulation of fishing has significantly curtailed and ultimately displaced the traditional freedom of fishing. Through the grant of sovereign rights and various discretionary powers, the EEZ regime is firmly biased towards the interests of coastal States. This bias is reinforced by the dispute settlement provisions of the Convention, which

---

[211] Patrick Shavloske, "The Canadian-Spanish Fishing Dispute: A Template for Assessing the Inadequacies of the United Nations Convention on the Law of the Sea and a Clarion Call for Ratification of the New Fish Stock Treaty," 7 *Ind. Int'l & Comp. L. Rev.* 223, 237 (1996).

[212] David Freestone, "The Effective Conservation and Management of High Seas Living Resources: Towards a New Regime?," 5 *Canterbury L. Rev.* 341, 347 (1994). Oda has also criticized the duty of cooperation imposed by the Convention in that it "seems rather abstract, and there is no provision describing how it can be performed in a concrete way." Oda, "Fisheries," at 751.

largely insulate the decisions of the coastal State from review. According to Article 297(3), disputes concerning the interpretation or application of the provisions of the Convention with regard to fisheries are to be settled in accordance with Section 2 of Part XV. Article 297(3) then proceeds to list the exceptions to this basic position. The exceptions only relate to fishing in the EEZ:

[T]he coastal State shall not be obliged to accept the submission to such settlement of any dispute relating to its sovereign rights with respect to the living resources in the exclusive economic zone or their exercise, including its discretionary powers for determining the allowable catch, its harvesting capacity, the allocation of surpluses to other States and the terms and conditions established in its conservation and management laws and regulations.[213]

The discussion below examines the operation of the dispute settlement system in the Convention in respect of fishing in the EEZ, on the high seas, and in respect of stocks and species that move between these two maritime zones.

Resolution of Disputes Relating to Fishing in the EEZ

The restrictions on the availability of mandatory dispute settlement entailing binding decisions for fishing disputes pertain only to areas where States exercise sovereign rights, namely, the EEZ and the continental shelf. Except for the reference to sedentary species in relation to the regime of the continental shelf, the regulation of States' sovereign rights over fishing is dealt with as part of the EEZ regime. The limitations on dispute resolution pertain to both conservation and utilization of the living resources of the zone by the coastal State. In constructing this regime, the Convention clearly favors the rights of the coastal State over those of other users. Many of the legal obligations imposed on coastal States fall more in the category of guidelines for their behavior as so many decisions are left within the power of the coastal State.[214] Considerable discretion is thus granted to the coastal State: it has the power to determine the quantity of the allowable catch; to judge the amount it has the capacity to harvest; decides if there is a surplus and

---

[213] UNCLOS, art. 297(3)(a).

[214] Kwiatkowska, *Exclusive Economic Zone*, p. 48 ("the nature of guideline should be ascribed to all detailed provisions related to allowable catch, maximum sustainable yield and surplus-scheme established with a view to implementation of the principle of optimum utilization and consisting of determining a harvesting capacity of the coastal state and granting other states access to the surplus catch which the coastal state has declared to exist").

what should be done with it; and is further empowered to develop a specific regime to control and reinforce all of these decisions. It is clearly difficult to determine the content of a legal obligation and insist on its enforcement when the level of discretion incorporated into the norm permits so much flexibility of action and decision-making.[215] The dispute settlement mechanism in UNCLOS reinforces these decisions through the near-complete insulation of the coastal State's discretionary powers from review. States evidently did not consider third-party review of their decisions to be necessary as part of the international regulation of fisheries. Instead, many developing countries considered that the increase in maritime space under coastal State jurisdiction was accompanied by an increase in jurisdiction for their respective national courts.[216] National court control could be preferable since it would presumably be more sensitive to a country's interests in protecting its fishing industry and thus more inclined to uphold the discretionary decisions of the government compared with an international institution. The only counter-trend to be discerned is through prompt release proceedings under Article 292.

Dispute Settlement and the Discretionary Powers of the Coastal State
Many States resisted the possibility that their powers in the EEZ could be challenged externally once legal recognition of coastal State rights had been achieved.[217] Discretionary powers of the coastal State with respect to both conservation and utilization, namely, the determination of the allowable catch; harvesting capacity; allocation of surplus; and terms and conditions of conservation and management laws and regulations, are all excluded from the mandatory regime in Section 2 of Part XV. These categories of discretionary powers vested in the coastal State (which will be discussed immediately below) are not considered exhaustive but are merely examples of the types of disputes that are excluded from compulsory procedures entailing binding decisions. Even beyond these specifically mentioned issues, "any dispute" relating to the

---

[215] Developing countries preferred this flexibility since the adoption of an EEZ gives rise to problems due "to the lack of technological capacity and financial resources to exploit (harvest) resources in the zone, to carry out scientific research therein, and obtain the necessary facilities to control and prevent external encroachment in the zone." Hamisi S. Kibola, "A Note on Africa and the Exclusive Economic Zone," 16 *Ocean Dev. & Int'l L.* 369, 375 (1986).

[216] See Pierce, at 349.

[217] De Mestral, at 184. ("The substantive discretion is so broad and plenary that it is not easy to imagine a situation in which third states would have the right to question the exercise of the sovereign rights of the coastal state.")

coastal State's sovereign rights over the living resources is excluded from the procedures in Section 2 of Part XV. As such, the dispute settlement procedures reinforce the preference in favor of coastal States rather than provide an effective means to temper or control this power.

Allowable Catch

The coastal State is obligated to determine the allowable catch of living resources within its EEZ.[218] The determination of the allowable catch is required in order to ensure through proper conservation and management measures that the living resources are not endangered by over-exploitation. Burke considers that this obligation is vaguely worded and is thus unlikely to impose a significant burden on the coastal State.[219] The assessment of allowable catch is to be made by taking into account "the best scientific evidence available" to the coastal State.[220] Coastal States must also consider the effects on species associated with or dependent upon harvested species when taking conservation and management measures.[221] A subjective standard for determining measures is incorporated into the text as there is an acknowledgement that not all coastal States will have an equivalent amount of scientific evidence about particular stocks available to it. Developing States have generally not adopted the specific goals of the Convention in their domestic legislation on the basis that they lack the technology to obtain the necessary scientific evidence.[222] To cater for this situation, the Convention anticipates the involvement of the appropriate international organizations by requiring the contribution and exchange of available scientific information, catch and fishing effort statistics, and any other data relevant to the conservation of fish stocks.[223] Yet the coastal State remains free to judge the appropriate allowable catch, subject only to its obligation to promote optimal utilization, and its decision may not be challenged through compulsory arbitration or adjudication.

---

[218] UNCLOS, art. 61(1). The reference to "living resources" thereby incorporates both targeted stocks as well as incidental catch.

[219] William T. Burke, "The Law of the Sea Convention Provisions on Conditions of Access to Fisheries Subject to National Jurisdiction," 63 *Oregon L. Rev.* 73, 81 (1984).

[220] UNCLOS, art. 61(2). Burke asserts that the term "available" includes data and evidence from sources beside the coastal State – such as foreign fleets, international organizations and other States involved in the fisheries under management. Burke, "Conditions of Access," at 85.

[221] UNCLOS, art. 61(4).   [222] Attard, p. 155.   [223] UNCLOS, art. 61(5).

In determining the appropriate conservation measures of the living resources of the EEZ, coastal States are required to maintain or restore populations in order to produce "the maximum sustainable yield."[224] "The Convention does not define the [maximum sustainable yield], but it is a well-known concept and is described by the maximum amount of fish that can be taken on a sustained basis without diminishing the species' reproductive capacity or adversely affect associated or dependent species."[225] The maximum sustainable yield is qualified by relevant environmental and economic factors "including the economic needs of coastal fishing communities and the special requirements of developing States, and taking into account fishing patterns, the interdependence of stocks and any generally recommended international minimum standards."[226] In this respect, maximum sustainable yield has not only a quantitative character but also a qualitative character.[227] The latter aspect can be used by coastal States as a way to vary the allowable catch assessment: "the coastal State may maintain a level of population abundance, short of endangering the resource, that meets its interests as it determines those interests."[228]

The concept of maximum sustainable yield has been criticized since it is based on what is beneficial for humans rather than fish and the methods of calculating the maximum sustainable yield "rest on tenuous assumptions and data which is often incomplete or speculative."[229] Economists have also criticized the maximum sustainable yield formula as causing economic waste of fishery resources and weakness of international fishing regulations.[230] Further criticism has been directed at the scope of the concept for being too narrow and ignoring recent developments in fisheries management.[231] Yet the wording of the Convention is "sufficiently flexible to allow coastal States to do otherwise."[232] The "sufficiently flexible" content of the maximum sustainable yield concept effectively strengthens the scope of action for coastal States in managing its fish resources. The discretionary powers of the coastal State are further buttressed through the insulation from formal third-party review.

---

[224] *Ibid.*, art. 61(3).   [225] Kwiatkowska, *Exclusive Economic Zone*, p. 48.
[226] UNCLOS, art. 61(3).   [227] See Castañeda, p. 617.
[228] Burke, "Conditions of Access," at 83.   [229] Attard, p. 153.   [230] *Ibid.*
[231] A. W. Koers, The Fishing Provisions of the 1982 Convention on the Law of the Sea, in *Proceedings of a Seminar in Jakarta 1983* (1984), p. 112, cited in Kwiatkowska, *Exclusive Economic Zone*, p. 49.
[232] *Ibid.*

Harvesting Capacity

Article 62 provides that the coastal State must determine its capacity to harvest the living resources. The determination of a coastal State's harvesting capacity is within the discretion of that State and is exclusive and non-reviewable. As part of the harvesting capacity calculation, Article 62 stipulates that coastal States are to promote the objective of optimum utilization without prejudice to the conservation measures to be taken. If a coastal State does not have the capacity to harvest the entire allowable catch, then other States must be given access. Such a system guarantees the sovereign rights of the coastal State because it ensures that the coastal State is still entitled to benefit economically even if it lacks the physical means fully to exploit its resources. In determining whether a surplus exists, a coastal State could simply establish an allowable catch that is equivalent to its capacity to harvest and thereby exclude all foreign exploitation of living resources within its EEZ.[233] In this respect, Burke has stated that a right to a portion of the surplus is not meaningful and that "a right that is dependent on another's discretion does not deserve the label 'right'."[234] O'Connell has instead argued that while the right to determine capacity is an exclusive right, it is not entirely subjective because of the obligation to allocate the surplus among other States.[235] "The coastal State could hardly be allowed to say that there is no surplus when manifestly it does not have the capacity to harvest the entire allowable catch."[236] In this regard, the coastal State "ostensibly does not have the right to permit less than full utilization of its resources."[237] Yet any external determination of the coastal State's assessment of its harvesting capacity – even where there is a gross discrepancy between the quantity of fish typically found in the relevant area and the capacity and advancement of the fishing industry of the relevant State – is not available under UNCLOS. It is only when the decision of the coastal State is "arbitrary" that it can be referred to compulsory conciliation procedures.

Allocation of Surpluses

Although third States have a right to the surplus, there is neither a legal obligation on the part of the coastal State to grant access to its

---

[233] Pierce, at 338 (arguing that the coastal State is granted unqualified sovereignty).
[234] William T. Burke, "Implications for Fisheries Management of U.S. Acceptance of the 1982 Convention on the Law of the Sea," 89 Am. J. Int'l L. 792, 800 (1995).
[235] D. P. O'Connell, 1 The International Law of the Sea (I. A. Shearer ed., 1982), p. 563.
[236] Ibid.
[237] Francis T. Christy, Jr., "Transitions in the Management and Distribution of International Fisheries," 31 Int'l Org. 235, 249 (1977).

EEZ nor is there a corresponding legal right in third States to claim a right of access.[238] States are not required to determine their policies for the development and use of their fish resources against any obligation to grant access but rather against their obligation to ensure the conservation and optimum utilization of the living resources.[239] In practice, most States have allowed for third-State access to the living resources of the EEZ in domestic legislation but have varied on the conditions for fishing in the zone.[240] Each coastal State is free to introduce foreign capital to obtain technical assistance from foreign States as well as allow any third State to engage in fishing agreements through concessionary agreements and to secure the maximum of the total allowable catch for itself.[241] If any controversy over foreign fishing in the EEZ is likely to arise, it is thus more probable that the dispute would be in relation to the conditions for fishing rather than the question of access to the EEZ.

Developing States have taken advantage of the flexible standards in the Convention as a means of obtaining scientific evidence to enhance or develop their utilization of living resources in the EEZ. What has often happened is that developing States grant foreign access in exchange for fisheries data and statistics, as well as for various forms of compensation that can be used to develop conservation and management capabilities.[242] Developing States may further use the grant of access as a means of ensuring continued control over their living resources:

For most developing states lacking the economic assets to directly and immediately make use of the resources in their EEZ, the effectiveness of their management and control efforts in their fisheries is largely dependent on their ability to strategically allocate their surplus to other foreign countries. Coastal states use their "access" powers to negotiate with those states that possess the economic and technical resources to help them exploit their fisheries. This area is where there exists a divergence between apparent legal authority and actual control over the resources. Ultimately, the party better able to efficiently exploit the resources has the actual control over them. In the case of many developing

---

[238] Kwiatkowska, *Exclusive Economic Zone*, p. 15. See also Phillips, at 606.

[239] Kwiatkowska, *Exclusive Economic Zone*, p. 60.

[240] Orrego Vicuña, *Exclusive Economic Zone Regime*, p. 157.

[241] Oda, "Fisheries," at 744.

[242] Kwiatkowska, *Exclusive Economic Zone*, p. 63 (citing various examples of such an arrangement). The fee system has been criticized because the amount paid rarely corresponds to the value of the resources harvested. The preferable approaches are joint venture arrangements in cooperation with enterprises from industrialized States or multinational joint ventures between developing States in the same region. Kibola, at 378. "It is essential, therefore, that more and more emphasis is put on cooperation in training and the transfer of latest fishing technology to the fishermen in the poor countries." Anand, at 289.

countries, it would seem that the nation able to negotiate the best access agreements with economically powerful distant water fishing nations will, in the long run, assume greater control over its resources.[243]

The reality of the actual process of allocation might be that the discretionary powers of the coastal State are minimized to some extent in light of the superior negotiating position of the more economically developed States. Certainly, it could well be expected that coastal States would take a variety of factors into account, and not necessarily factors solely pertaining to fishing. O'Connell has noted as much:

> The obligation to give other States access to the surplus is stated in Article 62(2), but this is made subject to "agreements or other arrangements", and "pursuant to the terms, conditions and regulations" referred to in paragraph 4, which concern licensing, fees, and other matters. The negotiation of such agreements could raise issues of general political and economic relations affecting the duty of allocation. Some countries have included a paraphrase of the catalogue of grounds for allocation in their legislation, but have added to it the competence of the Minister to take into account "other relevant matters." That portends a policy of denying allocations to countries which do not reciprocate in other matters even if they fall within the catalogue . . . The fact that Article 62(3) authorizes the coastal State to take into account "its other national interests" in giving access to its EEZ lends more plausibility to this. The problem is further complicated by the fact that [the Convention] envisages joint ventures, which could give bargaining over participating rights preference over allocations of the surplus.[244]

It is certainly quite foreseeable that a coastal State would rely on political interests in determining access to fish in its zone.[245] The political nature of these decisions renders them largely unsuitable for third-party review through international courts and tribunals.

While UNCLOS imposes obligations on a State to establish allowable catch levels, its domestic harvesting capacity, and the surplus catch, there is no indication that other States should be allowed to participate in such a determination.[246] In determining how to allocate the surplus

---

[243] M. Johanne Picard, "International Law of Fisheries and Small Developing States: A Call for the Recognition of Regional Hegemony," 31 *Texas Int'l L. J.* 317, 323 (1996).

[244] O'Connell, 1 *International Law of the Sea*, p. 566–67.

[245] For example, the United States denied Soviet and Polish access to its EEZ following, respectively, the Soviet invasion of Afghanistan and the Polish government's crackdown against Solidarity. See Lawrence Juda, "The Exclusive Economic Zone: Compatibility of National Claims and the UN Convention on the Law of the Sea," 16 *Ocean Dev. & Int'l L.* 1, 25 (1986).

[246] See Attard, p. 165. See also Burke, "Conditions of Access," at 102.

fish stock, coastal States are required under the Convention to take certain factors into account. Article 62, paragraph 3 requires the coastal State to take into account:

all relevant factors including, *inter alia*, the significance of the living resources of the area to the economy of the coastal State concerned and its other national interests, the provisions of articles 69 and 70, the requirements of developing States in the subregion or region in harvesting part of the surplus and the need to minimize economic dislocation in States whose nationals have habitually fished in the zone or which have made substantial efforts in research and identification of stocks.

This obligation is an attempt to balance the discretion of the coastal State with the rights of other users.[247] The difficulty in this provision lies in assessing which of the factors is to take priority. Once again, the discretion of the coastal State has preeminence. It has been noted that various proposals at the Third Conference did suggest a priority of interests but no such indication was ultimately included and thus "[t]he omission by the drafters raised the question of whether a list of priorities was rejected in favour of a free and possibly unordered competition."[248] Indeed, one of the possible reasons for not stipulating preferences could be that many States envisaged trading the right of access against non-marine concessions.[249]

Terms and Conditions in Conservation and Management
Laws and Regulations
Article 62, paragraph 4 permits the coastal State to establish laws and regulations, consistent with the Convention, relating to fishing by

---

[247] One group of States to be considered in the allocation process is landlocked and geographically disadvantaged States. This group of States had advocated during negotiations that the determination of the coastal State's harvesting capacity should include a reserve to meet the needs of the coastal State as well as its neighboring land-locked or geographically disadvantaged States. See Phillips, at 585 (describing a proposal submitted by Afghanistan, Austria, and Nepal). However, the rights of land-locked and geographically disadvantaged States are subject to the discretionary powers of the coastal State. Burke, "Conditions of Access," at 97. "Any actual participation by [landlocked and geographically disadvantaged States] is by agreement among the states concerned, again underlining that coastal states have the dominant decision-making position." Burke, "Implications for Fisheries Management," at 800. Little benefit is given to land-locked and geographically disadvantaged States in favor of other users.

[248] Attard, p. 167.

[249] *Ibid.*, p. 168. Christy agrees that the problem of distribution can only be resolved through negotiation, particularly by trading off one item of value for another. Christy, at 258.

nationals of third States in its EEZ. Beyond being consistent with the Convention, the nature of the terms and conditions is solely the decision of the coastal State. UNCLOS provides an inclusive list of topics to which these laws may relate. It has been suggested that the coastal State's power of regulation should be exercised in a reasonable manner in accordance with the duty to act with due regard for the rights and duties of other States.[250] Such an obligation would be a small concession in light of coastal States' resistance to any check on their powers through third-party review of allocation of fishing resources within the zone.[251] "The coastal State's authority to vary these conditions underscores the State's total control over access."[252]

Most typically, access to a coastal State's zone involves a system of licensing. Cooperation with a coastal State for scientific research into management and conservation of stocks of mutual concern as well as the condition of reciprocity are characteristic features of licensing systems.[253] Over 150 bilateral agreements have been concluded in the last twenty-five years providing for collaboration and cooperation between fishing activities in the EEZ, prescribing the terms and conditions under which the fishing vessels of one party may operate in waters under the EEZ of the other, or granting reciprocal fishing rights to vessels of both parties in their respective zones of jurisdiction.[254] The system of licensing may work to the disadvantage of some developing States as it is not necessarily a guarantee of adequate financial return compared with the value of the resources being taken from the coastal State's zone. Difficulties are compounded in regions of developing coastal States:

The nearby developing states will constantly compete among each other in their efforts to attract buyers for these licenses, and this competitive pressure undermines the negotiation leverage of any one state. Without strong regional cooperation in license price-fixing between these coastal states, there is a built-in incentive for them to compete and lower the prices to unprofitable levels.[255]

---

[250] Phillips, at 604.

[251] Ibid., at 605 (noting that coastal States "strenuously criticized" a proposal by European nations advocating a settlement procedure for this issue).

[252] Burke, "Conditions of Access," at 93.

[253] Kwiatkowska, Exclusive Economic Zone, p. 68. Picard notes that coastal States usually seek direct financial benefits, fishery development assistance, and general development assistance in access agreements. Picard, at 324–25.

[254] Anand, at 285.   [255] Picard, at 326.

UNCLOS does not impose any restraints or obligations on States in this regard, nor permit any differences to be submitted to compulsory procedures entailing a binding decision. Instead, States negotiating the Convention anticipated that the matter would continue to be resolved on a bilateral, or regional, basis.

Conclusion

Decisions on how much fish can be harvested from a coastal State's EEZ, who can fish when and according to what conditions are thus excepted from compulsory and binding dispute settlement. "Articles 61 and 62 are unequivocal in establishing the exclusivity of coastal State decision making authority, and article 297 both reinforces this exclusive authority and confirms the fact that decision making criteria are solely for the coastal State to determine in any specific instance."[256] Although coastal States have certain guidelines set out in the Convention, decisions relating to the exploitation, conservation, and management of the living resources of the EEZ are predominantly subjective and non-reviewable. Beyond national laws and regulations, coastal States will negotiate bilateral and regional agreements and potentially utilize these arrangements for technical or scientific information or economic benefits in other matters. If these separate agreements do not have their own dispute settlement procedures, States will typically rely on traditional consent-based methods of dispute resolution.[257] At most, a State wishing to fish in the EEZ of a coastal State may utilize conciliation as an external review process for limited categories of decisions.

Compulsory Conciliation for EEZ Fisheries Disputes

Article 297(3) provides that certain fisheries disputes relating to the sovereign rights of coastal States can be submitted to compulsory conciliation.[258] Settlement of fishing disputes must first be attempted in accordance with Section 1 of Part XV prior to the matter being submitted to conciliation under Annex V, Section 2. Article 297(3) specifies which disputes will be subject to compulsory conciliation rather than just submitting any dispute that falls within the terms of the exception. Conciliation can only be used when it is alleged that:

---

[256] Burke, "Conditions of Access," at 117.
[257] It is unlikely that decisions taken under the provisions of UNCLOS relating to harvesting capacity, maximum sustainable yield, and allocation would be justiciable in national courts.
[258] UNCLOS, art. 297(3)(b).

i) a coastal State has manifestly failed to comply with its obligations to ensure through proper conservation and management measures that the maintenance of the living resources in that exclusive economic zone is not seriously endangered;

ii) a coastal State has arbitrarily refused to determine, at the request of another State, the allowable catch and its capacity to harvest its living resources with respect to stocks which that other State is interested in fishing; or

iii) a coastal State has arbitrarily refused to allocate to any State, under articles 62, 69 and 70 and under the terms and conditions established by the coastal State consistent with this Convention, the whole or part of the surplus it has declared to exist.[259]

These three sorts of disputes may be broad enough to encompass disputes that would otherwise fall within the exception to submission of fisheries disputes to compulsory dispute settlement. However, the conciliation procedure under Article 297 has been structured "precisely to avoid the control and legal review of sovereign acts of the coastal State."[260] It is thus unsurprising that the conciliation formula received "widespread and substantial support."[261] Burke has concluded, "there is only a remote possibility that the conciliation process would ever be successfully invoked by a party and no possibility whatsoever that a conciliation commission could require a change in U.S. allocation policy."[262]

In determining the potential effectiveness of a conciliation procedure, it is evident that reference to States "manifestly" failing or "seriously" or "arbitrarily" refusing third States allows for subjective interpretations.[263] A State could, for example, argue that measures reasonably designed to promote the local harvesting industry are not inconsistent with UNCLOS and that the adoption and implementation of these measures would not amount to an "arbitrary refusal to allocate."[264] Such a determination is

---

[259] Ibid., art. 297(3)(b).   [260] Orrego Vicuña, Exclusive Economic Zone Regime, p. 130.

[261] Bernard H. Oxman, "The Third United Nations Conference on the Law of the Sea: The Seventh Session (1978)," 73 Am. J. Int'l L. 1, 19 (1979).

[262] Burke, "Implications for Fisheries Management," at 798.

[263] Shabtai Rosenne, "Settlement of Fisheries Disputes in the Exclusive Economic Zone," 73 Am. J. Int'l L. 89, 99 (1979); Singh, p. 138. Gamble argues that conciliation could be avoided if the coastal State is determined to do so. Gamble, "Binding Dispute Settlement?," at 50.

[264] Burke, "Implications for Fisheries Management," at 797 (arguing that the contention that conciliation proceedings would undesirably affect United States' decision-making is without serious foundation).

clearly biased and a matter within the discretion of the coastal State. Moreover, "because there are solid economic and environmental reasons for refusing to find a surplus, it is not an abuse of discretion to find the harvesting capacity is equal to the allowable catch."[265] Measures intended to promote local fishing industries that are consistent with the Convention are unlikely to be construed as an "arbitrary refusal to allocate."[266] Certain extreme conditions would need to be in effect to expect a conciliation commission to have jurisdiction. An example might be a State prohibiting any fishing of any stock for an indefinite period of time. These conditions are not indefensible, however. Even Oda has argued that terms such as "allowable catch," "capacity to harvest," and "surplus" are ambiguous and could be extremely difficult to implement.[267]

Assuming jurisdiction could be established, the impact of a conciliation process on State behavior is difficult to gauge. The process is limited because the conciliation commission may not substitute its discretion for that of the coastal State.[268] Moreover, the type of fisheries disputes to be referred to conciliation is specified in the Convention itself, rather than the procedure being available for all disputes excepted from arbitration or adjudication.[269] These limitations are then reinforced by the express stipulation in the Convention that the recommendations of the conciliation commission are not binding. The question of effectiveness ultimately revolves around the possible impact of any political pressure that could be derived from the recommendations of the commission. "Such political pressures as may be associated with conciliation proceedings, and this suggestion is speculative, may be expected to have varying weight depending on the nature of the recommendations, the parties to the dispute, and the general political context."[270]

Conciliation was nonetheless the best compromise that could be reached. Clearly the wide scope of powers accorded to the coastal State over living resources in the EEZ leaves opens the possibility of abuse where a State may neglect to follow the provisions relating to optimal

---

[265] Ibid., at 796.   [266] Ibid., at 797.
[267] Oda, "Fisheries," at 742–51.   [268] UNCLOS, art. 297(3)(c).
[269] A. D. Adede, The System for Settlement of Disputes Under the United Nations Convention on the Law of the Sea (1987), pp. 255–56.
[270] Burke, "Implications for Fisheries Management," at 797. Burke doubts that the United States would retreat from a particular policy because of an adverse, non-binding, recommendation by the conciliation commission. Ibid., at 798.

utilization, maximum sustainable yield, harvesting capacity, and allo-cations of surplus. To prevent certain arbitrary, serious, or manifest violations of these provisions, States included compulsory conciliation as an external source of review. Through conciliation, some impact is inevitable since the coastal State is at least required to pay part of the costs of the conciliation proceedings and it cannot prevent the comple-tion of the proceedings by refusing to participate.[271] There is no bar to the proceedings if the parties fail to reply to notification of institu-tion of proceedings or fail to submit to the proceedings.[272] The question of whether any recommendation could ever be enforced in the case of a default proceeding would again rest on political exigencies or other pressures that may be brought to bear. By insulating coastal State discre-tion and accepting the use of non-binding recommendations, the risk of third-party decisions being entirely ignored and thereby rendered redundant is reduced. The benefits of this process rest in the politically persuasive value of the recommendation. A State may opt to ignore a conciliation commission recommendation in furtherance of its own fish-ing policies. Otherwise, a State could conceive that it is in its interests to follow the recommendations of the commission as it is more likely to retain a good reputation in future negotiations over fishing capacity and access.

Disputes Relating to the Enforcement of Fisheries Laws and Regulations in the EEZ

If disputes arise between parties concerning measures taken by the coastal State for the enforcement of its laws and regulations relating to the exercise of its sovereign rights to explore, exploit, conserve, and manage the living resources in the EEZ and have not been resolved under Section 1 of Part XV, the matter can be referred to Section 2 of Part XV. The only exception to the availability of mandatory juris-diction, which will be considered further in Chapter 4, is where States have opted to exclude this type of law-enforcement dispute in accor-dance with Article 298 of the Convention.[273] Coastal States may board, inspect, arrest, and institute judicial proceedings against vessels found in violation of fishing laws and regulations.[274] In these circumstances,

---

[271] Burke, "Conditions of Access," at 90–91.   [272] UNCLOS, Annex V, art. 12.
[273] See further pp. 308–311.   [274] UNCLOS, art. 73(1).

disagreements over the exercise of this enforcement jurisdiction are more appropriately settled in the national courts of the coastal State.

Where a coastal State does not promptly release arrested vessels and their crews upon payment of a reasonable bond or other security,[275] the flag State may institute proceedings before ITLOS in accordance with Article 292. As discussed in Chapter 2, the Tribunal will take the coastal State's laws into account in assessing what constitutes a reasonable bond. Through this process, an assessment, albeit an indirect one, is made of coastal State laws. Although the Tribunal is not to address the merits of a case, to the extent that the Tribunal formulates an international standard for the prescription of bonds for arrested vessels and their crews, decisions that had formerly been the exclusive domain of national legislatures and courts have become part of an international process. This transfer of authority poses a rare constraint on coastal States' exercise of sovereign rights over living resources in the EEZ.

Conclusion

The role of international dispute settlement in the regulation of the exploitation, conservation, and management of the living resources of the EEZ is extremely limited. States are required to follow the rules of the Convention pertaining to optimal utilization, harvesting capacity, allocation of surplus, and so forth but the exact content of these decisions is dependent on the particular conditions of the coastal State and the relevant fish stock. A range of considerations can be taken into account in the course of the exercise of sovereign rights and these are within the discretionary power of the coastal State. Compulsory procedures entailing binding decisions were not necessary in this system. States have emphasized their national interests in the regulation of living resources in the EEZ and have most typically opted for bilateral or regional arrangements when dealing with States wishing to fish in their zone. International courts and tribunals are not perceived as having a role in this process. It is only when States have manifestly failed to comply with conservation and management obligations or arbitrarily refused to determine allowable catch, harvesting capacities, and allocation of surplus that external review is available. In such instances of gross violations of the Convention, the aggrieved State can refer the matter to conciliation. The use of conciliation allows for the continued insulation

[275] *Ibid.*, art. 73(2).

of the coastal State's discretion and does not create binding obligations on States. The only value of conciliation is to be found in the moral suasiveness of a recommendation in the diplomatic relations of the States concerned in resolving their differences. If the coastal State considers that the stakes are high, then the recommendations of the commission are likely to have significantly less effect and any differences can only be resolved through political means between the relevant States. The only third-party influence likely to impact on a coastal State's exercise of sovereign rights over its living resources may be through review of its enforcement activities – either because law enforcement activities were not selected for exclusion under Article 298 or indirectly through the prompt release proceedings in accordance with Article 292.

Resolution of Disputes Relating to Fishing on the High Seas

Fishing on the high seas is no longer governed by the *laissez-faire* policies inherent in the *mare liberum* philosophy of the past, but must now be conducted in accordance with certain obligations of cooperation and conservation through flag State control.[276] The duties of cooperation and conservation permit States a wide degree of action and incorporate flexible and subjective standards.[277]

With respect to conservation obligations, a wide scope of action is possible because only the flag State of the individual fishing vessel has the right to govern the activities of that vessel on the high seas. There is no provision in UNCLOS for one high seas fishing State to take action on the high seas to enforce a conservation obligation owed to it by another State.[278] The authority of the flag State to determine what measures it considers necessary for conservation can only be questioned under the dispute settlement system of the Convention (or through a separate international institution to which the State is a party). It is for this reason that Oda doubts the utility of mandatory procedures entailing binding decisions. He argues that there is no incentive for

---

[276] UNCLOS, arts. 117–19. Article 116 of UNCLOS further subjects the right to fish on the high seas to other treaty obligations and duties concerning straddling stock, highly migratory species, and catadromous and anadromous species.

[277] The only exception in this regard is the requirement that the conservation measures, whatever they might be, not discriminate in form or in fact against the fishermen of any State. See UNCLOS, art. 119(3).

[278] Edward L. Miles and William T. Burke, "Pressures on the United Nations Convention on the Law of the Sea of 1982 Arising from New Fisheries Conflicts," 20 *Ocean Dev. & Int'l L.* 343, 351 (1989) (also noting that no such obligation exists under customary international law either). See also Oda, "Fisheries," at 749.

States to refer a matter to a third-party mechanism to determine joint conservation measures where the lack of any binding determination permits States to continue to fish on the high seas without restriction.[279] Such an approach would countenance the view that the freedom of fishing on the high seas has not been altered in any way by the Convention, or by customary international law. It is non-controversial that conservation measures are now essential to ensure the continued existence of the long-distance fishing industry. Mandatory jurisdiction over disputes relating to fishing on the high seas provides an important avenue to indicate precisely what measures States are required to take.[280] In this instance, a special arbitral tribunal constituted under Annex VIII may be particularly well suited to this role in light of the technical or scientific expertise of the tribunal members.

Also contrary to Oda's assertion about the lack of incentive of a State in resorting to compulsory dispute settlement is the fact that the coastal State adjacent to the relevant high seas area is likely to have a greater interest in ensuring the conservation and management of the living resources of the high seas if many of its nationals are engaged in fishing that area. The compulsory resolution of high seas fisheries disputes could be a way of ensuring that over-fishing does not occur in waters adjacent to a coastal State's EEZ.[281] The coastal State may wish to rely on compulsory dispute settlement, or the threat of compulsory dispute settlement, as a means of protecting its interests. A further impetus for the resort to impartial third-party settlement is the possibility of avoiding lengthy disputes that cause significant economic and political loss through the failure to institute sufficient management controls.

With respect to the obligation to cooperate, States have great flexibility in deciding what action is sufficient to amount to cooperation since there is no determinate standard in the Convention by which that action can be measured. The difficulty in determining what the duty to cooperate actually involves was evident in the *Southern Bluefin Tuna* case. Japan took the view that it could not be in breach of its duty to cooperate simply by reason of the fact that the parties to the CCSBT had not at that point reached agreement as a result of their negotiations.[282] The

---

[279] Oda, "Fisheries," at 753.

[280] As discussed in Chapter 2, courts and tribunals also have the power to set fish catch totals on high seas fishing in prescribing provisional measures that bind the parties pending the resolution of a dispute. See notes 232–38 and accompanying text.

[281] Colson, 654. See also Burke, "Implications for Fisheries Management," at 803.

[282] Southern Bluefin Tuna, Japan's Memorial, para. 80.

Applicants contended that the duty of cooperation was not an abstract concept but had a clear objective of ensuring conservation and promoting the aim of optimum utilization.[283] While there can be no doubting the objective of cooperative measures, what actions are actually required remains unclear.[284]

Once fishing on the high seas is challenged through compulsory dispute settlement procedures, courts and tribunals are vested with broad power to determine what the appropriate standard is required to meet conservation and management goals. In this respect, UNCLOS transfers authority from States to international processes. The use of international processes to achieve cooperative goals is hardly novel for high seas fisheries. Such arrangements are necessary to attain conservation and allocation goals precisely because no single State has authority over the high seas.[285] This transfer of authority is more typically instituted in international organizations, rather than third-party dispute settlement, however. Examples of such international regimes include the Convention on the Conservation of Antarctic Marine Living Resources, 1980 as well as the International Convention for the High Seas Fisheries of the North Pacific Ocean, 1952, which is between the United States, Japan, and Canada. These organizations can be used to gather relevant scientific information in order to determine the best conservation measures to obtain the maximum sustainable yield for all the interested parties. Through these arrangements, the obligations under UNCLOS are given effect.[286] A result of establishing international organizations to regulate high seas fishing may be the exclusion of compulsory jurisdiction in Part XV of UNCLOS if the relevant States decide on alternative dispute settlement procedures in these separate agreements that come within the terms of Article 281. The *Southern Bluefin Tuna* case is an example of this situation.[287] Australia, New Zealand, and Japan had concluded the CCSBT to ensure the conservation and management of southern

---

[283] Southern Bluefin Tuna, Applicants' Reply, para. 110.

[284] Australia and New Zealand's arguments with respect to the duty of cooperation under Article 118 were similarly ambiguous. See *ibid.*, para. 56.

[285] Burke, *New International Law of Fisheries*, p. 88.

[286] UNCLOS anticipates the establishment and role of such international organizations.

[287] Southern Bluefin Tuna, Jurisdiction. Oxman has argued that this decision should be limited as a precedent on the basis that compulsory dispute settlement is the preferred method for resolving high seas fishing disputes and would promote the comprehensive coverage of Part XV of UNCLOS. Oxman, "Complementary Agreements," at 285–87 and 291–95.

bluefin tuna on the high seas. The majority of the Tribunal concluded that Article 16 of the CCSBT excluded recourse to the compulsory procedures in UNCLOS since the terms of Article 16 were intended to prevent disputes relating to the CCSBT from being included in the UNCLOS mechanism.[288] The rationale for this decision was that:

> To hold that disputes implicating obligations under both UNCLOS and an implementing treaty such as the [CCSBT] – as such disputes typically may – must be brought within the reach of section 2 of Part XV of UNCLOS would be effectively to deprive of substantial effect the dispute settlement provisions of those implementing agreements which prescribe dispute resolution by means of the parties' choice.[289]

If there are alternative means available to States to fulfill their obligations to cooperate in the conservation of the living resources of the high seas, mandatory dispute settlement under UNCLOS is not essential. The prevailing point is that the content of the duty to cooperate is to be determined through an international process controlled by third-party decision-making under UNCLOS unless States take actual steps to implement their obligations of conservation and management through a separate agreement.

While separate international institutions or the Convention's third-party procedures are indispensable to determine what measures should be taken to cooperate and to obtain conservation goals, there is no certainty that States will either join the relevant organization or comply with these decisions. Even if some fishing States do manage to reach agreement on the allocation of fish catch totals, their efforts may be thwarted by new entrants that do not submit to these arrangements.[290] This situation becomes particularly acute when vessels fly under the flag of a State that does not typically enforce fishing obligations. The problem of flags of convenience and the practice of reflagging could be challenged through the dispute settlement mechanism in UNCLOS to the extent that those actions affect States parties' obligations to cooperate to ensure conservation objections. Yet enforcement difficulties would clearly persist. On this basis, the limitations of international processes, and the extent of the contribution that compulsory dispute settlement can make to the legal regime of high seas fishing, remain apparent.

---

[288] Southern Bluefin Tuna, Jurisdiction, para. 57.   [289] *Ibid.*, para. 63.
[290] Burke, *New International Law of Fisheries*, pp. 89–90.

Resolution of Disputes Relating to Fisheries Occurring Across EEZs or Between an EEZ and the High Seas

The need for cooperative measures in order to achieve conservation objectives is particularly acute when dealing with stocks or species of fish that occur in more than one EEZ or in the EEZ of a coastal State and the high seas. "Most of the more intractable fisheries disputes occur because the stocks in question straddle two or more EEZs, or straddle the EEZ and the high seas."[291] This issue has been especially problematic because of the interests of the coastal State competing with those States that have long-distance fishing industries that fish the area or stock in question. In other words, the exclusive interests of the coastal State in exploiting and conserving the living resources of the EEZ compete with the inclusive interests of third States fishing on the high seas, subject only to obligations of cooperation and conservation. Neither conservation nor allocation objectives can usually be met through the independent action of one State. Instead, some sort of multilateral action is required.

While the Third Conference may have potentially offered a forum or prescribed a process for resolving these issues, the obligations imposed on States in UNCLOS for these fisheries are mostly exhortations to cooperate without specific standards or guidelines for decision-making processes. Christy has suggested several causes for the lack of attention to this problem during negotiations:

First, it may be that the problems of shared stocks are not fully appreciated by delegates who are not knowledgeable about fisheries and whose attentions are focused on the apparent immediate gains of extended jurisdictions. Second, the likely outcome of raising the issues of shared stocks is not at all clear. Both the states in regions of shared fisheries . . . and those outside these regions and that might be excluded . . . may feel they have more to lose by opening up the problems in an international arena than by dealing with them on a regional basis after the conference. And third, the complexity of the problems and the disparity in regional situations make it difficult to address the issues in the United Nations Conference.[292]

Clearly, if conservation goals are to be met, an arrangement between the relevantly affected States is necessary in this regard. Not only does

---

[291] Alan E. Boyle, "Problems of Compulsory Jurisdiction and the Settlement of Disputes Relating to Straddling Fish Stocks," 14 *Int'l J. Marine & Coastal L.* 1, 12 (1999).
[292] Christy, at 252–53.

this arrangement have to specify a system for determinations of catch allocation but methods for compliance with and enforcement of that system would also be required. Are compulsory dispute settlement procedures a necessary element of this regime? The Convention provides only a framework for the resolution of these issues. Moreover, there is considerable ambiguity as to whether the constricted system created for disputes over fisheries in the EEZ applies or whether the more comprehensive dispute settlement regime for high seas fisheries should control. These issues are considered below with respect to straddling stocks and highly migratory species and then with respect to anadromous and catadromous species.

Straddling Stock and Highly Migratory Species
Straddling stock and highly migratory species are now subject to two multilateral conventional regimes in addition to regional or bilateral agreements. The discussion below addresses the two multilateral regimes, which, in one instance, largely avoids many of the complex issues that arise with respect to this stock and species and, in the other instance, sets out a detailed regulatory regime.

Regulation under UNCLOS
Article 63 of the Convention addresses the problem of stocks occurring within the EEZ of two or more States or stocks that occur within the EEZ of a coastal State and in an area beyond and adjacent to it. UNCLOS simply specifies that States should seek to agree upon the measures necessary to coordinate and ensure the conservation and development of such stocks. This obligation "cannot fairly be described as very consequential."[293] The usual practice has been for neighboring coastal States to acknowledge their joint responsibility and seek an agreement on conservation and management of such stocks in conformity with the Convention.[294] Generally, "the advantages of joint management and agreed sharing of transboundary stocks . . . are so evident that in the long term neighbouring countries are almost bound to reach a settlement."[295]

---

[293] Burke, "Conditions of Access," at 106. See also Freestone, at 345 (citing the International Law Association's EEZ Committee as describing the provision as a minimalist solution).

[294] Kwiatkowska, *Exclusive Economic Zone*, p. 78.

[295] P. Copes, "The Impact of UNCLOS III on Management of the World's Fisheries," 5 *Mar. Pol'y* 217, 221 (1981).

Nonetheless, a number of disputes have arisen in respect of these types of species. "For international law purposes, the question is whether a sovereign can reach beyond its territories into the high seas for the purposes of protecting that sovereign's environment, or more cynically, its economy."[296]

States are also required to cooperate in the harvesting of highly migratory species under Article 64. The Convention sets out in Annex I what species are considered as "highly migratory species." These species are subject to coastal State authority in the EEZ but cooperation with other States fishing in the region is required. This cooperation is to be undertaken "with a view to ensuring conservation and promoting the objective of optimum utilization of such species throughout the region, both within and beyond the exclusive economic zone."[297] All States involved in the harvesting of highly migratory species are required to cooperate through international organizations in order to promote the optimum utilization of these species. If there is no preexisting international organization then States are to cooperate to establish such an organization and participate in its work. Unlike the provisions dealing with straddling stocks, the other provisions relating to the EEZ in Part V of the Convention are to apply with respect to highly migratory species.[298] On this basis, it could seem that greater coastal State control is authorized for highly migratory species than for straddling stocks. This emphasis could impact on the decision-making process for these species, including decisions by international courts and tribunals as to whether they have jurisdiction under Article 297.

UNCLOS on its own is insufficient to provide a normative framework for the regulation of these stocks and species. Multilateral cooperative efforts are required if both coastal and other States are to ensure adequate conservation and management of both straddling stocks and highly migratory species. To establish an effective multilateral organization, the relevant body should have control over the entire migratory range of the fish stocks; all States fishing the stocks must be part of the organization and there must be an effective allocation procedure among all fishing interests.[299] Moreover, the organization must be able to enforce the measures that are prescribed.[300] One State acting alone in restraining catch for conservation goals does so at short-term economic peril:

---

[296] Shavloske, at 233.   [297] UNCLOS, art. 64(1).
[298] Ibid., art. 64(2).   [299] Picard, at 332.   [300] Ibid.

Unless there is some type of effective coordination in conservation efforts between neighboring states, fishermen have no incentive to adhere to national conservation measures and restrain their catches in the interest of future return from the fishery, for what is not fished by one state today may be taken by others in the waters of the neighboring state.[301]

No one State has the authority to prescribe and enforce conservation measures for high seas areas unless there is agreement between all the States concerned. If multilateral agreements cannot be reached between these States, a coastal State may well face domestic pressure to extend its authority beyond the boundaries of the EEZ.[302] For these reasons, various regional or area-specific agreements have been reached to deal with straddling stocks – often at the instigation of the coastal State closest to the relevant high seas area.[303]

Fish Stocks Agreement
Efforts to identify and assess problems related to the conservation and management of straddling fish stocks and highly migratory species as well as the means of improving fisheries cooperation among States were initiated at a conference in 1992 under the auspices of the UN.[304] The work of this conference resulted in the adoption of the Agreement for the Implementation of the Provisions of the United Nations Convention on the Law of the Sea Relating to the Conservation and Management of Straddling Fish Stocks and Highly Migratory Fish Stocks ("Fish Stocks

---

[301] *Ibid.*, at 329.
[302] Barbara Kwiatkowska, "The High Seas Fisheries Regime: at a Point of No Return?," 8 *Int'l J. Marine & Coastal L.* 327, 337 (1993). The alternative to regional arrangements has been the proclamation of a "presential sea," a Chilean initiative. This concept involves coastal State participation in and surveillance of third-State activity in adjacent high seas areas. It also entitles the coastal State to undertake economic activities in the high seas that promote its national development as well as ensure that other activities do not harm this development. Only Chile has adopted this policy, and it has been met by protests from Belgium, France, and Spain. See *ibid.*, at 340–41. The presential sea concept thus provides an alternative approach to multilateral cooperation in a particular maritime area but is not yet an accepted concept in the law of the sea.
[303] State practice has tended to ensure that measures applicable to the high seas are consistent with those adopted by the coastal States in the EEZ. *Ibid.*, at 333 (referring to the "consistency rule" in a number of regional fisheries conventions).
[304] The United Nations Conference on Straddling Fish Stocks and Highly Migratory Fish Stocks was established by General Assembly Resolution 47/192 on December 22, 1992. See GA Res. 192, UN GAOR, 47th Sess., available at http://www.un.org/documents/ga/res/47/a47r192.htm.

Agreement" or "FSA") in 1995.[305] The objective of the FSA is "to ensure the long-term conservation and sustainable use of straddling fish stocks and highly migratory fish stocks through effective implementation of the relevant provisions of the Convention."[306]

The Fish Stocks Agreement applies primarily to the conservation and management of straddling and highly migratory stocks on the high seas.[307] "Attempts by coastal states to admit recognition of extended coastal state jurisdiction for the purpose of protecting (i.e. 'conserving') straddling stocks were rejected."[308] Only obligations under Articles 6 and 7, concerning the precautionary approach and compatible measures respectively, are applicable to both the high seas and the EEZ. Under Article 7, States must ensure compatibility between measures adopted for the high seas and those adopted for areas under national jurisdiction.

Part III of the Fish Stocks Agreement sets out a range of mechanisms to ensure compliance with conservation and management obligations. The FSA relies on the creation of regional organizations and provides that only States that are members of regional fisheries organizations or that agree to be bound by the conservation measures adopted by those organizations may fish in the relevant areas or for the relevant stocks. A number of the FSA provisions are intended to facilitate the establishment and functioning of these cooperative regimes.[309] To encourage participation in these regional organizations or cooperative arrangements, non-members may not authorize their national vessels to fish in areas subject to the organization's regime, but are under an obligation to cooperate in conservation and management efforts.[310] The onus is placed on flag States to introduce necessary measures to control their national vessels through licensing, record-keeping, marking vessels and gear, reporting fish catch, and other monitoring and surveillance techniques.[311] Flag

---

[305] The FSA is intended to implement the duties to cooperate set out in UNCLOS, and is to be "interpreted and applied in the context of and in a manner consistent with" UNCLOS. See FSA, art. 4. However, unlike the 1994 Agreement on Part XI of UNCLOS, becoming party to the FSA does not mean that State becomes party to UNCLOS at the same time, or vice versa.

[306] FSA, art. 2.

[307] Ibid., art. 3(1). General principles for the conservation and management of straddling and highly migratory fish stocks are set out in Article 5 of the FSA.

[308] Christopher C. Joyner, "Compliance and Enforcement in New International Fisheries Law," 12 Temp. Int'l & Comp. L.J. 271, 290 (1998).

[309] See FSA, arts. 8–16. These provisions are reinforced by specific duties relating to cooperation in enforcement. See ibid., arts. 20–21.

[310] Ibid., art. 17.   [311] Ibid., art. 18.

States are obliged to undertake a range of actions to ensure that their national vessels comply with regional conservation and management measures, and, if a member of a regional organization, have certain rights of inspection over other members, as well as non-members where those non-members are party to the FSA.[312] The Fish Stocks Agreement thus provides greater detail about the standards to which States should be held in their efforts to regulate fishing of straddling stock and highly migratory species. Although not binding on non-parties, it provides an indication of the appropriate international standards to be applied.

Dispute Settlement

The potential role for compulsory dispute settlement is obscure under both UNCLOS and the FSA. If States fail to reach agreement over the utilization and conservation of straddling stocks and highly migratory species, or in their efforts to form the appropriate organization for these activities, there may be an impetus for States to seek external review through the compulsory procedures available under the FSA or the Convention. Typically, States have not resorted to arbitration or adjudication in deciding on measures to regulate the stocks and species concerned. This avenue may, however, provide States with additional leverage in the negotiating process and potentially speed up the formulation of a cooperative mechanism.[313] In these respects, compulsory dispute settlement could have an essential role in enabling States to fulfil their obligations under the Convention and the FSA. Alternatively, the political risks involved in such a process (a State refusing to take part in the judicial or arbitral process and/or non-compliance with an award) could indicate that these legal rules are best formulated through diplomatic avenues and only consent-based methods of dispute settlement are appropriate.

Article 297 of UNCLOS allows for fishing disputes to be subject to the compulsory dispute settlement mechanism in Part XV and then sets out certain exceptions with respect to areas subject to the sovereign rights of the coastal State. There is no explicit provision addressing the issue of disputes over stocks or species occurring in both the high seas and the EEZ. A coalition of States at the Third Conference introduced a compromise proposal towards the end of the negotiations that attempted to link the failure to agree on conservation measures over straddling stocks with

---

[312] *Ibid.*, arts. 21–22.
[313] Ted L. McDorman, "The Dispute Settlement Regime of the Straddling and Highly Migratory Fish Stocks Convention," *Canadian Y.B. Int'l L.* 57, 62 (1997).

the compulsory dispute settlement provisions, thereby allowing ITLOS to determine the necessary measures.[314] However, distant-water fishing States resisted such a proposal and it was withdrawn by the sponsors.[315]

The dispute settlement mechanism in the FSA is then similar to UNCLOS. Part VIII of the FSA was based on the Part XV system in UNCLOS and includes a mandatory obligation to settle disputes by peaceful means and further stipulates that if no agreement can be reached on compatibility of conservation and management measures, then any of the relevant States may bring the issue to binding and compulsory dispute settlement. Part VIII of the FSA provides that the dispute settlement provisions of Part XV of UNCLOS apply *mutatis mutandis* to the FSA.[316] This arrangement allows for States Parties to utilize the same choice of procedure as selected under Article 287 of UNCLOS and States not party to UNCLOS may still choose one of the means set out in Article 287 as well. As with UNCLOS, the emphasis remains on States' free choice in selecting dispute settlement techniques and Article 28 of the FSA provides that States are to cooperate to avoid disputes. "Unilateral compulsory settlement is therefore again a residual measure of last resort."[317]

The scope of disputes subject to mandatory jurisdiction under the FSA is broader than UNCLOS in that it is not only available for disputes concerning the interpretation and application of the FSA but also for "any dispute concerning the conservation and management of such stocks."[318] The stocks in question are those that straddle the EEZ and the high seas, and not those that are shared across several zones.[319] However,

---

[314] Australia, Canada, Cape Verde, Iceland, Philippines, Sao Tome and Principe, Senegal and Sierra Leone: amendment to article 63, UN Doc. A/CONF.62/L.114, *reprinted in* 16 *Third United Nations Conference on the Law of the Sea: Official Records*, at 224, UN Sales No. E.84.V.2.

[315] See Miles and Burke, at 344.

[316] FSA, art. 30. Provisional measures are also available under the Fish Stocks Agreement by virtue of Article 31(2).

[317] Boyle, "Straddling Fish Stocks," at 20.

[318] FSA, art. 30(2). The inclusion of existing treaties within the scope of jurisdiction is reinforced by Article 30(5), which requires that the law to be applied in all disputes arising under the FSA or any other fishery treaty is UNCLOS, the FSA, any relevant regional, subregional, or global fisheries agreement, "as well as generally accepted standards for the conservation and management of living marine resources and other rules of international law not incompatible with the Convention."

[319] Boyle, "Straddling Fish Stocks," at 20. Boyle further states that Articles 5, 6, and 7 of the FSA, which are applicable to coastal States, are not subject to compulsory dispute settlement if properly characterized as involving the exercise of sovereign rights. *Ibid.*, at 21. *But see* Tullio Treves, "The Settlement of Disputes According to the Straddling Stocks Agreement of 1995," in *International Law and Sustainable Development*

the ambiguity as to the limitations of dispute settlement under the Convention (as to whether the restrictions for EEZ fishing disputes apply or not) is not resolved by the FSA. Under the heading "Limitations on applicability of procedures for the settlement of disputes," the FSA provides that Article 297(3) of the Convention also applies to the Fish Stocks Agreement.[320] As Articles 6 and 7 apply to both the EEZ and the high seas, the same questions as to the availability of mandatory jurisdiction thus arise with respect to the FSA as with respect to UNCLOS.

With no definite resolution of this question in the Convention or the Fish Stocks Agreement, commentators have reached different conclusions on the applicability of Section 2 of Part XV to these stocks. At one end of the spectrum, the particular interest of the coastal State has led some commentators to suggest that the limitations on dispute settlement pertaining to fishing in the EEZ should apply to fishing for stocks and species located in more than one EEZ or between the zones and the high seas.[321] With respect to the problem of straddling stocks, Orrega Vicuña argues that the limitations from Article 297 should apply equally since in relation to highly migratory species, catadromous and anadromous stocks, the Convention recognizes the coastal State's interest beyond the EEZ.[322] A degree of primacy in the management and conservation of straddling stocks could be implied to coastal States, it is argued, since these States are more likely to be motivated to preserve the straddling stock resources than a distant fishing State.[323] On this basis, disputes arising over straddling stock would be assimilated to disputes over the living resources of the EEZ and subjected to the same dispute resolution regime, namely, no compulsory or binding decision process at all. Burke notes that the coastal State does retain a dominant position since Article 116 makes the freedom of fishing on the high seas subject to provisions establishing coastal State rights, duties, and interests in the EEZ.[324] However, he does not argue that as a consequence,

(Alan Boyle and David Freestone eds, 1999), pp. 253, 259 (arguing that disputes concerning art. 7(4) may be referred to compulsory settlement).

[320] FSA, art. 32.

[321] See, e.g., Kwiatkowska, "First Award," at 276 (Article 297(3) "presumably applies as much to straddling and highly migratory stocks as to other fisheries, despite the fact that the coastal state's sovereign rights over the former stocks are inseparable from the high seas fishing for those stocks").

[322] Orrego Vicuña, *Exclusive Economic Zone Regime*, p. 131.

[323] Will Martin, "Fisheries Conservation and Management of Straddling Stocks and Highly Migratory Stocks under the UN Convention on the Law of the Sea," 7 *Geo. Int'l Envtl. L. Rev.* 765, 766 (1995).

[324] Burke, "Conditions of Access," at 113.

the limitations of compulsory dispute settlement relative to the EEZ also apply to high seas fisheries.[325] Boyle has suggested that in a conflict involving straddling stocks or highly migratory species, the disputant parties would have to agree separately on a forum for resolution or the high seas issues would have to be separated and submitted to compulsory settlement.[326] He notes, however, that agreeing on a forum may prove difficult and that fragmenting the dispute neglects dealing with it comprehensively and would probably fail in its effectiveness for that reason.[327] Boyle has also argued that the exception in Article 297(3) should be read narrowly to maintain the balance of interests in the Convention and in the FSA, "in the interests of equitable access to justice, and the effective management and sustainable use of straddling stocks."[328] At the other end of the spectrum, Rosenne has stated that because the scope of Article 297 is strictly limited to the EEZ, fisheries disputes relating to maritime spaces seaward of the outer limit of the EEZ would appear to come within the scope of the compulsory dispute settlement provisions.[329]

A court or tribunal faced with this question would need to consider certain features of State practice relating to the role ascribed to dispute settlement in the normative regulation of this issue area. It is noteworthy that States have not typically included mandatory dispute settlement provisions in their regional or multilateral arrangements dealing with the allocation and conservation of straddling stock and highly migratory species. Third-party dispute settlement has only been used with the agreement of the States concerned in a small number of cases.[330] Instead, States have preferred traditional methods of dispute resolution, such as negotiation or consent-based adjudication or arbitration when dealing with the regulation of this fishing activity.[331] When regional or

---

[325] *Ibid.*, at 114–15 and 118.   [326] Boyle, "Dispute Settlement," at 43.
[327] *Ibid.*   [328] Boyle, "Straddling Fish Stocks," at 25.
[329] Rosenne, "Settlement of Fisheries Disputes," at 98. See also Miles and Burke, at 352.
[330] One such example is *La Bretagne Arbitration* between Canada and France. See Filleting within the Gulf of St Lawrence between Canada and France (1986), 19 UN Rep. Int'l Arbitral Awards 225. Several maritime boundary cases have taken fisheries and/or fishing practice into account in allocating maritime space. See, e.g., Delimitation of the Maritime Boundary in the Gulf of Maine Area (*Canada* v. *United States*), 1984 ICJ 246 (October 12); Maritime Delimitation in the Area between Greenland and Jan Mayen (*Denmark* v. *Norway*), 1993 ICJ 38 (June 14). As a counter-example, the ICJ decided a case concerning the cod wars between Iceland and Britain even though Iceland did not participate in the proceedings. See Icelandic Fisheries.
[331] "[I]f past practice is a guide, states will be reluctant to make use of formal, binding third-party dispute settlement or other modes of formal dispute settlement and will prefer to rely on direct negotiations to heal rifts." McDorman, at 59.

multilateral organizations are formed, the treaties involved do not typically impose mandatory dispute settlement procedures on the participants.[332] The formulation of these regimes inevitably involves a range of concessions between competing interests, and could well be influenced by the power dynamic of the relevant participants. Furthermore, various problems of enforcement inevitably arise.[333] Many problems exist in the cooperative regimes developed by States, particularly because of the presence of States that are not participants in the regime and prefer immediate profit rather than long-term gain. A variety of factors are likely to come into play with respect to the enforceability of legal rules relating to fisheries:

The willingness of governments to obey international fishery rules can be affected by persuasion, inducement, or intimidation. The decision by a government to comply with a norm can be determined by that state's perceptions of how its national interests will be affected, irrespective of whether the incentive comes from opportunities or inducement, enforcement, sanctions or dispute settlement.[334]

States are relying on mutual benefits where incentives to cheat on the system are potentially reduced through availability of information. Participant States also rely on the reputational aspects involved in an ongoing arrangement and the accessibility of a forum for adjusting allocations in light of changing situations. Third-party intervention through an adversarial model would not seem to have a role here.[335]

---

[332] McDorman notes that the lack of dispute settlement processes has long been a criticism of regional fisheries management organizations such as the North Atlantic Fisheries Organization. *Ibid.*, at 67. The FSA stands in contrast in this regard.

[333] Christy writes:
> The difficulty of relinquishing national authority in favor of a regional agency is greatest with regard to the function of enforcement. The vital importance of the function lies in the fact that agreements over shared fisheries are fundamentally unstable. Once one state believes (rightly or wrongly) that another state is not abiding by the agreement, it loses all incentives to respect the agreement itself and the fishery will collapse to the point where all net benefits have been dissipated. There are no economic or other forces that will automatically impede or prevent the collapse since there is no stable equilibrium except at the point where no one stands to gain any net benefits.

Christy, at 264. See also Joyner, at 281–82 ("concerns over sovereign interests have made states reluctant to transfer substantial enforcement authority to international bodies and their secretariats").

[334] Joyner, at 280.

[335] Indeed, the FSA indicates that States should improve the decision-making procedures of regional organizations as a way of avoiding disputes. See McDorman, at 64.

If States do not rely on action through international organizations, could mandatory dispute settlement provide a new means to regulate State behavior in this regard? While third-party dispute settlement will not alleviate all compliance and enforcement issues in this problematic area, this avenue should enhance States' efforts in fulfilling their international obligations in fishing these stocks and species. Such a perspective is reinforced when the respective roles for dispute settlement in high seas and EEZ fishing regimes are recalled. The high seas fishing provisions rely on the availability of third-party procedures to elaborate on the content of obligations relating to cooperation and conservation. These same obligations are paramount with respect to highly migratory species and straddling stocks. Further, compulsory procedures entailing binding decisions for high seas fishing disputes would only be displaced in the event that States had formed international arrangements that incorporated a separate dispute settlement mechanism and would thus be applicable in accordance with Section 1 of Part XV. A similar emphasis on formation of separate agreements is found in UNCLOS for highly migratory species and straddling stock. The FSA is a prime example of an agreement specifically constructed to implement the Convention's obligations.[336] Finally, coastal State interests in fishing stocks that are found beyond their own EEZ must now be balanced with the interests of other States fishing these stocks and species. As such, complete insulation of coastal State decision-making is no longer appropriate in the face of inclusive interests of other States. The discretionary power of the coastal State is not the preeminent factor at stake here. Instead, mandatory jurisdiction may provide a check on coastal State power in this regard.[337] For these reasons, a court or tribunal would be justified in determining that it has jurisdiction under UNCLOS to resolve disputes relating to highly migratory species and straddling stock.

Catadromous and Anadromous Species
Catadromous and anadromous species provide a particular challenge to inter-State cooperation as they involve species of fish that can be severely

---

[336] The detailed regulations and heavy reliance on the operation of cooperative arrangements and regional organizations may have obviated the need for mandatory dispute settlement in the FSA. The Fish Stocks Agreement entered into force on December 11, 2001. It remains to be seen what use is made of its dispute settlement procedure.

[337] It must be acknowledged, however, that the need for mandatory dispute settlement as a check on the power of coastal States has been predominantly utilized to protect navigational interests, not fishing interests.

affected by the actions of one State while still being a shared resource with another State. Catadromous species are those fish that descend a river to spawn in the oceans whereas anadromous species proceed from the sea into rivers in order to spawn. It is the State in which the river is located that has the greater control over the conservation and utilization of these species and this situation calls for specific rules for the management of these species:

Because of the direct dependence of these species on the actions of individual states, these species require separate and special treatment in the law of the sea. If these stocks can be harvested freely and fully on the high seas by foreign states, then there is no incentive for the host states to invest in actions or programs that would enhance yields. The host states must be assured of satisfactory returns on their investments.[338]

For anadromous species, Article 66 grants the primary interest in and responsibility to States in whose rivers these stocks originate. The States of origin have the responsibility to take the appropriate conservation measures and to establish allowable catches after consultation with States that also fish the stock. Fishing of anadromous stock must take place within the EEZ unless it would result in the economic dislocation of another State.[339] The enforcement of regulations relating to anadromous stocks beyond the EEZ must be agreed upon between the State of origin and other concerned States.[340] Burke takes the view that if the relevant States fail to reach agreement, the coastal State could insist upon the termination of fishing of these species on the high seas and prescribe regulations that would apply in high seas areas.[341] In this case, "the best regime would be one that prohibits such fishing entirely, achieved by establishing an allowable catch of zero."[342]

As the fishing of anadromous species potentially occurs in both the EEZ and on the high seas, there is again ambiguity as to whether compulsory procedures entailing binding decisions are available in the event of disputes over the interpretation and application of the Convention. Burke clearly contemplates that these sorts of disputes would be subject to compulsory settlement.[343] The use of third-party review may provide

---

[338] Christy, at 255.   [339] UNCLOS, art. 66.   [340] *Ibid.*, art. 66(3)(d).

[341] Burke, "Implications for Fisheries Management," at 801.   [342] *Ibid.*

[343] "Any attempt to initiate a fishery targeting North Pacific Salmon would be a violation of the LOS Treaty. A dispute over whether the treaty allows such harvesting could be settled by the dispute settlement process in the treaty and there is no reason to doubt how that would turn out for any state foolhardy enough to attempt such a fishery." *Ibid.*, at 803.

a necessary control for States that have a historic interest in the species that is being denied by the coastal State. An international process may also delineate the terms and conditions for fishing beyond the EEZ while still giving due regard to the conservation requirements and needs of the State of origin. While compulsory dispute settlement could thus play an essential role in the maintenance of the normative regime created in the Convention for anadromous species, any decision would have to take due account of the preeminent role accorded to the coastal State in respect of these species. This favored position of the coastal State is relevant for interpreting the substantive principles, however, not to deny the existence of mandatory jurisdiction.

Priority is also accorded to the coastal State with respect to catadromous species. "A coastal State in whose waters catadromous species spend the greater part of their life cycle shall have responsibility for the management of these species and shall ensure the ingress and egress of migrating fish."[344] The Convention again limits the areas where these species can be fished by stipulating that harvesting must be conducted in the EEZ only. Harvesting is then to occur in accordance with the provisions of the Convention concerning fishing in the EEZ.[345] If the stock migrates through the zones of two or more States then those States must form an agreement for the management of the species in order to ensure its maintenance.[346]

As the fishing of catadromous species would occur only in the EEZ of a coastal State, disputes as to the harvesting of these species would fall within the limitations of Article 297(3). As catadromous species must be harvested within the EEZ and the Convention further specifies that fishing of these species is subject to other provisions of UNCLOS concerning EEZ fisheries,[347] a textual analysis suggests that the restrictions on dispute settlement for fishing of living resources within the EEZ would be applicable. If the stock is not located in the waters of another State and no protection of historic interests was considered necessary, then the discretionary decisions of the coastal State are insulated from third-party review under the Convention. The situation would be different when catadromous species migrate through the zones of other States and agreement between concerned States becomes necessary. It would then seem that the considerations attributable to dispute settlement for highly migratory species and straddling stock should be applicable for

---

[344] UNCLOS, art. 67(1).   [345] Ibid., art. 67(2).
[346] Ibid., art. 67(3).   [347] Ibid., art. 67(2).

these migrating catadromous species as well and thus tend in favor of inclusion of these disputes within mandatory jurisdiction.

Conclusion

Future decisions on jurisdiction by international tribunals and courts will determine how narrowly or broadly the exception in Article 297(3) will be drawn. The dispute settlement procedures reinforce the exclusive authority of the coastal State in the EEZ, rather than act as any control. So much is evident from Article 297(3): the limited avenues for conciliation; and the complete insulation of the coastal State's discretionary exercise of power from third-party review. Such an approach is appropriate since the majority of fisheries disputes may well be species or area specific. Further, these disputes could involve questions of a scientific nature or relate to essentially political decisions, rather than legal questions of interpretation and application. As Collier and Lowe have explained:

> The essence of such disputes would not be legal: there is relatively little room for argument over what the treaty obligations are. Rather it would concern the propriety of the State's exercise of discretion in determining the total allowable catch, its own harvesting capacity, and hence the surplus available to third States. Those are, clearly, matters requiring the expert interpretation of scientific evidence.[348]

The Convention clearly acknowledges the role that scientific and political considerations will play in the regulation of various fisheries in different EEZs and accordingly recognizes the preeminent position of the coastal State in this regard. Mandatory arbitration or adjudication does not have an essential role to play. Courts and tribunals should well be cautious in asserting jurisdiction in cases that run counter to this balance – overly ambitious interpretations of the scope of jurisdiction for third-party review could minimize the likelihood of compliance with decisions.

By comparison, regulation of fishing on the high seas under UNCLOS is far from detailed and negotiating States clearly anticipated that the practice of separate agreements would, and should, continue. These separate agreements can then include specific dispute settlement procedures. Otherwise, the compulsory procedures available under UNCLOS will perform the necessary role of elaborating on the duties imposed on States in their conservation efforts on the high seas.

[348] Collier and Lowe, p. 86.

For straddling stocks and highly migratory species, the basic provisions of the Convention have been implemented through the FSA. However, ambiguities persist with respect to the availability of mandatory jurisdiction for resolution of these disputes. Efforts at conservation have been hampered in assorted multilateral efforts undertaken thus far. The potential exists for third-party dispute settlement to maintain the balance of interests between coastal States and other fishing States. Such a solution could break an impasse in negotiations. Even the prospect of this process being resorted to by one of the States in dispute may prove sufficient in affecting State behavior. Whether these factors are enough to overcome problems of enforcement remains to be seen.

Marine Scientific Research

Marine scientific research has generally been considered as one of the freedoms of the high seas.[349] The utilization of scientific information has been essential since the start of the twentieth century for such activities as drawing up conventions on fisheries allocation and conservation as well as formulating control levels for pollution from ships. "The major contributions of marine scientific research include the acquisition of knowledge and development of understanding about the marine environment, its characteristics, properties and processes."[350] Marine scientific research has come to be regarded as a powerful tool for States because of the value that may be derived from this information for conservation purposes, military purposes, and, most importantly, for the exploitation of maritime resources. Developing States quickly recognized that marine scientific research was typically an activity undertaken by the wealthier, more technologically advanced States and that significant economic benefits could accrue with this knowledge. Developing coastal

---

[349] Such a view was taken during the formulation of the High Seas Convention at the First Conference. Only an implicit reference to scientific research was included in Article 2, which is not an exclusive list of high seas freedoms but allows for other general principles of international law to be incorporated amongst the assorted freedoms of the high seas. The International Law Commission intended such an inclusive approach and noted that the freedom to conduct scientific research would be another freedom. Report of the International Law Commission to the General Assembly, UN GAOR at 278, UN Doc. A/3159 (1956), reprinted in *ILC Yearbook*, (1956), vol. II.

[350] William T. Burke, *International Law of the Sea: Documents and Notes* (1995), p. 6. Marine scientific research has been defined as "any study or related experimental work designed to increase man's knowledge of the marine environment." Alfred H. A. Soons, *Marine Scientific Research and the Law of the Sea* (1982), p. 5.

States feared that if marine scientific research was undertaken by industrialized States to gather information for resource exploitation, then these States would be in an even stronger bargaining position during negotiations for concession contracts and other resource-related licenses.

Consequently, during negotiations at the Third Conference (and as had been foreshadowed at the First Conference), coastal States sought greater control over and involvement in marine scientific research activity, particularly in the EEZ and on the continental shelf. These interests were recognized through the inclusion of provisions on general goals to be achieved in respect of marine scientific research as well as specific details as to what conditions research would be subjected. The balance in the Convention is clearly in favor of coastal States over researching States and international organizations, and protection of the latter's interests is not very significant. The substantive provisions that deal with marine scientific research are summarized below. The discussion then turns to the role of dispute settlement in relation to these rules. Coastal State control is significantly reinforced by virtue of the exceptions incorporated into Article 297 and the use of compulsory conciliation as an alternative. The value of compulsory dispute settlement for researching States is minimal by comparison. As such, the limitations imposed through Article 297 raise questions about how effectively the normative regime relating to marine scientific research will function.

Regulation of the Freedom to Conduct Marine Scientific Research under UNCLOS

The provisions relating to marine scientific research are primarily located in Part XIII of the Convention.[351] Under UNCLOS, all States and competent international organizations enjoy the general right to conduct marine scientific research, subject to the rights and duties granted to other States in the Convention.[352] States and competent international organizations must promote and facilitate the development and conduct of marine scientific research in accordance with the Convention.[353] The duty to promote marine scientific research has been considered as implying certain obligations of cooperation as an "important means of realization of a just and equitable economic order in general, and the crucial means of implementation of the new EEZ regime in particular."[354]

---

[351] UNCLOS, arts. 238–65. See also *ibid.*, arts. 21(1)(g), 40, 56(1)(b)(ii), 143, 266, 275, 276, and 277.
[352] *Ibid.*, art. 238.   [353] *Ibid.*, art. 239.
[354] Kwiatkowska, *Exclusive Economic Zone*, p. 137.

Separate duties of cooperation are included in the Convention – including sharing information, creating favorable conditions for research, and integrating scientists' efforts, as well as the publication and dissemination of information, scientific data, and knowledge resulting from research.[355] Marine scientific research must be conducted exclusively for peaceful purposes; with appropriate scientific methods and means; not unjustifiably interfere with other legitimate uses of the oceans and be respected in the course of those uses; and be conducted in conformity with obligations for the protection and preservation of the marine environment.[356]

The Convention also sets out specific conditions in relation to the regulation, authorization, and conduct of marine scientific research in areas subject to coastal State sovereignty or jurisdiction. The express consent of the coastal State is required for research in the territorial sea of that State.[357] The conduct of research or survey activities during the course of passage through the territorial sea could be prejudicial to the peace, good order, or security of the coastal State thus negating the innocence of passage.[358] Instead, the coastal State may regulate innocent passage in respect of marine scientific research and hydrographic surveys.[359] Scientific research and hydrographic survey ships require prior authorization of States bordering on straits to carry out research or survey activities during transit passage.[360]

The issues raised with respect to marine scientific research in the EEZ and continental shelf were foreshadowed at the time States were codifying the freedoms of the high seas at the First Conference. There was already sensitivity to the impact such an explicit designation could have on coastal State control over the exploration and exploitation of the continental shelf. More attention was thus drawn to the question of marine scientific research for situations where the prospect of that research had the potential to threaten coastal State control over resources located in water areas adjacent to the territorial sea.[361] During the negotiations at the First Conference, the decisive role of the coastal State was emphasized.[362] Indonesia submitted a proposal on scientific research that required the consent of the coastal State for any such research.[363]

---

[355] UNCLOS, arts. 242–44.   [356] Ibid., art. 240.   [357] Ibid., art. 245.
[358] See ibid., art. 19(1) and (2)(j).   [359] Ibid., art. 21(1)(g).   [360] Ibid., art. 40.
[361] Such concern was never necessary over research in territorial waters as that maritime zone is subject to the sovereignty of the coastal State.
[362] See, e.g., First Conference, 4th Comm., at 28, ¶ 12 (United Arab Republic).
[363] Indonesia: Proposal, UN Doc. A/CONF.13/C.4/L.53, reprinted in ibid., at 140.

France modified this absolute requirement by specifying the circumstances by which States could not normally withhold their consent to scientific research.[364] The text had to find a compromise between two important aims: "first, that there must be no obstacle to bona fide scientific research and, secondly, that the coastal State must be protected against other activities that might be conducted under the guise of scientific research."[365] The text included in the Continental Shelf Convention provides that the consent of the coastal State is required for research by a qualified institution for purely scientific research and that this consent should not normally be withheld.[366]

Similar difficulties over the question of consent arose during the Third Conference.[367] By insisting on coastal State permission for marine scientific research, developing States considered that they would gain greater control over the research for their own political and economic development:

Claims to that end have been advanced in particular by the developing coastal states, which felt that all research generated knowledge on the availability of natural resources and which were apprehensive of the possible military repercussions of marine research. Since those states lack the technical and financial capabilities necessary to make use of the traditional freedom of scientific research, and regard a strong control over such research as a source of political strength and economic development, they advocated the absolute consent regime which could easily lead to complete elimination of the freedom of scientific research within the EEZ and on the [continental shelf].[368]

The compromise position reached during negotiations was the utilization of a combined absolute consent system for certain specified research projects whereas other research would be subject to qualified consent. Article 246 thus provides that marine scientific research in the EEZ and on the continental shelf must be conducted with the consent of the coastal State but that State must grant consent "in normal circumstances." Coastal States may, however, withhold consent at its discretion with respect to specific types of research projects.[369] The Convention also

---

[364] *Ibid.*, at 84, ¶ 2 (France).   [365] *Ibid.*, at 87, ¶ 24 (Iran).

[366] Continental Shelf Convention, art. 5(8).

[367] Soons, *Marine Scientific Research*, pp. 160–63.

[368] Kwiatkowska, *Exclusive Economic Zone*, p. 135. Kwiatkowska also considers that a culture of refusing permission for marine scientific research in the area adjacent to the territorial sea was borne of the fact that the First and Second Conferences failed to agree on a set breadth of the territorial sea. *Ibid.*, at 135. See also Phillips, at 595–96.

[369] UNCLOS, art. 246(5).

sets out the situations for which the consent of the coastal State may be implied.[370]

In addition to the consent requirements for marine scientific research in the EEZ and on the continental shelf, there is an obligation imposed on researching States and international organizations to provide the coastal State with certain information about the project.[371] Researching States and competent international organizations must further adhere to various conditions concerning participation and sharing of research data and results.[372] The Convention also addresses the legal status, deployment, and use of scientific research installations or equipment.[373] Once research is initiated, the coastal State has continuing control and is entitled to suspend or require cessation of marine scientific research activities if those activities are not in conformity with the project to which the coastal State consented or if there is a failure to comply with the provisions granting rights to the coastal State.[374] Although UNCLOS covers a range of issues, most States simply make general reference to marine scientific research in their EEZ legislation, if at all, rather than specifying the type of detail that is included in the Convention.[375] This practice persists even though Article 263 attributes responsibility to States and international organizations to ensure that marine scientific research is conducted in accordance with the Convention. The Convention further specifies that these actors are responsible for measures in contravention of the Convention and for damage caused by pollution arising out of research activities. If a dispute arises, then research activities cannot commence or continue without the express consent of the coastal State pending the settlement of a dispute under Part XV of UNCLOS.[376]

Compulsory Settlement of Disputes Relating to Marine Scientific Research

Article 264 of Part XIII provides that disputes concerning the interpretation or application of the Convention with regard to marine scientific research shall be settled in accordance with Part XV, Sections 2 and 3.[377] Earlier drafts of what is now Article 297 in Section 3 of Part XV did not

---

[370] *Ibid.*, art. 252.   [371] *Ibid.*, art. 248.
[372] *Ibid.*, art. 249.   [373] *Ibid.*, arts. 258–62.   [374] *Ibid.*, art. 253.
[375] Kwiatkowska, *Exclusive Economic Zone*, p. 147.   [376] UNCLOS, art. 265.
[377] Although Article 246 does not refer specifically to Section 1 of Part XV, Article 286 incorporates recourse to Section 1 for the applicability of the procedures available in Section 2 of Part XV.

distinguish between disputes relating to the marine environment and marine scientific research.[378] Instead, disputes concerning marine scientific research were subject to compulsory dispute settlement entailing binding decisions "when the coastal state had allegedly acted in contravention of specified international standards or criteria for the conduct of marine scientific research which were applicable to the coastal state."[379] This article was subsequently reformulated to provide that the compulsory dispute settlement procedure applies, with two exceptions, to the interpretation and application of the provisions relating to marine scientific research.[380]

As it stands, Article 297 more accurately reflects the compromise achieved in the substantive provisions. The majority of marine scientific research disputes will be referred to mandatory dispute settlement as a means of controlling coastal State authority over this inclusive use of the oceans. The potential utility of compulsory proceedings entailing a binding decision for the majority of marine scientific research disputes may be lessened because of the minor nature of the violation versus the costs of international judicial or arbitral proceedings and because of the scope of the exceptions to mandatory jurisdiction. Compulsory dispute settlement entailing binding decisions is not available with respect to research in the coastal State's EEZ or continental shelf in accordance with Article 246 or for decisions by a coastal State to order suspension or cessation of a research project. The scope of these exceptions has a considerable impact on the conduct of marine scientific research in a large expanse of water and favors the coastal States over those States and international organizations conducting marine research. The substantive rules that would require the coastal State to grant consent in normal circumstances for marine scientific research projects in the EEZ and on the continental shelf and that ensure that consent will not be delayed or denied unreasonably provide the researching State with some leverage over the coastal State.[381] However, this leverage is effectively undermined in the dispute settlement provisions of Part XV.

Marine Scientific Research Disputes Subject to Compulsory Dispute Settlement

Except for disputes arising in relation to the interpretation and application of Articles 246 and 253, all differences relating to marine scientific

---

[378] See Singh, p. 135; 5 *United Nations Convention on the Law of the Sea 1982: A Commentary*, pp. 97 *et seq.* (both describing the drafting history).
[379] See Singh, p. 135.   [380] UNCLOS, art. 297(2)(a).   [381] Roach, at 787.

research are subject to the procedures set out in Section 2 of Part XV. As Article 264 provides that disputes concerning the interpretation and application of provisions of UNCLOS with respect to marine scientific research shall be referred to Part XV, regard must also be had to provisions on marine scientific research that are found in the Convention, besides those in Part XIII. For example, Article 21 provides that the coastal State may adopt laws and regulations relating to innocent passage through the territorial sea in respect of marine scientific research and hydrographic surveys. By virtue of Article 264, disputes over the interpretation or application of this provision can be settled through the compulsory dispute settlement regime. Article 264 also encompasses the prohibition on research activities by foreign ships during transit passage through straits[382] and marine scientific research conducted in the Area if that research does not fall within the scope of "activities in the Area." "Activities in the Area" means all activities of exploration for, and exploitation of, the resources of the Area.[383] In that event, the dispute would fall within the exclusive jurisdiction of the Seabed Disputes Chamber of ITLOS.[384]

The substantive provisions on marine scientific research in Part XIII tend to reflect the preferences of coastal States in light of the many conditions imposed on researching States and international organizations. The burden is placed on States and international organizations conducting the research to share all results with the coastal State and even to allow the coastal State to participate or be represented in the particular project. The resulting obstacles that the researching States or organizations may confront are quickly summarized:

Delays in responding to requests for ship clearances; last minute denial of permission to conduct research; requiring all data, regardless of format, be provided immediately prior to departure from last port of call; requiring the data to be provided within a fixed time after leaving the coastal state's waters, rather than after completion of the cruise; requiring copies of data collected in international waters, or in waters under another country's jurisdiction; requiring data to be held in confidence and not placed into the public domain; requiring the cruise reports to be submitted in languages other than English; requiring more than one observer to be on board; requiring the observer to be on board during non-research legs of a voyage; requiring research and port call requests to be submitted other than through the Foreign Ministry; Foreign Ministry's failing to forward cruise reports to cognizant organization; finally, slow or incomplete staffing or coordination among interested coastal state bureaucracies.[385]

---

[382] UNCLOS, art. 40.   [383] Ibid., art. 1(3).
[384] Ibid., art. 187 and Annex VI, arts. 35–40.   [385] Roach, at 786.

When considering the range of difficulties that researching States and organizations may face in their research efforts, it may well seem that mandatory dispute settlement has a vital role to play in ensuring the proper interpretation and application of the substantive rules of UNC-LOS. Compulsory dispute settlement could be used to keep in check coastal State power over research activities to maintain a consistent international standard. Birnie argues that third-party interpretation is also necessary since many of the terms used are either ambiguous or opaque as a result of the political compromises necessary to achieve consensus.[386] The existence of possible third-party intervention may persuade coastal States to adhere to the standards in the Convention. Certainly without external avenues of review, coastal States have less impetus to adhere to the conditions of the Convention when violations may enable them to acquire additional knowledge from the research projects.

Yet for the conflicts that may arise over issues relating to the publication and dissemination of the objectives and results of research,[387] the sharing of all results with the coastal States or the participation of the coastal States,[388] resort to international judicial or arbitral settlement following the failure of negotiations or other peaceful methods may not be a realistic option. As a practical matter, the necessity of mandatory procedures entailing binding decisions is lessened when the resolution of a minor dispute becomes an expensive and laborious process before an international court or tribunal. If the level of interference is sufficiently grave, represents a consistent pattern of violations, or the interests at stake are generally important enough, then mandatory arbitral or adjudicative proceedings may provide the researching States and organizations with enough power to restrain the otherwise unchecked authority of the coastal State in controlling marine scientific research in the EEZ or on the continental shelf. In these particular situations, the need for compulsory dispute settlement again becomes evident.

Exclusion of Compulsory Dispute Settlement for Marine Scientific Research Conducted in the EEZ or on the Continental Shelf

Compulsory arbitration or adjudication is not available for conflicts concerning "the exercise by the coastal State of a right or discretion in accordance with article 246."[389] Article 246 grants to coastal States the

---

[386] Birnie, at 248.   [387] UNCLOS, art. 244.
[388] *Ibid.*, art. 249.   [389] *Ibid.*, art. 297(2)(a).

right to regulate, authorize, and conduct marine scientific research in their EEZ or on their continental shelf according to the terms of the Convention. Article 246 further subjects the right of all States to conduct marine scientific research in the EEZ and on the continental shelf to the consent of the relevant coastal State.[390] Coastal States are not to withhold their consent for research "in normal circumstances."[391] Soons considers that the Convention thus establishes the grant of consent as the norm and a requirement is imposed on the coastal State to explain its refusal if it deviates from the norm in refusing consent.[392] This balance indicates that the coastal State decision is not entirely subjective. The question then arises as to whether that explanation could be challenged through mandatory procedures entailing binding decisions. Does the coastal State have the sole right to determine whether normal circumstances exist? "Normal circumstances" could relate to a variety of situations entailing economic, political, and security factors that would not be relevant to the terms or activities of the actual research project. The sole express qualification on the discretion is that the absence of diplomatic relations does not necessarily preclude "normal circumstances."[393] In this situation, a challenge to the grant of consent could not be submitted to a third party for binding decision. At most, a conciliation commission could determine whether normal circumstances exist as a matter of fact but this determination would not necessarily require that consent for the relevant project be granted.

For the projects specified in paragraph 5 of Article 246, States are entitled to withhold their consent at their discretion. The types of projects subjected to discretionary consent include those relating to the exploration and exploitation of natural resources, activities involving drilling, or the introduction of harmful substances into the marine environment as well as projects involving artificial islands, installations, and structures.[394] The discretion then relates to the decision whether or not to

---

[390] *Ibid.*, art. 246(2). At the Third Conference, land-locked and geographically disadvantaged States unsuccessfully asserted a right to conduct marine scientific research in the EEZ of neighboring coastal States without that State's consent. See Phillips, at 612.

[391] UNCLOS, art. 246(3) and (4).

[392] Soons, *Marine Scientific Research*, p. 167.   [393] UNCLOS, art. 246(4).

[394] Article 246(5) reads:

> Coastal States may however in their discretion withhold their consent to the conduct of a marine scientific research project of another State or competent international organization in the exclusive economic zone or on the continental shelf of the coastal State if that project:

grant consent; not whether a particular project falls within the scope of paragraph 5.[395] A researching State or organization could thus dispute the characterization of a project as one falling under paragraph 5 through Section 2 of Part XV. The right of the coastal State that cannot be challenged through submission to a third party for binding decision is whether it will grant consent or not. Coastal State interests are well recognized through the variety of conditions that can be imposed and the inclusion of categories of research that are subject to discretionary consent. Mandatory jurisdiction could have been necessary to ensure that the substantive rights accorded for research in the EEZ or on the continental shelf are not abused to the detriment of the researching States. The exclusions in Article 297 undermine this balance and will decrease the likelihood of the Convention successfully regulating State behavior in this regard.

An interesting situation for dispute resolution may arise where marine scientific research activities in the EEZ or on the continental shelf interfere with the coastal State's exercise of jurisdiction. Under Article 246(8), research activities must not "unjustifiably interfere with activities undertaken by coastal states in the exercise of their sovereign rights and jurisdiction provided for in this Convention." Although this provision again indicates the primacy granted to the coastal State, no specific remedy is provided to the coastal State in this situation. The coastal State could not refer the matter to resolution under Section 2 of Part XV of UNCLOS because it arguably involves the exercise of the coastal State's rights under Article 246 (albeit the denial of the exercise of those rights). On the face of it, unjustifiable interference is not grounds for the suspension or the cessation of marine scientific research under Article 253. The interference would have to be cast in terms of a change of the method or means used from those initially stipulated in the information provided to the coastal State. This characterization would thus amount to a

(a) is of direct significance for the exploration and exploitation of natural resources, whether living or non-living;

(b) involves drilling into the continental shelf, the use of explosives or the introduction of harmful substances into the marine environment;

(c) involves the construction, operation or use of artificial islands, installations and structures referred to in articles 60 and 80;

(d) contains information communicated pursuant to article 248 regarding the nature and objectives of the project which is inaccurate or if the researching State or competent international organization has outstanding obligations to the coastal State from a prior research project.

[395] Soons, *Marine Scientific Research*, p. 170.

breach of Article 248 and would warrant a suspension or cessation order. Again, the coastal State would not be able to avail itself of binding arbitration or adjudication but only compulsory conciliation. Of course, it would depend on the exact scenario as to whether these limitations would prove a help or a hindrance to the interests of the coastal State. The example nevertheless indicates the necessary role that compulsory dispute settlement could have played in ensuring the successful functioning of the Convention in governing marine scientific research in areas subject to coastal State jurisdiction.

Exclusion of Compulsory Dispute Settlement for Orders of Suspension or Cessation of Marine Scientific Research

Under the second exception in Article 297(2), disputes involving Article 253, which addresses the suspension or cessation of marine scientific research, are not subject to Section 2 of Part XV. A coastal State has the right to suspend marine scientific research in its EEZ or on its continental shelf in only two situations. First, where the marine scientific research is not being conducted in accordance with the initial plans submitted to the coastal State and to which the coastal State consented.[396] Second, where the State or competent international organization fails to comply with certain conditions, such as ensuring the participation of the coastal State, supplying it with particular information, and removing installations and equipment upon completion of the research.[397] If either of these situations arises and is not rectified within a reasonable amount of time, the coastal State then has the right to require the cessation of the project.[398] The right to require cessation may also be exercised by the coastal State if there is a major change in the initial plan of the project.[399] A coastal State may not suspend or require the cessation for reasons other than those specified. In this respect, Article 253 has been considered as "primarily . . . a safeguard for research activities in progress against arbitrary acts of the coastal State."[400] Those States or international organizations conducting marine scientific research must terminate their activities if the coastal State notifies them of its decision

---

[396] States and international organizations undertaking marine scientific research must provide various details of their project to the coastal State six months prior to the start of the project. UNCLOS, art. 248.

[397] Ibid., art. 249 (setting out the duty of the State or international organization to comply with a range of conditions).

[398] Ibid., art. 253(3).   [399] Ibid., art. 253(2).

[400] Soons, *Marine Scientific Research*, p. 203.

to order suspension or cessation. The exercise of enforcement jurisdiction by the coastal State in this respect cannot be subjected to binding arbitration or adjudication. The exclusion from mandatory procedures thereby undermines the "safeguards" afforded researching States and organizations. At best, the research State or organization would have to rely on conciliation proceedings.

Compulsory Conciliation Procedure

If disputes arise over the interpretation and application of Articles 246 (consent for marine scientific research in the EEZ or on the continental shelf) and 253 (orders for suspension or cessation), the only form of mandatory dispute settlement available is conciliation.[401] The conciliation procedure under Annex V does not specify that only States may be parties to conciliation proceedings. An international organization conducting marine scientific research may thus submit a dispute to conciliation since the restrictions and requirements imposed by Articles 246 and 253 apply to both States and international organizations. Under Annex IX, international organizations that participate in the Convention may select either ITLOS or the arbitral tribunals for the settlement of its disputes.[402] Part XV applies *mutatis mutandis* to any dispute between parties to the Convention, one or more of which are international organizations.[403]

In the event of conciliation, a similar limitation is imposed on the competence of the commission for marine scientific research disputes as for fisheries disputes. The commission must not call into question the exercise of the coastal State's discretion. This limitation reaffirms the broad powers of the coastal State with respect to marine scientific research.[404] It also applies in relation to the coastal State withholding consent for the projects on the basis of Article 246(5). In addition, the commission must not question the coastal State's discretion to designate certain areas beyond the 200 nautical miles of the continental shelf as zones for exploitation or exploration.[405] Although the conciliation commission may not substitute its discretion for that of the coastal State in these two situations, Riphagen considers that the commission could report that the factual conditions for discretionary withholding

---

[401] UNCLOS, art. 297(2)(b).   [402] *Ibid.*, Annex IX, art. 7(1).
[403] *Ibid.*, Annex IX, art. 7(2).   [404] De Mestral, at 183. See also Brus, p. 19.
[405] UNCLOS, art. 297(2)(b). The actions of the coastal State may instead be assessed by the Commission on the Limits of the Continental Shelf under Article 76, but only if the relevant information is volunteered for that Commission's consideration.

of consent or for ordering suspension or cessation are clearly absent.[406] At most, the commission could determine whether or not a project is covered by Article 246(5), but could not question the motivation of the State to withhold consent.[407] The conciliation commission could also examine the coastal State's determination of "normal circumstances" for granting consent and the basis of its decision to order suspension or cessation of marine research as a question of fact without expressly judging the coastal State's discretion. In this way, the conciliation commission could potentially have greater impact on States' relations through these types of factual finding than it may otherwise have had. It is a small counterweight for a system that predominantly reflects the grant of very broad discretionary powers to the coastal State in the text of the Convention. Clearly, the primacy of coastal States' rights in the EEZ has been reinforced, as opposed to tempered, by dispute settlement. While the exclusions for marine scientific research disputes are more narrow than those for fishing in the EEZ and could provide factual findings that impact on resolution efforts, the sanctity of coastal State discretion and the non-binding nature of the conciliation commission's recommendations should underscore any enthusiasm for the use of compulsory conciliation.[408]

Conclusion

In sum, disputes over marine scientific research in the different maritime zones are nearly all subject to compulsory dispute settlement. The variety of conditions that may be imposed on States and organizations researching in areas subject to coastal State jurisdiction could be kept in check through the availability of external review, primarily, though, for large undertakings or in the face of consistent conduct in violation of the Convention. The exceptions to Section 2 of Part XV for marine scientific research disputes are limited in number and are still subject to compulsory conciliation. But these exceptions relate to two potentially controversial issues, namely, consent for marine scientific research in the EEZ and on the continental shelf and suspension and cessation orders for marine scientific research in the same areas. While the substantive provisions on these two issues are drafted in such

---

[406] Riphagen, p. 290.   [407] Soons, *Marine Scientific Research*, pp. 253–54.

[408] See also Adede, *System for Settlement of Disputes*, p. 257 (considering that scope of conciliation is limited because of the specification of the type of disputes to be alleged and the commission being unable to challenge the discretion of the coastal State).

a way to provide some protection to the interests of the researching States and organizations, the effect of Article 297 is to undermine these protections rather than provide a further check. The conciliation commission may issue findings on certain questions of fact in relation to the exceptions and even though the commission may not substitute its discretion for that of the coastal State, its findings may provide a positive influence in negotiations between States in dispute. While arguably less constrained than the role for conciliation ascribed to fishing disputes in the EEZ, the limitations of conciliation remain apparent. The exceptions in Article 297(2) relate to crucial aspects of research activities undertaken in large expanses of the oceans. At best, it would seem that States did not consider compulsory adjudication or arbitration to be necessary because the normative provisions are sufficient to balance the respective interests of the actors concerned. At worst, the absence of binding and mandatory jurisdiction for these questions will undermine the substantive regulation of marine scientific research in the EEZ and on the continental shelf.

Conclusion

This chapter has examined how disputes concerning the freedom of navigation, the protection and preservation of the marine environment, fishing activities, and marine scientific research are likely to be resolved under Part XV of the Convention. In particular, it has focused on the terms of Article 297, which sets forth a range of limitations and exceptions to compulsory procedures entailing binding decisions for conflicts arising in the maritime zones where States exercise sovereign rights and jurisdiction.

The first section considered the freedoms of navigation, overflight, and the laying of submarine cables and pipelines and set out how these traditional freedoms of the high seas have been affected through the recognition of the legal construct of the continental shelf and the institution of the EEZ. The attribution of exclusive rights over extended maritime zones was accorded in such a manner so as to cater for the existing freedoms of navigation, overflight, and the laying of submarine cables and pipelines. Substantive rules were thus formulated to balance the continuing rights of all States to exercise these freedoms of the high seas with the exclusive rights of coastal States to promote their economic well-being. The dispute settlement clause in Article 297, paragraph 1 provides further protection for the inclusive interests of States in the extended maritime zones. Dispute resolution procedures are available for specifically enumerated freedoms as well as "other internationally lawful uses of the sea" related to these freedoms. Mandatory third-party review is necessary to elaborate on requirements that coastal and flag States have due regard for their respective interests in the extended maritime zones and that conflicts should be resolved on the basis of equity and all other relevant circumstances when the Convention does not specifically attribute rights or jurisdiction to any specific State in the EEZ. International courts and tribunals established under Part XV should exercise their authority to reinforce the continuing inclusive rights in the extended maritime zones in the face of greater coastal State control over large ocean areas.

Article 297 also anticipates that measures taken for the protection and preservation of the marine environment in the EEZ or on the continental shelf should be subjected to compulsory procedures entailing binding decisions. Reliance on international decision-making is particularly acute for these questions. The determination of coastal State action as a violation of the Convention is dependent on the existence of international rules and standards that are found to be applicable to that coastal State. This approach permits a court or tribunal considerable flexibility in establishing international standards for the protection and preservation of the marine environment. Indeed, UNCLOS envisages that the guiding provisions included in the Convention are to be interpreted and applied without prejudice to the existence of specific obligations under other international agreements. Recourse to these other materials in this regard is also necessary in light of the use of hortatory standards in the Convention. Mandatory dispute settlement is required to elaborate on the normative content of obligations binding on States parties. In addition, these substantive provisions were drafted in such a way as to protect the freedom of navigation against arbitrary and excessive coastal State control over the protection and preservation of the marine environment. Compulsory third-party review is required to guarantee the continued exercise of the freedom of navigation.

The dispute settlement procedures needed for questions pertaining to the protection and preservation of the marine environment then stand in considerable contrast to those applicable to fisheries disputes in the dependence on international decision-making in shaping as well as protecting the actions of States. As described in the third section of this chapter, exclusive authority is ascribed to the coastal State to decide on the total allowable catch, harvesting capacity, the existence of a surplus, and to what State that surplus may be allocated with respect to the living resources in the EEZ. The coastal State is further entitled to prescribe and enforce a variety of laws and regulations relating to fishing activities in the zone. The rights of the coastal State have been insulated from review as Article 297(3) excludes from mandatory adjudication or arbitration all disputes arising with respect to the living resources in the EEZ. The only limitation on this exception is for a narrowly defined category of disputes that may be submitted to compulsory conciliation. The exercise of the coastal State's rights over its living resources may be submitted to international processes only to the extent that the action in question may impinge on the other freedoms of the high seas. In particular, the fisheries laws of the coastal State may be reviewed in the course of proceedings under Article 292 where a court or tribunal must assess the reasonableness of a bond for the release of vessels and crews violating fisheries laws.

By contrast, mandatory third-party dispute settlement is available for disputes relating to living resources in other maritime zones. The obligations dealing with fishing on the high seas are equivocal in that UNCLOS primarily anticipates that further agreements will be made to elaborate on the normative content of the obligations of cooperation. From the *Southern Bluefin Tuna* case, it is apparent that if these separate agreements have their own dispute settlement procedures then these latter procedures are likely to prevail over the compulsory means available under the Convention if no settlement has been reached by recourse to those other procedures and they do not exclude any further procedure. If no such subsequent agreements have been formulated, then the standard of cooperation required for the conservation and management of the living resources rests with the authority of the international court or tribunal constituted for the resolution of the particular dispute.

The situation of straddling stocks, highly migratory species, and catadromous and anadromous species seemingly falls, albeit appropriately, somewhere in between the procedures for EEZ and high seas fisheries disputes. The question is unresolved in the Convention as there is no indication as to whether disputes pertaining to these species fall within the mandatory procedures in Section 2 of Part XV or whether the limits for EEZ fisheries disputes apply. The Fish Stocks Agreement does not assist in this matter as it simply refers back to the dispute settlement mechanism in Part XV of the Convention. The element of control granted to the coastal State with regard to each type of fish species or stock may provide a determining characteristic for choosing the particular applicable procedure. For example, UNCLOS stipulates that catadromous species must be harvested within the EEZ and this obligation may require that the EEZ dispute settlement provisions be applied to these species. By contrast, where stocks are fished by both coastal and long-distance fishing States and that fishing is subjected to obligations of cooperation, these disputes may be more appropriately referred to the mandatory procedures in a similar fashion to high seas fishing disputes. The need for compulsory dispute settlement is particularly apparent in light of the balance to be attained between the exclusive and inclusive interests of the States concerned. Complete insulation of coastal State power is no longer appropriate for the conservation and management of these species.

The regulation of marine scientific research in the EEZ and on the continental shelf reflects a tendency to protect the interests of the coastal State in a manner similar to the exclusion of EEZ fisheries disputes from third-party review. Such protection is afforded for questions that relate to the coastal State's control of research activity in its EEZ or on the continental shelf. This exclusion prevents review through mandatory arbitration or adjudication of coastal State decision making in relation to the grant of consent for marine scientific research projects and as to the entitlement of coastal States to suspend or order the cessation of research projects. These questions are instead subjected to conciliation proceedings. Conciliation may of itself be sufficient to assist in dispute resolution if the matter of controversy is a question of fact that can indicate whether the basis of the coastal State's decision was legitimate. The failure to reaffirm the balance of interests of the substantive provisions in Part XV may indicate that binding third-party review is not necessary as part of the normative regime – or that these rules will not operate successfully without it. Aside from the two exceptions, all other disputes concerning marine scientific research are subjected to the procedures in Section 2 of Part XV. Questions relating to the principles for the conduct of marine scientific research, including the conditions that advantage the coastal State, and the deployment and use of scientific research installations or equipment are to be reinforced and upheld through international courts or tribunals. Consistent standards of conduct for marine scientific research could be reaffirmed through international processes if researching States or organizations are willing to pursue this avenue.

The analysis of Article 297 in relation to the regulation of maritime activities indicates the important role ascribed to compulsory dispute settlement procedures under the Convention. The carefully circumscribed availability of mandatory jurisdiction entailing binding decisions demonstrates when these procedures are required as a vital element of the normative regime as a whole. External third-party review was incorporated into the Convention when States considered this function to be an essential guarantee to protect inclusive rights when those rights coexist with exclusive rights accorded to coastal States. The freedom of navigation (and associated freedoms of communication) has faced considerable challenge in light of coastal States' increasing claims to jurisdiction and sovereignty in wider reaches of ocean space. The creation of the EEZ particularly highlighted the complex interrelationship of interests and functions between actors in the law of the sea. This development has resulted in the need for an international regime that incorporates a system of third-party review and decision-making to ensure that these freedoms of communication are upheld in the practice of States.

A study of Article 297 also reveals that international decision-making plays a requisite role for the substantive rules of the Convention that are set out in hortatory language, or that rely on future decisions by actors for the regulation of certain matters. For States to adhere to the goals of the Convention, an international process must be available to elaborate on the content of certain obligations. The international process does not necessarily have to be adjudication or arbitration, however. Through reference to separate agreements and future diplomatic conferences, States did not consider that compulsory dispute settlement procedures entailing binding decisions would be imperative. It is only in situations where these implementing agreements are not concluded that a court or tribunal could constitute an important element in determining what international standard should be applied in situations of conflict over the interpretation or application of UNCLOS. Although important, the availability of mandatory jurisdiction is not decisive to these normative regimes.

In light of the particular roles attributed to compulsory dispute settlement procedures in relation to specific substantive areas of the law of the sea, it is not surprising that the applicability of Section 2 of Part XV is so limited. The creation of the EEZ in UNCLOS signals a prevalent trend in favor of coastal State authority over the traditional *mare liberum* system. This emphasis has led to a range of coastal State decisions being placed outside the scope of review under Part XV of the Convention. A significant issue area excluded virtually entirely from third-party review is fishing in the EEZ. States clearly preferred that in dealing with the new regime in the Convention, traditional consent-based methods of dispute settlement would be more appropriate. Bilateral and regional approaches are more likely to ensure the effective operation of this regime due to the differing circumstances of various fisheries as well as differing circumstances relevant to coastal States themselves. Equally, the substantive provisions of the Convention may be sufficient in themselves to ensure the balance of interests appropriate for a particular issue and mandatory jurisdiction does not have a vital role to play in this regard. As a politically realistic instrument, compulsory dispute settlement is far from "comprehensive" in its application to the substantive rules of the Convention and clearly does not need to be so.

4 Optional Exceptions to Applicability of Compulsory Procedures Entailing Binding Decisions

Introduction

Article 298 of the Convention allows for States parties to exclude certain categories of disputes from compulsory procedures entailing binding decisions. States may declare when signing, ratifying, or acceding to the Convention, or at any time thereafter, that they do not accept the procedures available under Section 2 for those disputes specified in Article 298.[1] The declaration is without prejudice to the consent-based procedures set out in Section 1 of Part XV.[2] While a State is entitled to withdraw its declaration, a State may not submit a dispute subject to a declaration to any procedure under the Convention without the consent of the other State.[3]

Declarations permitted under Article 298 relate, first, to maritime delimitation disputes in relation to the territorial sea, EEZ, or continental shelf of States with opposite or adjacent coasts, as well as disputes involving historic bays or title. Second, States may opt to exclude disputes relating to military activities, as well as law enforcement activities relating to marine scientific research and fishing in the EEZ. Finally, disputes in respect of which the Security Council is exercising its functions under the UN Charter may also be excluded from compulsory procedures entailing binding decisions at the election of States. This chapter explores these categories of disputes and the role that dispute settlement is expected to play and what justifications can be posited for the possible exclusion of these disputes. While mandatory jurisdiction is either not

---

[1] UNCLOS, art. 298(1). Declarations and notices of withdrawals of declarations are to be deposited with the UN Secretary-General. *Ibid.*, art. 298(6).

[2] *Ibid.*, art. 298(1).

[3] *Ibid.*, art. 298(3). A State may agree to submit an otherwise excluded dispute to any procedure specified in the Convention. *Ibid.*, art. 298(2).

necessary in some cases, or not politically viable in others, it is notable that a small proportion of States parties has as yet availed themselves of these exceptions.[4] Such reticence, while a surprising deviation, may increase the likelihood of States using adjudication or arbitration for the future resolution of disputes on these issues, rather than just relying on consent-based modes of dispute settlement.

Maritime Delimitation and Historic Title Disputes

Maritime delimitation involves a determination of the outer boundary of a maritime zone as measured from a State's basepoints and baselines.[5] The delimitation may mark the point that the high seas begins or, in areas where there is insufficient water area for States to have their full entitlement to maritime zones, attributes zones of jurisdiction, sovereign rights, or sovereignty between States with opposite or adjacent coasts. When sufficient space exists for States to have their full entitlement then the question of delimitation is largely a unilateral act. However, as the claim of the coastal State in this instance involves allocation of areas that would otherwise be *res communis*, an international aspect to the claim remains.[6] When States have either adjacent or opposite coasts that create an overlapping entitlement, the area must be divided to determine the reach of each State's competence. Great efforts have been undertaken to devise international standards for this task but too many variables (geographic configurations, traditional patterns of usage, and social factors as well as economic and strategic considerations) come into play. These considerations have been amplified with the allocation of larger maritime zones through the creation of the EEZ and the legal recognition of the continental shelf. The formulation of legal rules for maritime delimitation has had to cater for all of these variations.

Delimitations of overlapping maritime zones have typically been left to negotiations between the relevant States. Problems may arise if States fail to reach an agreement and conflicts ensue over which State is entitled to exercise jurisdiction over particular activities. The problem may

---

[4] See United Nations, *Multilateral Treaties Deposited with the Secretary-General*, UN Doc. ST/LEG/SER.E/15, available at www.un.org/Depts/los/los_decl.htm (updated November 13, 2003).

[5] Baselines are lines drawn along a State's continental or insular coast from which maritime zones are measured. Basepoints are any point on the baseline.

[6] See Fisheries Case (*United Kingdom v. Norway*), 1951 ICJ 116, 132 (December 18).

become acute when companies wish to enter certain areas for the exploration and exploitation of hydrocarbons. Various avenues may be pursued in this situation – *de facto* or provisional arrangements could be developed or a joint project could be undertaken. This alternative may allow certain activities to proceed without prejudice to the fixing of a final boundary. If States are unable to agree on the boundary then it remains possible that no agreement could be reached on even a provisional or joint arrangement. Oil companies are less likely to invest in areas of questionable title and States thus have an incentive to resolve the question of the boundary. The matter could then be referred to third-party dispute settlement to resolve any impasse to agreement. The use of adjudication or arbitration is not unusual for maritime boundary disputes.[7]

The need to reach agreement and the variety of circumstances influencing States in the allocation of maritime areas have influenced the formulation of legal rules for maritime delimitation as well as the procedures available for differences arising over the interpretation or application of these rules. The first half of this section describes the principles and procedures dealing with the delimitation of maritime zones when there are overlapping entitlements, as well as with historic title, both prior to UNCLOS and in UNCLOS itself. The second half then analyzes the modes of dispute settlement available under the Convention for disputes relating to maritime delimitation. The Convention permits States to exclude at their election disputes relating to historic bays or title and maritime delimitation of the territorial sea, EEZ, and continental shelf. This optional exclusion potentially denies a range of advantages otherwise accruing to States in dispute but is a realistic reflection of State preferences for political, rather than third-party, settlement when dealing with an important matter such as title. Additional disputes arising with respect to maritime delimitation addressed in this section concern the application of straight baselines and the regime of islands

---

[7] See, e.g., North Sea Continental Shelf; Icelandic Fisheries; Tunisia/Libya; Gulf of Maine; Continental Shelf (*Libya/Malta*), 1985 ICJ 13 (June 3); Land, Island and Maritime Frontier Dispute (*El Salvador/Honduras; Nicaragua Intervening*), 1992 ICJ 351 (September 11); Report and Recommendations of the Conciliation Committee on the Continental Shelf Area between Iceland and Jan Mayen, 20 ILM 797 (1981); Beagle Channel Arbitral Award (*Argentina/Chile*), 52 ILR 93 (1979); Delimitation of the Continental Shelf (*United Kingdom/France*), 18 ILM 397 (1979); Arbitral Award of 19 October 1981 (*Emirates of Dubai/Sharjah*), 91 ILR 543 (1981); Maritime Boundary (*Guinea-Bissau/Senegal Maritime Delimitation Case*), 83 ILR 1 (1989); Delimitation of the Maritime Areas between Canada and France (St Pierre and Miquelon) (*France/Canada*), 95 ILR 645 (1992).

under UNCLOS. While these disputes will often be inherently linked to delimitation disputes between neighboring States, international review may well be necessary – and should be available – to protect inclusive interests.

Maritime Delimitation Prior to UNCLOS

Maritime delimitation prior to World War II mostly focused on the limits of coastal States' maritime zones as an indication of where the high seas began. This issue encompassed the question of the breadth of the territorial sea, drawing closing lines across the mouths of rivers, bays, ports, and other coastal features as well as the method for measuring the outer limit of the territorial sea. These questions were of considerable significance in light of the two contrasting legal regimes that applied in the territorial sea and on the high seas respectively. The question was one of where areas of sovereignty ended and areas of *res communis* began.

Methods of delimitation have long been grounded in notions of equality and proportionality.[8] When the limits of the territorial sea were quite narrow, there were few instances where the water areas between States with opposite coasts overlapped. In these cases, the typical approach was to apply a median line to allow for equal sharing; less often, the thalweg of a narrow strait would be used to preserve equal rights of navigation.[9] Delimitation of coastal waters between adjacent States initially varied between several approaches: utilizing a line of latitude, drawing a line perpendicular to the coast, or again employing a median line.[10] An early decision of the Permanent Court of Arbitration, *Grisbadarna*, devised a maritime boundary between Norway and Sweden that ran "perpendicularly to the general direction of the coast."[11] Some adjustment of this line was made in light of the Swedish tradition of lobster fishing in the area and various executive acts performed by Sweden.[12] The value of historic use was recognized in the statement that, "a state of things which actually exists and has existed for a long time should

---

[8] Sang-Myon Rhee, "Sea Boundary Delimitation Between States before World War II," 76 *Am. J. Int'l L.* 555, 556 (1982) (citing Pufendorf as the first to propose principles of sea boundaries in the middle of the seventeenth century).

[9] *Ibid.*, at 559–64.   [10] *Ibid.*, at 564–65.

[11] "Decision of the Permanent Court of Arbitration in the Matter of the Maritime Boundary Dispute between Norway and Sweden," 4 *Am. J. Int'l L.* 226, 232 (1910).

[12] *Ibid.*, at 233.

be changed as little as possible."[13] This decision thus utilized a variation on a median line, one that was modified for equitable considerations.[14]

At the 1930 Codification Conference, one of the Bases for Discussion concerned the delimitation of a strait that was less than twelve miles wide. The Preparatory Committee to this Conference had proposed the use of the median line "in principle."[15] However, during the debates at the Codification Conference, States did not want a specific rule set out but preferred to rely on special agreements between the relevant straits States. No uniform principle of delimitation for straits could be agreed upon at that time. States subsequently employed the median line in delimitations, but no uniform method of demarcation was actually formulated.[16] An approach to drawing the median line was devised in 1936 by S. Whittemore Boggs, who proposed a line "every point of which is equidistant from the nearest point or points on opposite shores."[17] This formula could be used for both adjacent and opposite coasts and was to prove influential in codification efforts after World War II. The debates prior to and at the First Conference remain of interest to the extent that they foreshadowed the views of States on dispute settlement procedures in relation to maritime delimitation in drafting UNCLOS. Well before UNCLOS was adopted, a potential role for compulsory dispute settlement was contemplated for maritime delimitation, but was ultimately resisted in favor of an optional procedure.

Delimitation of the Territorial Sea

The question of what method should be used to delimit the territorial sea between States with opposite or adjacent coasts was initially

---

[13] *Ibid.*

[14] Weil has noted that the *Grisbadarna* decision to apply a rule and then make exceptions to it was indicative of the trend in the method of maritime delimitations generally. See Prosper Weil, *The Law of Maritime Delimitation – Reflections* (1989), pp. 136–37.

[15] Bases of Discussion for the Conference drawn up by the Preparatory Committee, in 2 *Codification Conference*, at 227.

[16] Rhee, at 577–80.

[17] S. Whittemore Boggs, "Problems of Water-Boundary Definition: Median Line and International Boundaries Through Territorial Waters," 27 *Geographical Rev.* 445, 447 (1937). Boggs had earlier advocated the use of arcs of circles as the most practical method for drawing the outer limit of the territorial sea. See S. Whittemore Boggs, "Delimitation of the Territorial Sea: The Method of Delimitation Proposed by the Delegation of the United States at the Hague Conference for the Codification of International Law," 24 *Am. J. Int'l L.* 541, 544 (1930). The arcs of circles method is used to determine the equidistant points from baselines.

considered separately to the delimitation of the continental shelf within the International Law Commission prior to the First Conference.[18] Due to the technical nature of the question and the inability of the Commission to agree on one method, the Commission decided to refer the question of a delimitation method to experts.[19] The Committee of Experts formulated a detailed rule that provided for the application of an equidistance line with certain exceptions for the presence of islands as well as fishing and navigation interests.[20] In adopting a simplified version of this formula,[21] the Commission first considered that some provision for arbitration was needed.[22] However, no such dispute settlement clause was included in the texts submitted to the First Conference because of a general preference in the Commission to provide for compulsory dispute settlement only where extremely technical matters were involved and where it was expected that the majority of States would not accept certain obligations without the guarantee of compulsory adjudication or arbitration.[23] Presumably, the Commission did not consider these conditions were met for the delimitation of the territorial sea.

States at the First Conference accepted the use of an equidistant line for territorial sea delimitation and were primarily concerned with the

[18] The members of the International Law Commission canvassed alternative methods of delimitation between adjacent States in early drafts of the delimitation of the territorial sea. Régime of the Territorial Sea – Rapport par J. P. A. François, rapporteur spécial, UN Doc. A/CN.4/53, at 38, art. 13, reprinted in *Documents of the Fourth Session including the Report of the Commission to the General Assembly*, [1952] 2 Y.B. Int'l L. Comm'n 25, UN Doc. A/CN.4/SER.A/1952/Add.1, UN Sales No. 58.V.5, vol. II (1958). see also *Summary Records of the Fourth Session*, [1952] 1 Y.B. Int'l L. Comm'n, UN Doc. A/CN.4/Ser.A/1952, UN Sales No. 58.V.5, vol. I (1958) at 182, ¶ 13 (Yepes) (proposing the drawing of a line perpendicular and at right angles from the coast).

[19] *ILC Yearbook*, (1952), vol. I, at 185.

[20] Additif au deuxième rapport de M. J.P.A. François, rapporteur spécial, UN Doc. A/CN.4/61/Add.1, at 75, 77, reprinted in *Documents of the Fifth Session including the Report of the Commission to the General Assembly*, [1953] 2 Y.B. Int'l L. Comm'n, UN Doc. A/CN.4/Ser.A/1953/Add.1, UN Sales No. 59.V.4, vol. II (1959) at 57 (incorporating in its Annex the report of the Committee of Experts).

[21] *Report of the International Law Commission to the General Assembly*, UN GAOR, at 157, UN Doc. A/2693 (1954), reprinted in *Documents of the Sixth Session including the Report of the Commission to the General Assembly*, [1954] 2 Y.B. Int'l L. Comm'n, UN Doc. A/CN.4/Ser.A/1954/Add.1, UN Sales No. 59.V.7, vol. II (1960) at 140. The substance of this article was not subsequently altered before its submission to the First Conference.

[22] *Ibid.*, at 157–158.

[23] *First Conference*, 1st Comm., at 69–70, ¶¶ 16–17 (Statement by Mr. François, Expert to the Secretariat of the Conference).

exceptions, if any, to this rule.[24] States were willing to consider the possibility of historic usage as a reason for altering a boundary based on the median line as such circumstances had been considered in earlier delimitations.[25] However, the absence of a provision on arbitration or judicial settlement was used to reinforce arguments for the deletion of a reference to other special circumstances.[26] States supporting this view clearly considered that third-party dispute settlement was essential so that the maritime delimitation process was not rendered too indeterminate. The question was ultimately subsumed by the discussion on dispute settlement for all of the conventions being drafted at the First Conference and the adoption of the Optional Protocol. Even with optional jurisdiction, the reference to historic use and other special circumstances in the delimitation formula was retained. Article 12 of the Territorial Sea Convention sets forth the rule that the median line, which is equidistant from points on the respective coasts, is to be used for the delimitation of the territorial sea between opposite or adjacent States unless historic use or other special circumstances exist.[27]

Delimitation of the Continental Shelf

With the recognition of the continental shelf as a legal institution, States turned to consider the limits of this new maritime zone. The early discussions within the Commission focused on the need for States to reach agreement and what would happen in cases where no such agreement could be reached, rather than the actual method of delimitation. The Special Rapporteur to the International Law Commission had canvassed various delimitation methods and opted for calling on the relevant States to reach agreement and, in the absence of agreement, to

[24] Yugoslavia, for example, argued: "The granting of a right to establish an unspecified boundary line other than the median line would cause confusion and encourage States to claim special circumstances for reasons of self-interest." *Ibid.*, at 187, ¶ 8 (Yugoslavia). But see *ibid.*, at 189, 1136 (United Kingdom) (advocating the inclusion of a reference to special circumstances "for reasons of equity or because of the configuration of a particular coast," or to account for the presence of a navigation channel or small islands).

[25] Two earlier cases, *Grisbadarna* and *Anglo-Norwegian Fisheries*, had referred to historic use in deciding martime boundaries.

[26] *First Conference*, 1st Comm., at 192, ¶ 35 (Greece). See also *ibid.*, at 192, ¶ 22 (Netherlands).

[27] The final formulation largely followed the Commission's text with a slight change to take account of the fact that the specific breadth of the territorial sea had not been ascertained.

use a line extending the territorial boundary for cases of adjacency and a median line for opposite States.[28] Scelle suggested that exploitation could not begin until a settlement was reached but States would either have to maintain the *status quo* or be under an obligation to refer the dispute to the ICJ.[29] The compulsory nature of dispute settlement was viewed as somewhat inevitable on the basis that States would otherwise be unable to explore the seabed.[30] The issue of procedure became less pressing once the Commission settled on the use of equidistance-special circumstances for continental shelf delimitation following the report of the Committee of Experts. However, if the parties could not agree on a line then the matter was to be submitted to arbitration.[31]

At the First Conference, States accepted that priority had to be given to boundaries being delimited by agreement. Yet it was proposed that the matter could not simply be left to negotiations in a legal vacuum,[32] as this approach could too easily lead to disputes between States.[33] Instead,

---

[28] Deuxième rapport sur la haute mer par J. P. A. François, Rapporteur Spécial, Régime de the High Seas, UN Doc. A/CN.4/42, at 102, ¶ 162, reprinted in *Documents of the Third Session including the Report of the Commission to the General Assembly*, [1951] 2 Y.B. Int'l L. Comm'n, UN Doc. A/CN.4/Ser.A/1951/Add.1, UN Sales No. 1957.V.6, vol. II (1957) at 75.

[29] *Summary Records of the Third Session*, [1951] 1 Y.B. Int'l L. Comm'n 288, ¶ 5 (Scelle), UN Doc. A/CN.4/SER.A/1951, UN Sales No. 1957.V.6, vol. I (1957). See also *ibid.*, at 289, ¶ 16 (Scelle) ("Merely to exhort States to reach agreement was to leave the strong free to exert pressure on the weak.").

[30] *Ibid.*, at 291, ¶ 46 (Hsu). Cf. *ibid.*, at 289, ¶ 13 (Cordova). The members of the Commission agreed in 1951 that the draft text should provide for recourse to arbitration in the event of the interested States not reaching agreement. *Ibid.*, at 291 (by ten votes to two). It was further agreed that arbitration should be compulsory. *Ibid.*, at 292 (by eight votes to two, with two abstentions). Nonetheless, the draft article as a whole was rejected. *Ibid.*, at 293 (six votes in favor, six votes against). It was commented that:

> the votes cast against the inclusion of the word "compulsory" had not resulted from any dislike of the concept itself, but had been due to the fact that the members concerned had considered that it might offend the dignity of States. Nevertheless, a State refusing to reach an agreement had to be put under the obligation of submitting to arbitration.

Ibid., at 297, ¶ 22 (El Khoury). The Commission then adopted a proposal (by ten votes to two) reading: "Failing agreement, the parties are under the obligation to have boundaries fixed by arbitration". *Ibid.*, at 297, ¶ 23 (Spiropoulos).

[31] *Summary Records of the Fifth Session*, [1953] 1 Y.B. Int'l L. Comm'n 106, UN Doc. A/CN.4/SER.A/1953, UN Sales No. 59.V.4, vol. I (1959) (citing his report in UN Doc. A/CN.4/60). See also art. 73 of Articles 67 to 73 of the Draft of the International Law Commission, UN Doc. A/3159UN, reprinted in *First Conference*, 4th Comm., at 125.

[32] Venezuela: proposal, UN Doc. A/CONF.13/C.4/L.42, reprinted in *First Conference*, 4th Comm., at 138.

[33] *Ibid.*, at 94, ¶ 11 (Colombia).

States recognized that some sort of rule was required. The debates on continental shelf delimitation largely mirrored those on the delimitation of the territorial sea. Emphasis on the use of the median line was again apparent.[34] There was also more support for inclusion of the exception of special circumstances, as the rigid application of the median line would lead to inequitable results and considerable technical difficulties.[35] The final text of Article 6 of the Continental Shelf Convention required States with opposite or adjacent coasts to determine their boundary by agreement. It further provided, "In the absence of agreement, and unless another boundary is justified by special circumstances, the boundary shall be determined by application of the principle of equidistance from the nearest points of the baselines from which the breadth of the territorial sea of each State is measured."

Mandatory jurisdiction was not discussed as an elemental feature of the legal regime for delimitation of overlapping continental shelf entitlements specifically but was debated in relation to the legal regime of the continental shelf in its entirety. Some delegations strongly favored the inclusion of a mandatory dispute settlement mechanism,[36] particularly because of some of the vague expressions used in the articles relating to the continental shelf.[37] Other States doubted whether the ICJ, as proposed by the International Law Commission, was the preferable forum for dispute settlement in relation to the continental shelf. The very newness of the articles on the continental shelf suggested that compulsory adjudication was inappropriate since they had not "been put to the test of experience."[38] Moreover, in light of the technical character of the disputes that could be envisaged, an arbitral body similar to the one established for the conservation of living resources was suggested as

---

[34] *Ibid.*, at 92, ¶ 15 (United Kingdom) ("the median line would always provide the basis for delimitation").

[35] *Ibid.*, at 93, ¶ 5 (Italy). See also *ibid.*, at 92, ¶ 19 (Venezuela) (explaining that "failure to make due provision for special circumstances such as were frequently imposed by geography could not result in a solution which would be fair to all States").

[36] *Ibid.*, at 7, ¶ 18 (Netherlands); *ibid.*, at 7, ¶ 22 (Spain); *ibid.*, at 10, ¶ 13 (Colombia); *ibid.*, at 12, ¶ 9 (India) (provided it was subject to a declaration under Article 36 of the Court's Statute); *ibid.*, at 20, ¶ 14 (USA); *ibid.*, at 30, ¶ 31 (Canada) (acknowledging, however, that difficulties might arise for technical disputes); *ibid.*, at 101, ¶ 27 (Federal Republic of Germany); *ibid.*, at 100, ¶ 15 (Sweden); *ibid.*, at 101, ¶ 30 (Uruguay); *ibid.*, at 6, ¶ 8 (Greece) (stating that one of the conditions for its acceptance of the creation of the institution of the continental shelf was the inclusion of a provision on dispute settlement).

[37] *Ibid.*, at 9, ¶ 4 (Dominican Republic).   [38] *Ibid.*, at 99, ¶ 7 (USSR).

more appropriate.[39] Other delegations opposed the inclusion of a provision for mandatory jurisdiction in favor of dispute settlement according to Article 33 of the UN Charter.[40]

After the International Law Commission draft on dispute settlement was adopted narrowly,[41] the development of the Optional Protocol for dispute settlement rendered the article redundant.[42] States at the First Conference were satisfied with the inclusion of the equidistance-special circumstances formula for the delimitation of the continental shelf without any separate need to insist on the availability of compulsory dispute settlement in the event of failure to agree on a boundary. No cases concerning maritime delimitation were submitted to the processes of the Optional Protocol, but the formula adopted in the Continental Shelf Convention was discussed by the ICJ in the *North Sea Continental Shelf* cases and before an ad hoc tribunal in the *Channel Islands* case, which were both submitted on a consensual basis by the parties concerned.

North Sea Continental Shelf Cases

The Federal Republic of Germany, Denmark, and the Netherlands submitted cases by Special Agreement to the ICJ in 1967, asking the Court to state the principles and rules of international law that applied to the delimitation of the continental shelf appertaining to each of them. The Court was not asked to undertake the delimitation itself. Denmark and the Netherlands argued that the equidistance principle as defined in Article 6 of the Continental Shelf Convention was applicable to the delimitation of the North Sea. Although a signatory, Germany had not ratified the Continental Shelf Convention and was thus not a party. Denmark and the Netherlands submitted that this regime bound Germany either because it had assumed the obligations of the Continental Shelf Convention by virtue of public statements and proclamations, or because the equidistance-special circumstances rule was binding as a matter of general or customary international law. Germany resisted the application of the equidistance-special circumstances formula because its use on Germany's concave coast with respect to both Denmark and the Netherlands would have had the effect of cutting off Germany's entitlement to continental shelf area a short distance from its coast.

---

[39] *Ibid.*, at 3, ¶ 9 (South Africa).

[40] *Ibid.*, at 19, ¶ 8 (Pakistan) (arguing that "it was common knowledge that certain States did not accept the compulsory jurisdiction" and that Article 33 thus provided an acceptable alternative). See also *ibid.*, at 16, ¶ 16 (Chile); *ibid.*, at 21, ¶30 (Venezuela).

[41] *Ibid.*, at 106.   [42] *First Conference*, Plenary Meetings, at 55, ¶ 70 (India).

The Court determined that Germany was not bound by the terms of the Continental Shelf Convention by virtue of its conduct because only a very definite and consistent course of conduct could warrant a finding that a State had become bound by a treaty in the absence of its ratification.[43] Furthermore, the Court decided that equidistance-special circumstances was not binding on Germany as a matter of general or customary law. In discussing whether the formula amounted to a rule of law or just a method of delimitation, the Court noted that the method had practical convenience and certainty of application. These factors were not enough, however, to convert the method into a principle of law.[44] The equidistance-special circumstances formula had only been adopted as a matter of practical convenience and cartography rather than as a matter of legal theory. Equidistance-special circumstances was not of a "norm-creating character" – it was subject to reservations in the Continental Shelf Convention, it was a secondary obligation after the primary obligation of delimitation by agreement and there were controversies as to the exact meaning and scope of the notion of special circumstances.

The Court filled the vacuum left by this decision with "certain basic legal notions" that "delimitation must be the object of agreement between the States concerned, and that such agreement must be arrived at in accordance with equitable principles."[45] The Court referred to the standard that had been included in the Truman Proclamation – namely, that any dispute over maritime boundaries between adjacent or opposite States should be settled by mutual agreement and in accordance with equitable principles. No single method of delimitation was to be considered as obligatory in all cases. Instead, delimitation was to be effected by agreement in accordance with equitable principles and taking account of all relevant circumstances. "There is no legal limit to the considerations which States may take into account for the purpose of making sure that they apply equitable procedures."[46] In the present case, the Court considered that the factors to be taken into account were the general configuration of the coasts (including any special or unusual features), proportionality, the unity of the natural resources of the continental shelf, and any other continental shelf delimitations in the same region. The Court's decision was important for its impact on the legal regime of the continental shelf and the rights of States in relation thereto. However, in deciding on a different approach to maritime

---

[43] North Sea Continental Shelf, paras. 21–36.
[44] See Ibid., para. 23.   [45] Ibid., para. 85.   [46] Ibid., para. 93.

delimitation to that laid down in the Continental Shelf Convention, further uncertainty was introduced to the applicable substantive law and thus accorded States with additional discretion in determining their maritime boundaries.

Channel Islands Case

The second case to consider the possible application of Article 6 of the Continental Shelf Convention was the *Channel Islands* case, which was an arbitration between France and the United Kingdom over the delimitation of the Channel in the region around the Channel Islands. The Channel Islands archipelago is located within a rectangular gulf formed by the coasts of Normandy and Brittany. One of these islands lies within seven miles of the French coast. The task of the arbitral tribunal was to delimit the continental shelf of the Channel, which included the area lying to the north and to the west of the Channel Islands. With respect to this area, France argued that a median line should be drawn down the middle of the Channel with an enclave around the Islands.[47] France advanced this solution on the basis that the Channel Islands are situated close to the French coast, intrinsically linked with its continental land mass, and "on the wrong side of the median line."[48] France objected to the strict application of equidistance because it would grant to the United Kingdom a disproportionate area of the continental shelf in the Channel, impinge on French navigational interests, and negatively impact on the vital security and defense interests of France in separating the Channel into two zones.[49] The United Kingdom emphasized the proposition that every island is entitled to its own continental shelf and that the Channel Islands could not be viewed as "very small islands for the purpose of considering their effect on the delimitation of a median line between 'opposite' States."[50] The legal framework of the case was thus "that of two opposite States one of which possesses island territories close to the coast of the other State."[51]

Both France and the United Kingdom were parties to the Continental Shelf Convention but France had entered reservations to Article 6 to prevent its application in this area.[52] Although the United Kingdom

---

[47] Channel Islands, para. 156.   [48] *Ibid.*, paras. 157–59.
[49] *Ibid.*, paras. 161–62.   [50] *Ibid.*, para. 170.   [51] *Ibid.*, para. 187.
[52] France had declared that it would not accept a boundary by application of the equidistance principle where "special circumstances" existed and designated the Bay of Biscay, the Bay of Granville and the sea areas of the Straits of Dover and of the North Sea off the French coast as such.

had objected to this reservation, the Tribunal found that Article 6 was inapplicable as between the two parties to the extent of the reservations.[53] In applying customary international law, the Tribunal determined that the equidistance-special circumstances rule was indistinguishable from the general international law rule, which gave no special preference to equidistance.[54] The role of special circumstances was to ensure an equitable delimitation.[55] Article 6 of the Continental Shelf Convention produced no practical difference to the customary law in this case since the application of the equidistance-special circumstances method depended on geographical and other relevant circumstances.[56] Equidistance-special circumstances and the rules of customary law were said to have the same object of delimitation of a maritime boundary in accordance with equitable principles.[57]

The effect of this decision was to "subject the equidistance method to the primary goal of securing an equitable solution in delimitation agreements."[58] As such, this decision was significant for its timing during the UNCLOS negotiations. At the point that States were divided between reference to the equidistance-special circumstances or to equitable principles, the decision that the rule in the Continental Shelf Convention was the same as the customary law rule was hoped to have a moderating effect.[59]

Conclusion

Two legal formulae thus developed for the delimitation of both the territorial sea and the continental shelf prior to the negotiations and conclusion of UNCLOS. A more technical rule, equidistance-special circumstances, was adopted at the First Conference for both maritime areas. At the same time, States resisted the inclusion of a predetermined dispute settlement mechanism, or at least considered the availability of a mandatory jurisdiction as unnecessary in the formulation of this method. Subsequent to the adoption of the Territorial Sea Convention and the Continental Shelf Convention, two cases considered what method and legal principles applied to maritime delimitation. These

---

[53] Channel Islands, para. 61.
[54] Ibid., paras. 65–69. See also Jan Mayen, paras. 65–69. See further Malcolm D. Evans, "Maritime Delimitation and Expanding Categories of Relevant Circumstances," 40 Int'l & Comp. L.Q. 1, 4 (1990).
[55] Channel Islands, para. 70.   [56] Ibid., para. 97.   [57] Ibid., para. 68.
[58] Attard, p. 232.   [59] Oxman, "1977 New York Session," at 79.

decisions set the tone for the future resolution of maritime delimitation disputes by establishing a far more flexible (but indefinite) standard.

Maritime Delimitation and Historic Title under UNCLOS

It was against this background that States came to negotiate the delimitation clauses for the territorial sea and the extended maritime zones (the continental shelf and the EEZ) at the Third Conference. The delimitation of the territorial sea was far less controversial at the Third Conference as larger stakes had emerged in allocating maritime zones that extended even further from the coast. On this occasion, States not only had to take into account the delimitation of the continental shelf, but also that of the EEZ. Both the continental shelf and the EEZ may extend to a distance of 200 miles from a State's baselines.[60] With these greater distances, the likelihood of States' maritime entitlements overlapping is considerably increased. This part examines Articles 15, 74, and 83 of UNCLOS, which deal with the delimitation of the territorial sea, the EEZ, and the continental shelf respectively, as well as historic title. The application of some of these principles was considered in maritime delimitation awards rendered subsequent to the adoption of UNCLOS but prior to its entry into force.[61] *Eritrea/Yemen*,[62] which was decided in 1999, was the first case to use UNCLOS as the governing law for a maritime delimitation.[63] The discussion immediately below considers normative standards that may be applicable in the delimitation of the territorial sea, the EEZ,

---

[60] UNCLOS, art. 57 (setting the limit of the EEZ at 200 miles) and *ibid.*, art. 76 (allocating each State at least a 200-mile zone designated as continental shelf and allowing for extensions of up to 350 miles in certain circumstances). As the EEZ covers the seabed and subsoil, the two zones have thereby been linked, but the extent of this linkage has been the subject of debate among commentators. See, e.g., Kwiatkowska, *Exclusive Economic Zone*, pp. 6–18; Attard, pp. 136–45. In *Libya/Malta*, the Court stated: "This does not mean that the concept of the continental shelf has been absorbed by that of the exclusive economic zone; it does however signify that greater importance must be attributed to elements, such as distance from the coast, which are common to both concepts." Libya/Malta, para. 33.

[61] For example, an arbitral award between Dubai and Sharjah considered the 1980 draft of the Convention, which still included reference to equidistance-special circumstances where suitable, and considered this clause as well as customary law in determining the applicable law. Dubai/Sharjah, at 249–56.

[62] In the Matter of an Arbitration Pursuant to an Agreement to Arbitrate dated 3 October 1996 between the Government of the State of Eritrea and the Government of the Republic of Yemen (*Eritrea/Yemen*) (Award of the Arbitral Tribunal in the Second Stage of the Proceedings (Maritime Delimitation), December 17, 1999), available at http://pca-cpa.org/RPC/#Eritrea.

[63] This arbitration was not instituted under Part XV of UNCLOS but was conducted at the request of the parties under the auspices of the Permanent Court of Arbitration.

and the continental shelf as well as for historic title and the next part analyzes the interrelationship of this law with the dispute settlement mechanism in UNCLOS.

Delimitation of the Territorial Sea under UNCLOS

Article 15 of UNCLOS largely reproduces the text of the Territorial Sea Convention for territorial sea delimitation.[64] The use of an equidistance line unless another boundary was warranted by special circumstances had been accepted and applied in State practice.[65] Although various proposals were made to refer to equitable principles, there was widespread support for the retention of the provision, with only minor drafting amendments, during the UNCLOS negotiations.[66] Neither the substance of the provisions on territorial sea delimitation nor related questions of dispute resolution occupied a prominent position during deliberations at the Third Conference.[67] The equidistance-special circumstances formula was thus still considered acceptable for the narrower distances at stake in a territorial sea delimitation.

The Tribunal in the *Eritrea/Yemen* arbitration considered the application of Article 15 in the southern reaches of the Red Sea.[68] This arbitration involved two phases, where the first phase decided the sovereignty of some islands located roughly in the middle of the Red Sea and the second phase delimited the maritime boundary between the opposite coasts of the States. In the first phase, the Tribunal determined that Yemen

In the Agreement to Arbitrate, the parties agreed that UNCLOS would apply for the second stage of the proceedings for the purposes of the arbitration even though Eritrea was not a party to the Convention. See Arbitration Agreement, October 3, 1996, Eritrea-Yemen, available at http://www.pca-cpa.org/RPC/arbagreeER-YE.htm, art. 2(3).

[64] Article 15 reads:
> Where the coasts of two States are opposite or adjacent to each other, neither of the two States is entitled, failing agreement between them to the contrary, to extend its territorial sea beyond the median line every point of which is equidistant from the nearest points on the baselines from which the breadth of the territorial seas of each of the two States is measured. The above provision does not apply, however, where it is necessary by reason of historic title or other special circumstances to delimit the territorial seas of the two States in a way that is at variance therewith.

UNCLOS, art. 15.

[65] S. P. Jagota, *Maritime Boundary* (1985), pp. 56–57.

[66] Oxman, "Seventh Session," at 22. The suggestion to bring Article 15 into line with the articles on the delimitation of the EEZ and the continental shelf was not adopted. 2 *United Nations Convention on the Law of the Sea 1982: A Commentary*, p. 141.

[67] 2 *United Nations Convention on the Law of the Sea 1982: A Commentary*, p. 140.

[68] Territorial sea delimitations had previously been undertaken in the *Grisbardana* and *Beagle Channel* arbitrations.

had acquired title to the main mid-sea islands based on evidence from the decade prior to the arbitration. The Tribunal recognized Eritrea's sovereignty over some smaller islands extending from its coast to within ten miles of the mid-sea islands. In awarding sovereignty over the mid-sea islands to Yemen, the Tribunal considered that this title entailed the perpetuation of the traditional fishing regime in the region, including free access, for the fishermen of both Eritrea and Yemen.[69] This decision in the first phase of the arbitration then had to be taken into account in the second phase of the case. Article 15 was relevant because of the small distances between the Yemeni mid-sea islands and the Eritrean coastal islands. The Tribunal applied Article 15 in determining the international boundary in this area and took the view that there were no reasons of historic title or other special circumstances to vary the equidistant median line.[70] Neither the size, habitability, nor historic usage of the area from the western mainland altered the placement of the median line.[71] Instead, the importance of the shipping lane and the practicality of not enclaving these islands mediated in favor of its use.[72]

Another third-party decision to consider the application of Article 15 was *Qatar v. Bahrain*.[73] There, the ICJ noted that the parties had agreed that Article 15 of UNCLOS was part of customary law, and thus adopted the approach of drawing an equidistance line on a provisional basis and then considering whether that line should be adjusted in the light of the existence of special circumstances.[74] The presence of a tiny island midway between the island of Bahrain and the Qatar peninsula constituted a special circumstance to prevent a disproportionate effect being accorded to an insignificant maritime feature.[75] While the use of the equidistant line for the territorial sea was given preeminence in UNCLOS, and customary international law, territorial sea delimitation does not involve

---

[69] In the Matter of an Arbitration Pursuance to an Agreement to Arbitrate dated 3 October 1996 between the Government of the State of Eritrea and the Government of the Republic of Yemen (*Eritrea/Yemen*) (Award of the Arbitral Tribunal in the First Stage of the Proceedings (Territorial Sovereignty and Scope of the Dispute), October 9, 1998), available at http://pca-cpa.org/RPC/#Eritrea, para. 527 (vi).

[70] Eritrea/Yemen, Maritime Delimitation, para. 158.   [71] See *ibid.*

[72] *Ibid.*, para. 155. The arbitral tribunal in the *Beagle Channel* arbitration had previously taken issues of navigability into account in delimiting territorial sea areas. Beagle Channel, para. 110.

[73] Case Concerning Maritime Delimitation and Territorial Questions between Qatar and Bahrain, (*Qatar v. Bahrain*), 2001 ICJ (March 16), available at http://www.icj-cij.org/icjwww/idocket/iqb/iqbframe.htm.

[74] *Ibid.*, para. 176.   [75] *Ibid.*, para. 219.

much less flexibility than is inherent in the delimitation of the EEZ and the continental shelf.

Delimitation of the EEZ and the Continental Shelf under UNCLOS

Far more controversial than territorial sea delimitation has been the question of delimitation for overlapping entitlements to EEZ and the continental shelf. It was generally recognized at the Third Conference that the elements that had to be included in the delimitation provisions were delimitation by agreement; relevant or special circumstances; equity or equitable principles; and the median or equidistance line.[76] However, coastal States were, of course, aware of the impact that any particular method could have on their own maritime areas and therefore took different views on the respective weight to be attributed to these elements in the text because of their particular geographic situations vis-à-vis neighboring States.

Effected by Agreement on the Basis of International Law in Order to Achieve an Equitable Solution

The negotiating positions at the Third Conference were divided between those in favor of equidistance-special circumstances and those in favor of equitable principles. States did not consider that they were bound to retain the use of equidistance-special circumstances as set out in the Continental Shelf Convention, particularly as they were also considering the delimitation of the EEZ.[77] Moreover, as noted above, the ICJ had not accepted this rule as customary international law in the *North Sea Continental Shelf* cases and the arbitral tribunal in the *Channel Islands* case subsequently considered that equitable principles and relevant circumstances were equivalent to the method set out in Article 6 of the Continental Shelf Convention. Yet, the application of equitable principles was not considered as advancing the chances of a solution any further in light of their indeterminacy and the theoretically unlimited categories of relevant circumstances.[78] "Any precise formula will tend to divide the Conference, since for each coastal state that supports a particular

---

[76] Oxman, "Seventh Session," at 23. See also Jagota, p. 236.

[77] A Chamber of the ICJ noted the limitation of Article 6 was only applicable to the continental shelf and thus could not be used for the determination of a single maritime boundary. Gulf of Maine, paras. 115–21.

[78] Jonathan I. Charney, "Progress in International Maritime Boundary Delimitation Law," 88 *Am. J. Int'l L.* 227 (1994).

rule . . . another naturally reacts in fear that it will lose some area."[79] With a definite rule of delimitation, States would have a clearer idea of what factors could be used in delimitation agreements. "The purpose of including a substantive provision in the convention is to describe, and thereby to narrow, the range of choices available."[80] Otherwise, States would be free to choose any equitable principle and accord any weight to that principle based on the vagaries of geography.[81]

As no compromise could be reached on the use of the equidistance-special circumstances formulation or a reference to equitable principles, Articles 74 and 83 of the Convention provide that the delimitation of the EEZ and the continental shelf, respectively, shall be effected by agreement in accordance with international law in order to achieve an equitable solution. This position reaffirms the principle that the validity of a maritime boundary, even when unilaterally declared, is determined by international law.[82] Agreement is to be reached "on the basis of international law, as referred to in Article 38 of the Statute of the International Court of Justice."[83] The text was included at the final stages of the Third Conference despite significant criticism and hesitation.[84] It was disliked because it did not provide any "specific designation of which principles and rules from out of the entire panoply of customary, general, positive,

---

[79] John R. Stevenson and Bernard H. Oxman, "The Third United Nations Conference on the Law of the Sea: The 1974 Caracas Session," 69 *Am. J. Int'l L.* 1, 17 (1975). "The realization is growing that the Conference could become hopelessly bogged down if it tries to deal definitely with essentially bilateral delimitation problems." *Ibid.*

[80] Bernard H. Oxman, "The Third United Nations Conference on the Law of the Sea: The Eighth Session (1979)," 74 *Am. J. Int'l L.* 1, 31 (1980).

[81] L. D. M Nelson, "The Roles of Equity in the Delimitation of Maritime Boundaries," 84 *Am. J. Int'l L.* 837, 852 (1990).

[82] Anglo-Norwegian Fisheries, at 132. "The establishment of an international maritime boundary regardless of the legal position of other States is contrary to the recognized principles of international law." Attard, p. 223.

[83] UNCLOS, arts. 74(1) and 83(1).

[84] Bernard H. Oxman, "The Third United Nations Conference on the Law of the Sea, The Tenth Session," 76 Am. J. Int'l L. 1, 13 (1982). Oxman cites the comments of the American representative as follows:

> If "the main purpose of a Convention on the Law of the Sea is to reduce the possibility of disputes and conflict between States, and to help resolve differences that do arise by narrowing and reformulating them in generally acceptable legal terms," the U.S. representative observed, then this is not the time for the conference "to give up and move forward with an anodyne text that cannot achieve these purposes and that may indeed have the opposite effect of adding confusion to the law . . . a text that delegations on both sides privately look upon with embarrassment."

Ibid., at 15 (citing statement of Ambassador Malone in the plenary meeting of August 28, 1981).

and conventional law are of particular significance."[85] In this respect, neither States in favor of equidistance-special circumstances nor those that supported equitable principles received any satisfaction.

States are thus provided with minimal guidance from the Convention on what approach must be used in the delimitation of their extended maritime zones.[86] Articles 74 and 83 leave both negotiators and third-party decision-makers alike with considerable discretion in deciding on maritime boundaries. There is certainly room to doubt whether there is any legal rule at all. Oda has stated:

> The words "in order to achieve an equitable solution" cannot be interpreted as indicating anything more than a goal and a frame of mind, and are not expressive of a rule of law ... The deciding factors in such diplomatic negotiations are mainly the negotiating powers and the skills of each State's negotiator. In other words, there is *no* legal constraint, hence there is *no* legal rule, which guides negotiations on delimitation, even though the negotiations should be directed "to achiev[ing] an equitable solution."[87]

Sir Robert Jennings has questioned how the UNCLOS formula is different from a decision *ex aequo et bono*.[88] As it is the equitable solution that must predominate, principles could acquire an equitable quality if they lead to an equitable result.[89] The ICJ reached this conclusion in *Tunisia/Libya* when discussing the provisions in the 1981 draft of the Convention:

> Any indication of a specific criterion which could give guidance to the interested parties in their effort to achieve an equitable solution has been excluded. Emphasis is placed on the equitable solution which has to be achieved. The principles and rules applicable to the delimitation of the continental shelf areas are those which are appropriate to bring about an equitable result . . .[90]

---

[85] Tunisia/Libya, at 246 (Dissenting Opinion of Judge Oda). Cf. Oxman,"Eighth Session," at 31 (arguing that by referring to delimitation in accordance with international law there is some restraint on the claims available in a delimitation).

[86] As Charney notes, "If international law is supposed to be normative, this formulation fell far short of the ideal." Charney, "Progress," at 227.

[87] Oda, "Dispute Settlement Prospects," at 869 (emphasis in original).

[88] Robert Y. Jennings, "The Principles Governing Marine Boundaries," in *Staat und Völkerrechtsordnung: Festschrift für Karl Doehring* (Kay Hailbronner *et al.* eds., 1989), pp. 397, 408. ("Yet the obvious question, even if it be somewhat embarrassing, must in honesty be posed: how, then, does this differ from a decision *ex aequo et bono*, except indeed that this is not what the parties asked for nor sanctioned?")

[89] See Tunisia/Libya, para. 70. The Court subsequently clarified this approach to say that the matter was not one of abstract justice but justice according to the rule of law. Libya/Malta, para. 45. See also Charney, "Progress," at 227.

[90] Tunisia/Libya, para. 50.

The method to be followed for achieving the goal of an equitable solution is not specified. Instead, the Convention "restricts itself to setting a standard, and it is left to States themselves, or to the courts, to endow this standard with specific content."[91]

Courts and tribunals resolving maritime boundary conflicts since the adoption of the Convention have sought to attain an equitable result and have utilized a range of principles,[92] and relied on a diversity of factors in reaching such a result.[93] In assessing the application of Articles 74 and 83 in case law, one commentator has concluded:

The pronouncements of the International Court of Justice and the Court of Arbitration in the Guinea/Guinea Bissau arbitration indicate that Articles 74 and 83 are considered to be identical to the rules of customary international law on the matter. Application of either set of rules to the same case would result in the same outcome.[94]

Such a conclusion is possible in light of the very broad formulations in the Convention – so much flexibility is accorded to decision-makers, it is unlikely that the reasoning for and designation of a maritime boundary

[91] Libya/Malta, para. 28. See also Gulf of Maine, para. 95 ("Although the text is singularly concise it serves to open the door to continuation of the development effected in this field by international case law"); Guinea/Guinea-Bissau, para. 88 ("in each particular case, its application requires recourse to factors and the application of methods which the Tribunal is empowered to select").

[92] For example, in *Libya/Malta*, the Court states:
> The normative character of equitable principles applied as part of general international law is important because these principles govern not only delimitation by adjudication or arbitration, but also, and indeed primarily, the duty of Parties to seek an equitable result. That equitable principles are expressed in terms of general application, is immediately apparent from a glance at some well-known examples: the principle that there is to be no question of refashioning geography, or compensating for the inequalities of nature; the related principle of non-encroachment by one party on the natural prolongation of the other, which is no more than the negative expression of the positive rule that the coastal State enjoys sovereign rights over the continental shelf off its coasts to the full extent authorized by international law in the relevant circumstances; the principle of respect due to all such relevant circumstances the principle that although State are equal before the law and are entitled to equal treatment, "equity does not necessarily mean equality."

Libya/Malta, para. 46.

[93] Malcolm Evans has analyzed in detail the different circumstances utilized in the course of maritime delimitation arbitrations and adjudications. Malcolm D. Evans, *Relevant Circumstances and Maritime Delimitation* (1989).

[94] Alex G. Oude Elferink, "The Impact of the Law of the Sea Convention on the Delimitation of Maritime Boundaries," in *Order for the Oceans at the Turn of the Century* (Davor Vidas and Willy Østreng eds., 1999), pp. 457, 462.

would not be justified under Articles 74 and 83. When States are nego-tiating a boundary, there is no limit to the factors that may be taken into account,[95] and, consequently, more factors may be considered in the course of negotiations than in a decision process undertaken by a third-party tribunal. So long as the agreement is in accordance with international law and effects an equitable result, UNCLOS places no fur-ther constrictions on this practice.

In *Eritrea/Yemen*, the delimitation of the northern reaches of the mar-itime area was governed by Articles 74 and 83 of the Convention. The Tribunal decided that the "generally accepted view" was that the equidis-tance line normally provided an equitable boundary in delimitations between States with opposite coasts.[96] Considerations relating to the position of "barren and inhospitable" islands,[97] as well as the history of oil concessions in the area did not disturb the use of a median line (the latter consideration actually reinforced the use of the median line).[98] This decision was "in accord with practice and precedent in like situa-tions,"[99] as little guidance could otherwise be drawn from the Conven-tion for what specific method should be applied. The Tribunal noted as much: "there has to be room for differences of opinion about the interpretation of articles which, in a last minute endeavour at the Third United Nations Conference on the Law of the Sea to get agreement on a very controversial matter, were consciously designed to decide as little as possible."[100]

In sum, the latitude created under UNCLOS leaves States and third parties granted responsibility to devise a maritime boundary a wide scope for considering a range of sources for ascertaining what would be an equitable solution in the circumstances of each case. It is not possible to determine any uniform standard that must be applied in all maritime delimitations as what constitutes an equitable result varies in light of the geography of each of the relevant areas. At best, the cases may indicate what factors can be considered in a delimitation but no

---

[95] See UN Division for Ocean Affairs and the Law of the Sea, *Handbook on the Delimitation of Maritime Boundaries*, at 25, UN Sales No. E.01.V.2 (2000). The volumes edited by Charney and Alexander further illustrate the range of circumstances accorded weight by States in their agreements. See generally Jonathan I. Charney and Lewis M. Alexander, *International Maritime Boundaries* (1996).

[96] Eritrea/Yemen, Maritime Delimitation, para. 131.

[97] *Ibid.*, para. 147.   [98] *Ibid.*, para. 132.   [99] *Ibid.*, para. 132.

[100] *Ibid.*, para. 117. See also Oxman, "Eighth Session," at 30 (noting that judges or arbitrators were not likely to be influenced greatly by an inevitably flexible formulation).

guidance is provided on how factors relevant to a delimitation are to be balanced or weighed.[101] Consequently, the failure of States to arrive at an agreement on maritime delimitation is not usually because of a difference in interpretation over the rules of international law but a difference of opinion on what constitutes an equitable solution.[102]

Provisional Delimitations

Pending an agreement, "the States concerned, in a spirit of understanding and cooperation, shall make every effort to enter into provisional arrangements of a practical nature and, during this transitional period, not to jeopardize or hamper the reaching of the final agreement."[103] States resisted any reference to a median line pending agreement even though State practice had favored such a boundary as an interim measure.[104] The Chairman of the committee negotiating this question decided that reference to the median line as an interim arrangement should not be included without a compulsory dispute settlement procedure being available since the availability of the median line might not encourage agreements.[105] If States could employ the median line as the interim arrangement and this line was preferred by a State for the final boundary, there would be no incentive for that State to refer the matter to any further negotiations, or to third-party settlement.

Provisional arrangements are without prejudice to any final delimitation.[106] A claim based upon the conduct of one State alone reflects only what that State might consider equitable, not what might be an equitable solution for both.[107] The policy of allowing such arrangements rests in the promotion of stability in the relations between States:

Such arrangements enable states to make use of the disputed areas and to conduct normal relations there. In the absence of such arrangements, states may feel compelled at some cost, to forcefully challenge each other's actions in the area to maintain their legal rights.[108]

---

[101] See Evans, "Expanding Categories," at 27–28.
[102] Oda, "Dispute Settlement Prospects," at 870.
[103] UNCLOS, arts. 74(3) and 83(3).   [104] Attard, p. 227.
[105] See Oxman, "1976 Session," at 267 (citing the comments of the chairman).
[106] UNCLOS, arts. 74(3) and 83(3). See also Bernard H. Oxman, "International Maritime Boundaries: Political, Strategic, and Historical Considerations," 26 *U. Miami Inter-Am. L. Rev.* 243, 290 (1994–95). ("Fears that a *modus vivendi* may, for political or juridical reasons, evolve into a permanent boundary or boundary regime may limit the ability of the parties to find means to control the scope and intensity of their dispute.")
[107] Evans, "Expanding Categories," at 25.   [108] Charney, "Progress," at 227.

Nonetheless, reference to provisional measures "of a practical nature" has been criticized as "so vague that it can be of little practical assistance in establishing interim measures."[109] States are again left with considerable discretion in reaching agreement on what temporary measures should be taken and are under no obligation to make interim arrangements. It is when States are unable to reach agreement within a reasonable period of time that the States concerned are to resort to the procedures in Part XV, and the compulsory procedures may enable a State to seek an interim arrangement as a provisional measure if circumstances so require.[110]

Historic Title

Historic title is recognized in various contexts in UNCLOS – in relation to maritime delimitation, the status of bays as well as the rights of States in respect of archipelagic waters. The rationale for recognizing historic rights is clearly grounded in notions of stability. One commentator has stated that:

Longstanding practice evidenced by a strong historic presence should not be disturbed. Judicial bodies are ill-advised to disregard a situation that has been peacefully accepted over a long period of time. To justify a division based on historic presence over the area, coupled with affirmative action toward that end, should be apparent.[111]

Claims of historic title effectively seek to restrict the rights of the international community in those waters.[112] Historic waters have been defined as, "waters over which the coastal State, contrary to the generally applicable rules of international law, clearly, effectively, continuously, and over a substantial period of time, exercises sovereign rights with the acquiescence of the community of States."[113] While historic waters are typically internal waters, the exact status could depend on

---

[109] Attard, p. 228.

[110] See further pp. 59–85. But see Aegean Sea Continental Shelf Case, Request for Indication of Interim Measures of Protection (*Greece* v. *Turkey*), 1976 ICJ REP. 3 (September 11) (declining to issue an order that Turkey refrain from all exploration activity as the seismic tests undertaken were of a transitory nature and so there was no risk of irreparable prejudice to the rights in question).

[111] Marvin A. Fentress, "Maritime Boundary Dispute Settlement: The Nonemergence of Guiding Principles," 15 *Ga. J. Int'l & Comp. L.* 591, 622–623 (1985).

[112] Roach, at 777.

[113] L. J. Bouchez, *The Regime of Bays in International Law* (1964), p. 281. See also Andrea Gioia, "Tunisia's Claims over Adjacent Seas and the Doctrine of 'Historic Rights,'" 11 *Syracuse J. Int'l L. & Com.* 327, 328–29 (1984).

whether the right of innocent passage has been allowed through the area in question.[114]

The presence of historic title may affect the drawing of a maritime boundary. The delimitation of the territorial sea specifically requires an adjustment of the median line where it is necessary to take account of "historic title or other special circumstances." Historic rights were recognized in the determination of maritime boundaries by third parties in *Grisbadarna* and *Anglo-Norwegian Fisheries*. In the delimitation between Sweden and Norway, the Permanent Court of Arbitration decided that the Grisbadarna area should be assigned to Sweden. One of the reasons for this delimitation was the "circumstance that lobster fishing in the shoals of Grisbadarna has been carried on for a much longer time, to a much larger extent, and by much larger number of fishers by the subjects of Sweden than by the subjects of Norway."[115] The Court was willing to take this factor into account on the basis that, "it is a settled principle of the law of nations that a state of things which actually exists and has existed for a long time should be changed as little as possible."[116]

In *Anglo-Norwegian Fisheries*, which was decided in 1951, the United Kingdom accepted that Norway was allowed to claim certain maritime waters as internal waters or territorial seas on historic grounds. In the opinion of the United Kingdom, these claims constituted a derogation from general international law:

on the ground that she has exercised the necessary jurisdiction over them for a long period without opposition from other States, a kind of *possesio longi temporis*, with the result that her jurisdiction over these waters must now be recognized although it constitutes a derogation from the rules in force.[117]

The Court defined historic waters as "waters which are treated as internal waters but which would not have that character were it not for the existence of an historic title."[118] The majority of the Court accepted the

---

[114] Donat Pharand, *Canada's Arctic Waters in International Law* (1988), p. 93.
[115] Grisbadarna, at 233.   [116] *Ibid.*, at 233.
[117] Anglo-Norwegian Fisheries, at 130.
[118] *Ibid.* In a dissenting opinion, Sir Arnold McNair considered that for a claim of historic bay evidence is required of a long and consistent assertion of dominion over the bay and of the right to exclude foreign vessels except on permission of the relevant State. *Ibid.*, at 164 (Dissenting Opinion of Sir Arnold McNair). Judge Read, in his dissent, stated that the burden was upon Norway to prove the following facts: that the Norwegian system came into being as a part of the law of Norway; that it was made known to the world in such a manner that other nations, including that

argument that historic title should be taken into account in maritime delimitations: "Such rights, founded on the vital needs of the population and attested by very ancient and peaceful usage, may legitimately be taken into account in drawing a line which, moreover, appears to the Court to have been kept within the bounds of what is moderate and reasonable."[119] Although claims of historic rights have been raised in other maritime delimitation cases resolved by third parties, these claims have not prevailed to alter the course of the boundary.[120]

The Convention further envisages claims of historic title being asserted with respect to bays. Article 10, paragraph 6 provides that the rules for drawing closing lines across the mouths of bays do not apply for "so-called 'historic' bays." At the First Conference, a proposal was submitted for a request to the General Assembly to study the regime of historic bays.[121] Although a study was prepared on the juridical regime of historic waters, including historic bays,[122] the issue was not addressed at any length at the Third Conference and Article 10 replicates the relevant provision of the Territorial Sea Convention. The classification of certain areas as historic bays has been controversial because of the potential to close off bodies of water and thereby push exclusive maritime zones further into high seas areas. A notable example of this situation has been

Britain knew about it or must be assumed to have had knowledge; and that there has been acquiescence by the international community, including by the United Kingdom. *Ibid.*, at 194 (Dissenting Opinion of Judge Read).

[119] *Ibid.*, at 142. According to Judge Alvarez, in his Separate Opinion, for prescription to have effect the rights claimed to be based thereon should be well established; have been uninterruptedly enjoyed; not infringe rights acquired by other States; not harm general interests; and not constitute an *abus de droit. Ibid.*, at 152 (Separate Opinion of Judge Alvarez).

[120] In *Tunisia/Libya*, Tunisia claimed that a maritime boundary would have to take into account its historic rights in relation to the exploitation of the shallow inshore banks for fixed fisheries and the deeper banks for the collection of sponges. Tunisia/Libya, para. 98. The Court, however, was able to reach a decision on the position of the boundary without having to pass judgment on the validity of this claim. *Ibid.*, para. 105. Similarly, in *Eritrea/Yemen*, although the Tribunal had confirmed the perpetuation of the traditional fishing regime around the mid-sea islands, the boundary drawn did not specifically designate the location of these traditional fisheries.

[121] India and Panama submitted this proposal, which was adopted as Resolution VII, at the First Conference. See Resolutions Adopted by the Conference, UN Doc. A/CONF.13/L.56 (1958), reprinted in *First Conference*, Plenary Meetings, at 145. The General Assembly referred this request to the International Law Commission. GA Res. 1453, UN GAOR, 14th Sess., Supp. 16, at 57, UN Doc. A/4354 (1959). The UN Secretariat undertook the study instead.

[122] Juridical Regime of Historic Waters, including Historic Bays, UN Doc. A/CN.4/143, reprinted in [1962] 2 Y.B. Int'l L. Comm'n 1, UN Doc. A/CN.4/Ser.A/1962/Add.1, UN Sales No. 62.V.5 (1962).

the United States' military challenges to Libya's assertion that the Gulf of Sidra constitutes a historic bay and should be closed off as internal waters.[123]

Reliance on historic criteria is also permitted when considering whether a group of islands constitutes an archipelago for the purposes of the Convention,[124] and in the drawing of archipelagic baselines.[125] With respect to the latter:

> If a part of the archipelagic waters of an archipelagic State lies between two parts of an immediately adjacent neighboring State, existing rights and other legitimate interests which the latter State has traditionally exercised in such waters and all rights stipulated by agreement between those States shall continue and be respected.[126]

Traditional fishing rights and other legitimate activities of States that are immediate neighbors to archipelagic States are to be recognized.[127] The existence of other rights relating to archipelagoes will depend on the neighboring State establishing that it had traditionally exercised the rights or interests claimed. Historic rights of this kind permit States to exercise a limited authority over certain areas not usually subject to coastal State sovereignty; the sovereignty is limited to the activity in question and does not amount to full sovereignty over high seas areas.[128] For historic fishing rights, a tribunal would have to examine the validity, scope and opposability of those rights to the other party.[129]

One of the important reasons for asserting historic rights was to protect long-held economic interests in particular areas in the face of the *res communis* philosophy.[130] As such, it is arguable that historic rights should

---

[123] Libya's position has been strongly criticized by commentators. See, e.g., John M. Spinnato, "Historic and Vital Bays: An Analysis of Libya's Claim to the Gulf of Sidra," 13 *Ocean Dev. & Int'l L.* 65 (1983); Roger Cooling Haerr, "The Gulf of Sidra," 24 *San Diego L. Rev.* 751 (1987); Yehuda Z. Blum, "The Gulf of Sidra Incident," 80 *Am. J. Int'l L.* 668 (1986).

[124] UNCLOS, art. 46(b). A commentary on Article 46 notes:
    The expression "which historically have been regarded as such" was not elucidated at the Conference. This alternative historical method of qualification may not be very important in practice, because before an archipelagic State may draw archipelagic baselines it must satisfy the objective criteria prescribed in article 47 as well as the requirement that it consist of one or more archipelagos. Furthermore, it is improbable that an entity without geographic, economic and political unity would attempt to be considered an archipelagic State.
    2 *United Nations Convention on the Law of the Sea 1982: A Commentary*, pp. 414–15.

[125] UNCLOS, art. 47(6).   [126] *Ibid.*, art. 47(6).   [127] *Ibid.*, art. 51(1).

[128] Gioia, at 329.   [129] Attard, p. 267.   [130] Roach, at 777.

be admitted in a more restricted fashion now that coastal States have much broader entitlements to maritime jurisdiction.[131] States might be inclined to challenge declarations of historic title in certain areas if such a declaration impinges on inclusive uses of that region. Alternatively, a challenge may arise in a bilateral delimitation where the historic claim has the effect of enlarging the entitlement of States with an adjacent or opposite coast. Competing claims over the existence and opposability of historic title cannot easily be resolved under the terms of the Convention in light of the scant elaboration of principles on this matter. Specificity on the standard to be applied in determining claims to historic title was avoided in the Convention for similar reasons as maritime delimitation: the circumstances of individual cases varied too extensively to permit the formulation of a uniform standard.

Dispute Settlement Procedures for Maritime Delimitation and Historic Title

Compulsory dispute settlement under Section 2 of Part XV is available to States for disputes relating to the delimitation of the territorial sea, continental shelf, and EEZ, and to historic title unless States have opted to exclude these disputes by virtue of Article 298(1)(a). Articles 74 and 83 expressly stipulate that States shall resort to Part XV procedures in the event that no agreement is reached within a reasonable period of time.[132] There was support for some form of dispute settlement entailing a binding decision because "boundary disputes were likely to be more frequent when the zones under the jurisdiction of the coastal states were more extensive, and . . . those zones would create a danger to peace if they were not definitely settled by a binding decision."[133]

---

[131] See ibid.   [132] UNCLOS, arts. 74(2) and 83(2).

[133] 5 United Nations Convention on the Law of the Sea 1982: A Commentary, p. 117. Jacovides writes:

> The fact is that sea boundary delimitation, because of the high stakes involved due to the increase of the zones of maritime jurisdiction under the present Convention (as compared to the 1958 situation), because of the contentious potential since it touches sensitive nerves of national sovereignty and because of the vagueness of the substantive rules adopted in other parts of the convention – particularly in the case of Articles 74 and 83 on the delimitation of the exclusive economic zone and the continental shelf between states with opposite or adjacent coasts – especially lends itself to third party compulsory settlement if solutions are to be found peacefully and actual or potential disputes are not to escalate into confrontations, including in many instances even armed conflict.

Jacovides, at 167–68.

Further impetus to resort to adjudication or arbitration for determination of maritime boundaries may be derived from the highly flexible legal formulae prescribed under the Convention. UNCLOS provides no clear rule for States to apply in maritime delimitation of the EEZ and continental shelf beyond the exhortation that any agreement be based on international law. Similarly, no criteria are stated for establishing historic title in relation to territorial sea delimitation, bays, and fishing in archipelagic waters. The indeterminate nature of the substantive principles set out with respect to delimitation of the continental shelf and the EEZ, as well as the large degree of discretion accorded to States in asserting historic title, meant that mandatory jurisdiction would provide States with a procedure to facilitate agreement. Certainly, western States strongly favored the inclusion of a procedure entailing binding jurisdiction if the substantive rules were insufficiently determinative.[134] Moreover, the delimitation of maritime zones has been subject to third-party dispute settlement in the past despite the highly discretionary nature of the applicable legal principles.[135] It is nonetheless noticeable that the arbitral and adjudicative procedures that have been undertaken for the determination of maritime boundaries have lacked the zero sum result that is characteristic of litigated dispute resolution. The typical tactic is for States to submit maximalist claims to courts and tribunals and these bodies are left the task of devising a compromise position between these claims to achieve an "equitable result." This history could indicate that the subject of the dispute would be conducive to settlement under the compulsory procedures in Part XV of the Convention. It may well be another contributory factor as to why governments negotiating at the Third Conference did not insist on the complete exclusion of maritime delimitation and historic title disputes from the compulsory dispute settlement regime.

---

[134] Eero J. Manner, "Settlement of Sea-Boundary Delimitation Disputes According to the Provisions of the 1982 Law of the Sea Convention," in *Essays in International Law in Honour of Judge Manfred Lachs* (Jerzy Makarczyk ed., 1984), p. 625, at pp. 636–37. See also Brown, "Dispute settlement," at 24 (1997). ("The objective observer might well argue that the degree of need for compulsory settlement machinery is in inverse proportion to the degree of precision and certainty of the criteria of delimitation: the more imprecise and uncertain the criteria, the greater the need for some form of compulsory settlement.")

[135] "In spite of this indeterminacy, if not because of it, coastal states have found that third-party dispute settlement procedures can effectively resolve maritime boundary delimitation disputes." Charney, "Progress," at 227.

States also have an economic incentive to resolve maritime disputes in order to provide companies interested in exploring for hydrocarbons with certainty and exclusivity of title. Equally, States could only grant fishing licenses over certain areas, and undertake the necessary conservation and management enforcement measures, when it could be clearly ascertained which State was responsible for, and entitled to, a particular maritime area. The importance of international marketability illustrates why compulsory dispute settlement is an essential complement to maritime delimitation.[136] Dispute settlement procedures provide States with the chance to quiet their title to certain maritime areas, particularly in situations of overlapping entitlements. To the extent that resources in maritime areas cannot be harvested and sold without recognized legal title, there is an incentive to submit to third-party dispute resolution. Such a procedure is necessary in order to show investors and the international market that a State has good title to the resources in a particular maritime area. Without a legal resolution, a State may lose all capacity to harvest and market resources – or at best the questionable title will significantly diminish the value of the concession – and this is because it can no longer market exclusive rights to private fishing fleets or oil companies. Moreover, States are much more likely to comply with a third-party decision on the allocation of maritime areas. Due to the centrality of marketable title, there is little value in continuing to claim maritime areas when a tribunal has declared that a particular State is not the owner of a certain area. Third-party opinion carries substantial weight because a State will not be able to market resources profitably after an adverse ruling.

The economic motivations, indeterminate legal standards and history of adjudicated or arbitrated delimitations may have militated in favor of compulsory dispute settlement but the significant practice of settlement through agreement and the important interests at stake also impacted on the decision to include mandatory jurisdiction over these disputes. Coastal States may wish to negotiate boundary agreements rather than refer matters to third parties, as the States concerned are able to take into account human and resource conditions that have been ignored in boundaries settled through adjudication or arbitration.[137]

---

[136] See Brilmayer and Klein, at 732–36.

[137] See Charney, "Progress," at 227 (noting that such consideration was taken in *Jan Mayen* but criticizing the step as "unfortunate and likely to encourage greater conflict and uncertainty"). Oxman has similarly commented:

The fundamental importance of maritime delimitation has meant that conflicts relating to overlapping entitlements are "the most dangerous" disputes,[138] as they lie "at the very heart of sovereignty."[139] The significance of the national interests involved in allocation of maritime zones deterred States from transferring unconditionally this important decision to an international process. The socialist States indicated that, "they would not accept any formula – nor indeed the whole Convention – if it contained provisions on compulsory procedures entailing binding decisions relating to delimitation disputes."[140] This problem became particularly acute when the decision was reached that no reservations could be made to the Convention.[141] States were concerned as to whether the dispute settlement procedures would grant the parties autonomy to determine the contents of the reference for settlement or whether they would be compelled to submit the determination of the boundary itself.[142] The compromise reached was that maritime delimitation and historic title disputes would be included within the compulsory dispute settlement framework but States could optionally exclude these disputes, subject to an obligation to refer the matter to conciliation if certain conditions were met.[143]

> Provided they agree, the parties are largely free to divide as they wish control over areas and activities subject to their jurisdiction under international law. They may be guided principally, in some measure, or not at all by legal principles and legally relevant factors a court might examine, and by a host of other factors a tribunal might well ignore such as relative power and wealth, the state of their relations, security and foreign policy objectives, convenience, and concessions unrelated to the boundary or even to maritime jurisdiction as such.

Oxman, "Political, Strategic, and Historical Considerations," at 256.

[138] Stevenson and Oxman, "1975 Session," at 781.
[139] Gamble, "Dispute Settlement in Perspective," at 331.
[140] Manner, at 636–37. See also Jagota, p. 238 (noting that some delegations expressly reserved their position on the need for compulsory dispute settlement in their proposals).
[141] UNCLOS, art. 309. States were well aware of the connection between the exclusions to compulsory dispute settlement entailing binding decisions and the use of reservations. An earlier draft of the article on reservations was provisional on an agreement being reached on the rules relating to delimitation of the extended maritime zones and the dispute settlement procedures available for delimitation disputes. See Bernard H. Oxman, "The Third United Nations Conference on the Law of the Sea: The Ninth Session (1980)," 75 *Am. J. Int'l L* 211, 232 (1981).
[142] Jagota, p. 237.
[143] Earlier drafts of Article 298(1)(a) provided that declarations excluding maritime delimitation disputes from the Convention regime had instead to specify a regional or other third-party procedure entailing a binding decision. See 5 *United Nations Convention on the Law of the Sea 1982: A Commentary*, pp. 109–13.

The use of conciliation as an alternative to adjudication or arbitration allows States to consider a wide range of factors in their efforts to reach agreement. Conciliation may produce a more acceptable political and economic result than adjudication or arbitration because it is a highly flexible process that permits a comprehensive range of interests to be taken into account.[144] Compulsory conciliation was also considered as providing more protection for weaker parties compared with a free choice of procedure where, in practice, dispute settlement may remain in the realm of negotiations where bargaining positions would be unequal.[145] Although not a binding determination, the findings of the conciliation commission could carry weight as an impartial judgment.[146] The utility of conciliation reports lies in the elaboration of principles that could be applied by the parties in future negotiations. Such a method is not without precedent – the ICJ was charged with this responsibility in the *North Sea Continental Shelf* cases, rather than being asked to define the actual location of the boundary.[147] In this respect, the conciliation commission may take into account interests that have typically been excluded in third-party maritime delimitations. The ultimate weight that the conciliation report will have on the final agreement of the States may be limited because of its non-binding nature. The worth of the conciliation process will depend on the type of recommendations, the States involved in the delimitation process, and the overall political context.

Under Article 298(1)(a)(i), either party to a dispute excluded from mandatory adjudication or arbitration can submit the matter to conciliation provided certain conditions have been met. The first condition is that the dispute must be one that has arisen subsequent to the entry

---

[144] Brus, n. 19 (comparing the outcome of the conciliation procedures between Iceland and Norway concerning the delimitation in the Jan Mayen area and the International Court of Justice's delimitation in the dispute between Denmark and Norway in a neighboring area).

[145] *Ibid.*, p. 123. Cf. Jacovides, at 167–68. ("Such a situation – the relative vagueness of the substantive rules on the one hand and the absence of compulsory third party dispute settlement procedures of a binding nature on the other – is bound to create problems and to work an injustice at the expense of smaller and militarily weaker states because larger and stronger states may be tempted to claim the lion's share and are not obliged to accept third party adjudication.")

[146] Günther Jaenicke, "Dispute Settlement under the Convention on the Law of the Sea," 43 *Zeitschrift für ausländisches öffentliches Recht und Völkerrecht* (1983), pp. 813, 827.

[147] North Sea Continental Shelf, para. 2. Norway advocated this approach in *Jan Mayen*, but the Court decided against Norway on this point. Jan Mayen, at 77–78. The argument was also made, and rejected, in *Tunisia/Libya*. Tunisia/Libya, at 38–40.

into force of UNCLOS between the parties to the dispute. The inclusion of this condition is a natural consequence of paragraph 4 of Articles 74 and 83, which states: "Where there is an agreement in force between the States concerned, questions relating to the delimitation of the [EEZ or continental shelf, respectively] shall be determined in accordance with the provisions of that agreement." This condition significantly reduces the number of delimitations that could be subject to the Convention's regime.[148] It excludes disputes that arise prior to the entry into force of the Convention for the particular States in dispute, not just disputes that arise after the entry into force of the Convention in general. This condition is grounded in the presumption against retroactivity in the law of treaties and prevents any longstanding disputes being made subject to Part XV of UNCLOS.[149] Furthermore, only addressing disputes that arise subsequent to the entry into force of the Convention prevents States from attempting to reopen disputes that had previously been settled in the hope that a more favorable outcome (a more "equitable result") would be achieved.

A point of contention here could well be deciding at what point in time the dispute arose. The Third Conference had considered three different formulae for this exception – one that excepted disputes; another that excepted disputes that related to situations or facts existing prior to the entry into force of the Convention; and a composite of these two.[150] Reference to existing facts and situations created a highly subjective test that would be dependent on the circumstances of each individual case.[151] Otherwise, the dispute can be deemed to arise at the time that opposing views of the States concerned take definite shape.[152] While Singh argues that the "crystallization of disagreement between the dispute States" model would add certainty to the operation of the

---

[148] Manner, p. 642. ("Accordingly, these provisions will not cover important old and pending delimitation disputes.")

[149] The presumption against retroactivity will not operate to bar the exercise of jurisdiction where there is a continuing violation of international law, however. See Joost Pauwelyn, "The Concept of a 'Continuing Violation' of an International Obligation: Selected Problems," 66 Brit. Y.B. Int'l L. 415, 435 (1995). ("The general rule is that in these cases the international tribunal will be allowed to exercise jurisdiction over the alleged breach for the period which continues to elapse after the critical date, even though the breach came into existence before that date.")

[150] Singh, p. 144.   [151] Ibid., p. 145.

[152] This test was used in the Mavrommatis Palestine Concessions case (Greece v. Britain) (Jurisdiction), 1924 PCIJ, Series A, No. 2, p. 28; 2 AD 27 et al. and the Interhandl case. Ibid., p. 145.

conciliation procedure,[153] this test does not advance a more objective formula. The question will clearly depend on the facts of any case in order to determine when the dispute concerning the location of the boundary or the challenge to the existence of historic title first occurred.

The second condition precedent is that no agreement has been reached in negotiations between the parties after a reasonable period of time. This condition reinforces the importance the Convention places on the peaceful settlement of disputes as a precursor to settlement under the compulsory UNCLOS regime. It further reaffirms the obligation to reach agreement found in Articles 15, 74, and 83. A question, of course, arises as to what constitutes a "reasonable period of time" and whether a State could challenge the competence of the conciliation commission on the basis that efforts at negotiations have not been exhausted or that a "reasonable" time for negotiations has not lapsed. The ICJ has considered that for maritime delimitations, States "are under an obligation to enter into negotiations with a view to arriving at an agreement, and not merely to go through a formal process of negotiation."[154] A decision on whether efforts at negotiation constitute more than a "formal process" will depend on the facts of each case. Undoubtedly, a reasonable period of time lapses if one party refuses to negotiate.[155] Another question is whether a disputant State would have to wait a "reasonable" period of time when it considers as soon as the dispute arises that negotiations would be unlikely to yield a result or it would be forced to accept a particular result through economic or political pressure that would have less impact in conciliation proceedings. In the provisional measures stage of *Southern Bluefin Tuna*, ITLOS considered that requirements to take efforts to resolve a dispute were met at the decision of one of the States that the possibilities for settlement were exhausted.[156] This decision referred to the conditions under Section 1 of Part XV. If a unilateral decision is sufficient for determining when negotiations are exhausted in relation to maritime delimitation, then this condition is unlikely to pose a significant hurdle.

---

[153] *Ibid.*, p. 146.
[154] North Sea Continental Shelf, para. 85. See also Railway Traffic between Lithuania and Poland (*Lithuania* v. *Poland*) 1931 PCIJ (ser. A/B) No. 42, at 116 (stating that the obligation was not just to enter into negotiations, but to pursue them as far as possible with a view to concluding agreements).
[155] See United States Diplomatic and Consular Staff in Tehran (*United States* v. *Iran*) 1980 ICJ 3, paras. 49 and 52 (May 24).
[156] Southern Bluefin Tuna, Provisional Measures, paras. 60 and 61.

A dispute submitted for conciliation cannot involve "concurrent consideration of any unsettled dispute concerning sovereignty or other rights over continental or insular land territory."[157] This clause limits the scope of a dispute, rather than serving as a condition precedent to the submission of the matter to conciliation.[158] If two States seeking to delimit their maritime boundary also dispute sovereignty over particular territory, the boundary could still be drawn to the extent that the delimitation would not be influenced by the disputed territory.[159] For example, a maritime boundary could be drawn up to the point that the maritime zone of a disputed island would begin to influence the line. This approach would be consistent with maritime boundary cases that have had to account for third-party interests becoming impacted in the delimitation of a bilateral boundary.[160]

If a State submits the matter to conciliation in accordance with Annex V, Section 2 of the Convention, the other party to the dispute is obliged to submit to such proceedings.[161] The function of the conciliation commission is to "hear the parties, examine their claims and objections, and make proposals to the parties with a view to reaching an amicable settlement."[162] The parties are then required to negotiate an agreement on the basis of the commission's report.[163] Article 298(1)(a)(ii) provides that "if these negotiations do not result in an agreement, the parties shall, by mutual consent, submit the question to one of the procedures provided for in Section 2, unless the parties otherwise agree." This provision is quite peculiar as it imposes a mandatory obligation ("shall") to submit the dispute to procedures in Section 2 but this referral is to be through "mutual consent," which would indicate that the use of Section 2 is not so mandatory. In addition, it purports to require the use of the procedures entailing a binding decision under Section 2 even though the whole purpose of the optional exception and the use of conciliation was to exclude resort to these sorts of mechanisms. This provision has been described as "one of the most bizarre passages in the entire Convention."[164] Gamble further writes:

---

[157] UNCLOS, art. 298(1)(a)(i).

[158] But see UN Handbook, p. 99 (considering this issue as a third condition precedent).

[159] See Oxman, Political, Strategic, and Historical Considerations, at 268.

[160] See, e.g., Libya/Malta, para. 78 (accounting for the maritime zones of Italy), and Eritrea/Yemen, Maritime Delimitation, para. 164 (accounting for the maritime zones of Saudi Arabia and Djibouti).

[161] UNCLOS, Annex V, art. 11.   [162] Ibid., Annex V, art. 6.   [163] Ibid., art. 298(1)(a)(ii).

[164] Gamble, "Binding Dispute Settlement?," at 51.

It is difficult to ascertain if anything is gained by this provision or others like it. The passage declares that the disputants "shall negotiate an agreement" but then immediately provides an alternative if no agreement can be reached. By mutual consent, the parties can submit the question to one of the procedures from section 2. The quintessence of the Montego Bay Convention's dispute settlement regime is the right of disputants to settle any dispute, at any time, by any mutually acceptable legal mode. Thus, the above provision would seem to contribute absolutely nothing.[165]

Perhaps one could have reference here to the decision of the ICJ in delimiting the maritime boundary between Greenland and the Norwegian island of Jan Mayen. Denmark had submitted the case to the Court on the basis of the optional clause whereby Norway and Denmark had agreed in advance to the compulsory jurisdiction of the Court.[166] Norway argued that the Court should not delimit the actual boundary but merely indicate the principles on which the delimitation should be based.[167] Such an approach had to be adopted by the Court, Norway argued, since States are only required to settle their maritime boundary disputes by agreement and not according to any specific rule or principle.[168] However, the Court decided to delimit the boundary.[169] Charney has stated: "Thus, the obligation to establish the maritime boundary by agreement was construed as merely a preliminary obligation; once efforts to negotiate a settlement were exhausted, the substantive international maritime boundary law became applicable and provided the rules pursuant to which the boundary must be delimited."[170] The question could then be posed as to whether the UNCLOS procedure should be approached in a similar way. Once the conciliation procedure has run its course, the States can thus consider their efforts to reach agreement exhausted and the compulsory procedures are then available to allow the matter to be settled through a third party. Such an argument is unlikely to succeed, however. The wording was intended to reinforce the paramountcy of State discretion in deciding how to settle maritime boundary disputes as well as the importance of a consensual resolution. Accounts of the negotiations at the Third Conference affirm this perspective: "The reference to 'mutual consent' was considered an essential additional element of compromise because it excluded

---

[165] *Ibid.*   [166] ICJ Statute, art. 36.   [167] See Jan Mayen, paras 88–89.
[168] Oral Presentation by Mr. Highet, Agent for Norway, Maritime Delimitation in the Area between Greenland and Jan Mayen (*Denmark v. Norway*), ICJ Verbatim Record, at 58–78 (January 21, 1993), cited in Charney, "Progress," at 227.
[169] Jan Mayen, para. 89.   [170] Charney, "Progress," at 227.

the interpretation that the parties had to accept a third-party decision in the event that the conciliation did not result in an agreement."[171] On this basis, it would seem more likely that the awkward phrasing of "shall, by mutual, consent," was intended to reinforce the idea that compulsory third-party arbitration or adjudication was not available for maritime boundary or historic title disputes if excluded at the option of the States parties. Thus, if States so elect, maritime delimitation and historic title disputes can be excluded from compulsory procedures entailing a binding decision and reliance is thereby placed on diplomatic methods and other consent-based forms of dispute settlement.

In sum, maritime delimitation and historic title disputes may be subject to compulsory dispute settlement procedures. While this decision may have been desirable for economic reasons and to provide a means to give the substantive principles of delimitation some content, the interests at stake were too great to surrender these matters entirely to international arbitration or adjudication. The variety of political, strategic, social, and economic factors involved in allocation of maritime areas and the resultant malleable legal principles have lent support for resolution through political channels rather than third-party decision. States have more typically delimited their maritime boundaries through agreement and have been able to take into account a wide range of factors that are peculiar to the geography of the area as well as the political relations between the relevant States. It is ultimately this tradition of negotiated agreement that is reinforced in UNCLOS.

Disputes relating to Articles 15, 74, and 83 between States with opposite or adjacent coasts, as well as historic title, may be excluded if a State chooses to make a declaration to that effect. When this declaration is made, a State will only be obliged to submit to conciliation proceedings if the dispute arose after the entry into force of the Convention for the parties and no agreement has been reached within a reasonable period of time. Furthermore, any conciliation process is to be limited to the extent that the dispute necessarily involves consideration of disputes over land territory. Once the commission has presented its report, States are to resort to negotiations again and cannot refer the matter to compulsory procedures entailing a binding decision unless they so agree. Article 298 also repeats limitations on dispute settlement under the Convention that are found in Section 1 of Part XV as well as in the

[171] Manner, p. 638.

articles on maritime delimitation themselves.[172] The end result is that if States cannot reach agreement and one State has opted to exclude compulsory jurisdiction, there is no mandatory mechanism for decision and the dispute can be left unresolved. While the availability of compulsory dispute settlement may be essential to the delimitation of maritime zones in accordance with the Convention, political realities have prevented the compulsory use of third-party decision-making.

Other Disputes Relating to Maritime Delimitation and Historic Title

The disputes concerning maritime delimitation that may be expressly excluded from compulsory dispute settlement involve States with adjacent or opposite coasts. The question arises as to whether maritime delimitation disputes between States that do not have opposite or adjacent coasts could be settled under Section 2 of Part XV regardless of any declaration under Article 298. Disputes may well arise in situations where a coastal State makes an excessive maritime claim thereby appropriating areas that would otherwise constitute high seas. These claims have been viewed as potentially impinging on the freedoms of navigation and overflight and could subsequently threaten the security interests of other users.[173] To counter excessive maritime claims, the United States has continuously protested and operated in contested areas under the Freedom of Navigation Program, which emphasizes the use of naval exercises to protect freedom of navigation and to discourage State claims inconsistent with customary international law.[174] Dispute resolution under UNCLOS may be preferable in view of the increasing political, economic, and military costs of the Program.[175] These sorts of disputes are most likely to arise in the context of how coastal States have

---

[172] Article 298(1)(a)(iii) reads: "This subparagraph does not apply to any sea boundary dispute finally settled by an arrangement between the parties, or to any such dispute which is to be settled in accordance with a bilateral or multilateral agreement binding upon those parties." UNCLOS, art. 298(1)(a)(iii).

[173] John H. McNeill, "The Strategic Significance of the Law of the Sea Convention," 7 *Geo. Int'l Envtl. L. Rev.* 703, 705 (1995).

[174] United States Department of State, Pub. No. 112, *Limits in the Seas: United States Responses to Excessive Maritime Claims* (1992), pp. 2–4. McNeill cites the example of the United States continuing to operate in the Persian Gulf despite the 1993 Iranian Maritime Areas law that attempts to inhibit uses of the area. McNeill, at 705–06.

[175] See George Galdorisi, "The United Nations Convention on the Law of the Sea: A National Security Perspective," 89 *Am. J. Int'l L.* 208, 210–212 (1995) (highlighting the challenges facing the Freedom of Navigation Program because of the large number of excessive maritime claims).

drawn their baselines or in a State's use of certain terrestrial features as islands to justify extending maritime zones as far as possible.

Straight Baselines

Baselines and closing lines have a fundamental importance in determining areas of maritime jurisdiction for they fix the points from which maritime areas are measured. Closing lines may be drawn across certain areas of water, such as bays and the mouths of rivers, and the enclosed waters have the status of internal waters, as opposed to territorial sea or high seas. Internal waters are identified where there is a "more or less close relationship existing between certain sea areas and the land formations which divide or surround them."[176] These waters must be "sufficiently closely linked to the land domain to be subject to the regime of internal waters."[177] Internal waters are juridically indistinguishable from a State's land territory (except for the requirement of allowing access to international ports) and are not typically subject to the regime of innocent passage.

In addition to closing lines, the Convention establishes two types of baselines from which the various maritime zones are to be measured. First, there is the normal baseline, which is the low-water line along the coast.[178] Second, the Convention includes the concept of the straight baseline in Article 7.[179] The straight baselines system was developed by the ICJ in the *Anglo-Norwegian Fisheries* case. In this case, the United Kingdom challenged the baselines used in a Norwegian decree that delimited a zone in which the fisheries were reserved to its own nationals. The Court determined that the drawing of straight baselines was not

---

[176] Anglo-Norwegian Fisheries, at 133.   [177] *Ibid.*

[178] The Second Sub-Committee at the 1930 Conference had agreed that the baseline from which the territorial sea would normally be measured was a line of low-water mark along the entire coast. Report of the Second Sub-Committee, Report Adopted by the Committee on April 10, 1930, Appendix, reprinted in 4 *Codification Conference*, at 1419. The use of the low-water line was also adopted in Article 3 of the Territorial Sea Convention and Article 5 of UNCLOS.

[179] In addition to the matter of normal baselines, the Preparatory Committee to the 1930 Conference asked States to consider if baselines were drawn following the sinuosities of the coast or whether islands, islets, or rocks could be considered as points for drawing lines. Point IV, Bases of Discussion, reprinted in 2 *Codification Conference*, at 253. The latter resembles an early formulation of straight baselines but the concept was not included as a possible basis for discussion at this time on the grounds that it "would necessitate detailed information as regards the choice of the salient points and the distance determining tha [sic] base line between these points." *Ibid.*, at 256.

unlawful if certain geographic – and possibly economic – conditions were met. The Territorial Sea Convention codified the conditions set out in *Anglo-Norwegian Fisheries* in order for straight baselines to be lawfully drawn.[180]

Article 7 of UNCLOS now allows for straight baselines to be used in "localities where the coastline is deeply indented and cut into, or if there is a fringe of islands along the coast in its immediate vicinity."[181] Where straight baselines are used, they "must not depart to any appreciable extent from the general direction of the coast, and the sea areas lying within the lines must be sufficiently closely linked to the land domain to be subject to the regime of internal waters."[182] Under the Convention, the drawing of straight baselines must therefore take into account geographical features.[183] In determining whether the lawful situation for straight baselines exists, consideration may further be given to particular economic interests in the relevant region, provided that the reality and importance of these interests are clearly evidenced by a long usage.[184] Economic interests only can be used in drawing straight baselines once it is clear that such lines are permissible on geographic

---

[180] The main divergence between the text adopted and the rule espoused in *Anglo-Norwegian Fisheries* is that the Territorial Sea Convention does not permit straight baselines to be drawn to and from low-tide elevations unless there are lighthouses or other installations on them that are permanently above sea level. See Territorial Sea Convention, art. 4(3). The Court had permitted Norway to draw baselines between low-tide elevations. Anglo-Norwegian Fisheries, at 133 and 144.

[181] UNCLOS, art. 7(1). Questions were raised during the debates at the First Conference about the use of the term "immediate vicinity." The delegation from the Philippines considered the definition of that phrase "should be left to the courts to decide." *First Conference*, 1st Comm., at 160, ¶ 66 (Philippines). The United States has proposed criteria for determining whether a coast is deeply indented or whether islands constitute a "fringe." To be "deeply indented" the coast must have three or more indentations in close proximity to one another and the depth of each indentation must be greater than one-half the length of its proposed baseline. For a "fringe," the islands must mask 50 percent of the coastline in the given location, lie within twenty-four miles of the coast and each baseline must not exceed twenty-four miles in length. Department of State, Bureau of Oceans and International Environmental and Scientific Affairs, *Developing Standard Guidelines for Evaluating Straight Baselines* (Limits in the Sea, No. 106) (1987), cited in John Astley III and Michael N. Schmitt, "The Law of the Sea and Naval Operations," 42 *Air Force L. Rev.* 119, 123 (1997).

[182] UNCLOS, art. 7(3).

[183] The geographical conditions necessary to warrant the drawing of straight baselines was one of the major controversies of the First Conference because of their effect of decreasing high seas areas. Dean, "Geneva Conference," at 617.

[184] UNCLOS, art. 7(5).

grounds.[185] When straight baselines are used "they should be drawn conservatively to reflect the one rationale for their use that is consistent with the Convention, namely the simplification and rationalization of the measurements of the territorial sea and other maritime zones off highly irregular coasts."[186]

Straight baselines may also be used to enclose the outermost islands of archipelagic States. The method for drawing these straight baselines is specified in Article 47, which sets out criteria for the length of the baselines and what basepoints may be used. The drawing of these baselines has the effect of transforming the waters within those lines into archipelagic waters and consequently further reduces the amount of high seas available to other users. In view of this appropriation, States that have used these waters will be concerned with the size of the area that will be subject to the sovereignty of archipelagic States.

The recognition of the straight baselines system had considerable repercussions for international navigation and overflight as the waters thereby enclosed became subject to the regime of internal waters. The Special Rapporteur to the International Law Commission had recognized prior to the First Conference, "the system was primarily aimed at increasing the zone of internal waters wherein navigation might be restricted by the coastal State."[187] The compromise solution adopted by the Commission, and endorsed in both the Territorial Sea Convention and in UNCLOS, was to allow for the right of innocent passage in areas used for international navigation and newly closed off by the application of straight baselines.[188]

Systems of straight baselines also have the effect of extending all other areas subject to coastal State sovereignty or jurisdiction significantly seaward. The accrual of exclusive interests for the coastal State may provide an incentive for States to use straight baselines in a manner that is not

---

[185] Dean, "Geneva Conference," at 618 (highlighting this wording as a success of the United States since the Soviet Union wished the economic and geographic factors to be alternatives rather than cumulative conditions). See also Fitzmaurice, at 77.

[186] Roach, at 780.

[187] *Summary Records of the Seventh Session*, [1955] 1 Y.B. Int'l L. Comm'n, at 196–97, ¶ 25 (François), UN Doc. A/CN.4/SER.A/1955, UN Sales No. 60.V.3, vol. I (1960).

[188] Report of the International Law Commission to the General Assembly, UN GAOR at 267, UN Doc. A/3159 (1956), reprinted in *ILC Yearbook*, (1956), vol. II, at 253. (dealing with para. 3 of the article and commentary). See also Territorial Sea Convention, art. 5 and UNCLOS, art. 8(2). A special regime was created in the Convention for passage through archipelagic waters. See notes 361–76 below and accompanying text.

entirely consistent with the terms of the Convention.[189] The Convention itself grants coastal States a large degree of discretion with respect to this issue. The possible abuse that may arise with the use of straight baselines was anticipated during the initial codification efforts. Prior to the First Conference, the International Law Commission considered whether there would be a maximum length imposed on a straight baseline as a possible way to control the use of straight baselines. Such a limitation had been recommended by the Committee of Experts, and adopted by the Special Rapporteur.[190] Scelle considered a maximum length acceptable if the principle of compulsory arbitration was accepted for the purpose of determining the baseline of the territorial sea.[191] Lauterpacht also wondered if the ICJ would have jurisdiction over exceptions to the low-water line,[192] and went so far as to propose an amendment to the draft article on straight baselines whereby the ICJ would be given the power to maintain, modify, or annul the lines drawn.[193] These comments indicate that when a subjective decision is left to the coastal State,

[189] Reisman and Westerman have identified two categories of claims that are not in entire conformity with the formula for determining straight baselines as set out in Article 7 of the Convention. W. Michael Reisman and Gayl S. Westerman, *Straight Baselines in Maritime Boundary Delimitation* (1992), p. 118. The first category of disputable claims is where straight baselines have been drawn along coasts that are neither deeply indented and cut into nor fringed with islands in the immediate vicinity and the second category is where a State does have this type of coast but the basepoints selected for drawing the baseline are inappropriate. *Ibid.*, p. 118. Controversy may also arise over what constitutes a bay or island or low-tide elevation for the purpose of drawing a baseline. See Astley and Schmitt, at 122 (noting that baselines constitute a "critical point of departure" and are thus the focus of many law of the sea disputes).

[190] Additif au deuxième rapport de M. J. P. A. François, Rapporteur Spécial, UN Doc. A/CN.4/61/ Add.1, at 77, reprinted in *ILC Yearbook*, (1953), vol. II, at 75. The Special Rapporteur voiced the fears left by discretion (without suggesting dispute settlement was the answer):

> The matter of the territorial sea concerned not merely the interests of one State; it was a possible source of abuse and the Commission should endeavour to secure acceptance of a rule applicable to all countries. If the Commission wished to codify international law, or establish its rules by means of conventions, it could not leave unlimited discretion to Governments in all matters.

Summary Records of the Sixth Session, [1954] 1 Y.B. Int'l L. Comm'n, UN Doc. A/CN.4/SER.A/1954, UN Sales No. 59.V.7, vol. I (1959), at 70, ¶ 26 (François).

[191] *ILC Yearbook*, (1954), vol. I, at 69, ¶ 20 (Scelle).   [192] *Ibid.*, at 68, ¶ 4 (Lauterpacht).

[193] *Ibid.*, at 75, ¶ 27 (Lauterpacht). Scelle considered this "extremely valuable," as the ICJ had the power "to rule *ex aequo et bono* and hence the freedom to evolve new law on the particular subject." *Ibid.*, at 75, ¶¶ 35–36 (Scelle). This proposal was criticized by several members of the Commission and ultimately withdrawn. See *ibid.*, at 83–85. A later proposal was to refer the matter to the same international organ that would have considered claims to different breadths of territorial sea. Amendements

then third-party dispute settlement might be necessary to balance the discretion granted.[194]

The delimitation of the territorial sea or the extended maritime zones by a coastal State can therefore be a controversial issue if straight baselines are drawn in such a way as to increase the size of the coastal State's internal waters and thereby restrict the rights and freedoms of other users.[195] As with other aspects of maritime delimitation, the exercise of a State's discretion in fixing its baselines may be subject to international scrutiny and the validity of the delimitation will depend on international law.[196] It is most typical that a challenge to baselines will ensue in the context of a delimitation between States with opposite or adjacent coasts.[197]

The question of straight baselines arose in the *Eritrea/Yemen* arbitration when the Tribunal delimited the northern reaches of the maritime area in dispute. Each country had relied on different basepoints in drawing straight baselines around the Dahlak islands, a fringe of islands off the Eritrean mainland coast. Although the Tribunal noted that it was not called upon to decide the reality, validity, or definition of the straight baseline system that had been established under Ethiopian legislation,[198]

proposés par M. J. P. A. François, Spécial Rapporteur, sur la base des observations des gouvernements au projet d'articles provisoires adopté par la Commission à sa sixième session, UN Doc. A/CN.4/93, reprinted in *Documents of the Seventh Session including the Report of the Commission to the General Assembly*, [1955] 2 Y.B. Int'l L. Comm'n 5, UN Doc. A/CN.4/SER.A/1955/Add.1, UN Sales No. 60.V.3, vol. II (1960).

[194] The only proposal for a dispute settlement mechanism relating to baselines at the First Conference came from the Japanese delegation, which proposed, without success, a new article for the Territorial Sea Convention that would have required disputes arising out of Article 5 (straight baselines) and Article 7 (bays) be submitted to the ICJ unless the parties agreed on another method of dispute settlement. Japan: Proposal, UN Doc. A/CONF.13/C.1/L.130, reprinted in *First Conference*, 1st Comm., at 246.

[195] Roach gives the example of Myanmar's 222-mile straight baseline across the Gulf of Martaban that effectively claims 14,300 square miles (an area the size of Denmark) as internal waters. Roach, at 780.

[196] Anglo-Norwegian Fisheries, at 132.

[197] Reisman has noted that courts or tribunals deciding maritime boundaries have been more inclined to ignore exorbitant straight baseline systems rather than criticize them. W. Michael Reisman, "Eritrea-Yemen Arbitration (Award, Phase II: Maritime Delimitation)," 94 *Am. J. Int'l L.* 721, 732 (2000). The approach taken has been to fix the maritime boundary without taking into account the basepoints or baselines utilized by the parties. See Tunisia/Libya, at 76, para. 104; Gulf of Maine, at 332, para. 210; Libya/Malta, at 48, para. 64; Channel Islands, para. 19; Guinea/Guinea-Bissau, para. 96.

[198] Legislation that had been adopted by Ethiopia during the period of Ethiopia's annexation of Eritrea continued in force after Eritrea's formal independence in 1993.

it still had responsibility for deciding on the basepoints that would control the course of the international boundary.[199] In this context, the Tribunal rejected the use of a particular feature, called Negileh Rock, as a basepoint on the basis that a British Admiralty Chart had shown the feature to be an underwater reef. Although rejecting Eritrea's submission in this regard, the Tribunal did not use the Eritrean islands suggested by Yemen as basepoints but determined itself what basepoints to use.[200] When considering the basepoints on the Yemeni coast, the Tribunal again considered the possible application of a straight baseline system. As Yemen had argued that the mid-sea islands should be used as basepoints, rather than its mainland coast, Yemen had not made any submissions on the application of a straight baseline system around the islands immediately adjacent to its coast. The Tribunal thus decided that the "intricate system of islands, islets and reefs which guard this part of the coast" constituted a "'fringe system' of the kind contemplated by Article 7 of the Convention, even though Yemen does not appear to have claimed it as such."[201] In making this decision, the Tribunal effectively assumed the power to assess the legitimacy of straight baselines in the context of a maritime delimitation dispute.

The decision in *Qatar v. Bahrain* may further signal a new trend in international courts and tribunals to assess the lawfulness of straight baselines. Bahrain alleged that the islands off the coast of the main islands could be assimilated to a fringe of islands that constituted a whole with the mainland.[202] While the ICJ considered that these features were part of the overall geographical configuration, the geographic conditions did not qualify as a fringe of islands along the coast for the purpose of applying the straight baselines method.[203] Instead, each maritime feature would have its own effect for the determination of baselines. The Court clearly stated in *Qatar v. Bahrain* that, as an exception to the normal rules for the determination of baselines, the straight baselines method had to be applied restrictively.[204]

To the extent that a dispute over baselines involves allocation of overlapping maritime zones between States with opposite or adjacent coasts or relates to historic title, the dispute could be excluded from compulsory procedures entailing a binding decision by virtue of Article 298. However, a third State may wish to challenge baselines if they are drawn

---

[199] Eritrea/Yemen, Maritime Delimitation, para. 142.   [200] *Ibid.*, para. 146.
[201] *Ibid.*, para. 151.   [202] *Qatar v. Bahrain*, para. 213.
[203] *Ibid.*, para. 214.   [204] *Ibid.*, para. 212.

in such a manner to allocate areas that would otherwise be part of the high seas. The *Anglo-Norwegian Fisheries* case involved such a challenge by the United Kingdom in respect of Norway's baselines.[205] On a textual analysis, the optional exception would not preclude States from instituting compulsory procedures under Section 2 of Part XV, if a State has filed an optional exclusion of jurisdiction on this question, as Article 298(1)(a)(i) refers explicitly to Articles 15, 74, and 83, and historic bays and titles. A dispute simply concerning the drawing of straight baselines in contravention of Article 7 falls outside the scope of the optional exception and could thus be resolved within the framework of Part XV.[206] Reisman and Westerman suggest that ITLOS could be used to "reinforce the intended purpose of straight baselines as mechanisms to rationalize ('smooth out') the ocean boundaries of irregular coastlines rather than as mechanisms to extend a nation's territorial waters."[207]

The situations where a dispute could be isolated in such a manner are limited, however. If a State is complaining that its high seas rights are being denied because of the coastal State's assertions of jurisdiction, sovereign rights, or sovereignty over a maritime area then it is likely that the dispute involves questions concerning resource exploitation (such as an assertion of enforcement jurisdiction over unlawful fishing) or allegations of unauthorized marine scientific research. A dispute could thus be characterized in such a manner that it would still fall within the limitations or exceptions to Section 2 of Part XV. If the drawing of baselines is the preliminary, or base, issue involved, a tribunal or court may be justified in proceeding to answer that question. To the extent that the question of baselines is subsumed or inherently linked to other substantive questions, the court or tribunal must decide what characterization is to take precedence in deciding on jurisdiction. If the dispute over the use of straight baselines arises because of interference with the freedoms of navigation or overflight then an important role for third-party dispute resolution remains in protecting these inclusive interests, and should warrant the exercise of jurisdiction.

---

[205] As noted above, the United Kingdom challenged the legality of Norwegian baselines that delimited a zone in which the fisheries were reserved to Norwegian nationals.

[206] See Roach, at 781.

[207] Reisman and Westerman, p. 219. But see Noyes, "ITLOS," at 155. ("One ought not assume that a 'binding' decision against a state's straight baseline claim by the ITLOS [or another court or tribunal] will automatically lead the political authorities of that state to reverse their position.")

The existence of a means to challenge the drawing of straight baselines through the Convention's dispute settlement mechanism may discourage States from making excessive claims in the future as well as encourage States to revise existing claims to ensure that they are in accord with the criteria in UNCLOS.[208] The question of the international legality of straight baselines may well be resolved through processes other than mandatory dispute settlement. For example, as coastal States are required to deposit copies of charts marking geographical coordinates of baselines with the UN Secretary General,[209] the resulting publicity may cause States to reassess their drawings of baselines. As Reisman notes, "[g]iven the discretionary and somewhat subjective character of straight baselines, this requirement would appear to have been designed as a necessary component of their validity and opposability to third states."[210] The Division of Ocean Affairs and the Law of the Sea in the UN Secretariat has established the necessary facilities to receive and disseminate this information.[211] In addition, the Division has a Geographic Information System that "helps . . . to identify any inconsistencies in the information submitted."[212]

Another possible way to rectify unlawful baselines may be through the Commission on the Limits of the Continental Shelf.[213] The Commission is the body created under the Convention to make recommendations to coastal States that want to claim extended continental shelf jurisdiction.

---

[208] "In discharging this obligation, states may either re-examine the outer limit lines previously defined in their national legislation or have to establish these lines, if they have not yet done so. The publicity resulting from these coastal state actions may provoke reactions from interested states". Oude Elferink, p. 458.

[209] UNCLOS, art. 16. The General Assembly requested the Secretary-General to establish the appropriate facilities for the deposit by States of maps, charts and geographic coordinates concerning national maritime zones and establishing a system for their recording and publicity. GA Res. 28, UN GAOR, 49th Sess. (1994), available at http://www.un.org/documents/ga/res/49/a49r028.htm, para. 15(f).

[210] Reisman, "Eritrea-Yemen," at 732. See also *ibid.*, at 733 ("But how can international users, availing themselves of the freedom of navigation, know of unpublished straight baselines and their consequent projection of different legal regimes *vers le large*?"); Oude Elferink, p. 459 ("non-compliance with the obligation to give due publicity to the limits of maritime zones may make these unopposable against other states if a conflict over their location arises").

[211] UN Handbook, p. 11.   [212] *Ibid.*

[213] This Commission was established on March 14, 1997 in accordance with Article 76, which addresses the limits of the continental shelf. Under Article 77, the coastal State exercises sovereign rights over the continental shelf for the purpose of exploring and exploiting its natural resources to a distance of 200 miles from its baselines. Provided certain technical criteria are met, coastal States may claim up to 350 miles of jurisdiction over areas where the actual shelf extends beyond 200 miles.

Its functions are to consider the data and other material submitted by coastal States concerning the outer limit of the continental shelf in areas where those limits extend beyond 200 miles and to provide scientific and technical advice, if requested, during the preparation of such data.[214] The Commission makes recommendations to establish the limit of the continental shelf and any recommendation could take account of the baselines drawn by the States wishing to extend their continental shelf and whether those baselines are in accordance with the terms of the Convention. It could be argued that experts in the field of geology, geophysics, or hydrography are not qualified to address such an issue, or it is outside the scope of the Commission's jurisdiction. However, the Commission is responsible for assisting States in the lawful extension of their continental shelf and without considering the position of the baselines, the Commission could well be perpetuating a violation of the Convention. The instances where the Commission may be able to function in this way are undoubtedly limited, however.

Although mechanisms besides compulsory dispute settlement exist within the Convention as a means of regulating the lawful drawing of straight baselines, these alternative processes are limited in their lack of authoritative control and restricted availability. Compulsory dispute settlement entailing binding decisions is available under the Convention and may serve the role of modifying State discretion to ensure conformity with international legal standards. An additional procedure may fill a gap in a viable normative regime for the drawing of lawful straight baselines. Lacunae still remain, though. Questions may arise as to whether a dispute over baselines relates to delimitation disputes under Articles 15, 74, and 83 or to historic bays and titles. If so, the optional exception may exclude the dispute from the Section 2 process. Even when a third State is challenging straight baselines because of the impact on inclusive uses of ocean space, the matter may be linked to disputes that would otherwise be excluded from mandatory jurisdiction by virtue of Article 297. In the latter situation, where the drawing of straight baselines is somehow inherently linked to issues that would otherwise be outside the scope of mandatory jurisdiction, the question for the tribunal or court is how to characterize the dispute. The issue of straight baselines may be the predominant or preliminary question and may warrant the intervention of an international court or tribunal. Respect for the exercise of coastal State discretion would have to be

---

[214] UNCLOS, Annex II, art. 3(1).

balanced against the need to affirm the criteria set out for the lawful drawing of straight baselines, and to protect the inclusive interests of other users. If coastal States have not been prepared to register their baselines in accordance with Article 16, the responsibility for maintaining the international standards under the Convention falls to international courts and tribunals. Courts and tribunals constituted under Part XV should not hesitate to exercise jurisdiction to enforce the standards for straight baselines set out in the Convention and thereby reaffirm and uphold the normative content of these rules.

Islands

Disputes may arise over islands in different contexts. Issues may concern the definition of an island and whether a particular feature may be so defined. This question is relevant for the use of islands in drawing baselines to determine the extent of coastal State jurisdiction or sovereignty as well as the impact an island may have in drawing maritime boundaries between opposite and adjacent States. The legal definition of an island is also relevant where a State may wish to claim rights to maritime space by virtue of the presence of a tiny, isolated, barren island in the middle of the high seas.[215] An island is defined in Article 121 of the Convention as "a naturally formed area of land, surrounded by water, which is above water at high tide."[216] These three criteria must be met for a State to claim the territorial sea, contiguous zone, EEZ, and continental shelf surrounding the land formation.[217] Article 121 applies to natural land formations and individual islands, rather than groups of islands, which are covered by the provisions on archipelagoes in Article 46.

---

[215] Barbara Kwiatkowska and Alfred H. A. Soons, "Entitlement to Maritime Areas of Rocks Which Cannot Sustain Human Habitation or Economic Life of Their Own," 21 *Neth. Y.B. Int'l L.* 139, 145–46 (1990) (describing islands that are so located).

[216] UNCLOS, art. 121 (1). Islands are also mentioned in the Convention in reference to the drawing of baselines (*ibid.*, arts. 6, 7(1), and 10(3)), navigation through straits (*ibid.*, art. 38(1)), archipelagic states (*ibid.*, art. 46 and Part IV generally), and artificial islands (*ibid.*, arts. 11, 60, 80, and 147(2)(e)).

[217] *Ibid.*, art. 121(2). This definition was first formulated at the 1930 Codification Conference where the Sub-Committee's Report refers to an island being an area of land, surrounded by water, which is permanently above the high-water mark. This definition was subsequently followed by the International Law Commission and adopted in Article 10 of the Territorial Sea Convention. The definition of an island, and particularly the meaning of "above water at high tide," was considered in *United States v. Alaska*, 117 S. Ct. 1888 (1997).

Islands are entitled to the same maritime areas as continental land unless they constitute "rocks," as defined under the Convention. Rocks do not generate continental shelf or EEZ rights if they "cannot sustain human habitation or economic life of their own."[218] The exact meaning of this qualification has been rightly queried.[219] No further explanation could be agreed upon during the Third Conference and so the definition was deliberately left ambiguous.[220] Charney has rightly noted that the two conditions are directly linked to human activities and development and that they may well vary over time as technology and resource use change.[221] He further considers that permanent habitation or year-long economic use are not necessary but there must just be proof that the rock has "some capacity" for human habitation or economic value.[222] The words "cannot sustain" reinforce that the question is one of capacity rather than a factual situation of sustaining human habitation or economic life or not.[223] This assessment may involve consideration of the history of the maritime feature to determine whether it qualifies as an island or a rock.[224] In addition, Attard has argued that the words "of their own" ensure that no State can artificially create conditions for human habitation or economic life.[225] These considerations should all be relevant in applying the definition in Article 121. Any decision on whether a particular landform is an island or a rock will have more significance if the question arises in the context of a maritime delimitation

---

[218] UNCLOS, art. 121(3). As an interesting forerunner to this qualification, several States responded to questions prepared for the Codification Conference regarding the definition of islands that islands should be defined by reference to whether they were capable of effective use and occupation. See, e.g., South Africa, Germany, Australia, Great Britain, India, New Zealand, Point VI, Bases of Discussion, reprinted in 2 *Codification Conference*, at 270–71. This criterion was not included as part of the bases of discussion, however, and was thus not ultimately considered at the 1930 Conference. Point VI, Bases of Discussion, reprinted in *ibid.*, at 272.

[219] See, e.g., Jonathan I. "Charney, Rocks that Cannot Sustain Human Habitation," 93 *Am. J. Int'l L.* 863 (1999); Kwiatkowska and Soons; Jonathan L. Hafetz, "Fostering Protection of the Marine Environment and Economic Development: Article 121(3) of the Third Law of the Sea Convention," 15 *Am. U. Int'l L. Rev.* 584 (2000).

[220] Jon M. Van Dyke and Robert A. Brooks, "Uninhabited Islands: Their Impact on the Ownership of the Oceans' Resources," 12 *Ocean Dev. & Int'l L.* 265, 282 (1983).

[221] Charney, "Rocks," at 867–68.

[222] *Ibid.*, at 868. This opinion is consistent with the decision of the Jan Mayen Conciliation Commission, which took the view that the maintenance of an economic life of its own would not necessarily exclude external support for a population that was not always permanent. See Report and Recommendations of the Conciliation Commission on the Continental Shelf Area between Iceland and Jan Mayen, 20 ILM 797, 803–04 (1981). See also Kwiatkowska and Soons, at 168–69.

[223] Kwiatkowska and Soons, at 160.   [224] *Ibid.*, at 161.   [225] Attard, pp. 259–60.

between States with adjacent or opposite coasts or whether the question is one of the legality of baselines and exertion of coastal State jurisdiction or sovereignty over maritime areas.

Islands and rocks have been discussed in third-party decisions delimiting boundaries between opposite or adjacent States. These features typically constitute "special" or "relevant" circumstances and have differing impact on the drawing of the maritime boundary depending on their geographic location and their importance as well as the overall geography of the maritime area being delimited.[226] There has not been any consideration of whether a particular feature was a "rock" under the terms of UNCLOS and thereby reduced the entitlement of a State to extended maritime zones.[227] In *Eritrea/Yemen*, the Tribunal had to delimit the southern areas between the small Eritrean islands and the Yemeni mid-sea islands. Due to the narrow distances involved,[228] the Tribunal did not need to consider whether the particular features were rocks or islands under Article 121.[229] By negative implication, rocks are entitled to a territorial sea and contiguous zone.[230] The other implication to be drawn here is that a rock must still be a "naturally formed area of land, surrounded by water, which is above water at high tide," because it would otherwise constitute a low-tide elevation, which is not accorded territorial sea if it is situated outside the territorial sea of a coastal State.[231] The question may have arisen in the northern Red Sea area given

---

[226] "It may thus be necessary, in the delimitation of a boundary, to abate the effect of an island which forms an incidental special feature." Dubai/Sharjah, at 676. See also Tunisia/Libya, at 89, para. 129 ("a number of examples are to be found in state practice of delimitations in which only partial effect has been given to islands situated close to the coast; the method adopted has varied in response to the varying geographical and other circumstances of the particular case"); Channel Islands, paras. 183–84 and 187 (considering the geographic situation of two opposite States with islands of one State close to the coast of the other State, the islands' political relationship with the mainland, their economy, and population as well as each State's territorial sea limits and coastal fisheries).

[227] In *Jan Mayen*, Denmark argued that Jan Mayen was not capable of sustaining human habitation or economic life but did not go so far as to assert that the island had no entitlement to continental shelf or fishing zones. Jan Mayen, para. 80.

[228] The combined territorial seas of each State in this area were no more than five miles wide.

[229] If wider distances had been at stake, then the question would probably have arisen given the descriptions of the different southern islands as "rocky islets which amount to little more than navigational hazards" and "uniformly unattractive, waterless, and habitable only with great difficulty." Eritrea/Yemen, Territorial Sovereignty, paras. 467, 93 (respectively).

[230] UNCLOS, art. 121(3). See also Charney, "Rocks," at 864.

[231] UNCLOS, art. 13. See also Kwiatkowska and Soons, at 150.

the greater distances involved and the barren and inhospitable nature of the mid-sea islands there located. However, the Tribunal elected to ignore these features in delimiting the boundary line between Eritrea and Yemen without casting the question in terms of entitlement of rocks or islands.[232]

To the extent that the status of islands is part of the overall settlement of territorial sea, EEZ and/or continental shelf boundaries, disputes over the qualification of certain landforms as islands will be subjected to the same procedures as specified in Article 298(1)(a). A State may try to raise the specific question of whether a particular feature is a rock or an island under Article 121 without asking a tribunal or court to be involved in the actual maritime delimitation. Such a decision could then be used by a State in influencing negotiations over the boundary. Article 298 does not *prima facie* exclude disputes over the interpretation or application of Article 121 from compulsory procedures entailing a binding decision if a State has otherwise so elected. There may be an advantage in referring a question of interpretation of "human habita-tion or economic life of their own" to an international body as a means of developing and clarifying the law on this issue. However, a challenge to the jurisdiction of the tribunal or court would certainly be warranted on the basis that the question is inherently related to maritime delim-itation and should be excluded due to the optional exception of one (or both) of the disputant States. A consistently recognized principle of maritime delimitation has been effecting a boundary by agreement between the parties concerned. This principle has been affirmed in the Convention in the articles dealing with the substantive law of delim-itation as well as the dispute settlement procedures.[233] To isolate one particular question pertaining to the maritime delimitation for manda-tory adjudication or arbitration deprives States from reaching agree-ment on their own accord. A decision by a court or tribunal on this specific issue denies States the full benefit of a right granted under the Convention.

The other context in which disputes over the definition of islands may arise is in the designation of basepoints for the determination of the outer limit of maritime zones. The position of islands may provide another means for littoral States to designate basepoints beyond the

---

[232] Eritrea/Yemen, Maritime Delimitation, para. 147.

[233] See UNCLOS, arts. 15, 74, 83, 298, and Part XV, Section 1 generally. This principle was also reaffirmed in the *North Sea Continental Shelf* cases. See discussion at notes 43–46 and accompanying text.

mainland coast. The ownership of islands is also important when a State with sovereignty over a small island in the middle of the high seas or a long distance from its coast but still within its extended maritime zone uses the existence of that island to claim an even greater entitlement to maritime areas. The claim to maritime space may be controversial if third States consider that the "island" causing the maritime boundary to be extended is actually a "rock." A confrontation could further result between a State with a long-distant fishing fleet fishing outside the territorial sea of a "rock" and a State seeking to exclude those fishing vessels from the area that it alleged was the EEZ of its "island." The potential for such a dispute has already been raised before ITLOS. In a decision relating to the prompt release of a vessel that was seized in the EEZ of Kerguelen Islands, Judge Vukas in a separate declaration doubted whether the establishment of an EEZ for those "uninhabitable and uninhabited" islands was in accordance with UNCLOS.[234] This statement in a prompt release proceeding was an unusual moment of judicial activism.[235] At the least, it indicates the potential for a dispute over the interpretation and application of Article 121 being raised in proceedings instituted under Article 286.

It would thus seem that in situations where a dispute arises over the definition of an island under Article 121 between the State with sovereignty and third States then these conflicts are subject to the compulsory procedures in Section 2, once the requirements of Section 1 are fulfilled. However, the fact that the dispute may arise in the context of the exercise of enforcement jurisdiction by the coastal State in its EEZ in respect of fishing activities may bring into play other limitations to compulsory jurisdiction. The question is then similar to that posed with respect to straight baselines. Any court or tribunal would have to decide whether the dispute concerning Article 121 was preliminary to a determination on the exercise of jurisdiction on other aspects of the dispute. A segregation of the dispute in this manner may be sufficient to resolve the conflict in question. However, the division of the dispute may not be possible or viable if the court or tribunal considers the question of the entitlement of the landform to extended maritime zones as integral to a decision on a State's exercise of enforcement jurisdiction. As with straight baselines, it may be preferable for an international standard to

---

[234] Monte Confurco, Declaration of Judge Vukas.

[235] Judge Anderson noted his surprise at Judge Vukas' Declaration as, *inter alia*, the Tribunal is only meant to deal with questions of release in considering applications under Article 292 of the Convention. *Ibid.*, Dissenting Opinion of Judge Anderson, n. 1.

be further elaborated through international processes to provide greater clarity in the law and to protect the inclusive uses of the oceans.

Conclusion

The law of maritime delimitation and historic title as set out in the Convention brings to the fore the importance of State decision-making power. So much is evident by States' discretion to determine what areas are subject to the regime of historic rights, what features constitute islands, what coastlines qualify for the drawing of straight baselines. However, these acts have an international dimension because of their impact on the entitlement of other States – either to their own maritime areas or to the freedoms of the high seas. The delimitation of overlapping entitlements to maritime areas also permits a large degree of discretion between the States concerned. For the delimitation of the territorial sea, States with opposite or adjacent coasts may reach their own agreement. Failing agreement between them, they are entitled to extend their territorial sea to an equidistant line. This boundary will not apply, however, if another boundary is justified by historic title or other special circumstances. What will constitute special circumstances will depend on the conditions pertaining to each area. For the delimitation of the EEZ and the continental shelf between States with opposite or adjacent coasts, delimitation is to be effected by agreement. No precise rule is applied to delimitation efforts but States may rely on the panoply of international law articulated in treaties, customary, and general international law, and as recognized in arbitral and judicial decisions, as a means of achieving an equitable solution. No interim boundary is specified before final agreement is reached but States must attempt to enter into provisional arrangements of a practical nature.

What becomes rapidly evident is that UNCLOS does not dictate how maritime boundaries are to be drawn in cases of overlapping entitlement. Beyond what could best be described as guiding principles (to effect an agreement on the basis of international law and to achieve an equitable solution), States are entitled to devise their own boundaries as appropriate for their individual circumstances. Given the scant normative criteria set out in the Convention for maritime delimitation and for historic bays and titles, an external international process could have conceivably formed a vital element in the application of the law. Moreover, the economic incentives and the earlier case law may have rendered mandatory jurisdiction as requisite for the functioning of the maritime delimitation provisions in the Convention. However, the normative framework is designed to leave the matter largely within the control of the relevant States. The high stakes involved in maritime territory rendered complete acquiescence in compulsory procedures entailing binding decisions as unacceptable to some States. A desire to avoid compulsory procedures entailing binding decisions is obvious. Even the convoluted conciliation process in Article 298(1)(a) returns States to negotiation. The inclusion of an optional exception for disputes relating to Articles 15, 74, 83, and historic bays and titles thus retains the emphasis on State decision-making and agreement.

By contrast, the legal regimes for straight baselines and for islands do require compulsory dispute settlement. Article 7, which draws on earlier case law and the Territorial Seas Convention, sets out the criteria for drawing straight baselines. While some external review is possible under Article 16 in the process of registering and publicizing baselines used for maritime delimitation (or perhaps through the work of the Continental Shelf Commission), States could well interpret the language of the Convention somewhat loosely in order to augment their exclusive maritime space. Where this action impacts on areas that would otherwise constitute high seas, all States have an interest in ensuring that the legal standards are maintained and upheld. Mandatory jurisdiction plays an essential role in this regard. Similarly, Article 121 creates standards that impact on States' entitlement to maritime areas. Unlike Article 7, Article 121 is an innovation in the Convention in that it expressly excludes rocks as generating rights to an EEZ and continental shelf. The standard for what constitutes a rock remains to be elucidated in the practice of States and in third-party decisions. Compulsory dispute settlement provides a check on the power of States through the interpretation and application of Article 121, paragraph 3 and thereby prevents the unlawful extension of exclusive rights into the high seas. The necessity of this role should color the characterization of a dispute that may otherwise be excluded from mandatory jurisdiction by means of another exception or limitation.

Use of Force, Military Activities, and Law Enforcement

Naval power has long been one of the pillars of States' military policies. States with significant naval fleets have relied on the traditional freedoms of the high seas to undertake a range of missions to promote national policies.[236] In addition to naval warfare, maritime military activities encompass naval exercises; weapons tests; naval presence missions; installation of military structures and devices; and declaring security zones. While specific legal regimes were developed to govern the conduct of naval warfare, many other military activities, which do not amount to armed conflict, remain to be regulated under the law of the sea.

UNCLOS provides little detail on what military conduct is allowed in different maritime zones or how that conduct, if allowed, is to be regulated. The desire to exclude this activity from the scope of international regulation and review in UNCLOS is further evident in Part XV of the Convention. The Convention permits States to exclude from mandatory adjudication or arbitration disputes relating to the military activities of warships and government vessels and aircraft engaged in non-commercial service,[237] as well as disputes relating to certain law enforcement activities in accordance with Article 298(1)(b). States may further choose to exclude disputes in respect of which the Security

---

[236] Hedley Bull outlined the importance of naval power in 1976 when writing for the International Institute of Strategic Studies:

> The first of these advantages is its flexibility: a naval force can be sent and withdrawn, and its size and activities varied, with a higher expectation that it will remain subject to control than is possible when ground forces are committed. The second is its visibility: by being seen on the high seas or in foreign ports a navy can convey threats, provide reassurance, or earn prestige in a way that troops or aircraft in their home bases cannot do. The third is universality or pervasiveness: the fact that the seas, by contrast with the land and the air, are an international medium allows naval vessels to reach distant countries independently of nearby bases and makes a state possessed of sea power the neighbor of every other country that is accessible by sea.

Hedley Bull, "Sea Power and Political Influence," in *Power at Sea I: The New Environment*, Adelphi Paper No. 122, Spring 1976, p. 6, cited in Richardson, "Power," at 907. The primary missions for the United States Navy are strategic deterrence, sea control, projection of power ashore, naval presence, and scientific research. See Mark W. Janis, "Dispute Settlement in the Law of the Sea Convention: The Military Activities Exception," 4 *Ocean Dev. & Int'l L.* 51, 57 (1977).

[237] Article 29 defines a warship as, "a ship belonging to the armed forces of a State bearing the external marks distinguishing such ships of its nationality, under the command of an officer duly commissioned by the government of the State and whose name appears in the appropriate service list or its equivalent, and manned by a crew which is under regular armed forces discipline." UNCLOS, art. 29. For the purposes of this discussion, warships and government vessels engaged in non-commercial service shall be referred to as "military and government vessels" unless comments are specifically related to either warships or government vessels engaged in non-commercial service.

Council is exercising the functions assigned to it by the UN Charter.[238] The exact contours of the exclusions are not immediately evident from the text of Article 298 but they potentially allow for the exclusion of a wide range of disputes.

This half of Chapter 4 examines the variety of disputes that are excepted from mandatory jurisdiction at the option of States under Article 298(1)(b) and (c), and considers what the absence of compulsory dispute settlement may mean for the international rules governing these activities. The first section analyzes the possible application of UNCLOS during times of armed conflict as well as military activities that do not amount to armed conflict. Both the military activities and the Security Council exceptions may be relevant here in addition to certain questions of admissibility. The second section discusses the various rights of passage accorded to military and government vessels in areas subject to coastal State sovereignty and the role of dispute settlement for these legal regimes. The third section turns to the question of law enforcement and addresses the particular law enforcement disputes specifically envisaged under Article 298 as well as other law enforcement activities under the Convention. With respect to the latter, difficulties may arise in determining where a line should be drawn between what constitutes law enforcement that is subject to mandatory jurisdiction and what constitutes military activities for the purposes of the optional exceptions.

Resolution of Disputes Relating to Armed Conflict at Sea

The role of Part XV in relation to armed conflict at sea depends on the general applicability of UNCLOS, in part or in its entirety, during times of armed conflict. Traditionally, the international rules governing the conduct of naval warfare have been derived from a series of conventions adopted in The Hague in 1907.[239] The conditions by which States may lawfully resort to force have altered significantly since the adoption

---

[238] *Ibid.*, art. 298(1)(c).

[239] Convention [No. VI] Relating to the Statue of Enemy Merchant Ships at the Outbreak of Hostilities, October 18, 1907, 100 *Brit. & Foreign St. Papers* 365 (1906–07), *reprinted in The Law of Naval Warfare: A Collection of Agreements and Documents with Commentaries* 96 (N. Ronzitti ed., 1988); Convention [No. VII] Relating to the Conversion of Merchant Ships to Warships, October 18, 1907, 100 *Brit. & Foreign St. Papers* 377 (1906–07), reprinted in *The Law of Naval Warfare: A Collection of Agreements and Documents with Commentaries* 114 (N. Ronzitti ed., 1988); Convention [No. VIII] Relative to the Laying of Automatic Submarine Contact Mines, October 18, 1907, 36 Stat. 2332, 1 Bevans 669; Convention [No. IX] Concerning Bombardment by Naval Forces in Time of War, October 18, 1907, 36 Stat. 2351, 1 Bevans 681; Convention [No. XI] Relative to Certain Restrictions with Regard to the Exercise of the Right of Capture in Naval War,

of these conventions. In particular, the UN Charter now prohibits the use or threat of force unless in the exercise of self-defense,[240] or unless authorized by the Security Council under Chapter VII of the UN Charter.[241] The change in the justifications for the resort to force raises the question of whether the laws governing the means and methods of warfare, as developed from the 1907 conventions, remain equally applicable. The exact interplay between the principles in the UN Charter and the laws of war is far from evident.[242] Churchill and Lowe suggest that the principles of the laws of war and neutrality, if not their specific details, continue to apply to international armed conflicts.[243]

The question then arises as to what extent UNCLOS may be applicable during times of armed conflict. A spectrum of views on this issue can be identified. It has been suggested that UNCLOS now replaces many of the rights and responsibilities drawn from the laws of naval warfare and that those laws are generally no longer valid due to the prohibition on the use of force in the UN Charter.[244] Alternatively, Astley and Schmitt consider that the law of the sea is mostly consistent with the laws of war, particularly those rules relating to neutrality.[245] Finally, it has been argued that UNCLOS was envisaged, like the 1958 Conventions before it, as a treaty for times of peace and is thus not applicable at all during armed conflict.[246] If UNCLOS were intended to govern the conduct of naval warfare, it would remain applicable between the warring parties.[247] However, some rights enshrined in UNCLOS, particularly

---

October 18, 1907, 36 Stat. 2396, 1 Bevans 711; Convention [No. XIII] Concerning the Rights and Duties of Neutral Powers in Naval War, October 18, 1907, 36 Stat. 2415, 1 Bevans 723.

[240] See UN Charter, arts. 2(4) and 51.

[241] See UN Charter, arts. 39–42.

[242] George P. Politakis, *Modern Aspects of the Laws of Naval Warfare and Maritime Neutrality* (1998), p. 7 (describing three views on the interrelationship of these bodies of law).

[243] R. R. Churchill and A. V. Lowe, *The Law of the Sea* (3rd ed., 1999), p. 423.

[244] See A. V. Lowe, "The Commander's Handbook on the Law of Naval Operations and the Contemporary Law of the Sea," in 64 *International Law Studies: The Law of Naval Operations* (Horace B. Robertson ed., 1991), pp. 111, 130–133. See *ibid.*, at 141. ("The very idea that the Laws of War, in particular the eighty-year old Hague Conventions, remain binding is one which is open to serious doubt.")

[245] Astley and Schmitt, at 138 ("the maritime rights and duties States enjoy in peacetime continue to exist, with minor exceptions, during armed conflict").

[246] Rauch, at 233. ("To be sure, the new Convention constitutes part of the law of peace and is not intended to regulate the law of naval warfare.")

[247] There is no clear line on what treaties remain applicable during times of armed conflict and what treaties are suspended as between the warring parties. See Michael K. Prescott, "How War Affects Treaties between Belligerents: A Case Study of the Gulf

those related to passage, are unlikely to apply between the warring States during an armed conflict.[248]

It seems most likely that the minimal regulation of military activities in the Convention indicates that it was not intended to replace the customary laws regulating the use of naval force under the UN Charter during times of armed conflict. Certainly, the Preamble to UNCLOS affirms that matters not regulated by the Convention continue to be governed by the rules and principles of general international law.[249] Instead, the Convention simply reiterates in Article 301 the proscriptions of the UN Charter on the use of force. Article 301 requires:

In exercising their rights and performing their duties under this Convention, States parties shall refrain from any threat or use of force against the territorial integrity or political independence of any State, or in any other manner inconsistent with the principles of international law embodied in the Charter of the United Nations.

Although suggested during the debates at the Third Conference that there should be a complete prohibition of all military activities in the oceans, most States accepted that some broader, more general understanding would be the most likely compromise position.[250] When Article 301 is considered in light of the UN Charter, the Definition of Aggression,[251] and the Declaration on Friendly Relations,[252] the only military acts prohibited at sea are those that are either directed against the sovereignty, territorial integrity, or political independence of another State or constitute a blockade or an attack on the sea forces or the

---

War," 7 *Emory Int'l L. Rev.* 192 (1993); Christine M. Chinkin, "Crisis and the Performance of International Agreements," 7 *Yale J. World Pub. Ord.* 177 (1981); Harvard Research in International Law, "Law of Treaties," 29 *Am. J. Int'l L. Supp.* 653 (1935); "The Effects of Armed Conflicts on Treaties," 61-II *Y.B. Inst. Int'l L.* 199 (1986).

[248] See Chinkin, at 196.

[249] Regard can also be had in this respect to Article 311, paragraph 2 which reads: "This Convention shall not alter the rights and obligations of States Parties which arise from other agreements compatible with this Convention and which do not affect the enjoyment of other States Parties of their rights or the performance of their obligations under this Convention." UNCLOS, art. 311(2).

[250] See Boleslaw A. Bozcek, "Peaceful Purposes Provisions of the United Nations Convention on the Law of the Sea," 20 *Ocean Dev. & Int'l L.* 359, 369 (1989). See also Rauch, at 239–40.

[251] Definition of Aggression, GA Res. 3314, UN GAOR, 29th Sess., Supp. No. 31, at 142, UN Doc. A/9631 (1975).

[252] Declaration of Principles on International Law concerning Friendly Relations and Co-operation among States in accordance with the Charter of the United Nations, GA Res. 2625, UN GAOR, 25th Sess., Supp. No. 28, at 121, UN Doc. A/2890 (1970).

marine fleets of another State.[253] In line with this view, "the high seas may legally be used for a whole panoply of military purposes as long as none of them are aggressive."[254] If the requirements to reserve the oceans for peaceful purposes mean that States must abide by the UN Charter obligations regarding the threat or use of force, then these articles add little substance to obligations already binding States.[255] No further regulation of naval warfare is provided in the Convention.[256] On this basis, UNCLOS cannot be viewed as creating any new substantive obligations with respect to the use of force at sea. What is significant here is the new procedural aspect whereby compulsory arbitration or adjudication is available, subject to the optional exceptions, for disputes concerning any threat or use of force during the exercise of rights or performance of duties under the Convention.[257]

For situations of armed conflict, the optional exclusion under Article 298(1)(c) may take effect if the Security Council is seized with the matter and measures are being prescribed in relation to the conflict as part of the Council's exercise of its functions. This provision avoids a conflict between any procedures of dispute resolution started under the Convention and any action that the Security Council may be taking with respect to the same matter to maintain or restore international peace and security.[258] If the Security Council decides to remove the matter from its agenda or calls upon the parties to settle the dispute by the procedure in the Convention, then the compulsory dispute settlement

---

[253] Rüdiger Wolfrum, "Restricting the Use of the Sea to Peaceful Purposes: Demilitarization in Being?," 24 *German Y.B. Int'l L.* 200, 217 (1981).

[254] Rex J. Zedalis, "Military Uses of the Ocean Space and the Developing International Law of the Sea: An Analysis in the Context of Peacetime ASW," 16 *San Diego L. Rev.* 575, 613 (1979).

[255] Bozcek, at 370–71. See also Oxman, "The Regime of Warships," at 814 and 831. Wolfrum argues that the legislative history of this article indicates that it was not an essential part of the Convention and should not be over-emphasized nor used to limit military activities at sea that are recognized under customary international law. Wolfrum, at 213.

[256] Politakis writes, UNCLOS "can offer dim guidance at best as to the normative substance of modern rules governing armed conflict at sea." Politakis, at 7.

[257] See Oxman, "Regime of Warships," at 815.

[258] 5 *United Nations Convention on the Law of the Sea 1982: A Commentary*, p. 138. There was some resistance to this exclusion because it would be unclear as to when the Security Council was exercising its functions. However, as the wording reflects Article 12 of the UN Charter, which prevents the General Assembly from making recommendations in respect of any dispute or situation when the Security Council is exercising the functions assigned to it, this formulation was considered sufficiently specific. *Ibid.*, at 138–40.

mechanism can be used.[259] While the Convention anticipates a possible overlap in jurisdiction between courts and tribunals constituted under the Convention and the Security Council, no such allowance is made when a matter is before a different political body. A question of admissibility as to the proper forum may be raised in this context if one of the warring parties attempted to bring a matter that constituted one aspect of a wider conflict under the UNCLOS system as part of its overall political campaign. Such a tactic may be viewed as an abuse of process. Also in this situation, the relevant court or tribunal could properly determine under the circumstances that the dispute did not actually relate to the interpretation or application of the Convention and it thus lacked jurisdiction to resolve the dispute.

If any of the States involved in the armed conflict had opted for the military activities exception, it is clear that a dispute arising out of the context of an armed conflict will fall under this exception. Such a characterization would only be avoided if, for example, States pointed to failures to cooperate in respect of fishing conservation, denying passage, or unlawfully suspending marine scientific research as violations of the Convention without citing the conflict as possible reason for this alleged transgression. Again, a court or tribunal would have to decide if the dispute was truly one relating to the interpretation or application of the Convention. Furthermore, a question of admissibility might be raised in this instance to challenge the political character of the dispute. The political nature of the dispute could well be reaffirmed if the entirety of the conflict was being addressed by a regional organization or in another political forum. A court or tribunal may reason that it is dealing with the legal dimensions of the dispute and that its holding might contribute to the overall resolution of the conflict. The political question may not create too much pause, particularly in light of the tendency of the ICJ to exercise jurisdiction in these cases.[260] The risk is that the misuse of the compulsory dispute settlement mechanism in this manner could undermine the authority of the tribunal or court and diminish the likelihood of compliance with the decision.

Military Activities on the High Seas and in the EEZ

A range of military activities can be undertaken on the high seas or in EEZ areas that do not amount to armed conflict. As O'Connell notes:

[259] UNCLOS, art. 298(1)(c).
[260] See, e.g., Military and Paramilitary Activities (*Nicaragua* v. *United States*), 1984 ICJ 392, 434–35 (November 26); Teheran Hostages, at 19.

the occasion for navies to be employed to influence events will be multiplied because the increasing complexities of the law of the sea, with its proliferation of claims and texts and regimes covering resources, pollution, security and navigation, are multiplying the opportunities for disputes and the circumstances for the resolution of disputes by the exertion of naval power.[261]

In these cases, the laws of war would not govern an "exertion of naval power" and so the focus then becomes how UNCLOS might govern these sorts of uses of the oceans. Naval activities on the high seas and in the EEZ are generally not regulated specifically under the terms of the Convention. States deliberately minimized debate on military uses to avoid controversy and to incorporate sufficient ambiguity within the Convention to allow for differing interpretations.[262] The tactical reason for this approach was to retain considerable flexibility in the military uses of the oceans and thereby allow States to pursue their assorted strategic objectives.

States with considerable naval fleets were particularly anxious to preserve their rights on the high seas. The freedoms of the high seas listed under Article 87 are not exclusive and may be interpreted as including implicitly a variety of military activities. The inclusive listing of categories (signaled by the phrase "*inter alia*") was also used in the High Seas Convention.[263] In neither convention is any express reference made to military activities, although the freedom of navigation has traditionally encompassed the free movement of warships across the high seas.[264]

---

[261] D. P. O'Connell, *The Influence of Law on Sea Power* (1975), p. 10. See also Scott C. Truver, The Law of the Sea and the Military Use of the Oceans in 2010," 45 *La. L. Rev.* 1221 (1985). ("Sea power will be a fundamental tool of coercive and supportive diplomacy employed by coastal and maritime states alike to safeguard all their interests in the oceans, particularly in light of the potential for international tension and crisis to arise over ocean rights and obligations.")

[262] Majula R. Shyam, "The UN Convention on the Law of the Sea and Military Interests in the Indian Ocean," 15 *Ocean Dev. & Int'l L.* 147, 149 (1985). Booth considers that the drafters of the Convention deliberately followed the tactic of silence, and that a number of rights for navies are hidden within that silence. Booth, at 340. See also Rauch, at 231 (noting that all substantive discussion of questions with security policy or military implications was off the record and that assorted euphemisms are used to refer to military uses).

[263] High Seas Convention, art. 2.

[264] O'Connell writes:

So, battle fleets in past ages steamed in formations, conducted manoeuvres, and engaged in gunnery practice extending over hundreds of square miles. Provided that the rules of the road were observed and the range was kept clear, this was a lawful use of the high seas because other ships in the area continued to navigate without being diverted.

One of the few requirements in UNCLOS that may impact on the conduct of high seas military maneuvers is that the freedoms of the high seas are to be exercised with due regard for the interests of other States in their exercise of high seas freedoms.[265] How this obligation of due regard is likely to influence State conduct on the high seas is unclear. A due regard requirement had not been included in the High Seas Convention. Instead, Article 2 of that treaty had set out a test of reasonableness whereby the freedoms of the high seas were to be exercised "with reasonable regard to the interests of other states."[266] Therefore, in the past, the high seas have been used by naval powers for extended military exercises as well as weapons tests and these States have claimed these acts to be lawful uses of the oceans as they meet a standard of reasonableness.[267] This previous standard could arguably be read into a standard of "due regard" under UNCLOS. However, the change in terminology and the use of the due regard standard in respect of activities in the EEZ indicate that a balancing test of subjective interests may be undertaken in the event of a dispute, rather than an objective assessment of reasonableness *writ large*. The shift in emphasis should not be over-emphasized, however.

A further limitation on military activities on the high seas could be Article 88 of the Convention, which reserves the high seas for peaceful purposes. Larson, however, considers that the reservation of the high seas for peaceful purposes is virtually redundant. He argues:

Exactly what this means in practice is rather difficult to define, since the superpowers in particular use the [high seas] to deploy sub-surface submarines and surface vessels and use the air space above for naval and other military purposes. As a result, the practical effect of reserving the [high seas] for peaceful purposes is almost non-existent.[268]

From this perspective, it would seem that little clarity on the authorization of military activities is provided through the reference to peaceful

---

O'Connell, 2 *International Law of the Sea*, p. 809. See also P. Sreenivasa Rao, "Legal Regulation of Maritime Military Uses," 13 *Indian J. Int'l L.* 425, 435 (1973).

[265] UNCLOS, art. 87(2).

[266] High Seas Convention, art. 2.

[267] At the time of the First Conference, States were unable to agree on legal rules for these military activities, beyond a reasonable regard test.

[268] David L Larson, "Security Issues and the Law of the Sea: A General Framework," 15 *Ocean Dev. & Int'l L.* 99, 116 (1985). See also Truver, at 1242 (stating that Article 88 "seems to have very little substance"); Booth, at 341 (describing Article 88 as, "a familiar piece of pious rhetoric, calculated to degrade respect for the document rather than legitimize new patterns of behavior").

purposes. The reservation of areas for "peaceful purposes" has been used in other multilateral treaties to refer to complete demilitarization or to excluding certain types of military activities – either as conventional obligations or as goals for States parties.[269] In the UNCLOS context, the proscription is limited to threats or use of force as set forth in the UN Charter.[270] No further curtailment can be drawn from the peaceful purposes provisions of the Convention.[271] As noted above, the States with the superior military strength will presumably conduct military exercises or weapons tests and rely on their rights under the freedoms of the high seas for such acts. These States would expect to protect these rights by excluding the possibility of review by international courts or tribunals.

The lack of normative guidelines on military activities on the high seas then carries over to the EEZ. Through the cross-reference in Article 58, paragraph 2, the reservation of the high seas for peaceful purposes is extended to the EEZ, to the extent that this obligation is not incompatible with the provisions of the Convention governing the EEZ. As with the high seas, a due regard requirement is incorporated into Article 58 whereby:

States shall have due regard to the rights and duties of the coastal State and shall comply with the laws and regulations adopted by the coastal State in accordance with the provisions of the Convention and other rules of international law in so far as they are not incompatible with this Part [dealing with the EEZ].

The rights and duties of the coastal State are those set out in Article 56 and relate to issues such as the conservation and management of the natural resources, artificial islands, marine scientific research, and the marine environment. The Convention does not specifically authorize coastal States to control conduct relating to military activities in the EEZ.

---

[269] See Bozcek, "Peaceful Purposes Provisions," at 361–63 (discussing the use of "peaceful purposes" provisions for the regimes governing Antarctica, the moon and other celestial bodies and the seabed). See also James C. F. Wang, *Handbook on Ocean Politics and Law* (1992), pp. 367–88; Wolfrum, at 201–02.

[270] UNCLOS, art. 301.

[271] The Convention designates both maritime zones and activities as subject to the peaceful purposes requirement. See *ibid.*, art. 88 (reservation of high seas for peaceful purposes); *ibid.*, art. 141 (Area is only to be used for peaceful purpose); *ibid.*, art. 143 (marine scientific research in the Area is only to be for peaceful purposes); *ibid.*, art. 147 (installations in the Area only for peaceful purposes); *ibid.*, art. 240 (marine scientific research is to be conducted for peaceful purposes). These activities must similarly fall short of threats or use of force under the UN Charter to be for "peaceful purposes" under the Convention.

The fulfillment of the requirement of due regard will ultimately depend on what activities are being undertaken by the respective States. A number of commentators have taken the view that Article 58 was intended to ensure for third States that the rights enjoyed in the EEZ were quantitatively and qualitatively the same as the traditional freedoms of the high seas.[272] Rauch has argued that the freedom of navigation associated with the "operation of ships" allows for a range of internationally lawful military activities, including maneuvers, deployment of forces, exercises, weapons tests, intelligence gathering, and surveillance.[273] Some governments argue, however, that various military activities, such as weapons exercises and testing, may not be conducted without coastal State consent.[274] This view is based on an interpretation of Article 58 that focuses on the listing of the specific freedoms and that not all military activities are related to the specified freedoms.[275] Furthermore, it is quite likely that a naval presence mission or military exercises in the EEZ of another State could well interfere with coastal State economic rights.[276] An attempt to introduce a requirement of coastal State consent for naval operations other than navigation in the EEZ during the drafting of the Convention did not succeed.[277] Francioni instead remarks, "[f]rom the text and legislative history of article 58, it seems difficult to infer that the establishment of the EEZ has involved a limitation on military operations of foreign navies other than pure navigation

---

[272] Richardson, "Navigation and National Security," at 573. See also Walter F. Doran, "An Operational Commander's Perspective on the 1982 LOS Convention," 10 *Int'l J. Marine & Coastal L.* 335 (1995) ("The Convention does not permit the coastal state to limit traditional non-resources related high seas activities in this EEZ, such as task force manoeuvring, flight operations, military exercises, telecommunications and space activities, intelligence and surveillance activities, military marine data collection, and weapons' testing and firing."); Oxman, "Regime of Warships," at 838 ("It is essentially a futile exercise to engage in speculation as to whether naval maneuvers and exercises within the economic zone are permissible. In principle, they are."); Francesco Francioni, "Peacetime Use of Force, Military Activities, and the New Law of the Sea," 18 *Cornell Int'l L.J.* 203, 214 (1985) (noting that the majority of authors believe that military uses of the seas remain unaffected by the establishment of the EEZ).

[273] Rauch, at 252.

[274] Brazil, Cape Verde, and Uruguay have taken this view. United Nations, Office of the Special Representative of the Secretary-General for the Law of the Sea, *Law of the Sea Bulletin*, No. 5 (1985), at 6–7, 8, 24. Singh has argued that military activities in the EEZ are subject to the national jurisdiction of the relevant coastal States. See Singh, p. 148. However, this interpretation cannot be correct because it would attribute to coastal States jurisdiction over non-economic activities.

[275] See Lowe, "Commander's Handbook," at 113.

[276] See Mark Janis, *Sea Power and the Law of the Sea* (1976), p. 84.

[277] Francioni, at 215.

and communication."[278] Sufficient ambiguity in the text means that interpretations can be made both in favor of and against the right of warships to conduct military maneuvers in a foreign EEZ.[279] A similar vagueness is evident with regard to the legality of military installations and devices.[280] In light of the deliberate ambiguity in relation to this issue and the specific grant of sovereign rights and jurisdiction in the EEZ, the better interpretation does seem to be in favor of the legality of military activities in the EEZ, subject to due regard requirements only.

The want of precision as to what military activities are permissible on the high seas and in the EEZ may constitute good reason to allow for third-party dispute resolution. A court or tribunal could set out the appropriate legal standards based on UNCLOS provisions and specify what conduct is or is not acceptable under the Convention. In addition, the inclusion of military activities within the scope of mandatory jurisdiction is also necessary as a consequence of the doctrine of sovereign immunity of warships.[281] Articles 95 and 96 provide for the complete immunity of warships as well as ships owned or operated by a State and used only on government non-commercial service on the high seas. Immunity is also accorded to these vessels in the territorial sea of a State, subject to certain rules relating to innocent passage.[282] Any claims brought before the national courts of States, other than the relevant flag State, can be excluded from national jurisdiction on the basis of sovereign immunity. Reference to sovereign immunity was not

---

[278] *Ibid.*, at 216.

[279] Bozcek, "Peaceful Purposes Provisions," at 372. Robertson argues that the right to conduct naval manoeuvres is seemingly incompatible with coastal State interests in the EEZ. He believes the only possible restriction is found in Article 88, which is applicable to the EEZ by virtue of Article 58(2), providing that the high seas are reserved for peaceful purposes. However, if these maneuvres are restricted in the zone, then it would also follow that such maneuvres are similarly restricted on the high seas and this latter interpretation is contrary to the established position permitting such naval activities on the high seas. See Robertson, at 885–87. By contrast, Shyam has noted that none of the littoral States on the Indian Ocean have enacted legislation prohibiting naval exercises by other States. Shyam, Military Interests, at 164. The negative implication to be drawn from this practice is that naval exercises are not viewed as activities that can be regulated under the EEZ regime.

[280] Bozcek, "Peaceful Purposes Provisions," at 373.   [281] See Janis, at 56.

[282] See UNCLOS, art. 32. See also notes 296–334 and accompanying text. Moore argues that warships transiting straits are also subject to immunity through a reading of Articles 31, 32, 42(4) and (5), 233, and 236. John Norton Moore, "The Regime of Straits and the Third United Nations Conference on the Law of the Sea," 74 *Am. J. Int'l L.* 77, 99 (1980) ("coastal states shall not interfere with or take enforcement action against warships or other vessels entitled to sovereign immunity"). See also *ibid.*, at 106.

included in Article 298, as it was considered inappropriate – and would be anomalous – for international courts and tribunals that hear disputes between sovereign States.[283] The continued exemption of military vessels or aircraft from national jurisdiction was a strong reason not to exclude their activities entirely from the scope of international jurisdiction.[284]

However, the highly political nature of naval activities on the high seas has typically meant that the role of courts and tribunals has been marginal in the legal regulation of military uses of the oceans.[285] The minimal substantive regulations along with an optional exclusion covering military activities on the high seas and in the EEZ are indicative of a preference on the part of States not to use compulsory third-party procedures for resolving disputes about military activities. The optional exclusion is beneficial to naval powers not wishing to have their military activities questioned through an international process. The exclusion satisfies "the preoccupation of the naval advisors . . . that activities by naval vessels should not be subject to judicial proceedings in which some military secrets might have to be disclosed."[286] An optional exclusion is also beneficial to coastal States that could use the exception to prevent review of any of their interference with naval exercises in their EEZ. The deliberate obfuscation of rights and duties in different maritime areas provides States with considerable leeway in deciding what actions to take and how certain disputes should be resolved. The intention of the States parties is respected through Article 298 in this regard. Permitting "military activities" to be excluded from compulsory dispute settlement reinforces the versatility allowed for this issue: "It is obvious that states can define military matters as broadly as they wish."[287] Such

---

[283] "Doubts were raised . . . as to whether any vessels are entitled to sovereign immunity in a case brought before an international tribunal, as that doctrine applies only to domestic courts which are not allowed to bring before them a foreign sovereign, and as the very purpose of international tribunals is to deal with disputes between sovereign States." 5 *United Nations Convention on the Law of the Sea 1982: A Commentary*, p. 135. The question should be raised, however, as to whether the same considerations should automatically apply to disputes involving non-State entities before international tribunals.

[284] Singh, p. 168, n. 21; and 5 *United Nations Convention on the Law of the Sea 1982: A Commentary*, p. 136 (referring to the views of the New Zealand delegate).

[285] The constrained judgments in the *Nuclear Tests* cases are exemplary in this regard. See Nuclear Tests (*Australia v. France; New Zealand v. France*), 1974 ICJ 253, 457 (December 20).

[286] 5 *United Nations Convention on the Law of the Sea 1982: A Commentary*, at 135. See also Noyes, "Compulsory Adjudication," at 685 (noting that an exception was required for military activities because naval advisers were concerned about exposing military secrets in the course of judicial proceedings).

[287] Gamble, "Dispute Settlement in Perspective," at 331.

choices can be made in accordance with strategic policies and protects States from formal international review through legal processes if they so elect.

Passage through Territorial Seas, Straits, and Archipelagic Waters

The military activities exception could encompass the acts of military and government vessels as they traverse maritime areas subject to coastal State sovereignty. Unlike military activities on the high seas, the Convention contains detailed provision for the passage of different types of foreign ships through territorial seas, straits, and archipelagic waters. The law of the sea has addressed the question of rights and duties relating to the passage of foreign vessels through territorial seas because of the rights of the coastal State over this body of water as well as third States' interests in ensuring the passage of all vessels through the safest and most expeditious route. In addition, navigation through territorial seas and straits has always had considerable military importance.[288] Straits, particularly narrow bodies of water between coasts, are essential for passage between larger bodies of water and are typically high-traffic areas for commercial, military, and government vessels alike.[289] These coastal States then have interests in protecting their security as well as their economic and environmental interests in the areas directly adjacent to their land. Such interests have been balanced through the recognition of a right of innocent passage through waters subject to coastal State sovereignty.

A threat to the mobility of vessels, especially military vessels, arose when coastal States advocated for a territorial sea wider than the traditionally accepted three-mile limit. The States with large naval fleets particularly faced this challenge during the First and Second Conferences. An increase in breadth would have reduced the high seas area available for the exercise of the freedom of navigation. A broader territorial sea

---

[288] Naval vessels need to be able to traverse all areas of the oceans in order to fulfill their strategic objectives. As Richardson writes: "To fulfill their deterrent and protective missions these forces must have the manifest capacity either to maintain a continuing presence in farflung areas of the globe or to bring such a presence to bear rapidly. An essential component of this capacity is true global mobility – mobility that is genuinely credible and impossible to contain." Richardson, "Power," at 907.

[289] Straits of strategic importance for United States' commercial and military interests include Gibraltar, Dover, Malacca (in the Indonesian archipelago), Hormuz (the gateway to the Persian Gulf), Bab al Mamdab (in the south of the Red Sea), and Bonifacio (between Corsica and Sardinia). Mark E. Rosen, "Military Mobility and the 1982 UN Law of the Sea Convention," 7 Geo. Int'l Env. L. Rev. 717, 720 (1995).

belt meant greater coastal State control over the passage of naval vessels and thus affected the strategic policies of some of the major maritime States. An extension of the breadth of the territorial sea also had the effect of turning over a hundred international straits into territorial seas.[290] One of the reasons coastal States agitated for the wider belt of territorial sea was to frustrate the military objectives of the maritime States. This security aspect arose with respect to the threat of force that could be used against a State as a means of applying pressure on that State, rather than just protection from a full-scale war.[291] States were therefore keen to prevent naval ships from posing a threatening presence just off their coast.[292]

When both the First and Second Conferences failed to reach agreement on the breadth of the territorial sea for inclusion in a convention, the matter was left unresolved for a number of years. The United States and the Soviet Union both wished to have the question resolved and began sounding out various governments on their views on holding

---

[290] Carl M. Franklin, "The Law of the Sea: Some Recent Developments (With Particular Reference to the United Nations Conference of 1958)," 53 Int'l L. Studies 1, 90 (1959–60).

[291] See D. W. Bowett, "The Second United Nations Conference on the Law of the Sea," 9 Int'l & Comp. L.Q. 415, 417 (1960). This concern was certainly valid for a time when weaponry was less powerful. Latvia, for example, had expressed the view in 1930 that a sixty mile territorial sea was necessary "to prevent, for at least at that distance, attempts upon its national security." Acts of the Conference for the Codification of International Law, Meetings of the Committee, vol. III, Minutes of the Second Committee, Territorial Waters, reprinted in 4 Codification Conference, at 1335. In 1958, States argued that extensions of the territorial sea would not assist defensive measures because of the vastly increased range of modern armaments. See, e.g., First Conference, 1st Comm., at 150, ¶ 11 (New Zealand). Canada, for instance, dismissed claims for extending the breadth of the territorial sea on this basis: "Carrier task forces, rocket-firing submarines, heavy bombers and long-range nuclear weapons had long since moved such matters on to another plane." Ibid., at 167, ¶ 3 (Canada).

[292] Franklin, at 122–23 (estimating that "the deterrent effect and stabilizing influence of a display of naval force in a trouble-area of the world where a three-mile territorial sea exists would be reduced by at least 50% if the limit were extended to six miles; it would be reduced to nil with a 12-mile territorial sea"). At the Second Conference, Albania stated: "In Albania's case the limit that would best safeguard the security of the State was that of twelve miles; it had often happened that maritime powers had carried out demonstrations of force off the shores of a weaker country, in order to intimidate it." Second Conference, at 101, ¶ 14 (Albania). See also ibid., at 105, ¶ 32 (Byelorussian Soviet Socialist Republic); ibid., at 125, ¶¶ 6 and 7 (Romania); ibid., at 77, ¶ 24 (India); ibid., at 39, ¶ 4 (Soviet Union) (the latter arguing that a flexible breadth of territorial sea had "an important bearing on the security of coastal States, some of which were at present vulnerable to intimidation by demonstrations of force in their coastal waters, even in time of peace").

another conference.[293] "[P]rotecting the mobility and use of warships was a central motivating force in organizing the Third United Nations Conference on the Law of the Sea."[294] At the Third Conference, there was little controversy about the breadth of the territorial sea being extended to twelve miles. The focus of discussions in relation to territorial seas and straits was what passage would be permissible for both commercial and different military vessels.[295] Two separate regimes were established depending on the body of water. Innocent passage would apply for the territorial sea and for certain types of straits while a new form of passage, transit passage, would apply in all other international straits. A third form of passage also had to be contemplated with the agreement that archipelagic States would be able to close off the waters inside their outer most islands. The system of passage existing within archipelagic waters incorporates both innocent and transit passage. These three forms of passage are discussed immediately below, with particular reference to the effect on warships and other government vessels operated for non-commercial service, and to the role of dispute settlement.

Territorial Sea and Innocent Passage

The territorial sea is a belt of water adjacent to a coastal State over which that State exercises sovereignty. The sovereignty of the coastal State extends to the bed, subsoil, and the airspace over the territorial sea.[296] The sovereignty of the littoral State is subject to the right of ships of all States to enjoy innocent passage.[297] The right of innocent passage also applies to straits where the right of transit passage is not accorded,

---

[293] Rauch, at 233. See also Oxman, "Tenth Session," at 4 (noting that the Soviet Union and the United States circulated draft articles on the territorial sea and straits).

[294] Oxman, "Regime of Warships," at 810.

[295] Buzan writes:

> During UNCLOS, a strong contingent of coastal states tried various ways of restricting the activity of foreign warships in their coastal waters . . . part of a general attempt to extend sovereignty and jurisdiction into oceans, but in this sector they met extremely determined opposition from the maritime powers. While the maritime powers were prepared to concede very large areas of control over resources and associated activities, they refused to yield almost anything on the rights of warships.

> Barry Buzan, "Naval Power, the Law of the Sea, and the Indian Ocean as a Zone of Peace," 5 *Marine Pol'y* 194 (1981).

[296] UNCLOS, art. 2.

[297] *Ibid.*, art. 17. "As a general principle, the right of innocent passage requires no supporting argument or citation of authority, it is firmly established in international law . . ." Phillip Jessup, *The Law of Territorial Waters and Maritime Jurisdiction* (1927), p. 120.

or where a strait is used for international navigation between a part of the high seas or an EEZ and the territorial sea of a foreign State.[298] The right of innocent passage applies to both merchant and military vessels. Some particular restrictions are imposed on nuclear-powered vessels and submarines. The coastal State is entitled to designate sea lanes within its territorial sea and may restrict nuclear-powered vessels, or vessels carrying nuclear material, to these lanes.[299] Submarines are required to navigate on the surface and show their flag while in the territorial sea.[300] Warships, though not required to comply with traffic separation schemes, must still operate with "due regard" to other vessels.[301] The coastal State is further permitted to adopt laws and regulations that may indirectly impinge on the passage of military vessels.[302] If a warship fails to comply with these laws and regulations during passage, then the coastal State may require it to leave the territorial sea immediately,[303] and the flag State is responsible for any damage caused by the warship.[304]

Coastal States have attempted to subject military vessels to further regulation by requiring either prior authorization or prior notification before the exercise of their right of innocent passage. State practice has varied on whether prior notice or authorization is required for a warship to traverse a coastal State's territorial sea in exercise of the right of innocent passage.[305] In 1930, the Legal Sub-Committee at the Codification Conference had decided that as a general rule, a coastal State could not forbid the passage of foreign warships in its territorial sea nor could it require previous authorization or notification.[306] The International Court of Justice subsequently adopted this approach in the *Corfu Channel* case.[307] Prior to the First Conference, the International Law Commission noted during its debates that, "while it was obligatory in international

---

[298] UNCLOS, art. 45.

[299] *Ibid.*, art. 22. These vessels must carry documents and observe special precautionary measures established for such ships by international agreements. *Ibid.*, art. 23.

[300] *Ibid.*, art. 20.   [301] Astley and Schmitt, at 134.

[302] See UNCLOS, art. 21 (permitting coastal States to adopt laws and regulations relating to, *inter alia*, the safety of navigation).

[303] *Ibid.*, art. 30.   [304] *Ibid.*, art. 31.

[305] See Astley and Schmitt, at 132 (noting that over twenty-five States require prior permission, thirteen require prior notification and five States place special restrictions on nuclear-powered submarines).

[306] Report Adopted by the Committee on April 10, 1930, Appendix 1, reprinted in 4 *Codification Conference*, at 1418.

[307] The Court there decided:
> It is, in the opinion of the Court, generally recognized and in accordance with international custom that States in time of peace have a right to send their warships through straits used for international navigation between two parts

law to grant the right of passage without authorization, notification had always been the practice except in urgent cases of vessels in distress."[308] At the First Conference, objections were raised to any requirement that would make the passage of warships or government ships through the territorial sea liable to previous authorization.[309] In the final voting stage at the Plenary Meeting, the inclusion of a reference to "authorization" was deleted and, as a result, a provision requiring notification was deemed unnecessary.[310] It was ultimately decided that there should not be a special regime for the passage of warships and Article 23 of the Territorial Sea Convention simply provided that coastal States may require warships to leave if those ships do not comply with its regulations. Reservations were entered to this provision to the effect that a coastal State had the right to establish procedures for the authorization of the passage of foreign warships through its territorial waters.[311]

Similar to the Territorial Sea Convention, UNCLOS also provides that coastal States may require warships to leave their territorial seas for non-compliance with coastal State regulations.[312] No express reference is made to a requirement of prior notice or authorization within the scope of the coastal State's competence to adopt laws and regulations.[313] Although amendments were proposed at UNCLOS that would have enabled a coastal State to require prior notice or authorization, these amendments were not pressed to a vote.[314] No clarification on the issue

of the high seas without the previous authorization of a coastal State, provided that the passage is innocent. Unless otherwise prescribed in an international convention, there is no right for a coastal State to prohibit such passage through straits in time of peace.

Corfu Channel (*United Kingdom* v. *Albania*), 1949 ICJ 28 (April 9).

[308] *ILC Yearbook*, (1955), vol. I, at 143–44, ¶ 96 (Liang, Secretary to the Commission).

[309] *First Conference*, 1st Comm., at 133–34, ¶¶ 22 and 32 (United Kingdom).

[310] *First Conference*, Plenary, at 67.

[311] See, e.g., reservations by Bulgaria, Byelorussian SSR, Romania, Ukrainian SSR UN, *Multilateral Treaties Deposited with the Secretary-General*, available at http://untreaty.un.org/ENGLISH/bible/englishinternetbible/partI/chapterXXI/treaty1.asp (August 13, 2001). Some reservations stated this need specifically. See, e.g., reservations by Colombia, Czechoslovakia, Hungary. *Ibid.*

[312] UNCLOS, art. 30. The flag State also bears responsibility for damage caused by military vessels. *Ibid.*, art. 31.

[313] See *ibid.*, art. 21 (listing the subjects of laws and regulations that the coastal State may adopt).

[314] See Karin M. Burke and Deborah A. DeLeo, "Innocent Passage and Transit Passage in the United Nations Convention on the Law of the Sea," 9 *Yale J. World Pub. Ord.* 389, 398–99 (1983) (considering the requirement of notice or prior authorization and what support it received during the negotiations of UNCLOS).

was possible in UNCLOS. While contrary views still exist in practice,[315] the major naval powers have maintained that no such notice or authorization is required under international law. For example, in 1989 a Joint Statement issued by the USSR and the United States stipulated that neither prior notification nor authorization would be required for the passage of warships through territorial seas.[316]

If prior authorization or notification is not a requirement, the only other possible impediment to the passage of military vessels through the territorial sea comes from the characterization of innocent passage. Passage will be considered innocent if it is not prejudicial to the peace, good order, or security of the coastal State.[317] Article 19 of the Convention sets out a number of activities that could be considered as prejudicial to the peace, good order, or security of the State and its final clause sets a fairly low threshold for the entire range of activities by stipulating that any activity "not having a direct bearing on passage" could mean the passage is not innocent.[318] A number of these activities bear specifically on warships and other military vessels – including threats of the use of force in violation of the UN Charter, weapons exercises, launching and landing of aircraft and military devices as well as the collection of information or the dissemination of propaganda.[319] On this basis, the acts that are undertaken by the vessel inform the nature of the passage rather than simply the character or type of vessel.[320]

---

[315] For example, Bangladesh, China, Croatia, Egypt, Iran, Malta, Oman, Serbia and Montenegro, and Yemen still maintain the need for prior notification or authorization according to declarations submitted at the time of signing or ratifying UNCLOS. See United Nations, *Multilateral Treaties Deposited with the Secretary-General*, UN Doc. ST/LEG/SER.E/15, available at www.un.org/Depts/los/los_decl.htm (Apr. 11, 2003).

[316] Joint Statement with Attached Uniform Interpretation of Rules of International Law Governing Innocent Passage, September 23, 1989, US-USSR, 28 ILM 1444. The President of the Third Conference is also reported as stating that there is no need for warships to acquire the prior consent or even notification from the coastal State. See Rauch, at 245. Germany, Italy, the Netherlands, and the United Kingdom also agreed with this interpretation in their declarations submitted at the time of signing or ratifying UNCLOS. United Nations, *Multilateral Treaties Deposited with the Secretary-General*, UN Doc. ST/LEG/SER.E/15, available at www.un.org/Depts/los/los_decl.htm (April 11, 2003).

[317] UNCLOS, art. 19. The Territorial Sea Convention had not specified what acts would be prejudicial to the peace, good order or security of a State. See Territorial Sea Convention, art. 14. Moore has commented: "This 'Innocent Passage' section of the territorial sea chapter is rooted in the provisions of the 1958 Geneva Territorial Sea Convention but in important respects modernizes and improves it." Moore, at 116.

[318] UNCLOS, art. 19(2)(l).   [319] See ibid., art. 19 (a)–(f).

[320] But see Robert C. Reuland, "The Customary Right of Hot Pursuit onto the High Seas: Annotations to Article 111 of the Law of the Sea Convention," 33 *Va. J. Int'l L.* 557, 578

The ICJ took this approach in *Corfu Channel* when addressing issues related to damage caused to British warships by mines in Albanian waters. The primary issue in *Corfu Channel* was the right of States to pass through international waterways without the prior consent of the littoral State.[321] Nonetheless, the discussion on innocent passage through the North Corfu Channel is still pertinent to the regime of innocent passage through territorial waters as the Court addressed the manner in which passage should be conducted to constitute innocent passage.[322] The United Kingdom had sent its warships to test the resolve of Albania during a time of political tension between the countries, and to demonstrate the strength of the British naval power. Albania fired on these ships as they passed through the North Corfu Channel. In deciding whether the passage was innocent, the Court had regard to the manner in which the passage was carried out.[323] In so doing, the Court took into account the facts that the guns of the warships were trimmed fore and aft, not loaded, and that the flotilla did not proceed in combat formation.[324] The Court concluded that the United Kingdom had not violated Albania's sovereignty by reason of the British Navy's acts in Albania's territorial waters.[325]

The acts of the United Kingdom may now be viewed differently in light of the list set out in Article 19 of UNCLOS, but the *Corfu Channel* judgment remains indicative of the need to analyze the character of the passage and thereby prevents coastal States from discriminating against warships *per se* in their territorial seas. The determination as to whether passage is innocent or not is left to the discretion of the coastal State though,[326] as the coastal State is entitled to take any necessary steps

---

(1993) (stating that the very presence of a ship may prejudice the coastal State, without committing any particular act).

[321] Corfu Channel, at 27–30.

[322] Innocent passage would still be required under UNCLOS because the North Corfu Channel falls under Article 38, which provides that "if the strait is formed by an island of a State bordering the strait and its mainland, transit passage shall not apply there if there exists seaward of the island a route through the high seas or through an exclusive economic zone of similar convenience with respect to navigational and hydrographical characteristics."

[323] Corfu Channel, at 30.   [324] *Ibid.*

[325] *Ibid.*, at 32. From this decision, McDougal and Burke note that a "technical state of war" (involving a high expectation of violence and the passage of warships that were principal supporters of the strait State's opponents) was not a sufficient justification to deny access to foreign warships. Myres S. McDougal and William T. Burke, *Public Order of the Oceans* (1962), pp. 206–208.

[326] A joint Soviet and United States statement provides that if a coastal State questioned whether passage was innocent, then the ship had to be given the opportunity to

to prevent passage that is not innocent.[327] The implications of this discretionary power to determine subjectively the innocence of passage and unilaterally prescribe limitations on such passage have rightly been described as far-reaching.[328] If the passage of a warship can be characterized as "non-innocent" and the coastal State requests it to leave its territorial sea,[329] the coastal State may use minimum force to compel its departure.[330] Coastal States are further permitted to suspend innocent passage temporarily if essential for the protection of security, including for weapons exercises.[331]

Potential exists for disputes to arise in respect of innocent passage when warships violate the laws and regulations of the coastal State (including issues of prior notice or authorization); when coastal States require a warship to leave its waters for violations of those laws and regulations; and in respect of the characterization of the passage. A court or tribunal would need to consider whether the military activities exception, if chosen by one of the disputant States, extends to all questions pertaining to the passage of military and government vessels. It seems likely that it would so apply. Many of the reasons that led to the inclusion of the optional exception in relation to military activities on the high seas and EEZ are equally applicable to the passage of military and government vessels through the territorial sea. States may wish to have their naval missions left outside the purview of legal processes and may prefer not to disclose information relating to national security in adjudication or arbitration. The military activities exception could work to the advantage of both coastal States and flag States to the extent that their actions are put beyond review by the international legal

clarify its intentions or to correct its conduct. Joint Statement with Attached Uniform Interpretation of Rules of International Law Governing Innocent Passage, September 23, 1989, US-USSR, 28 ILM 1444.

[327] UNCLOS, art. 25(1). Reisman considers that coastal States have been given too much latitude in this regard thereby posing a threat to national security. W. Michael Reisman, "The Regime of Straits and National Security: An Appraisal of International Lawmaking," 74 Am. J. Int'l L. 48, 60–65 (1980).

[328] Charles E. Pirtle, "Transit Rights and U.S. Security Interests in International Straits: The "Straits Debate" Revisited," 5 Ocean Dev. & Int'l L. 477, 481 (1978).

[329] UNCLOS, art. 30. "The power to require departure from its territory is of course the classic remedy for a State that lacks enforcement jurisdiction over the sovereign agent or instrumentality of a foreign State, be it a diplomat or a warship." Oxman, "Regime of Warships," at 817.

[330] Astley and Schmitt, at 131 (rationalizing that although specific remedies are not included in the Convention, the right to employ the minimum necessary force is a reasonable derivation of State sovereignty over the territorial sea).

[331] UNCLOS, art. 25(3).

system. A dispute relating to the characterization of innocent passage may involve a warship acting in a manner contrary to the peace, good order, and security, or it may involve an allegation of coastal State interference with the passage of warships in unjustified circumstances. The Convention has tilted the balance in favor of the coastal State, however. The broadness of interpretation permissible in characterizing passage as innocent or not rests within the "unfettered discretion" of the coastal State.[332] This discretion applies in favor of the coastal State for commercial as well as military vessels – yet it is the coastal State that may be able to exclude its actions from review if the enforcement of these rules involves acts by military vessels. Rights of navigation in the territorial sea are clearly subjected to the control of the coastal State, both substantively and procedurally.

Given the discretion vested in the coastal State in these circumstances, it could well be argued that the availability of compulsory dispute settlement is important to provide a check on the exercise of these powers. Access to external review may provide a valuable tool in the way that coastal States exercise their sovereignty over their territorial seas. These reasons may indicate why disputes concerning military activities as applied to passage through the territorial sea are optionally excluded, rather than entirely excluded. The availability of mandatory dispute settlement in respect of innocent passage through the territorial sea may not be imperative, however. In addressing the question of prior authorization or notification, Lowe considers the matter somewhat of a non-issue:

few international incidents have occurred, largely because of the *practice* of giving low-level and informal notice of passage on the occasions when naval vessels are sent into the territorial seas of States requiring notification or authorization, which may be followed by a purported "authorization" not sought by the passing ships: such ambiguous procedures save honor on both sides. Important as the controversy is as an academic matter, in practice the world has lived more or less happily with the contradictory interpretation of the law now for many years . . .[333]

---

[332] "A recalcitrant state could thus couch its interference with, for example, the rights of innocent passage, in terms of military activities so as to fit within the escape provisions of article 298(1)(b). The [Convention] does not define what constitutes a military activity; thus, the claiming state would appear to have unfettered discretion when arguing its actions were military activities." Pierce, at 342. See also Reisman, "Regime of Straits," at 58–59.

[333] Lowe, "Commander's Handbook," at 119 (emphasis in original). See also D. P. O'Connell, *The Influence of Law on Sea Power* (1975), p. 140; Lawrence Wayne Kaye, "The Innocent

Typically, the common interest in the freedom of navigation for all ships has worked without resulting in any significant abuses of the right of innocent passage.[334] This reciprocity may provide a satisfactory basis to regulate future exercise of the right of innocent passage without reliance on compulsory dispute settlement.

International Straits and Transit Passage

The naval powers' interests in maintaining freedom of passage through straits became more acute in the face of claims to increasing coastal State jurisdiction.[335] Prior to the extension of the territorial sea to twelve miles, an area of high seas was typically located in international straits allowing passage without coastal State control. This situation changed with the increase in the breadth of the territorial sea. For States with large military fleets, the naval interest was to maintain a right of passage through international straits for naval forces that could not be limited, especially in a time of crisis, by the littoral State.[336] During the drafting of UNCLOS, the interest of maintaining this freedom of movement had to be balanced with the concerns of States bordering straits relating to the proximity and density of traffic, along with the possible adverse effects of this traffic on their security and economic interests.[337] From the start of negotiations, the United States asserted that straits were quite distinct from other areas of territorial waters as a functional matter.[338] It was with this functional perspective in mind that an acceptable balance could be struck through the creation of the right of transit passage. The regime of transit passage only applies in respect of straits between one part of the high seas or an EEZ and another part of the high seas or an EEZ.[339]

Passage of Warships in Foreign Territorial Seas: A Threatened Freedom," 15 *San Diego L. Rev.* 573, 583 (1978).

[334] Rao, at 446.   [335] Janis, at 57.

[336] *Ibid.*, at 58. See also Richard J. Grunawalt, "United States Policy on International Straits," 18 *Ocean Dev. & Int'l L.* 445, 447 (1987). ("The flexibility and mobility of naval forces are dependent upon their ability to transit choke points in sea lines of communication, and to do so as a matter of right rather than at the sufferance of the coastal or island nations concerned.") But see Pirtle, at 489 (arguing that unimpeded passage through straits was not a necessary requisite for United States' security).

[337] Burke and DeLeo, at 400–01. See also Rauch, at 246.

[338] Special Report of the UN Law of the Sea Conference, Off. of Media Services, Bureau of Pub. Aff., 70 DEPT. STATE BULL. 398 (1974), cited in Richardson, "Navigation and National Security," at 563.

[339] UNCLOS, art. 37.

As a new creation of UNCLOS, the question arises as to the extent of freedom of navigation that transit passage accords. Some commentators consider that transit passage is equivalent to the high seas freedom of navigation but applied to international straits.[340] The range of competences accorded to the coastal State with respect to transit passage tends to detract from any argument that the freedom of navigation, as exercised on the high seas, is equivalent to transit passage. Moreover, the new regime has been criticized as "a neologism; it lies somewhere between 'freedom of navigation' on the one hand, and 'innocent passage' on the other. It is a compromise, a concession or a second-best solution."[341] The compromise was inevitable, however, because of the irreversible trend towards the appropriation of larger maritime areas by coastal States. Furthermore, some limitation had to be imposed on the traditional freedom of navigation to prevent overt military exercises and weapons testing, surveillance and intelligence gathering, and refueling in international straits.[342]

Any analysis of transit passage must account for its character as a species of passage lying somewhere between innocent passage and the freedom of navigation. All ships and aircraft enjoy the right of unimpeded transit passage through straits that lie between one part of the high seas or an EEZ and another part of the high seas or an EEZ.[343] Transit passage requires ships and aircraft to proceed without delay through or over the strait.[344] Compared with innocent passage, transit passage allows for greater surface navigation rights. Transiting warships are permitted to perform activities that are incidental to passage through the strait and consistent with the security of the unit (such as, the use of radar, sonar, and air cover).[345] Ships and aircraft exercising the right of

---

[340] See, e.g., David A. Larson, "Innocent, Transit, and Archipelagic Sea Lanes Passage," 18 *Ocean Dev. & Int'l L.* 411, 414–15 (1987) (also suggesting that transit passage is a codification and development of the customary rule set out in *Corfu Channel*); Rauch, at 233 ("the right of transit passage is a specific formulation of the high seas freedoms of navigation and overflight"). But see Reisman, "Regime of Straits," at 70 (arguing that "transit passage" is more a species of innocent passage than a high seas freedom because of the coastal State's legal duties and consequent entitlement to assess the character of the passage).

[341] Reisman, "Regime of Straits," at 68.   [342] *Ibid.*, at 72.

[343] UNCLOS, art. 38. Four categories of straits to which transit passage does not apply are also listed in the Convention as part of the necessary compromise to reach consensus on the overall concept of transit passage. See *ibid.*, arts. 35(c), 36, 37, and 45.

[344] *Ibid.*, art. 39(1)(a).

[345] Bruce A. Harlow, "UNCLOS III and Conflict Management in Straits," 15 *Ocean Dev. & Int'l L.* 197, 201 (1985). As with innocent passage, it is the manner of the passage that is relevant rather than the purpose of the passage. Lowe, "Commander's Handbook," at 126.

transit passage must refrain from any threat or use of force against the territorial integrity or political independence of the littoral State.[346] This prohibition, while still being broad, is much more flexible than the list of activities that may be prejudicial to the peace, good order, or security of a coastal State for innocent passage through the territorial sea.[347] Moreover, the right of transit passage cannot be suspended.[348] States bordering straits subject to transit passage are entitled to designate sea lanes and prescribe traffic separation schemes for navigation through the strait (provided they are established in conformity with generally accepted international regulations)[349] and may also adopt laws and regulations relating to navigation, pollution, fishing, and fiscal, immigration, and sanitary laws.[350] Research and survey activities must not be carried out by foreign ships during transit passage without the authorization of the States bordering the strait.[351]

A controversial issue regarding transit passage has been whether there is a right of submerged passage for submarines. The Convention specifically stipulates that submarines must navigate on the surface and show their flag while exercising the right of innocent passage,[352] but no express provision is made for transit passage. The absence of a prohibition on submerged passage in respect of passage through straits can be interpreted as permissive or proscriptive. The only guide on this matter is in Article 39, which provides that ships and aircraft must "refrain from any activities other than those incident to their normal modes of continuous and expeditious transit."[353] As submarines "normal mode" of passage is submerged, then that passage is presumably permitted through straits.[354] The reference to "normal mode" may impact on other military vessels. The "normal mode" permitted for transit passage has been interpreted to include launching and recovering aircraft and helicopters and thus allows carrier task forces to put up combat air patrols as a defensive measure.[355]

---

[346] UNCLOS, art. 39(1)(b). See also Larson, "Security Issues," at 117 (noting that threats to the sovereignty, territorial integrity or political independence of the straits States is distinct from the peace, good order, and security of the coastal State).

[347] See UNCLOS, art. 19.   [348] Ibid., art. 44.   [349] Ibid., art. 41.

[350] Ibid., art. 42.   [351] Ibid., art. 40.   [352] Ibid., art. 20.   [353] Ibid., art. 39(1)(c).

[354] Burke and DeLeo, at 403–04. See also Lowe, "Commander's Handbook," at 122; International Maritime Organization, Guidance for Ships Transiting Archipelagic Waters, IMO SN/Circ.206, January 8, 1999.

[355] Astley and Schmitt, at 133. See also Grunawalt, at 453; Doran, at 340 (defining the term "normal modes" to include surface warships being permitted to launch and recover aircraft as well as formation steaming). But see Lowe, "Commander's Handbook," at 122 (arguing that the right of overflight does not seem sufficient to warrant the launching and recovery of aircraft in international straits).

Overall, the articles in UNCLOS on transit passage contain "sufficient vagueness, so that both the straits states and the major maritime powers can read into it what they want."[356] Transit passage was one way to satisfy the needs of the naval military powers but given the importance of guaranteeing this freedom of navigation, "[w]hy permit the straits states to interpret, if they care to, transit passage to mean something very close to innocent passage?"[357] Compulsory dispute settlement is a means to maintain the nature of the compromise formed at the time of the drafting of the Convention. A third-party process is preferable to establish international standards for transit passage, rather than allow straits States to establish and maintain their own unilateral standards.[358] This role for dispute settlement is most likely blocked by the military activities exception, however, as the most controversial questions regarding transit passage concern the rights of military and government vessels. If the exception is elected, these disputes are then left for resolution through traditional methods. In this respect, the legal regime governing access to straits could be less important than the political context in which transit occurs.[359] Straits could be closed to military transit where the political will exists regardless of a regime of unimpeded transit or innocent passage.[360] Nonetheless, in light of the fact that transit passage is a creation of UNCLOS and designed for the specific purpose of balancing the interests of States possessing large naval military fleets with the interests of the straits States, mandatory dispute settlement is a necessary element in this system. There is distinct potential to undermine the legal regime of transit passage if third-party involvement is not available to maintain the system created by the Convention. The use of the military activities exception to prevent the institution of proceedings where necessary will impair the viability of transit passage in the law of the sea.

Archipelagic Waters and Archipelagic Passage

UNCLOS affords a recognized legal status to archipelagic States. The Convention creates a regime for the recognition of archipelagic States

---

[356] Larson, "Passage," at 418. Richardson has taken this approach and thus argues: "The text [on transit passage] emphasizes the rights of transiting states, placing on them only reasonable obligations that do not impair, *inter alia*, the execution of military missions." Richardson, "Power," at 915.

[357] Janis, at 59.   [358] *Ibid.*, at 60.   [359] Pirtle, at 489.

[360] *Ibid.*, at 490. The reality of this political will is evident in the purchase of particular antiship missiles as well as offshore mines by various straits States after witnessing their success during the Falkland Islands conflict. David L. Larson, "Naval Weaponry and the Law of the Sea," 18 *Ocean Dev. & Int'l L.* 125, 144 (1987).

and their rights as well as those of third States within the waters of these States. Under UNCLOS, an archipelago means "a group of islands, including parts of islands, interconnecting waters and other natural features which are so closely interrelated that such islands, water and other natural features form an intrinsic geographical, economic and political entity, or which historically have been regarded as such."[361] An archipelagic State is then a State that is constituted wholly by one or more archipelagos and may include other islands.[362] Archipelagic States may enclose their outermost islands with straight baselines. The drawing of these baselines has the effect of transforming the waters within those lines into archipelagic waters and consequently further reduces the amount of ocean space available to other users.

All States enjoy the right of innocent passage through archipelagic waters in line with the right of innocent passage through territorial seas.[363] On this basis, submarines must navigate on the surface and passage may only be suspended temporarily. In addition to the right of innocent passage, the Convention establishes archipelagic sea lanes passage, which means "the exercise in accordance with this Convention of the right of navigation and overflight in the normal mode solely for the purpose of continuous, expeditious and unobstructed transit between one part of the high seas or exclusive economic zone and another part of the high seas of an exclusive economic zone."[364] Passage in archipelagic sea lanes is thus at least as broad with respect to navigation and overflight as transit passage through straits. As with transit passage, the creation of archipelagic sea lanes passage is a compromise between the regime of innocent passage and freedom of navigation on the high seas.[365] Transit passage was an acceptable passage regime because archipelagic sea lanes are not necessarily close to land territory.[366]

Designation of archipelagic sea lanes rests with the archipelagic State. Although the Convention specifies how these lanes should be defined,[367] it is within the discretion of the archipelagic State to determine how many sea lanes will traverse its waters. As such, the archipelagic State has a large degree of control over the amount of traffic that may pass

---

[361] UNCLOS, art. 46.   [362] Ibid., art. 46.   [363] Ibid., art. 52.   [364] Ibid., art. 53(3).

[365] Noegroho Wisnomoerti, Indonesia and the Law of the Sea, in The Law of the Sea: Problems from the East Asian Perspective (Choon-ho Park and Jae Kyu Park eds., 1987), p. 392, at pp. 395–96.

[366] J. Peter A. Bernhardt, "The Right of Archipelagic Sea Lanes Passage: A Primer," 35 Va. J. Int'l L. 719, 727 (1995).

[367] UNCLOS, art. 53(5), which provides: "Such sea lanes and air routes shall be defined by a series of continuous axis lines from the entry points of passage routes to the exit points."

through its waters. In balance to this control, if the archipelagic State fails to designate sea lanes through and air routes over its waters, the right of archipelagic sea lanes passage may be exercised through the routes normally used for international navigation.[368] This provision has been described as supplying "the lowest common denominator or 'safety valve' which enabled the maritime states to accept the concept of archipelagic sea lanes passage."[369] Controversy could well arise as to what passage regime applies in certain areas of archipelagic waters unless sea lanes are clearly delimited. When they have designated sea lanes, archipelagic States may prescribe traffic separation schemes.[370] The archipelagic State's power to prescribe traffic separation schemes is more limited than straits States' power to do so because the archipelagic State may only prescribe these schemes "for the safe passage of ships through narrow channels in such sea lanes"[371] rather than for any sea lanes. The rights of archipelagic States are further limited in that, similarly to transit passage, they are not permitted to close archipelagic sea lanes.[372] An express closure of the normal passage routes used for international navigation through archipelagic waters as well as conduct that has the effect of denying navigation rights would constitute a violation of UNCLOS.[373] Archipelagic States may suspend innocent passage through archipelagic waters temporarily only if essential for protection of security.[374]

---

[368] *Ibid.*, art. 53(12).   [369] Bernhardt, at 755.

[370] UNCLOS, art 53(6). This right is also granted to straits States "where necessary to promote the safe passage of ships." *Ibid.*, art. 41.

[371] *Ibid.*, art. 53(6).

[372] Article 54 provides that Article 44 applies *mutatis mutandis* to archipelagic sea lanes passage. *Ibid.*, art. 54. As such, archipelagic States must not hamper or suspend passage.

[373] In response to Indonesia's closure of the Straits of Lombok and Sunda for naval exercises, the US Department of State wrote:
> No nation may, consistent with international law, prohibit passage of foreign vessels or aircraft or act in a manner that interferes with straits transit or archipelagic sea lanes passage . . . While it is perfectly reasonable for an archipelagic state to conduct naval exercises in its straits, it may not carry out those exercises in a way that closes the straits, either expressly or constructively, that creates a threat to the safety of users of the straits, or that hampers the right of navigation and overflight through the straits or archipelagic sea lanes.

Marian Nash Leich, "U.S. Practice, Indonesia: Archipelagic Waters," 83 *Am. J. Int'l L.* 558, 560 (1989).

[374] UNCLOS, art. 52 (unlike the suspension rights in the territorial sea, no suspension of archipelagic passage is permitted for military exercises).

The archipelagic regime created in the Convention is clearly intended to balance the interests of archipelagic States with the continuing interests in international navigation through these maritime areas. The hybrid passage regime manifests this balance through the provision of transit passage in areas that are designated by the archipelagic State or in areas that are normally used for international navigation. The Convention anticipates that the selection of sea lanes, as well as traffic separation schemes, will entail the involvement and approval of the competent international organization (typically the International Maritime Organization).[375] The axis of sea lanes as well as traffic separation schemes must further be indicated on charts that are given due publicity.[376] These external processes may count for adequate review to ensure that archipelagic States conform to the rules set out in the Convention. Otherwise, compulsory dispute settlement could provide an accessible avenue to protect the rights and duties of both archipelagic and third States in respect of passage through archipelagic waters as balanced in UNCLOS. There is no doubt that to the extent that commercial navigation is affected, compulsory dispute settlement is available. With respect to the passage of military and government vessels, similar considerations apply as for transit passage. Compulsory dispute settlement is necessary in order to maintain the balance produced in the Convention and to provide a check on the exercise of States' powers. Third-party involvement, in the form of review by international organizations or dispute settlement proceedings, is necessary to maintain the system created by the Convention. The archipelagic regime could be less viable if the military activities exception prevents recourse to international proceedings.

Law Enforcement

Law enforcement activities were first considered in the context of an optional exception to mandatory jurisdiction as a way of describing the extent of the military activities exception.[377] The exclusion of "military activities" from compulsory dispute settlement was included in early drafts of the Convention on the understanding that law enforcement activities pursuant to the Convention would not be considered as military activities.[378] A State could exclude disputes "concerning military activities, including those by government vessels and aircraft engaged

---

[375] *Ibid.*, art. 53(9).   [376] *Ibid.*, art. 53(10).   [377] Singh, p. 148.
[378] See *ibid.* (referring to the Single Negotiating Text and the Revised Single Negotiating Text).

in non-commercial service, but law enforcement activities pursuant to this Convention shall not be considered military activities."[379] Objections were raised that this provision would allow for a situation where "in the exclusive economic zone of a State, the military activities of foreign States' would be excluded from third-party settlement, but the coastal State's law enforcement activities would be subject to compulsory international settlement."[380] As originally drafted, the optional exception would have favored the naval power States in excluding their actions in the zones of third States while subjecting the actions of coastal States to possible third-party review. Law enforcement activities related to the exercise of sovereign rights or jurisdiction provided for in the Convention were then included as a possible optional exclusion in the Informal Composite Negotiating Text.[381] The final text of the Convention narrowed the exclusion to law enforcement activities related to fishing and marine scientific research.

Law Enforcement Optionally Excluded from Compulsory Dispute Settlement

Article 298(1)(b) refers, in relevant part, to "disputes concerning law enforcement activities in regard to the exercise of sovereign rights or jurisdiction excluded from the jurisdiction of a court or tribunal under article 297, paragraph 2 or 3." A direct link is thus made between Article 298 and Article 297. These paragraphs of Article 297 respectively relate to marine scientific research and fishing in the EEZ. As discussed in Chapter 3, disputes concerning marine scientific research are subject to the compulsory procedure in Section 2 of Part XV except for disputes relating to marine scientific research in the EEZ and on the continental shelf of a coastal State and for decisions by a coastal State to order suspension or cessation of a research project.[382] Along with these specified exclusions, a State may choose to exclude law enforcement activities with respect to marine scientific research as well.[383] Similarly, disputes concerning fisheries are subject to compulsory dispute settlement except for those disputes relating to the exercise of sovereign rights over living resources

---

[379] *Single Negotiating Text*, UN Doc. A/CONF. 62/WP. 9/Rev. 1, art. 18(2)(b), cited in Singh, p. 148.

[380] 5 *United Nations Convention on the Law of the Sea 1982: A Commentary*, p. 136.

[381] Singh, p. 148 (referring to UN Doc. A/CONF.62/WP.10, 15 July 1977, art. 297(1)(b)).

[382] UNCLOS, art. 297(2)(a).

[383] There is no specific provision in UNCLOS addressing law enforcement activities with respect to marine scientific research.

in the EEZ. For those disputes that are still covered by Section 2, States may also choose to exclude law enforcement activities with respect to fisheries.

Article 73, paragraph 1 allows the coastal State to take various measures to ensure compliance with its laws and regulations relating to the exploration, exploitation, conservation, and management of the living resources in the EEZ. The Convention anticipates that coastal States may board, inspect, arrest, and institute judicial proceedings against vessels found in violation of fishing laws and regulations. Burke has considered a range of other measures that coastal States have taken, or may take, to enhance enforcement of their fishing laws and regulations including prescribing sea lanes for transiting fishing vessels; requiring report of entry and exit together with route used; and stowage of fishing gear during passage.[384] In addition, coastal States will often include enforcement procedures in access agreements so that the flag State of foreign fishing fleets given access to the EEZ is responsible for monitoring and policing of its own ships.[385] The penalties imposed by the coastal State may not include imprisonment, in the absence of agreements to the contrary by the States concerned, or any form of corporal punishment.[386] In cases of arrest or detention of foreign vessels, the coastal State must promptly notify the flag State through appropriate channels of the action taken and of any penalties subsequently imposed.[387]

Coastal States are required promptly to release arrested vessels and their crews upon the posting of a reasonable bond or other security.[388] Although this action is part of the enforcement powers vested in the coastal State and could thus seemingly be excluded from mandatory proceedings, Article 292 permits the institution of proceedings against the detaining State when it is alleged that the detaining State has not complied with the prompt release requirement of, *inter alia*, Article 73, paragraph 2.[389] The prompt release proceedings under Article 292 can only deal with the question of release and the posting of a reasonable bond or other financial security, and not inquire into obligations relating to coastal State penalties or notification.[390] Oda has argued that a

---

[384] Burke, *New International Law of Fisheries*, pp. 315–35. See also Attard, pp. 180–81 (describing the enforcement measures exercised by various States and the validity of those measures under customary international law).

[385] Picard, at 336 (1996). See also Burke, *New International Law of Fisheries*, pp. 315–35; and Kwaitkowska, *Exclusive Economic Zone*, pp. 87–88.

[386] UNCLOS, art. 73(3).   [387] *Ibid.*, art. 73(4).

[388] *Ibid.*, art. 73(2).   [389] See further pp. 85–119.

[390] See Camouco, para. 59; Monte Confurco, para. 63.

problem of overlapping issues may arise with respect to proceedings for the prompt release of vessels, commenting that it is "inevitably linked with the content of the rules and regulations of the coastal State concerning the fisheries in its exclusive economic zone, and the way in which these rules are enforced."[391] However, in light of the limited jurisdiction of ITLOS in prompt release proceedings, any challenge to the particular enforcement measures prescribed by the coastal State would have to be made pursuant to a challenge on the merits and would only then risk being excluded by virtue of Article 298. The creation of a special procedure specifically for the prompt release of vessels was justified on the basis of the potential for too much interference with rights of navigation through the EEZ. Consequently, the optional exception for law enforcement should not be considered as excluding the application of Article 292.[392]

A problem may arise when the law enforcement powers of the coastal State in the EEZ clash with the rights of navigation of third States. The coastal State may prescribe measures, such as the designation of sea lanes or applying territorial sea authority to fishing vessels, that could interfere with the freedom of navigation. Burke argues that the enforcement of fishing laws and regulations should be done in such a way to minimize the negative impact on navigation since the fishing industry is only of vital importance to the economies of a small number of States.[393] The difficulty for the operation of the dispute settlement system in Part XV is that Article 297 subjects allegations that a coastal State has acted in contravention of the freedom of navigation to the mandatory procedures in Section 2 while States have the option to exclude law enforcement disputes under Article 298. The interaction of these provisions is not explained in the text of UNCLOS so the question may well become one of characterization of the dispute. Riphagen considers that the question is really one of degree – a foreign fishing vessel should not be arrested merely because it is equipped for fishing, as opposed to actually fishing, because that would seriously impair the freedom of navigation.[394] He argues that, "[o]ne could hardly assume that 'law enforcement' of such a kind could be made immune from compulsory dispute settlement by a court or tribunal."[395] Since a limited range of law

---

[391] Oda, "Dispute Settlement Prospects," at 866.   [392] Riphagen, pp. 293–94.
[393] Burke, *New International Law of Fisheries*, pp. 309–10.
[394] Riphagen, pp. 293–94. He takes the same view with respect to enforcement of laws and regulations relating to marine scientific research. *Ibid.*
[395] *Ibid.*, at 293–94.

enforcement activities are only excluded from mandatory jurisdiction at the option of the State whereas Article 297 expressly includes navigation disputes relating to the EEZ and the continental shelf, the balance in the Convention would appear to be in favor of resolving navigation disputes through compulsory procedures entailing binding decisions. The aim of accommodating the competing interests of coastal and third States in navigation can "best be attained, and disruptive confrontation avoided, if the navigational articles are interpreted in a manner to give continuing efficacy to that balance."[396] As compulsory dispute settlement is necessary for the operation of the navigation regime established in UNCLOS, these interests should be weighted accordingly.

Settlement of Other Law Enforcement Disputes

Other aspects of the Convention that relate to the powers of States parties to enforce various laws relating to the uses of the oceans are not excluded from compulsory procedures entailing binding decisions, unless some other exception applies. Articles 27 and 28 relate to the exercise of civil and criminal jurisdiction over vessels (and jurisdiction over persons on those vessels) passing through territorial seas. Enforcement activities may also be undertaken in the contiguous zone. According to Article 33, States may exercise the control necessary to prevent and punish the infringement of their customs, fiscal, immigration, or sanitary laws and regulations within their territory or territorial sea in a zone extending twenty-four miles from their baselines. Enforcement activities may also be undertaken on the high seas in respect of fishing, piracy, slave trading, and unauthorized broadcasting through the right of visit and the right of hot pursuit.

The right of visit is exclusively available to warships on the high seas,[397] and "exists as an exception to the general principle of the exclusive jurisdiction of the flag State over ships flying its flag, set out in article 92."[398] The right of hot pursuit has long been accepted as part of the law of the sea.[399] "The right of hot pursuit – an exception to the freedom of the high seas – is at the same time a right of the littoral State established for the effective protection of areas under its

---

[396] Grunawalt, at 456.   [397] UNCLOS, art. 110(1).

[398] 3 *United Nations Convention on the Law of the Sea 1982: A Commentary*, pp. 238–39.

[399] See O'Connell, 2 *International Law of the Sea*, pp. 1078–79 (describing the entrenched position of the right and consequent lack of controversy over the right during the progressive codification of the law of the sea). See also Reuland, at 557.

sovereignty or jurisdiction."[400] Article 111 sets out the basic right and a number of qualifications on the way the right may be exercised.[401] The right of visit is only ascribed to warships whereas the right of hot pursuit may be undertaken by warships as well as ships or aircraft clearly marked and identifiable as being on government service and authorized to that effect. In this regard, it may be possible to discern some overlap between law enforcement activities and military activities. The distinction between law enforcement and military activities may become relevant since many enforcement activities are undertaken by military vessels. The question thus arises as to what extent the military activities exception may exclude disputes relating to law enforcement activities undertaken by military vessels.

The right of visit for the enforcement of various laws under the Convention must be distinguished from the right of visit and search that may be exercised by a belligerent State against all merchant ships during time of war.[402] "The right of visit and search is a war right; it can only be expressed in time of peace by virtue of an express stipulation in an international treaty, or in the course of maintaining the security of navigation by a generally recognised usage in the interests of all nations."[403] The right of visit granted under UNCLOS is expressly for the enforcement of designated prescriptions set out in the Convention with respect to vessels that are not accorded immunity. Unlike the right of visit, the Convention does not specify that the right of hot pursuit may not be exercised against foreign military and government vessels. McDougal and Burke take the view that in light of the immunity of these vessels, the enforcing ship should not be authorized to pursue and seize warships or other government vessels not engaged in commercial service.[404] The right of hot pursuit is necessary to ensure the effective application and enforcement of coastal regulations and "as such, is merely ancillary to the substantive measures intended to be applied."[405]

It is difficult to assert that the right of hot pursuit and the right of visit are not law enforcement activities rather than military activities as both acts involve the enforcement of specific laws. The mere fact that

---

[400] Nicholas M. Poulantzas, *The Right of Hot Pursuit in International Law* (1969), p. 39.
[401] O'Connell notes that these qualifications, which were included in the drafting of the High Seas Convention, were more detailed than customary doctrine but could be viewed as reasonable corollaries of it. O'Connell, 2 *International Law of the Sea*, p. 1079.
[402] See C. John Colombos, *The International Law of the Sea* (6th ed., revisd, 1967), pp. 753–54.
[403] *Ibid.*, p. 311.   [404] McDougal and Burke, p. 895.
[405] *Ibid.*, p. 896. See also *ibid.*, pp. 894 and 902.

these rights are exercised by military and government vessels does not justify a characterization of "military activities" for the purposes of Article 298. Clearly, from the terms of Article 298(1)(b), only law enforcement activities pertaining to fishing or marine scientific research in the EEZ may be excluded as "law enforcement." Furthermore, the drafting history of this provision would indicate that all law enforcement activities besides those specified are subject to compulsory procedures entailing binding decisions.[406] The military activities exception is not intended, and not needed, to insulate from mandatory jurisdiction disputes that are more properly construed as law enforcement activities.

Conclusion

The use of force, military activities, and law enforcement are subject to minimal normative regulation under the Convention. The application of all provisions of UNCLOS in times of armed conflict is unclear (but unlikely) and deliberate vagueness was preferred with respect to a range of naval activities on the high seas and in the EEZ of coastal States. Part XV nonetheless anticipates that these disputes will arise in relation to the interpretation and application of the Convention as Article 298 permits States to exclude disputes relating to military activities as well as disputes that are threats to international peace and security and are thus subject to the functions of the Security Council. The implication from this procedural device is that international legal processes are not necessarily required as the means to resolve disputes relating to armed conflict and naval activities in maritime areas where the freedoms of the high seas are exercised. The military activities exception and the Security Council exception can work to the advantage of States with greater naval power if they wish to resolve these disputes through political avenues.[407] Coastal States can also take advantage of the military activities exception if they have the capability to interfere with naval operations of third States in their territorial sea and EEZ and do not wish to have their actions subject to adjudication or arbitration.[408]

---

[406] See notes 377–81 and accompanying text. Singh, p. 148 ("military activities" were initially excluded from compulsory dispute settlement on the understanding that law enforcement activities pursuant to the Convention would not be considered as military activities).

[407] "From a military point of view the new LOS Convention protects to the fullest extent the security interests of the naval powers." Rauch, at 230.

[408] Janis, at 56–57 (noting that this would not be detrimental for the naval power if it was in a position to exert its relative physical advantage).

Greater regulation is evident for maritime areas subject to coastal State sovereignty. The traditional regime of innocent passage has been subject to increasing codification, first in the Territorial Sea Convention and now in UNCLOS. However, as a mutually beneficial system, States have long resolved disputes relating to innocent passage through diplomatic channels without typically resorting to international arbitration or adjudication. This system of reciprocity was jeopardized when coastal States began to agitate for a wider breadth of territorial sea. States with considerable commercial and strategic interests espoused greater concern about the freedoms of navigation. To respond to these concerns in particular maritime areas, namely, certain straits used for international navigation as well as archipelagic waters, new regimes of passage were created in the Convention. As true of many provisions in UNCLOS, some ambiguity was left within the terms of the Convention in order to allow for a range of interpretations to accord with the different interests of States. The systems of passage created in the Convention are delicate balances and are susceptible to erosion if misused by either the coastal State or the States in passage. To maintain a control on the powers of States in this regard, compulsory dispute settlement plays a vital role. Referral of a dispute to international adjudication or arbitration (or at least the threat of so doing) guarantees the balance of the Convention. The systems of transit and archipelagic passage could well break down without recourse to dispute settlement being available. To this end, the military activities exception, if held applicable, could undermine the viability of these passage regimes. Perhaps the passage of military and government vessels should not even be considered as "military activities" in this regard. Such a characterization would be less plausible when a tribunal or court was dealing with a question of rights of passage being suspended or denied unlawfully. Special conditions attached to passage (such as a levy or inspection) should also be deemed outside the exception of "military activities." Only acts that are tantamount to a threat or use of force in the course of passage – by either the coastal State or the State passing through the strait or archipelagic waters – should be viewed as falling within the category of disputes that could be excluded from mandatory jurisdiction of an international court or tribunal. This interpretation would be in line with the exclusions appropriate for military actions on the high seas or in the EEZ.

Finally, the exclusion of law enforcement activities is limited to disputes that relate to the exercise of sovereign rights or jurisdiction excluded from the jurisdiction of a court or tribunal under Article 297, paragraph 2 or 3. All other law enforcement activities will be subject to mandatory procedures entailing a binding decision, unless one of the other exceptions or limitations applies. There may be some overlap between law enforcement activities relating to fishing in the EEZ and the right of navigation of third States through the EEZ. If the dispute is characterized as one relating to law enforcement then it could be excluded from jurisdiction by virtue of Article 298. Equally, if the dispute is characterized as one relating to the rights of navigation then it is included for resolution under Section 2 of Part XV in accordance with Article 297. In determining how to characterize the dispute, any court or tribunal should heed the essential role accorded to international arbitration and adjudication in respect of the regime of navigation in the EEZ. The need judicially to resolve disputes relating to the interpretation and application of the provisions on navigation in the EEZ should be taken into account in determining what characterization best fulfills the purposes of the Convention. A potential overlap between law enforcement and military activities is less problematic. The right of visit and the right of hot pursuit, as well as the enforcement powers exercisable in the territorial sea and contiguous zone, are quintessentially law enforcement activities even if undertaken by military and government vessels. The military activities exception was not intended to cover law enforcement acts, except for those expressly included in Article 298.

5   Deep Seabed Mining

Development of the Deep Seabed Mining Regime

The existence of mineral-rich nodules on the floor of the deep seabed has been known about since the oceanographic expedition of HMS *Challenger* of 1872–76,[1] but it was only in the second half of the twentieth century that commercial interest in the deep seabed evolved.[2] This interest centered on the presence of an estimated 22 billion tons of polymetallic nodules, which contain fine-grained oxides of copper, nickel, cobalt, and manganese, located on the bed of the ocean at depths of approximately three miles.[3] The exploitation of polymetallic nodules from the deep seabed had not been technically possible at the time of the First and Second Conferences. This situation rapidly changed in the 1960s as the range of ocean uses significantly increased through improvements in technology.[4] At the time that the exploitation of manganese nodules became technically possible, the minerals found in the nodules were important to developing and developed countries alike where the

[1] John Alton Duff, "UNCLOS and the New Deep Seabed Mining Regime: The Risks of Refuting the Treaty," 19 *Suffolk Transnational L. Rev.* 1, 5 (1995); William C. Brewer, "Deep Seabed Mining: Can An Acceptable Regime Ever be Found?," 11 *Ocean Dev. & Int'l L. J.* 25, 27 (1982).

[2] See Duff, at 5–7.

[3] James H. Breen, "The 1982 Dispute Resolving Agreement: The First Step Toward Unilateral Mining Outside the Law of the Sea Convention," 14 *Ocean Dev. & Int'l L. J.* 201, 204 (1984); Brewer, at 28 (1982) (estimating depths of 3,000 to 5,000 meters).

[4] "Technological developments spurred by the arms race, space exploration, and economic growth were to have inevitable and lasting effects that transcended local and national interests." Euripides L. Evriviades, "The Third World's Approach to the Deep Seabed," 11 *Ocean Dev. & Int'l L. J.* 201, 207 (1982). See also *ibid.*, at 207–09 (describing the effect of technological advancements on continental shelf exploration and exploitation, fishing, deep seabed mining, merchant shipping, and protection of the marine environment).

latter were the greatest consumers and the former were the greatest producers.[5] These resources were important for iron and steel production, in applications requiring high temperature resistant alloys, for corrosion resistance, and to strengthen alloy steel.[6]

The development of the technology to recover manganese nodules coincided with the international movement to devise a New International Economic Order ("NIEO"), which was spearheaded by developing countries.[7] Creating a legal regime for a new and important resource was an opportunity for these States to further the aims of the NIEO. The economic potential in the development of deep seabed mining technology prompted Ambassador Arvid Pardo of Malta to propose that the UN declare the seabed and ocean floor "underlying the seas beyond the limits of present national jurisdiction" to be "the common heritage of mankind," not subject to appropriation by any State for its sole use.[8] The concept of the common heritage of mankind was entirely new. It did not establish a *res communis*, allowing all States to exploit common property with reasonable regard for the rights of other users, nor was it *res nullius*, which would permit the acquisition of exclusive rights by occupation or appropriation.[9] Ambassador Pardo suggested that a body should be

[5] Brewer, at 29. Around the time of the adoption of UNCLOS, the United States was importing "98 percent of its cobalt, principally from Zaire; 97 percent of its manganese, principally from Gabon and South Africa; and 73 percent of its nickel, principally from Canada." Breen, at 205 (citing *Impediments to US Involvement in Deep Ocean Mining can be Overcome*, GAO Rep. EMD/82/31, at 5 [February 3, 1982]). Japan had to import 100 percent of its nickel and cobalt requirements, 96 percent of its copper, and over 90 percent of its manganese needs. Moritaka Hayashi, "Japan and Deep Seabed Mining," 17 *Ocean Dev. & Int'l L. J.* 351, 356 (1986). The European Community was entirely dependent on imports of mineral ores and imported 90 percent of its required metals. Michael Hardy, "The Law of the Sea and the Prospects for Deep Seabed Mining: The Position of the European Community," 17 *Ocean Dev. & Int'l L. J.* 309, 313 (1986). By comparison, India was self-sufficient in manganese but imported between 65 and 90 percent of its copper requirements and 100 percent of its nickel and cobalt needs. Manjula R. Shyam, "Deep Seabed Mining: An Indian Perspective," 17 *Ocean Dev. & Int'l L. J.* 325, 327 (1986).

[6] Mark S. Bergman, "The Regulation of Seabed Mining Under the Reciprocating States Regime," 30 *Am. Univ. L. Rev.* 477, 485 (1981); Breen, at 205.

[7] The basic goals of the NIEO were the reconstruction of the existing international economic system in order to improve development and welfare in developing countries; narrow disparities between developing and developed States; and giving developing countries more control over their political, social and economic destinies. See Reubens, at 1.

[8] The complete address is in UN GAOR, 1st Comm., 22d Sess., 1515th mtg., at 1–15, UN Doc. A/C.1/PV.1515 (1967), and UN GAOR, 1st Comm., 22d Sess., 1515th mtg., at 1–3, UN Doc. A/C.1/PV.1516 (1967). See also UN Doc. A/6695 (August 18, 1967) (Malta's Memorandum to the Secretary-General).

[9] Brewer, at 32.

established in order to study the possibility of an international regime, including an international agency, and that it should draft a comprehensive treaty to safeguard the international character of the seabed.[10] In enthusiasm for the possible transformation of the world economy, the "figures were uncritically accepted by many at the time, although they assumed, wrongly as it turned out, that the continental slope would lie beyond the limits of national jurisdiction, and they took little account of the extent of risk capital needed, the economics of marketing, or the effect of seabed recoveries upon the price of land-recovered minerals."[11] Nonetheless, "the Maltese Initiative provided both the impetus and the legal rationale for the need to establish a cooperative organization to control, manage and operate an international area reserved specifically for the benefit of mankind."[12]

Industrialized States were aware of the economic demands of developing States and were sensitive to the numerical strength that the Group of 77 could command in international conference settings. At the same time, the developed States had their own economic needs to obtain vital minerals used in industry without being dependent on developing countries for their supply. This concern deepened following the oil crisis of the early 1970s. Moreover, industrialized countries faced domestic pressure from wealthy mining consortia and interested constituents in developing a stable legal regime that would promote investment in deep sea mining ventures.

In an attempt to create some sort of interim protection for developing countries' interests before the creation of an international authority and to forestall commercial exploitation by developed States, the General Assembly adopted a Moratorium Resolution in 1969. This resolution declared that "pending the establishment of the . . . international regime," States were "bound to refrain from all activities of exploitation of the resources . . . of the sea-bed and ocean floor . . . beyond the limits of national jurisdiction."[13] This resolution has been described as "one of

[10] Annick de Marfy, "The Pardo Declaration and the Six Years of the Sea-Bed Committee," in 1 *A Handbook on the New Law of the Sea* (René-Jean Dupuy and Daniel Vignes eds., 1991), p. 144.

[11] O'Connell, 1 *International Law of the Sea*, p. 459. Pardo's statement was also criticized for offering "limitless mineral resources, a bonanza in the oceans" without considering the associated costs. Guilio Pontecorvo, "Musing About Seabed Mining, or Why What We Don't Know Can't Hurt Us," 21 *Ocean Dev. Int'l L.* 117 (1990).

[12] Wang, p. 243.

[13] GA Res. 2574D, UN GAOR, 24th Sess., Supp. No. 30, at 11, UN Doc. A/7630 (1969) (notably only exploitation, not exploration, was prohibited).

the most concise and powerful statements evidencing the strong senti-ment calling for a new international economic order."[14] Unsurprisingly, developed countries voted against the resolution. A second resolution, which received wider support, was the 1970 Declaration of Principles Regarding the Sea-Bed.[15] This Declaration affirmed that the deep seabed area was part of the common heritage of mankind. Moreover, it pro-vided that this area could not be subject to appropriation or claims of sovereignty and that all exploration and exploitation activities would be governed by the international regime to be established.

When preparations for the Third Conference began in 1967, it was considered to be a prime opportunity for developing States to create a regime that would uphold the philosophy of the NIEO and thereby estab-lish a precedent in other wealth-distribution negotiations.[16] It could not be predicted at the time of the drafting of the Convention whether the different interests of developing and developed countries would in fact be reconciled. The financial interests in deep seabed mining at stake at the start of the Third Conference were already considerable.[17] Conse-quently, the successful establishment of a deep seabed regime, premised on the notion of the common heritage of mankind, had to accommodate competing economic philosophies. Part XI of UNCLOS sets out an inter-national regime for the exploration and exploitation of the deep seabed through the International Seabed Authority ("Authority"). Embedded in the principles of the NIEO, Part XI largely reflected the views of develop-ing States. The ongoing controversy over the deep seabed mining regime caused a number of industrialized States to vote against the adoption of the Convention,[18] and subsequently refuse to sign or ratify it.

The United States voted against the Convention when it was adopted in April, 1982, primarily because of the provisions relating to deep seabed

---

[14] John King Gamble, Jr., "Assessing the Reality of the Deep Seabed Regime," 22 *San Diego L. Rev.* 779, 780 (1985).

[15] GA Res 2749, UN GAOR, 25th Sess., Supp. No. 28, at 24, UN Doc. A/8028 (1970).

[16] Robert L. Friedham and William J. Durch, "The International Seabed Resources Agency Negotiations and the New International Economic Order," 31 *Int'l Org.* 343, 344 (1977). The impact of the NIEO ideology had already been felt at the First and Second Conferences where questions of resources were already perceived as a crucial issue, and a point of division between industrialized and developing States. *Ibid.*

[17] "It is said in excess of $100 million already has been spent on preliminary work by developed state mining companies and multinational consortia interested in establishing a seabed nodule mining industry." *Ibid.*, at 351.

[18] The States abstaining at that time included the United Kingdom, the Netherlands, Belgium, the Federal Republic of Germany, Italy, Spain, and the majority of eastern European countries.

mining.[19] The restrictive provisions of Part XI on the entry into the market, the ceiling on annual production and the mandatory transfer of technology were all viewed as inconsistent with free market principles.[20] The institutions created under Part XI were called "an OPEC of the oceans,"[21] as the impact on the United States economy during the OPEC oil crisis had highlighted its dependence on maintaining availability of oil and gas resources.[22] The European Community also considered that Part XI was defective since the mechanism was "too heavy and weighted against the individual firms and consortia that wish to engage in seabed mining."[23] The result of developed countries' dissatisfaction with Part XI was the development of an alternative regime that was more in line with the market philosophies of these States. The interested developed States acted through domestic legislation and formulated a reciprocating arrangement to resolve issues of competing claims.

At the same time, steps began under the auspices of the UN to prepare for the entry into force of the Convention.[24] The number of ratifications gradually increased throughout the 1980s, but did not generally include the major industrialized States. The UN Secretary-General acknowledged

---

[19] The United States considered that the Convention was contrary to its vital national interests, and was thus:

> unwilling to compromise those interests for the sake of world opinion or American participation in a global regime structured with an institutional bias against the interests of the United States and its allies; a regime at odds with important principles of political liberty, private property, and free enterprise; an experiment viewed as a prototype for future multilateral arrangements.

James L. Malone, "The United States and the Law of the Sea," 24 *Va. J. Int'l L.* 785, 785–86 (1984).

[20] Steven J. Molitor, "The Provisional Understanding Regarding Deep Seabed Matters: An Ill-Conceived Regime for U.S. Deep Seabed Mining," 20 *Cornell Int'l L. J.* 223, 235 (1987).

[21] Northcutt Ely, "One OPEC is Enough," 5 *Regulation* 19 (1981), cited in Susan M. Banks, "Protection of Investment in Deep Seabed Mining: Does the United States have a Viable Alternative to Participation in UNCLOS?," 2 *Boston Univ. Int'l L. J.* 267, 280 (1983).

[22] Banks, at 278. Another commentator (who was the United States representative in the final years of the Third Conference negotiations) confirms this view:

> An essential component of the President's national security program was to ensure America's access to vital energy and mineral resources by encouraging domestic production and reducing dependence on foreign suppliers.

Malone, at 786.

[23] Hardy, at 314.

[24] In accordance with Resolution I of the Final Act of the Conference, a Preparatory Commission ("Prepcom") was established with broad discretionary authority to draw up rules, regulations, and procedures for the Authority and for ITLOS. It began its work immediately after the adoption of the Convention.

in 1990 that certain aspects of Part XI had deterred States from becoming party to UNCLOS and consequently raised the question of whether that regime could be reviewed in order to gain universal participation in the Convention.[25] The Secretary-General decided to convene informal consultations with a number of interested States, including the United States, the Soviet Union, Germany, and the United Kingdom, in order to address the outstanding problems relating to deep seabed mining with the hope of ensuring widespread ratification and to avoid the possibility that UNCLOS would enter into force without the participation of the major industrialized States.[26] This revision was possible as both enthusiasm for the NIEO and expectations about the riches to be obtained from deep seabed mining had waned. As a result, States formulated a new agreement in 1994 that significantly altered the Part XI regime. The Agreement relating to the Implementation of Part XI of the United Nations Convention on the Law of the Sea ("1994 Agreement") was adopted on July 28, 1994, and entered into force on July 28, 1996. While some fundamental changes to Part XI were made, one commentator nonetheless noted: "What is interesting, now that the changes have been made, is how much of Part XI was not regarded as posing serious problems requiring revision."[27] This new regime is currently in operation and the Authority has signed contracts with most of the seven pioneer investors.

This chapter first sets out the normative regime under the Convention and the 1994 Agreement, with a particular emphasis on the availability and role ascribed to dispute settlement. The last section of this chapter describes the alternative regime that was devised by developed States as an alternative to UNCLOS, and highlights a different dispute settlement function as well as the potential interplay between the Convention

---

[25] Consultation of the Secretary-General on Outstanding Issues Relating to the Deep Seabed Regime Provisions of the United Nations Convention on the Law of the Sea: Report of the Secretary-General, UN GAOR, 48th Sess., Agenda Item 36, at 2, UN Doc. A/48/950 (1994).

[26] A number of motivations have been identified for the drafting of a new agreement to modify the provisions in Part XI of UNCLOS that industrialized States considered so objectionable. See Bernard H. Oxman, "The 1994 Agreement relating to the Implementation of the UN Convention on the Law of the Sea," in *Order for the Oceans at the Turn of the Century* (Davor Vidas and Willy Östreng eds., 1999), pp. 15, 17 (citing the need for a global constitution of the oceans; the move to free market philosophies in a greater number of countries; recognition that deep seabed mining was not as lucrative as first imagined; and the realization that international organizations had to be cost effective for competent functioning).

[27] Oxman, "1994 Agreement relating to Implementation," p. 35.

system and alternative substantive principles and dispute settlement mechanisms.

Regime Established under Part XI of UNCLOS and the 1994 Agreement

The deep seabed regime established in Part XI of the Convention has been described as "one of the most elaborate systems ever envisioned for controlling the use of a natural resource."[28] The seabed and ocean floor and subsoil thereof, beyond the limits of national jurisdiction to which this regime applies, is referred to as the "Area" in the Convention and the 1994 Agreement. The basic principles governing the Area relate to its status as the common heritage of mankind and its use for the benefit of all mankind. In this regard, it is provided that no State may claim or exercise sovereignty or sovereign rights over any part of the Area or its resources nor may any such area be appropriated.[29] Any attempt to do so will not be recognized.[30] Part XI preserves the status of the superjacent waters as the high seas, thereby focusing solely on the resources of the seabed.[31] General obligations pertaining to marine scientific research, the transfer of technology, and the protection of the marine environment are also included. Article 147 sets out a provision of mutual accommodation whereby activities in the Area must be carried out with reasonable regard for other activities in the marine environment and vice versa. These guiding principles were relatively noncontroversial.

The main point of contention with respect to Part XI revolved around the system of exploration and exploitation of the seabed. In this regard, there were three central issues involved: who may explore and exploit the area; the conditions of exploration and exploitation; and the economic aspects.[32] For each of these issues there were a number of interests to be taken into account. States all had diverse visions of what the international regime should look like. There were differences as to the level of detail in rules and regulations, the amount of control of the institution, the control exercised by States within the institution, and external mechanisms for influencing the actions of the Authority. The

---

[28] Gamble, "Deep Seabed Regime," at 783.

[29] UNCLOS, art. 137(2).   [30] *Ibid.*, art. 137(3).

[31] This principle was non-controversial. See Friedham and Durch, at 366.

[32] See A. O. Adede, "The System for Exploitation of the 'Common Heritage of Mankind' at the Caracas Conference," 69 *Am. J. Int'l L.* 31, 37 (1975).

1994 Agreement sought to resolve these differences, particularly in light of the shift in views on economic ideology that had occurred since the adoption of the Convention.[33] The 1994 Agreement is to be interpreted and applied together with Part XI as a single instrument,[34] and in the event of any inconsistency between the 1994 Agreement and UNCLOS, the 1994 Agreement is to prevail.[35]

In light of the reconfiguration of the legal regime in Part XI, the discussion below focuses on the principal features of the new legal system for deep seabed mining as altered by the 1994 Agreement and as relevant to issues of dispute settlement. Focus is therefore on: the Authority; transfer of technology; competition with land-based mineral producers; financing; and pioneer investment.

International Seabed Authority

The Convention provides that "[a]ctivities in the Area shall be organized, carried out and controlled by the Authority on behalf of mankind as a whole . . ."[36] The Authority is "the organization through which States parties shall, in accordance with this Part, organize and control activities in the Area, particularly with a view to administering the resources of the Area."[37] The Enterprise was established as an organ of the Authority to "[c]arry out activities in the Area directly . . . as well as the transporting, processing and marketing of minerals recovered from the Area."[38] In developing the resources of the Area, the Enterprise was to operate in accordance with "sound commercial principles."[39] Under Part XI, activities in the Area were to be carried out by the Enterprise (the operating arm of the Authority) and by States parties in association with the Authority.

One of the most controversial issues in relation to the establishment of the Authority was the division of responsibility between the relevant bodies and the amount of control that each of these bodies would have. The Authority was created with an Assembly, of which all States

---

[33] The Preamble states that the 1994 Agreement reflected "political and economic changes, including in particular a growing reliance on market principles."

[34] 1994 Agreement, art. 1.   [35] Ibid., art. 2.

[36] UNCLOS, art. 153(1).   [37] Ibid., art. 157.   [38] Ibid., art. 170.

[39] Ibid., Annex IV, art. 1(3). In addition, the Enterprise "shall not interfere in the political affairs of any State Party; nor shall it be influenced in its decisions by the political character of the State Party concerned. Only commercial considerations shall be relevant to its decisions, and these considerations shall be weighed impartially in order to carry out [its] purposes." Ibid., Annex IV, art. 12(7).

parties were members, and a Council, which was composed of States representing particular interests. Such a structure is quite typical of international organizations and the Authority was initially modeled on the International Civil Aviation Organization, "the archetype of successful international regulatory agencies."[40] The developing States wanted the Assembly to be the "truly supreme decision-making organ of the Authority,"[41] as all States were equally represented in the Assembly and this scenario would give the Group of 77 a majority. The Council would then carry out the day-to-day activities of the Authority along with the other organs. By contrast, the developed countries preferred that the Assembly would simply approve very broad policy lines and the Council would have wide executive powers and some flexibility in managing the business of the Authority.[42] The 1994 Agreement has qualified the broad power of the Assembly in Part XI by requiring collaboration with the Council for decisions on administrative, budgetary, or financial matters.[43]

Apart from the composition of the Authority, States at the Third Conference had fundamentally divergent views as to the role of the Authority in the exploration and exploitation of the resources of the deep seabed.[44] In line with the common heritage of mankind and the NIEO philosophy, developing countries were interested in granting this international entity exclusive rights to mine the seabed. In contrast, developed States envisaged the role of the Authority as facilitating a licensing system whereby licenses would be granted to States and to its nationals to conduct the mining operations. As a compromise, the United States proposed a "parallel system" whereby States and corporations would be placed on an equal footing with the Authority.[45] The proposal envisaged that such a system would grant the Authority effective administrative and financial supervision over activities in the Area in order to ensure compliance with the Convention and the Authority's rules and regulations but not restrict activities in the Area to the Authority exclusively. This parallel system is set out in Article 153(2) and Annex III of the Convention, and was retained in the 1994 Agreement.

---

[40] Oxman, "1994 Agreement relating to Implementation," at 27 and n. 57.
[41] Evriviades, at 233.   [42] See Stevenson and Oxman, "1975 Session," at 767.
[43] See Bernard H. Oxman, "The 1994 Agreement and the Convention," 88 *Am. J. Int'l L.* 687, 689 (1994) (citing White House Fact Sheet).
[44] See Adede, "Common Heritage," at 37–38.
[45] See generally Evriviades, at 218; Oxman, "1976 New York Session," at 254.

Authorization to Explore and Exploit the Area

In order to explore and exploit the Area in accordance with UNCLOS, an applicant had to nominate a single continuous area, divide this area into two separate areas of equal commercial value, and submit all data obtained with respect to these areas. The Authority would then designate one of these areas to be reserved solely for the conduct of activities by the Authority through the Enterprise or in association with developing States upon approval of the plan of work while the applicant was accorded exclusive rights to the non-reserved area.[46] The Enterprise was allowed to decide whether it would carry out activities in the reserved area or not and could act on its own or as a joint venture with an interested State or entity.[47] Developing States were entitled to submit plans of work for a reserved area in the event that the Enterprise decided not to carry out activities in that area.[48] The system established under Part XI would have resulted in the Enterprise being entitled to claim mining sites, funding, and activities equal to the combined total of all competing private consortia and State-sponsored mining concerns authorized to operate in the Area.[49] The 1994 Agreement has deferred indefinitely the creation of the Enterprise.[50] It is only to come into operation upon a vote that there is a market demand for a reserved area and that progress in deep seabed mining warrants its functioning. In the event that the Enterprise does begin to function, it is required to operate on the basis of sound commercial principles and the obligations that apply to private contractors are equally applicable to the Enterprise.

The 1994 Agreement also changed the convoluted and detailed requirements in Part XI for authorization to explore and exploit the area so that the conditions for access to mining sites were rendered more neutral and stipulated less undertakings to which miners would have to adhere. Instead of the discretionary approach to the grants of mining licenses under UNCLOS, the 1994 Agreement sets up a system whereby an application must be approved if the application fee is paid, procedural and environmental conditions are met, the area applied for is not already taken, and if the sponsoring State would not

---

[46] See UNCLOS, Annex III, art. 8.

[47] *Ibid.*, Annex III, art. 9, and Annex III, art. 11 (providing for joint arrangements between the Enterprise and other contractors).

[48] *Ibid.*, Annex III, Art. 9(4).   [49] Wang, p. 219.

[50] The changes in the operation of the Enterprise are set forth in Section 2 of the Annex to the 1994 Agreement.

exceed the maximum limits specified in the Convention.[51] Developed States were anxious to prevent the possibility that qualified applications would be rejected because of onerous voting requirements or for political reasons.[52]

"Where a dispute arises relating to the disapproval of a plan of work, such dispute shall be submitted to the dispute settlement procedures set out in the Convention."[53] The Seabed Disputes Chamber, which is part of ITLOS, only has jurisdiction over disputes between the Authority and a prospective miner in relation to the refusal of a contract when all of the necessary conditions for authorization have been fulfilled.[54] In other words, the Chamber does not have jurisdiction over disputes as to whether the necessary conditions have been fulfilled, but only when the conditions are met and the contract is nonetheless refused. Jurisdiction may also be exercised over disputes relating to a legal issue that arises in the negotiation of a contract; there is no mechanism for resolving disputes in relation to technical or financial requirements. The Chamber may not review any decisions taken by the Authority for refusing an application.[55] Although the availability of dispute settlement procedures is limited with respect to challenging the authorization process, this restriction is now less important. With the shift in the substantive principles in the 1994 Agreement, the need for States to utilize dispute settlement procedures to counter-balance the power of the Authority is reduced.

Regulation of Mining Operations

In awarding the contract, the Authority must accord to an operator "the exclusive right to explore and exploit the area covered by the plan of work in respect of a specified category of resources and shall ensure that no other entity operates in the same area for a different category of resources in a manner which might interfere with the operations of the operator."[56] In seeking an exclusive right to mine the seabed, the rights accorded were similar to the continental shelf regime in that the right was for the purposes of exploration and exploitation of resources. However, unlike the continental shelf, the exclusive right to use the deep

---

[51] 1994 Agreement, Annex, Section 1, paras. 7, 13.

[52] Oxman, "1994 Agreement relating to Implementation," at 30.

[53] 1994 Agreement, Annex, Section 3, para. 12.   [54] UNCLOS, art. 187.

[55] Judicial review is limited to a determination of whether the Authority's actions were an excess of jurisdiction or misuse of power. UNCLOS, art. 187.

[56] *Ibid.*, Annex III, art. 16.

seabed is temporary and does not include a right not to use the Area.[57] The grant of mining rights is further dependent on stated performance requirements.[58]

One of the main legislative tasks of the Authority has been the adoption of the regulations on prospecting and exploration for polymetallic nodules.[59] These Regulations are largely an elaboration of Annex III of UNCLOS, and not only detail regulations for these activities on the deep seabed, but also annex forms to be used in notifying of intention to engage in prospecting, the application for approval of a plan of work, and a model contract for exploration. Now that the regulations have been adopted, the Authority has been able to enter into contracts for exploration with registered pioneer investors whose plans of work were approved by the Council in August 1997.[60] These contracts incorporate a series of standard clauses annexed to the regulations.

For disputes arising during the operation of the contract, UNCLOS anticipates compulsory procedures for disputes between States parties regarding the interpretation or application of Part XI and Annexes III and IV of UNCLOS as well as for disputes between States parties and the Authority with respect to acts or omissions of either in violation of the Convention.[61] States may also refer disputes to commercial arbitration, with certain limitations. The developed States supported the use of commercial arbitration for the resolution of contractual disputes at the request of either party but the Group of 77 was concerned about questions of interpretation and application of the Convention being referred to commercial arbitration as well.[62] The compromise position was to allow for commercial arbitration for contract disputes unless otherwise agreed in the contract and that this tribunal would not be competent to determine questions of interpretation of the Convention

---

[57] See Oxman, "1976 New York Session," at 256.

[58] This approach was consonant with domestic mining legislation. *Ibid.*, at 256–57.

[59] Decision of the Assembly relating to the regulations on prospecting and exploration for polymetallic nodules in the Area, UN Doc. ISBA/6/A/18 (October 4, 2000) (annexing the regulations). See also Decision of the Council relating to the regulations and prospecting and exploration for polymetallic nodules in the Area, UN Doc. ISBA/6/C/12 (July 13, 2000).

[60] See Report of the Secretary-General of the International Seabed Authority under Article 166, paragraph 4 of the United Nations Convention on the Law of the Sea, June 7, 2002, UN Doc. ISBA/8/A/5, para. 36.

[61] UNCLOS, art. 187. See also 1994 Agreement, Annex, Section 8, para. 1(8). Disputes concerning the Regulations on prospecting and exploration for polymetallic nodules in the Area are also subject to this dispute settlement regime. See Regulations for the Area, Regulation 39.

[62] Evriviades, at 238.

but if such questions arose, they were to be referred to the Seabed Disputes Chamber.[63] The types of contract disputes that could be resolved by the Seabed Disputes Chamber are those involving interpretation of the contract; financial matters; performance of a contract in relation to acts or omissions relating to activities in the Area and affecting the parties legitimate interests; refusal of a contract or legal issue arising in relation to negotiation of the contract; and liability for damages as a result of wrongful acts.[64] These disputes could also be referred to a special chamber of ITLOS or to an *ad hoc* chamber of the Seabed Disputes Chamber.[65]

Given the use of standard clauses in exploration contracts and the detailed regulation of deep seabed mining activity, the availability of dispute settlement is limited to the enforcement of rights and duties of the participants in this specific legal regime. International regulation is dependent on State action through the Authority; internal control is preferred to external control. In this regard, it is notable that the discretion of the Authority has been preserved, as is evident from the provisions on the scope of judicial review. Industrialized States wanted the Chamber to have the power to review the actions of the Authority but developing nations were opposed to such a provision.[66] It was instead considered that the Chamber could only resolve disputes over decisions or measures taken by the Authority on the basis of those decisions or measures being in violation of Part XI in individual cases,[67] or being outside the relevant organ's jurisdiction or being a misuse of power. However, the Chamber cannot determine whether the procedures adopted by the Assembly or by the Council are in conformity with the Convention nor declare whether any such rules are invalid. Furthermore, the Chamber does not have jurisdiction over the exercise of discretionary jurisdiction of the Authority nor may it substitute its discretion for that of the Authority. "This limitation upon the competence of the Chamber . . . is consistent with the view maintained by those seeking to protect the Authority from what they consider as unacceptable judicial encroachment upon the legislative and discretionary powers of the Authority."[68]

---

[63] See *ibid*.   [64] See Wang, p. 78.
[65] UNCLOS, art. 188.   [66] Evriviades, at 238.
[67] The Chamber may also consider claims for damages to be paid or other remedy to be given to a claimant for the failure of another party to comply with either its Convention or contractual obligations. UNCLOS, art. 189.
[68] A. O. Adede, "The Law of the Sea – The Integration of the System of Settlement of Disputes Under the Draft Convention as a Whole," 72 *Am. J. Int'l L.* 84, 90 (1978). See also Gaertner, at 589–90.

The Convention also sets out the penalties that the Authority may impose for non-compliance if a contractor has "conducted his activities in such a way as to result in serious, persistent and wilful violations of the fundamental terms of the contract, Part XI and the rules, regulations and procedures of the Authority" or if the contractor has not complied with a binding order from a dispute settlement procedure.[69] The available penalties include suspension or termination of the contractor's rights.[70] For violations other than "serious, persistent and wilful violations," or as an alternative to suspension or termination, the Authority may impose upon the contractor "monetary penalties proportionate to the seriousness of the violation."[71] The prescription of penalties is a rare feature in the UNCLOS dispute settlement system. It is particularly unusual in international law for stating a penalty in the event of non-compliance with orders issued under the UNCLOS dispute settlement mechanism. Presumably, such penalties were acceptable to the drafters of the Convention since they are directed at contractors, not States.

Transfer of Technology

At the Third Conference, the developing countries sought comprehensive provisions on technology transfer to the Authority and to developing countries generally, including that the transfer be a condition of obtaining a contract so as to help the Enterprise begin business with equal abilities at the same point as other miners. Transfer of technology was intended to enable the Enterprise to exploit seabed resources itself, as well as to redress the economic imbalance in the world.[72] The approach preferred by the developed countries was that technology transfer would be negotiated separately to a mining contract, that it would be contingent on whether the miner had the right lawfully to transfer the technology and that such a transfer would only occur for a limited period.[73] Developed States wanted to avoid the situation whereby the Authority could delay issuance of a contract indefinitely, pending agreement on technology transfer.[74]

The requirements of developing States resulted in the formulation of both substantive and dispute settlement provisions in UNCLOS that are slanted tremendously in favor of the Authority acquiring the necessary

---

[69] UNCLOS, Annex III, art. 18.   [70] *Ibid.*, Annex III, art. 5.   [71] *Ibid.*, Annex III, art. 5.

[72] Gamble, "Deep Seabed Regime," at 784. "[T]he ironclad right to buy seabed mining technology was an essential ingredient in spelling out the full meaning of the common heritage." Brewer, at 47.

[73] See Oxman, "Seventh Session," at 9–10.   [74] *Ibid.*, at 9.

technology. In the event of any disputes arising with respect to the provisions on the transfer of technology, the dispute was to be referred to the compulsory procedures envisaged under Part XI.[75] With respect to disputes over the contracts with the owners of technology and whether offers were within the range of fair and reasonable commercial terms and conditions, these disputes were to be submitted to binding commercial arbitration in accordance with the UNCITRAL Arbitration Rules.[76] The Convention anticipated resistance on the part of the contractor in that it specifically provided for the situation where a finding was made that the contractor's terms were not fair and reasonable. The contractor then had forty-five days to revise the offer before the Authority took action to impose penalties.

The provisions on the transfer of technology were significantly altered by the 1994 Agreement.[77] Instead of an obligation to transfer technology to the Enterprise and developing States, there is a general obligation to cooperate so that technology can be obtained on fair and reasonable commercial terms on the open market or through joint ventures. The goal of availability of technology is retained but the means of achieving it have been considerably weakened. The 1994 Agreement provides for effective protection of intellectual property related to deep seabed mining. Any assistance to developing States is now to be derived from the scientific and technical cooperation of States parties by training or special programs. The replacement of mandatory conditions for the transfer of technology with duties of cooperation means that there is less opportunity for the demands of the Authority conflicting with mining companies. Even if a matter is referred to dispute settlement, the normative standard to be applied by the tribunal or Chamber is now less onerous and no longer involves any analysis of what consists of fair and reasonable terms. Requirements dealing with the transfer of technology were thus weakened on both a procedural and a substantive level.

Competition with Land-Based Producers

A number of developing States were major producers of the minerals found in polymetallic nodules and recognized that "[u]ncontrolled seabed mineral production could have a direct and in some cases, catastrophic impact on the foreign exchange earnings of Third World

---

[75] UNCLOS, Annex III, art. 5(4).   [76] Ibid., Annex III, art. 5(4).
[77] 1994 Agreement, Annex, Section 5 (expressly stating that the provisions of Annex III, Article 5, of UNCLOS are not to apply).

land-based producers."[78] However, the interests of the land-based producers of the different minerals were "varied and complicated."[79] Land-based
producers sought protection from unfair competition from seabed-based
producers. The Convention allowed the Authority to set quantity limits
on seabed mining production based on increased supply by land-based
mining operators.[80] The imposition of production controls is a common
device used to deal with the price fluctuations of the raw materials upon
which many developing States depend for hard currency.[81] As a result, a
number of concessions were made to States with land-based production
industries and once these controls on production were incorporated into
the Convention, there was effectively no way for them to be challenged
subsequently.

Unsurprisingly, the regulations relating to production policies were
also targeted in the review of Part XI of the Convention.[82] The Convention was criticized because it:

reflected a protectionist bias and discouraged development of the resources in an
efficient manner by setting production ceilings that would limit the availability
of minerals for global consumption; limiting the number of mining operations
that could be conducted by any one state or its nationals; and granting broad
discretionary powers to the International Seabed Authority, which could further
deter deep seabed mining.[83]

The 1994 Agreement requires that the development of the resources
of the Area take place in accordance with sound commercial principles.
Land-based producers no longer receive special consideration under the
1994 Agreement as there is to be no discrimination for access to markets
or for imports between minerals derived from the Area and those derived
from other sources. Instead, the General Agreement on Tariffs and Trade,
and its successor agreements, are to apply to activities relating to the
deep seabed, particularly disallowing the possibility of subsidization.
This change creates a balance by eliminating the discrimination in favor
of land-based producers but also prohibits States from using subsidies,

---

[78] Evriviades, at 222. See also Jon Van Dyke and Christopher Yuen, "'Common Heritage' v.
  'Freedom of the High Seas': Which Governs the Seabed?," 19 *San Diego L. Rev.* 493, 531
  (1982).
[79] Evriviades, at 223.   [80] UNCLOS, art. 151(5), (9) and (10).
[81] Friedham and Durch, at 358. It has been suggested that these limits were not
  incompatible with free market ideology because it was unlikely that the limits would
  in practice obstruct commercial seabed development by the developed States' mining
  consortia. Steven J. Molitor, at 231.
[82] 1994 Agreement, Annex, Section 6.   [83] Duff, at 28.

trade barriers, and similar intervention in the market that would have the effect of protecting sea-based producers.[84] These changes reflect the shift to market-oriented economic philosophy, rather than the protectionism inherent in the NIEO.

For disputes that arise concerning the provisions of GATT or the WTO in relation to the deep seabed, States parties must have recourse to the WTO dispute settlement mechanism. If one or more of the States in dispute are not party to the GATT or WTO then the dispute must be referred to the dispute settlement procedures in UNCLOS. Clearly, the WTO procedures have precedence over the compulsory jurisdiction in UNCLOS. This priority is consistent with the emphasis in Section 1 of Part XV for parties to use other dispute settlement procedures, including those producing a binding result, before resorting to compulsory arbitration or adjudication under UNCLOS.

Financing

The financing of the Enterprise was another of the controversial issues in the UNCLOS debates on Part XI. In order to establish the initial operations of the Enterprise, it was proposed that half of the funds required would come from States parties in the form of long-term, interest-free loans to the Authority. The remaining funds would then be procured from borrowings on the financial market guaranteed by the Authority's members. Article 171 of UNCLOS provides that the funds of the Authority were to be derived from assessed contributions from States parties, funds from activities in the Area (including from the Enterprise), loans, voluntary contributions, and payments to a compensation fund. The funds from States parties were to be assessed according to the UN scale of assessments, could only be used for the administrative expenses of the Authority, and were to be supplied for as long as it was necessary for the Authority to generate its own income from mining operations.

Developed States were concerned about the broad discretion resting in the Assembly with respect to transferring funds from the Enterprise to the Authority, as this arrangement had the potential of varying greatly the financial obligations of the Enterprise from other miners.[85] The financial arrangements for the Authority were generally criticized for being unrealistic. They were "merely assumptions under the most favorable international conditions for the mining operations in the Area"

[84] See Oxman, "1994 Agreement relating to Implementation," at 24.
[85] Oxman, "Seventh Session," at 11.

and "did not take into account a number of difficulties which may well arise if and when deep seabed operation in the Area [was to] begin."[86] In the 1994 Agreement, major changes to financial arrangements were made.

With regard to the financing of the Authority itself, the costs to be attributed to States parties have been altered in light of the requirement that the Authority and its organs operate on a cost-effective basis.[87] Economic assistance to developing countries that export the minerals to be recovered from the Area will be derived from funds that exceed the administrative costs of the Authority and funds from payments received from contractors.[88] Furthermore, the application fee is halved in the 1994 Agreement, and the detailed financial obligations imposed on miners, including the annual fee, have been eliminated.[89] Disputes concerning the financial terms of the contract are subject to the same procedures that are applicable to contract regulations more generally.[90] In particular, disputes over the financial terms of the contract may also be referred to commercial arbitration.[91]

Pioneer Mining Activities

A further issue to be addressed in creating an international regime for the exploration and exploitation of the seabed was the status of the entities that had engaged in what was called "preparatory investment in pioneer activities."[92] Developed States sought recognition of these acts within the framework of UNCLOS to ensure that the Authority would not usurp mine sites established prior to the conclusion of the Convention.[93] This issue was addressed in resolutions added to the final act adopted at the Third Conference. These resolutions established a program to protect preparatory investment prior to the Convention's entry into force. Pioneer investors were defined as State enterprises or mining consortia that by 1983 had spent at least $30 million, with 10 percent going toward the location, survey, and evaluation of a mining area.[94] In accordance with the parallel system established in UNCLOS, the pioneer activities had to be large enough to cover two mining operations so that

---

[86] Wang, p. 228.   [87] 1994 Agreement, Annex, Section 1.

[88] Ibid., Annex, Section 7.   [89] Ibid., Annex, Section 8, paras. 2, 3.

[90] See ibid., Annex, Section 8, para. 1(f).   [91] UNCLOS, Annex III, art. 13(15).

[92] See Final Act of Conference, Annex I, Resolution II. These preparatory activities are encompassed by "grandfather provisions," which recognize activities that take place prior to the Convention entering into force.

[93] See Banks, at 281.

[94] Final Act of Conference, Annex I, Resolution II, para. 1(a).

half could be allocated to the Enterprise.[95] Qualified pioneer investors were required to register with the Preparatory Commission ("Prepcom") established at the end of the Third Conference. Consortia could be registered as a pioneer investor if one of the consortium partners belonged to a country that had signed the Convention. Upon registration, the mining consortia acquired the exclusive right to explore the specific mine site. Only certain activities were permissible under the pioneer investors scheme – such as exploration, mapping, and some processing operations. Once the Convention entered into force, it was intended that the pioneer investor would then have an automatic right to a contract to mine that specific site, provided it complied with the requirements of UNCLOS. In this fashion, pioneer investors would be ensured site protection and tenure under the Convention but at the same time were still subject to the many undertakings for the conduct of operations. The grant of such limited rights was considered as insufficient to promote investment in the deep seabed mining industry.[96]

In granting access to sites, the 1994 Agreement makes allowance for mining activities undertaken prior to the entry into force of the Convention whereby a sponsoring State can certify that certain applicants have met the necessary financial and technical qualifications.[97] In this regard, the investments made pursuant to national regulatory regimes receive recognition as well as protection within the UNCLOS framework. These activities are entitled to arrangements similar to and no less favorable than those accorded investors of other countries that registered as pioneers with the Prepcom.[98]

Conflicts could not only arise with respect to the contracts for pioneer investors, but also with regard to overlapping areas claimed as pioneer mining sites. For the latter, States were to resolve their conflicts by negotiations within a reasonable period and then, if no resolution was reached, to refer the matter to binding arbitration.[99] In light of the overlapping claims that existed between the pioneer investors registered under the Prepcom, the Prepcom adopted an Understanding on Resolution of Conflicts among Applicants for Registration as Pioneer Investors in 1984. This Understanding was an attempt to solve conflicts by exchanging pioneer area coordinates, identifying of overlaps, and initiating discussions on "non-poaching" agreements. The pioneer investor

---

[95] Final Act of Conference, Annex I, Resolution II, para. 3(a) and (b).
[96] Bergman, at 505–06.   [97] 1994 Agreement, Annex, Section 1, para. 6.
[98] *Ibid.*, Annex, Section 1, para. 6.
[99] Final Act of Conference, Annex I, Resolution II, para. 5(c).

regime provided that overlapping claims for mine sites had to be resolved through a system of conflict resolution, including binding arbitration, before the registration was approved. "[W]ithout such a process to resolve the overlapping claims, there would be no 'security of tenure' for the mining enterprises 'to prevent claim jumping' and to make major mining investments."[100] The need for a compulsory dispute settlement system to resolve conflicts of overlapping claims is thus comparable with the need for mandatory procedures for maritime boundary disputes.[101]

Conclusion

The biases and philosophies underlying the deep seabed mining regime in UNCLOS shifted considerably with the adoption of the 1994 Agreement. The fundamental structure did not change inasmuch as deep seabed mining is regulated through an international institution, the Authority. The retention of this institutional framework meant that the core role for third-party dispute settlement has not greatly changed. The Convention's mandatory dispute settlement procedures constitute a separate procedural mechanism needed for extreme situations in the functioning of this discrete legal system. Moreover, the substantive changes to the Authority and the distribution of power therein has reinforced the reliance on States to regulate behavior within the institutional framework. Although the discretion of the Authority is insulated from third party review, the decision-making power of the Authority is now more representative of the States involved in deep seabed mining. The more that this legal regime could be self-regulating, the less the requirement for compulsory dispute resolution. This dynamic can be contrasted with the role for dispute settlement in the alternative deep seabed mining regime, discussed in the next section.

Alternative Deep Seabed Mining Regime

The dissatisfaction of developed States with Part XI emerged during the Third Conference. Before the conclusion of negotiations on UNCLOS, mining companies had completed sufficient development and research to be able to commence substantial exploration but were loath to make the necessary investment in the absence of a legal regime to protect claims to specific sites.[102] It was suggested also that even participation

---

[100] Wang, p. 212.
[101] See Chapter 4, notes 133–143 and accompanying text.   [102] Brewer, at 34.

in the Convention would not bring adequate investment security since there was no history of stability of the Authority nor was it possible to predict the manner in which it would exercise its discretion.[103]

The course of negotiations indicated to domestic constituents what the final form of Part XI could look like and intensified agitation for domestic action to create an alternative regime. An initial question to be considered in this regard was what legal regime governed the exploitation of the deep seabed prior to the adoption of UNCLOS; had any customary rules developed? The controversy over the existence of any such rules meant that developed States had to proceed carefully in establishing any sort of legal regime separate to the international institution being created at the Third Conference. Domestic legislation was adopted first and was drafted in a way to conform to some extent to the views being expressed at the Third Conference. Industrialized States also sought reciprocal recognition of their domestic laws and the means to resolve possible conflicts concerning overlapping claims. Any steps taken had to be as acceptable as possible to the largest number of States in order to secure the necessary investment. The alternative regime was driven by the developed States and it was therefore designed to meet their mutual needs. However, the claims of States with the same capability but excluded from the reciprocating agreements, as well as the claims of developing States, necessarily impacted on the feasibility of the alternative regime.

The alternative regime is discussed here for two reasons. First, it illustrates how States created a specific law of the sea regime separate to UNCLOS and what comparable role was designated to dispute settlement procedures in that alternative regime. Second, the alternative regime is also exemplary of the procedural problems that may be encountered when more than one avenue for dispute settlement is available, and one of those avenues is compulsory. This section first considers the substantive principles applicable in the alternative regime – both as a matter of customary law and under domestic legislation. It then turns to issues of dispute settlement, within the alternative regime and between that regime and other dispute settlement procedures.

Customary Law Regulation of Deep Seabed Mining

While UNCLOS was not in force, some States were provided with the opportunity to maximize their benefits from the deep seabed on a

---

[103] *Ibid.*, at 42.

unilateral basis. Any restraints on States' actions were dependent on the extent that the principles incorporated in the Convention represented customary international law – both during the course of the negotiations and then subsequent to its adoption. One of the main views advanced on this issue was that the exploitation of the deep seabed was governed by the principles of the freedom of the high seas. Article 2 of the High Seas Convention sets out an inclusive list of high seas freedoms,[104] and so even though mining was not specifically listed it was arguably implicit in the terms of the article.[105] The only limits to be imposed on States' activities in this area were those inherent in the exercise of the high seas freedoms. In particular, States could only carry out mining "with reasonable regard to the interests of other States in their exercise of the freedom of the high seas."[106]

Another view was that the status of the deep seabed as the common heritage of mankind had already passed into customary international law and so could only be exploited within an international regime, namely, the system being established under UNCLOS. Support for such an argument was drawn from the General Assembly resolutions adopted with respect to a moratorium and on the principles regarding the seabed.[107] The status of these resolutions as reflecting or creating custom was questionable, however, in light of the inconsistent practice of States with capacity to mine and because of the nebulous concepts included in the resolutions.[108]

Domestic Legislation

Pressure from mining companies and the need for the nodule minerals meant that several industrialized nations could not afford to wait for the final outcome of the Third Conference negotiations. The United States, the United Kingdom, France, Germany, Japan, and the Soviet

---

[104] Article 2 provides that the freedom of the high seas "comprises, *inter alia*," which allows for the possibility of freedoms additional to those listed.

[105] A number of commentators took this approach. See, e.g., Kathryn Surace-Smith, "United States Activity Outside of the Law of the Sea Convention: Deep Seabed Mining and Transit Passage," 84 *Columbia L. Rev.* 1032, 1037 (1984); Breen, at 207.

[106] 1958 High Seas Convention, art. 2. See also T. Kronmiller, 1 *The Lawfulness of Deep Seabed Mining* (1980), pp. 388–91; Brewer, at 31; Bernard H. Oxman, "The High Seas and the International Seabed Area," 10 *Mich. J. Int'l L.* 538 (1989).

[107] See Van Dyke and Yuen, at 524–25.

[108] Surace-Smith, at 1041–43. But see Van Dyke and Yuen, at 521–22 (asserting that even though the exact meaning of "common heritage of mankind" was unclear, there was still agreement in the international community on the policy objective).

Union passed domestic legislation in order to permit and regulate seabed mining pending the adoption of UNCLOS. Commentators have suggested that one of the reasons for proceeding with the adoption of domestic legislation was to influence the course of negotiations by demonstrating clearly what was acceptable to developed countries.[109] Nonetheless, the various statutes were generally cast in such a way so as to avoid overly antagonizing developing countries (mainly by setting up a levying system where funds would be available for the international regime when it came into effect and by not claiming any rights over the deep seabed area itself). However, the Group of 77 challenged the legality of domestic legislation, claiming that it violated the rule of good faith in negotiations and that rights acquired through mining under domestic law would only be recognized under certain conditions in the international regime.[110]

The United States Congress passed the Deep Seabed Hard Mineral Resources Act ("DSHMR Act") in 1980 in order to authorize mining of the deep seabed by United States multinationals pending adherence to a comprehensive treaty.[111] The DSHMR Act established a system for granting licenses and permits to United States citizens for the purposes of exploration and exploitation of seabed sites. "The exploration license gives a company the necessary 'security of tenure' to make substantial capital investments without the threat of claim-jumping by other United States companies."[112] Licenses were not required for scientific research, mapping, measuring, or random sampling of the seabed. Licenses or permits would only be issued to applicants that had adequate financial resources to meet licensing and permit requirements; had the technological capability to fulfill proposed exploration and recovery work plans; provided information on environmental protection procedures; specified the size and location of the site; projected the volumes of minerals to be recovered; and gave other facts indicating the viability of the mining proposal.

The drafters of the DSHMR Act equally attempted to justify the legislation in terms of international law as well as cater for the views of other

---

[109] See, e.g., Brewer, at 34; Oxman, "Seventh Session," at 32–33 (discussing the impact of domestic legislation on negotiating positions at the Conference).

[110] See Oxman, "Eighth Session," at 8; and Oxman, "Seventh Session," at 32–33.

[111] Public Law No. 96–283, Title I, 94 Stat. 553 (1980); 30 USC Sec. 1401–1473 (1982). The Act prohibited significant commercial exploitation until January 1, 1988, to allow a certain period of time for UNCLOS to be concluded and to enter into force.

[112] J. M. Broadus and Porter Hoagland III, "Conflict Resolution in the Assignment of Area Entitlements for Seabed Mining," 21 *San Diego L. Rev.* 541, 549 (1984).

actors in the international system. The legislation was based on the freedoms of the high seas and provided that licenses would be issued under such conditions as to prevent unreasonable interference with the interests of other States in their exercise of the freedoms of the high seas. In addition, the proposed mining activity could not conflict with international obligations imposed on the United States nor could it threaten international peace. To remain consistent with traditional principles of the freedom of the high seas – and also in accordance with the notion of the common heritage of mankind – it further stipulated that the United States was not asserting sovereignty, sovereign or exclusive rights, or jurisdiction over any area or resources of the seabed. The United States could thus only exercise jurisdiction over its nationals and ships flying its flag. The DSHMR Act, anticipating the finalization of UNCLOS and its adoption, provided for a revenue-sharing system whereby a certain percentage was to be deposited in a distinct fund for a particular purpose. In adopting these provisions, the United States took action in order to advance the interests of the mining constituents but still sought to minimize the potential for conflict in so doing.

Legislation was also adopted in France,[113] Germany,[114] Japan,[115] the Soviet Union,[116] and the United Kingdom.[117] These laws shared a number of similarities.[118] All were intended to be temporary measures, designed to have interim application pending the conclusion and entry into force of UNCLOS. When these developed States decided not to sign UNCLOS, the domestic regimes provided a legal framework for their own nationals. The legislation prohibited any unlicensed exploration and established systems for the granting of licenses. Further, these laws stipulated fees to be levied on license holders and, like the DSHMR Act, placed in special funds to be paid to the international regime upon its creation. Finally, the laws provided that if a person held a license with one State

---

[113] Law on the Exploration and Exploitation of Mineral Resources of the Deep Seabed, 1981 Journal Officiel de la Republique Française 3499, 1982 Dalloz-Sirey, Legislation 11, reprinted in 21 ILM 808 (1982).

[114] Act of Interim Regulation of Deep Seabed Mining, § 14, Bundesgesetzblatt, Teil 1, 9080 (no. 50), at 1457, reprinted in 20 ILM 393 (1981).

[115] Law on Interim Measures for Deep Seabed Mining, Horei Zensho, reprinted in 22 ILM 102 (1983).

[116] Edict on Provisional Measures to Regulate Soviet Enterprises for the Exploration and Exploitation of Mineral Resources, reprinted in 21 ILM 551 (1982).

[117] Deep Sea Mining (Temporary Provisions) Act 1981, ch. 53, reprinted in 20 ILM 1217 (1981).

[118] See Breen, at 212–13.

then there was no need to seek authorization from another State. While the different laws set out conditions for the grant of licenses, there were differences in the types and number of criteria included.[119] States had an incentive to offer less rigorous conditions in order to exercise jurisdiction over as many mining operations as possible.[120]

Dispute Settlement under the Alternative Regime

While the domestic legislation provided mining companies with a legal framework for operation, conflicts were still possible between States with shared interests in mining. By 1984, at least nine entities (four multinational industrial groups, three State-sponsored programs, and two French and Japanese enterprises) were engaged in deep seabed mining activities.[121] To avoid, or to minimize, any controversy or antagonism between these actors, efforts at coordination and cooperation were favored. In order for operations to be undertaken within an international regulatory framework, a reciprocal regime was required to ensure the orderly development of the seabed while UNCLOS was not in force.[122] Such an international cooperative scheme was viewed as necessary in order to enforce claims to particular sites against other States with mining capability.[123] The economic incentives for settling deep seabed mining disputes are similar to those for settling maritime boundary disputes between opposite and adjacent States in order to facilitate the exploration and exploitation of the continental shelf – a recognized legal regime is essential to quiet title and warrant considerable financial investment.[124]

The United States, the United Kingdom, France, and West Germany concluded an agreement to facilitate the identification and resolution of conflicts arising from the filing and processing of applications for authorization to exploit a mining site under each countries'

---

[119] The British legislation was viewed as less onerous than the United States and German legislation in this regard. Breen, at 213; James Lyall Stuart, "Law of the Sea: Unilateral Licensing of Seabed Mining – *Deep Sea Mining (Temporary Provisions) Act 1981*, ch. 53," 23 *Harv. J. Int'l L.* 155, 160 (1982). The regulations promulgated by the United States Department of Commerce have been described as "lengthy, complex and quite burdensome." Michael R. Molitor, "The U.S. Deep Seabed Mining Regulations: The Legal Basis for an Alternative Regime," 19 *San Diego L. Rev.* 599, 603 (1982).

[120] Van Dyke and Yuen, at 546–47.   [121] Breen, at 204.   [122] Bergman, at 483.

[123] "Deep seabed miners want assurance of control over resources located on their sites and protection from interference by other claimants to those sites once exploration begins." Banks, at 283.

[124] Brilmayer and Klein, at 736–40.

legislation.[125] Such an agreement was viewed as a necessary corollary to their domestic legislation.[126] This Dispute Resolving Agreement applied to all "Pre-enactment Explorers," which were entities engaged in nodule exploration through substantial surveying activity with respect to the area applied for prior to the earliest date of enactment of domestic legislation by any party. The parties to the Dispute Resolving Agreement first had an obligation to consult with each other before issuing any authorizing license or entering into any other agreement concerning deep seabed mining.[127] If there were conflicting claims to the same area, then domestic conflicts were to be settled according to the domestic legislation of each party. For international conflicts, the parties were obliged to assist the applicants in resolving any dispute by voluntary procedures. It was only if no resolution was reached that the matter had to be referred to binding arbitration. For the determination of the priority of claims through arbitration, the tribunal was to apply "principles of equity," which closely resembled the factors to be taken into account with respect to disputes over pioneer areas registered under UNCLOS.[128]

In light of the significant potential for conflicting claims, interested companies did not wish to rely uniquely on the mechanisms in domestic legislation or in the Dispute Resolving Agreement. Some seabed mining consortia, comprising both public and private companies, signed an Industry Arbitration Agreement to resolve overlaps of exploration areas.[129] It was reported that the companies involved agreed to apportion on a voluntary basis the areas identified as the most promising but if such a decision was not feasible then binding arbitration could be invoked by any of the parties.[130] Several conflicts were resolved on this basis of "equal sharing."[131]

Subsequent to the Dispute Resolving Agreement, Belgium, France, Germany, Italy, Japan, the Netherlands, the United Kingdom, and the United States entered into a Provisional Understanding Regarding Deep Seabed Mining.[132] This agreement was also designed to prevent

---

[125] Agreement Concerning Interim Arrangements Relating to Polymetallic Nodules of the Deep Sea Bed, September 2, 1982, 21 ILM 950 (1982) ("Dispute Resolving Agreement"). The National Oceanic and Atmospheric Administration formulated regulations to resolve possible conflicting claims in the United States. See Broadus and Hoagland, at 550.

[126] Breen, at 203.   [127] Dispute Resolving Agreement, Section 4(c) and (d).

[128] See Broadus and Hoagland, at 552.   [129] See ibid., at 553–54.   [130] Ibid., at 554.

[131] Ibid. (but noting that this system potentially violated antitrust laws).

[132] Provisional Understanding Regarding Deep Seabed Mining, August 3, 1984, 23 ILM 1354 (entered into force September 2, 1984).

overlapping deep seabed mine site claims. In accordance with domestic legislation, it provided that actual mining was not to commence until 1988, which was the date envisaged for the entry into force of UNCLOS. A subsequent agreement was signed in 1987,[133] which, in substantive part:

defines the boundaries of the area where cooperation is sought. Further, it requires the States to respect those boundaries, refrain from interfering with the registration of each other's application for sites within the area; avoid further "practical problems" regarding the area; refrain from physically interfering with each other's exploration and exploitation of the area; and consult with each other on issues governed by the Agreement.[134]

The Understanding did not purport to claim sovereignty or sovereign rights over the seabed nor did it attempt to grant exclusive rights that could be enforceable against non-signatory States. It was very much grounded in an emphasis on extensive communication and cooperation among the parties. Nonetheless, developing States were opposed to this agreement as it was viewed as regulating exploration and exploitation, which was the role of the Authority, rather than simply creating a mechanism for resolving claims.[135] The Understanding had the further difficulty that it did not include India or the Soviet Union, which were both involved in large-scale research and development.[136] Ultimately, "the Understanding has not brought United States deep seabed miners any closer to development. Not only is this mining not economically competitive, but the Understanding fails to provide a sufficiently secure right to the mine sites necessary to attract bank loans and investment capital."[137] One of the prime incentives for establishing the deep seabed mining regime was thus unfulfilled. Given the coexistence of UNCLOS and the expectation of its entry into force, the viability of the alternative regime was undermined and could not prove reliable enough.

[133] Agreement of the Resolution of Practical Problems With Respect to Deep Seabed Mining Areas, and Exchange of Notes Between the United States and the Parties to the Agreement, August 14, 1987, 26 ILM 1502.

[134] Duff, at 10. It has been described as "a 'non-poaching' agreement, imposing upon its parties an obligation of self-restraint." Steven J. Molitor, at 243.

[135] See David L. Larson, "Deep Seabed Mining: A Definition of the Problem," 17 *Ocean Dev. & Int'l L. J.* 271, 281 (1986).

[136] It was believed that one of the Soviet Union's sites overlapped with a site claimed by France and Japan. *Ibid.*, at 281–82.

[137] Jonathan I. Charney, "The United States and the Revision of the 1982 Convention on the Law of the Sea," 23 *Ocean Dev. Int'l L.* 279, 287 (1992).

Another potential problem with the alternate regime was that mining could be conducted under the UNCLOS provisions or pursuant to the reciprocal regime.[138] A range of conflicts were imaginable in the event that the mining consortia established to mine a particular area included nationals of States, or State entities, that were party to UNCLOS. For example:

An interesting problem would arise if an American corporation or corporations forms a consortium under a reciprocal states agreement with corporate entities from other non-signing states, only to have one or more of those states decide to adhere to the Convention while mining operations were in progress. The power of the Authority could then be asserted, transfers of technology could be mandated, and some sort of punishment for past mining outside of the Convention might be imposed.[139]

Such a scenario was possible in light of the fact that, in 1984, the seabed mining operations in existence all included at least some participation by national governments through State companies.[140] Article 137 of UNCLOS stipulates that States parties were not to recognize any "claim, acquisition, or exercise of . . . rights" with respect to minerals recovered from the deep seabed. This provision meant that a State faced conflicting obligations if party to both the Convention and a reciprocating States' arrangement. France, for example, signed UNCLOS and was party to the Dispute Resolving Agreement, and, if it had ratified UNCLOS, France and those entities registered in France or French companies part of international consortia registered in a third country, would have been exposed to conflicting obligations and dispute settlement regimes. Japan, Belgium, Italy, the Netherlands, and Canada could have been in a similar position as they finally signed UNCLOS in order to achieve pioneer status at the Prepcom and continued their involvement in the alternative regime.[141] Mining companies themselves were aware of the potential danger of conflicting legal regimes and sought to minimize

---

[138] Such a problem arose when the Soviet Union registered a mining site with the Preparatory Commission, established pursuant to the Final Act of the Conference, and the Soviet Union was not part of the multilateral agreements that had been created. See Duff, at 9–10.

[139] William B. Jones, "Risk Assessment: Corporate Ventures in Deep Seabed Mining Outside the Framework of the UN Convention on the Law of the Sea," 16 *Ocean Dev. & Int'l L.* 341, 348 (1986).

[140] Broadus and Hoagland, at 556.

[141] See Hayashi, "Japan," at 352; Lee Kimball, "Turning Points in the Future of Deep Seabed Mining," 17 *Ocean Dev. & Int'l L. J.* 367, 379 (1986).

this problem by registering coordinates with non-States parties as well as States parties.[142] In addition, problems could have arisen with the Dispute Resolving Agreement whereby a State not party to this agreement had taken advantage of the research and development of another nation and moved into the same area that had demonstrated considerable financial promise.[143] The Provisional Understanding and Dispute Resolving Agreement were only binding between the signatories and "such a narrow guarantee of mine site security [would] probably be unsatisfactory to risk-conscious lenders."[144]

The risks inherent in proceeding to mine the deep seabed outside of a universal treaty regime included the possibility of international judicial proceedings. The President of the Third Conference announced an intention to ask the ICJ for an Advisory Opinion on the legality of deep sea mining under a mini-treaty.[145] Such an action was viewed with skepticism, however. It has been suggested that there was insufficient legal interest preventing the depletion of the common heritage of mankind to be able to found an action.[146] Furthermore, an Advisory Opinion on unilateral licensing of deep seabed mining could constitute a political question or affect certain States so closely that their consent would be required to give the Opinion.[147] Even if the Court did announce that mining outside of the UNCLOS regime was unlawful, mining companies would only be affected if the Advisory Opinion was enforced through domestic mechanisms.[148]

Consideration also had to be given to domestic litigation against mining companies. If an action could be founded on irreparable environmental damage to the ocean's seabed or that the unilateral exploitation

---

[142] For example, Kennecott and INCO groups both filed coordinates with Canada to preserve future options as well as seeking licenses under the United States legislation. These coordinates were withdrawn from Canada when the United States government criticized the companies for undermining the position that the companies had urged the government to take. See Lee Kimball, "Turning Points in the Future of Deep Seabed Mining," 17 Ocean Dev. & Int'l L. J. 367, 375 (1986).

[143] Breen, at 218. See also Van Dyke and Yuen, at 545.

[144] Steven J. Molitor, at 248.

[145] Koh, President of the Law of the Sea Conference, Statement Delivered at Press Conference (May 3, 1982), p. 2, cited in Surace-Smith, at n. 8.

[146] Jesper Grolin, "The Future of the Law of the Sea: Consequences of a Non-Treaty or Non-Universal Treaty Situation," 13 Ocean Dev. & Int'l L. J. 1, 21 (1983).

[147] Ronald Scott Moss, "Insuring Unilaterally Licensed Deep Seabed Mining Operations Against Adverse Rulings by the International Court of Justice: An Assessment of the Risks," 14 Ocean Dev. & Int'l L. J. 161, 165–75 (1984).

[148] Ibid. at 175.

of the deep seabed was a violation of international law then companies could be forced to pay large penalties or be forced to close offices in that particular jurisdiction.[149] Attempts could also be made to challenge the title of a mining company to any recovered nodules through domestic litigation.[150]

Other risks to be encountered in proceeding with deep seabed mining on a unilateral basis could evolve from the political organs of the UN and its specialized agencies. Although actions within these fora would be extremely unlikely to have a binding effect,[151] it would be possible for this question to be linked to other questions in which the mining States had a greater interest.[152] Furthermore, if anger was sufficiently roused, mining companies and equipment could be subject to terrorist attack.[153]

While the alternative regime was an obvious response to the dissatisfaction of developed States towards Part XI, it failed to resolve the key question for the most interested actors: was the legal regime sufficiently stable to warrant large-scale investment? To this end, the Dispute Resolving Agreement and Provisional Understanding sought to allay concerns about the risks of overlapping claims and the lack of international mechanisms to resolve this issue. The dispute settlement procedures created were needed as an essential element to the alternative regime if it was to have any viability at all. Overall, the incomplete participation in the alternative regime and its dispute settlement procedures, the diplomatic pressure from developing and other States parties to UNCLOS, and the potential for conflicting legal obligations all contributed to the ulimtate downfall of the alternative regime.

Conclusion

The establishment of international regimes for the exploration and exploitation of the deep seabed represents another way that States have attempted to allocate maritime resources. Certainly, one trend at the time of the formulation of UNCLOS was that "the interdependence

---

[149] See Jones, at 349.

[150] H. G. Knight, *Consequences of Non-Agreement at the Third UN Law of the Sea Conference* (1976), pp. 34–35.

[151] Only the Security Council can issue binding decisions under Chapter VII of the Charter but as the United States has the veto power, along with other States interested in deep sea mining, it would be almost impossible to expect that any resolution would be adopted.

[152] See Jones, at 344.   [153] *Ibid.*, at 344–45. See also Breen, at 219.

of peoples and their problem of survival made inevitable the appearance of a globalizing and unifying concept: the common heritage of mankind."[154] However, States were ultimately more determined to secure resources for their own populations. Even Ambassador Pardo, who initiated the application of the common heritage concept to the deep seabed, considered that the Authority would not "play a significant role in establishing a new legal and economic order in ocean space."[155] He reached such a conclusion because it was clear from the negotiating text that the Authority would not have a monopoly over manganese nodules due to the extension in areas under coastal State jurisdiction.[156] Basically, "coastal states were able to ensure that virtually all geological structures associated with significant deposits of oil and gas are likely to be found within coastal state jurisdiction, not in the international seabed."[157]

For the interests that remain in the deep seabed, the primary concern has been to create a stable legal regime in order to allow for financial investment in mining operations. This investment was crucial regardless of whether the mining occurred through an international institution or by private mining consortia. All actors concerned needed an initial supply of funds for the final goal of profiting from the extraction of the nodules. The various regimes created in the international system were designed to reflect and enhance these interests. The alternative regime could not provide complete answers. It created a legal regime that permitted some exploration and other research to begin, but as it was generated as a matter of domestic law and dealt with an issue of international concern, the actions of other interested nationals and States could not be ignored. This awareness meant that recognition for the different domestic regimes had to be sought. Furthermore, the range of actors involved under the different domestic regimes, and the multinational character of the entities initially interested in deep seabed mining, meant that an additional mechanism was needed to resolve disputes over conflicting claims to certain deep seabed areas. A dispute settlement procedure was one of the requisite elements for the alternative regime. The lack of comprehensiveness of the formulated procedures and the potential

---

[154] de Marfy, pp. 158–59.
[155] Arvid Pardo and Elizabeth Mann Borgese, *The New International Economic Order and the Law of the Sea* (1976), p. 98.
[156] *Ibid.*
[157] John R. Stevenson and Bernard H. Oxman, "The Future of the United Nations Convention on the Law of the Sea," 88 *Am. J. Int'l L.* 488, 490 (1994).

for conflict with parties acting under UNCLOS, or through political or diplomatic avenues, undermined the viability of the alternative regime.

The legal regime created under Part XI of UNCLOS only became feasible upon the adoption of the 1994 Agreement (which was also when interest in deep seabed mining had generally decreased and there was less support for the NIEO). As described earlier in this chapter, the 1994 Agreement served to overcome many of the objections towards Part XI of UNCLOS upon that Convention's adoption. By contrast to the alternative regime, UNCLOS and the 1994 Agreement regulate deep seabed mining through an international institution and provide for recourse to compulsory dispute settlement in a range of defined situations. While the jurisdiction of the courts or tribunals hearing deep seabed disputes is limited in some respects, this fact should not undermine the overall legal regime. Instead, the institutional framework permits changes or adjustments to be made within the functioning of the different organs and does not create dependence on the availability of any third-party mechanism to a comparable extent as the alternative regime. UNCLOS and the 1994 Agreement are still hampered by lack of universal participation, but given the ability of nationals of States not party to these agreements to form conglomerations with other entities that are operating in accordance with the UNCLOS and 1994 Agreement regime, this abstinence has not yet proved detrimental to the operation of this discrete legal system within the law of the sea.

6   Conclusion

UNCLOS is one of the most important constitutive instruments in international law. It represents the creation and codification of a substantial body of law that impacts on a variety of economic, political, military, and social interests of States, international organizations, companies, and individuals. Every State, landlocked or coastal, relies on the oceans as a supply of resources as well as for communication and security, and can thus benefit from the way that this global resource is regulated. The rights and obligations embodied in UNCLOS affect the decisions and relationships of all States. While the Convention is firmly grounded in traditional principles of the law of the sea, it also marks important developments in ocean use (the clearest examples being the institution of the EEZ, the creation of the transit passage regime, and a special international regime for the exploration and exploitation of the deep seabed). This book has focused on one particularly unusual feature in UNCLOS: the inclusion of a compulsory dispute settlement system as an integral feature of the Convention. When States become parties to the Convention, as over 140 States are, they also take the unique step of agreeing to mandatory jurisdiction for certain disputes relating to the interpretation and application of this instrument.

The inclusion of a mandatory dispute settlement system in such a significant constitutive document was hailed by delegates at the Third Conference and by commentators as significant progress in international law. Certainly, the use of a mandatory mechanism for dispute resolution was uncharacteristic of international law generally, and law of the sea specifically, where the preference has typically been for political resolution of differences between States or, at most, for consent-based modes of adjudication and arbitration. Given this counter-trend in international relations, some commentators have questioned the extent that international dispute settlement has been transformed through the conclusion of UNCLOS. Such skepticism is warranted in view of the continuing emphasis on consent-based dispute settlement procedures as well as the number of exceptions and limitations to the applicability of the compulsory procedures entailing binding decisions. Indeed, as the discussion here has demonstrated, it is doubtful that compulsory dispute settlement is necessary for the regulation of many issue areas addressed in the Convention.

Focusing on the designated exceptions and limitations, I have examined in which situations the dispute settlement procedures have constituted an elemental part of the substantive rules of the Convention as well as when the availability of compulsory dispute settlement, or lack thereof, is inconsequential for the functioning of the provisions of the Convention. This Conclusion summarizes these findings with respect to the dispute settlement procedure itself and with respect to the disputes potentially excepted from mandatory procedures. Undoubtedly, UNCLOS is a significant advancement in international law, but it does not contain a comprehensive dispute settlement system in view of the remaining gaps and ambiguities. This overview highlights why compulsory dispute settlement was or was not necessary for the functioning of the substantive provisions of the Convention. From this analysis, the following questions can be examined: What significance does this complex dispute settlement system have for the law of the sea? What problems are associated with the use of mandatory jurisdiction? And, what impact will these changes in the law of the sea have for other areas of international law as well as for international relations?

In Part XV, UNCLOS sets out a mechanism that combines traditional modes of peaceful dispute settlement with the availability of mandatory jurisdiction for certain disputes relating to the interpretation and application of the Convention. Section 1 of Part XV emphasizes the freedom of choice allowed to States in selecting methods to resolve disputes through peaceful means. States are fully entitled to utilize a range of traditional dispute settlement processes prior to resorting to compulsory procedures entailing binding decisions. States are specifically obligated to proceed to an exchange of views under Article 283 in the event of a dispute in order to facilitate the negotiation process. Section 1 thus acknowledges the continuing importance of diplomatic and political avenues for resolving differences.

States are further entitled, and, in some instances, required, to resolve disputes through mechanisms available under other agreements. If

States select their own means of dispute settlement then Part XV will only apply if no resolution is reached through that means and if the parties did not exclude any further procedure in so choosing.[1] Further, States may refer disputes to procedures that produce a binding decision under general, regional, or bilateral agreements, unless the parties agree that procedures under Section 2 of Part XV should be used.[2] The continuing availability of alternative dispute settlement processes under other agreements was a necessary arrangement so as not to deprive these other means of dispute settlement of any effect.[3] Priority is thus accorded to the preference of States to avoid mandatory arbitral or adjudicative proceedings.

In the event that States have not resolved their differences through the variety of procedures available under Section 1 of Part XV, disputes concerning the interpretation or application of the Convention may be referred to compulsory procedures entailing binding decisions (subject to the exceptions and limitations set out in Section 3 of Part XV). Establishing a dispute settlement system that would prove acceptable to the States negotiating the Convention required not only deference to preferences for alternative methods, but also flexibility in the choice of procedure. To this end, the Convention permits States a choice between four different institutions for adjudication or arbitration of disputes. This choice of procedure was necessary not only to account for differing attitudes toward international courts and arbitral tribunals but also as a reflection of the different types of disputes that could arise under the terms of the Convention.

The role that these courts and tribunals may play in the resolution of a variety of disputes dealing with different substantive issues has been foreshadowed in the preliminary proceedings that have been undertaken under Article 290. Article 290 permits courts and tribunals with *prima facie* jurisdiction to order provisional measures to preserve the respective rights of the parties or to prevent serious harm to the marine environment prior to the final resolution of the dispute. Most notably, ITLOS decided in the provisional measures phase of *Southern Bluefin Tuna* to prescribe fish catch totals for the parties to the dispute pending its resolution thereby arrogating a matter that would normally rest with coastal States or be resolved through a cooperative arrangement between the States concerned.[4] The provisional measures decisions in *MOX Plant* and

---

[1] UNCLOS, art. 281. [2] *Ibid.*, art. 282.
[3] See Southern Bluefin Tuna, Jurisdiction, para. 63.
[4] Southern Bluefin Tuna, Provisional Measures, para. 90(c).

Land Reclamation have demonstrated the facilitative role that ITLOS is prepared to play in setting forth measures of cooperation to be taken by the parties pending the resolution of the disputes through arbitration.[5]

The transfer of national authority to international processes has also been evident in prompt release proceedings, which form part of the compulsory procedures entailing binding decisions. The inclusion of this provision was part of the overall framework of legal protection for the freedom of navigation. Some effort has been evinced to formulate an international standard for the determination of a reasonable bond or other financial security. The *Grand Prince* (as well as the decision on the merits in *M/V "Saiga" (No. 2)*) has also indicated that international review is available for determinations of the nationality of vessels and that it is not solely a decision of national authorities. A further feature of the Article 292 proceedings that may be indicative of trends in decisions on the merits is that ITLOS has taken into consideration the role it must play in balancing inclusive rights of navigation with exclusive interests of coastal States in the conservation and management of living resources. These decisions demonstrate what role dispute settlement must play as an integral function in the normative regimes set out in the Convention.

Rather than establishing a comprehensive dispute settlement system, important limitations and exceptions to mandatory proceedings entailing binding decisions are included in Section 3 of Part XV of UNCLOS. The availability of compulsory procedures was clearly considered a vital element in the normative regimes for some issue areas whereas others did not require mandatory jurisdiction in the same way as traditional methods of consent-based dispute settlement would suffice. Articles 297 and 298 set out a system designating certain disputes as subject to mandatory and binding decisions, others to mandatory procedures without binding decisions, and still others to no third-party review at all. The lack of compulsory arbitration or adjudication reflects the political reality of what States were willing to surrender to third-party processes. In most instances (but certainly not all), where mandatory jurisdiction entailing binding decisions is not available, the substantive regime will likely function as intended under the Convention. The limitations and exceptions in Articles 297 and 298 predominantly relate to the exercise of sovereign rights and jurisdiction in the EEZ and on the continental shelf. This book has followed the structure of Section 3 of Part XV in analyzing the limitations on the applicability of Section 2 addressed

---

[5] See further pp. 79–85.

in Article 297 (relating to the freedoms of navigation, overflight, the laying of submarine cables and pipelines; the protection and preservation of the marine environment; fishing and marine scientific research) and then the optional exceptions of Article 298 (dealing with maritime delimitation and historic title as well as military activities, law enforcement, and disputes over which the Security Council is exercising its functions). Dispute settlement and the deep seabed mining regime was then addressed. The discussion of these different subjects in Chapters 3, 4, and 5 is summarized immediately below.

The rights and freedoms of navigation, overflight, the laying of submarine cables and pipelines, and related internationally lawful uses of the oceans have traditionally been exercised over extensive high seas areas in accordance with *mare liberum*. Even in areas subject to coastal State sovereignty, rights of navigation were guaranteed through the regime of innocent passage. Gradually, encroachment on high seas areas for different purposes increased. The first major movement in this direction was for the exploration and exploitation of resources found in the seabed and subsoil. This change was quickly followed by claims over the superjacent waters in 200-mile zones for the conservation and management of living resources. Coastal States were keen to claim these rights over larger areas of the ocean to enhance their economic interests. Their efforts culminated in the legal recognition of the continental shelf at the First Conference and then in the institution of the EEZ in UNCLOS. With these developments, States that had traditionally profited from the freedoms of communication demanded that their interests be protected as part of the international system recognizing the claims of coastal States over the natural resources of the extended maritime zones. Rules were thus set out in the Convention to protect the freedoms of navigation, overflight, and the laying of submarine cables and pipelines in the EEZ and on the continental shelf. States recognized at the Third Conference that with the uncertain status of the EEZ (as either *sui generis* or as a high seas area with a new overlay of rights and duties) disputes could well arise in light of coexisting rights and duties in this maritime area. Rules of due regard to the interests of States as well as a formula for resolving differences were included within the body of the Convention. In addition, Section 3 of Part XV specifically stipulates that disputes relating to the freedoms and rights of navigation, overflight, or the laying of submarine cables and pipelines, or in regard to other internationally lawful uses of the sea specified in Article 58 are subject to compulsory procedures entailing binding decisions. Compulsory dispute settlement was necessary as part of the normative regime for these freedoms of communication to give content to the guidelines for dispute resolution relating to unattributed rights and duties and relating to conflicting interests in areas subject to the sovereign rights of coastal States. External third-party review was also necessary to ensure that the balance between inclusive and exclusive interests in the extended maritime zones is maintained as envisaged in the Convention.

Concern about ensuring the continued rights and freedoms of navigation also resulted in the necessity of mandatory dispute settlement procedures for differences arising over the exercise of coastal State jurisdiction in relation to the protection and preservation of the marine environment. Part XII of the Convention sets out general obligations imposed on all States for the protection and preservation of the marine environment and for the prevention, reduction, and control of pollution of the marine environment. The inclusion of a Part on this topic is a reflection of the recognized need for conservation as a way to protect and preserve the resources of the marine environment as well as the oceans in their entirety. In addition to addressing the right of States to prescribe and enforce laws relating to various sources of pollution, a number of obligations of cooperation are imposed on States in subjective and hortatory language. These obligations are clearly in the nature of soft law and indicate the way that States are to deal with this issue in the future. Mandatory dispute settlement is specifically designed to allow for the hortatory aspects of Part XII as well as ensuring the maintenance of international standards that can be applied to the coastal State. Article 297(1)(c) stipulates that the procedures under Section 2 of Part XV are applicable when a coastal State is alleged to have acted in contravention of international rules and standards established either by the Convention or through the appropriate fora in accordance with the Convention and when those rules and standards are applicable to that coastal State. Mandatory dispute settlement may not be essential for this regime if a separate agreement is formulated and applicable between the States concerned. If no such agreement exists, compulsory adjudication or arbitration fills a lacuna in the substantive rules through the elaboration of what conduct conforms to international rules for the protection and preservation of the marine environment as well as determining to what standard the particular coastal State must adhere. If more than general guidelines are needed to regulate State conduct for the protection and preservation of the marine environment, then mandatory jurisdiction is requisite to implement the international standards and rules of Part XII.

The role of dispute settlement for the protection and preservation of the marine environment is comparable with that for fishing on the high seas. No exclusion to mandatory jurisdiction is specified in the Convention for disputes relating to high seas fishing. The freedom of fishing on the high seas has gradually been transformed as methods of fishing significantly improved through technological developments and as concerns over conservation have increased. One response to these developments has been an augmentation in the areas over which coastal States are entitled to exercise authority – first with the extension of the territorial sea to a breadth of twelve miles and then with the institution of the EEZ in the Convention, which accords coastal States with sovereign rights over the exploitation, conservation and management of the living resources in a 200-mile zone. Even in high seas areas, the freedom of fishing may no longer be practiced without regard to conservation and management practices. This high seas freedom is now subject to treaty obligations, certain rights and interests of coastal States as well as the duty to adopt conservation measures. States are to determine allowable catches for their nationals in accordance with Article 119 and cooperate with other States whose nationals fish the same stock or in the same area. The decisions for appropriate conservation measures rest with the States whose nationals fish on the high seas. Yet there is some ambiguity as to what this duty of cooperation involves and what measures are to be taken to conserve the living resources of the high seas. In the event of dispute, third-party decision-making through Part XV procedures provides an avenue to elaborate on the appropriate conduct of States and to ascertain what would constitute "any generally recommended international minimum standards."[6] It is only in situations where States have entered into an agreement implementing the obligations of the Convention that an alternative dispute settlement system may prevail over that in UNCLOS, in accordance with the decision on jurisdiction in *Southern Bluefin Tuna*.

The situation is entirely different when examining the exercise of sovereign rights of coastal States over the living resources of the EEZ. The exclusive interests of the coastal State are of paramount importance and virtually all avenues for international review of national decision-making are unavailable. The emphasis in the substantive rules regulating the exploitation, conservation and management of the living resources of the EEZ is on the decision-making power of the coastal State.

---

[6] UNCLOS, art. 119(1)(a).

Such an emphasis was justified because of the economic importance of the fishing industry and the variety of conditions existing with respect to different stocks and species of fish as well as the differing circumstances of States regulating such stocks and species. Coastal States are to determine what quantity of fish may be harvested, what its own capacity for harvesting is, and what allocations shall be made to other States in the event of a surplus existing. Coastal States are further entitled to prescribe and enforce rules and regulations for the conservation and management of their living resources. These decisions are insulated nearly entirely from any form of third-party review. Only conciliation proceedings may be instituted in limited circumstances but even then, the commission is not to substitute its discretion for that of the coastal State and its recommendations are not binding on the States in dispute. Mandatory and binding jurisdiction clearly does not have a role to play in the regulation of the living resources of the EEZ. Coastal State decision-making power has preeminence and the rights of other States to participate in fishing in the zone are subject to the sovereign rights of the coastal State. Arrangements are to be made through negotiations and coastal State decisions could well be influenced by factors that do not solely relate to marine resources. If disputes arise, they are to be resolved through traditional, consent-based methods rather than require mandatory arbitration or adjudication. It is unclear from the terms of the Convention whether a similar role for dispute settlement is necessary for fish that are located in more than one zone or in an EEZ and the high seas. It has been proposed that any decision on jurisdiction for disputes involving these different stocks and species should be guided by the roles accorded to dispute settlement in respect of fishing in the EEZ and on the high seas.

Dispute settlement procedures for conflicts relating to marine scientific research are available except for two important categories of decision-making. Marine scientific research was formerly considered as falling within the freedoms of the high seas. With the movement towards greater coastal State control over resources and the concomitant recognition that research projects could yield important information about these resources, a more detailed system was elaborated to account for coastal State interests in acquiring this knowledge. Part XIII of UNCLOS sets out the duties and obligations of States in relation to the conduct of marine scientific research in different ocean areas. Both general obligations are imposed on States as well as more detailed rules according coastal States certain rights in the EEZ in relation to the grant of consent for specific types of projects and entitlement to participate in different ways in research activities. The substantive rules of the Convention set out a carefully balanced regime to cater for the interests of coastal States as well as States and competent international organizations conducting marine scientific research. It is arguable on this basis that mandatory dispute settlement does not have a role to play for marine scientific research. Nonetheless, Article 297 stipulates that marine scientific research disputes are subject to the procedures in Section 2 of Part XV, except for the exercise by the coastal State of a right or discretion in relation to marine scientific research in the EEZ or on the continental shelf or for decisions of the coastal State to order suspension or cessation of a research project. The availability of compulsory procedures entailing binding decisions could constitute a guarantee for the balance of interests established in the substantive provisions, in a similar manner to the protection of the freedom of navigation, overflight, the laying of submarine cables and pipelines, and other related uses. Similar to fisheries disputes, though, an important category of conflicts is excluded from mandatory and binding jurisdiction and a limited form of conciliation is available as an alternative. The availability of conciliation is not subject to constraints related to the manifest or arbitrary conduct of the coastal State and so any dispute excluded by virtue of Article 297(2)(a) may be submitted at the request of either party to conciliation. Compulsory conciliation may prove more useful for marine scientific research disputes than fishing disputes on the basis that the commission can reach certain factual determinations in relation to the positions of the parties. The presentation of the report has greater potential here to influence future negotiations between the relevant States. The protection of national decision-making is not as comprehensive and international processes retain a relevant role in ensuring the functioning of the marine scientific research regime.

The different roles attributed to compulsory dispute settlement under Article 297 are also apparent upon an examination of Article 298, which sets out the optional exceptions to compulsory procedures entailing binding decisions. An emphasis on State decision-making power is again evident for the delimitation of maritime areas. Maritime delimitation has long been an important issue in the law of the sea because it marks the limitations of areas subject to a State's sovereignty and jurisdiction. Delimitation always has an international aspect because it either allocates areas between States with opposite or adjacent coasts or defines the seaward extent of a coastal State's maritime space with the area beyond constituting high seas. The provisions on delimitation of the territorial sea, EEZ, and continental shelf between States with opposite or adjacent coasts reflect that a variety of factors can be relevant in the delimitation process. It was not possible for States to agree on a global rule that would be strictly applicable in all situations. For the delimitation of the territorial sea, allowance is made for "historic title or other special circumstances" whereas the provisions on delimitation of the extended maritime zones simply requires States to effect delimitation through agreement and on the basis of international law to achieve an equitable solution. These provisions constitute guiding principles at best, according States a large measure of discretion in what boundary to choose in cases of overlapping entitlements. States have an incentive to reach agreement (or at least a provisional arrangement) in order to settle the limits of jurisdiction or sovereignty and allow for the issuing of fishing licenses, enforcement of environmental regulations, or entering into concession agreements with oil companies. While external third-party review could conceivably form a vital element in the delimitation process, particularly in assessing claims to historic title, States considered the political stakes too high to accept mandatory adjudication or arbitration. Instead, States may elect to exclude these decisions from compulsory procedures entailing binding decisions. While a conciliation process may be undertaken if certain conditions are met, the end result is to lead the parties in dispute back to negotiations. States have typically settled their maritime boundaries through agreement and the continuation of this practice will undoubtedly be preferred under the Convention rather than trusting in international courts or tribunals. States may also fix their own straight baselines or determine what landforms constitute rocks or islands in accordance with the Convention. These decisions may be taken into account in the process of negotiations when they affect the extent of overlap between States' entitlements to maritime areas. However, these decisions will be subject to international review if the determinations result in an unlawful extension of maritime zones into high seas areas. The role of dispute settlement is necessary here to guarantee that inclusive interests in high seas freedoms are not jeopardized.

Further disputes that may be excluded from compulsory procedures entailing binding decisions are those relating to military activities, acts subject to the exercise of the functions of the Security Council, and specific law enforcement activities. The exercise of naval power has long been a feature of ocean use – either in offensive or defensive measures or for activities such as naval exercises or weapons tests. Whether the Convention applies in times of armed conflict and to what extent the Convention governs military activities not amounting to armed conflict is unclear as States deliberately preferred ambiguity for questions relating to military uses of the oceans. Generally, military activities will fall within the exercise of the freedom of navigation and are thus allowable in the EEZ as well as on the high seas. The only limitations are the duty of due regard for the interests of other users as well as a stipulation that the oceans are to be used for peaceful purposes thereby prohibiting all military activities that constitute a threat or use of force against the political independence or territorial integrity of any State or are in any other manner inconsistent with the principles of international law embodied in the UN Charter. The very fact that Part XV anticipates disputes arising with respect to the acts of warships and other government vessels used for non-commercial purposes suggests that UNCLOS does regulate military activities on the oceans. The extent of ambiguity in the text and the tendency to require mandatory third-party review to protect the freedom of navigation may indicate that compulsory dispute settlement could play a vital role in stipulating what rules apply in relation to military activities. International dispute settlement may also be necessary because of the attribution of sovereign immunity to these vessels. However, the absence of mandatory and binding legal proceedings will not hamper the regulation of uses of the oceans beyond areas subject to coastal State sovereignty. The activities of military and government vessels have not traditionally been subject to third-party adjudication or arbitration but have been regulated under customary international law and differences resolved through consent-based methods of dispute resolution. The preference of States to keep these questions largely outside the normative regime in UNCLOS indicates that States will continue to favor traditional modes of dispute resolution to compulsory procedures. Whether this situation is desirable in the long term must be questioned as the number of claims to and uses of ocean space continue to increase. In such a situation, the need for third-party intervention to balance the different interests may become crucial.

Less ambiguity is found with respect to the acts of military and government vessels in areas subject to coastal State sovereignty. The military activities exception may encompass disputes relating to the passage of military and other government vessels used for non-commercial service through territorial seas, straits, and archipelagic waters. Foreign vessels have the right to traverse the territorial sea of a coastal State provided that the passage is not prejudicial to the peace, good order, or security of that State. Threats to the freedom of navigation posed by coastal State claims to extended breadths of territorial seas were derived from the potential applicability of the regime of innocent passage in larger areas of ocean space. This possible limitation was viewed as hampering not only commercial voyages but also a range of naval missions. States with considerable naval fleets did not want their passage subjected to coastal State control in any manner. Such control was inevitable based on the range of acts that could result in a determination by the coastal State that passage was not innocent. The Convention favors the coastal State in granting to it the authority to determine the character of passage and in prescribing laws for the regulation of passage. To exclude external third-party review of coastal State decision-making relating to the passage of warships and other government vessels operated for non-commercial services has the effect of reinforcing the power of the littoral State in respect of its authority over territorial seas. The exception could be read narrowly to exclude these questions of passage from the scope of military activities. This approach would enable the dispute settlement procedures to fulfill a valuable role in the regulation of this regime by guaranteeing the balance of rights. However, the history of the regime of innocent passage functioning relatively effectively based on reciprocity with any differences most typically resolved through political methods or diplomatic channels indicates that there is rarely need to resort to international adjudication or arbitration.

This situation is then contrasted with the regimes of transit passage and archipelagic passage. These rules were specifically developed in the Convention as a balance to the recognition of twelve-mile breadths of territorial sea. Coastal State sovereignty could be recognized over waters in straits and within the outer islands of archipelagic States because the Convention included guarantees for the rights of navigation. The need for third-party dispute resolution is far more evident with these rules of passage because the normative regimes are designed for the specific purpose of balancing the interests of third States with the straits States and archipelagic States concerned. Third-party intervention is necessary to uphold the balance devised in the Convention and the viability of the rules pertaining to transit and archipelagic passage could well be undermined if the military activities exception is utilized to prevent recourse to international decision-making processes.

The possible exclusion of military activities from the scope of compulsory procedures entailing binding decisions was initially considered on the understanding that law enforcement activities undertaken pursuant to the Convention would not fall within that exception. Coastal States feared, however, that an imbalance would be created in favor of foreign vessels operating in their extended maritime zones. An exception was thus incorporated to permit the exclusion of disputes concerning law enforcement activities in respect of fishing and marine scientific research in the EEZ to be excluded from the procedures set out in Section 2 of Part XV. This exception reinforces those in Article 297 that emphasize coastal State authority. Difficulties in the application of this optional exception may arise when there is a conflict between the freedom of navigation of third States and the exercise of enforcement jurisdiction by the coastal State. In light of the requisite role of mandatory jurisdiction for the functioning of the navigation regime in the EEZ, a court or tribunal should weight inclusive interests accordingly in characterizing the dispute and deciding whether jurisdiction can be exercised under Part XV. A further overlap is possible in respect of other acts that involve law enforcement activities that are undertaken by military and government vessels. The rights of visit and hot pursuit are relevant here. These acts may be excluded from compulsory dispute settlement as law enforcement activities to the extent that the vessels are acting to enforce laws and regulations relating to fishing and marine scientific research in the EEZ. For other laws and regulations, the question still remains as to whether these acts are "military activities" for the purposes of the optional exception. To the extent that these activities are properly viewed as law enforcement, then the exclusions should not be applicable.

As discussed in Chapter 5, the deep seabed mining regime evolved on parallel tracks, with the international institutional approach endorsed and developed in the Convention and the alternative regime initiated by individual developed States. The alternative regime was heavily dependent on reciprocity between interested States as well as third-party mechanisms as a means of legitimizing their claims. Part XI of the Convention consisted of a highly regulated regime to be pursued through the Authority, an international institution, and was driven by the concerns of developing States in upholding the NIEO and the concept of common heritage. As a result, the regulation of deep seabed mining under UNCLOS was never accepted by developed States and was finally modified through the adoption of the 1994 Agreement. While the system established under the Convention and the 1994 Agreement permits access to compulsory dispute settlement procedures with respect to a range of issues that may arise in respect of the granting and exercising of rights in the Area, its role is ultimately marginal. Prior to the adoption of the

1994 Agreement, the primary exclusions to mandatory jurisdiction centered on the Authority's exercise of discretion and non-reviewability of certain of its actions. The 1994 Agreement did not revise these jurisdictional limits specifically, but the modifications to the powers, role, and composition of the Authority and its constituent organs had the effect of minimizing their detrimental impact. The transfer of authority to an international institution has meant that States do not need to rely on courts or tribunals to guarantee the balance of interests or to flesh out the normative content of international rights and obligations. Instead, the international institution provides the framework for these processes to occur without necessitating resort to external dispute settlement bodies.

This examination has demonstrated that the compulsory dispute settlement system is not comprehensive, nor is it "the cement which should hold the whole structure together."[7] Nonetheless, Part XV is an indispensable and politically realistic component of UNCLOS. Mandatory procedures entailing binding decisions have primarily been necessary as a complement to the system for protecting the rights and freedoms of communication in the face of greater coastal State authority over ocean spaces. Compulsory dispute settlement has been an elemental part of this normative regime as a way to guarantee the balances created in the Convention. This need for dispute settlement in respect of navigation rights is evident not only with respect to the preservation of high seas freedoms in the EEZ and on the continental shelf but also in relation to passage through straits and archipelagic waters, prompt release proceedings, and the enforcement of laws dealing with the protection and preservation of the marine environment. A similar role for compulsory dispute settlement was arguably needed in relation to the rights of researching States and organizations in the provisions dealing with marine scientific research.

The only other reason for compulsory dispute settlement being requisite in the Convention would be when the substantive provisions require future agreement between States or are simply broad guidelines that establish the goals in the legal development of the law of the sea. Third-party review could provide one avenue for the elaboration of these rules and would be necessary to the extent that no other international decision making process is available for this task. If States are able to form separate regimes to implement these provisions of the

---

[7] Boyle, "Dispute Settlement," at 38.

Convention, the availability of either an international forum or the traditional modes of dispute settlement may be sufficient in the regulation of State conduct without resort to either arbitral or adjudicative proceedings.

Alternatively, States may prefer to rely on traditional modes of dispute settlement, operating through political means or diplomatic channels, as has been the custom with respect to the law of the sea in the past. It is evident that mandatory jurisdiction was not perceived as necessary for some issue areas addressed in the Convention. States will clearly favor political or diplomatic means of dispute settlement for issues that are more easily settled on a bilateral or regional basis. While disadvantages to this system can be envisaged, coastal State interest in the economic resources of the EEZ resulted in a strong resistance to third-party review of national decision-making. Participation in fisheries in the EEZ, differences over the conduct of military activities, and delimiting maritime boundaries are matters that are more likely to be resolved through negotiations between the concerned States rather than through an arbitral or adjudicative process. Compulsory dispute settlement is not requisite for the functioning of these activities under the Convention.

In the Convention, there are a number of regimes that deal with different maritime areas and different maritime activities. This book has analyzed the functional importance of the dispute settlement procedures for the operation of these discrete sets of substantive provisions. These regimes will function in different ways and will not necessarily require any form of external third-party review to operate in the way intended in the drafting of the Convention. Instead, reliance will be placed on other techniques in international relations for ensuring compliance and enforcement – as has happened in other multilateral regimes. The power dynamic between the relevant actors, the benefits derived from reciprocity, the importance of information, and the iteration of dealings on particular issues will all influence the way the Convention regulates the conduct of States and other international actors. While these factors will be of continuing relevance in the relationships of States, for the regimes that do require third-party decision-making, a new phase in the evolution of the law of the sea has definitely begun. To the extent that compulsory dispute settlement is not needed for various issue areas, there will be no significant change in the way the law of the sea has operated for these issues in the past.

When considering the impact that compulsory dispute settlement may have on the law of the sea generally, it is not enough to consider the essential role that these procedures may (or may not) have in the regulation of each of these specific issue areas. Regard must also be had to the interrelated nature of the Convention and the coexistence of interests and activities. The division between those new regimes that comprise compulsory dispute settlement and those that are norm-based without this procedural element is far from evident. The factual basis of a dispute may result in difficulties of characterization for determination of whether a limitation or exception to jurisdiction applies. The way a case is formulated is critical to a decision on whether a court or tribunal constituted under the Convention has jurisdiction.[8] The problem of overlap was apparent at the provisional measures stage of M/V "Saiga" (No. 2) when Guinea argued that the Tribunal lacked prima facie jurisdiction because the case concerned the exercise of sovereign rights relating to living resources in the EEZ. Guinea pursued this argument since the Tribunal had decided in the earlier prompt release proceedings that the request for release on payment of a reasonable bond or other financial security related to enforcement proceedings under Article 73. The Tribunal made short shrift of this argument in basing its jurisdiction for the prescription of provisional measures on Article 297(1), concerning the right of navigation in the EEZ. Although Guinea was entitled to raise challenges to jurisdiction at subsequent proceedings, this argument was not pursued. Given the uncertain legal status of bunkering of fishing vessels in the EEZ, a challenge to jurisdiction may still have been worthwhile at the subsequent hearing. Oda considers that the problem of overlapping issues is particularly evident with respect to proceedings for the prompt release of vessels. He argues that these proceedings are "inevitably linked with the content of the rules and regulations of the coastal State concerning the fisheries in its exclusive economic zone, and the way in which these rules are enforced."[9] This issue would have been before ITLOS in the Grand Prince if the Tribunal had not been confronted with the problem of nationality of the vessel. The parties to the dispute themselves could well avoid questions of overlap in the formulation of their submissions. Otherwise, the court or tribunal hearing the dispute will have to decide on its jurisdiction through a proper

---

[8] As Boyle notes:

> [E]verything turns in practice not on what each case involves but on how the issues are formulated. Formulate them wrongly and the case falls outside compulsory jurisdiction. Formulate the same case differently and it falls inside.

Ibid., at 44–45.

[9] Oda, "Dispute Settlement Prospects," at 866.

characterization of the dispute in light of the claims of the parties. This process of characterization should entail consideration of the role that third-party review was intended to play for the substantive issues involved.

The risk of overlap not only arises with respect to the merits of a case but also in provisional measures decisions or prompt release proceedings. Decisions on nationality of vessels, such as in *Grand Prince*, and prescription of duties related to conservation and management of fish stock, as in *Southern Bluefin Tuna*, influence States' understandings of their rights and obligations under the Convention. The inter-connected interests, rights, and duties of States and other international actors in their activities and functions in relation to maritime space mean that the effect of many international decisions will reverberate in other areas of the law of the sea. As such, the necessity of compulsory dispute settlement for certain subjects, and its concomitant availability, could impact on areas where mandatory jurisdiction is not typically necessary. As a formal matter, the decisions of courts and tribunals are only binding on the parties before it. Nonetheless, a decision by a court or tribunal constitutes an authoritative interpretation of the provisions of the Convention and that meaning could then be relevant to all other States parties. While the possibility remains that a State may prefer its own interpretation if a decision does not conform to its understanding of the Convention, a judicial or arbitral decision is likely to carry weight in future national decision-making.

The existence of mandatory dispute settlement under UNCLOS further has the potential to create novel complications in international dispute settlement. Cases ostensibly relating to the interpretation or application of the Convention may be brought before the courts or tribunals under Part XV when they either are being or could be settled in a different forum. The interaction of domestic courts with international courts is not new in this respect. The Convention affirms the application of the exhaustion of local remedies rule in Article 295. However, the availability of proceedings under Article 292 for the prompt release of vessels and crews upon the payment of a reasonable bond or other financial security has posed a more complicated situation in this regard. In its early cases on this question, ITLOS has considered the impact of its decisions on the process being undertaken in a national court. Bond amounts have been readjusted and factual determinations have been reassessed while criminal proceedings were still being pursued in the national courts. The *Grand Prince* decision signals that questions will arise regarding the availability of prompt release proceedings before an international body when decisions on merits have been reached in domestic courts.

Dispute settlement proceedings under the Convention could also be run in parallel with efforts undertaken in political forums for resolution of the dispute (or of a wider dispute of which the case under UNCLOS is one aspect). The Convention anticipates this situation in Article 298(1)(c) with respect to disputes concurrently before the Security Council. No such allowance is made for the involvement of regional organizations, issue-specific international organizations (such as the International Maritime Organization), or other political bodies in the UN system. The exclusion of regional organizations may be particularly harmful when multilateral cooperative regimes are established to regulate certain issue areas. Decision-making within these organizations might be structured on a consultative basis, or require changes in the regime by consensus. An external third-party decision could be quite disruptive to this process. The confrontational nature of adjudication may force the parties to solidify their positions or, more commonly, to maximize their claims, rather than move towards an acceptable compromise where neither party is a clear winner or loser.

Even more complicated is when a dispute is brought before different international tribunals – the dispute may be characterized differently depending on the jurisdictional limitations of the respective tribunals but address essentially the same problem. This situation could arise when a dispute is before a court or tribunal constituted under UNCLOS as well as a court of general jurisdiction (perhaps a regional court), or another tribunal with mandatory jurisdiction (such as the dispute settlement panels established under the auspices of the WTO). The overlap of jurisdiction between different adjudicative bodies could again depend on how the dispute is characterized. Rules of *res judicata* and *lis pendens* cannot easily apply between different international tribunals as the parties and the bases of the claims will not usually be identical (as required for the application of these principles). As there are few international tribunals or courts with mandatory jurisdiction, there are as yet no clear rules in international law to address these problems.

The final question to consider is what impact these changes in the law of the sea will have for other areas of international law, and for international relations generally. What impact can be anticipated given the inclusion of a mandatory dispute settlement system in an important constitutive instrument? Such a transgression from the norm in international relations deserves attention, but does it mark a new era in international dispute settlement? It could be argued that the significance of this development in international law is that it represents part of the trend to form more international courts and tribunals, particularly the tendency to establish courts and tribunals that are topic-specific as an alternative to the ICJ. Yet these new tribunals, such as the International Criminal Court, are not typically accorded mandatory jurisdiction.

As the discussion in this book has shown, compulsory dispute settlement was not actually essential for all issues relating to the law of the sea that were being regulated under the Convention. The ongoing reliance on traditional forms of dispute settlement is also evident in the fact that not all States have signed on to UNCLOS, the United States being the most noticeable non-party in this regard. These non-parties exercise the rights and adhere to obligations in the Convention to the extent that those rights and obligations represent customary international law. In this respect, the substantive principles are in no way dependent on the availability of mandatory jurisdiction for their operation or effectiveness. There is no deviation from the norm in this respect.

Finally, the conditions existing during the drafting of UNCLOS were quite unique. States were dealing with one of the most significant resources of the planet, a resource that had already been governed by a body of law for several centuries, and were both codifying as well as adapting this law to cater for new technologies, concerns, and interests. The law-making process undertaken at the Third Conference was highly complex because it sought to address a wide range of issues and to create a package that would be acceptable to all States. Compromises could be reached because of the diversity of interests involved – in some instances, but certainly not all, compulsory dispute settlement was needed as part of the compromise. While the importance of UNCLOS should not be underestimated because of the significance of the resource and the interests at stake, its uniqueness means that the wider lessons to be drawn from the role of dispute settlement in the international law-making process are ultimately quite limited.

Bibliography

TREATISES, CHAPTERS, AND JOURNAL ARTICLES

Abbot, Kenneth W., "Modern International Relations Theory: A Prospectus for International Lawyers," 14 *Yale J. Int'l L.* 335 (1989).

Adede, A. O., "The System for Exploitation of the 'Common Heritage of Mankind' at the Caracas Conference," 69 *Am. J. Int'l L.* 31 (1975).

"Settlement of Disputes Arising under the Law of the Sea Convention," 69 *Am. J. Int'l L.* 795 (1975).

"Settlement of Disputes Arising under the Law of the Sea Convention," 71 *Am. J. Int'l L.* 305 (1977).

"Prolegomena to the Dispute Settlement Part of the Law of the Sea Convention," 10 *NYU J Int'l L & Pol.* 253 (1977–78).

"Settlement of Disputes Arising under the Law of the Sea Convention," 72 *Am. J. Int'l L.* 84 (1978).

"Toward the Formulation of the Rule of Delimitation of Sea Boundaries between States with Opposite or Adjacent Coasts," 19 *Va. J. Int'l L.* 209 (1978–79).

"Streamlining the System for Settlement of Disputes under the Law of the Sea Convention," 1 *Pace L. Rev.* 15 (1980).

"Environmental Disputes under the Law of the Sea Convention," 7 *Envtl. Pol'y & L.* 63 (1981).

"The Basic Structure of the Disputes Settlement Part of the Law of the Sea Convention," 11 *Ocean Dev. & Int'l L.* 125 (1982).

The System for Settlement of Disputes Under the United Nations Convention on the Law of the Sea (1987).

Alexander, Lewis M., "International Straits," in 64 *International Law Studies: The Law of Naval Operations* (Horace B. Robertson ed., 1991), p. 91.

Anand, R. P., "The Politics of a New Legal Order for Fisheries," 11 *Ocean Dev. & Int'l L.* 265 (1982).

Astley III, John, and Schmitt, Michael N., "The Law of the Sea and Naval Operations," 42 *Air Force L. Rev.* 119 (1997).

Attard, David Joseph, *The Exclusive Economic Zone in International Law* (1987).

Banks, Susan M., "Protection of Investment in Deep Seabed Mining: Does the United States have a Viable Alternative to Participation in UNCLOS?," 2 *Boston Univ. Int'l L. J.* 267 (1983).

Barkenbus, J., *Deep Seabed Resources* (1979).

Bergman, Mark S., "The Regulation of Seabed Mining Under the Reciprocating States Regime," 30 *Am. Univ. L. Rev.* 477 (1981).

Bernhardt, J. P. A., "Compulsory Dispute Settlement in the Law of the Sea Negotiations: A Reassessment," 19 *Va. J. Int'l L.* 69 (1978–79).

"The Right of Archipelagic Sea Lanes Passage: A Primer," 35 *Va. J. Int'l L.* 719 (1995).

Bilder, R. B., "Some Limitations of Adjudication as a Dispute Settlement Technique," 23 *Va. J. Int'l L.* 1 (1982–83).

Birnie, Patricia, "Law of the Sea and Ocean Resources: Implications for Marine Scientific Research," 10 *Int'l J. Marine & Coastal L.* 229 (1995).

Bishop, William W., Jr., "International Law Commission Draft Articles on Fisheries," 50 *Am. J. Int'l L.* 627 (1956).

Blum, Yehuda Z., "The Gulf of Sidra Incident," 80 *Am. J. Int'l L.* 668 (1986).

Boggs, S. Whittemore, "Delimitation of the Territorial Sea: The Method of Delimitation Proposed by the Delegation of the United States at the Hague Conference for the Codification of International Law," 24 *Am. J. Int'l L.* 541 (1930).

"Problems of Water-Boundary Definition: Median Line and International Boundaries Through Territorial Waters," 27 *Geographical Rev.* 445 (1937).

Booth, Kenneth, "The Military Implications of the Changing Law of the Sea," in *Law of the Sea: Neglected Issues* 328 (John King Gamble, Jr., ed., 1979).

Bouchez, L. J., *The Regime of Bays in International Law* (1964).

Bowett, D. W., "The Second United Nations Conference on the Law of the Sea," 9 *Int'l & Comp. L.Q.* 415 (1960).

Boyle, A. E., "Problems of Compulsory Jurisdiction and the Settlement of Disputes Relating to Straddling Fish Stocks," 14 *Int'l J. Marine & Coastal L.* 1 (1999).

Boyle, Alan E., "Marine Pollution under the Law of the Sea Convention," 79 *Am. J. Int'l L.* 347 (1985).

"Dispute Settlement and the Law of the Sea Convention: Problems of Fragmentation and Jurisdiction," 46 *Int'l & Comp. L.Q.* 37 (1997).

"UNCLOS, the Marine Environment and the Settlement of Disputes," in *Competing Norms in the Law of Marine Environmental Protection – Focus on Ship Safety and Pollution Prevention* (Henrik Ringbom ed., 1997), p. 241.

Boyle, Francis Anthony, *Foundations of World Order: The Legalist Approach to International Relations, 1898–1922* (1999).

Bozcek, Boleslaw A., "Peacetime Military Activities in the Exclusive Economic Zones of Third Countries," 19 *Ocean Dev. & Int'l L.* 445 (1988).

"Peaceful Purposes Provisions of the United Nations Convention on the Law of the Sea," 20 *Ocean Dev. & Int'l L.* 359 (1989).

Breen, James H., "The 1982 Dispute Resolving Agreement: The First Step Toward Unilateral Mining Outside the Law of the Sea Convention," 14 *Ocean Dev. & Int'l L. J.* 201 (1984).

Brewer, William C., "Deep Seabed Mining: Can An Acceptable Regime Ever be Found?," 11 *Ocean Dev. & Int'l L. J.* 25 (1982).

Briggs, Herbert W., "The Optional Protocols of Geneva (1958) and Vienna (1961, 1963) Concerning the Compulsory Settlement of Disputes," in *Recueil D'études de Droit International: en Hommage à Paul Gugenheim* (1968), p. 628.

Brilmayer, Lea and Klein, Natalie, "Land and Sea: Two Sovereignty Regimes in Search of a Common Denominator," 33 *NYU J. Int'l L & Pol.* 703 (2001).

Broadus, J. M., and Hoagland III, Porter, "Conflict Resolution in the Assignment of Area Entitlements for Seabed Mining," 21 *San Diego L. Rev.* 541 (1984).

Brooke, Robert L. "The Current Status of Deep Seabed Mining," 24 *Va. J. Int'l L.* 361 (1984).

Brown, E. D., and Churchill, R. R., eds., *The UN Convention on the Law of the Sea: Impact and Implementation* (1989).

Brown, E. D., "Dispute settlement and the law of the sea: the UN Convention regime," 21 *Marine Pol'y* 17 (1997).

"The M/V 'Saiga' case on prompt release of detained vessels: the first Judgment of the International Tribunal for the Law of the Sea," 22 *Marine Pol'y* 307 (1998).

Brownlie, Ian, "The Relation of Law and Power," in *Contemporary Problems of International Law: Essays in Honour of Georg Schwarzenberger* (Bin Cheng and E. D. Brown eds., 1988), p. 19.

"The Peaceful Settlement of International Disputes in Practice," 7 *Pace Int'l L. Rev.* 257 (1995).

Brus, Marcel M. T. A., *Third Party Dispute Settlement in an Interdependent World* (1995).

Burke, Karin M., and DeLeo, Deborah A., "Innocent Passage and Transit Passage in the United Nations Convention on the Law of the Sea," 9 *Yale J. World Pub. Ord.* 389 (1983).

Burke, William T., "Some Comments on the 1958 Conventions," in *Proceedings of the American Society of International Law at its Fifty-Third Annual Meeting, April 30–May 2, 1959* (1959), p. 197.

"National Legislation on Ocean Authority Zones and the Contemporary Law of the Sea," 9 *Ocean Dev. & Int'l L.* 289 (1981).

"Exclusive Fisheries Zones and Freedom of Navigation," 20 *San Diego L. Rev.* 595 (1983).

"The Law of the Sea Convention Provisions on Conditions of Access to Fisheries Subject to National Jurisdiction," 63 *Oregon L. Rev.* 73 (1984).

The New International Law of Fisheries: UNCLOS 1982 and Beyond (1994).

"Implications for Fisheries Management of U.S. Acceptance of the 1982 Convention on the Law of the Sea," 89 *Am. J. Int'l L.* 792 (1995).

International Law of the Sea: Documents and Notes (1995).

"Evolution in the Fisheries Provisions of UNCLOS," in *Liber Amicorum Judge Shigeru Oda* (N. Ando *et al.* eds., 2002), p. 1355.

Buzan, Barry, *Seabed Politics* (1976).

"Naval Power, the Law of the Sea, and the Indian Ocean as a Zone of Peace," 5 *Marine Pol'y* 194 (1981).

Carlston, Kenneth S., *The Process of International Arbitration* (1946).

"Codification of International Arbitral Procedure," 47 *Am. J. Int'l L.* 218 (1955).

Cassese, Antonio, *International Law in a Divided World* (1986).

Castañeda, Jorge, "Negotiations on the Exclusive Economic Zone at the Third United Nations Conference on the Law of the Sea," in *Essays in International Law in Honour of Judge Manfred Lachs* 605 (Jerzy Makarczyk ed., 1984).

Chappell, D., "Conference on the Law of the Sea," 1 *Tasm. U. L. Rev.* 323 (1959).

Charney, Jonathan I., "Ocean Boundaries between Nations: A Theory for Progress," 78 *Am. J. Int'l L.* 582 (1984).

"The Law of the Deep Seabed Post UNCLOS III," 63 *Oregon L. Rev.* 19 (1984).

"The Exclusive Economic Zone and Public International Law," 15 *Ocean Dev. & Int'l L.* 233 (1985).

"The United States and the Revision of the 1982 Convention on the Law of the Sea," 23 *Ocean Dev. Int'l L.* 279 (1992).

"Progress in International Maritime Boundary Delimitation Law," 88 *Am. J. Int'l L.* 227 (1994).

"The Marine Environment and the 1982 United Nations Convention on the Law of the Sea," 28 *Int'l Law.* 879 (1994) [Charney, "Marine Environment"].

"U.S. Provisional Application of the 1994 Deep Seabed Agreement," 88 *Am. J. Int'l L.* 705 (1994).

"Entry into Force of the 1982 Convention on the Law of the Sea," 35 *Va. J. Int'l L.* 381 (1995).

"The Protection of the Marine Environment by the 1982 United Nations Convention on the Law of the Sea," 7 *Geo. Int'l Envtl. L. Rev.* 731 (1995) [Charney, "Protection of the Marine Environment"].

"The Implications of Expanding International Dispute Settlement Systems: The 1982 Convention on the Law of the Sea," 90 *Am. J. Int'l L.* 69 (1996).

"Third Party Dispute Settlement and International Law," 36 *Colum. J. Transnat'l L.* 65 (1997).

"Rocks that Cannot Sustain Human Habitation," 93 *Am. J. Int'l L.* 863 (1999).

Charney, Jonathan I., and Alexander, Lewis M., *International Maritime Boundaries* (1996).

Cheng, Bin, *General Principles of Law as Applied by International Courts and Tribunals* (1987).

Chinkin, Christine M., "Crisis and the Performance of International Agreements," 7 *Yale J. World Pub. Ord.* 177 (1981).

Christy, Jr., Francis T., "Transitions in the Management and Distribution of International Fisheries," 31 *Int'l Org.* 235 (1977).

Churchill, R. R., and Lowe, A. V., *The Law of the Sea* (1983).
  The Law of the Sea (3rd ed., 1999).
Clark, M. Wesley, *Historic Bays and Waters: A Regime of Recent Beginnings and Continued Usage* (1994).
Clingan, Thomas A., *The Law of the Sea: Ocean Law and Policy* (1994).
Collier, John, and Lowe, Vaughan, *The Settlement of Disputes in International Law: Institutions and Procedures* (1999).
Colombos, C. John, *The International Law of the Sea* (6th ed., revised, 1967).
Colson, David A., "United States Accession to the United Nations Convention on the Law of the Sea," 7 *Geo. Int'l Envtl. L. Rev.* 651 (1995).
Cooling Haerr, Roger, "The Gulf of Sidra," 24 *San Diego L. Rev.* 751 (1987).
Copes, P., "The Impact of UNCLOS III on Management of the World's Fisheries," 5 *Mar. Pol'y* 217 (1981).
Cory, Helen May, *Compulsory Arbitration of International Disputes* (1932).
Curtis, Clifton E., "The United Nations Convention on the Law of the Sea and the Marine Environment: A Non-Governmental Perspective," 7 *Geo. Int'l Envtl. L. Rev.* 739 (1995).
D'Amato, Anthony, "An Alternative to the Law of the Sea Convention," 77 *Am. J. Int'l L.* 281 (1983).
Damrosch, L. F., ed., *The International Court of Justice at a Crossroads* (1987).
De Mestral, A. L. C., "Compulsory Dispute Settlement in the Third United Nations Convention on the Law of the Sea: A Canadian Perspective," in *Contemporary Issues in International Law, Essays in Honor of Louis B. Sohn* (Thomas Buergenthal ed., 1984).
Dean, Arthur H., "The Geneva Conference on the Law of the Sea: What was Accomplished," 52 *Am. J. Int'l L.* 607 (1958).
  "Achievements at the Law of the Sea Conference," in *Proceedings of the American Society of International Law at its Fifty-Third Annual Meeting, April 30–May 2, 1959* (1959), p. 186.
  "The Second Geneva Conference on the Law of the Sea: The Fight for Freedom of the Sea," 54 *Am. J. Int'l L.* 751 (1960).
Doran, Walter F., "An Operational Commander's Perspective on the 1982 LOS Convention," 10 *Int'l J. Marine & Coastal L.* 335 (1995).
Doswald-Beck, Louise ed., *San Remo Manual on International Law Applicable to Armed Conflicts at Sea* (1995).
Duff, John Alton, "UNCLOS and the New Deep Seabed Mining Regime: The Risks of Refuting the Treaty," 19 *Suffolk Transnational L. Rev.* 1 (1995).
Dupuy, René-Jean and Vignes, Daniel, eds., *A Handbook on the New Law of the Sea* (1991).
Elias, T. O., "The Commission of Mediation, Conciliation and Arbitration of the Organization of African Unity," 40 *Brit. Y. B. Int'l L.* 336 (1964).
Evans, Malcolm D., *Relevant Circumstances and Maritime Delimitation* (1989).
  "Maritime Delimitation and Expanding Categories of Relevant Circumstances," 40 *Int'l & Comp. L.Q.* 1 (1990).

"The Southern Bluefin Tuna Dispute: Provisional Thinking on Provisional Measures?," 10 Y. B. Int'l Envtl L. 7 (1999) [Evans, "Southern Bluefin Tuna"].

Evriviades, Euripides L., "The Third World's Approach to the Deep Seabed," 11 Ocean Dev. & Int'l L. J. 201 (1982).

Fabra, Adriana, "The LOSC and the Implementation of the Precautionary Principle," 10 Y.B. Int'l Envtl L. 15 (1999).

Falk, R. A., "Realistic Horizons for International Adjudication," 11 Va. J. Int'l L. 314 (1970–71).

Fentress, Marvin A., "Maritime Boundary Dispute Settlement: The Nonemergence of Guiding Principles," 15 Ga. J. Int'l & Comp. L. 591 (1985).

Fitzmaurice, Gerald, "Some Results of the Geneva Conference on the Law of the Sea: Part 1 – The Territorial Sea and Contiguous Zone and Related Topics," 8 Int'l & Comp. L.Q. 73 (1959).

Fox, H., "States and the Undertaking to Arbitrate," 37 Int'l & Comp. L.Q. 1 (1988).

Francioni, Francesco, "Peacetime Use of Force, Military Activities, and the New Law of the Sea," 18 Cornell Int'l L. J. 203 (1985).

Franckx, Eric, "'Reasonable Bond' in the Practice of the International Tribunal for the Law of the Sea," 32 Cal. W. Int'l L. J. 303 (2002).

Franklin, Carl M., "The Law of the Sea: Some Recent Developments (With Particular Reference to the United Nations Conference of 1958)," 53 Int'l L. Studies 1 (1959–60).

Freestone, David, "The Effective Conservation and Management of High Seas Living Resources: Towards a New Regime?," 5 Canterbury L. Rev. 341 (1994).

Friedham, Robert L., and Durch, William J., "The International Seabed Resources Agency Negotiations and the New International Economic Order," 31 Int'l Org. 343 (1977).

Friedman, A. G., and Williams, C. A., "The Group of 77 at the United Nations: An Emergent Force in the Law of the Sea," 16 San Diego L. Rev. 555 (1978–79).

Gaertner, Marianne P., "The Dispute Settlement Provisions of the Convention on the Law of the Sea: Critique and Alternatives to the International Tribunal for the Law of the Sea," 19 San Diego L. Rev. 577 (1982).

Galdorisi, George, "The United Nations Convention on the Law of the Sea: A National Security Perspective," 89 Am. J. Int'l L. 208 (1995).

"The United States Freedom of Navigation Program: A Bridge for International Compliance with the 1982 United Nations Convention on the law of the Sea," 27 Ocean Dev. & Int'l L. 399 (1996).

Gamble, Jr., John King, "The Law of the Sea Conference: Dispute Settlement in Perspective," 9 Vand J. Int'l L. 323 (1976).

"Assessing the Reality of the Deep Seabed Regime," 22 San Diego L. Rev. 779 (1985).

"The 1982 UN Convention on the Law of the Sea: Binding Dispute Settlement?," 9 B. U. Int'l L.J. 39 (1991).

Gautier, Phillipe, "Interim Measures of Protection Before the International Tribunal for the Law of the Sea," in Current Marine Environmental Issues and *the International Tribunal for the Law of the Sea* (Myron H. Nordquist and John Norton Moore eds., 2001), p. 243.

Gioia, Andrea, "Tunisia's Claims over Adjacent Seas and the Doctrine of 'Historic Rights,'" 11 *Syr. J. Int'l L. & Com.* 327 (1984).

Gonsiorowski, M., "Political Arbitration under the General Act of Pacific Settlement of Disputes," 27 *Am. J. Int'l L.* 469 (1933).

Gray, Christine, and Kingsbury, Benedict, "Developments in Dispute Settlement Inter-State Arbitration Since 1945," 63 *Brit. Y.B. Int'l L.* 97 (1992).

Grolin, Jesper, "The Future of the Law of the Sea: Consequences of a Non-Treaty or Non-Universal Treaty Situation," 13 *Ocean Dev. & Int'l L. J.* 1 (1983).

Grotius, Hugo, *The Freedom of the Seas or the Right which Belongs to the Dutch to Take Part in the East Indian Trade* (Ralph Magoffin trans., James Brown Scott ed., Oxford Univ. Press 1916) (1633).

   The Rights of War and Peace (A. C. Campbell trans., Introduction by David J. Hill, Universal Classic Library ed., 1901) (1646).

Grunawalt, Richard J., "United States Policy on International Straits," 18 *Ocean Dev. & Int'l L.* 445 (1987).

Guillaume, Gilbert, "The Future of International Judicial Institutions," 44 *Int'l & Comp. L.Q.* 849 (1995).

Gutteridge, J. A. C., "The 1958 Geneva Convention on the Continental Shelf," 35 *Brit. Y.B. Int'l L.* 102 (1959).

Hafetz, Jonathan L., "Fostering Protection of the Marine Environment and Economic Development: Article 121(3) of the Third Law of the Sea Convention," 15 *Am. U. Int'l L. Rev.* 584 (2000).

Haggard, Stephan, and Simmons, Beth A., "Theories of International Regimes," 41 *Int'l Org.* 491 (1987).

Hardy, Michael, "The Law of the Sea and the Prospects for Deep Seabed Mining: The Position of the European Community," 17 *Ocean Dev. & Int'l L. J.* 309 (1986).

Harlow, Bruce A., "UNCLOS III and Conflict Management in Straits," 15 *Ocean Dev. & Int'l L.* 197 (1985).

Hayashi, Moritaka, "Japan and Deep Seabed Mining," 17 *Ocean Dev. & Int'l L. J.* 351 (1986).

   "The Southern Bluefin Tuna Cases: Prescription of Provisional Measures by the International Tribunal for the Law of the Sea," 13 *Tul. Envtl L. J.* 361 (2000).

Heintschel von Heinegg, Wolff, "The Law of Armed Conflict at Sea," in *Handbook of Humanitarian Law in Armed Conflicts* (Dieter Fleck ed., 1995), p. 403.

Horowitz, Deborah, "The Catch of Poseidon's Trident: The Fate of High Seas Fisheries in the Southern Bluefin Tuna Case," 25 *Melb. Univ. L.R.* 810 (2001).

Howe, Nick, "ITLOS – A Practitioner's Perspective," in *Current Marine Environmental Issues and the International Tribunal for the Law of the Sea* (Myron H. Nordquist and John Norton Moore eds., 2001), p. 159.

Hudson, Manley O., "The First Conference for the Codification of International Law," 24 *Am. J. Int'l L.* 447 (1930).

International Tribunals: Past and Future (1944).

Hurst, Sir Cecil, "Whose is the Sea Bed?," 4 *Brit. Y.B. Int'l L.* 34 (1923–24).

Hutchinson, D. N., "The seaward limit to continental shelf jurisdiction in customary international law," 56 *Brit. Y.B. Int'l L.* 112 (1986).

International Maritime Organization, *Guidance for Ships Transiting Archipelagic Waters*, IMO SN/Circ.206, January 8, 1999.

Irwin, P. C., "Settlement of Maritime Boundary Disputes: An Analysis of the Law of the Sea Negotiations," 8 *Ocean Dev. & Int'l L.* 51 (1980)

Jacovides, Andreas J., "Peaceful Settlement of Disputes in Ocean Conflicts: Does UNCLOS III Point the Away?," in *Contemporary Issues in International Law, Essays in Honor of Louis B. Sohn* (Thomas Buergenthal ed., 1984), p. 165.

Jaenicke, Günther, "Dispute Settlement under the Convention on the Law of the Sea," 43 *Zeitschrift für ausländisches öffentliches Recht und Völkerrecht* 813 (1983).

Jagota, S. P., *Maritime Boundary* (1985).

Janis, Mark, *Sea Power and the Law of the Sea* (1976).

Janis, Mark W., "Dispute Settlement in the Law of the Sea Convention: The Military Activities Exception," 4 *Ocean Dev. & Int'l L.* 51 (1977).

Jenks, C. Wilfred, *The Prospects of International Adjudication* (1964).

Jennings, Robert Y., "The Principles Governing Marine Boundaries," in *Staat und Völkerrechtsordnung: Festschrift für Karl Doehring* (Kay Hailbronner *et al.* eds., 1989), p. 397.

Jessup, Philip, *The Law of Territorial Waters and Maritime Jurisdiction* (1927).

Jessup, Philip C., "The International Law Commission's 1954 Report on the Regime of the Territorial Sea," 49 *Am. J. Int'l L.* 221 (1955).

"Geneva Conference on the Law of the Sea: A Study in International Law-Making," 52 *Am. J. Int'l L.* 730 (1958).

"The United Nations Conference on the Law of the Sea," 59 *Colum. L. Rev.* 234 (1959).

"The Law of the Sea Around Us," 55 *Am. J. Int'l L.* 104 (1961).

Johnson, D. H. N., "The Preparation of the 1958 Geneva Conference on the Law of the Sea," 8 *Int'l & Comp. L.Q.* 123 (1959).

"International Arbitration Back in Favour?," 34 *Y.B. World Aff.* 305 (1980).

Johnston, Douglas M., "Fishery Diplomacy and Science and the Judicial Function," 10 *Y.B. Int'l Envtl L.* 33 (1999).

Jones, William B., "Risk Assessment: Corporate Ventures in Deep Seabed Mining Outside the Framework of the UN Convention on the Law of the Sea," 16 *Ocean Dev. & Int'l L.* 241 (1986).

Joyner, Christopher C., "Compliance and Enforcement in New International Fisheries Law," 12 *Temp. Int'l & Comp. L.J.* 271 (1998).

Juda, Lawrence, "The Exclusive Economic Zone: Compatibility of National Claims and the UN Convention on the Law of the Sea," 16 *Ocean Dev. & Int'l L.* 1 (1986).

Kass, S. L., "Obligatory Negotiations in International Organisations," 3 *Can. Y.B. Int'l L.* 36 (1965).

Kaye, Lawrence Wayne, "The Innocent Passage of Warships in Foreign Territorial Seas: A Threatened Freedom," 15 *San Diego L. Rev.* 573 (1978).

Keohane, Robert O., *After Hegemony: Cooperation and Discord in the World Political Economy* (1984).

International Institutions and State Power: Essays in International Relations Theory (1989).

Kibola, Hamisi S., "A Note on Africa and the Exclusive Economic Zone," 16 *Ocean Dev. & Int'l L.* 369 (1986).

Kimball, Lee, "Turning Points in the Future of Deep Seabed Mining," 17 *Ocean Dev. & Int'l L. J.* 367 (1986).

"The Law of the Sea Convention and Marine Environment Protection," 7 *Geo. Int'l Envtl. L. Rev.* 745 (1995).

Kindt, John Warren, "Dispute Settlement in International Environmental Issues: The Model Provided by the 1982 Convention on the Law of the Sea," 22 *Vand. J. Transnat'l L.* 1097 (1989).

Knight, H. G., *Consequences of Non-Agreement at the Third UN Law of the Sea Conference* (1976).

Koh, Kwang Lim, "The Continental Shelf and the International Law Commission," 35 *B.U. L. Rev.* 523 (1955).

Koh, Tommy T. B., "Negotiating a New World Order for the Sea," 24 *Va. J. Int'l L.* 761 (1984).

Krasner, Stephen D., "Structural Causes and Regime Consequences: Regimes as Intervening Variables," in *International Regimes* (Stephen D. Krasner ed., 1983), p. 1.

Kronmiller, T., *The Lawfulness of Deep Seabed Mining* (1980).

Kwiatkowska, Barbara, *The 200 Mile Exclusive Economic Zone in the New Law of the Sea* (1989).

"The High Seas Fisheries Regime: at a Point of No Return?," 8 *Int'l J. Marine & Coastal L.* 327 (1993).

"Inauguration of the ITLOS Jurisprudence: The Saint Vincent and the Grenadines v. Guinea M/V Saiga Case," 30 *Ocean Dev. & Int'l L.* 43 (1999).

"The Southern Bluefin Tuna (New Zealand v Japan; Australia v Japan) Cases," 15 *Int'l J. Marine & Coastal L.* 1 (2000) [Kwiatkowska, "Southern Bluefin Tuna Cases"].

"Southern Bluefin Tuna (Australia and New Zealand v. Japan). Jurisdiction and Admissibility," 95 *Am. J. Int'l L.* 162 (2001) [Kwiatkowska, "Jurisdiction and Admissibility"].

"The Australia and New Zealand v. Japan Southern Bluefin Tuna (Jurisdiction and Admissibility) Award of the First Law of the Sea Convention Annex VII Arbitral Tribunal," 16 *Int'l J. Marine & Coastal L.* 239 (2001) [Kwiatkowska, "First Award"].

Kwiatkowska, Barbara, and Soons, Alfred H. A., "Entitlement to Maritime Areas of Rocks Which Cannot Sustain Human Habitation of Economic Life of Their Own," 21 *Neth. Y.B. Int'l L.* 139 (1990).

Laing, Edward Arthur, "ITLOS Procedures and Practices: Bonds," in *Current Marine Environmental Issues and the International Tribunal for the Law of the Sea* (Myron H. Nordquist and John Norton Moore eds., 2001), p. 113.

Larson, David L., "Security Issues and the Law of the Sea: A General Framework," 15 *Ocean Dev. & Int'l L.* 99 (1985).

"Deep Seabed Mining: A Definition of the Problem," 17 *Ocean Dev. & Int'l L.* 271 (1986).

"Innocent, Transit, and Archipelagic Sea Lanes Passage," 18 *Ocean Dev. & Int'l L.* 411 (1987).

"Naval Weaponry and the Law of the Sea," 18 *Ocean Dev. & Int'l L.* 125 (1987).

Laslo, Ervin *et al.*, *The Objectives of the New International Economic Order* (1979).

Lauterpacht, Eli, "The First Decision of the International Tribunal for the Law of the Sea: The M/V Saiga," in *Liber Amicorum Professor Ignaz Seidl-Hohenveldern* (Gerhard Hafner *et al.* eds., 1998), p. 395.

Lauterpacht, Hersch, "Sovereignty Over Submarine Areas," 27 *Brit. Y.B. Int'l L.* 376 (1950).

Leich, Marian Nash, "U.S. Practice, Indonesia: Archipelagic Waters," 83 *Am. J. Int'l L.* 558 (1989).

Lillich, Richard B., and Brower, Charles N., eds., *International Arbitration in the 21st Century: Towards "Judicialization" and Uniformity?: the Twelfth Sokol Colloquium* (1994).

Lowe, A. V., "The Commander's Handbook on the Law of Naval Operations and the Contemporary Law of the Sea," in 64 *International Law Studies: The Law of Naval Operations* (Horace B. Robertson ed., 1991), p. 111.

Lowe, Vaughan, "The Impact of the Law of the Sea on Naval Warfare," 14 *Syracuse J. Int'l L. & Comm.* 657 (1988).

"The M/V Saiga: The First Case in the International Tribunal for the Law of the Sea," 48 *Int'l & Comp. L. Q.* 187 (1999).

Malia, Gerald A., "The New 'International Tribunal for the Law of the Sea': Prospects for Dispute Resolution at the 'Sea Court,'" 7 *Geo. Int'l Envtl. L. Rev.* 791 (1995).

Malone, James L., "The United States and the Law of the Sea," 24 *Va. J. Int'l L.* 785, 785–86 (1984).

Mangone, Gerard J., "Straits Used for International Navigation," 18 *Ocean Dev. & Int'l L.* 391 (1987).

Manley, Robert H., "The Geneva Conferences on the Law of the Sea as a Step in the International Law-Making Process," 25 *Alb. L. Rev.* 17 (1961).

Manner, Eero J., "Settlement of Sea-Boundary Delimitation Disputes According to the Provisions of the 1982 Law of the Sea Convention," in *Essays in International Law in Honour of Judge Manfred Lachs* (Jerzy Makarczyk ed., 1984), p. 625.

de Marfy, Annick, "The Pardo Declaration and the Six Years of the Sea-Bed Committee," in 1 *A Handbook on the New Law of the Sea* (René-Jean Dupuy and Daniel Vignes eds., 1991), p. 144.

Martin, Will, "Fisheries Conservation and Management of Straddling Stocks and Highly Migratory Stocks under the UN Convention on the Law of the Sea," 7 *Geo. Int'l Envtl. L. Rev.* 765 (1995).

Max Planck Institute, *Judicial Settlement of International Disputes* (1974).

McConnell, Moira L., and Gold, Edgar, "The Modern Law of the Sea: Framework for the Protection and Preservation of the Marine Environment?," 23 *Case W. Res. J. Int'l L.* 83 (1991).

McDorman, Ted L., "The Dispute Settlement Regime of the Straddling and Highly Migratory Fish Stocks Convention," *Canadian Y.B. Int'l L.* 57 (1997).

McDougal, Myres S., and Burke, William T., "Crisis in the Law of the Sea: Community Perspectives Versus National Egoism," 67 *Yale L. J.* 539 (1958).

The Public Order of the Oceans: A Contemporary International Law of the Sea (1962).

McDougal, Myres S., and Schlei, Norbert A., "The Hydrogen Bomb Tests in Perspective: Lawful Measures for Security," 64 *Yale L. J.* 648 (1955).

McNees, Richard B., "Freedom of Transit Through International Straits," 6 *J. Mar. L. & Com.* 175 (1974–75).

McNeill, John H., "The Strategic Significance of the Law of the Sea Convention," 7 *Geo. Int'l Envtl. L. Rev.* 703 (1995).

Meltzer, Evelyne, "Global Overview of Straddling and Highly Migratory Fish Stocks: The Nonsustainable Nature of High Seas Fisheries," 25 *Ocean Dev. & Int'l L.* 255 (1994).

Merrills, J. G., *International Dispute Settlement* (3rd ed., 1998).

Miles, Edward, "The Structure and Effects of the Decision Process in the Seabed Committee and the Third United Nations Conference on the Law of the Sea," 31 *Int'l Org.* 159 (1977).

Miles, Edward L., and Burke, William T., "Pressures on the United Nations Convention on the Law of the Sea of 1982 Arising from New Fisheries Conflicts," 20 *Ocean Dev. & Int'l L.* 343 (1989).

Mirvahabi, Farin, "Fishery Disputes Settlement and the Third United Nations Conference on the Law of the Sea," 57 *Revue de Droit Int'l de Sciences Diplomatiques et Politiques* 45 (1979).

Molitor, Michael R., "The U.S. Deep Seabed Mining Regulations: The Legal Basis for an Alternative Regime," 19 *San Diego L. Rev.* 599 (1982).

Molitor, Steven J., "The Provisional Understanding Regarding Deep Seabed Matters: An Ill-Conceived Regime for U.S. Deep Seabed Mining," 20 *Cornell Int'l L. J.* 223 (1987).

Moore, John Norton, "The Regime of Straits and the Third United Nations Conference on the Law of the Sea," 74 *Am. J. Int'l L.* 77 (1980).

"The United Nations Convention on the Law of the Sea and the Rule of Law," 7 *Geo. Int'l Envtl. L. Rev.* 645 (1995).

Morgan, Donald L., "A Practitioner's Critique of the Order Granting Provisional Measures in the Southern Bluefin Tuna Cases," in *Current Marine Environmental Issues and the International Tribunal for the Law of the Sea* (Myron H. Nordquist and John Norton Moore eds., 2001), p. 173.

"Emerging Fora for International Litigation (Part 1): Implications of the Proliferation of International Legal Fora: The Example of the Southern Bluefin Tuna Cases," 43 *Harv. Int'l L.J.* 541 (2002).

Morgenthau, Hans, *Politics Among Nations* (5th ed., 1973).

Morris, Hugh G., "The Continental Shelf – An International Dilemma," 1 *Osgoode Hall L. J.* 37 (1958).

Morris, Michael A., "The New International Economic Order and the New Law of the Sea," in *The New International Economic Order – Confrontation or Cooperation between North and South?* (Karl P. Sauvant and Hajo Hasenpflug eds., 1977), p. 175–89.

Morrison, Fred L., "The Future of International Adjudication," 75 *Minn. L. Rev.* 827 (1991).

Moss, Ronald Scott, "Insuring Unilaterally Licensed Deep Seabed Mining Operations Against Adverse Rulings by the International Court of Justice: An Assessment of the Risks," 14 *Ocean Dev. & Int'l L. J.* 161 (1984).

Munkman, A. L. W., "Adjudication and Adjustment – International Judicial Decision and the Settlement of Territorial and Boundary Disputes," 46 *Brit. Y.B. Int'l L.* 1 (1972–73).

Murphy, C. F., "The World Court and the Peaceful Settlement of Disputes," 7 *Ga. J. Int. & Comp. L.* 551 (1977).

Nandan, Satya N., "Legislative and Executive Powers of the International Seabed Authority for the Implementation of the Law of the Sea Convention," in *Order for the Oceans at the Turn of the Century* (Davor Vidas and Willy Østreng eds., 1999), p. 73.

Ndiaye, Tafsir Malick, "Provisional Measures Before the International Tribunal for the Law of the Sea," in *Current Marine Environmental Issues and the International Tribunal for the Law of the Sea* (Myron H. Nordquist and John Norton Moore eds., 2001), p. 95.

Nelson, L. D. M., "The Roles of Equity in the Delimitation of Maritime Boundaries," 84 *Am. J. Int'l L.* 837 (1990).

Nordquist, Myron H. *et al.* eds., *United Nations Convention on the Law of the Sea 1982: A Commentary* (1989).

Northedge, F. S., and Donelan, M. D., *International Disputes: The Political Aspects* (1971).

Noyes, John E., "Compulsory Third-Party Adjudication and the 1982 United Nations Convention on the Law of the Sea," 4 *Conn. J. Int'l L.* 675 (1989).

"The International Tribunal for the Law of the Sea," 32 *Cornell Int'l L.J.* 109 (1999).

O'Connell, D. P., "The Geneva Conference on the Law of the Sea: Possible Implications for Australia," 32 *Australian L. J.* 134 (1958).

The Influence of Law on Sea Power (1975).

The International Law of the Sea (I. A. Shearer ed., 1984).

Oda, Shigeru, "The Territorial Sea and Natural Resources," 4 *Int'l & Comp. L.Q.* 415 (1955).

"A Reconsideration of the Continental Shelf Doctrine," 32 *Tul. L. Rev.* 21 (1957).

"Fisheries under the United Nations Convention on the Law of the Sea," 77 *Am. J. Int'l L.* 739 (1983).

"Some Reflections on the Dispute Settlement Clauses in the United Nations Convention on the Law of the Sea," in *Essays in International Law in Honour of Judge Manfred Lachs* (Jerzy Makarczyk ed., 1984), p. 645.

"Dispute Settlement Prospects in the Law of the Sea," 44 *Int'l & Comp. L.Q.* 863 (1995).

Oellers-Frahm, Karin, "Interim Measures of Protection," in 1 *Encyclopedia of Public International Law* (Rudolph Bernhardt ed., 1986), p. 70.

Örebech, Peter, Sigurjonsson, Ketill, and McDorman, Ted L., "The 1995 United Nations Straddling and Highly Migratory Fish Stocks Agreement: Management, Enforcement and Dispute Settlement," 13 *Int'l J. Marine & Coastal L.* 119 (1998).

Orrego Vicuña, Francisco ed., *The Exclusive Economic Zone: A Latin American Perspective* (1984).

"The Contribution of the Exclusive Economic Zone to the Law of Maritime Delimitation," 31 *German Y.B. Int'l L.* 120 (1988).

The Exclusive Economic Zone: Regime and Legal Nature under International Law (1989).

Oude Elferink, Alex G., "The Impact of the Law of the Sea Convention on the Delimitation of Maritime Boundaries," in *Order for the Oceans at the Turn of the Century* (Davor Vidas and Willy Østreng eds., 1999), p. 457.

Oxman, Bernard H., "The Third United Nations Conference on the Law of the Sea: The 1976 New York Session," 71 *Am. J. Int'l L.* 247 (1977).

"The Third United Nation's Conference on the Law of the Sea: The 1977 New York Session," 72 *Am. J. Int'l L.* 57 (1978).

"The Third United Nations Conference on the Law of the Sea: The Seventh Session (1978)," 73 *Am. J. Int'l L.* 1 (1979).

"The Third United Nations Conference on the Law of the Sea: The Eighth Session (1979)," 74 *Am. J. Int'l L.* 1 (1980).

"The Third United Nations Conference on the Law of the Sea: The Ninth Session (1980)," 75 *Am. J. Int'l L.* 211 (1981).

"The Third United Nations Conference on the Law of the Sea: The Tenth Session," 76 *Am. J. Int'l L.* 1 (1982).

"The Regime of Warships Under the United Nations Convention on the Law of the Sea," 24 *Va. J. Int'l L.* 809 (1984).

"The High Seas and the International Seabed Area," 10 *Mich. J. Int'l L.* 526 (1989) [Oxman, "International Seabed Area"].

"Commentary," in *Implementation of the Law of the Sea Convention Through International Institutions* (Alfred H. A. Soons ed., 1990), p. 648 [Oxman, "Commentary"].

"International Law and Naval and Air Operations," in 64 *International Law Studies: The Law of Naval Operations* (Horace B. Robertson ed., 1991), p. 19.

"The 1994 Agreement and the Convention," 88 *Am. J. Int'l L.* 687 (1994) [Oxman, "1994 Agreement and the Convention"].

"International Maritime Boundaries: Political, Strategic, and Historical Considerations," 26 *U. Miami Inter-Am. L. Rev.* 243 (1994–95).

"Observations on Vessel Release under the United Nations Convention on the Law of the Sea," 11 *Int'l J. Marine & Coastal L.* 201 (1996).

"The 1994 Agreement relating to the Implementation of the UN Convention on the Law of the Sea," in *Order for the Oceans at the Turn of the Century* (Davor Vidas and Willy Østreng eds., 1999), p. 15 [Oxman, "1994 Agreement relating to Implementation"].

"Complementary Agreements & Compulsory Jurisdiction," 95 *Am. J. Int'l L.* 277 (2001).

Oxman, Bernard H., and Bantz, Vincent P., "The 'Camouco' (Panama v. France) (Judgment)," 94 *Am. J. Int'l L.* 713 (2000).

Pardo, Arvid, and Borgese, Elizabeth Mann, *The New International Economic Order and the Law of the Sea* (1976).

Pauwelyn, Joost, "The Concept of a 'Continuing Violation' of an International Obligation: Selected Problems," 66 *Brit. Y.B. Int'l L.* 415, 435 (1995).

Pharand, Donat, *Canada's Arctic Waters in International Law* (1988).

Phillips, J. C., "The Exclusive Economic Zone as a Concept in International Law," 26 *Int'l & Comp. L. Q.* 585 (1977).

Picard, M. Johanne, "International Law of Fisheries and Small Developing States: A Call for the Recognition of Regional Hegemony," 31 *Texas Int'l L.J.* 317 (1996).

Pierce, George A., "Dispute Settlement Mechanisms in the Draft Convention on the Law of the Sea," 10 *Denv. J. Int'l L. & Pol.* 331 (1981).

Pirtle, Charles E., "Transit Rights and U.S. Security Interests in International Straits: The 'Straits Debate' Revisited," 5 *Ocean Dev. & Int'l L.* 477 (1978).

Politakis, George P., *Modern Aspects of the Laws of Naval Warfare and Maritime Neutrality* (1998).

Pontecorvo, Guilio, "Musing About Seabed Mining, or Why What We Don't Know Can't Hurt Us," 21 *Ocean Dev. & Int'l L.* 117 (1990).

Poulantzas, Nicholas M., *The Right of Hot Pursuit in International Law* (1969).

Powers, Jr., Robert D., and Hardy, Leonard R., "How Wide the Territorial Sea?," 53 *Int'l L. Studies*, Appendix N, p. 305 (1959–60).

Prescott, Michael K., "How War Affects Treaties between Belligerents: A Case Study of the Gulf War," 7 *Emory Int'l L. Rev.* 192 (1993).

Ralston, Jackson H., *The Law and Procedure of International Tribunals* (1926).

Rao, P. Sreenivasa, "Legal Regulation of Maritime Military Uses," 13 *Indian J. Int'l L.* 425 (1973).

Rauch, Elmar, "Military Uses of the Oceans" [1984] 28 *German Y.B. Int'l L.* 229 (1985).

Reeves, Jesse S., "The Codification of the Law of Territorial Waters," 24 *Am. J. Int'l L.* 486 (1930).

Reisman, W. Michael, "The Regime of Straits and National Security: An Appraisal of International Lawmaking," 74 *Am. J. Int'l L.* 48 (1980).

"Eritrea-Yemen Arbitration (Award, Phase II: Maritime Delimitation)," 94 *Am. J. Int'l L.* 721 (2000) [Reisman, *Eritrea-Yemen*].

Reisman, W. Michael, and Westerman, Gayl S., *Straight Baselines in Maritime Boundary Delimitation* (1992).

Reubens, Edwin P., "An Overview of the NIEO," in *The Challenge of the New International Economic Order* (Edwin P. Reubens ed., 1981), p. 1.

Reuland, Robert C., "The Customary Right of Hot Pursuit onto the High Seas: Annotations to Article 111 of the Law of the Sea Convention," 33 *Va. J. Int'l L.* 557 (1993).

Rhee, Sang-Myon, "Sea Boundary Delimitation Between States before World War II," 76 *Am. J. Int'l L.* 555, 556 (1982).

Richardson, Elliot L., "Power, Mobility and the Law of the Sea," 58 *Foreign Aff.* 902 (1979–80).

"Law of the Sea: Navigation and Other Traditional National Security Considerations," 19 *San Diego L. Rev.* 553 (1982).

"Dispute Settlement under the Convention on the Law of the Sea: A Flexible and Comprehensive Extension of the Rule of the Law to Ocean Space," in *Contemporary Issues in International Law, Essays in Honor of Louis B. Sohn* (Thomas Buergenthal ed., 1984), p. 149.

"The Case for the Convention," in *The 1982 Convention on the Law of the Sea* (Albert W. Koers and Bernard H. Oxman eds., 1984), p. 4.

Riphagen, W., "Dispute Settlement in the 1982 United Nations Convention on the Law of the Sea," in *The New Law of the Sea* (C. L. Rozakis and C. A. Stephanou eds., 1983), p. 281.

Roach, J. Ashley, "Dispute Settlement in Specific Situations," 7 *Geo. Int'l Envtl. L. Rev.* 775 (1995).

Robertson, Horace B., "Navigation in the Exclusive Economic Zone," 24 *Va. J. Int'l L.* 865 (1984).

Romano, Cesare, "The Southern Bluefin Tuna Dispute: Hints of a World to Come . . . Like It or Not," 32 *Ocean Dev. & Int'l L.* 313 (2001).

Ronzitti, N., ed., *The Law of Naval Warfare: A Collection of Agreements and Documents with Commentaries* (1988).

Rosen, Mark E., "Military Mobility and the 1982 UN Law of the Sea Convention," 7 *Geo. Int'l Envtl L. Rev.* 717 (1995).

Rosenne, Shabtai, ed., *League of Nations, Conference for the Codification of International Law [1930]* (1975).

"Settlement of Fisheries Disputes in the Exclusive Economic Zone," 73 *Am. J. Int'l L.* 89 (1979).

"Establishing the International Tribunal for the Law of the Sea," 89 *Am. J. Int'l L.* 806 (1995).

"International Tribunal for the Law of the Sea: 1998 Survey," 14 *Int'l J. Marine & Coastal L.* 453 (1999).

"Historic Waters in the Third United Nations Conference on the Law of the Sea," in *Reflections on Principles and Practice of International Law: Essays in Honour of Leo J. Bouchez* (Terry D. Gill and Wybo P. Heere eds., 2000), p. 191.

"The International Tribunal for the Law of the Sea: Survey for 1999," 15 *Int'l J. Marine & Coastal L.* 443 (2000).

"The Case-Law of ITLOS (1997–2001): An Overview," in *Current Marine Environmental Issues and the International Tribunal for the Law of the Sea* (Myron H. Nordquist and John Norton Moore, eds., 2001), p. 127.

Sands, Phillipe, "ITLOS: An International Lawyer's Perspective," in *Current Marine Environmental Issues and the International Tribunal for the Law of the Sea* (Myron H. Nordquist and John Norton Moore, eds., 2001), p. 141.

Schachte, Jr., William L., "National Security: Customary International Law and the Convention on the law of the Sea," 7 *Geo. Int'l Envtl L. Rev.* 709 (1995).

Schwebel, Stephen M., "The Southern Bluefin Tuna Case," in *Liber Amicorum Judge Shigeru Oda* (N. Ando *et al.* eds., 2002), p. 743.

Scott, James Brown, *Judicial Settlement of International Disputes* (1927).

Seeberg-Elverfeldt, Niels-J, *The Settlement of Disputes in Deep Seabed Mining: Access, Jurisdiction and Procedure Before the Seabed Disputes Chamber of the International Tribunal for the Law of the Sea* (1998).

Selden, John, *Of the Dominion, Or, Ownership of the Sea* (Marchamont Nedham trans., 1972) (1635).

Sharma, Surya P., "Framework of Likely Disputes under the Law of the Sea Convention – Some Thoughts," 45 *Zeitschrift für ausländisches öffentliches Recht und Völkerrecht* 465 (1985).

Shavloske, Patrick, "The Canadian-Spanish Fishing Dispute: A Template for Assessing the Inadequacies of the United Nations Convention on the Law of the Sea and a Clarion Call for Ratification of the New Fish Stock Treaty," 7 *Ind. Int'l & Comp. L. Rev.* 223 (1996).

Shyam, Majula R., "The U. N. Convention on the Law of the Sea and Military Interests in the Indian Ocean," 15 *Ocean Dev. & Int'l L.* 147 (1985).

"Deep Seabed Mining: An Indian Perspective," 17 *Ocean Dev. & Int'l L.* 325 (1986).

Simpson, J. L. and Fox, Hazel, *International Arbitration: Law and Practice* (1959).

Singh, Gurdip, *United Nations Convention on the Law of the Sea Dispute Settlement Mechanisms* (1985).

Sohn, Louis B., "Exclusion of Political Disputes from Judicial Settlement," 38 *Am. J. Int'l L.* 694 (1944).

"The Role of International Institutions as Conflict Adjusting Agencies," 28 *U. Chi. L. Rev.* 205 (1960–61).

"The Role of International Arbitration Today," 108 *Hague Recueil des Cours* 1 (1963).

"The Role of Arbitration in Recent International Multilateral Treaties," 23 *Va. J. Int'l L.* 171 (1982–83).

"The Future of Dispute Settlement," in *The Structure and Process of International Law: Essays in Legal Philosophy, Doctrine, and Theory* (Ronald St. J. MacDonald and Douglas M. Johnston eds., 1983), p. 1121.

"Peacetime Use of Force on the High Seas," in 64 *International Law Studies: The Law of Naval Operations* (Horace B. Robertson ed., 1991), p. 38.

"International Law Implications of the 1994 Agreement," 88 *Am. J. Int'l L.* 698 (1994).

"Settlement of Law of the Sea Disputes," 10 *Int'l J. Marine & Coastal L.* 205 (1995).

Soons, Alfred H. A., *Marine Scientific Research and the Law of the Sea* (1982).

Implementation of the Law of the Sea Convention Through International Institutions (1990).

International Arbitration: Past and Prospects (1990).

Sorensen, Max, "Law of the Sea," 520 *Int'l Conciliation* 195 (1958).

Spinnato, John M., "Historic and Vital Bays: An Analysis of Libya's Claim to the Gulf of Sidra," 13 *Ocean Dev. & Int'l L.* 65 (1983).

Stephens, Dale G., "The Impact of the 1982 Law of the Sea Convention on the Conduct of Peacetime Naval/Military Operations," 29 *Calif. W. Int'l L. J.* 283 (1999).

Stevenson, John R., and Oxman, Bernard H., "The Preparations for the Law of the Sea Conference," 68 *Am. J. Int'l L.* 1 (1974).

"The Third United Nations Conference on the Law of the Sea: The 1974 Caracas Session," 69 *Am. J. Int'l L.* 1 (1975).

"The Third United Nations Conference on the Law of the Sea: The 1975 Geneva Session," 69 *Am. J. Int'l L.* 763 (1975).

"The Future of the United Nations Convention on the Law of the Sea," 88 *Am. J Int'l L.* 488 (1994).

Stuart, James Lyall, "Law of the Sea: Unilateral Licensing of Seabed Mining – Deep Sea Mining (Temporary Provisions) Act 1981, ch. 53," 23 *Harv. J. Int'l L.* 155 (1982).

Surace-Smith, Kathryn, "United States Activity Outside of the Law of the Sea Convention: Deep Seabed Mining and Transit Passage," 84 *Columbia L. Rev.* 1032 (1984).

Swan, Charles, and Ueberhorst, James, "The Conference on the Law of the Sea: A Report," 56 *Mich. L. Rev.* 1132 (1958).

Taniguchi, Chad, "Jurisdiction, Enforcement and Dispute Settlement in the Law of the Sea Convention," in *Consensus and Confrontation: the United States and the Law of the Sea Convention* (Jon M. Van Dyke ed., 1985), p. 462.

Treves, Tullio, "The Settlement of Disputes According to the Straddling Stocks Agreement of 1995," in *International Law and Sustainable Development: Past Achievements and Future Challenges* (Alan Boyle and David Freestone eds., 1999), p. 253.

  "Preliminary Proceedings in the Settlement of Disputes under the United Nations Law of the Sea Convention: Some Observations," in *Liber Amicorum Judge Shigeru Oda* (N. Ando *et al.* eds., 2002), p. 749.

Truver, Scott C., "The Law of the Sea and the Military Use of the Oceans in 2010," 45 *La. L. Rev.* 1221 (1985).

UN Division for Ocean Affairs and the Law of the Sea, *Handbook on the Delimitation of Maritime Boundaries,* UN Sales No. E.01.V.2 (2000).

US Department of State, Pub. No. 112, *Limits in the Seas: United States Responses to Excessive Maritime Claims* (1992).

Van Dyke, Jon M., *Consensus and Confrontation: the United States and the Law of the Sea Convention* (1985).

Van Dyke, Jon M., and Brooks, Robert A., "Uninhabited Islands: Their Impact on the Ownership of the Oceans' Resources," 12 *Ocean Dev. & Int'l L.* 265 (1983).

Van Dyke, Jon, and Yuen, Christopher, "'Common Heritage' v. 'Freedom of the High Seas': Which Governs the Seabed?," 19 *San Diego L. Rev.* 493 (1982).

Vorah, L. C., Askin, Kelly Dawn, and Mundis, Daryl A., "Contemporary Law Regulating Armed Conflict at Sea," in *Liber Amicorum Judge Shigeru Oda* (N. Ando *et al.* eds., 2002), p. 1523.

Waldock, C. M. H. ed., *International Disputes: The Legal Aspects* (1972).

Wang, James C. F., *Handbook on Ocean Politics and Law* (1992).

Weil, Prosper, *The Law of Maritime Delimitation – Reflections* (1989).

Whiteman, Marjorie M., "Conference on the Law of the Sea: Convention on the Continental Shelf," 52 *Am. J. Int'l L.* 629, 637 (1958).

Wilson, Robert R., "Reservation Clauses in Agreements of Obligatory Arbitration," 23 *Am. J. Int'l L.* 68 (1929).

Wisnomoerti, Noegroho, "Indonesia and the Law of the Sea," in *The Law of the Sea: Problems from the East Asian Perspective* (Choon-ho Park and Jae Kyu Park eds., 1987), p. 392.

Wolfrum, Rüdiger, "Restricting the Use of the Sea to Peaceful Purposes: Demilitarization in Being?," 24 *German Y.B. Int'l L.* 200 (1981).

Yankov, Alexander, "Current Fisheries Disputes and the International Tribunal for the Law of the Sea," in *Current Marine Environmental Issues and the International Tribunal for the Law of the Sea* (Myron H. Nordquist and John Norton Moore eds., 2001), p. 223.

  "Irregularities in Fishing Activities and the Role of the International Tribunal for the Law of the Sea," in *Liber Amicorum Judge Shigeru Oda* (N. Ando *et al.* eds., 2002), p. 773.

Young, Oran R., "International Regimes: Toward a New Theory of Institutions," 39 *World Pol.* 104 (1986).

Young, Richard, "The Geneva Convention on the Continental Shelf: A First Impression," 52 *Am. J. Int'l L.* 733 (1958).

Zedalis, Rex J., "Military Uses of the Ocean Space and the Developing International Law of the Sea: An Analysis in the Context of Peacetime ASW," 16 *San Diego L. Rev.* 575 (1979).

    "'Peaceful Purposes' and Other Relevant Provisions of the Revised Composite Negotiating Text: A Comparative Analysis of the Existing and Proposed Military Regime for the High Seas," 7 *Syracuse J. Int'l L and Com.* 1 (1979).

"Harvard Research in International Law, Law of Treaties," 29 *Am. J. Int'l L. Supp.* 653 (1935).

"Statement by Expert Panel: U.S. Policy on the Settlement of Disputes in the Law of the Sea," 81 *Am. J. Int'l L.* 438 (1987).

"Territorial Seas and Fisheries Disputes," *Solicitors J.* 849 (1959).

"The Effects of Armed Conflicts on Treaties," 61-II *Y.B. Inst. Int'l L.* 199 (1986).

UNITED NATIONS MATERIALS

GA Res. 900, UN GAOR, 9th Sess., Supp. No. 21, at 51, UN Doc. A/2890 (1954).

Report of the International Technical Conference on the Conservation of the Living Resources of the Sea to the International Law Commission, UN Doc. A/CONF.10/5/Rev.2 (1955).

Documents of the Second Session including the Report of the Commission to the General Assembly, [1950] 2 Y.B. Int'l L. Comm'n, UN Doc. A/CN.4/Ser.A/1950/Add.1, UN Sales No. 1957.V.3, vol. II (1957).

Summary Records of the Second Session, [1950] 1 Y.B. Int'l L. Comm'n, UN Doc. A/CN.4/SER.A/1950, UN Sales No. 1957.V.3, vol. I (1958).

Summary Records of the Third Session, [1951] 1 Y.B. Int'l L. Comm'n, UN Doc. A/CN.4/SER.A/1951, UN Sales No. 1957.V.6, vol. I (1957).

Documents of the Third Session including the Report of the Commission to the General Assembly, [1951] 2 Y.B. Int'l L. Comm'n, UN Doc. A/CN.4/Ser.A/1951/Add.1, UN Sales No. 1957.V.6, vol. II (1957).

Summary Records of the Fourth Session, [1952] 1 Y.B. Int'l L. Comm'n, UN Doc. A/CN.4/Ser.A/1952, UN Sales No. 58.V.5, vol. I (1958).

Documents of the Fourth Session including the Report of the Commission to the General Assembly, [1952] 2 Y.B. Int'l L. Comm'n, UN Doc. A/CN.4/SER.A/1952/Add.1, UN Sales No. 58.V.5, vol. II (1958).

Summary Records of the Fifth Session, [1953] 1 Y.B. Int'l L. Comm'n, UN Doc. A/CN.4/SER.A/1953, UN Sales No. 59.V.4, vol. I (1959).

Documents of the Fifth Session including the Report of the Commission to the General Assembly, [1953] 2 Y.B. Int'l L. Comm'n, UN Doc. A/CN.4/Ser.A/1953/Add.1, UN Sales No. 59.V.4, vol. II (1959).

Summary Records of the Sixth Session, [1954] 1 Y.B. Int'l L. Comm'n, UN Doc. A/CN.4/SER.A/1954, UN Sales No. 59.V.7, vol. I (1959).

Documents of the Sixth Session including the Report of the Commission to the General Assembly, [1954] 2 Y.B. Int'l L. Comm'n, UN Doc. A/CN.4/Ser.A/1954/Add.1, UN Sales No. 59.V.7, vol. II (1960).

Summary Records of the Seventh Session, [1955] 1 Y.B. Int'l L. Comm'n, UN Doc. A/CN.4/SER.A/1955, UN Sales No. 60.V.3, vol. I (1960).

Documents of the Seventh Session including the Report of the Commission to the General Assembly, [1955] 2 Y.B. Int'l L. Comm'n, UN Doc. A/CN.4/SER.A/1955/Add.1, UN Sales No. 60.V.3, vol. II (1960).

Summary Records of the Eighth Session, [1956] 1 Y.B. Int'l L. Comm'n, UN Doc. A/CN.4/SER.A/1956, UN Sales No. 1956.V.3, vol. I (1956).

Documents of the Eighth Session including the Report of the Commission to the General Assembly, [1956] 2 Y.B. Int'l L. Comm'n, UN Doc. A/CN.4/Ser.A/1956/Add.1, UN Sales No. 1956.V.3, vol. II (1957).

GA Res. 1105, UN GAOR, 11th Sess., Supp. No. 17, at 54, UN Doc. A/3572 (1957).

GA Res. 1307, UN GAOR, 13th Sess., Supp. No. 18, at 54, UN Doc. A/4090 (1958).

United Nations Conference on the Law of the Sea, Preparatory Documents, UN Doc. A/CONF.13/37, UN Sales No. 58.V.4, vol. I (1958).

United Nations Conference on the Law of the Sea, Plenary Meetings, UN Doc. A/CONF.13/38, UN Sales No. 58.V.4, vol. II (1958).

United Nations Conference on the Law of the Sea, 1st Comm., UN Doc. A/CONF.13/39, UN Sales No. 58.V.4, vol. III (1958).

United Nations Conference on the Law of the Sea, 2nd Comm., UN Doc. A/CONF.13/40, UN Sales No. 58.V.4, vol. IV (1958).

United Nations Conference on the Law of the Sea, 3rd Comm., UN Doc. A/CONF.13/41, UN Sales No. 58.V.4, vol. V (1958).

United Nations Conference on the Law of the Sea, 4th Comm., UN Doc. A/CONF.13/42, UN Sales No. 58.V.4, vol. VI (1958).

United Nations Second Conference on the Law of the Sea – Official Records, Summary Records of Plenary Meetings and of Meetings of the Committee of the Whole, Annexes and Final Act, UN Doc. A/CONF.19/8, UN Sales No. 60.V.6 (1960).

Juridical Regime of Historic Waters, including Historic Bays, UN Doc. A/CN.4/143, reprinted in *Documents of the Thirteenth Session including the Report of the Commission to the General Assembly*, [1962] 2 Y.B. Int'l L. Comm'n 1, UN Doc. A/CN.4/Ser.A/1962/Add.1, UN Sales No. 62.V.5 (1962).

UN GAOR 1st Comm., 22d Sess., 1515th mtg, at 1–68, UN Doc. A/C.1/PV.1515 (1967).

UN GAOR 1st Comm., 22d Sess., 1515th mtg., at 1–6, UN Doc. A/C.1/PV.1516 (1967).

UN GAOR 1st Comm., 22d Sess., UN Doc. A/6695 (1967).

GA Res. 2340, UN GAOR, 22d Sess., Supp. No. 16, at 14, UN Doc. A/6716 (1967).

GA Res. 2574D, UN GAOR, 24th Sess., Supp. No. 30, at 11, UN Doc. A/7630 (1969).

GA Res. 2749, UN GAOR, 25th Sess., Supp. No. 28, at 24, UN Doc. A/8028 (1970).

Declaration of Principles on International Law concerning Friendly Relations and Co-operation among States in accordance with the Charter of the United Nations, GA Res. 2625, UN GAOR, 25th Sess., Supp. No. 28, at 121, UN Doc. A/2890 (1970).

Definition of Aggression, GA Res. 3314, UN GAOR, 29th Sess., Supp. No. 31, at 142, UN Doc. A/9631 (1975).

3 *Third United Nations Conference on the Law of the Sea: Official Records*, UN Sales No. E.75.V.5 (1974).

5 *Third United Nations Conference on the Law of the Sea: Official Records*, UN Sales No. E.76.V.8 (1984).

16 *Third United Nations Conference on the Law of the Sea: Official Records*, UN Sales No. E.84.V.2 (1984).

17 *Third United Nations Conference on the Law of the Sea: Official Records*, UN Sales No. E.84.V.3 (1984).

United Nations, Office of the Special Representative of the Secretary-General for the Law of the Sea, *Law of the Sea Bulletin*, No. 5 (1985).

United Nations Conference on Straddling Fish Stocks and Highly Migratory Fish Stocks was established by General Assembly Resolution 47/192 on 22 December 1992. See GA Res. 192, UN GAOR, 47th Sess., available at http://www.un.org/documents/ga/res/47/a47r192.htm.

Consultation of the Secretary-General on Outstanding Issues Relating to the Deep Seabed Regime Provisions of the United Nations Convention on the Law of the Sea: Report of the Secretary-General, UN GAOR, 48th Sess., Agenda Item 36, at 2, UN Doc. A/48/950 (1994).

GA Res. 28, UN GAOR, 49th Sess., (1994), available at http://www.un.org/documents/ga/res/49/a49r028.htm, para. 15(f).

Oceans and the law of the sea: law of the sea; results of the review by the Commission on Sustainable Development of the sectoral theme of "oceans and seas," UN Doc. A/54/429, (September 30, 1999).

Decision of the Assembly relating to the regulations on prospecting and exploration for polymetallic nodules in the Area, UN Doc. ISBA/6/A/18 (October 4, 2000).

Decision of the Council relating to the regulations and prospecting and exploration for polymetallic nodules in the Area, UN Doc. ISBA/6/C/12 (July 13, 2000).

Report of the Secretary-General of the International Seabed Authority under Article 166, paragraph 4 of the United Nations Convention on the Law of the Sea, UN Doc. ISBA/8/A/5 (June 7, 2002).

Lists of Experts for the purposes of article 2 of Annex VIII (Special Arbitration) to the Convention, available at http://www.un.org/Depts/los/settlement_of_disputes/experts_special_ arb.htm (as at June 24, 2003).

Multilateral Treaties Deposited with the Secretary-General, UN Doc. ST/LEG/SER.E/15, available at http://www.un.org/Depts/los/los_decl.htm (updated November 13, 2003).

CASES AND PLEADINGS

Decision of the Permanent Court of Arbitration in the Matter of the Maritime Boundary Dispute between Norway and Sweden, 4 *Am. J. Int'l L.* 226 (1910) [Grisbadarna].

Status of Eastern Carelia, Advisory Opinion No. 5, 1923 P.C.I.J. (ser. B) No. 5 (July 23).

Railway Traffic between Lithuania and Poland (Lith. v. Pol.) 1931 P.C.I.J. (ser. A/B) No. 42.

Treatment of Polish Nationals and Other Persons of Polish Origin or Speech in the Danzig Territory, Advisory Opinion, 1932, P.C.I.J., Series A/B, No. 44, p. 4.

Free Zones of Upper Savoy and the District of Gex, Judgment, 1932, P.C.I.J., Series A/B, No. 46, p. 167.

Corfu Channel (U.K. v. Alb.) 1949 ICJ 28 (Apr. 9).

Fisheries Case (U.K. v. Nor.) 1951 ICJ 116 (Dec. 18).

Ambatielos (Greece v. U.K.) 1953 ICJ 10 (May 19).

Interhandl Case (Switz. v. U.S.A) 1957 ICJ 105 (Oct. 24).

South West Africa (Second Phase) (Eth. v. S. Afr.; Liber. v. S. Afr.) 1966 ICJ 6 (July 18).

North Sea Continental Shelf (FRG/Den.; FRG/Neth.), 1969 ICJ 3 (Feb. 20).

Fisheries Jurisdiction (U.K. v. Ice.; FRG v. Ice.), Request for the Indication of Interim Measures of Protection, Order, 1972 ICJ 12, 30 (Aug. 17).

Fisheries Jurisdiction (U.K. v. Ice.; FRG v. Ice.) 1974 ICJ 3, 175 (July 25).

Nuclear Tests (Austl. v. Fr.; N.Z. v. Fr.) 1974 ICJ 253, 457 (Dec. 20).

Aegean Sea Continental Shelf Case, Request for Indication of Interim Measures of Protection, (Gr. v. Turk.) 1976 ICJ 3 (Sept. 11).

Delimitation of the Continental Shelf (U.K. /Fr.), 18 ILM 397 (1979).

Beagle Channel Arbitral Award (Arg./Chile), 17 ILM 632 (1978), 52 ILR 93 (1979).

United States Diplomatic and Consular Staff in Teheran (U.S. v. Iran), 1980 ICJ 3 (May 24).

Arbitral Award of 19 October 1981 (Emirates of Dubai/Sharjah), 91 ILR 543 (1981).

Report and Recommendations of the Conciliation Commission on the Continental Shelf Area between Iceland and Jan Mayen, 20 ILM 797 (1981).

Continental Shelf (Tunis./Libya), 1982 ICJ 18 (Feb. 24).

Delimitation of the Maritime Boundary in the Gulf of Maine Area (Can. v. U.S.) 1984 ICJ 246 (Oct. 12).

Military and Paramilitary Activities (Nicar. v. U.S.), 1984 ICJ 392 (Nov. 26).

Continental Shelf (Libya/Malta), 1985 ICJ 13 (June 3).

SPP(ME) Ltd. v. Egypt (First Decision on Jurisdiction), Nov. 27, 1985, 106 ILR 502.

Filleting within the Gulf of St Lawrence between Canada and France (1986), 19 UN Rep. Int'l Arbitral Awards 225 (July 17).

Maritime Boundary (Guinea/Guinea-Bissau), 25 ILM 252 (1986), 83 ILR 1 (1989).

Land, Island and Maritime Frontier Dispute (El Sal./Hond.; Nicar. Intervening), 1992 ICJ 351 (Sept. 11).

Delimitation of the Maritime Areas between Canada and France (St Pierre and Miquelon), 31 ILM 1149 (1992), 95 ILR 645 (1992).

Maritime Delimitation in the Area between Greenland and Jan Mayen (Den. v. Nor.), 1993 ICJ 38 (June 14).

US v. Alaska 117 S. Ct. 1888 (1997).

The M/V "Saiga", Request for Prompt Release (St. Vincent v. Guinea) (Dec. 4, 1997), *available at* http://www.itlos.org/start2_en.html.

The M/V "Saiga" (No. 2), Order on Provisional Measures (St. Vincent v. Guinea) (Mar. 11, 1998), Verbatim Record, ITLOS/PV.98/2, pp. 7–8 *available at* http://www.itlos.org/start2_en.html.

The M/V "Saiga" (No. 2), Order on Provisional Measures (St. Vincent v. Guinea) (Mar. 11, 1998) *available at* http://www.itlos.org/start2_en.html.

Vienna Convention on Consular Relations (Para. v. U.S.A.), Request for the Indication of Provisional Measures, Order, 1998 ICJ, (Apr. 9).

In the Matter of an Arbitration Pursuance to an Agreement to Arbitrate dated 3 October 1996 between the Government of the State of Eritrea and the Government of the Republic of Yemen (Eri./Yemen) (Award of the Arbitral Tribunal in the First Stage of the Proceedings (Territorial Sovereignty and Scope of the Dispute), Oct. 9, 1998), *available at* http://pca-cpa.org/RPC/#Eritrea.

LaGrand (F.R.G. v. U.S.), Request for the Indication of Provisional Measures, Order, 1999 ICJ, (Mar. 3).

Difference Relating to Immunity from Legal Process of a Special Rapporteur of the Commission on Human Rights, Advisory Opinion, 1999 ICJ (Apr. 29).

M/V "Saiga" (No. 2), Merits (St. Vincent v. Guinea) (Judgment of July 1, 1999), *available at* http://www.itlos.org/start2_en.html.

In the Matter of an Arbitration Pursuant to an Agreement to Arbitrate dated 3 October 1996 between the Government of the State of Eritrea and the Government of the Republic of Yemen (Eri./Yemen) (Award of the Arbitral Tribunal in the Second Stage of the Proceedings (Maritime Delimitation), Dec. 17, 1999) *available at* http://pca-cpa.org/RPC/#Eritrea.

Southern Bluefin Tuna, Requests for Provisional Measures (N.Z. v. Japan; Austl. v. Japan) (Order of Aug. 27, 1999), *available at* http://www.itlos.org/start2_en.html.

Southern Bluefin Tuna, Requests for Provisional Measures (N.Z. v. Japan; Austl. v. Japan) (Order of Aug, 27, 1999), Verbatim Records, ITLOS/PV.99/20, p. 23, *available at* http://www.itlos.org/start2_en.html.

Southern Bluefin Tuna, Requests for Provisional Measures (N.Z. v. Japan; Austl. v. Japan) (Order of Aug. 27, 1999), Verbatim Records, ITLOS/PV.99/21, p. 24 *available at* http://www.itlos.org/start2_en.html.

Southern Bluefin Tuna, Requests for Provisional Measures (N.Z. v. Japan; Austl. v. Japan) (Order of Aug. 27, 1999), Verbatim Records, ITLOS/PV.99/23, p. 9 *available at* http://www.itlos.org/start2_en.html.

"Camouco," Application for Prompt Release (Pan. v. Fr.) Verbatim Record, ITLOS
   PV-00/1, p. 26 *available at* http://www.itlos.org/start2_en.html.
"Camouco," Application for Prompt Release (Pan. v. Fr.) Verbatim Record, ITLOS
   PV-00/2, p. 17 *available at* http://www.itlos.org/start2_en.html
"Camouco," Application for Prompt Release (Pan. v. Fr.) Verbatim Record, ITLOS
   PV-00/3, p. 5 *available at* http://www.itlos.org/start2_en.html'
"Camouco," Application for Prompt Release (Pan. v. Fr.) (Judgment of Feb. 7,
   2000) *available at* http://www.itlos.org/start2_en.html.
In the Dispute Concerning Southern Bluefin Tuna, Australia v. Japan,
   Statement of Claim and Grounds on Which it is Based, para. 69 *available at*
   http://www.worldbank.org/icsid/bluefintuna/main.htm.
Southern Bluefin Tuna Case – Australia and New Zealand v. Japan, Government
   of Japan, Memorial on Jurisdiction, *available at* http://www.worldbank.org/
   icsid/bluefintuna/main.htm.
Southern Bluefin Tuna Case – Australia and New Zealand v. Japan, Australia
   and New Zealand, Reply on Jurisdiction, Volume 1, Text, Mar. 31, 2000
   available at http://www.worldbank.org/icsid/bluefintuna/main.htm.
Southern Bluefin Tuna Cases – Australia and New Zealand v. Japan, Award on
   Jurisdiction and Admissibility, (Austl. v. Japan; N.Z. v. Japan) (Arbitral
   Tribunal constituted under Annex VII of the United Nations Convention
   on the Law of the Sea, Aug. 4, 2000), 39 ILM 1359 (2000).
"Monte Confurco," Application for Prompt Release (Sey. v. Fr.), (Judgment of
   Dec. 18, 2000), Verbatim Record, ITLOS PV.00/8, p. 11, *available at*
   http://www.itlos.org/start2_en.html.
"Monte Confurco," Application for Prompt Release (Sey. v. Fr.), (Judgment of
   Dec. 18, 2000), *available at* http://www.itlos.org/start2_en.html.
Case Concerning Maritime Delimitation and Territorial Questions between
   Qatar and Bahrain (Qatar v. Bahr.), 2001 ICJ (Mar. 16).
"Grand Prince," Application for Prompt Release, (Belize v. Fr.) (Judgment of
   Apr. 20, 2001) *available at* http://www.itlos.org/start2_en.html.
LaGrand (F.R.G. v. U.S.) 2001 ICJ (June 27), *available at*
   http://www.icj-cij.org/icjwww/idocket/igus/igusframe.htm.
In the Dispute Concerning the MOX Plant, International Movements of
   Radioactive Materials, and the Protection of the Marine Environment of
   the Irish Sea, (Ireland v. U.K.) Request for Provisional Measures and
   Statement of Case of Ireland, Nov. 9, 2001 *available at*
   http://www.itlos.org/start2_en.html.
The MOX Plant Case (Ir. v. U.K.), Request for Provisional Measures (Order of Dec.
   3, 2001) *available at* http://www.itlos.org/start2_en.html.
"Volga," Application for Prompt Release, (Russ. v. Austl.), Memorial of the
   Russian Federation, *available at* http://www.itlos.org/start2_en.html.
The "Volga" Case, Statement in Response of Australia, Dec. 7, 2002, *available at*
   http://www.itlos.org/start2_en.html.
"Volga," Application for Prompt Release, (Russ. v. Austl.) (Judgment of Dec. 23,
   2002) *available at* http://www.itlos.org/start2_en.html.

In the Dispute Concerning the MOX Plant, International Movements of Radioactive Materials, and the Protection of the Marine Environment of the Irish Sea, Part II, para. 6.7 (July 26, 2002), *available at* http://www.pca-cpa.org/PDF/Ireland%20Memorial%20Part%20II.pdf.

The MOX Plant Case, (Ir. v. U.K.) Counter-Memorial of the United Kingdom, Jan. 9, 2003, *available at* http://www.pca-cpa.org/ENGLISH/RPC/.

In the Dispute Concerning the MOX Plant, International Movements of Radioactive Materials, and the Protection of the Marine Environment of the Irish Sea, (Ir. v. U.K.) Reply of Ireland, Mar. 7, 2003 *available at* http://www.pca-cpa.org/ENGLISH/RPC/.

The MOX Plant Case, (Ir. v. U.K.) Rejoinder of the United Kingdom, Apr. 24, 2003, *available at* http://www.pca-cpa.org/ENGLISH/RPC/.

MOX Plant, Day 2 Transcript, *available at* http://www.pca-cpa.org/PDF/MOX%20-%20Day%20Two.pdf.

Case Concerning Land Reclamation by Singapore In and around the Straits of Johor (Malay. v. Sing.), Request for the Prescription of Provisional Measures under Article 290, Paragraph 5, of the United Nations Convention on the Law of the Sea, Response of Singapore (Sept. 20), *available at* http://www.itlos.org/start2_en.html.

Case Concerning Land Reclamation by Singapore in and around the Straits of Johor (Malay. v. Sing.), Request for Provisional Measures, Verbatim Record, ITLOS/PV.03/02/Corr.1, p. 23, *available at* http://www.itlos.org/start2_en.html.

Case Concerning Land Reclamation by Singapore in and around the Straits of Johor (Malay. v. Sing.), Request for Provisional Measures, Verbatim Record, ITLOS/PV.03/03, *available at* http://www.itlos.org/start2_en.html.

Case concerning Land Reclamation by Singapore in and around the Straits of Johor, Request for Provisional Measures, Malay. v. Sing., Verbatim Record, ITLOS/PV.03/05, p. 10. *available at* http://www.itlos.org/start2_en.html.

Case concerning Land Reclamation by Singapore in and around the Straits of Johor (Malay. v. Sing.), Request for Provisional Measures (Order of Oct. 8, 2003) *available at* http://www.itlos.org/start2_en.html.

MOX Plant, Statement of the President, June 13, 2003, *available at* http://www.pca-cpa.org/ENGLISH/RPC/.

Arbitral Tribunal Constituted Pursuant to Article 287, and Article 1 of Annex VII, of the United Nations Convention on the Law of the Sea for the Dispute Concerning the MOX Plant, International Movements of Radioactive Materials, and the Protection of the Marine Environment of the Irish Sea, The MOX Plant Case (Ir. v. U.K) Order No. 3, Suspension of Proceedings on Jurisdiction and Merits, and Request for Further Provisional Measures, June 24, 2003 *available at* http://www.pca-cpa.org/ENGLISH/RPC/.

Arbitral Tribunal Constituted Pursuant to Article 287, and Article 1 of Annex VII, of the United Nations Convention on the Law of the Sea for the Dispute Concerning the MOX Plant, International Movements of

Radioactive Materials, and the Protection of the Marine Environment of the Irish Sea, The MOX Plant Case (Ir. v. U.K) Order No. 4, Further Suspension of Proceedings on Jurisdiction and Merits, Nov. 14, 2003 available at http://www.pca-cpa.org/ENGLISH/RPC/.

TREATIES AND OTHER INTERNATIONAL INSTRUMENTS

Treaty of Amity, Commerce and Navigation, Nov. 19, 1794, U.S.-U.K., 1794, 8 Stat. 116 [Jay Treaty].

Convention [No. I] Regarding the Pacific Settlement of International Disputes, July 29, 1899, 32 Stat. 1779, 1 Bevans 230.

Convention [No. VI] Relating to the Status of Enemy Merchant Ships at the Outbreak of Hostilities, Oct. 18, 1907, 100 Brit & Foreign St. Papers 365 (1906–07), reprinted in The Law of Naval Warfare: A Collection of Agreements and Documents with Commentaries 96 (N. Ronzitti, ed., 1988).

Convention [No. VII] Relating to the Conversion of Merchant Ships to Warships Oct. 18, 1907, 100 Brit & Foreign St. Papers 377 (1906–07), reprinted in The Law of Naval Warfare: A Collection of Agreements and Documents with Commentaries 114 (N. Ronzitti, ed., 1988).

Convention [No. VIII] Relative to the Laying of Automatic Submarine Contact Mines, Oct. 18, 1907, 36 Stat. 2332, 1 Bevans 669.

Convention [No. IX] Concerning Bombardment by Naval Forces in Time of War, Oct. 18, 1907, 36 Stat. 2351, 1 Bevans 681.

Convention [No. XI] Relative to Certain Restrictions with Regard to the Exercise of the Right of Capture in Naval War, Oct. 18, 1907, 36 Stat. 2396, 1 Bevans 711.

Convention [No. XIII] Concerning the Rights and Duties of Neutral Powers in Naval War, Oct. 18, 1907, 36 Stat. 2415, 1 Bevans 723.

Treaty between Great Britain and the United States for the Protection of Fur Seals, Feb. 7, 1911, U.K.-U.S., 37 Stat. 1538. Modified by Convention between Great Britain, Japan, Russia and the United States respecting Measures for the Preservation and Protection of Fur Seals in the North Pacific Ocean, July 7, 1911, 37 Stat. 1542.

Covenant of the League of Nations (1919).

Statute of the Permanent Court of International Justice (1919).

Treaty between His Majesty in Respect of the United Kingdom and the President of the United States of Venezuela Relating to the Submarine Areas of the Gulf Paria, Feb. 26, 1942, 1942 U.K.T.S. No. 10.

United Nations Charter (1945).

Statute of the International Court of Justice (1945).

Presidential Proclamation No. 2667, 28 Sept., 1945, 59 Stat. 884.

Presidential Proclamation No. 2668, 28 Sept., 1945, 59 Stat. 885.

International Convention for the Prevention of the Pollution of the Sea by Oil, May 12, 1954, 12 UST 2989; 327 UNTS 3.

Treaty Establishing the European Economic Community, Mar. 25, 1957, art. 186, 298 UNTS 3.

Convention on the Territorial Sea and Contiguous Zone, Apr. 29 1958, 15 UST 1606, 516 UNTS 205.

Convention on the High Seas, Apr. 29 1958, 13 UST 2312, 450 UNTS 82.

Convention on Fishing and Conservation of the Living Resources of the High Seas, Apr. 29 1958, 17 UST 138, 559 UNTS 285.

Convention on the Continental Shelf, Apr. 29 1958, 15 UST 1171, 499 UNTS 311.

Optional Protocol of Signature Concerning the Compulsory Settlement of Disputes, Adopted by the United Nations Conference on the Law of the Sea, Apr. 29 1958, 450 UNTS 172.

International Convention for the Prevention of Pollution from Ships, May 18, 1967, 17 UST 1523, 600 UNTS 332, *as modified by* Protocol of 1978 relating thereto, June 1, 1978, 17 ILM 546 (1978).

International Convention Relating to Intervention on the High Seas in Cases of Oil Pollution Casualties, Nov. 29, 1969, 26 UST 765.

Convention on the Prevention of Marine Pollution by Dumping of Wastes and Other Matter, Dec. 29, 1972, 26 UST 2403, 1046 UNTS 120.

Convention on the Conservation of Antarctic Marine Living Resources, May 21, 1980, 33 UST 3476.

Agreement Concerning Interim Arrangements Relating to Polymetallic Nodules of the Deep Sea Bed, Sept. 2, 1982, 21 ILM 950 (1982).

United Nations Convention on the Law of the Sea, *opened for signature* December 10, 1982, 1833 UNTS 397.

Final Act of the Third United Nations Conference on the Law of the Sea, *available at* http://www.un.org/Depts/los/convention_agreements/texts/final_act_eng.pdf.

Agreement on the United States' Actions Concerning the Conference on the Law of the Sea, II PUB. PAPERS 911 (July 9, 1982).

Provisional Understanding Regarding Deep Seabed Mining, Aug. 3, 1984, 23 ILM 1354 (entered into force Sept. 2, 1984).

Agreement of the Resolution of Practical Problems With Respect to Deep Seabed Mining Areas, and Exchange of Notes Between the United States and the Parties to the Agreement, Aug. 14, 1987, 26 ILM 1502.

Joint Statement with Attached Uniform Interpretation of Rules of International Law Governing Innocent Passage, Sept. 23, 1989, US-USSR, 28 ILM 1444.

International Convention on Oil Pollution Preparedness, Response and Co-operation, Nov. 30 1990, 30 ILM 773 (1991).

Treaty on European Union (Maastricht) Feb. 7, 1992, (1992) 31 ILM 247.

Convention for the Conservation of Bluefin Tuna, May 10, 1993, Austl.-N.Z.-Japan, May 10, 1993, 1819 UNTS 360 (entered into force May 30, 1994).

Agreement on Trade-Related Aspects of Intellectual Property Rights, Apr. 15, 1994, Marrakesh Agreement Establishing the World Trade Organization,

Annex 1C, *Legal Instruments – Results of the Uruguay Round* vol. 31; 33 ILM 81 (1994).

Agreement Relating to the Implementation of Part XI of the United Nations Convention on the Law of the Sea, Nov. 16, 1994, S. TREATY DOC. No. 104–24, 1836 UNTS 3 (1995).

Arbitration Agreement, Oct. 3, 1996, Eri.-Yemen, *available at* http://www.pca-cpa.org/RPC/arbagreeER-YE.htm.

Declaration concerning the competence of the European Community with regard to matters governed by the United Nations Convention on the Law of the Sea of 10 December 1982 and the Agreement of 28 July 1994 relating to the implementation of Part XI of the Convention, (April 1, 1998) *available at* http://www.un.org/Depts/los/convention_ agreements/convention_declarations.htm#European%20Community% 20Declaration%20made%20upon%20formal%20confirmation.

Rules of the Tribunal (ITLOS/8), as amended on 15 March and 21 September 2001, *available at* http://www.itlos.org/start2_en.html.

Index

Note: Reference should also be made to the Table of Treaties and Other International Instruments. Unless otherwise indicated, article references are to UNCLOS

[1] including material common to UNCLOS Part VI provisions on the continental shelf

CAMBRIDGE STUDIES IN INTERNATIONAL AND COMPARATIVE LAW

Lightning Source UK Ltd.
Milton Keynes UK
UKHW041503141121
393833UK00007B/307